Conflict of Laws

The International Library of Essays in Law and Legal Theory
Series Editor: Tom D. Campbell

Schools

Natural Law, Vols I & II *John Finnis*
Justice *Thomas Morawetz*
Law and Economics, Vols I & II *Jules Coleman and Jeffrey Lange*
Critical Legal Studies *James Boyle*
Marxian Legal Theory *Csaba Varga*
Legal Reasoning, Vols I & II *Aulis Aarnio and D. Neil MacCormick*
Legal Positivism *Mario Jori*
American Legal Theory *Robert Samuel Summers*
Postmodernism and Law *Dennis Patterson*
Law in History, Vols I & II *David Sugarman*
Law and Language *Fred Schauer*
Sociological Theories of Law *Kahei Rokumoto*
Rights *Carlos Nino*
Law and Psychology *Martin Lyon Levine*
Feminist Legal Theory, Vols I & II *Frances Olsen*
Law and Society *Roger Cotterrell*
Contemporary Criminological Theory *Francis T. Cullen and Velmer S. Burton Jr.*

Areas

Criminal Law *Thomas Morawetz*
Tort Law *Ernest J. Weinrib*
Contract Law, Vols I & II *Larry Alexander*
Anti-Discrimination Law *Christopher McCrudden*
Consumer Law *Iain Ramsay*
International Law *Martti Koskenniemi*
Property Law, Vols I & II *Elizabeth Mensch and Alan Freeman*
Constitutional Law *Mark V. Tushnet*
Procedure *D.J. Galligan*
Evidence and Proof *William Twining and Alex Stein*
Company Law *Sally Wheeler*
Privacy, Vols I & II *Raymond Wacks*
Lawyers' Ethics *David J. Luban*
Administrative Law *D.J. Galligan*
Child Law *Harry D. Krause*
Family Law, Vols I & II *Harry D. Krause*
Welfare Law *Peter Robson*
Medicine and the Law *Bernard M. Dickens*
Commercial Law *Ross Cranston*
Environmental Law *Michael C. Blumm*
Conflict of Laws *Richard Fentiman*
Law and Religion *Wojciech Sadurski*
Human Rights Law *Philip Alston*
European Community Law, Vols I & II *Francis Snyder*
Tax Law, Vols I & II *Patricia D. White*
Media Law *Eric Barendt*
Labour Law *David L. Gregory*
Alternative Dispute Resolution *Michael D.A. Freeman*

Legal Cultures

Comparative Legal Cultures *Csaba Varga*
Law and Anthropology *Peter Sack*
Hindu Law and Legal Theory *Ved Nanda*
Islamic Law and Legal Theory *Ian Edge*
Chinese Law and Legal Theory *Michael Palmer*
Russian Legal Theory *W. Butler*
Common Law *Michael Arnheim*
Japanese Law and Legal Theory *Koichiro Fujikura*
Law and Development *Anthony Carty*
Jewish Law and Legal Theory *Martin P. Golding*
Legal Education *Martin Lyon Levine*
Civil Law *Ralf Rogowski*
African Law and Legal Theory *Gordon Woodman and Akintunde Obilade*

Future Volume
Cumulative index

Conflict of Laws

Edited by

Richard Fentiman

Fellow and Director of Studies in Law
Queens' College, University of Cambridge

NEW YORK UNIVERSITY PRESS
REFERENCE COLLECTION

First published in the U.S.A. in 1996 by
NEW YORK UNIVERSITY PRESS
Washington Square
New York NY 10003

Library of Congress Cataloging-in-Publication Data
Conflict of laws / edited by Richard Fentiman.
p. cm. – (International library of essays in law and legal theory. Areas ; 28)
Includes bibliographical references.
ISBN 0-8147-2608-9
1.Conflict of laws. I. Fentiman, Richard. II. Series.
K7040.C66 1996
340.9–dc20 96-1073
CIP

Contents

PART II COMMON LAW TRADITIONS IN CHOICE OF LAW

The Theoretical Tradition in America

The Pragmatic Tradition in England

Acknowledgements

The editor and publishers wish to thank the following for permission to use copyright material.

American Association for the Comparative Study of Law for the essays: Friedrich K. Juenger (1988), 'The Recognition of Money Judgments in Civil and Commercial Matters', *The American Journal of Comparative Law*, **36**, pp. 1–39; Trevor C. Hartley (1987), 'Comity and the Use of Antisuit Injunctions in International Litigation', *The American Journal of Comparative Law*, **35**, pp. 487–511.

Boston University Law Review for the essay: Arthur Taylor von Mehren (1983), 'Adjudicatory Jurisdiction: General Theories Compared and Evaluated', *Boston University Law Review*, **63**, pp. 279–340. Copyright © 1983 by Arthur Taylor von Mehren. Permission given by the Author and Boston University Law Review.

The British Institute of International and Comparative Law, 17 Russell Square, London WC1B 5DR, for the essay: J.J. Fawcett (1982), 'Is American Governmental Interest Analysis the Solution to English Tort Choice of Law Problems?', **31**, *The International and Comparative Law Quarterly*, **31**, pp. 150–66.

P.B. Carter (1985), 'Rejection of Foreign Law: Some Private International Law Inhibitions', *British Yearbook of International Law*, **55**, pp. 111–31. Copyright © P.B. Carter, 1985.

Cornell Law Review and Fred B. Rothman & Company for the essay: Rudolf B. Schlesinger (1973), 'A Recurrent Problem in Transnational Litigation: The Effect of Failure to Invoke or Prove the Applicable Foreign Law', *Cornell Law Review*, **59**, pp. 1–26. Copyright © 1973 by Cornell University. All rights reserved.

Duke University School of Law for the essays: Willis L.M. Reese (1963), 'Conflict of Laws and the Restatement Second', *Law and Contemporary Problems*, **28**, pp. 679–99; Paul Heinrich Neuhaus (1963), 'Legal Certainty Versus Equity in the Conflict of Laws', *Law and Contemporary Problems*, **28**, pp. 795–807.

Harvard Law Review for the essays: David F. Cavers (1933), 'A Critique of the Choice-of-Law Problem', *Harvard Law Review*, **XLVII**, pp. 173–208. Copyright © 1933 by The Harvard Law Association. Erwin N. Griswold (1938), 'Renvoi Revisited', *Harvard Law Review*, **51**, pp. 1165–1208. Copyright © 1938 by The Harvard Law Association. J.H.C. Morris (1951), 'The Proper Law of a Tort', *Harvard Law Review*, **64**, pp. 881–95. Copyright © 1951 by The Harvard Law Association.

King's College Law Journal for the essay: P.M. North (1992), 'Choice in Choice of Law', *The King's College Law Journal*, **3**, pp. 29–48.

The Michigan Law Review Association for the essays: Albert A. Ehrenzweig (1960), 'The Lex Fori – Basic Rule in the Conflict of Laws', *Michigan Law Review*, **58**, pp. 637–88; Lea Brilmayer (1980), 'Interest Analysis and the Myth of Legislative Intent', *Michigan Law Review*, **78**, pp. 392–431.

New York University Law Review for the essay: Robert A. Leflar (1966), 'Choice-Influencing Considerations in Conflicts Law', *New York University Law Review*, **41**, pp. 267–327.

Oxford University Press for the essay: A.J.E. Jaffey (1982), 'The Foundations of Rules for the Choice of Law', *Oxford Journal of Legal Studies*, **2**, pp. 368–92.

University of Chicago Law School for the essay: Brainerd Currie (1958), 'Married Women's Contracts: A Study in Conflict-of-Laws Method', *University of Chicago Law Review*, **25**, pp. 227–68.

The Yale Law Journal and Fred B. Rothman for the essay: Ernest G. Lorenzen (1941), 'The Qualification, Classification, or Characterization Problem in the Conflict of Laws', *Yale Law Journal*, **50**, pp. 743–61.

Every effort has been made to trace all the copyright holders but if any have been inadvertently overlooked the publishers will be pleased to make the necessary arrangement at the first opportunity.

Series Preface

The International Library of Essays in Law and Legal Theory is designed to provide important research materials in an accessible form. Each volume contains essays of central theoretical importance in its subject area. The series as a whole makes available an extensive range of valuable material which will be of considerable interest to those involved in the research, teaching and study of law.

The series has been divided into three sections. The Schools section is intended to represent the main distinctive approaches and topics of special concern to groups of scholars. The Areas section takes in the main branches of law with an emphasis on essays which present analytical and theoretical insights of broad application. The section on Legal Cultures makes available the distinctive legal theories of different legal traditions and takes up topics of general comparative and developmental concern.

I have been delighted and impressed by the way in which the editors of the individual volumes have set about the difficult task of selecting, ordering and presenting essays from the immense quantity of academic legal writing published in journals throughout the world. Editors were asked to pick out those essays from law, philosophy and social science journals which they consider to be fundamental for the understanding of law, as seen from the perspective of a particular approach or sphere of legal interest. This is not an easy task and many difficult decisions have had to be made in order to ensure that a representative sample of the best journal essays available takes account of the scope of each topic or school.

I should like to express my thanks to all the volume editors for their willing participation and scholarly judgement. The interest and enthusiasm which the project has generated is well illustrated by the fact that an original projection of 12 volumes drawn up in 1989 has now become a list of some 60 volumes. I must also acknowledge the vision, persistence and constant cheerfulness of John Irwin and the marvellous work done by Mrs Margaret O'Reilly and Ms Sonia Hubbard.

TOM D. CAMPBELL
Series Editor
The Faculty of Law
The Australian National University

Introduction

The conflict of laws is a subject of enduring interest and practical importance. In a world of increasing personal mobility, global trade and enhanced communications, law's transnational aspects have seldom mattered more. Concerned with the foreign elements in private legal relations, with questions of jurisdiction, international civil procedure[1] and the applicable law, the issues at the subject's core are as immutable as they are often intractable. When, for example, should a court entertain claims against foreign parties, perhaps involving acts abroad? What substantive law governs such foreign-linked matters? What, in a given case, is the issue in dispute, given that a different law may apply depending on the answer? If foreign law applies, by what means is its content to be proved? What if the issue is already subject to a binding foreign judgment?

That such questions are persistent does not make them stale. The multicultural nature of many societies, for example, casts in a new light old questions concerning public policy, the validity of marriage and the recognition of foreign divorce.[2] So too, such developments as the burgeoning market in intellectual property and the growth in information technology give fresh impetus to fundamental questions concerning the proper treatment of intangibles in the conflict of laws.[3] Again, such diverse matters as the globalization of communications[4] and the increasing incidence of transnational products liability[5] pose urgent questions concerning the location of tortious wrongs and the law which should govern them.

Against this background the present collection has a straightforward purpose. Its task is to fix the conceptual coordinates of the conflict of laws by reference to its extensive periodical literature. Chosen because they illuminate the subject's central issues, the selected essays are drawn exclusively from English and American writing and illustrate each jurisdiction's distinctive approach to the subject. Localized as they are, however – offering an insight into the common law tradition in the conflict of laws – the issues which this collection addresses are far from being parochial. Although expressed in a common law idiom, the selected papers address problems of universal interest, their concern being not so much with the Anglo-American experience as with the inherent logic of the conflict of laws.

Indicative as it is of the subject's scope, such a selection cannot do justice to its complexity, nor to the richness of its literature. The very fact that it is a collection of essays itself distorts our impression of the conflicts canon, much of which derives from textbooks and monographs.[6] By including, moreover, only pieces which engage primarily with issues of theory and principle, much exemplary work of a technical nature is omitted, chiefly because of its mainly local resonance.[7]

More particularly, those familiar with the American conflicts experience will notice how much is excluded concerning the continuing debate over the design of choice of law rules and the search for principled flexibility in such matters.[8] Some major works which define what has come to be called the American conflicts revolution are included, but much interstitial writing of interest and importance is not. English lawyers may see a different omission. They will detect little evidence of the current English trend to focus on the subject's procedural aspects and to collapse the distinction between private international law and international civil procedure.[9] The growing sophistication of English law's discretionary approach to jurisdiction, and the emergence of extraterritorial forms of interim relief, are only hinted at. This is not to deny that such contemporary concerns have yielded a rewarding and suggestive literature. Nor do these omissions imply that such matters, because topical (even fashionable), are ephemeral. It is merely that such trends are of largely local interest and, for all their importance, are founded on a more fundamental conceptual basis which is the focus of this collection.

The chapters which follow are organized within two groups. Part I is concerned with identifying the principal issues which underlie the subject. Part II distinguishes different approaches to resolving choice of law questions as reflected in the American and English literature.

Central Issues in the Conflict of Laws

Essays in the first group address the subject's central issues. They are concerned with the four principal aspects of the conflicts process: the question of jurisdictional competence; the mechanics of selecting the applicable law; the relationship between foreign law and that of the forum; and the proper response to proceedings in foreign courts.

The initial question in all cross-border proceedings is whether a court will entertain proceedings with a foreign element. This is the subject of von Mehren's seminal study of the different grounds for accepting jurisdiction in multistate cases (Chapter 1). Although rooted in American practice,[10] it highlights a universal theme in the practical alliance between a court's standards of jurisdiction and the recognition of its judgments abroad. It describes two approaches to jurisdiction – one based upon power over the defendant, the other on considerations of convenience and fairness – thus identifying the tension at the core of any reflection about jurisdictional competence. It also foreshadows the problem which has come to dominate the Anglo-American experience: to what extent should justiciability depend on immutable rules or on judicial discretion?

Once a court's competence is established, a host of substantive issues arise, all concerning how best to identify the applicable law. The very nature of the choice of law process is subjected to searching analysis in Cavers's influential paper of 1933 (Chapter 2). Reacting to what he perceived as the mechanical formalism of American conflicts scholarship, Cavers sees the process contextually – part of the search for acceptable results in particular cases. In doing so he invites us to engage with the consequences of applying conflicts rules and to weigh the results of different solutions. But he requires us to proceed in a principled way, thus posing the question at the core of the choice of law process: how is law selection possible which is neither mechanically formalistic nor crudely instrumental, but is at once discretionary and structured?[11]

Such questions concern the form of conflicts rules. Equally important are the criteria for selecting the governing law. The tension here is between approaches which seek to establish an objective connection between an issue or event and a given country's law, and those which operate subjectively, seeking to give effect to the intentions of those involved. The role of intention in the conflicts process is the theme of North's 'Choice in Choice of Law'

(Chapter 5).[12] This wide-ranging study surveys the different ways in which party choice affects that process, through forum selection, pleading and direct choice of law. It highlights the antagonism between, on the one hand, the conception of conflicts rules as mandatory and, on the other, the fairness and utility of allowing individuals to shape the legal consequences of their actions. It also poses the question whether choice of law rules should primarily guide the adjudication of disputes or instead assist in the prospective planning of people's legal affairs.

A further cluster of problems concerns calibrating the choice of law process, refining the question 'which law governs'? One such problem concerns the classification of legal issues for conflicts purposes. Given that different laws may be applied depending on how an issue is categorized, it is critically important to know whether, for example, a given dispute is one in tort, perhaps, or in contract. Similarly, once an issue's nature is known and the correct choice of law rule applied, there may be a question as to whether a particular rule of the chosen law in fact belongs to that category, such that it is caught by the relevant choice of law rule. This important process of classification is described in Chapter 3 by Lorenzen[13] who exposes the abiding conflict between foreign law and the law of the forum in classifying legal issues. He also identifies the important truth that the result of any enquiry into the applicable law depends critically on how the question is posed.

If the problem of classification concerns how the choice of law question should be posed, the problem of *renvoi* concerns how the answer should be understood. As Griswold's influential essay shows (Chapter 4), the question is whether the law applicable to a given issue is the domestic law of the chosen country or its private international law. Although Griswold favoured wider use of the doctrine which advocates applying the 'whole law' of the *lex causae*, his optimism about its future has been fulfilled neither in England nor in America. In both countries the general rule is that a state's local law will be applied without reference to its conflicts rules, although, in some cases (where to do so would introduce flexibility into an otherwise rigid choice of law rule, or where policy considerations justify doing so), the whole law may be applied.[14] Whatever the law's present state, however, the possibility of *renvoi* creates a nagging ambiguity at the heart of the conflicts process.

Chapters 6 to 8 by Ehrenzweig, Carter and Schlesinger traverse different aspects of the relationship between foreign law and the law of the forum. Carter is concerned with the circumstances in which the public policy of the forum may exclude the application of an otherwise applicable foreign law.[15] Schlesinger writes of how litigants in the common law tradition may generally choose whether or not to plead foreign law in a case with a foreign element, thus excluding foreign law by election.[16] In describing how the interests of the forum may intrude into the conflicts process, effectively disabling it, both authors highlight the important truth that conflicts rules are part of the *lex fori*, subject to such restrictions as the forum may impose upon them. This general theme is articulated and explored in Ehrenzweig's important and challenging defence of the *lex fori*'s role. He touches on such defining features of the conflicts process as the distinction between substance and procedure, the pleading of foreign law, the doctrine of *renvoi*, the 'incidental question' and the role of public policy. More generally, by presenting the conflicts process as an exception to the application of the forum's law, he illuminates the process as a whole.

Cases with foreign elements generally involve proceedings in the forum concerned. But in two principal ways a court may be asked to respond to proceedings elsewhere. Most obviously, this arises when it is asked to recognize a judgment given in a foreign forum. Less often it may occur when it is asked to restrain proceedings elsewhere. The recognition and enforcement of foreign judgments are the subject of Juenger's encyclopaedic account in Chapter 9 of the response of different legal systems to the problem.[17] As his survey indicates, there is considerable disparity between the approaches adopted by different systems. This stems partly from the greater willingness of some countries to protect their nationals or to assert their national interests in the face of hostile foreign judgments, and partly from the extent to which the recognition of foreign judgments is firmly rooted in their distinctive procedural traditions.

The restraint of foreign proceedings, the subject of Chapter 10 by Hartley, is a different matter. But like the recognition question, it raises important issues concerning the role of international comity in the conflict of laws. As Hartley's account implies, it once again begs questions about how far a court may assert its distinctive policies – in this case the policy of preventing the harassment of individuals through foreign proceedings – in a situation in which another state's interests are implicated.

Common Law Traditions in Choice of Law

Despite a common legal heritage, a shared juristic idiom and, at one time, a common caselaw, the English and American traditions in the conflict of laws are strikingly different. At least with regard to choice of law issues, with which we are presently concerned, the former is predominantly pragmatic, the latter more theoretical. It is arresting how differences of opinion in English conflicts scholarship amost exclusively concern the solution to specific, technical problems. In the United States, by contrast, they reflect fundamental doctrinal differences concerning the design of conflicts rules and the subject's nature and purpose.

English commentators generally see their role in this field as being the exposition and critique of existing law. New approaches are crafted from old ones and the law's progress is seen as organic, incremental and piecemeal. As one leading textbook says of theoretical approaches to the subject,

> ... such theoretical analyses are unsupported by English private international law. They are alien to the common law tradition and if offered in argument would be a matter of surprise to an English judge. The instinct of the English lawyer is to test a proposed rule by its practical bearing on normal activities and expectations. ... He is nothing if not an empiricist and a pragmatist.[18]

Admittedly, recent legislative reform has prompted a more speculative discourse but, even here, the discussion is singularly pragmatic.[19] Even at its most speculative, utility and common sense are the benchmarks of the English approach.

The American tradition has a very different appearance. More theoretical in nature, this has tended to strive for ideal solutions in the design of conflicts rules. Led by considerations of policy and fairness, less by concern with precedent and practice, American scholars, freed from such constraints, have produced a variety of divergent theories on the choice of law question.[20]

That England and America should differ in their perspective on the conflict of laws is at first sight surprising. Dicey, who did so much to shape the English approach, freely acknowledged his debt to Story, his American precursor.[21] So too, Beale's 1935 *Restatement of the Conflict of Laws* owed much in turn to Dicey's work, both in its endorsement of the 'vested rights' theory[22] and in its dogmatic, positivist style. One source of the divergence may be the very different circumstances in which the subject operated – and still operates – in each jurisdiction. Most obviously, conflicts of law in the United States are predominantly of an inter-state nature while those in England are international. This may explain the invariable tendency of English choice of law rules to be jurisdiction-selecting, such that a given country's law is selected as the *lex causae* and its rules applied (public policy apart) whatever their content. By contrast, most American techniques are variants on a rule-selecting (or result-selecting) approach whereby the substantive appropriateness of applying a foreign or a local rule is assessed. Where, as in England, the applicable law is that of a foreign sovereign state, it is both impractical and inappropriate to examine its scope and the interests which might be served by its application. Comity also makes it hard to do anything other than give effect to its rule without question, extreme cases involving public policy aside. Such inhibitions do not obtain in American inter-state conflicts. Indeed, the fundamental similarity between state laws allows something like a sensible weighing of state interests to be accomplished.

More importantly perhaps, England never experienced in any significant form the revolution in legal thought which has come to be identified with American legal realism.[23] Indeed, it is striking that, although Beale's *Restatement* was a prime target for realist commentators, Dicey and Morris's *Conflict of Laws*,[24] which it so much resembles, remains the cornerstone of English conflicts thinking. Characterized by a distrust for traditional common law reasoning, a suspicion of rule-led thinking and a desire for policy-orientated decisions, the instrumentalism of the American approach contrasts sharply with the (relatively) formalistic style of English law. Indeed, American scholarship in this area is in large part a continuous meditation on the implications of such instrumentalism: how can law both bind and serve at the same time?

The selected studies illustrate these differences and depict various aspects of both the English and the American traditions. The contrast is put into perspective in Chapter 15 by Neuhaus's essay on legal certainty in the conflict of laws. In highlighting the familiar dichotomy between certainty and equity in legal thinking and in describing its particular implications for the conflicts process, he lays bare the matrix of issues which lie at the subject's core. Should conflicts rules be fair or certain, discretionary or fixed? Should they be designed for use by courts or by those wishing to plan their affairs prospectively? Should they be imposed *a priori* or honed in practice? To what extent is uniformity an objective, such that discretionary approaches should be disparaged?

Such questions are not without importance for English lawyers; indeed, are of greater importance than might be supposed. But English commentators, never having lost faith with traditional legal reasoning, are not required to engage with them constantly. For American commentators, by contrast, they are a persistent concern.

The Theoretical Tradition in America

The essays which exemplify the American tradition in this collection are no more than samples of the perspectives on offer. Some distinguished alternative views have been developed largely in book form, which prevents their inclusion here.[25] Others may be seen as variants on the theories presented in the chosen pieces.[26] Each of the three selected writers argue, however, for important approaches to the choice of law process.

Currie represents the chief exponent of what has become known as governmental interest analysis, although he shares much with Cavers, whose influential essay on the choice of law process has already been mentioned.[27] The essence of Currie's approach in Chapter 11 is that a court should investigate whether a conflict truly exists between the policies expressed by the competing rules of local and foreign law. If it does, the *lex fori* should be preferred. As such, it is, in a sense, the apogee of the American perspective. Indifferent to comity and requiring a court to assess the substantive applicability of its law against that of another jurisdiction, it is largely inappropriate to international (as distinct from inter-state) conflicts of law. Moreover, by leaving the question of the applicable law to a court's discretion, it offers little comfort to those who wish to structure their legal relations without recourse to litigation.

Other writers have focused on how to structure the discretion associated with a flexible, instrumental approach to choice of law. Unlike Currie, who sought to replace the choice of law process with the principled application of the *lex fori*, they have engaged directly with how to choose the most appropriate law. Reese, the reporter responsible for the *Second Restatement*, and Leflar, whose approach has received some judicial support, have each sought to supply effective law-selection criteria (see Chapters 12 and 13). Superficially similar in their enumeration of such criteria, Reese and Leflar differ in two important ways. First, Reese's approach, as embodied in the *Second Restatement*,[28] seeks to connect a given issue with the legal system with which it has the most significant relationship. As such it remains at least tenuously true to the traditional idea that an issue should be localized in some way in a particular jurisdiction whose law will be applicable. Leflar, by contrast, does not seek such a connection between issue and *lex causae*. His approach is result-led, his criteria being designed to secure the best result, not the application of the best connected law.

The second important difference between Reese and Leflar concerns where they stand on the dichotomy (so well illuminated by Neuhaus) between certainty and discretion, flexibility and constraint. The criteria suggested by Reese and embodied famously in the *Second Restatement* are relatively specific. Moreover, his approach assumes that the principled discretion which it provides offers a process whereby clear and fixed choice of law rules will eventually emerge. It is less a substitute for such rules than a means of creating them.[29] Leflar's theory is, by contrast, open-textured in the extreme. The generality of his criteria, their tendency to lead to conflicting results and the deference he would pay to the application of the best rule of law all encourage a high degree of uncertainty and discretion. Indeed, if Reese's may be characterized as the most orthodox of modern American conflict's theories, Leflar's is the most avant garde. The former, it might be said, cleaves to the notion that, however open-textured in formulation, a test may be posited whereby the connection between an issue and a given law may be established. The latter, by contrast, assumes that it is for a judge to answer the choice of law question; abjuring any objective relationship between an issue and its governing law, it entirely replaces the idea of a choice of law rule with that of an 'approach'.[30]

Although such writers define the issues at stake in the American conflicts debate, their work is far from being the end of the matter. Commentators have come to doubt many of their assumptions, especially the notion that courts are capable of weighing state interests and policies. Indeed, if writers such as Currie, Reese and Leflar represent the modernist school in American conflicts scholarship, that scholarship has now entered a post-modern phase. Of the many writings which represent the new orthodoxy, Brilmayer's assault on interest analysis (Chapter 14) is especially instructive.[31] It serves as a convincing critique of the idea that interest analysis actually reflects legislative intent, impugning any objectivity to which such theories lay claim. But it speaks to wider issues too. It reminds us how seldom legislators articulate the territorial scope of statutes, a fact which generally leaves to courts the onerous task of determining a statute's international scope. It suggests also how incoherent any theory becomes the more it tries to accommodate exceptional cases or to achieve flexibility. And, importantly, it prompts the thought that such certainty as is possible in the conflicts process may only be found in traditional, territorial connecting factors which link laws to events by reference to the parties' personal connections or to the locus of an act or event.

The Pragmatic Tradition in England

A feature of English conflicts scholarship – perhaps a signal of its distinctive pragmatism – is that rival accounts of the subject appear more often in textbooks than in periodicals. Differences of opinion between the editors of Dicey and Morris's *Conflict of Laws* and of Cheshire and North's *Private International Law* for many years represented the axis of debate on conflicts questions, albeit that their differences were more technical than doctrinal.[32] That such works have long dominated the subject does not mean that an influential journal literature does not exist. It tends, however, to be more concerned with technical matters than with the subject's nature and design. Amongst those articles which are exceptions to this predominantly black-letter approach, three are included here.[33] Each in different ways offers an English response to the American revolution in conflicts thinking. Each is essentially pragmatic because, although sometimes speculative, each is firmly rooted in the practice of the courts and in the requirements of sound adjudication.

In Chapters 17 and 18, Fawcett and Jaffey attempt in different ways to relate American approaches to the English experience, sharpening and narrowing the choice of law problem as perceived by English lawyers. Fawcett's analysis of choice of law in tort engages directly with the difficulty of transplanting it.[34] Rejecting interest analysis, he argues that rule-selecting approaches, in so far as they depend on a weighing of competing state policies, are inappropriate in resolving international conflicts in the English context. Jaffey offers a different ground for rejecting such approaches. He sees most domestic laws as protecting private interests (perhaps because the legal and the political are more sharply differentiated in England), thus only exceptionally expressing considerations of public policy. As such, justice to the parties is for Jaffey a more appropriate aspiration for the conflicts process than is the implementation of state interests.

A third example of the English approach, Morris's influential essay entitled 'The Proper Law of a Tort' (Chapter 16), is interesting for its resemblance to the approach of the *Second Restatement*. The author famously advocates extending to tortious conflicts the existing English approach for ascertaining a contract's governing law. He provides no particular formulation for this 'proper law' approach and may have meant merely that there should be flexibility in deciding such cases – that no single rule is capable of applying soundly in every case. It is apparent, however, that Morris would have wished the applicable law to be, in general terms, that with which the issue has the most significant connection.[35]

Despite the apparent similarity between this approach and that of the *Second Restatement*, care must be exercised in making a comparison. Certainly, the gap between English and American conflicts thinking is at its narrowest when comparing Morris's position on tort with the *Restatement*. But if the former is decidedly open-ended by English standards, just as the latter is relatively traditional in American terms, telling differences emerge between them. It is unclear, for example, how readily Morris would have endorsed the assessment of state policies and interests embodied in the *Restatement* approach. Certainly, although he assumed that the *Restatement* had adopted his own position, Morris appears to have seen it as primarily embodying a test for establishing a territorial connection between an issue and its governing law based on such traditional elements as the parties' connections and the place of the wrong.[36] It is unclear how far state interests and policies – features of the *Restatement* test – were accommodated in Morris's approach.

It is also revealing that Morris envisaged his approach as a solution to the distinct problems raised by choice of law in tort, not as a universal template in the fashion of the *Restatement*. Arrestingly, seeing it perhaps as no more than a useful solution to a specific difficulty, he never sought to expand it into anything like a general theory of the conflict of laws. He was, indeed, reluctant to employ it elsewhere, even in areas of the subject in which it might have seemed suitable.[37] Morris's proper law approach is also firmly rooted in his perception of its success in the area of contract conflicts. Far from being an *a priori* theory, his approach keeps faith with the common law principle of reasoning by analogy, thereby confirming its pragmatic credentials.

Conclusion

Although offering no more than a sample of an extensive literature, the present collection serves to plot the subject's parameters. In part, as the first section shows, these are technical in nature, concerning the subject's inherent logic, the issues which potentially arise whenever foreign elements touch private legal relations. But the metes and bounds of the subject are also doctrinal. As the selected essays illustrate, the literature represents a continuous debate between different visions of the conflicts process. Should connecting factors be objective or subjective? Should comity or the forum's interests take priority? Should choice of law rules be jurisdiction-selecting or rule-selecting? Should conflicts rules, whether concerned with choice of law or jurisdiction, generally be fixed and certain or discretionary and flexible?

Different writers, many of them not represented in this collection, will address such issues in different ways. So too, different jurisdictions – civil law as well as common law – will regard some as more pressing than others. There is, however, a universal quality about such matters which makes them, perhaps, the common currency of the conflict of laws.

Notes

1 Civil lawyers customarily distinguish private international law from international civil procedure, the latter comprising matters of evidence and jurisdiction: see, for example, Ulmer (1970),

Intellectual Property Rights and the Conflict of Laws, 14. For present purposes the conflict of laws is taken in its widest sense to encompass all international aspects of private legal relations.
2 North *supra*, Chapter 5, 188.
3 European Commission (1995), *Green Paper on Copyright and Related Rights in the Information Society*, 38–44.
4 Ibid.
5 Fawcett (1993), *Products Liability in Private International Law: a European Perspective*.
6 In English law such works as Dicey and Morris's *The Conflict of Laws* (12th ed., 1994) and Cheshire and North's *Private International Law* (12th ed., 1992) have been singularly influential. See, in the American context, works such as von Mehren and Trautman (1965), *The Law of Multistate Problems* and (for a comparative approach) Ehrenzweig and Jayme (1967–77), *Private International Law*, Vols I–III.
7 See, for example, in the English context, the influential pieces by Lawrence Collins, collected in his (1994), *Essays in International Litigation and the Conflict of Laws*.
8 For the nature of the continuing debate in America, see (1985), 'Symposium on Interest Analysis in the Conflict of Laws', *Ohio St. L.J.*, **46**; (1991), 'New Directions in Choice of Law: Alternatives to Interest Analysis', *Cornell Intl. L.J.*, **24**. See also, von Mehren (1975), *Cornell L. Rev.*, **60**, 927; Juenger (1985), *Hague Recueil*, **IV**, 123.
9 Briggs (1989), *Oxford Journal of Legal Studies*, **9**, 251.
10 For a contemporary account of the international jurisdiction of US courts see, Born and Westin (2nd ed., 1993), *International Civil Litigation in United States Courts*.
11 This problem is exemplified in different approaches to choice of law in tort: see Reese, *Vand. L. Rev.*, **33**, 717; Fentiman (1995), *Memorandum of Evidence*, Proceedings of the Special Public Bill Committee on the Private International Law (Miscellaneous Provisions) Bill, HL Paper 36.
12 An extended version appears in North (1993), *Essays in Private International Law*, Ch. 7.
13 See further, Beckett (1934), *B.Y.B.I.L.*, 46; Robertson (1940), *Characterisation in the Conflict of Laws*.
14 Cheshire and North, *Private International Law*, op.cit., Ch. 5; *Restatement, Second, Conflict of Laws*, Ch. 1, section 8.
15 See also Kahn-Freund (1953), 39 *Grotious Society*, 39.
16 See also Fentiman (1993), *L.Q.R.*, **108**, 142.
17 The 1968 Brussels Convention on Jurisdiction and the Enforcement of Judgments regulates enforcement within European Union states. For treatments of this topic see Collins (1983), *The Civil Jurisdiction and Judgments Act 1982*; Hartley (1984), *Civil Jurisdiction and Judgments*.
18 Cheshire and North, op.cit., 39.
19 See, for example, the comprehensive survey of the relevant theories in Law Commission Working Paper No. 87, 'Choice of Law in Tort' (1984).
20 For a masterly account of the American tradition see Juenger, op.cit., Ch. III.
21 Dicey (2nd ed., 1914), *Law and Opinion in England*, 365.
22 Juenger, op.cit., 208–9.
23 See generally, Summers (1982), *Instrumentalism and American Legal Theory*.
24 Dicey and Morris, op.cit.
25 See especially von Mehren and Trautman, op.cit. (advocating a 'functional approach'); Ehrenzweig and Jayme, op.cit. (advocating a consideration of the forum's interests as the dominant test). See also Walter Wheeler Cook (1942), *Logical and Legal Bases of the Conflict of Laws*. A powerful critic of the first Restatement, his 'local law theory' has not endured.
26 An important variant on interest analysis is Baxter's 'comparative impairment' approach: see (1963), *Stan. L.R.*, **16**, 1.
27 The approach of Cavers, especially in his later work, differs from Currie's in supplying 'principles of preference' for resolving 'true conflicts': (1965), *The Choice of Law Process*; (1970), *Hague Recueil*, **III**, 75; (1985), *The Choice of Law, Selected Essays*. On interest analysis generally, see Shapira (1970), *The Interest Approach to Choice of Law*.
28 This position originated in Cheatham and Reese (1952), *Col. L.R.*, **52**, 959.
29 Reese (1976), II *Hague Recueil*, **1**, 180.

30 Reese also saw the *Restatement* as embodying an approach, rather than rules, but he kept faith with the idea that rules might emerge: ibid., 44–65.

31 Other critiques include: Rosenberg (1967), *Columbia L. Rev.*, **67**, 459; von Mehren (1965), *Cornell L. Rev.*, **60**, 927; (1974), *Harvard L. Rev.*, **88**, 347; Juenger (1985), *Hague Recueil*, **IV**, 123, 227–52.

32 See, for example, the debate over choice of law in marriage described in Cheshire and North, op.cit., 586–90.

33 Another prominent example is North's 'Choice in Choice of Law', see n.12 supra; see also Graveson (1962), *L.Q.R.*, **78**, 337.

34 English law's traditional approach to choice of law in tort has subsequently undergone radical change, although the difference in the perspective of English and American writers, depicted by Fawcett, remains: Private International Law (Miscellaneous Provisions) Act 1995, Part III; *Red Sea Insurance Co. Ltd.* v. *Bouygues S.A.* [1995] 1 A.C. 190 (P.C.). The new law is not founded on interest analysis.

35 At 888.

36 Morris (4th ed., 1993), *The Conflict of Laws*, 280. For the present law see Private International Law (Miscellaneous Provisions) Act 1995, Part III.

37 Such as in connection with marriage; ibid., 152 et seq.

Part I
Central Issues in the Conflict of Laws

Jurisdiction

[1]

VOLUME 63 NUMBER 2 MARCH 1983

BOSTON UNIVERSITY LAW REVIEW

ADJUDICATORY JURISDICTION: GENERAL THEORIES COMPARED AND EVALUATED†

ARTHUR TAYLOR VON MEHREN*

TABLE OF CONTENTS

 This Article is based on a lecture, entitled "A General Theory of Adjudicatory Jurisdiction," delivered at Tel-Aviv University, Faculty of Law, on January 1, 1981. A revised version of that lecture appears in 6 TEL-AVIV STUDIES IN LAW 9 (1982), under the same title as this Article.

* Story Professor of Law, Harvard Law School. B.S., 1942, LL.B., 1945, Ph.D., 1946, Harvard University.

I. Introduction

Relations and transactions can have significant connections either with one politically organized society or with two or more such societies. Those falling within the first category are fully domestic in that they have no significant nondomestic aspect. For example, two persons who are nationals, domiciliaries, and habitual residents of State *A* enter into an agreement in that state whereby one agrees to convey Blackacre, located in State *A*, to the other in exchange for Greenacre, also located in State *A*, and the payment of an additional amount in the local currency of *A*. This transaction, viewed from a social, economic, or legal perspective, has significant connections with only one politically organized society. Accordingly, although difficulties and ambiguities may be encountered in applying State *A*'s law, that law should govern all disputes that may arise between the parties. Furthermore, State *A*'s adjudicatory institutions are appropriate for the ventilation of such disputes and any ensuing decision is legally effective within State *A*. The legal order of State *A* is properly concerned with all problems relating to the administration of justice in situations that are fully domestic to State *A*.

In the contemporary world, however, there are many relations and transactions that have significant connections with more than one politically organized society. If one party to the transaction just described were, for example, a national of State *B*, if Greenacre were located in State *B*, or if the contract were concluded there, the situation would no longer be fully domestic but would take on interstate or international aspects. The discipline of private international law is concerned with the resolution of various issues that arise with respect to transactions that have interstate or international characteristics. Basically, three distinct, though interrelated, problems are posed: (1) in what circumstances is it appropriate for a legal order's juridical institutions to adjudicate multistate or international controversies; (2) from what source or sources are the rules and principles that regulate such controversies to be derived; and (3) in what circumstances and to what extent should a legal order accord respect to adjudications of interstate or international controversies by the juridical institutions of a foreign legal order? These problems are addressed by the three branches of private international law: adjudicatory jurisdiction, choice of law, and recognition and enforcement of foreign judgments.

There are various and complex interrelations, some of which are mentioned in this Article, among these branches.[1] Furthermore, each faces, in

[1] For a discussion of the interrelations between (1) jurisdiction to adjudicate and choice of law and (2) jurisdiction to adjudicate and recognition practice, see A. von Mehren & D. Trautman, The Law of Multistate Problems 599-615, 836-40 (1965); see also von Mehren, *Recognition and Enforcement of Foreign Judgments—General Theory and the Role of Jurisdictional Requirements*, 167 Académie de droit international, Recueil des Cours 9, 39-41 (1980 II).

one guise or another, certain issues common to all: Is the attainment of justice inherently more difficult in relations or transactions that have significant connections with two or more legal orders? If so, what causes this difficulty? Finally, how closely can the measure of justice achieved in interstate or international cases approximate that realized in fully domestic cases, and through what methods and doctrines is this approximation to be pursued?[2]

This Article considers only adjudicatory jurisdiction in the interstate or international sense. The primary concern is to develop a general theory for evaluating the propriety of adjudicating in a given legal order a controversy involving other legal orders as well. (If the legal orders in question all belong to one federal system, the controversy is interstate; otherwise, it is international. The term "multistate" is used hereinafter to refer generically to interstate and international situations.) In this endeavor, the logical implications of the several premises upon which jurisdictional practices can rest are explored in order to explain the theoretical basis for various jurisdictional practices. At any given time, these practices may rest on more than one premise, and these premises may ultimately be incompatible. When such is the case, considerations of principle and consistency will, in the long run, usually lead the legal system to prefer one premise. Thus jurisdictional thinking and practice in the United States during the three decades between *International Shoe Co. v. Washington*[3] and *Shaffer v. Heitner*[4] relied alternatively on power and on convenience, fairness, and justice. Finally, however, the tension inherent in this double allegiance was found intolerable and the power premise was relegated to a subordinate position in American theory and practice.[5]

Most of the examples used in this Article are drawn from cases decided by state or federal courts in the United States, both because of the great richness and variety of the American experience with the subject and because of the author's familiarity with this body of material. However, the theoretical analysis proposed is intended to have general application and to illuminate any contemporary legal order's efforts to address the problem of adjudicatory jurisdiction in principled terms. Of course, if a legal order's institutions and practices are significantly different from those found in the United States, the problems and issues that stand in high relief may be different from those that have preoccupied American courts and jurists.

---

[2] For discussions of these problems with particular reference to choice of law, see von Mehren, *Choice of Law and the Problem of Justice*, 41 LAW & CONTEMP. PROBS. 27 (1977); von Mehren, *The Significance of the State for Choice of Law*, in FESTSCHRIFT FÜR KONRAD ZWEIGERT 287 (Bernstein, Drobnig & Kötz eds. 1981). These issues, as they relate to the recognition and enforcement of foreign judgments, are considered in von Mehren, *supra* note 1.

[3] 326 U.S. 310 (1945).

[4] 433 U.S. 186 (1977).

[5] *See infra* Part IV B.

These problems and issues should nonetheless yield, as do those encountered in American practice, to the analysis proposed in this Article.

One peculiarity of the American experience, as compared to that of most other legal orders, is the power of the Supreme Court to establish general canons of state-court jurisdiction under the due process clause.[6] Moreover, state-court judgments that rest on a proper jurisdictional basis are entitled to recognition and enforcement in sister states under the full faith and credit clause.[7] These constitutional controls affect jurisdictional practice in various ways. In the first place, ultimate authority over jurisdictional practice does not rest with each state; unlike practice in an international setting, state practice must respect a body of principle that applies to all the states that make up the federal polity. Furthermore, the linkage between the assumption of jurisdiction and the recognition and enforcement of the resulting judgment is more direct in sister-state practice than in international practice. These and other differences between an international and a federal context affect specific rules and results. But these differences do not require significant changes in general theory and analysis; the same analytical tools can be applied to international and interstate situations, although in some cases the results appropriate in an interstate context differ from those appropriate in a comparable international setting.

II. Terminology; Three General Theories

Our topic is sometimes called "judicial jurisdiction."[8] However, the adjudicatory agency need not be a court. For example, in many legal orders divorce was formerly the province of the executive or the legislature. And today commissions typically adjudicate claims under workers' compensation statutes. Consequently, the term "adjudicatory jurisdiction"—which emphasizes the function rather than the agency—is to be preferred.[9]

The expression used in this Article—"adjudicatory jurisdiction"—is at

---

[6] U.S. Const. amend. XIV, § 1. Similarly, general canons of federal-court jurisdiction must comport with the due process clause of the fifth amendment. *Id.* amend. V; *cf.* Texas Trading & Milling Corp. v. Nigeria, 647 F.2d 300, 315-16 n.37 (2d Cir. 1981) (adopting fourteenth amendment due process analysis in a fifth amendment due process case).

[7] U.S. Const. art. IV, § 1.

[8] *See, e.g.*, 1 Restatement (Second) of Conflict of Laws, ch. 3. (1969) (entitled "Judicial Jurisdiction").

[9] *Cf.* Restatement of the Foreign Relations Law of the United States (Revised) § 441 (Tent. Draft No.2, 1981) (using the term "jurisdiction to adjudicate"). Another synonym for "adjudicatory jurisdiction" is "territorial jurisdiction." *See* 1 Restatement (Second) of Judgments § 4 (1982). This usage is defective in at least two respects: the term does not suggest the function in question, and it can cover problems, such as the source of the governing law, that are distinct from jurisdiction to adjudicate.

times applied to two problems that can arise when a State has adjudicatory jurisdiction in the international or interstate sense. The first is that of subject-matter jurisdiction: Is a matter properly handled by the civil or the administrative courts in systems that provide both; by the regular courts or specialized tribunals, such as probate or labor courts, where these exist? The second problem is venue—the territorial allocation of judicial business within subdivisions, such as districts or counties, of a single legal order. In this Article, however, the term "adjudicatory jurisdiction" is used exclusively in an international or interstate sense; it describes the willingness of a given politically organized society to furnish the law-applying agency—usually, but not necessarily, a court—for the adjudication of a matter involving significant elements that are not domestic to that society.

Historically, the exercise of adjudicatory jurisdiction has been justified in terms of at least three general theories. Jurisdiction—literally the capacity of law (or right) saying—can be viewed as resting on the relationship of lord (or king) and tenant (or subject), on physical power, or on considerations of convenience, fairness, and justice.

In the feudal systems of medieval Europe, the administration of justice was viewed as a function of a personal bond between the lord and his tenant. The lord had a personal and inescapable duty to render justice to the tenant. This duty could be delegated, but the delegate's authority to adjudicate derived from the personal bond between tenant and lord. As kings grew strong, concepts of society and politics changed. But the notion of the king as the fountain of justice still rested, to some extent, on a personal relation between subject and king.

With the rise of the sovereign State another explanation of adjudicatory authority became widely accepted. A personal bond or relation between subject and ruler—or party and State—was no longer central. Instead, as Justice Holmes put it in a famous aphorism: "The foundation of jurisdiction is physical power . . . ."[10]

In much contemporary thinking, the propriety of adjudication rests neither on a personal or political relationship between parties and a legal order, nor on a legal order's sheer physical power over the parties. Instead, the exercise of adjudicatory authority is explained and justified primarily by considerations of convenience, fairness, and justice. For the most part, contemporary analysis assesses the propriety of a legal order's assertion of adjudicatory jurisdiction by reference to two sets of considerations—the parties' relation to the forum community independent of the underlying controversy, and the underlying controversy's litigational relation to the forum community. In some special situations, the controversy's substantive relation to that community—that is, the forum's interest in applying its law to the controversy—may have decisive importance.[11]

---

[10] McDonald v. Mabee, 243 U.S. 90, 91 (1917).

[11] Considerations of the governing law assume special importance when the

The general theory used to approach the topic of adjudicatory jurisdiction profoundly influences not only jurisdictional practices but also the concepts used to describe and analyze those practices. A general theory of adjudicatory jurisdiction based on power inevitably differs fundamentally from one based on a personal relation or on considerations of convenience, fairness, and justice.

This Article develops and compares general theories of adjudicatory jurisdiction based on power and on fairness. (The latter term as used hereinafter comprehends convenience, fairness, and justice.) A general theory based on relation or allegiance is also possible. However, exercises of jurisdiction on such bases are relatively rare in the contemporary world. The French practice of basing jurisdiction on the French nationality of either plaintiff or defendant can be seen as a contemporary expression of an allegiance theory.[12] But exercises of adjudicatory jurisdiction are today based, for the most part, either on power or on fairness. Typically, exercises of jurisdiction can be explained on either ground. Only the extreme or limiting case need raise, therefore, the issue of which theory is, in the final analysis, determinative.

Neither power theories nor fairness theories set limits to the exercise of jurisdiction through a purely logical analysis. A legal order may, in practice, decline to assert jurisdiction that can be justified theoretically. For example, a power theory could justify the assertion of jurisdiction when a legal order has no present hold over the defendant on the ground that, at some future time, it may acquire power over him or his property. Section 23 of the German Code of Civil Procedure,[13] which provides for jurisdiction where the defendant has property within the power of the court when the action is initiated without limiting a resulting judgment to the value of the property, is presumably to be explained along these lines.[14] Conversely, multistate situations in which only one legal order can exercise power over the defendant or his property are rare. Accordingly, the result of one legal order's exercise of jurisdiction can ordinarily be undone in whole or in part by other legal orders. Similarly, a legal order that bases jurisdiction on fairness could emphasize the *plaintiff's* convenience to the exclusion of other considerations and assert jurisdiction in every case.[15] In many such cases, however, the legal order may well not be able to enforce the resulting judgment; moreover, even when the judgment is enforceable, other legal orders can ordinarily undo what has been accomplished.

---

choice-of-law process either can not operate or may not operate properly. *See infra* Part V D.

[12] *See* CODE CIVIL [C. CIV.] arts. 14, 15 (France).

[13] ZIVILPROZESSORDNUNG § 23 (W. Ger.).

[14] *See* A. VON MEHREN & D. TRAUTMAN, *supra* note 1, at 673-74.

[15] *See, e.g.*, C. CIV. art. 14 (basing jurisdiction on the plaintiff's French nationality). *But cf. supra* note 12 and accompanying text (noting that art. 14 can be viewed as an expression of the relation theory of jurisdiction).

The analysis and solution of legal problems are subtly and importantly shaped by the premises and intellectual structure in terms of which the problems are perceived and addressed. In multistate situations, therefore, much can turn on the differences between the premises and intellectual structure and terminology appropriate for a general theory of adjudicatory jurisdiction based on power and those appropriate for a general theory based on fairness. What, then, are the paradigmatic characteristics of each of these conceptual systems?

III. The Premises and Structures of General Theories of Jurisdiction

A. *Power Theories*

In essence, a power theory justifies the exercise of jurisdiction if the legal order has, directly or indirectly, an effective hold over the defendant. The legal order always has a hold over the plaintiff because he has placed himself within its power; the decisive question, therefore, is whether there is power over the defendant. When the power is clear and complete, the claim to adjudicatory jurisdiction is strongest; when the power is contingent or incomplete, the jurisdictional claim is correspondingly problematical. In a jurisdictional calculus based entirely on power, nothing turns on the convenience of the parties or on the forum's concern, if any, for the parties or the underlying transaction.

It follows that, for a power theory, service upon the defendant while he is physically present within the state is a clear basis for adjudicatory jurisdiction. A defendant could be detained to await the outcome of the proceedings and forced to obey the resulting judgment. Thus it has been said of the common law that "[o]rdinarily jurisdiction over a person is based on the power of the sovereign asserting it to seize that person and imprison him to await the sovereign's pleasure."[16] In practice, because of the inconvenience and hardship involved, "we dispense with the necessity of maintaining the physical power, and attribute the same force to the judgment or decree whether the party remain within the jurisdiction or not. This is one of the decencies of civilization that no one would dispute."[17]

A sovereign's power over a temporarily absent resident is, in a sense, more contingent than the power over a physically present nonresident. But, in such cases, the high probability that the sovereign will be able to exercise power over the absent resident satisfies the requirements of a power theory.

The presence within the State's territory either of property belonging to the defendant or of the defendant's debtor likewise constitutes a hold over the defendant; this power is, of course, limited by the value of the property or the amount of the debt. If the property has a fixed location—land, for

[16] Michigan Trust Co. v. Ferry, 228 U.S. 346, 353 (1913) (Holmes, J.).
[17] *Id.*

example—and the judgment sought can be satisfied by proceeding against the property, a State's claim to jurisdiction under a power theory is of overwhelming strength. If the property's location is not fixed but the property is within the State—or if the defendant's debtor is there—when jurisdiction is to be established, the rationale of a power theory is satisfied—within the limits set by the value of the property or debt—in essentially the same way as when jurisdiction is based upon personal service on the defendant. If property ordinarily located in the State is temporarily absent, jurisdiction is available under a power theory by analogy to the rationale that supports jurisdiction over a temporarily absent resident defendant.

Power theories draw what is, from the perspective of the premises on which they are based, a natural distinction between jurisdiction over "persons" (jurisdiction *in personam*) and jurisdiction over "things" (jurisdiction *in rem* and *quasi in rem*). As long as jurisdictional thinking ultimately rests on power, jurisdictional rules can conveniently and accurately be ordered and presented in terms of these categories.

Power theories, in their pure form, have little room for the exercise of *specific* jurisdiction—that is, assertions of adjudicatory authority that are not all-embracing but are limited to controversies grounded in particular situations. Power theories utilize a form of specific jurisdiction to adjudicate ownership of property with respect to the entire world on the basis of the property's location (or "situs") within the state. Specific jurisdiction is also asserted—although its propriety is open to doubt when tested in terms of power alone—when a status such as marriage is reified and adjudicatory authority is claimed on the theory that the status is "present" within the forum community because, for example, the spouse who initiated the proceedings lives there.

Because a power theory justifies jurisdiction if power can be asserted either directly or indirectly over particular defendants, the form of jurisdiction typically established is *general;* that is, the adjudicatory authority extends, in principle, to any claim against the defendant. Two types of general jurisdiction can be claimed. *Unlimited* jurisdiction is asserted if the judgment will not be restricted to any specific property. If the judgment can affect only specified property, *limited* general jurisdiction is claimed. The logic of a power theory strongly supports the maintenance of this distinction. Jurisdiction *in personam*—that is, power over the defendant's person—logically entails a claim of unlimited general jurisdiction. The various forms of *in rem* jurisdiction, on the other hand, under which power exists only over property belonging to the defendant, logically find their limit in the particular property or fund.

A general theory of jurisdiction based on power has little place for considerations of litigational fairness and convenience. (The doctrine of forum non conveniens, under which many power theories take these considerations into account in egregious cases, represents a concession to considerations of fairness and convenience.[18]) Consequently, jurisdiction is sometimes exercised even though the exercise is plainly improper when tested in terms of convenience, fairness, and justice. Conversely, even if the exercise is justifiable in these terms, a State that remains faithful to a power theory will refuse to exercise jurisdiction when the State lacks power over the defendant.

B. *Fairness Theories*

The premises and intellectual structure of a jurisdictional theory based on fairness are very different from those appropriate for a power theory. Furthermore, because the concepts of jurisdiction *in personam, in rem,* and *quasi in rem* do not serve well, different terminology is needed.[19]

A jurisdictional theory resting on fairness does not focus on the object, human or otherwise, over which power is exercised. Accordingly, a fundamental objection to the power theory's equating of persons and things for jurisdictional purposes—that persons have rights and duties while things are the subjects of rights and duties—can no longer be overlooked.[20] The traditional terminology has no logical or psychological connection with a jurisdictional theory based on fairness. Indeed, use of the terminology supports intellectual biases—in particular, the central importance of power in jurisdictional thinking—that are inconsistent with a fairness theory. More importantly, traditional terminology sometimes obscures the policy issues that such a theory faces in connection with the assertion of adjudicatory jurisdiction.

Use of the terms "jurisdiction *in rem*" and "jurisdiction *quasi in rem*" suggests that the basis for asserting jurisdiction will be the same for every situation falling within these two categories. This suggestion is correct while a power theory holds sway; in a theory based on fairness, however, the reasons justifying the exercise of jurisdiction in situations that can be described as "*in rem*" typically differ profoundly from those that justify

---

[18] *See infra* note 25 and accompanying text.

[19] For an earlier discussion of the terminological question, see von Mehren & Trautman, *Jurisdiction to Adjudicate: A Suggested Analysis,* 79 HARV. L. REV. 1121, 1135-36, 1164-66 (1966).

[20] The second *Restatement of Conflicts* tries to overcome the difficulty by explaining the phrase "jurisdiction over a thing" as "a customary elliptical way of referring to jurisdiction over the interests of persons in a thing." 1 RESTATEMENT (SECOND) OF CONFLICT OF LAWS, Introductory Note to ch. 3, topic 2, tit. A, at 192 (1969).

The second *Restatement of Judgments* abandons the power theory of jurisdiction, but retains the traditional distinctions on the ground that "the terminology remains useful for descriptive purposes." 1 RESTATEMENT (SECOND) OF JUDGMENTS § 6 comment *a* (1980); *see id.* § 5 comment *b*. Presumably the *Restatement of Judgments* sought to carry forward, insofar as feasible, terminology used in the second *Restatement of Conflicts,* which was still significantly influenced by the power theory. *See infra* page 304.

jurisdiction when the situation can be described as "*quasi in rem.*" For example, the exercise of jurisdiction when property is located in the State and rights in that property are in issue—as in an action to partition land or to quiet title—is justified by the importance of clear titles for commerce, a reason not available when the effort is to apply property to satisfy in whole or in part a claim unrelated to any direct interest in the property.

A theory of jurisdiction based on fairness is better and more appropriately served by terminology that distinguishes between general jurisdiction—that is, assertion of general power to adjudicate any kind of controversy—and specific jurisdiction—the power to adjudicate with respect to claims grounded in the particular situation. These terms can, of course, be used to describe assertions of jurisdiction based on a power theory;[21] in this sense, the terminology is doctrinally neutral. However, it is clearly more congenial to fairness than to power theories.

Fairness theories, unlike power theories, must explicitly weigh the various considerations—including power—that can rationally influence a legal order's decision whether to assert adjudicatory jurisdiction over controversies involving nondomestic elements.[22] Several aspects of the situation can have relevance in this connection.

In the first place, close or strong ties between the litigants and the forum, existing independently of the underlying controversy, may establish the fairness of an assertion of jurisdiction. The kind and intensity of the ties between the parties and forum vary greatly. Perhaps the closest and strongest ties are those of the habitually resident citizen; far less significant for general jurisdictional purposes are such connections as temporary presence, activity, or the ownership of property. To the extent that one party can be said to belong to the forum community, various reasons support the taking of jurisdiction to adjudicate. One that is always present is the community's interest in providing its members with an orderly process for the resolution of disputes. A separate range of considerations, also related to the ties between the forum and the litigants, involves questions of convenience, impartiality, and expense. If one party is a member of the community and the other is not, these considerations are often Janus-faced, looking both toward and away from the taking of jurisdiction. Is the forum, either typically or in the particular case, reasonably convenient for one or both parties? Will one or both parties be put to unusual expense—for example, because of the high cost of transportation—if litigation proceeds in the forum? Does the foreignness of one party raise a substantial issue of possible prejudice?

---

[21] *See supra* page 286.

[22] In deciding whether to exercise jurisdiction, a fairness approach may, on occasion, properly consider the ability to enforce a judgment locally. Indeed, when the forum or forums that would normally be considered appropriate are closed to the plaintiff, the possibility of local enforcement may be decisive for the assumption of jurisdiction. *Cf.* Fragistas, *La Compétence internationale en droit privé,* 104 ACADÉMIE DE DROIT INTERNATIONAL, RECUEIL DES COURS 159, 173 (1961 III).

A second group of relevant considerations relates to litigational concerns that involve the underlying controversy. Even if the parties are closely connected with the forum community, evidence not within the parties' immediate control may be difficult and expensive to produce if the relevant conduct occurred, or its consequences were felt, abroad. In such situations the cost of litigation increases, with a resulting burden on the parties and severe inconvenience to witnesses asked to travel long distances. Difficulties flowing from litigational considerations related to the underlying controversy are often hard to evaluate when litigation is initiated. Even in classes of cases, such as personal injury actions, in which nonparty testimony is ordinarily important, both the complexity of the factual issues and the number of essential witnesses can vary considerably.

The third group of relevant considerations is the substantive relation of the underlying controversy to the forum: Is the forum vitally interested in ensuring that its domestic rules or, at least, its choice-of-law rules are applied? To the extent that the forum is prepared to assume that the choice-of-law process operates satisfactorily, this factor is marginal except perhaps when a true conflict—a situation in which the legitimate concerns of interested legal orders can not be accommodated in a fashion considered appropriate by all these legal orders—is involved. The difficulties, uncertainties, and burdens of applying a rule other than the forum's ordinary domestic rule can conduce in slight measure to a refusal of jurisdiction to adjudicate; on the other hand, trade and other activities having important nondomestic aspects can be assisted by the assumption of jurisdiction and the consequent development of a fully articulated body of rule and principle by reference to which conduct can be oriented and regulated. To the extent that there are fears that the choice of law will not be satisfactory, in particular when true conflicts are likely, the substantive relation of the underlying transaction to the forum becomes increasingly significant for the jurisdictional problem.[23] When the relation is such that the forum's substantive policies call for vindication, the assumption of jurisdiction may be proper in spite of countervailing considerations;[24] otherwise, a reason, which may not be decisive because of countervailing considerations, is provided for refusing jurisdiction on forum non conveniens grounds.

These three sets of considerations—the parties' relation to the forum community independent of the underlying controversy, the underlying con-

---

[23] It might be thought that the probability of a true conflict would weigh in favor of the assertion of jurisdiction by an interested forum regardless of whether that forum perceives the choice-of-law process as operating satisfactorily or unsatisfactorily. In either situation, the forum's policies can be vindicated, in the particular case, only by taking jurisdiction. But, when the choice-of-law process is considered satisfactory, the forum's interest in having its law applied to a particular controversy may be outweighed by its interest in promoting cooperative resolution of multistate controversies generally.

[24] *See infra* Part V D.

troversy's litigational relation to the forum community, and the controversy's substantive relation to the forum—furnish the basic analytical framework within which a legal order using a fairness theory will determine the propriety of asserting adjudicatory jurisdiction.

Approaching jurisdictional issues in power terms results, as has already been pointed out, in general jurisdiction being the form of jurisdiction normally claimed. Fairness theories are, in contrast, very receptive to assertions of specific jurisdiction. Jurisdiction justified by the controversy's litigational or substantive relationship to the forum is specific rather than general jurisdiction. On the other hand, jurisdiction justified by the parties' relation to the forum community independent of the underlying controversy is general jurisdiction.

IV. Pervasive Problems and Major Issues

The basic features of these two general theories of jurisdiction having been discussed, a more detailed consideration of some aspects of thinking and practice under the aegis of each can be undertaken. The discussion that follows explores the major issues that power theories generate, traces the transition from a power theory to a fairness theory in the United States, and then raises issues posed by fairness theories that do not arise under power theories. The effort is to explain why the theories focus on quite different problems and reach, in the limiting cases, significantly different results.

A. *In Power Theories*

As has already been remarked, a basic characteristic of a power theory is that it has little or no place for general considerations of fairness. This is not to say, of course, that assertions of jurisdiction justified by a power theory are typically unfair. However, fairness as such does not enter into the jurisdictional equation; it is, at best, taken into account at a second stage through the doctrine of forum non conveniens.[25] Thus, in the common law,

---

[25] For discussions of this doctrine, see A. Anton, Private International Law 148-54 (1967); G. Chesire & P. North, Private International Law 119-22 (P. North 10th ed. 1979); F. James & G. Hazard, Civil Procedure 657-60 (2d ed. 1977); E. Sykes & M. Pryles, Australian Private International Law 60-62 (1979); R. Weintraub, Commentary on the Conflict of Laws 205-12 (2d ed. 1980); Comment, *Forum Non Conveniens and American Plaintiffs in the Federal Courts*, 47 U. Chi. L. Rev. 373 (1981).

It seems that no comparable doctrine is known on the continent of Europe. *See* Schima, *La giurisdizione e lo straniero: Considerazioni comparative e tendenze evolutive*, 2 Revista di diritto internazionale privato e processuale 681, 684 (1966); Braucher, *The Inconvenient Federal Forum*, 60 Harv. L. Rev. 908, 909 (1947). *But see* J. Schröder, Internationales Zuständigkeit 486-504 (1971); *id.* at 491 ("The dismissal where jurisdiction is inappropriate is not, despite what is said, unusual [in continental European] . . . judicial practice."). Originally, the Supreme

service of process on a defendant casually present establishes jurisdiction; fairness and convenience are irrelevant except, of course, for the plaintiff's judgment that instituting the action serves his purposes.

In *Peabody v. Hamilton,*[26] the plaintiffs were English citizens who resided in London; the defendant was a citizen of the United States living in New York who owned no property in Massachusetts. An action was brought in the Massachusetts courts for breach of a contract that had no connection with Massachusetts. The defendant, a passenger on an English steamer, which he had boarded in Halifax, Nova Scotia, on a voyage to New York, was served with process while the steamer was docked in East Boston. The defendant sought to quash the service on the ground that "the circumstances set forth are not sufficient to give jurisdiction" to the court.[27] The Supreme Judicial Court, reasoning in power terms, gave the objection short shrift. "When the party is in the state, however transiently, and the summons is actually served upon him there, the jurisdiction of the court is complete, as to the person of the defendant."[28] One can imagine circumstances—for example, when the defendant's domicile or residence would not entertain the action—in which considerations of fairness would justify Massachusetts's assumption of jurisdiction in *Peabody*. However, the court's rationale for assuming jurisdiction clearly rested on considerations of power alone.

A modern version of the *Peabody* case is *Grace v. MacArthur.*[29] Jurisdiction was based on service made aboard a "non-stop flight from Memphis, Tenn. to Dallas, Texas," when the "airplane was in the Eastern District of Arkansas and directly above Pine Bluff, Arkansas . . . ."[30] The argument that the court lacked jurisdiction because the defendant had "not been properly served with process in this action *within the State of Arkansas*"[31] was rejected. To the extent that the court looked behind the ritual of service

---

Court of the United States also took the view that a court had no discretionary power to refuse to exercise jurisdiction. *See* Cohens v. Virginia, 19 U.S. (6 Wheat.) 264 (1821) (Marshall, C.J., dictum).

Special problems, not considered in this Article, arise when forms of equitable relief—for example, specific performance where supervision abroad may be involved or foreign land is affected—are sought in multistate situations. In such cases, the issue posed for the court is analogous to that in forum non conveniens cases; however, public interest factors—the burden on the forum and comity problems—are decisive and private interest factors—the litigational burden on the defendant, for example—are not in the forefront as they are in forum non conveniens cases.

[26] 106 Mass. 217 (1870).

[27] *Id.* at 218.

[28] *Id.* at 220.

[29] 170 F. Supp. 442 (E.D. Ark. 1959).

[30] *Id.* at 443.

[31] *Id.* (emphasis in original).

of process, it discussed the propriety of asserting jurisdiction in terms of power:

> It may be conceded, perhaps, that a time may come, and may not be far distant, when commercial aircraft will fly at altitudes so high that it would be unrealistic to consider them as being within the territorial limits of the United States or of any particular State while flying at such altitudes.[32]

A power theory logically supports not only personal jurisdiction but also various forms of *in rem* jurisdiction. Again, the analysis does not address considerations of fairness. The insensitivity to the unfairness to the defendant when power is the jurisdictional touchstone is perhaps most acute when a form of so-called *quasi in rem* jurisdiction is employed. The logic of a power theory establishes limited general jurisdiction over a defendant wherever he can sue his debtors. Thus, if the debtor lives in one state and travels through several others, the defendant is potentially subject to the jurisdiction of each of these states.

The logic and practice of this form of jurisdiction are exemplified by the well-known decision of the Supreme Court of the United States in *Harris v. Balk.*[33] Harris and Balk were both residents of North Carolina. In 1896, Balk loaned Harris $180. From an entirely unrelated transaction, Balk was indebted to Epstein, a resident of Maryland, in the sum of over $300. In the late summer of 1896, Harris went to Maryland on business. Epstein served Harris in Maryland and obtained "a foreign or non-resident writ of attachment against Balk, attaching the debt due Balk from Harris."[34] The purpose of the attachment was to apply the $180 that Harris owed Balk in partial satisfaction of the larger amount that Epstein claimed Balk owed him.

In the proceedings in Maryland, in which Balk did not appear, Harris admitted his indebtedness to Balk. Judgment was entered against Harris as garnishee for $180, the amount he owed Balk. Pursuant to the judgment, Harris paid $180 to Epstein. Thereafter, Balk brought an action against Harris in North Carolina to compel payment of the $180 that he had loaned

---

[32] *Id.* at 447.

The result reached in *Grace* is problematical under a strict power analysis because the forum had no present hold over the defendant. Accordingly, unless the possibility of power at some future date is to be considered sufficient, Arkansas lacked jurisdiction under a power theory. The difficulty is concealed because the Arkansas judgment would be entitled to full faith and credit within the United States if Arkansas had jurisdiction. It is doubtful, however, that the mere possibility that a legal order may establish, at a later date, power over the defendant or his property is sufficient to give its judgment the benefit of the full faith and credit clause. *See* Pennoyer v. Neff, 95 U.S. 714 (1878). In the final analysis, therefore, *Grace* may illustrate how personal service, originally an expression of power and a condition for its exercise, had declined by the 1950's into an arbitrary ritual.

[33] 198 U.S. 215 (1905).

[34] *Id.* at 216.

Harris. Harris pleaded in bar the Maryland judgment, asserting that North Carolina was required to recognize it under the full faith and credit clause. Judgment for Balk was affirmed by the Supreme Court of North Carolina on the ground "that the Maryland court obtained no jurisdiction to attach or garnish the debt due from Harris to Balk, because Harris was but temporarily in the State, and the *situs* of the debt was in North Carolina."[35]

Harris thereupon brought the North Carolina judgment to the Supreme Court. Under well-established constitutional doctrine, if Maryland had properly asserted jurisdiction over the debt Harris owed Balk (and thus indirectly over Balk), the resulting judgment in Epstein's favor was entitled to full faith and credit, with the consequence that Harris's obligation to Balk was extinguished. Accordingly, the Supreme Court squarely faced the issue of whether Maryland had jurisdiction to adjudicate Epstein's claim against Balk.

The Court viewed the problem in terms of the power theory:

> [I]f the garnishee [Harris] be found in that State, and process be personally served upon him therein, we think the court thereby acquires jurisdiction over him, and can garnish the debt due from him to the debtor [Balk] of the plaintiff [Epstein] and condemn it, provided the garnishee could himself be sued by his creditor [Balk] in that State. We do not see how the question of jurisdiction *vel non* can properly be made to depend upon the so-called original *situs* of the debt, or upon the character of the stay of the garnishee, whether temporary or permanent, in the State where the attachment is issued. Power over the person of the garnishee confers jurisdiction on the courts of the State where the writ issues. . . . If, while temporarily there, his creditor might sue him there and recover the debt, then he is liable to process of garnishment, no matter where the *situs* of the debt was originally.[36]

An interesting variation of the type of power-based jurisdiction exemplified by *Harris v. Balk* was used in *Seider v. Roth*.[37] The plaintiffs, New York residents, were injured in an automobile accident in Vermont. The allegedly negligent driver of the other car, a Quebec resident, was insured under a policy issued in Quebec by an insurance company that was incorporated in Connecticut and did business in many jurisdictions, including New York. Jurisdiction was asserted by the New York courts on the basis of an attachment of the insurer's contractual obligation to defend and indemnify the driver. As the insurer did business in New York, the Quebec driver could have sued the company in New York to enforce this obligation; accordingly, the plaintiffs urged that they could attach the "debt" and apply the proceeds to satisfying their personal injury claims against the Quebec driver.

A majority of the Court of Appeals accepted the argument: "Jurisdiction is properly acquired by this attachment since the policy obligation is a debt

[35] *Id.* at 217.

[36] *Id.* at 222.

[37] 17 N.Y.2d 111, 216 N.E.2d 312 (1966).

owed to the defendant by the insurer, the latter being regarded as a resident of this State . . . ."[38] Three judges of the seven-judge court dissented. They, like the majority, reasoned in terms of power: because the insurer's promise to indemnify was contingent on an award of damages against the insured, "there was nothing in this State to which the levy could apply."[39]

In one respect, the exclusion of considerations of fairness from the power theory's jurisdictional equation is relaxed in situations of the kind represented by *Harris v. Balk.* A sovereign's power is rarely, if ever, complete; what one sovereign does, another may be able to undo in whole or in part. Had *Harris v. Balk* arisen in an international setting lacking the full-faith-and-credit compulsion available in the federal system of the United States, North Carolina could have compelled Harris to pay Balk even though another sovereign had already required payment by Harris to Epstein. The potential unfairness to garnishees, who have no responsibility for the dispute between the real parties in interest, has caused sovereigns to renounce the use of this type of jurisdiction when the garnishee would be exposed to a substantial risk of having to pay twice. For example, the Supreme Court of Arizona concluded that where "the [defendant's] services were all rendered in the Republic of Mexico for a [garnishee] corporation whose plant is entirely in that country, and . . . the debt was made and payable therein, the [garnishee] ought not to be compelled to pay such debt to an Arizona creditor when it is not only possible but probable it would have to pay it again."[40]

Power theories take fairness into account in other contexts in which persons not parties to the underlying dispute are directly affected. For example, courts have refused to base jurisdiction on the sovereign's power over persons controlling property belonging to another when the property is situated in another state; "in the absence of any fraud or connivance on the part of the garnishee to aid the debtor in defrauding his creditors, personal property or real estate which is lawfully in the possession or under the control of the garnishee outside of this state is not the subject of garnishment . . . ."[41] Likewise, a common carrier is usually not required to stop and hold

---

[38] *Id.* at 114, 216 N.E.2d at 315.

[39] *Id.* at 115, 216 N.E.2d at 315.

[40] Weitzel v. Weitzel (Southern Pac. R.R. of Mexico, garnishee), 29 Ariz. 117, 125, 230 P. 1106, 1108 (1924); *see also* Parker, Peebles & Knox, Inc. v. National Fire Ins. Co., 111 Conn. 383, 150 A. 313 (1930) (unlikelihood of Haiti's recognizing Connecticut judgment led to court's refusal to order garnishee to pay insurance proceeds to plaintiff); RESTATEMENT (SECOND) OF THE FOREIGN RELATIONS LAW OF THE UNITED STATES § 40 (1962) (requiring moderation in the exercise of enforcement jurisdiction in light of the hardship imposed by inconsistent enforcement actions).

[41] Bates v. Chicago, Milwaukee & St. Paul Ry., garnishee, 60 Wis. 296, 302, 19 N.W. 72, 75 (1884). The court further remarked: "It is unnecessary to intimate the

in the state property in transit when it is sought to establish limited general jurisdiction over the property's owner.[42]

> The nature of the possession and control which the railroad company has of and over personal property in actual transit, the interruption of business, and the general inconvenience which must necessarily result from holding such property the subject of the garnishee process . . . are amply sufficient to justify us in making such property an exception to the general rule, in the absence of any positive declaration of the legislature subjecting such property to the process . . . .[43]

If one of the characteristics of power theories is that when jurisdiction is fully justified in power terms it will—subject to very rare exceptions—not be relinquished because of considerations of fairness, the converse is also true; when jurisdiction is problematic in power terms, considerations of fairness will not remove the difficulty. This characteristic of power theories can be seen by comparing *Harris v. Balk* with *Seider v. Roth*. The contingent nature of the insurance company's obligation makes *Seider* jurisdiction much more problematical for a power theory than *Harris* jurisdiction. Indeed, the latter was widespread in the United States while the former was exceptional. Yet, viewed in terms not of power but of fairness, *Seider* jurisdiction seems clearly the more acceptable.[44] An insurance company is better able than an ordinary garnishee to bear the burden of litigating in the forum selected by the plaintiff; the principal debtor's position vis-à-vis the plaintiff is much less prejudiced since, even if the plaintiff could not prevail in another forum, the insured is not out of pocket; and, finally, the garnishee runs no risk of having to pay twice as any payments under the policy redound to the insured's

---

difficulties and hardships which would result from the enforcement of a rule against garnishees compelling them to deliver up to the processes of the courts of this state any property they may have under their control, belonging to the principal debtor, situated in another state." *Id.* at 304, 19 N.W. at 76. *But cf.* United States v. First Nat'l City Bank, 379 U.S. 378 (1965) (district court has jurisdiction to grant, in aid of the enforcement of internal revenue laws, a temporary injunction "freezing" a foreign corporation's account in respondent bank's foreign branch pending establishment of jurisdiction over the corporation).

[42] *See, e.g.*, Bates v. Chicago, Milwaukee & St. Paul Ry., garnishee, 60 Wis. 296, 305-10, 19 N.W. 72, 76-78 (1884).

[43] *Id.* at 306, 19 N.W. at 77; *see* Annot., 46 A.L.R. 933 (1927). An early Massachusetts case, Adams v. Scott, 104 Mass. 164 (1870), reached the opposite result: "There is no reason why a common carrier should not be liable to the trustee process, in the same manner as other bailees are . . . ." *Id.* at 165.

[44] This is not to say, of course, that either type of jurisdiction should be acceptable to a fairness theory. Indeed, the Supreme Court has since held both *Harris* and *Seider* jurisdiction unconstitutional. *See* Rush v. Savchuk, 444 U.S. 320 (1980), *discussed infra* note 83; Shaffer v. Heitner, 433 U.S. 186 (1977), *discussed infra* text accompanying notes 71-80.

benefit and reduce the insurer's obligations under the policy. (The insured can, however, sometimes be adversely affected—for example, under collateral estoppel principles or by exhaustion of the policy if there are other claimants—by an action brought by the third party against the insurance company.)

A more dramatic example of the unwillingness of power theories to use considerations of fairness as a basis for asserting jurisdiction is furnished by the decision of the Supreme Court in *New York Life Insurance Co. v. Dunlevy.*[45] In 1907, Boggs & Buhl recovered a valid judgment in the Pennsylvania courts against Mrs. Dunlevy, at the time a resident of Pennsylvania. In 1909, some $2,500 became due under a life insurance policy that New York Life, an insurance company doing business in Pennsylvania, had issued to Gould, a resident of Pennsylvania. Boggs & Buhl, asserting that Gould had assigned the policy in 1893 to his daughter, Mrs. Dunlevy, sought to enforce their 1907 judgment against her out of the proceeds that were due. Gould, protesting that no assignment had been made, also claimed the proceeds. New York Life, faced by two claims to the same fund, asked the Pennsylvania court to decide which claimant was entitled to the proceeds. The court took jurisdiction. Dunlevy, who was by now a California resident, was notified of the proceedings but did not enter an appearance. The issue of whether Gould had assigned the policy to his daughter was litigated and judgment was given for Gould. New York Life thereupon paid Gould the proceeds of the policy.

Subsequently, Dunlevy sued New York Life in California to recover the proceeds of the policy. The insurance company urged that Dunlevy was bound by the judicial proceedings in Pennsylvania which had adjudged the policy to be Gould's property. Judgment for Dunlevy was affirmed by the Supreme Court. It was recognized that the Pennsylvania courts could, if New York Life's indebtedness to Dunlevy were not controverted, compel her debtor to pay to Boggs & Buhl their claim against her. But the logic of the power theory led the Court to conclude without hesitation that, since the Pennsylvania courts found that New York Life was not her debtor, she had neither a debtor nor property in Pennsylvania. It followed that, as—in the view of the Pennsylvania courts—neither a debtor of hers nor property belonging to her was present in Pennsylvania, that state could not claim personal, *quasi in rem,* or *in rem* jurisdiction with respect to her or her property.

A strict power theory thus finds no room for the argument that justice requires that at least one forum have jurisdiction to adjudicate conflicting claims in cases where otherwise the debtor, through no fault of his own, will be exposed to the risk of having to pay twice. The forums that could reasonably come into question on the facts of the *Dunlevy* case are Pennsylvania, California, and the state in which the insurance company was incor-

---

[45] 241 U.S. 518 (1916).

porated or had its head office. Among these, litigational fairness and overall convenience probably favor Pennsylvania. Accordingly, there is a strong argument in terms of convenience and fairness in favor of Pennsylvania jurisdiction to determine which claimant was entitled to the proceeds of the insurance policy.[46]

The results and reasoning in *Harris v. Balk* and *Dunlevy* call attention to what might be called the metaphysical side of power theories. The idea of power and such concepts as "presence" are usually reasonably manageable in both practical and theoretical terms when natural persons and tangible objects are in question. Difficulties arise, however, when these notions are applied to legal persons or to intangibles. Where are legal persons and intangibles present? In what sense can a sovereign have power over them? Similar problems arise when jurisdiction is to be exercised over complex relations involving two or more natural persons, for example, the marriage relation.

The metaphysical problem of whether intangibles have a situs was considered in *Harris v. Balk*. Balk argued that the situs of the debt Harris owed him was in North Carolina; accordingly, the Maryland court's hold over Harris due to his temporary presence in that state did not give control over Balk's property. This argument was rejected on the ground that Balk could have sued Harris in Maryland for payment; "[t]he obligation of the debtor to pay his debt clings to and accompanies him wherever he goes."[47] It follows, as the second *Restatement of Conflicts* notes, that "[i]ntangible things that are not embodied in a document, such as simple contract and tort claims, have no location in space."[48]

The proposition that intangibles do not have a situs also explains the result in *Dunlevy*. If the insurance company's obligation had a location in space—a situs—then a power theory could take the view, by analogy to tangible property, that the courts of the situs had jurisdiction to decide to whom the property belonged. However, the company's obligation having no situs, a court with jurisdiction over the company can order it to pay one claimant but lacks power to extinguish the rights of another claimant because to do so the sovereign must have a hold either over that claimant or over his property. The first condition is not satisfied because the claimant neither lives nor is physically present in the territory. Nor can the second be met; the determination that, in the court's view, no obligation is owed to a given claimant necessarily means that the sovereign has no hold over him. All this is rather metaphysical and mysterious but either these propositions or their

[46] *Cf.* Atkinson v. Superior Court, 49 Cal. 2d 338, 316 P.2d 960 (1957) (upholding, on the basis of fairness reasoning, the assertion of state-court jurisdiction to adjudicate claims of resident plaintiffs against a resident defendant for certain royalty payments also claimed by a third party who, but for the need to protect the defendant against the probability of having to pay twice, would not be subject to jurisdiction).

[47] 198 U.S. at 222.

[48] 1 RESTATEMENT (SECOND) OF CONFLICT OF LAWS § 56 comment *a* (1969).

converse—for example, that an intangible has a location in space—are necessary if the jurisdictional problems that these situations pose are to be analyzed in terms of power over parties or things.

Another issue that has metaphysical overtones is the significance that a power theory should attach to the "embodiment" of an intangible in a document.

> A debt or mere right of action with nothing more is wholly incorporeal, with no evidence or representative which can give it habitation anywhere. As to such property, whether it seeks to tax or adjudicate, sovereign power must proceed in personam simply because there is nothing to take hold on for proceeding in rem or quasi in rem. Hence there can be no jurisdiction to adjudge ownership save as there is jurisdiction in personam over the persons who must be bound in order to settle that issue. . . . But, when debtor and creditor create such a corporeal thing as bearer bonds, they have created something upon which jurisdiction of any kind may act. They have made more than mere symbol. They have fabricated a matrix-like container for the property, wherein it is to be carried from place to place, jurisdiction to jurisdiction, at the will of the possessor.[49]

Another area in which the notional apparatus required by a power theory encounters metaphysical problems is that of jurisdiction over legal persons, particularly corporations. An initial issue is whether a corporation can be present outside its State of incorporation. At one time, courts answered this question in the negative because a corporation "can have no legal existence out of the boundaries of the sovereignty by which it is created."[50] As a consequence of this view, in the early decades of the nineteenth century in the United States a corporate defendant could ordinarily be sued only in its state of incorporation unless it had property in another state.[51] The resulting situation, however satisfactory from a purely doctrinal perspective, was unacceptable as a practical matter. Corporate defendants could hardly enjoy greater protection than natural persons with respect to the assumption of jurisdiction over them.

During the age in which power theories were dominant, the first efforts to find a solution utilized the idea of consent. Legislation was passed which, resting upon a state's power to exclude a foreign corporation from doing business within the state, required as a condition for the doing of business that the corporation submit to jurisdiction by consenting to being sued in the state's courts on causes of action arising from business done in the state.[52]

[49] First Trust Co. v. Matheson, 187 Minn. 468, 474, 246 N.W. 1, 3 (1932).

[50] Bank of Augusta v. Earle, 38 U.S. (13 Pet.) 519, 588 (1839) (Taney, C.J.).

[51] *See* G. Henderson, The Position of Foreign Corporations in American Constitutional Law 77 (1918).

[52] *Cf.* Warren Mfg. Co. v. Etna Ins. Co., 29 F. Cas. 294 (C.C.D. Conn. 1837) (No. 17,206) (Maryland default judgment against Connecticut corporation doing business there not entitled to full faith and credit because Maryland consent statute, enacted after the cause of action arose, not given retrospective effect).

Because personal service is of basic importance in power theory, the problem of where a legal person is present remained insistent. As a practical matter, a corporation clearly has

> existence, vitality, efficiency, beyond the jurisdiction of the sovereign which created it, provided it be voluntarily exercised. If it be said that all these acts are performed by its agents, as they may be in the case of a private individual, and that the corporation itself is not present, the answer is, that a corporation [unlike a natural person] acts nowhere, except by its officers and agents. It has no tangible existence, except through its officers. . . . Its existence anywhere and everywhere is but ideal.[53]

But such an illusory or theoretical presence did not suffice for a power theory; accordingly, another tack was taken, one that foreshadowed a jurisdictional theory based on fairness. It was asked whether "the service of process . . . is so unreasonable, so contrary to natural justice and the principles of natural law, that it ought not to be sanctioned."[54] The corporation "having voluntarily entered th[e] jurisdiction, and transacting business there; having invoked the comity and the protection of the laws of that sovereign for their own benefit, can[not] . . . complain that the contracts there made are enforced within that sovereignty and in accordance with its laws[.]"[55]

If analysis along these lines had been generally accepted in the latter half of the nineteenth century, a jurisdictional theory based on fairness would have challenged the power theory, at least where corporate defendants were concerned, much earlier than in fact occurred. However, instead of working out a competing theory, jurists, faced with the proposition that a legal person's presence—even in its state of incorporation—is only "ideal," rendered the proposition manageable by equating "presence" with activity.

In the latter decades of the nineteenth century, therefore, American courts asserted jurisdiction over legal persons on the basis of either "consent" or "presence." Because of various complications and difficulties inherent in the consent approach, by the end of the second decade of the twentieth century, consent had for most practical purposes been supplanted by presence. Justice Brandeis formulated the proposition succinctly: "A foreign corporation is amenable to process to enforce a personal liability, in the absence of consent, only if it is doing business within the State in such manner and to such extent as to warrant the inference that it is present there."[56]

But difficulties remained for the power theory even after the metaphysical proposition that a legal person is present where activities are done on its

---

[53] Moulin v. Trenton Mut. Life & Fire Ins. Co., 25 N.J.L. 57, 60-61 (1885).

[54] *Id.* at 62.

[55] *Id.* at 62-63.

[56] Philadelphia & Reading Ry. v. McKibbin, 243 U.S. 264, 265 (1917).

behalf was accepted. Does any activity in the State constitute presence? Moreover, must the activities be going on when the litigation is initiated? In the final analysis, jurisdiction over legal persons was never fully or comfortably explained in strict power terms. When Justice Brandeis spoke of a legal person "doing business within the State in such manner and to such extent as to warrant the inference that it is present there," he raised considerations that cannot be analyzed or evaluated in terms of a general theory of jurisdiction based on power. It is understandable, therefore, that Chief Justice Stone's opinion in *International Shoe Co. v. Washington*[57]—the decisive step in the emergence in the United States of an alternative general theory of jurisdiction based on fairness—involved jurisdiction over legal rather than natural persons.

B. *The Passage from a Power Theory to a Fairness Theory*

The emergence in the United States of a jurisdictional theory based on fairness was due more to the constraints that the power theory imposed than to the excesses that it permitted. In order to allow assertions of jurisdiction when intuitively held standards of fairness required, the strict logic of power was, in the manner just described, first subtly undermined in the case of legal persons. By the second decade of this century symptoms of a somewhat comparable development with respect to adjudicatory jurisdiction over natural persons began to appear.

In *Hess v. Pawloski*[58] the Supreme Court considered whether Massachusetts could assert jurisdiction over a Pennsylvania resident who, while driving his car in Massachusetts, struck and injured the plaintiff. A state's claim to jurisdiction must comport with the standards of the due process clause. The due-process test traditionally applied to assertions of jurisdiction was whether the claim could be squared with a power theory. The Massachusetts jurisdictional statute invoked in *Hess* understandably sought, therefore, to fit the situation within the logic of a power theory. The statute provided that:

> The acceptance by a nonresident of the rights and privileges conferred by section three or four, as evidenced by his operating a motor vehicle thereunder . . . shall be deemed equivalent to an appointment by such nonresident of the registrar or his successor in office, to be his true and lawful attorney upon whom may be served all lawful processes in any action or proceeding against him, growing out of any accident or collision in which said nonresident may be involved while operating a motor vehicle on [a public] way, and said acceptance or operation shall be a signification of his agreement that any such process against him which is so served shall be of the same legal force and validity as if served on him personally.[59]

---

[57] 326 U.S. 310 (1945).

[58] 274 U.S. 352 (1927).

[59] *Id.* at 354.

In effect, Massachusetts sought to apply to natural persons a version of the consent-based-on-activity theory that had been developed to justify assertions of adjudicatory jurisdiction over legal persons. However, as Justice Butler pointed out in his opinion for a unanimous Court,

> [a] personal judgment rendered against a nonresident, who has neither been served with process nor appeared in the suit, is without validity. . . . The mere transaction of business in a state by nonresident natural persons does not imply consent to be bound by the process of its courts. . . . The power of a State to exclude foreign corporations, although not absolute, but qualified, is the ground on which such an implication is supported as to them. . . . But a State may not [in view of the privileges and immunities clause of the Constitution] withhold from nonresident individuals the right of doing business therein.[60]

His opinion then entered into a discussion that was, under the strict logic of a power theory, irrelevant:

> Motor vehicles are dangerous machines, and, even when skillfully and carefully operated, their use is attended by serious dangers to persons and property. In the public interest the state may make and enforce regulations reasonably calculated to promote care on the part of all, residents and nonresidents alike, who use its highways. The measure in question operates to require a nonresident to answer for his conduct in the state where arise causes of action alleged against him, as well as to provide for a claimant a convenient method by which he may sue to enforce his rights. Under the statute the implied consent is limited to proceedings growing out of accidents or collisions on a highway in which the nonresident may be involved.[61]

An argument having thus been made in terms of fairness, the opinion sought to bring the situation within the ambit of a power theory of jurisdiction.

> [I]n advance of the operation of a motor vehicle on its highway by a nonresident, the state may require him to appoint one of its officials as his agent on whom process may be served in proceedings growing out of such use. . . . [T]he state [has the power] to exclude a nonresident until the formal appointment is made. And, having the power so to exclude, the state may declare that the use of the highway by the nonresident is the equivalent of the appointment of the registrar as agent on whom process may be served. . . . The difference between the formal and implied appointment is not substantial, so far as concerns the application of the due process clause of the Fourteenth Amendment.[62]

---

[60] *Id.* at 355.

[61] *Id.* at 356.

[62] *Id.* at 356-57 (citing Kane v. New Jersey, 242 U.S. 160, 167 (1916)).

Thus, the Massachusetts statute was sustained under an analysis that strained but did not abandon the power theory of jurisdiction.[63]

In the United States, an alternative to a general theory of jurisdiction based on power first decisively emerged in *International Shoe Co. v. Washington.*[64] The State of Washington brought an action in its courts against a Delaware corporation to recover unpaid contributions to the state unemployment compensation fund. Because a tax claim was involved, the suit might well not have been entertained by the courts of states such as Missouri and Delaware which clearly had, under a power theory, adjudicatory authority over the corporation.[65]

The corporation, whose principal place of business was St. Louis, Missouri, had arranged its activities—the manufacture and sale of shoes and other footwear—in such a fashion as to reduce to a minimum—or even entirely avoid—the doing of business in Washington. It maintained no office in the state and made no contracts for either the sale or the purchase of merchandise there. No stock of merchandise was maintained and all orders were filled by f.o.b. shipments from points outside Washington to purchasers within the state. During the years for which unemployment contributions were claimed, the corporation employed about a dozen salesmen who were under the direct supervision and control of sales managers located in St. Louis. The salesmen resided in Washington and their principal activities were in that state. The corporation supplied them with samples and reimbursed them for the rent of inventory display rooms. The salesmen exhibited samples and solicited orders but had no authority to enter into contracts or make collections. All orders were accepted or rejected in St. Louis.

The Washington courts found that the corporation's activities, in particular the regular and systematic solicitation of orders within the state by its salesmen, which resulted in a continuous flow of the corporation's products into the state, were sufficient to constitute doing business in the state. The corporation brought the matter to the Supreme Court, arguing "that its activities within the state were not sufficient to manifest its 'presence' there" so that the assertion of jurisdiction violated due process.[66]

Chief Justice Stone's opinion for the Court, after stating the facts and the arguments, which were couched in terms of the power theory, treated the problem in other terms:

---

[63] For a discussion of how the jurisdictional basis asserted in *Hess* can be justified under a fairness theory, see *infra* Part V C.

[64] 326 U.S. 310 (1945).

[65] *See* Moore v. Mitchell, 30 F.2d 600 (2d Cir. 1929), *aff'd on other grounds*, 281 U.S. 18 (1930). *But cf.* State *ex rel.* Oklahoma Tax Comm'n v. Rodgers, 238 Mo. App. 1115, 193 S.W.2d 919 (1946) (revenue law of foreign state enforced against former resident of that state). *See generally* Scoles, *Interstate and International Distinctions in Conflict of Laws in the United States*, 54 CALIF. L. REV. 1599, 1607-08 (1966).

[66] 326 U.S. at 315.

> Historically the jurisdiction of courts to render judgment *in personam* is grounded on their de facto power over the defendant's person. Hence his presence within the territorial jurisdiction of a court was prerequisite to its rendition of a judgment personally binding him. . . . But now that the *capias ad respondendum* has given way to personal service of summons or other form of notice, due process requires only that in order to subject a defendant to a judgment *in personam*, if he be not present within the territory of the forum, he have certain minimum contacts with it such that the maintenance of the suit does not offend "traditional notions of fair play and substantial justice." . . .
>
> Since the corporate personality is a fiction, . . . it is clear that unlike an individual its "presence" without, as well as within, the state of its origin can be manifested only by activities carried on in its behalf by those who are authorized to act for it. To say that the corporation is so far "present" there as to satisfy due process requirements . . . is to beg the question to be decided. For the terms "present" or "presence" are used merely to symbolize those activities of the corporation's agent within the state which courts will deem to be sufficient to satisfy the demands of due process. . . . Those demands may be met by such contacts of the corporation with the state of the forum as make it reasonable, in the context of our federal system of government, to require the corporation to defend the particular suit which is brought there. An "estimate of the inconveniences" which would result to the corporation from a trial away from its "home" or principal place of business is relevant in this connection.[67]

The Chief Justice then explained certain solutions reached under the aegis of the power theory in terms of convenience, fairness, and justice:

> [I]t has been generally recognized that the casual presence of the corporate agent or even his conduct of single or isolated items of activities in a state in the corporation's behalf are not enough to subject it to suits on causes of action unconnected with the activities there. . . . To require the corporation in such circumstances to defend the suit away from its home or other jurisdiction where it carries on more substantial activities has been thought to lay too great and unreasonable a burden on the corporation to comport with due process.[68]

In his view, the mechanical or quantitative test of presence that an approach in terms of a power theory required was not decisive. "Whether due process is satisfied must depend rather upon the quality and nature of the activity in relation to the fair and orderly administration of the laws which it was the purpose of the due process clause to insure."[69] Stone continued:

> Applying these standards, the activities carried on in behalf of appellant in the State of Washington were neither irregular nor casual. They

---

[67] *Id.* at 316-17.

[68] *Id.* at 317.

[69] *Id.* at 319.

> were systematic and continuous throughout the years in question. They resulted in a large volume of interstate business, in the course of which [the corporation] received the benefits and protection of the laws of the state, including the right to resort to the courts for the enforcement of its rights. The obligation which is here sued upon arose out of those very activities. It is evident that these operations establish sufficient contacts or ties with the state of the forum to make it reasonable and just, according to our traditional conception of fair play and substantial justice, to permit the state to enforce the obligations which appellant has incurred there.[70]

International Shoe announced a new theory of jurisdiction but did not declare the power theory unacceptable. For some three decades, the new and the old coexisted as apparent equals. Thus section 24(1) of the second *Restatement of Conflicts,* promulgated in 1969, speaks in terms of the new theory: "A state has power to exercise judicial jurisdiction over a person if that person's relationship to the state is such as to make the exercise of such jurisdiction reasonable." Section 56(1) announces the same standard: there is "judicial jurisdiction to affect interests in a thing if the relationship of the thing to the state is such as to make the exercise of such jurisdiction reasonable." However, section 28 of the *Restatement* provides that "[a] state has power to exercise judicial jurisdiction over an individual who is present within its territory, whether permanently or temporarily." And section 68 restates the rule of *Harris v. Balk:* "A state has power to exercise judicial jurisdiction to apply to the satisfaction of a claim an obligation owed to the person against whom the claim is asserted if the obligor is subject to the judicial jurisdiction of the state . . . ."

The authors of the *Restatement* were fully aware, of course, of the tension between the jurisdictional theory set out in sections 24(1) and 56(1) and the jurisdictional bases recognized by sections 28 and 68. However, as the courts were using both the older and the newer jurisdictional rationales, the *Restatement* accepts both. The ambivalence that results is recognized in Comment *a* to section 28:

> The rule that physical presence is a basis of judicial jurisdiction may result at times in a defendant being compelled to stand suit in a state to which he has no relationship other than the fact that he was served with process while passing through that state's territory. It can also be contended that the rule is inconsistent with the basic principle of reasonableness which underlies the field of judicial jurisdiction (see § 24).

Likewise, Comment *c* to section 68 notes that "[t]he rule that the temporary presence of the garnishee in the state provides an adequate basis of garnishment jurisdiction might be thought inconsistent with the basic principle of reasonableness which underlies the field of judicial jurisdiction (see §§ 24, 56)."

---

[70] *Id.* at 320.

This theoretical ambivalence came to an end, at least in blatant form, in 1977 with the Supreme Court's decision in *Shaffer v. Heitner*.[71] Heitner, a nonresident of Delaware, brought suit in Delaware against Greyhound Corporation, Greyhound Lines, a wholly owned subsidiary, and various present and former officers and directors of one or both of the foregoing. Greyhound is incorporated in Delaware, Greyhound Lines in California; the principal place of business of both is Phoenix, Arizona. Heitner "alleged that the individual defendants had violated their duties to Greyhound by causing it and its subsidiary to engage in actions that resulted in the corporations being held liable for substantial damages in a private antitrust suit and a large fine in a criminal contempt action."[72] The conduct in question took place in Oregon.

Jurisdiction was established over the individual defendants by sequestering, as Delaware law permitted, stock and stock options belonging to them. The certificates representing the stock were not physically present in Delaware but, under Delaware law, the "situs of ownership of all stock in Delaware corporations" is Delaware.[73] The individual defendants challenged this assertion of jurisdiction on several grounds, including "that under the rule of *International Shoe Co. v. Washington* . . . they did not have sufficient contacts with Delaware to sustain the jurisdiction of that State's courts."[74] This argument was given short shrift by the Delaware Supreme Court. In a brief, two paragraph discussion, that court took the position that jurisdiction can be based either on considerations of fairness or on power, and that the jurisdiction asserted plainly rested on the latter theory and satisfied the constitutional standards traditionally applicable when that theory is invoked.[75]

As Justice Marshall noted in his opinion for the Supreme Court, "[t]his . . . analysis assumes the continued soundness of the conceptual structure founded on the century-old case of *Pennoyer v. Neff* . . . ."[76] After careful analysis, Marshall concluded that

---

[71] 433 U.S. 186 (1977). Of course, not all elements of the power theory have been extirpated from the jurisprudence of jurisdiction. In the first place, effectiveness, though linked to power, is also relevant for nonpower theories of jurisdiction. Secondly, certain jurisdictional bases—for example, jurisdiction based on physical presence—that can be seen as resting on a power-based analysis are still in general use in the United States. Finally, the language and anaylsis used by the courts in approaching jurisdictional issues still exhibit not insignificant elements that derive from power theory. *See, e.g.*, World-Wide Volkswagen Corp. v. Woodson, 444 U.S. 286 (1980), *discussed infra* notes 91-93 & 115-24 and accompanying text.

[72] 433 U.S. at 190.

[73] *Id.* at 192 (citing DEL. CODE ANN. tit. 8, § 169 (1975)).

[74] *Id.* at 193.

[75] *See id.* at 195 (quoting Greyhound Corp. v. Heitner, 361 A.2d 225, 229 (Del. 1976)).

[76] *Id.* at 196.

[t]he fiction that an assertion of jurisdiction over property is anything but an assertion of jurisdiction over the owner of the property supports an ancient form without substantial modern justification. Its continued acceptance would only serve to allow state-court jurisdiction that is fundamentally unfair to the defendant.

We therefore conclude that all assertions of state-court jurisdiction must be evaluated according to the standards set forth in *International Shoe* and its progeny.[77]

Justice Rehnquist took no part in the consideration or decision of *Shaffer v. Heitner*. All the other justices—except Justice Powell on a limited issue[78] and Justice Stevens on a broader basis[79]—agreed with the proposition that

---

[77] *Id.* at 212.

[78] Justice Powell's possible qualification was limited to the question of whether the ownership of some forms of property whose situs is indisputably and permanently located within a State may, without more, provide the contacts necessary to subject a defendant to jurisdiction within the State to the extent of the value of the property. In the case of real property, in particular, preservation of the common-law concept of *quasi in rem* jurisdiction arguably would avoid the uncertainty of the general *International Shoe* standard without significant cost to "traditional notions of fair play and substantial justice."

Id. at 217 (Powell, J., concurring).

[79] Justice Stevens' basic position was apparently that an exercise of jurisdiction is constitutionally acceptable as long as the "requirement of fair notice" is met. For Justice Stevens, fair notice "includes fair warning that a particular activity may subject a person to the jurisdiction of a foreign sovereign." *Id.* at 218 (Stevens, J., concurring in the judgment). Accordingly, he would apparently uphold jurisdiction in the following circumstances: "If I visit another State, or acquire real estate or open a bank account in it, I knowingly assume some risk that the State will exercise its power over my property or my person while there. My contact with the State, though minimal, gives rise to predictable risks." *Id.* It follows that Justice Stevens would not "invalidate *quasi in rem* jurisdiction where real estate is involved" nor "other long-accepted methods of acquiring jurisdiction over persons with adequate notice of both the particular controversy and the fact that their local activities might subject them to suit." *Id.* at 219.

Justice Stevens went on to say, regarding the case at hand, that "[p]erhaps the same consequences should flow from the purchase of stock of a corporation organized under the laws of a foreign nation, because to some limited extent one's property and affairs then become subject to the laws of the nation of the domicile of the corporation." However, this conclusion does not follow when one purchases shares of stock of a corporation organized under the laws of a state of the United States as one "can hardly be expected to know that he has thereby become subject to suit in a forum remote from his residence and unrelated to the transaction." *Id.* The risk and burden are especially great in the case of Delaware because it, "[u]nlike the 49 other States . . . treats the place of incorporation as the situs of the stock, even though both the owner and the custodian of the shares are elsewhere." *Id.*

exercises of adjudicatory jurisdiction can no longer be based on a conceptual structure that rests on a power theory.[80]

C. *In Fairness Theories*

When the jurisdictional problem is approached in terms of convenience, fairness, and justice, several issues arise that a power theory, in view of its premise, does not face. The first, and most fundamental, is when, if ever, considerations of the plaintiff's convenience can be decisive for the assertion of jurisdiction. In other words, should the plaintiff be made to seek out the defendant or should the defendant be made to come to the plaintiff? The problem does not, of course, arise in these terms under a power theory; at least formally, the plaintiff must go to the defendant as the litigation can proceed only where power can be exercised over the defendant or his property. In fairness theories, however, the issue is squarely posed. For example, should the habitual residence or domicile of *either* party be a basis of jurisdiction, or only the defendant's domicile or habitual residence?

For purely domestic situations, a general and almost universally accepted maxim favors the challenged over the challenger, at least when the parties enjoy relatively equal economic strength and social standing. The status quo between the parties is not to be lightly changed; the burden rests on the plaintiff. A specific application of the general domestic-law policy of favoring defendants is seen in venue provisions developed for domestic litigation. These normally favor the defendant by allowing suit at his domicile or residence, but not at the plaintiff's domicile or residence.[81]

The issue of which party must go to the other is normally much more significant in litigation presenting multistate elements than in litigation involving only local parties, transactions, or situations. In the former type of litigation, one party often must incur significant expense in transporting himself and his witnesses to another community. Moreover, on occasion one party will have to face institutions, attitudes, and values that are strange or

---

[80] Justice Brennan "fully agree[d]" with the portion of the Court's opinion discussed above but dissented from the Court's conclusion that Delaware's assertion of jurisdiction did not satisfy the *International Shoe* standard. *Id.* at 219-20 (Brennan, J., concurring in part and dissenting in part).

[81] "In most instances, the purpose of statutorily specified venue is to protect the *defendant* against the risk that a plaintiff will select an unfair or inconvenient place of trial. For that reason, Congress has generally not made the residence of the plaintiff a basis for venue in nondiversity cases." Leroy v. Great Western United Corp., 443 U.S. 173, 183-84 (1979) (emphasis in original); *see also* Stafford v. Briggs, 444 U.S. 527, 543-44 (1980) (construing venue statute, 28 U.S.C. § 1391(e) (1976), providing that suits against federal officers may be brought in the district in which the plaintiff resides, as not covering suits in which the individual officer may be held personally liable). *See generally* Sunderland, *The Provisions Relating to Trial Practice in the New Illinois Civil Practice Act,* 1 U. CHI. L. REV. 188, 192 (1933).

even hostile. It is thus understandable that a community may choose to give greater weight to the plaintiff's than to the defendant's convenience so that its members will be able to litigate locally controversies with significant multistate elements.[82]

An additional consideration that is not present in local controversies, but which militates against giving equal weight to the plaintiff's and the defendant's convenience, is that doing so would increase the forum-shopping advantage already enjoyed by the plaintiff. In multistate controversies—even if the plaintiff must seek out the defendant—usually two or more forums are open. Of these, the plaintiff will choose the one that is the more advantageous for him in terms of litigational convenience and expense, procedural arrangements—for example, the availability of pretrial discovery and jury trial—, and choice of law.[83] Making an additional forum available

---

[82] Thus the draft Swiss Federal Law on Private International Law provides in article 3 that a Swiss national living abroad can sue in Switzerland when "in the circumstances a proceeding abroad cannot be reasonably required." Eidg. Justizabteilung, Bundesgesetz über das internationale Privatrecht (IPR-Gesetz) (no date). Among the situations article 3 is intended to cover is the case in which the defendant and the Swiss plaintiff live in countries that are geographically remote from each other and the plaintiff can not establish jurisdiction under the rules of his domicile. *See* Schlussbericht der Expertenkommission zum Gesetzesentwurf, *Bundesgesetz über das internationale Privatrecht (IPR-Gesetz)*, 13 SCHWEIZER STUDIEN ZUM INTERNATIONALEN RECHT 44 (1979).

[83] For an egregious example of the great advantage a plaintiff can enjoy if he has a free choice between his and the defendant's forum, see Savchuk v. Rush, 311 Minn. 480, 245 N.W.2d 624 (1976). In *Rush*, two Indiana residents were involved in a single-car accident in Indiana. The Rush car was insured by the State Farm Mutual Insurance Co., which does business in every state of the United States. Savchuk, the passenger in the car, was injured, but his claim was barred by the Indiana guest statute. Six months after the accident, Savchuk moved to Minnesota. About a year later, he sued Rush in the Minnesota courts, seeking to establish jurisdiction by garnishing State Farm's obligation under the insurance policy to defend and indemnify Rush in connection with such suits. The Minnesota courts, adopting the position of *Seider v. Roth*, *see supra* text accompanying notes 37-39, upheld jurisdiction. Rush appealed to the Supreme Court which, in the light of its 1977 decision in *Shaffer v. Heitner*, *see supra* text accompanying notes 71-80, vacated the judgment and remanded the case for further consideration. Rush v. Savchuk, 433 U.S. 902 (1977). On remand, the Minnesota Supreme Court held the assertion of jurisdiction compatible with the *Shaffer* standard. Savchuk v. Rush, 272 N.W.2d 888 (Minn. 1977). Rush again appealed to the Supreme Court, which held the asserted jurisdiction unconstitutional. Rush v. Savchuk, 444 U.S. 320 (1980).

Why was the plaintiff-guest so anxious to litigate in Minnesota? Is it not plain that the Minnesota court would, as a choice-of-law matter, apply the Indiana guest statute? The answer is that Minnesota's views with respect to choice of law are such that its courts might well have applied the Minnesota rule, which allows the guest to sue, even though Minnesota's only connections with the situation arose after the accident occurred. *Cf.* Hague v. Allstate Ins. Co., 289 N.W. 2d 43 (Minn. 1979)

thus necessarily increases the substantial advantage that the plaintiff typically already enjoys over the defendant.

Theoretically, of course, a legal order that serves the plaintiff's convenience by permitting him to call the defendant to his forum could seek to redress the balance by not allowing the plaintiff to litigate in the defendant's forum. However, the general arguments in favor of allowing the plaintiff to pursue the defendant in the latter's forum seem far too strong to make this course acceptable.[84] Accordingly, the question that fairness theories face is whether to base general jurisdiction on a close relationship between the forum community and *either* the plaintiff or the defendant or, instead, to require the plaintiff to go to the defendant so that general jurisdiction can be asserted only by a legal order with which the defendant is closely connected either directly or through the underlying transaction. Justice Brennan has suggested that a jurisdictional principle almost exclusively "focus[ed] on the rights of defendants, may be outdated."[85]

> The model of society on which the [jurisdictional preference for defendants is based] is no longer accurate. Business people, no matter how local their businesses, cannot assume that the goods remain in the business' locality. Customers and goods can be anywhere else in the country usually in a matter of hours and always in a matter of a very few days.[86]

Brennan would, therefore, treat the plaintiff and defendant equally for jurisdictional purposes. For him the "contacts between [the defendant and the forum State] should not be determinative."[87]

This position has not been accepted by a majority of the Supreme Court of the United States. In *Shaffer v. Heitner,* Justice Marshall observed in passing that after *International Shoe* "the relationship among the defendant, the forum, and the litigation . . . became the central concern of the inquiry

---

(upholding application of local law to a controversy arising from a foreign accident involving residents of the foreign state). And it is quite possible that the Supreme Court would not have held a choice of Minnesota law unconstitutional. *Cf.* Allstate Ins. Co. v. Hague, 449 U.S. 302 (1981) (plurality opinion) (affirming Minnesota's application of its own substantive law). For a discussion of *Hague,* see Symposium, *Choice-of-Law Theory After* Allstate Insurance Co. v. Hague, 10 HOFSTRA L. REV. 35 (1981).

[84] *See supra* page 307.

[85] World-Wide Volkswagen Corp. v. Woodson, 444 U.S. 286, 308 (1980) (Brennan, J., dissenting to both *World-Wide Volkswagen* and *Rush v. Savchuk*). Justice Brennan may have had the point in mind, but did not develop it, in his opinion in *Shaffer. See infra* note 88. For an earlier discussion of the question, see von Mehren and Trautman, *supra* note 19, at 1127-28.

[86] World-Wide Volkswagen Corp. v. Woodson, 444 U.S. 286, 309 (1980).

[87] *Id.* at 310.

into personal jurisdiction."[88] Three years later, in his opinion for the Court in *Rush v. Savchuk*,[89] Marshall emphasized the proposition that it is the defendant's, not both parties', connections with the forum that are significant for purposes of jurisdiction: "In determining whether a particular exercise of state-court jurisdiction is consistent with due process, the inquiry must focus on the 'relationship among the defendant, the forum, and the litigation.'"[90] And in *World-Wide Volkswagen Corp. v. Woodson*,[91] Justice White wrote for the Court that "[a]s has long been settled, and as we reaffirm today, a state court may exercise personal jurisdiction over a nonresident defendant only so long as there exist 'minimum contacts' between the defendant and the forum State."[92] One of the two functions served by the concept of minimum contacts, White continued, is to protect "the defendant against the burdens of litigating in a distant or inconvenient forum."[93]

However, neither those who take the position that, in principle, the plaintiff must go to the defendant nor those who, like Justice Brennan, seem prepared to require the defendant to go to the plaintiff have considered what effect the comparative litigational capacity of a class of plaintiffs or defendants should have for this issue.[94] There are a few examples—the French is the best known—of legal systems that ground general jurisdiction to adjudicate on a close connection between *either* party and the forum. However, most legal systems, perhaps influenced by an approach in power terms, give preference to the challenged over the challenger for jurisdictional purposes.[95] In theories for which the exercise of jurisdiction turns on consid-

---

[88] 433 U.S. at 204. In his partial concurrence and partial dissent in *Shaffer*, Justice Brennan equally casually remarked that the "primary teaching of [Justice Marshall's opinion for the Court] is that a State, in seeking to assert jurisdiction over a person located outside of its borders, may only do so on the basis of minimum contacts among the *parties*, the contested transaction, and the forum State." *Id.* at 220 (emphasis added).

[89] 444 U.S. 320 (1980).

[90] *Id.* at 327.

[91] 444 U.S. 286 (1980).

[92] *Id.* at 291 (citing *International Shoe*, 326 U.S. at 316).

[93] *Id.* at 292. The other function is "to ensure that the States, through their courts, do not reach out beyond the limits imposed on them by their status as coequal sovereigns in a federal system." *Id.* Here Justice White recognized the role that choice-of-law concerns can play in jurisdictional thinking. *See infra* Part V D. He emphasized, however, respect for sovereign power rather than fairness to parties. In this sense, an element of the metaphysics of power theory persists in his analysis.

[94] For a discussion of the importance of comparative litigational capacity, see *infra* Part V B.

[95] *See* Fragistas, *supra* note 22, at 199-200; *see also* J. SCHRÖDER, *supra* note 25, at 229-40.

erations of fairness, however, this preference cannot be absolute but must rest on the assumption that, in the general run of cases, the preferred class of parties is not significantly better able than the nonpreferred class to bear the burden of litigating in the other's forum. It follows that these theories, unlike those that rest on power, can rationally prefer the plaintiff class for jurisdictional purposes where a particular class of defendants is significantly better able than the related plaintiff class to assume the burden of litigating abroad. For example, the plaintiff class might be preferred where it is essentially localized in its activities while the related defendant class regularly engages in extensive multistate activity. The argument for reversing the traditional jurisdictional preference is especially strong when the plaintiff class—for example, consumers—is not typically engaged in commercial activity but the defendant class—for example, insurance companies or manufacturers—is.

A second range of issues that does not arise under a power theory but which a fairness theory must face is whether general jurisdiction should be recognized at all and, if so, what balance should be struck between recourse to this form of jurisdiction and to specific jurisdiction. The power theory's equation of jurisdiction with power, as has already been remarked, makes claims of general jurisdiction commonplace for it; a theory based on fairness, on the other hand, must explain the use of general jurisdiction on the ground that there should be a certain and predictable place where a person can be reached by those having claims against him. To the extent that fairness theories encourage, as they must, the emergence of various forms of specific jurisdiction, this justification loses some of its force. Accordingly, in the long run, general jurisdiction is likely to have relatively less importance in a regime informed by fairness than in one dominated by a power theory. Consequently, a fairness theory will tend to claim general jurisdiction only when, as in the case of jurisdiction based on habitual residence or principal place of business, the arguments supporting the forum's claim are clearly persuasive. This is not to say that general jurisdiction should, in principle, disappear in fairness theories. It is justified by ease of administration and predictability.

V. Jurisdictional Bases Acceptable to Fairness Theories

A. *In General*

In fairness theories, claims of jurisdiction can plausibly be made in five basic situations:

(1) Unless the forum is one of the few that assert jurisdiction on the basis of a relationship between the State and the plaintiff, general jurisdiction is claimed where the defendant has a close and continuing relation with the forum.

The remaining situations involve claims of specific jurisdiction:

(2) Where the defendant class in question is, relatively speaking, sig-

nificantly better able to litigate in the plaintiff's forum than is the plaintiff's class in the defendant's forum, specific jurisdiction may be asserted in view of either the plaintiff's or the controversy's close relation with the forum. Probably the most numerous and important claims of specific jurisdiction made by fairness theories rest in large measure on this consideration. Accordingly, this type of jurisdiction is further discussed below.[96]

(3) Litigation or enforcement considerations flowing from the particular class of controversies in question may lead to the assertion of specific jurisdiction. For example, the assertion of jurisdiction by the legal order in which immovable property or tangible movable property is located or in which an accident involving only nonresidents occurs is presumably to be justified, at least in part, on this ground.[97]

(4) Choice-of-law considerations—the forum's view that the subject matter is one to which forum law must be applied or its belief that choice of law is, generally speaking, not reliable for the subject matter in question—can in some but by no means all cases justify the assertion of specific jurisdiction.[98] The assumption of jurisdiction to divorce by the moving spouse's domicile[99] analytically must rest in considerable measure on assigning decisive importance to making the forum's family law available to all members of the community.[100]

---

[96] *See infra* Part V B.

[97] *See infra* Part V C.; *cf.* Hess v. Pawloski, 274 U.S. 352 (1927), *discussed supra* text accompanying notes 58-63; Hague Convention on the Recognition and Enforcement of Foreign Judgments in Civil and Commercial Matters, art. 10(4) (adopted Apr. 25, 1966; became effective Feb. 1, 1971), CONFÉRENCE DE LA HAGE DE DROIT INTERNATIONAL PRIVÉ, ACTES ET DOCUMENTS DE LA SESSION EXTRAORDINAIRE, No. 53, at 324, 326 (1966).

[98] *See infra* Part V D.

[99] *See* Estin v. Estin, 334 U.S. 541, 546-47 (1948); 1 RESTATEMENT (SECOND) OF CONFLICT OF LAWS § 71 (1969); *cf.* Stewart v. Stewart, 32 Idaho 180, 186, 180 P. 165, 166 (1919) (moving spouse's domicile applies its divorce law even though act constituting ground for divorce was committed in the state where parties were domiciled at the time and was not a ground for divorce under its law).

The practice in common law systems of always applying forum law in divorce cases may require the refusal of jurisdiction even when considerations of the parties' convenience support its exercise. *Cf.* Alton v. Alton, 207 F.2d 667, 684-85 (3d Cir. 1953) (Hastie, J., dissenting) (suggesting that jurisdiction over both parties is a sufficient basis for jurisdiction to divorce but that choice-of-law doctrine may require application of the law of the parties' domicile).

[100] The Supreme Court has justified the exercise of specific jurisdiction to divorce as follows: "Marital status involves the regularity and integrity of the marriage relation. . . . The interest of the State extends to its domiciliaries. The State should have the power to guard its interest in them by changing or altering their marital status . . . . [Only by exercising jurisdiction to divorce] could the State of the domicile have and maintain effective control of the marital status of its domiciliaries." Estin v. Estin, 334 U.S. 541, 546-547 (1948).

(5) Specific jurisdiction may be asserted because the controversy implicates multiple or indeterminate parties, all of whom cannot be brought before a single forum on other jurisdictional bases.[101] In such cases, if two or more jurisdictions have roughly equal claims in terms of litigational convenience, it may be appropriate, with a view to limiting forum-shopping possibilities, to recognize jurisdiction only in the forum that offers intrinsic guarantees against an aberrational or unfair choice-of-law process.[102]

B. *The Significance of the Parties Relative Abilities to Bear Litigational Burdens*

A jurisdictional analysis resting on the principle of relative party ability to bear litigational burdens considers the ability not of the parties actually involved in the litigation but of the *class* of plaintiffs or defendants to which the parties belong. Considerations of administrability, planning, predictability, and objectivity require this approach to jurisdictional rules generally.[103] Thus, in deciding whether jurisdiction should be claimed, it is relevant that the plaintiff is a consumer or an insured but not that he is a pauper or a millionaire. Jurisdictional rules based on the relative ability principle could, however, give weight to the individualized situation of the plaintiff or the defendant in deciding whether to refuse to exercise jurisdiction under the doctrine of forum non conveniens.

Many important claims of specific jurisdiction made by legal orders that approach jurisdiction in terms of fairness can be explained as resting, at least in large measure, on the defendant *class*'s relatively greater ability, as compared with that of the related plaintiff *class*, to bear the litigational burdens of litigating in the other party's forum. It is interesting, therefore, to explore how jurisdictional standards designed to give significant weight to the parties' relative litigational abilities might be developed and to consider the form that such standards might take. The basic proposition is that a class

---

Where the forum's choice-of-law concern is less compelling, this form of specific jurisdiction has been rejected. *See, e.g.*, Vanderbilt v. Vanderbilt, 354 U.S. 416 (1957) (domicile of moving party in divorce proceeding lacks jurisdiction over nonappearing respondent with respect to property arrangements such as alimony); *cf.* Kulko v. Superior Court, 436 U.S. 84 (1978) (no jurisdiction in forum where mother and child were living over action for increased child support against father who lived elsewhere). *But cf.* Simons v. Miami Beach First Nat'l Bank, 381 U.S. 81 (1965) (domicile of moving party has jurisdiction to extinguish dower rights of nonappearing respondent in property located in the forum state).

[101] *See* von Mehren & Trautman, *supra* note 19, at 1162-63; *infra* Part V E.

[102] *See* von Mehren & Trautman, *supra* note 19, at 1174-75; *infra* Part V E.; *cf. infra* note 178 (discussing Hanson v. Denckla, 357 U.S. 235 (1958)).

[103] Were it not for these considerations, a forum-conveniens theory of jurisdiction might be acceptable. *See generally* Ehrenzweig, *The Transient Rule of Personal Jurisdiction: The "Power" Myth and Forum Conveniens*, 65 YALE L.J. 289 (1956).

of plaintiffs whose ability to bear the burden of litigation is clearly significantly less than that of the related class of defendants should receive special treatment for jurisdictional purposes. Further analysis of the characteristics of classes of plaintiffs and defendants that affect their respective abilities to bear litigational burdens is thus needed.

For reasons of administrability, planning, predictability, and objectivity, a relative ability analysis should be structured in terms of the localized or multistate character of the activities of the class of parties normally related to the type of controversy in question. The premise is that a party's economic and psychological ability to litigate in the other party's forum, as well as his expectations with respect to the possibility that he may have to do so, decrease as a direct function of the degree to which his normal activities are localized and have only local effects. Accordingly, for jurisdictional purposes the following situations can be distinguished: (1) multistate plaintiff, localized defendant; (2) both parties localized; (3) both parties multistate; (4) localized plaintiff, multistate defendant. These situations proceed from the one in which a jurisdictional preference for the defendant is most plausible to the situation in which the preference is least plausible.

How a relative ability analysis might work in practice can be suggested by examining several cases that have considered claims of specific jurisdiction. To some extent, the courts' rhetoric in these cases derives from power theory; in none of them is the structure for analysis suggested above more than implicit. Nonetheless, the results reached in most of them are consistent with a claim of adjudicatory jurisdiction by the plaintiff's forum when the plaintiff class in question is typically less able to bear the burden of litigating abroad than is the related defendant class.

McGee v. International Life Insurance Co.[104] is a classic example of a claim of specific jurisdiction that can be explained in terms of the relatively greater ability of multistate defendants, as compared with localized plaintiffs, to bear the burden of litigating abroad. A resident of California purchased a life insurance policy from an Arizona corporation in 1944. In 1948, International Life assumed the original insurer's obligation. Thereafter, premiums were paid by mail to the defendant's Texas office. The insured died in 1950. The company refused to pay the beneficiary on the ground that the insured had committed suicide. Neither the original insurer nor the defendant had ever had an officer or agent in California, and as far as the record showed, the defendant had "never solicited or done any insurance business in California apart from the policy involved."[105] California "based its jurisdiction on a state statute which subjects foreign corporations to suit in California on insurance contracts with residents of that State . . . ."[106]

The beneficiary, who was unable to collect the judgment in California

[104] 355 U.S. 220 (1957).

[105] *Id.* at 222.

[106] *Id.* at 221.

because the company had no assets there, sought to enforce it in Texas. Enforcement was refused by the Texas courts on the ground that California lacked jurisdiction over the defendant company. The matter was brought to the Supreme Court, which held that Texas had improperly denied full faith and credit to the California judgment because, in the circumstances of the case, there was no constitutional bar to California's exercise of jurisdiction over the defendant.

Justice Black wrote for a unanimous Court:

> It is sufficient for purposes of due process that the suit was based on a contract which had substantial connections with [California]. . . . The contract was delivered in California, the premiums were mailed from there and the insured was a resident of that State when he died. It cannot be denied that California has a manifest interest in providing effective means of redress for its residents when their insurers refuse to pay claims. . . . When claims were small or moderate individual claimants frequently could not afford the cost of bringing an action in a foreign forum—thus in effect making the company judgment proof. Often the crucial witnesses—as here on the company's defense of suicide—will be found in the insured's locality. Of course there may be inconvenience to the insurer if it is held amenable to suit in California where it had this contract but certainly nothing which amounts to a denial of due process.[107]

The Court's analysis gave some weight to litigational considerations—the presence in California of witnesses on the issue of suicide—but the result rests, for the most part, on the significantly greater capacity of the class of defendants in question, as compared with the plaintiff class, to bear the burden of litigating in the other's forum. The same general approach is seen in litigation against manufacturers to recover damages suffered because of defective products. In *Certisimo v. Heidelberg Co.,*[108] the plaintiff brought an action in New Jersey against the distributor of a printing press to recover for injuries received due to defects in the press. The distributor thereupon sought to join the German manufacturer of the press. Jurisdiction over the latter was asserted on the basis of a New Jersey statute which permitted assertion of adjudicatory jurisdiction when "consistent with due process of law."[109]

The manufacturer did not carry on any manufacturing or selling activities in the United States. Title to its presses was taken in Germany by the

[107] Id. at 223-24; *cf.* EEC Convention on Jurisdiction and Enforcement of Judgments in Civil and Commercial Matters, art. 8 (as amended by the 1978 Convention on Accession), 21 O.J. Eur. Comm. (No. L 304) 77, 80 (1978) ("An insurer domiciled in a contracting State may be sued: . . . 2. in another Contracting State, in the courts for the place where the policy-holder is domiciled . . . .").

[108] 122 N.J. Super. 1, 298 A.2d 298 (Law Div. 1972).

[109] *Id.* at 3, 298 A.2d at 299.

distributor; the manufacturer had no financial interest in the distributor nor did it control or supervise the distributor's operations in the United States. "In short, the only contact on which personal jurisdiction may be based in this case is the fact that a printing press sold to the [distributor] with the obvious expectation that it would be resold in the United States eventually caused injury to plaintiff in New Jersey."[110]

The court held that assertion of adjudicatory jurisdiction over the manufacturer did not not violate due process. Even though the distributor was entirely independent, in the circumstances New Jersey could assert jurisdiction over the manufacturer.

> The economic reality of the situation is that these distributors . . . provide the same service of distribution . . . as if they were the [manufacturer's] agents. . . . [T]o prevent recovery by an injured [party] because the manufacturer had no "contacts" in that it handled all transactions through a middleman-distributor, is to allow a legal technicality to subvert justice and economic reality in the worst sense.[111]

The court then noted the "clear and weighty" "need for a citizen of New Jersey to be able to sue for injuries he sustains here . . . . New Jersey has pioneered in the field of products liability and in the endeavor to have the rights of all parties decided where constitutionally permissible in a single forum."[112] In considering whether the exercise of jurisdiction by New Jersey represented an "undue inconvenience" for the manufacturer, the court emphasized that the defendant's products were distributed throughout the world. "If [the defendant] wishes to benefit from American markets . . . it is not unreasonable or fundamentally unfair for [it] to be required to submit to the jurisdiction of a state whose resident has allegedly been injured by its product."[113]

The decision in *Certisimo* rests in part on the proposition that specific jurisdiction is properly asserted when a controversy involves multiple parties—all of whom cannot be brought before a single forum on a more usual jurisdictional basis—and the putative forum is, in comparison to other forums that might seek to exercise jurisdiction in the particular circumstances, at least as plausible as any of the other forums. However, the central theme in the court's analysis is the relative ability of the customer and the manufacturer to bear the burden of litigating in the other's forum. In effect, the localized plaintiff was permitted to call the multistate defendant to his forum.

Both *McGee* and *Certisimo* thus fall into the fourth group of situations mentioned earlier as they involve essentially localized plaintiffs and defendants that can be characterized as highly multistate. Moreover, in neither

---

[110] *Id.* at 4-5, 298 A.2d at 300.

[111] *Id.* at 12, 298 A.2d at 304.

[112] *Id.*, 298 A.2d at 304.

[113] *Id.* at 14, 298 A.2d at 305.

case was the plaintiff's forum outside the geographical area which the defendant knew, or could reasonably anticipate, would be directly affected by its multistate activity. In *McGee,* California was not within the area of the defendant's activities; however, the defendant knowingly continued to insure the California resident on whose policy the claim rested. In *Certisimo,* the defendant manufacturer did not deal directly with the New Jersey customer but the geographical area in which the manufacturer's products were sold included New Jersey.

The philosophy that underlies these American decisions is generalized for consumer contracts in the European Economic Community (EEC) Convention on Jurisdiction and Enforcement of Judgments in Civil Matters.[114] A "consumer," as defined in article 13 of the Convention, is normally a member of a localized class with respect to the transaction in question since he must have contracted "for a purpose which can be regarded as being outside his trade or profession." The other contracting party is likely to be less localized in his or its activities since article 13 requires that the transaction relate to:

1. a contract for the sale of goods on installment credit terms, or
2. a contract for a loan repayable by installments, or for any other form of credit, made to finance the sale of goods, or
3. any other contract for the supply of goods or a contract for the supply of services, and
   (a) in the State of the consumer's domicile the conclusion of the contract was preceded by a specific invitation addressed to him or by advertising, and
   (b) the consumer took in that State the steps necessary for the conclusion of the contract.

If these conditions are satisfied, then, under article 14, the "consumer may bring proceedings against the other party to a contract either in the courts of the Contracting State in which that party is domiciled or in the courts of the Contracting State in which he is himself domiciled."

The EEC Convention answers a question that *McGee* and *Certisimo* left open: Must the defendant's multistate activities either predictably or normally involve the plaintiff's forum before the defendant can be called to that forum? The three contract types described in article 13 involve situations in which the other party will know, at the time of contracting, where the potential consumer-plaintiff is domiciled. In the case of installment sales and sales on credit, a change in the consumer's domicile after the contract is concluded will establish jurisdiction in a forum that was not foreseeable by the other party at the time of contracting. However, it seems fair and reasonable to require, as the Convention does, the nonconsumer party to go to the consumer's new domicile as the type of contract in question will

---

[114] 21 O.J. Eur. Comm. (No. L 304) 77 (1978).

require the nonconsumer to keep in touch with the consumer. When the contract does not involve such a continuing relationship between the parties, the consumer's change of domicile presumably prevents his calling the other party to either the old or the new domicile. It follows, therefore, that the consumer-plaintiff cannot call the defendant to his forum unless the latter's activities either predictably or normally involve that forum.

The question that the EEC Convention thus seems to answer in the affirmative was posed for the United States by the facts of *World-Wide Volkswagen Corp. v. Woodson.*[115] New York residents purchased an Audi automobile from Seaway, a Volkswagen dealer in New York. A year later, they left New York in their car for a new home in Arizona. While passing through Oklahoma, their Audi was struck in the rear by another car, causing a fire which severely burned three members of the family. A products liability action was subsequently brought in the Oklahoma courts; it was alleged that the injuries resulted from defective design and placement of the Audi's gas tank and fuel system. Joined as defendants were the automobile's manufacturer, the importer, the regional distributor (World-Wide Volkswagen Corporation), and the retail dealer (Seaway). The latter two defendants objected that the assertion of jurisdiction violated the due process clause. The Oklahoma Supreme Court upheld jurisdiction. The Supreme Court of the United States granted certiorari and reversed.

The relationships of Seaway and World-Wide with the manufacturer and importer were contractual. Seaway's activities were local in that it was a retail dealer, incorporated in New York and serving a local market. Although World-Wide was incorporated and had its business office in New York, its activities had an interstate dimension; it distributed vehicles, parts, and accessories, under contract with the importer, to retail dealers in New York, New Jersey, and Connecticut. There was, however, "no evidence that either World-Wide or Seaway does any business in Oklahoma, ships or sells any products to or in that State, has an agent to receive process there, or purchases advertisements in any media calculated to reach Oklahoma."[116] Seaway could be viewed, therefore, as a localized defendant while World-Wide was an interstate defendant whose interstate activities neither normally nor predictably involved Oklahoma.

Justice White's majority opinion approached the jurisdictional issue in terms for the most part different from those developed in the foregoing discussion. The decisive question for White was whether there were "minimum contacts" between the defendant and the forum state. This formula, articulated by Chief Justice Stone in *International Shoe,*[117] has echoes of the power theory of jurisdiction.[118] Thus Justice White wrote that "[t]he con-

---

[115] 444 U.S. 286 (1980).

[116] *Id.* at 289.

[117] 326 U.S. at 316.

[118] *See generally* Cassad, Shaffer v. Heitner: *An End to Ambivalence in Jurisdiction Theory?*, 26 KAN. L. REV. 61 (1977).

cept of minimum contacts . . . can be seen to perform two related, but distinguishable, functions. It protects the defendant against the burdens of litigating in a distant or inconvenient forum. And it acts to ensure that the States, through their courts, do not reach out beyond the limits imposed on them by their status as coequal sovereigns in a federal system."[119] Protecting the defendant from undue burdens of litigating in a distant forum is, of course, a proper concern of a jurisdictional theory based on fairness. On the other hand, as Justice White's remarks regarding the second purpose served by the "minimum contacts" requirement may suggest, choice-of-law considerations should not justify the assumption of jurisdiction at least where the choice-of-law process can be expected to operate appropriately.[120]

Perhaps Justice White had this problem in mind or was still partially under the influence of a power theory when he wrote:

> Even if the defendant would suffer minimal or no inconvenience from being forced to litigate before the tribunals of another State; even if the forum State has a strong interest in applying its law to the controversy; even if the forum State is the most convenient location for litigation, the Due Process Clause, acting as an instrument of interstate federalism, may sometimes act to divest the State of its power to render a valid judgment.[121]

Justice White's opinion focused only in part on the question of when a defendant's activities are of such a nature as to justify depriving him of the benefit of the jurisdictional advantage that would be given to a defendant whose activities were entirely local. His opinion does indicate, however, that an interstate defendant may not be subject to suit in every jurisdiction with which a localized plaintiff or the underlying controversy has a significant connection.

> [T]he foreseeability that is critical to due process analysis is not the mere likelihood that a product will find its way into the forum State. Rather, it is that the defendant's conduct and connection with the forum State are such that he should reasonably anticipate being haled into court there. . . . The Due Process Clause . . . gives a degree of predictability to the legal system that allows potential defendants to structure their primary conduct with some minimum assurance as to where that conduct will and will not render them liable to suit.[122]

Under this test, Oklahoma could not properly assert jurisdiction over either Seaway or World-Wide; although World-Wide unlike Seaway engaged in interstate activities, these neither normally nor predictably involved Oklahoma to such a degree as to permit Oklahoma to treat World-Wide as an interstate defendant for jurisdictional purposes.

---

[119] 444 U.S. at 291-92.

[120] *See infra* Part V D.

[121] 444 U.S. at 294 (citing Hanson v. Denckla, 357 U.S. 235, 251, 254 (1958)).

[122] *Id.* at 297.

Some of the views expressed by the dissents in *World-Wide Volkswagen* can be understood as presenting various arguments as to why World-Wide and Seaway are properly considered interstate defendants. Thus Justice Marshall wrote:

> Manifestly, the "quality and nature" of commercial activity is different, for purposes of the *International Shoe* test, from actions from which a defendant obtains no economic advantage. Commercial activity is more likely to cause effects in a larger sphere, and the actor derives an economic benefit from the activity that makes it fair to require him to answer for his conduct where its effects are felt. The profits may be used to pay the costs of suit, and knowing that the activity is likely to have effects in other States the defendant can readily insure against the costs of those effects, thereby sparing himself much of the inconvenience of defending in a distant forum.[123]

Justice Blackmun argued that, as far as interstate activity is concerned, no distinction need be drawn between World-Wide and Seaway, on the one hand, and the manufacturer and the importer, on the other. He saw

> nothing more unfair for them [in upholding jurisdiction in Oklahoma] than for the manufacturer and the importer. All are in the business of providing vehicles that spread out over the highways of our several States. It is not too much to anticipate at the time of distribution and at the time of retail sale that this Audi would be in Oklahoma.[124]

To the extent that Justice Blackmun was considering the relative ability of the several classes of defendants in *World-Wide Volkswagen* to litigate in the plaintiff's chosen forum, his analysis is plainly wrong. Clearly, in economic as well as other terms, the manufacturer and the importer-distributor could more easily bear the burden of litigating in the plaintiff's forum than could the local distributor and the retailer. Neither Justice Blackmun's opinion nor those of the other Justices addressed the issue of the relative ability of the plaintiffs and the several classes of defendants to bear litigational burdens. By failing to do so, the Court passed up an excellent opportunity to explore and develop the principle of relative litigational ability.

Of course, if a court believes that the jurisdictional preference traditionally accorded the defendant is outmoded in today's world, it may express this view indirectly by treating a defendant as multistate as soon as its activities are, with respect to the underlying controversy, no longer entirely localized. *Cornelison v. Chaney*[125] is perhaps explainable along these lines. The husband of the plaintiff, a California resident, was killed in a highway collision with the defendant's truck in Nevada. The accident occurred at a point close to the California border. The defendant lived in Nebraska. The

---

[123] *Id.* at 317.

[124] *Id.* at 318.

[125] 16 Cal. 3d 143, 545 P.2d 264, 127 Cal. Rptr. 352 (1976).

plaintiff brought an action in California to recover damages for her husband's death. The defendant challenged jurisdiction and the trial court dismissed the action. Upon the plaintiff's appeal, the California Supreme Court, with three judges dissenting, held that the exercise of jurisdiction satisfied due-process requirements.

The defendant was licensed to haul freight in several states, including California. The accident occurred while he was en route to California with a large cargo of dry milk for delivery in Long Beach. The court concluded that the plaintiff's cause of action had "a substantial connection with a business relationship defendant has purposely established with California."[126] The court then asked "whether it would be fair and reasonable to subject defendant to the jurisdiction of California in light of the inconvenience to him in defending an action in this state, when balanced against the interests of plaintiff in suing locally and of the state in assuming jurisdiction."[127] In this connection the Court considered "the interstate character of defendant's business" significant.

> A necessary incident of [the defendant's] business was the foreseeable circumstance of causing injury to persons in distant forums. While the existence of an interstate business is not an independent basis of jurisdiction which, without more, allows a state to assert its jurisdiction, this element is relevant to considerations of fairness and reasonableness. The very nature of defendant's business balances in favor of requiring him to defend here.[128]

To the extent that a theory of jurisdiction is prepared to deny a class of defendants—on the ground that their activities are, with respect to the given forum, multistate—the jurisdictional preference otherwise accorded defendants, the further question arises of the importance, if any, to be assigned the fact that the plaintiff's activities are likewise multistate. Several solutions are possible: In the case of multistate plaintiffs, all defendants—whether localized or multistate—could enjoy the preference normally accorded defendants. On the other hand, the principle of comparative ability to bear the litigational burden could be applied, with defendants enjoying the preference unless the plaintiffs are, with respect to the particular controversy, significantly less multistate. Finally, multistate defendants could, regardless of whether plaintiffs are localized or multistate, be denied the preference. Various arguments can be advanced for and against these positions.

The defendant's jurisdictional preference rests on the advantages that a plaintiff typically enjoys in selecting among several forums and on the proposition that, other things being equal, burdens that must rest on either

---

[126] *Id.* at 149, 545 P.2d at 267, 127 Cal. Rptr. at 355.

[127] *Id.* at 150, 545 P.2d at 268, 127 Cal. Rptr. at 356.

[128] *Id.* at 151, 545 P.2d at 269, 127 Cal. Rptr. at 357. There is a strong dissent. *Id.* at 152, 545 P.2d at 269, 127 Cal. Rptr. at 357 (Clark, J.).

the challenger or the challenged are to be borne by him who seeks to change the status quo. If a legal order accepts these rationales, the principle of relative litigational ability is, within the present realm of discourse, the only fully persuasive basis for denying a given defendant class the preference.[129] However, difficulties in administering a relative ability standard, the advantage of bright-line tests in jurisdictional matters, plus, perhaps, lurking doubts as to the propriety of according the preference at all, could lead to its denial whenever the defendant class is not localized.[130] On the other hand, a bright-line test could also take the form of a rule that all multistate plaintiffs should, regardless of relative litigational ability, be required to come to the defendant's forum. Use of this test requires, in cases where the plaintiff class is localized, consideration of the characteristics of the defendant class. The test—and the additional inquiry that its application involves in some cases—seems appropriate, however, if one is convinced that the principle of defendant preference is generally correct.

C. *The Significance of the Controversy's Litigational Relation to the Forum*

What significance should jurisdictional theories based on fairness give to the controversy's litigational relation to the forum community? In principle, litigational considerations such as the convenience of witnesses ordinarily should not be of decisive importance in the contemporary world. As the overall impact of litigation is normally much greater on parties than on witnesses, jurisdictional solutions need not give special attention to the convenience of the latter if travel is rapid and convenient. On the other hand, if crucial testimony, for reasons other than party obdurateness, is available in only one jurisdiction, what would amount to jurisdiction by necessity might well be recognized in that forum.

Standing alone, litigational considerations thus only rarely justify the exercise of adjudicatory jurisdiction. If litigational considerations alone are not decisive, how then is the assumption of jurisdiction by the place where an automobile accident occurs[131] or a heater explodes[132] to be explained? If

---

[129] *Cf.* Erlanger Mills, Inc. v. Cohoes Fibre Mills, Inc., 239 F.2d 502 (4th Cir. 1956) (holding that exercise of jurisdiction violates due process when an interstate corporation sues another interstate corporation in a forum where the latter does not transact business).

[130] *Cf.* In-Flight Devices Corp. v. Van Dusen Air, Inc., 466 F.2d 220, 234 (6th Cir. 1972) (both parties interstate; court remarked, *inter alia,* that assertion of jurisdiction is not "unfair in this respect as such assertion over a consumer or small local business might be").

[131] *See, e.g.,* Hess v. Pawloski, 274 U.S. 352 (1927), *discussed supra* text accompanying notes 58-63.

[132] *See, e.g.,* Gray v. American Radiator & Standard Sanitary Corp., 22 Ill.2d 432, 176 N.E.2d 761 (1961); *cf.* Hague Convention, *supra* note 97, art. 10(4).

the plaintiff is a member of the community in which the accident or explosion occurs, the jurisdictional claim can rest on the principle of comparative litigational ability since, with respect to the activities that give rise to the controversy, the plaintiff class is localized while the defendant class is multistate unless the defendant also belongs to the local community in which event general jurisdiction can be exercised over him.

When, on the other hand, neither party belongs to the local community, both are to some extent multistate with respect to the controversy. As between such parties, the defendant's claim to have the plaintiff come to his forum is weaker than when both parties are localized. (Moreover, where the defendant is typically insured and the insurer will handle the case and bear the loss up to the policy limits—as in the case of automobile accidents—or can spread the loss as a cost of doing business—as in the case of a manufacturer of heaters—the defendant is presumably better able to bear litigational burdens than is the plaintiff.) But as both parties are multistate with respect to the activity, perhaps the plaintiff should not enjoy the advantage of litigating in his home forum. If so, specific jurisdiction can reasonably be assumed by the legal order with which both parties' multistate activity was connected when the claim arose. This legal order presumably has no reason to be biased in favor of one of the parties and offers, in addition, litigational advantages in that witnesses and evidence are likely to be more readily available there.

D. *The Significance of the Forum's Choice-of-Law Concerns*

This subtle and complex problem has already been briefly touched upon in several contexts but requires further discussion: What significance should a putative forum's choice-of-law concerns have for the assumption of adjudicatory jurisdiction in theories based on fairness? The issue does not arise for power theories; since the applicability of forum law to the controversy does not affect the forum's power over the defendant or his assets, choice-of-law considerations are irrelevant for jurisdictional practice under these theories.

1. In General

For at least two reasons choice of law and adjudicatory jurisdiction can not be kept entirely apart in fairness theories. In the first place, when foreign law is applied, an adjudicator must normally both assume an additional burden and run a greater risk of misunderstanding. At some point this risk or burden may provide a basis for refusing to assume jurisdiction that would otherwise be taken. Conversely, where a forum has a strong or vital interest in having its law (or perhaps the law of a third state) apply to a matter, this interest may justify the taking of specific jurisdiction where it would otherwise be refused. Choice-of-law concerns are not, therefore, entirely ignored by fairness theories. What scope should be accorded to these concerns in jurisdictional practice and theory?

Although not necessarily excluded by theoretical considerations, a strong tendency exists in fairness theories to assign relatively little importance to choice-of-law considerations in working out jurisdictional standards. Generally speaking, the primary concern is to assign fairly between or among the parties the litigational burdens inherent in multistate litigation.[133] In considering what is fair, most of these theories accept the proposition that the allocation of burdens should redress, at least in part, the advantage that the plaintiff inevitably enjoys, when several forums with different choice-of-law practices are available, of choosing the law most favorable to his cause.

Jurisdictional theory is thus largely concerned with the problem of what is the appropriate balance of *party* risk, burden, and opportunity;[134] adjustment and vindication of a *legal order*'s choice-of-law concerns—in particular, the appropriate reach of its substantive policies—is seen as primarily the responsibility of choice-of-law practice.

A first proposition is clear: a legal order's assumption of specific—or, *a fortiori,* general—jurisdiction should not necessarily imply that its domestic law will be applied to at least one of the substantive issues to be decided. Conversely, a legal order may well decline to assume jurisdiction even though the forum would, if the matter came before it on a proper jurisdictional basis, apply its domestic law to one or more of the substantive issues raised. These conclusions follow from the premise that, generally speaking, different considerations are decisive for the assumption of jurisdiction, whether general or specific, and for the application of forum law.

In special circumstances there may be, however, a close link in principle between *specific* jurisdiction and choice of law. Where the subject matter is one for which choice of law is not available in the sense that, if the forum adjudicates, it can apply only its domestic rules and principles, jurisdiction should not be assumed unless the putative forum considers that these rules and principles can, in the circumstances of the case, appropriately be applied.[135]

---

[133] *See* Insurance Company of Ireland, Ltd. v. Compagnie des Bauxites de Guinee, 102 S. Ct. 2099, 2104 (1982) ("The requirement that a court have personal jurisdiction . . . recognizes and protects a personal liberty interest. It represents a restriction on judicial power not as a matter of sovereignty, but as a matter of individual liberty.").

[134] In this connection it is instructive to note that a motion to dismiss on the ground of forum non conveniens, *see supra* note 25 and accompanying text, cannot be defeated, at least in federal court practice, "merely by showing that the substantive law that would be applied in the alternative forum is less favorable to the plaintiffs than that of the present forum. [Indeed, t]he possibility of a change in substantive law should ordinarily not be given conclusive or even substantial weight in the *forum non conveniens* inquiry." Piper Aircraft Co. v. Reyno, 454 U.S. 235, 247 (1981).

[135] An unwillingness to utilize the choice-of-law process can be based on various grounds. If the relevant foreign law is unknowable either because it is not on public

In private-law matters, perhaps the best known example of this phenomenon is the unwillingness of common law courts to assert jurisdiction to divorce on such jurisdictional bases as personal service, occurrence within the jurisdiction of the conduct on which the claim for divorce is based, or consent. (Instead, courts in the United States always apply their domestic law rules in divorce cases[136] and assume jurisdiction only when either the moving party or the respondent is domiciled in the jurisdiction.[137])

This linkage of the jurisdictional and choice-of-law issues in divorce cases is not inevitable;[138] indeed, these issues are separated in many continental European legal systems.[139] The explanation for such linking can only be a belief that serious difficulties would be encountered in applying correctly another legal order's divorce laws. The argument presumably runs along the following lines: These laws typically set down rather general standards; the content that is given them in the administration of justice reflects to a large extent the attitudes and experiences of the local community. Consequently,

---

record or because it is completely ad hoc, there is no way in which the forum can consider it. Taking foreign law into account may pose special difficulties in understanding or risks of misunderstanding. Finally, involvement in a matter in which another legal order is concerned to such a degree that its views should be decisive may expose the forum to possible embarrassment or require large expenditures of resources that ultimately redound largely to the benefit of another society. For a discussion of the problem in general and with particular reference to criminal law, divorce, and workmen's compensation, see A. von Mehren & D. Trautman, *supra* note 1, at 84-90, 98-100.

[136] This rule has prevailed for at least a century and a half.

> Upon the whole, the doctrine now firmly established in America upon the subject of divorce is, that the law of the place of the actual, *bona fide* domicil of the parties gives jurisdiction to the proper Courts to decree a divorce for any cause allowed by the local law, without any reference to the law of the place of the orginal marriage, or the place where the offence for which the divorce is allowed was committed.

J. Story, Commentaries on the Conflict of Laws § 230a (2d ed. Boston 1841) (1st ed. Boston 1834); *see also supra* note 99.

[137] In the United States, special jurisdictional bases have been accepted to handle the problem that arises when a spouse lives in one place for an extended period of time under conditions that normally preclude the acquisition of domicile there—e.g., military personnel under orders. By statute, the place of extended residence may be permitted to exercise jurisdiction to divorce. *See, e.g.*, Craig v. Craig, 143 Kan. 624, 56 P.2d 464 (1936); Crownover v. Crownover, 58 N.M. 597, 274 P.2d 127 (1954); Wood v. Wood, 159 Tex. 350, 320 S.W.2d 807 (1959). Under these statutes, the forum's domestic divorce law is applied.

[138] *See* Alton v. Alton, 207 F.2d 667, 684-85 (3d Cir. 1953) (Hastie, J., dissenting).

[139] For example, the French courts are willing to take jurisdiction to divorce and apply the divorce law of another legal order. *See, e.g.*, Gould v. Gould, 235 N.Y. 14, 138 N.E. 490 (1923) (recognition accorded to French divorce decree applying New York law as the parties' national law).

even though the black-letter rule is readily ascertained, a foreign court will find it difficult to determine the meaning that the rules have in practice.

Although these refusals to apply nondomestic law in the divorce area may be questionable, the common law practice illustrates the proposition that when the forum considers the application of foreign law infeasible, jurisdiction can only be assumed if, in the forum's view, local law applies. In these situations, the considerations that justify the application of the local law will normally also justify the assumption of specific jurisdiction. A legal order will hesitate to impose further requirements for the assumption of jurisdiction; any such requirement constitutes a *pro tanto* relinquishment of the opportunity to have the controversy in question regulated under the forum's domestic-law rules unless other putative jurisdictions are prepared to apply nondomestic rules.

The handling of workers' compensation litigation under commission-administered statutes illustrates the situation that results when only domestic rules can be applied.[140] The normally available bases of general jurisdiction are not utilized; instead, jurisdiction turns on relations between the controversy and the forum, such as the place where the employment contract was concluded or the place of injury, relations which also give a plausible basis for applying the forum's workers' compensation statute.

Although, for the reason discussed above, specific jurisdiction and choice of law are not linked in principle, the question remains whether a legal order should include among its accepted bases for assuming jurisdiction the applicability of its domestic law. Order 11 of the English Supreme Court of Judicature provides for discretionary jurisdiction over nonresidents for suits in contract if the contract "by its terms, or by implication" is "governed by English law."[141] The Montevideo Treaty on International Civil Law of 1940 provides more generally for jurisdiction in the place whose law governs the subject matter of the action.[142] And Justice Brennan argued for the adoption of the jurisdictional basis under discussion in his dissent in *Shaffer v. Heitner:*

---

[140] *See* A. von Mehren & D.Trautman, *supra* note 1, at 87-90; *see also supra* note 135.

[141] Rules of the Supreme Court (1962), Order 11 r.1(1)(f)(iii), [1962] Stat. Instr., No. 2145, at 2529, 2552.

[142] The first paragraph of Article 56—contained in Title XIV, Of Jurisdiction—provides that "Personal actions should be instituted before the judges of the place whose law governs the juridical act that constitutes the subject-matter of the action." The next paragraph provides that such actions "may likewise be instituted before the judges of the defendant's domicile." 37 Am. J. Int. L. Supp. 141, 149 (1943); *see* A. Boggiano, Derecho Internacional Privado 67-71 (1978). The Treaty has been ratified by Argentina, Paraguay, and Uruguay. *See* 1 R. Sapena Pastor, Derecho Internacional Privado 63 (2d ed. 1980).

> [W]hen a suitor seeks to lodge a suit in a State with a substantial interest in seeing its own law applied to the transaction in question, we could wisely act to minimize conflicts, confusion, and uncertainty by adopting a liberal view of jurisdiction, unless considerations of fairness or efficiency strongly point in the opposite direction.[143]

On the other hand, Chief Justice Warren, writing for the majority in *Hanson v. Denckla,*[144] remarked that a state "does not acquire . . . jurisdiction by being the 'center of gravity' of the controversy . . . . The issue is . . . jurisdiction, not choice of law."[145] In *Kulko v. Superior Court,*[146] Justice Marshall, writing for the majority, expressly took the position that the applicability of a putative forum's domestic law need not justify the exercise of jurisdiction:

> [W]hile the presence of the children and one parent in California arguably might favor application of California law in a lawsuit in New York, the fact that California may be the "center of gravity" for choice-of-law purposes does not mean that California has personal jurisdiction over the defendant.[147]

What arguments are to be made in fairness theories for—and against—the proposition that applicability of a putative forum's domestic law is a basis for its assumption of jurisdiction? If fairness for jurisdictional purposes is primarily viewed from the *perspective of the parties,* the only situation in which the applicability of a given legal order's law would, in itself, justify the assumption of jurisdiction by that legal order is when establishing the applicable law before a foreign forum would be difficult or expensive. But the problem should, at least on occasion, also be viewed from the *perspective of the interested legal order.* When do its choice-of-law concerns justify the assumption of jurisdiction?

In principle, private international law adjusts competing choice-of-law concerns through the choice-of-law process. There are, however, situations in which the legitimate concerns of all interested legal orders cannot be accommodated; the policies held by some must be preferred at the expense of those held by others. In such cases, the argument for basing jurisdiction on the applicable law is that only in this way can a legal order vindicate policies which, in its view, should regulate the controversy in question. Where the choice-of-law process does not operate—e.g., the common law position respecting divorce or the situation presented by commission-administered workers' compensation statutes—such "true conflicts" are perhaps especially likely because the normal process for working out an accommodation between potentially conflicting substantive views is simply not available. Accordingly, where the choice-of-law process does not oper-

[143] 433 U.S. at 225-26.

[144] 357 U.S. 235 (1958).

[145] *Id.* at 254.

[146] 436 U.S. 84 (1978).

[147] *Id.* at 98 (citing Hanson v. Denckla, 357 U.S. at 254).

ate, the argument in favor of the assumption of jurisdiction is strong if, in the forum's view, its domestic law applies.

It is more debatable whether jurisdiction should be assumed where the choice-of-law process is available but the putative forum would apply its domestic law. This broad rule is undesirable for several reasons. In the first place, by expanding the plaintiff's choice of forums it significantly undermines the traditional preference for the defendant in jurisdictional practice without clear justification from either the plaintiff's or the putative forum's point of view. Furthermore, adoption of such a rule expresses a general lack of confidence in the choice-of-law process and may, therefore, encourage the development of parochial choice-of-law practices, thereby weakening the legal framework needed to ensure that multistate social and economic activities are conducted in a tolerably just and efficient fashion.

The question remains whether a putative forum can properly assume jurisdiction whenever, in its view, there are both weighty reasons to apply its domestic law and a significant likelihood of a true conflict. The argument in favor of such a rule is that, in these situations, the forum must take jurisdiction in order to vindicate its choice-of-law concerns. The first argument against the rule is the difficulty involved in its administration; adherence to the requirement that there be a fair likelihood of a true conflict would often require the court to complete a complex choice-of-law analysis in order to resolve the jurisdictional issue. A second argument is that full vindication of a legal order's choice-of-law concerns is not—except where the concerns are of unusual weight—of sufficient importance to justify departing from the general principle that the plaintiff should go to the defendant's forum. Furthermore, claims of jurisdiction by legal orders on the ground that their domestic law should apply and a true conflict may be involved would probably bring into operation of a kind of Gresham's law; parochial choice-of-law practices would increasingly take the place of more cosmopolitan practices. Finally, recognition and enforcement of judgments with this jurisdictional basis might well be refused internationally. Tying jurisdiction to choice of law in this way would, therefore, conduce to a less cooperative and more disorderly international order.

2. In Federal Systems

Additional considerations affect the propriety of jurisdiction based on choice-of-law concerns in a federal system such as that of the United States. Although the law has not so developed in the United States, there are strong arguments that choice of law in a federal polity should ultimately be regulated under uniform rules administered by a national supreme court. In principle, the over-arching central authority—not the individual states—should be responsible for accommodating the conflicting views of member states bound together by the political, economic, and historical ties that federalism implies. The central authority, by resolving choice-of-law issues in an impartial fashion that fairly considers and mediates the legitimate claims and interests of each state, can achieve for the federation a larger measure of conflicts justice than is possible when these decisions are left to the individual states.

However, perhaps largely because of the enormity of the task, the Supreme Court of the United States has refused to assume even modest direct control over state choice-of-law practice.[148] Of course, if *full* federal control were assumed over state choice of law, the argument for assuming jurisdiction on the basis of the applicability of the forum's domestic law would, as far as interstate situations are concerned, largely disappear. Each state would be assured that, where the choice-of-law process operated, its concerns would receive appropriate attention under the applicable federal choice-of-law rule regardless of the state in which the matter was litigated. Accordingly, jurisdictional practice could turn exclusively on considerations of litigational convenience without regard to choice-of-law considerations.[149]

In the absence of effective federal control over state choice-of-law practices, applicability of local law should not, as a matter of general theory, establish the propriety of state assumption of jurisdiction. By keeping jurisdiction and choice of law separate, the Supreme Court can fashion for the federal polity a jurisdictional theory that rests on a principled elaboration of propositions concerning fairness to the parties and their litigational convenience. Accepting the applicability of the putative forum's domestic law as a jurisdictional basis would undermine federal control of jurisdictional practice; in view of the Supreme Court's unwillingness or inability to control choice of law, constitutional control over the scope of adjudicatory jurisdiction would largely disappear.[150]

---

[148] *See, e.g.*, Allstate Ins. Co. v. Hague, 444 U.S. 320 (1980); Symposium, *supra* note 83.

[149] Professor Hazard's "interstate venue" theory of state-court jurisdiction would be appropriate in these circumstances; however, as the situation now stands, the theory is fatally flawed because it does not take into account each state's essentially independent control of choice of law. The proposal is that

> state court jurisdiction should be considered a problem of venue in a national court system that is managed primarily by the states. Hence, a state court should be regarded as having territorial jurisdiction of a controversy if that state is an appropriate forum according to the criteria employed in typical venue provisions.

Hazard, *Interstate Venue*, 74 Nw. U.L. Rev. 711, 711 (1979). Of course, choice-of-law considerations do not influence venue provisions because the spatial allocation is within a single legal order.

[150] It has been suggested that in the United States "[t]he differing standards for choice of law and jurisdiction seem to be an accident of history." Martin, *Personal Jurisdiction and Choice of Law*, 78 Mich. L. Rev. 872, 873 (1980). But, for the reasons discussed above, differing standards seem appropriate both internationally and within federal systems. Were choice of law unitary, jurisdictional standards

These arguments might have to yield if each member state had the constitutional right to resolve choice-of-law issues for itself, at least when a true conflict is potentially involved, because the assumption of jurisdiction would be essential to the vindication of this right. However, the existing unrestrained state control over choice-of-law does not rest on principle but rather on convenience and historical practice. Accordingly, a state has no principled claim to assume jurisdiction because of choice-of-law concerns. It follows that when state choice-of-law concerns seek expression through assertions of jurisdiction, the federal authority properly considers—as the majority did in *Kulko*—whether the state's interest in applying its domestic rule outweighs general federal policies with respect to the exercise of adjudicatory jurisdiction. Further, from the point of view of the federal system as a whole, the views on choice of law of a state whose claim to adjudicatory jurisdiction rests largely on choice-of-law considerations have no greater claim to wisdom or objectivity than do those of a state whose jurisdictional claim rests on other considerations. Accordingly, sacrificing specifically jurisdictional policies—in particular, considerations of party convenience and of the proper allocation of litigational risks and burdens—would not ensure "wiser" or more "objective" choice-of-law decisions.

Perhaps a federal system should give greater weight to state choice-of-law concerns when, for one reason or another, the choice-of-law process can not operate. In these circumstances, denying jurisdiction to a state that would apply its domestic law results in another state regulating the matter under its domestic law even though, if the choice-of-law process operated, the second state arguably should have applied the first state's law. In such cases, the inability of the forum to take the substantive concerns of other legal orders into account argues with some force for jurisdiction based on choice-of-law concerns.

One further observation remains to be made regarding the question of whether, in a federal system such as the United States, applicability of the putative forum's domestic law should provide an independent basis for assuming adjudicatory jurisdiction. Where, as is today the case in the United States, the federal authority does not control state choice-of-law practices, accepting such a jurisdictional basis would significantly increase the impact of parochial practices insofar as these favor plaintiffs. A well-advised plaintiff will, unless his litigational burden would be disproportionately increased, always litigate in the forum in which the choice-of-law rules are most favorable to his cause.[151] A defendant can, on occasion, escape from these

---

arguably could be assimilated to venue standards, *see supra* note 149; where it is not, jurisdictional theory's concern to minimize forum-shopping stands in the way of accepting, in principle, applicability of forum law as a basis for asserting jurisdiction except when the forum has especially weighty reasons for applying its own law.

[151] "Ordinarily, . . . plaintiffs will select that forum whose choice of law rules are most advantageous." Piper Aircraft Co. v. Reyno, 454 U.S. 235, 263 (1981).

practices because the state lacks jurisdiction. This restraint on parochial rules that favor plaintiffs would disappear, however, were the Supreme Court to accept the view expressed by Justice Brennan in *Shaffer v. Heitner*,[152] while the restraint on parochial rules favoring defendants—the plaintiff's right to choose the forum—would not be affected. Accepting Justice Brennan's position would thus disturb significantly—and without any principled basis—the balance of risk and opportunity between plaintiff and defendant in multistate litigation now struck by the Supreme Court of the United States under the due process clause.[153]

E. *The Significance of Multiple Parties*

The foregoing discussion of when fairness theories consider assertions of adjudicatory jurisdiction appropriate has assumed litigation in which, as in two-party controversies, a jurisdictional basis available against one defendant is available against all. In more complex litigation, the jurisdictional problem may be complicated because not only has no putative forum a common jurisdictional basis with respect to all defendants but, indeed, no forum can claim as to each defendant one of the jurisdictional bases so far discussed. The question then arises whether jurisdiction can appropriately be claimed over all defendants because practical necessity requires that some forum be able to speak with respect to the situation as a whole. The jurisdictional problem posed by this class of cases is complicated in international situations by sovereign sensibilities and the diversity of legal systems.

Litigation involving multiple or indeterminate parties presents complications even when no nondomestic elements are involved. When multistate elements must be taken into account, problems of adjudicatory jurisdiction frequently produce additional difficulties. Complex litigation that is not fully domestic can raise a variety of issues, including the availability of class suits,[154] the possible preclusive effect of decisions in related litigation, and the availability of impleader[155] and interpleader.[156] These matters may affect the problem of how general theory should address the jurisdictional issue in multiple-party litigation.

---

[152] *See supra* text accompanying note 143.

[153] On occasion a defendant can obtain relief from forum-shopping by invoking the doctrine of forum non conveniens. *See, e.g.*, Piper Aircraft Co. v. Reyno, 454 U.S. 235 (1981). However, dismissal on the ground that the forum is inconvenient is discretionary and will, in practice, be accorded in only a very small percentage of the cases in which choice-of-law considerations were decisive for the plaintiff's choice of forum.

[154] *See* von Mehren & Trautman, *supra* note 19, at 1153-55.

[155] On federal impleader in the United States and the use of the "ancillary concept" to obtain jurisdiction over a third-party defendant, see C. WRIGHT, HANDBOOK OF THE LAW OF FEDERAL COURTS 375-80 (3d ed. 1976).

[156] On federal interpleader in the United States, see *id.* at 362-68.

In the United States, the federal courts have jurisdiction in interpleader actions in which "money or property of the value of $500 or more" in the custody or possession of the party filing the action, or the benefits arising by virtue of "any obligation [of the filing party] written or unwritten to the amount of $500 or more," are or may be claimed by "[t]wo or more adverse claimants, of diverse citizenship."[157] In order to exercise the subject-matter jurisdiction thus conferred on the federal courts, two further requirements must be satisfied. In the first place, the federal legal order must have jurisdiction in the international sense;[158] secondly, venue must lie in the federal district court in which the interpleader action is brought. The provisions relating to federal interpleader do not provide special rules for adjudicatory jurisdiction. Consequently, there must be an independent basis of adjudicatory jurisdiction with respect to each of the adverse claimants. However, since the relevant legal order is the United States considered as a whole rather than a member state, there is much more likely to be adjudicatory jurisdiction over each claimant than if the interpleader action were to proceed, as it did in the *Dunlevy* case,[159] in a state court. Venue is unlikely to raise difficulties because the interpleader action "may be brought in the judicial district in which one or more of the claimants reside"[160] or, if all the claimants are aliens, "in any district."[161]

To the extent that techniques such as federal interpleader make it possible to handle multiple-party litigation in a single forum under existing jurisdictional bases, special jurisdictional bases need not be made available for such litigation.[162] Where jurisdictional difficulties remain, however, the need for unified administration of litigation involving multiple or indeterminate parties may justify the assumption of a special form of specific jurisdiction. Thus, the Supreme Court held in *Mullane v. Central Hanover Bank & Trust Co.*[163] that the state in which a common trust fund was created and is administered can, with respect to all questions concerning its management, exercise jurisdiction over every person, known or unknown, who is or may later be interested in the fund. As Justice Jackson wrote,

> the interest of each state in providing means to close trusts that exist by the grace of its laws and are administered under the supervision of its

---

[157] 28 U.S.C. § 1335(a) (1976).

[158] *See* Japan Gas Lighter Ass'n v. Ronson Corp., 257 F.Supp. 219 (D.N.J. 1966).

[159] *See supra* text accompanying notes 45-46.

[160] 28 U.S.C. § 1397 (1976). For venue purposes, a corporation is deemed to reside "in any judicial district in which it is incorporated or licensed to do business or is doing business . . . ." *Id.* § 1391(c).

[161] *Id.* § 1391(d).

[162] The passage of federal interpleader legislation handled, for example, the problem that resulted from the Supreme Court's refusal in *Dunlevy* to permit state interpleader. *See* Chafee, *Interstate Interpleader*, 33 YALE L.J. 685, 722-23 (1924).

[163] 339 U.S. 306 (1950).

> courts is so insistent and rooted in custom as to establish beyond doubt the right of its courts to determine the interests of all claimants, resident or nonresident, provided its procedure affords full opportunity to appear and be heard.[164]

In the case of ordinary trusts, considerations of convenience and practical necessity are less compelling but seem sufficient to justify specific jurisdiction to determine the interests of the beneficiaries and the liability of the trustee.[165]

The argument for basing specific jurisdiction on the need for a unified administration of complex and interrelated matters is strongest when injustice may result if litigation must proceed in several forums. The claim of jurisdiction is thus compelling in situations such as *Mullane*, and would be in *Dunlevy* but for the availability of federal interpleader.

The situs of land likewise has strong reasons for claiming specific jurisdiction in actions to quiet title to land. Here, of course, a power theory had no difficulty in asserting jurisdiction, but the result is equally appropriate for theories based on fairness. *Tyler v. Judges of the Court of Registration*[166] upheld against federal and state constitutional objections a statute providing that a decree of registration, obtained after proceedings designed to give as extensive notice as was feasible, "shall bind the land and quiet the title thereto."[167] In his opinion for the Massachusetts court, Chief Justice Holmes found no difficulty in this assertion of jurisdiction against the whole world. His opinion explained the result in terms both of power and of convenience, fairness, and justice. "Jurisdiction is secured by the power of the court over the *res*."[168] But, Holmes noted: "All proceedings, like all rights, are really against persons. Whether they are proceedings or rights *in rem* depends on the number of persons affected."[169] In any event, as the opinion pointed out, the assertion of adjudicatory jurisdiction in question was justified by practical necessity:

> If [this proceeding] does not satisfy the Constitution, a judicial proceeding to clear titles against all the world hardly is possible; for the very meaning of such a proceeding is to get rid of unknown as well as known claims,—indeed certainty against the unknown may be said to be its chief end,—and unknown claims cannot be dealt with by personal service upon the claimant.[170]

---

164 *Id.* at 313.

165 *See* Cocke v. Duke Univ., 260 N.C. 1, 131 S.E.2d 909 (1963) (charitable foundation); *cf. infra* note 178 (discussing *Hanson v. Denckla*).

166 175 Mass. 71, 55 N.E. 812, *appeal dismissed,* 179 U.S. 405 (1900).

167 *Id.* at 72, 55 N.E. at 812.

168 *Id.* at 75, 55 N.E. at 813.

169 *Id.* at 76, 55 N.E. at 814.

170 *Id.* at 73, 55 N.E. at 813. In context, this observation focuses upon the notice problem, but the argument seems relevant also for the problem of adjudicatory jurisdiction.

The problem of the *Tyler* case also arises with respect to chattels. When the situs is relatively permanent and was established with the consent of all concerned, the exercise of specific jurisdiction can often be justified on grounds of practical necessity. The argument for specific jurisdiction—though less compelling than in *Tyler* because the location of chattels is not fixed—is basically the same as that discussed above in connection with that case.[171]

The necessity argument for specific jurisdiction where trusts, land, and chattels are concerned applies in many other situations. For example, the argument justifies specific jurisdiction in the chartering legal order to determine whether assessments can be levied against stockholders. In *Bernheimer v. Converse,*[172] the receiver of a Minnesota corporation had obtained a determination of stockholders' liability—provided for by the constitution and statutes of Minnesota—in a proceeding in Minnesota against all stockholders, including those who were nonresident and absent. In an action to enforce the judgment in New York, the jurisdictional basis of the Minnesota decision was challenged. The Supreme Court brought Minnesota's assertion of jurisdiction within the then prevailing power theory by using a consent rationale.[173] Today the same result would presumably be rationalized in terms of practical necessity and the unique appropriateness of having litigation binding all stockholders proceed in the chartering legal order.

The argument for specific jurisdiction in multiple party cases is less com-

---

[171] *See, e.g.*, Educational Studios, Inc. v. James Cruze Prods., Inc., 112 N.J. Eq. 352, 164 A. 24 (Ct. Err. & App. 1933). In *Educational Studios,* the litigation involved rather complicated contractual arrangements for producing and distributing a motion picture. Several parties were involved, some of which were not directly affiliated by residence or incorporation with New Jersey. The picture had been produced in California; financing was obtained in New York; the negatives and sound track were deposited, as provided for by the contract, in the New Jersey warehouse of a Delaware corporation; distribution was to be handled by New York firms. "The court of chancery has jurisiction to settle as between parties, some of whom are nonresidents, their conflicting equitable liens upon a chattel physically in the state and in the possession of a resident party, and upon the moneys to be realized by marketing the chattel." *Id.* at 355, 164 A. at 26.

[172] 206 U.S. 516 (1907).

[173] *See id.* at 533; *see also* Hartford Life Ins. Co. v. Ibs, 237 U.S. 662 (1915) (upholding adjudicatory jurisdiction in the chartering legal order over assessments made by a fraternal benefit society on members to meet death claims, on the basis of the practical necessity of allowing the matter to proceed against all members in one forum so as to assure uniform assessments); Eminent Household of Columbian Woodmen v. Bryant, 62 Ga. App. 167, 8 S.E.2d 438 (1940) (holding that Tennessee, where the company had its principal offices, did not have jurisdiction to make assessments on holders of fraternal benefit policies but that an assertion of such jurisdiction by Mississippi, the chartering state, would have been recognized).

pelling when it rests on convenience alone. For example, unified administration of decedents' estates—presumably by the last domicile—is desirable for reasons of convenience but is usually not required to avoid injustice. Accordingly, the propriety of an assertion of specific jurisdiction is more problematical although the claim is on occasion made by one legal order—and recognized by others.[174]

The decision in *World-Wide Volkswagen*[175] has been criticized on the ground that in such circumstances specific jurisdiction should be available so that complete relief can be granted and possibly conflicting results avoided.[176] This criticism ignores several considerations. In the first place, there is no reason to believe that the just adjudication of the plaintiff's products-liability claim in *Volkswagen* required that the regional distributor and the retail dealer be before the court that decided the claim against the manufacturer and the importer. Indeed, Justice Blackmun remarked in dissent that he was

> somewhat puzzled why the plaintiffs in this litigation are so insistent that the regional distributor and the retail dealer . . . who handled the ill-fated Audi automobile involved in this litigation, be named defendants. It would appear that the manufacturer and the importer, whose subjectability to Oklahoma jurisdiction is not challenged before this Court, ought not to be judgment-proof.[177]

Secondly, if a just adjudication of the whole controversy required the presence of defendants other than the manufacturer and the importer, jurisdiction was available over all under conventional standards in New York. Accordingly, Oklahoma's claim to jurisdiction could not be justified by the

---

[174] *See, e.g.*, Jones v. Jones, 301 S.W.2d 310, 317 (Tex. Civ. App. 1957).

[175] 444 U.S. 286 (1980); *see supra* text accompanying notes 115-24.

[176] *See* Kamp, *Beyond Minimum Contacts: The Supreme Court's New Jurisdictional Theory*, 15 GA. L. REV. 19, 44-51, 53-54 (1980).

[177] 444 U.S. at 317-18.

A possible explanation for the plaintiffs' joining the regional distributor and the retailer was to preclude removal by the defendants to the federal district court. *See* Strawbridge v. Curtis, 7 U.S. (3 Cranch) 267 (1806) (construing statutory grant of subject-matter jurisdiction to federal courts in diversity actions as applicable only to suits in which there is complete diversity, that is, no two adverse parties are residents of the same state). Plaintiffs have the choice of initiating an action that meets the diversity requirement in either a court of a state that has adjudicatory jurisdiction or in the federal courts sitting in that state. In many cases, a plaintiff may prefer to litigate in the state court because, for example, he believes that it tends to give larger awards than does the federal court. The plaintiffs in *Volkswagen* were, when the accident occurred, en route from New York, their residence to Arizona, where. they intended to establish a new residence. If a new residence had not been established before the action was begun in the Oklahoma courts, removal would be precluded by the presence in the litigation of defendants—the regional distributor and the wholesaler—whose residence was in New York.

proposition that justice required that one legal order, at least, have jurisdiction over the multiple defendants.

The issue remains whether jurisdiction in Oklahoma over the manufacturer and the importer should, in the circumstances, attract jurisdiction over the regional distributer and the retailer although jurisdiction could not be asserted over the latter but for the related action against the former two defendants. The answer turns on whether, in the circumstances, the latter two defendants' claim to have the plaintiffs come to them is, when weighed against countervailing considerations that the plaintiffs can advance, of sufficient strength to require that the plaintiffs be put to the choice of pursuing two defendants in one forum (Oklahoma) or pursuing all four in another (New York). Theories which accord a jurisdictional preference to defendants presumably should require plaintiffs who wish to avoid such a choice to establish that convenience, fairness, and justice support their position. In *World-Wide Volkswagen* "attracted" jurisdiction in Oklahoma over the regional distributor and the dealer was not—and probably could not have been—established under this standard. However, in a case in which—unlike *Volkswagen*—there were strong reasons why the entire controversy should be litigated in a single forum, a plaintiff's legitimate claim to call to his forum a multistate defendant together with a litigational relation such as existed in *Volkswagen* between that forum and the controversy might properly "attract" jurisdiction over other defendants who are localized.

The problem of the significance of multiple parties for the assertion of jurisdiction arises in a simpler form when the defendants, though geographically dispersed, are all localized. In such a situation the plaintiff cannot rely on the argument that, unless all the defendants can be sued in one forum, his right to call multistate defendants to his forum will be frustrated. These simpler situations raise the question, however, of what—if any—legal order should be able to assume jurisdiction and whether, in principle, specific jurisdiction should be recognized in only one legal order. The basic argument for limiting—perhaps to one—the number of legal orders that may assume jurisdiction is that the plaintiff's choice-of-law advantage increases as a direct function of the number of forums open to him. The plaintiff's claim to specific jurisdiction because fairness requires that interconnected controversies be adjudicated by a single forum does not justify according him choice-of-law advantages that he would not otherwise enjoy—or depriving defendants of jurisdictional protections from which they would otherwise benefit—except to the extent required to provide a forum in which all defendants can be sued. Because this ground can justify only one forum, this form of specific jurisdiction should—unless no principled basis can be advanced for choosing between or among the two or more forums in question—be recognized only in the most appropriate forum.

The issue of appropriateness turns on the circumstances of the particular case. For example, if a high proportion of the defendants are closely connected with one forum, that forum might be accepted. When the defendants are many and widely dispersed, the controversy's litigational relation to a given forum may be decisive. Finally, if the choice-of-law practices of certain forums are less likely to be parochial than those of others, the former should be preferred so as to minimize the possibility that this form of specific jurisdiction will be utilized to obtain unwarranted choice-of-law advantages. Thus, in litigation involving competing claims to a trust fund, jurisdiction over all those actually or potentially having rights to income or corpus might well be limited to the legal order in which the trust was established on the ground that this legal order is at least as likely as any other to have choice-of-law practices that are, with respect to the issues raised, not parochial.[178]

VI. Conclusion

Much more could be said about the two theories of jurisdiction considered in this Article. We can appropriately conclude, however, with a brief discussion of which theory is, in principle, to be preferred. At first blush, the

[178] *Hanson v. Denckla*, 357 U.S. 235 (1958), can be viewed as supporting this proposition. The case turned on the issue of whether a trust, established under Delaware law and there administered, was invalid because the testator had reserved too much power over the trustee and the trust corpus. If the trust was invalid, the trust assets would fall under the residuary clause of the settlor's will. Those who took under this clause brought an action in Florida, where the settlor was living when she died—she had been a Pennsylvania resident when the trust was established—to have the trust held invalid. Jurisdiction was obtained over some of the trust beneficiaries on conventional bases for assuming general jurisdiction. Jurisdiction on such bases could not be established, however, over some beneficiaries or over the trustees.

The Florida court asserted specific jurisdiction as to these beneficiaries and the trustees on the ground "that the circumstances of th[e] case amount to sufficient affiliation with the State of Florida to empower its courts to exercise personal jurisdiction over" the trustee. *Id.* at 250. If the propriety of this jurisdictional claim turns only on a weighing of party convenience, the argument for recognizing jurisdiction in Florida is strong. The corporate trustee was essentially only a stake-holder and was less localized in its activities than were the other parties and, in addition, most of the beneficiaries were living in Florida. However, the Florida court had, in holding the trust testamentary, applied Florida domestic law; this choice of law was, in the circumstances, extremely parochial. Indeed, Chief Justice Warren indicated that the choice of Florida law might well constitute a denial of due process under *Home Ins. Co. v. Dick*, 281 U.S. 397 (1930). *See Hanson*, 357 U.S. at 254 n.27. (Since *Allstate Ins. Co. v. Hague*, 449 U.S. 303 (1981), presumably the Supreme Court would not hold Florida's choice of law in *Hanson* unconstitutional.) The Court did not reach the *Dick* issue but the majority's views on the jurisdictional question may well have been influenced by Florida's choice of law.

The place in which a trust was established and is administered is likely to have a balanced choice of law rule with respect to issues such as whether the trust is testamentary. Accordingly, where a jurisdictional claim in litigation involving such issues ultimately rests on the practical necessity that some forum be able to speak with respect to the situation as a whole, specific jurisdiction can appropriately be limited to the legal order in which the trust is established and administered.

answer seems obvious; when the choice is between practices based on power and practices that reflect the rational elaboration of goals and values, the latter command our allegiance. Reflection soon suggests, however, that the equation is more complex. Adjudication is not a self-contained event in the administration of justice; unless an adjudication can be enforced and given other appropriate effects, the exercise of adjudicatory power serves little or no purpose.

It follows that the theory and practice of adjudicatory jurisdiction in controversies with multistate elements cannot ignore general practices concerning the recognition and enforcement of foreign judgments. The nature of the influence of recognition practice upon jurisdictional theory can be suggested by considering two paradigms, that of an autarchical world in which foreign judgments are given little preclusive effect and that of a more cooperative world in which foreign judgments are, by and large, recognized and enforced.

In an era of autarchy there is little sense in taking adjudicatory jurisdiction unless the forum can enforce the resulting judgment. Power is thus a prerequisite to the assertion of jurisdiction; however, even in an autarchical world, the existence of power need not always require the assumption of jurisdiction. The choice among various possible bases of jurisdiction, all of which involve an element of power, can be made on grounds of effectiveness alone—the greater the forum's control over the parties and the situation as a whole, the more appropriate is the exercise of jurisdiction. Alternatively, where power exists, choices can be based on fairness and litigational convenience.

The attitudes and concerns that produce and sustain an autarchical world may also cause legal orders to view assumptions of jurisdiction largely in terms of effectiveness or power. In such a world, a legal order will simply want to ensure that its arsenal of jurisdictional bases is sufficiently large and varied to permit the legal order to assume jurisdiction whenever it has power and is concerned with a party or the underlying controversy. No jurisdictional basis that meets the criterion of effectiveness is likely to be put aside except on the ground that the jurisdictional arsenal is already fully stocked with other equally effective bases.

Perhaps two qualifications must be made, however. Even in a paradigmatic autarchical world, a legal order will not want to exercise power to adjudicate and to enforce the resulting judgment if such action may prompt reprisals from other legal orders that also have power and are concerned with the parties or the underlying controversy. In multistate situations, no single legal order can claim exclusive authority over the parties or the subject matter of the controversy. For example, when one legal order, having assumed jurisdiction on the basis of power over the defendant or his property, awards damages to the plaintiff, another legal order, with power over the plaintiff or his property, can require the plaintiff to return the amount so awarded. Accordingly, even in an autarchical world, there must be a degree of tolerance and forbearance. An awareness of this necessity may operate to prevent exercises of power when the sensibilities of other legal orders would be deeply offended.

Furthermore, even in an autarchical world, a legal order may refuse to exercise power over a defendant if the ultimate consequence of the exercise would be to penalize an innocent third party. The form of *quasi in rem* jurisdiction exemplified by *Harris v. Balk* is hardly acceptable unless the garnishee will not have to pay twice, once to the defendant's creditor and once to the defendant. A legal order that applies an amount owed the defendant by a third party in order to satisfy the plaintiff's claim has only an indirect hold over the defendant; therefore, the defendant's debtor is subject to a substantial risk of having to pay his debt twice unless the original judgment is recognized abroad. In these circumstances, even in an autarchical world, considerations of justice may well cause a forum not to exercise its power.[179]

Subject to the rather modest qualifications suggested above, however, the power principle naturally and perhaps inevitably dominates jurisdictional theory in an autarchical world. Accordingly, a theory of jurisdiction based on convenience, fairness, and justice can hardly emerge and prosper unless the international order is cooperative and ready to recognize and enforce foreign judgments. The first effect of the emergence of a more cooperative order can, it is true, be to remove certain restraints that a more autarchical order imposes on power theory. Thus, in the American federal system, the compulsion to recognize sister-state judgments that flows from the full faith and credit clause removed the objection, discussed above, to the form of *quasi in rem* jurisdiction exercised in *Harris v. Balk*.

In the long run, however, the existence of a cooperative interstate or international order stimulates and nourishes jurisdictional thinking in terms of convenience, fairness, and justice. Once a legal order can assume that its adjudications will be given preclusive effect abroad, power is no longer a *sine qua non* for claiming jurisdiction. It becomes possible to consider the principles on which adjudicatory authority should be allocated within a community of cooperating legal orders. To the extent that cooperation exists, power is largely irrelevant and other considerations become decisive.

The theories of adjudicatory jurisdiction that result will be closely linked to decent, nonparochial practices with respect to the recognition and enforcement of foreign judgments. It is, therefore, understandable why in the last quarter century a theory of this nature has come to dominate jurisdictional thinking in the United States with respect to both the federal and the international context. Of course, American experience with multistate controversies derives, in large part, from matters that are federal rather than international in nature. But, though the transfer is not inevitable, in the absence of clear countervailing considerations there is a strong and natural tendency in American practice to approach problems of both adjudicatory

---

[179] *See supra* page 294.

jurisdiction and recognition of foreign judgments, arising in an international context, in the way that comparable problems arising in an interstate context are handled.[180]

Both history and logic suggest that power theories of jurisdiction prosper when legal orders look inward and give little support or encouragement to economic and social activities that have significant nondomestic aspects. Conversely, as legal orders give effective legal support to such activities, power theories are displaced by theories based on considerations of fairness. A legal order's approach to the problem of adjudicatory jurisdiction may provide, therefore, an insight into its hopes or fears for a just international order sustained, in its legal aspects, by the discipline and practices of private international law.

---

[180] It is most regrettable that, in the Brussels Convention on Jurisdiction and Enforcement of Judgments in Civil and Commercial Matters, the European Economic Community has accepted jurisdictional bases for certain international situations that it rejects as exorbitant for situations in which the defendant is closely connected with a member of the Community. *See generally* von Mehren, *Recognition and Enforcement of Sister-State Judgments: Reflections on General Theory and Current Practice in the European Economic Community and the United States*, 81 COLUM. L. REV. 1044 (1981).

The Choice of Law Process

[2]

HARVARD
LAW REVIEW

VOL. XLVII DECEMBER, 1933 No. 2

A CRITIQUE OF THE CHOICE-OF-LAW PROBLEM

FOR the commentator on the conflict of laws, it is an article of faith, attested by works if not avowed in words, that its proper study will disclose rules or principles which, like the hazel wand of the diviner, will indicate the "appropriate" jurisdictions whose laws are to determine those controversies that, in one way or another, have failed to respect state lines. But what that "proper study" may be has long been matter for dispute, and the methods championed by the disputants have produced fruits so diverse that pragmatic appraisal is impossible. Moreover, as the quest for jurisdiction-selecting rules continues, there steals upon one who finds his zeal flagging before this diversity the suspicion that perhaps it points not to the need for the task but to the futility of its doing. A suspicion so subversive will not easily down. Doubt breeds inquiry, and inquiry is the mother of monographs.

I

To students of the conflict of laws, Dicey's dichotomy wherein he opposes the "theoretical" to the "positive" method is familiar. In his hand, the distinction seems to depend on nothing more significant than the relative proportions of "ought" and "is" in the blend of both that is characteristic of legal thought in this and every other field of law.[1] That dichotomy, as employed

[1] Dicey describes as "two common characteristics" of devotees of the "theo-

by Cook and Lorenzen, gains sharpness. The theoretical method becomes a survival of scholasticism; the positive method is identified with experimental science.[2] To the distrust of deductions from " self-evident principles of right " and the need for constant reference to the decisions of the courts, stressed by Dicey, there is added Professor Cook's determination " to adopt the procedure which has proved so fruitful in other fields of science, *viz.*, to observe concrete phenomena first and to form generalizations afterwards ".[3] And Professor Lorenzen has asserted, " The cor-

retical " method the views (1) that rules for choice of law constitute " in some sense 'a common law' tacitly adopted by all civilized nations ", from which " deviations ought to be avoided ", and (2) that " the object of a writer on the conflict of laws is to discover the principles which either do or should determine this common law of Europe ". DICEY, CONFLICT OF LAWS (5th ed. 1932) 11. However, it is conceded that their method " is normally based upon careful investigation into the rules as to the conflict of laws which in fact prevail in given countries ". *Id.* at 13. (This concession was not made until the fourth edition of his work, and its authorship remains uncertain. See note 53, *infra.*)

The writers of the " positive " school " make it the object of their labors to ascertain what is the law of a given country with regard to the extra-territorial recognition of rights. . . . When they have done this, they may proceed to formulate the fundamental principles on which the rules in question avowedly or tacitly rests ". *Id.* at 13–14.

[2] Professor Cook notes the distinction in the physical sciences between " the deductive method of ascertaining truth " and " the inductive method of modern science " to which the former has given way and observes that Dicey's theoretical and positive methods " correspond exactly to the two methods " whose rivalry in the physical sciences he describes. Cook, *The Logical and Legal Bases of the Conflict of Laws* (1924) 33 YALE L. J. 457–58. Lorenzen, too, identifies the theoretical method with that of *a priori* deduction. Lorenzen, *Territoriality, Public Policy and the Conflict of Laws* (1924) 33 YALE L. J. 736.

Neither Professor Cook nor Professor Lorenzen have remained content with the narrow rôle allotted by Dicey to the positivists. See, *e.g.*, Cook *" Substance " and " Procedure " in the Conflict of Laws* (1933) 42 YALE L. J. 333; Lorenzen, *Validity and Effects of Contracts in the Conflict of Laws* (1921) 30 YALE L. J. 655, 672 (where the author concedes in regard to a proposal made by him, " no case has gone quite so far as this "). Nor do they repudiate the virtue which Dicey ascribes, at p. 13, to the theoretical method, namely, the belief " that the choice of one system of law rather than of another for the decision of a particular case is dictated by reasons of logic, of convenience, or of justice ". *Cf.* Cook, *The Logical and Legal Bases of the Conflict of Laws*, *supra*, at 486 *et seq.*; Lorenzen, *Territoriality, Public Policy, and the Conflict of Laws*, *supra*, at 748.

[3] Cook, *The Logical and Legal Bases of the Conflict of Laws* (1924) 33 YALE L. J. 457, 460. The " concrete phenomena " chosen for observation are " what [the] courts have *done*, rather than . . . the description they have given of the reasons for their action ". *Ibid.*

rect mode of approach to this subject would strip it of all fictions and deal with all phenomena *a posteriori* ".[4]

The immediate contributions attributable to these resolutions to be positive have thus far been negative, but they are important nonetheless. The notion that the law applicable to a given controversy might be deduced from principles of the territoriality of law, embodied in the common law, was the first point of attack. Both Professor Cook and Professor Lorenzen, heeding Dicey's admonition to look to the cases, found that American and English were not consistently consonant with any such principles. Their conclusion, reached with evident satisfaction, was that no such principles existed in the common law.[5] The second point of attack was the " vested rights " theory which had been regarded as essential to explain the paradoxical apparition of a territorially-limited rule of law in a foreign forum. Proceeding from the assumptions that " law " is a prophecy of what courts will do and that " rights " are hypostases of that prophecy, Professor Cook demonstrated[6] that courts in conflicts cases were not engaged " in the recognition and enforcement of foreign created rights ",[7] the conception of their function basic to that explanation. Professor Cook's conclusion was, of course, no sounder than those assumptions,[8] but the wide acceptance that they enjoy today has served to establish his position firmly as the view of at least a substantial minority. Indeed, one may now wonder how any juristic construct such as " right " could have been accepted

[4] Lorenzen, *Territoriality, Public Policy, and the Conflict of Laws* (1924) 33 YALE L. J. 736, 748.

[5] Cook, *supra* note 3, at 484; Lorenzen, *supra* note 4, at 743. In a recent article, Professor Cook subjects Story's propositions as to the territorial limitations of law to analytical scrutiny, demonstrating that if Story meant what it seems reasonably clear he did not mean, then he would have been still more clearly wrong. See Cook, *The Jurisdiction of Sovereign States and The Conflict of Laws* (1931) 31 COL. L. REV. 369.

[6] Cook, *supra* note 3.

[7] Beale, *Summary of the Conflict of Laws* in 3 CASES ON THE CONFLICT OF LAWS (1902) 501. *Cf.* Dicey's reference to the conflicts of laws as " the part of the law of England which regulates the extra-territorial recognition of rights ". DICEY, CONFLICT OF LAWS 14.

[8] Professor de Sloovère has attacked their utility in the conflict of laws. See de Sloovère, *The Local Law Theory and Its Implications in the Conflict of Laws* (1928) 41 HARV. L. REV. 421.

as fundamental in the explanation of any important aspect of judicial activity.[9]

The refusal to recognize as binding the limitations which the territorial theory and its corollary had fastened upon those important problems in the conflict of laws designated by the phrase, "choice of law",[10] effected their emancipation from deductive methodology. Indeed, in the eight years which have followed the publication of the articles in which these views were voiced, scepticism as to the fruitfulness of all deductive methodologies has become endemic among American legal scholars. One would, accordingly, have anticipated that this freedom would have been used to considerable advantage by scholars in this branch of conflicts. Generally speaking, such has not been the case. This is in part attributable to the fact that the lines of conduct out of which springs the litigation presenting this problem are not well defined. The opportunity for any form of institutional approach to a question which owes its existence to the accidental interposition of state lines and to the equally accidental differences in state laws is definitely limited. There is, however, another obstacle to the profitable employment of the positive method which is not inherent in the subject but which is a heritage of the theoretical method, deriving as much from the "vested rights" as from the territorial theory. It is with that obstacle that this article is concerned.

II

A change in methodology invites a re-inspection of the problem to be attacked, for the formulation of a problem is likely to be as much the product of an approach as the approach is the product of the problem. A positive methodology applied to a problem which for it, at least, is false will not yield a fair return; and the

---

[9] The elliptical nature of the term is too frequently forgotten in doctrinal discourse. Its usefulness for descriptive purposes does not justify resort to it in explanation of that which it describes.

[10] The problem of defining in a phrase the fact situations presenting choice-of-law problems is insuperable, since what the operative facts are depend on the rules for choice of law adopted. Until these rules are definitely ascertained, who can be sure that a given case is wholly "domestic"? An alternative approach is the procedural. This again is not susceptible of succinct statement in view of the variety of methods by which the question as to the appropriate law may be raised.

situation disclosed by the state of authority in cases involving a choice of laws is symptomatic of a false problem.

Where a problem which courts have set themselves is false, one of two results is inevitable. The courts may adhere consistently to a broad principle beneath the shelter of which a variety of results will be concealed, or they may take refuge in a diversity of doctrines.[11] Whether in either event the decisions themselves may be subsumed under some inarticulate premises is another matter. Complete optimism on this count would point the superfluity of much legal study. Since the courts will usually escape the check of criticism directed to these premises, one is justified, perhaps, in suspecting the worst. We have been too ready, I suggest, to trade the dogma of the automatic and inflexible rule for the myth of the rule freely and deliberately manipulated by the courts.

In American conflicts cases, the alternative of diversity in doctrines has probably been resorted to the more frequently. This is in part due to the coincidence of the development of the federal union with the rapid expansion of international and interstate trade. These events brought to the courts an influx of conflicts cases for which adequate authority did not exist. Story's treatise, designed to meet this need, brought to their attention the works of Continental jurists, adepts of the theoretical method, from whose writings Story had selected those views most consonant with his own. But no embargo could be laid on future imports, and when, subsequently, the hard pragmatism of common law jurisprudence could not be reconciled to the result dictated by one of Story's principles, another doctrine was ready to the judge's hand. Rules proliferated, each fashionably tagged with its appropriate Latin phrase. *Lex loci contractus, lex loci solutionis, lex rei sitae, locus regit actum, mobilia sequuntur personam,* — each phrase bears testimony to our common law judges' dalliance with civilian doctrine.

All this is an old story. More significant is the fact that the conditions of whose origin it offers some explanation have persisted to the present time. Lines of decision have hardened here and there, but the article on a conflict of laws topic which does not deplore a current " confusion of authority " is still a rarity.

[11] *Cf.* Arnold, *Criminal Attempts — The Rise and Fall of an Abstraction* (1930) 40 YALE L. J. 53.

And to account for its origin does not explain its continuance. That same pragmatism of the common law has effected many times before this the absorption of those elements of an alien theory which were congenial to it while it rejected the rest. Why has a century not worked this result in the conflict of laws? The explanation, it is submitted, lies in the nature of the problem which a choice of law case is thought to pose.

When a case arises in which a foreign law is offered in evidence or in which the applicability of the law of the forum is denied, a court faithful to the conventional approach will turn in search of a conflicts of laws rule to determine the *jurisdiction* whose law should govern the question at issue. The conflicts rule indicates in which jurisdiction the appropriate law may be found. Assuming the law offered to be from that jurisdiction, the court will then proceed with the case, employing that law as a rule of decision. Not until its admission for that purpose does the content of that law become material. Both the territorial and the "vested rights" theories sanctioned its disregard. So long as deduction from territorial postulates could indicate only one jurisdiction as a source of law in a given case, the content of that law would be logically irrelevant. Again, so long as the court was in search of a "foreign-created right", it would seek an appropriate jurisdiction, not an appropriate substantive rule, for metaphorical consistency demands that the creation or non-creation of rights be attributed only to states and not to their legal rules. That rules for the determination of the appropriate jurisdiction would ignore the content of its law may not be inevitable as a matter of logic; actually it has seemed inescapable.

With the reaction against the restrictions of theory, there has come a recognition that considerations of justice and social expediency should be, and in many cases have been, the dominant determinants of problems in this field. Yet these considerations are still harnessed to the old task of devising (or justifying) rules for selecting the appropriate jurisdiction whose law should govern a given case. Like the forms of action, in Maitland's telling phrase, the territorial and vested rights theories rule us from their graves,[12] and this dominion is maintained by the problem which they have set and with which we have not broken.

[12] It may be objected that this constitutes premature burial. The territorial

A willingness to convert the positive methodology to the uses of the old problem is evident even in the writings of Professor Lorenzen. He concludes an uncompromisingly realistic depiction of the court's task in a " choice of law " case with this statement: " The general problem is, therefore, always the same: What are the demands of justice in the particular situation; what is the controlling policy? " But the succeeding sentences suggest that he, too, sees the problem in terms of rules for choice of jurisdiction.

> " If the situation is one admitting of the application of ' foreign ' law, the choice of the rule to be applied will be determined again in many instances by general social or economic considerations. For example, if the question relates to capacity, a state may conclude that the principal interest involved is the protection of its citizens or of persons domiciled within its territory, wherever they may be. If this be so, it will probably say that the *lex patriae* or the *lex domicilii* governs ' capacity '. On the other hand, it may conclude that its principal interest in the matter is the security of local transactions. In this event it will say that the *lex loci contractus* governs capacity ".[13]

This passage, insofar as it is not merely descriptive of judicial practice, may not be representative of its author's present views.[14] However, in its acceptance of the conventional formulation of solutions to choice-of-law problems, it is characteristic of most current comment on case law in this field, however restive the commentators may be under the limitations which this search for the appropriate jurisdiction places upon judicial realism. What those

---

and vested rights theories seem to constitute the theoretical basis of the American Law Institute's Restatement and are accepted by the author of the most recent treatise in the field. See GOODRICH, CONFLICT OF LAWS (1927) 11. The figure employed above must, therefore, be restricted in its application to those who disavow allegiance to these theories.

[13] Lorenzen, *supra* note 4, at 748.

[14] Thus, in his more recent *Tort Liability and the Conflict of Laws* (1931) 47 L. Q. REV. 483, 490 Professor Lorenzen states: " Much may be said in favor of greater elasticity in the rules of the conflict of laws. Just what the qualifications to the *lex loci delicti* should be it is difficult to say. What is wanted are decisions that appeal to one's sense of justice ". But the *obligatio* theory remains the villain of the piece. Nowhere does he seem to have dealt explicitly with what to me seems the insuperable obstacle to their satisfactory formulation, the disregard of the content of the law chosen. *Cf.*, however, his proposal with respect to contract cases involving conflicts of law, discussed pp. 182–83.

limitations are may be made more evident by the use of a hypothetical case.

A salesman induces a married lady, not yet 21, in state *A* to order several feet of *belles lettres*. Her order is received and accepted by the publishers at their office in state *B*, and they express the books to her residence in state *A*. After reading through two inches and paying for six, the customer repents of her bargain. The publishers sue in state *A*. The lady pleads want of capacity to contract. If the problem is to find a rule to determine the law of what state governs capacity to contract, the fact that the law of state *A* is reminiscent of those days when husband and wife were one is no more material than the fact that the law of state *B* mirrors the latest views of the National Woman's Party on sex equality before the law. It is equally immaterial that in state *A* infants' protection may, in Professor Chafee's phrase, cause infantile paralysis, while in state *B* married minors are emancipated. The court is seeking a rule which, if it already has the pedigree of precedent, may have arisen in a case where the competing domestic laws were, with relation to the facts of the transaction, the reverse of those now before it. Moreover, the court must contemplate the use of its decision in the instant case as a precedent for the decision of some subsequent "capacity" case which will present still another pattern of local laws. Now, however pragmatic the considerations may be which move the court in its determination of the rule for choice of law, the fact remains that as to this case, and all subsequent cases in which that rule will be involved, the court is employing the divining rod, or, to use a more modern metaphor to symbolize fortuitous selection, it is engaging in a blindfold test. The court must blind itself to the content of the law to which its rule or principle of selection points and to the result which that law may work in the case before it. The conflicts rule having pointed out the jurisdiction in which the appropriate law may be found, judicial scrutiny of that law, except for the purpose of its application, is henceforth proscribed.

But the fabric of this blindfold is a legal theory. The court will, of course, actually know the provisions of the law proffered to it as the appropriate one and may well be familiar with the content of the competing laws of other jurisdictions. Perhaps the discipline of authority, where precedent happens to point in a single direction, will effect the insulation of this knowledge from the process of decision. Devotion to a single theory of choice of law may work a similar compartmentation. But where both the state of authority and the absence of cherished principles of conflicts theory leave the court relatively free to determine the applicability of the foreign law, only a judge in whom the legal mind, as defined by Professor Powell,[15] has hypertrophied could exclude from consideration the consequences of the application of the proffered law to the facts of the given case.

That this consideration will determine the issue of the case cannot be predicted. The court, conscious of its duty to formulate a rule applicable equally to situations where the patterns of laws are different, may devise or adopt a rule which in its judgment will accommodate itself most successfully to those various patterns, deploring the while whatever harshness this rule may work in the case at bar. Yet it seems more likely that the court's deliberations will disclose a happy coincidence between the dictates of justice in the instant case and factors decisive of the proper conflicts rule. False problems are not likely to lead to unsatisfactory results when first they are posed. They are more likely to owe their origin to the facile solutions which they afford to embarrassing issues. It is only when subsequent cases arise that the penalty is exacted. The court faced with a new case in which the only variation from its predecessor lies in the pattern of local laws may find the rule, which seemed so persuasive once, compelling it to a decision repugnant to its sense of justice. And this may happen even though the court had employed in the first case a methodology as exactingly " positive " as the character of the problem would permit.[16] A " positive " methodology charged

[15] Professor Arnold, in the article cited in note 11, *supra*, at 58, quotes from an unpublished manuscript of Professor T. R. Powell the following definition: " If you think you can think about something which is attached to something else without thinking about what it is attached to, then you have what is called a legal mind ".

[16] It must be remembered also that the opinions of courts are not the only ingredients entering into the composition of legal rules. The opinions of commentators as to what decisions " hold " are often equally influential, and the commentator is not controlled, as are the courts, by the realities of actual controversies which must be decided. Recently the New York Court of Appeals decided the first important American case squarely posing a problem as to the creation of a living trust of personalty. The trust in question offended the law of the settlor's domicil on

with ascertaining a rule of law capable of working satisfactory results in two cases wherein facts decisive of the judgments reached (the applicable domestic laws) may be diametrically opposed is set an impossible task.

III

There have been a few avenues of escape from this entanglement which from time to time have been tried by the courts. Among these are the following:

1. The conflict of laws rule may itself be couched in terms of a result regarded as proper in litigation of a given sort. The most familiar example is the rule generally adopted to govern the choice of a usury law. The decline of the defense of usury in judicial esteem has led many courts to uphold any contract alleged to be usurious when it would be valid by the law of any jurisdiction to which the transaction was materially related.[17] It has been suggested by Professor Lorenzen that this rule be ex-

marital property but was valid under the laws of the forum where the trust estate (securities) was situated at the time of its creation, where the trust was to be administered, and whose laws, it seems apparent, were regarded by the parties as applicable. Hutchison v. Ross, 262 N. Y. 381, 187 N. E. 65 (1933). In an able opinion by Lehman, J., far more "positive" in character than is usually found in choice-of-law cases, the court (two judges *dubitantibus*) held the New York law applicable. Considerable attention was devoted in the opinion to the conflicting claims of the domicil and the *situs*, but significance was accorded the parties' intention and the policy of the state, as declared in a statute passed after the transaction at issue. I predict, however, that this decision will very generally be taken to confirm § 315 of the Conflict of Laws Restatement that the law of the *situs* governs the validity of an *inter vivos* trust of personalty. This simplification will, I believe, utterly distort the decision, and it is not difficult to imagine cases where, because of the differences in the pattern of laws and "contacts", its application will work results wholly out of harmony with the spirit which informs the opinion. This distortion will be the consequence of the search for a jurisdiction-selecting rule and of the premium placed upon certainty in this field, to which Judge Lehman himself pays tribute. See 262 N. Y. 381 at 389, 187 N. E. at 68. If the case were confined to the circumstances which gave rise to it, its significance as the basis of a rule would be greatly circumscribed. Its significance as an evaluation of the various factors involved therein would, however, remain, and as such its contribution to the law would be of very considerable value.

[17] See GOODRICH, CONFLICT OF LAWS 238. This result is generally attributed to the intention of the parties and, therefore, the illustration might be classed with ordinary cases where the parties' intention has been adopted as the proper guide in the choice of law. However, where no intent is expressed, the parties are "presumed to have chosen the law which will sustain the contract". *Id.* at 238–39.

tended wherever the " intrinsic validity " of a contract is in question.[18] This view represents a drastic simplification of the problem and places a low appraisal on the significance of the variations in domestic laws relating to contracts. Perhaps such an estimate is justifiable. In any event, this means of escaping the artificiality of conflicts rules will not be available generally [19] and is itself subject to the qualification implicit in the recognition accorded by its sponsor to the doctrine immediately following.

2. The conflict of laws rule may be disregarded when the foreign law it selects dictates a result repugnant to the public policy of the forum.[20] In this situation we have a frank discarding of the blindfold. There is, however, no disavowal of the choice-of-law rule which is preserved for use when the results it produces do not run counter to local standards of justice and policy. The invocation of the doctrine has been deprecated quite generally.[21]

---

[18] Professor Lorenzen formulates his suggestion as follows: ". . . the intrinsic validity of contracts should be recognized if the local law of any state with which the contract has a substantial connection be satisfied ". Lorenzen, *Validity and Effect of Contracts in the Conflict of Laws* (1921) 30 YALE L. J. 655, 673.

[19] The rule as to usury is not uniformly followed, and Professor Lorenzen concedes that no case has gone as far as his suggestion. However, the statutes changing common law rules seek usually to effectuate a given result, not merely to furnish a guide for selecting a jurisdiction whose law is unknown. See, *e.g.*, *Uniform Marriage Evasion Act* § 1; *Uniform Wills Act, Foreign Executed* § 1.

[20] A valuable survey of cases involving the public policy of the forum is to be found in Note (1933) 33 COL. L. REV. 508, in which it is pointed out that resort is often had to the public policy doctrine without a determination of the choice-of-law problem at issue. *Id.* at 513.

Recourse to the " public policy " escape is facilitated by the doctrine of " comity " which competes in judicial opinions with the " vested-rights " theory as an explanation of the enforcement of a foreign law whose extra-territorial operation is denied. The formula, " comity is not a right but a courtesy ", Ulman, Magill & Jordan Woolen Co. v. Magill, 155 Ga. 555, 557, 117 S. E. 657, 658 (1923), is the customary prelude to a decision to be discourteous.

[21] A vigorous criticism is to be found in Beach, *Uniform Interstate Enforcement of Vested Rights* (1918) 27 YALE L. J. 656, approved by GOODRICH, CONFLICT OF LAWS 11. Judge Beach over-simplifies the issue by his failure to appreciate the difficulties inherent in a determination of what law " created " the " vested right " whose unquestioning enforcement he urges. Professor Lorenzen, who would leave some scope for the operation of the doctrine (see Lorenzen, *supra* note 18, at 673), charges that the inordinate indulgence in the public policy doctrine has resulted from " the notion that the rules of the Conflict of Laws can be derived from some general formula or theory ". Lorenzen, *supra* note 4, at 746. With this charge I agree in part, but I do not share his optimism that this situation may be remedied by devising rules with regard to " general social or economic considerations " so

In certain instances, its employment may be controlled by the Supreme Court.[22] Its very facility is its most unfortunate trait. In its somewhat cavalier dismissal of a foreign law, it dispenses with the necessity for close analysis, for an affirmative appraisal of the situation upon which judgment must be passed. On the Continent efforts have been made to systematize the doctrine of public policy, but the variety of circumstances which may evoke its use is such that generality in the principle evolved has been inescapable.[23] This opens the door to a practice, familiar enough throughout our law, of shifting the focus of inquiry from the narrow issue of policy raised by the case at bar to the broad issue of determining with respect thereto the limits of the principle. Its generality compels resort to other and different cases for aid in its definition.

3. The conflict of laws rule may refer the court to the intention of the parties as a guide to the selection of the appropriate law.[24] Where this intention has been expressed, as is not infrequent in contracts when at least one party is regularly engaged in interstate

---

long, at least, as the operation of those rules is to select jurisdictions without regard to the rules of law thereby selected.

[22] *Cf.* Bradford Elec. Light Co. v. Clapper, 286 U. S. 145 (1932); Bond v. Hume, 243 U. S. 15 (1917). See Dodd, *The Power of the Supreme Court to Review State Decisions in the Field of Conflict of Laws* (1926) 39 HARV. L. REV. 533, 557.

[23] A Dutch jurist has criticized these efforts as follows: " It is impossible to give an enumeration of the legal rules of public policy; to classify them is difficult and not worth while. . . . Every case must be considered separately ". Kosters, *Public Policy in Private International Law* (1920) 29 YALE L. J. 745, 756, 758. Westlake, in his PRIVATE INTERNATIONAL LAW (7th ed. 1925) 51, has said of the reservation in favor of public order and morals that no attempt to define its limit has ever succeeded.

[24] This rule has been resorted to by American courts chiefly in cases involving the validity of contracts. See GOODRICH, CONFLICT OF LAWS 235. The difficulty of ascertaining an unexpressed intent, from which the courts have sought to escape by the employment of various presumptions, has laid it open to criticism on the score of uncertainty. See Beale, *What Law Governs the Validity of a Contract* (1910) 23 HARV. L. REV. 260, 264. It has been attacked on the theoretical ground that it " involves a delegation of sovereign power to private individuals ". Lorenzen, *supra* note 18, at 656, where the views of Professors Beale and Dicey are presented. Judge Learned Hand in a recent case characterized an attempt to determine by a declaration of intention the law governing the contract as an effort " to pull on one's bootstraps ". Gerli & Co. v. Cunard S. S. Co., 48 F.(2d) 115, 117 (C. C. A. 2d, 1931). But this method of levitation actually works in many jurisdictions, both here and abroad.

business [25] or in wills and trust settlements of importance,[26] the parties themselves will probably have appraised the consequences of an application of the law intended to the controversy in question. If the court is willing unquestioningly to accept their intention as its guide, the blindfold, if preserved, is without consequence. Where, however, the court considers that expressed intent as only one of the factors to be weighed in the selection of an appropriate law, or where the absence of any such expression obliges the court to speculate as to an intention which may never have been conceived, then it should become necessary to take into careful account the results which the competing laws would work in the case at bar. To the extent that the intention rule compels this consideration of the domestic laws, it avoids the anomaly of the blindfold test. To me, this seems a factor in its favor of greater consequence than a preservation of "autonomy of the will," where at least that will becomes well-defined only after conferences with counsel. But the rule trades one false problem for another where intention has not been expressed and is not palpably inferable from the circumstances. A conjectural intent, especially where this is directed to a generality such as "the law of the contract" and not to the consequences of the controversy in litigation, may result in the selection of a different law from that which a considered appraisal of all the factors would have indicated.

4. The conflict of laws rule may make the choice of jurisdiction depend on the "nature" of the domestic law whose application is in question. A significant instance of such a rule is the familiar doctrine that the forum's rules of procedure will always be employed. If a foreign rule of law is found, when offered, to be

[25] Such declarations are common in contracts for carriage. New York brokerage house with branches throughout the country provide, frequently, in their form contracts, that New York law shall govern the transactions under them.

[26] This practice has been given legislative sanction by a New York statute providing that New York law shall govern trusts of personal property situated in that state at the creation thereof if the parties to the trust instrument, wherever resident, so declare. N. Y. PERS. PROP. LAW § 12a, N. Y. Laws 1930, c. 849. I have elsewhere urged the adoption of such a view in the absence of statute where there is some point of contact between the transaction and the state whose law is thus designated. See Cavers, *Trusts Inter Vivos and the Conflict of Laws* (1930) 44 HARV. L. REV. 161.

procedural in character, it is rejected for the analogous rule of the forum.[27] Recently Professor Cook has convincingly revealed the inutility of an approach which seeks to derive a solution to this question from pre-existing concepts of "procedure" and "substantive law".[28] But the courts in these cases must at least examine the competing rules of law as a means of determining the appropriate law to be applied. Professor Cook's insistence that this examination include a consideration of the results worked by such rules in the cases [29] would make possible, if heeded, a thoroughly realistic handling of the problem.

These devices are either limited in scope [30] or, although useful at times, more likely to preserve the situation from which on occasion they afford a means of escape than to lead to its ultimate elimination. If the conflict of laws is to keep pace with the development in other fields of the law, courts and commentators alike must abandon the quest for rules which will work justice equally in two contradictory situations. So long as that is the goal of their inquiry, it may be doubted how significant is the choice between the theoretical and the positive methods. Whatever rules may be worked out will in some cases reach results which seem

[27] See GOODRICH, CONFLICT OF LAWS 157.

[28] See Cook, *"Substance" and "Procedure" in the Conflict of Laws* (1933) 42 YALE L. J. 333.

[29] Professor Cook's thesis is that in classifying legal rules as substantive or procedural, the courts have failed to consider the purpose for which the classification is made and have tended, as a consequence, to draw without discrimination upon cases posing quite different basic problems wherein the same terminology is employed to designate the classes. In the conflict of laws cases, the purpose of the classification is to relieve the forum of the burden of taking over "all the machinery of the foreign court for the 'enforcement' . . . of the 'substantive rights'". Cook, *supra* note 28, at 343. There being no sharp distinction between the "substantive" and the "procedural", the question is to determine how far the forum can go in importing foreign rules without undue hindrance to itself. This can be answered only by a reference to the situations in which the rules are to be employed. Thus it may "turn out that in some cases the question of the 'form of action' has so little relation to 'substance' that the *lex fori* ought to govern, but that in others the real problem has so much to do with whether the plaintiff shall be given an effective right that the views of the 'place of wrong' or of the 'place of contracting', *etc.*, with reference to the 'form of action' ought to be the decisive ones". *Id.* at 352–53.

[30] Thus, the doctrine of public policy, the most comprehensive of the four, is negative in its operation. Reference to the intention of parties is useful only in consensual transactions and, as to some of these, marriage, for example, it is obvious that social interest cannot be subordinated to the desires of the individual.

eminently desirable and just as surely will compel courts in others to call upon hitherto undeclared policies of the state or unsuspected intentions of the parties to extricate them from the necessity of pronouncing intolerable judgments.

IV

How then should a court regard the problem raised by a controversy of which a foreign law or laws are alleged to be determinative? A diagnosis having been advanced, a prescription is called for. In medicine alone have these functions usually been looked upon as sufficiently differentiated to justify a division of labor. It should be evident, however, that the difficulty is one for which no specific stands ready. For this reason it seems more profitable to commence not with the definition of an issue but with the suggestion of a way of attack to a problem no less general than that posed by Professor Lorenzen: " What are the demands of justice in the particular situation; what is the controlling policy? "

The decision of a case of this nature is one of the most delicate of judicial functions. Not infrequently, in the administration of domestic law, there arise situations in which two lines of authority, pointing in opposite directions, seem open to a court. Those situations may at times be clarified by the precipitant of judicial intuition, but more often they bring to the fore the finest manifestations of judicial intellection. They demand a penetrating analysis of the controversy and the transaction out of which it arose, an exacting inquiry into and appraisal of the competing rules, a deliberate weighing of the equities. In such a case there may be consequent on the decision the growth of one rule, the stunting of the other. But regardless of whether this be so, there is very definitely a heightening of the court's responsibility to the parties. The decision cannot be attributed to the wisdom of judges of times past, for it must disregard the wisdom of judges equally dead and equally wise. Compare the situation which a novel conflicts case presents.[31] Two rules of law are invoked;

[31] What constitutes a " novel " conflicts case must, of course, depend on the range of facts which the observer deems significant. If the *situs* of personalty determines the choice of law in all cases affecting title thereto, then obviously " novel " cases are certain to be infrequent. If other facts in the title-affecting transaction

usually the selection of either will determine the case in favor of the party urging its choice.[32] That selection will probably not contribute materially to the development of the rule of law so chosen. In that sense the case differs from its domestic analogue. From the standpoint of the parties, however, is there not a comparable responsibility upon the court? Their transaction, because of its interstate character, has placed them in a position where each may, with some justification, urge the protection of a recognized rule of law. The choice between these rules, even as a precedent for future choices, may not be of great social significance. But does this discharge the court from a painstaking examination of the same factors whose materiality would be admitted were the case a purely local one, together with those additional factors which the interstate character of the transaction raises into prominence?

At present it is customary in a conflicts case to scrutinize the transaction or occurrence from which it springs only to ascertain the existence of those facts which bring into play whatever rules for choice of law may be urged by counsel. For this purpose it may be material to ascertain, in accordance with the laws of the forum, a party's domicil, the *situs* of property at the time of an alleged transfer of an interest therein, the place at which an alleged contract would be regarded as having been created. Sometimes the determination of these questions compels the presentation of much testimony and not a little argument on points of local law, but once the determination is made, its effect upon the choice of law is mechanical.

The alternative approach suggested would require an equally complete depiction of these facts, but to determine what their effect upon the choice of the competing laws should be, would necessitate their careful appraisal with this end in view. To recur to the hypothetical case, the fact that the publisher's agent went

may be regarded as pertinent to the choice of law, then the possibility of encountering significant differences in new cases is correspondingly increased.

[32] It seems highly probable that the number of cases involving possible conflicts of law is far greater than the number in which such conflicts are actually considered. The presumption of similarity as to the law of other jurisdictions is doubtless indulged by counsel far more frequently than by the courts. It is a fair prediction, therefore, that when a conflicts point is pressed, its determination will be vital to, or at least of considerable consequence in, the decision of the case.

to the defendant's home would be material. Had she first "clipped the coupon" that fact might be accorded some weight. It might also be material that his sale was part of a sales campaign waged in that state and not an isolated transaction. Certainly such a case presents quite a distinct picture from one where the bargain is struck by mail, either solely as a consequence of correspondence or as a result of preliminary negotiations in the seller's state. The fact that the transaction comprises a sale of books might lead to its being viewed in a different light than if its subject were, on the one hand, shares of stock whose edges alone were gilt, or, on the other hand, some article, a vacuum cleaner perhaps, which barely lay beyond the concept of the "necessary".[33]

So far the inquiry might be looked upon merely as an attempt to delimit the scope of the decision by selecting for emphasis and inclusion, among the operative facts of the case, certain facts which would be of no significance in the conventional approach to a conflicts problem.[34] Such discrimination would perhaps be helpful, but it is difficult to see how the facts so selected could be properly appraised except in relation to the provisions of the laws whose application is at issue. The court is not idly choosing a law; it is determining a controversy. How can it choose wisely without considering how that choice will affect that controversy?

In the hypothetical case, state *A*, where the defendant was resident, is a jurisdiction which persists in classifying together, for purposes of contractual capacity, the married woman, the infant, and the lunatic. Now, to reverse the hypothesis as to the domestic laws, if state *A's* law had been less indulgent to its minor

---

[33] Such discriminations are not material, it is true, when the domestic law relating to an infant's capacity to contract is at issue. From the great mass of commodities of commerce, we select a few, dub them "necessaries", and accord their sellers favored treatment. The need for further differentiation is not felt. But when the question is whether that domestic law should be applied or whether, instead, a law from which this basic distinction has been eliminated, is that distinction, concededly valid for its purpose, still the only pertinent one?

[34] Emphasis on the significance of social and economic factors in the construction of rules leads inevitably to the narrowing of issues and the restriction in scope of rules. The categories of life are less sweeping than those of jurisprudence. One might, perhaps, anticipate one rule for insurance contracts, another for negotiable instruments, a third for contracts of employment, and still others for other transactions if the views of the foes of deductive methodology were comprehensively developed.

femes coverts and had recognized their capacity to contract, would there have been any good reason for invoking the stricter law of state *B* to defeat such a contract? Should enterprising publishing houses in state *B* be penalized in their extra-state business, because of the anachronistic legislation of that commonwealth? The rhetorical nature of these questions is evident. Obviously, on this hypothesis, the law of state *A* should be applied, not because it is the *lex domicilii* or the *lex loci contractus* or because all contracts should be sustained if a law can be found to turn the trick, but because its application here so clearly produces an eminently sensible result. But let us return to the original hypothesis as to the domestic laws wherein state *A's* law is the stringent one. Of what real importance is it now that state *A's* law should have been applied had its provisions been exactly the reverse of what they are? The fact that now the application of state *A's* law will defeat the contract confers a radically different aspect upon the problem. The degree to which sustaining this bargain would impair the protection which state *A* insists is due its infant matrons must be measured against the degree to which its avoidance will frustrate the reasonable expectations of business men from without the state. And inasmuch as the courts still dispense justice between individuals as well as enunciate social policies, it becomes important to inquire to what extent this particular lady merited judicial solicitude and whether the plaintiff seller's acts were representative of the type of interstate business to be fostered in cases of conflicting laws. Very possibly the individualization of this decision would seem appropriate, and, if so, this might be effectuated by a stressing, in the court's opinions, of the differentiating facts.

Be that as it may, in the course of this evaluation, the court's opinion as to the desirability of limitations upon the contractual capacity of infants and married women will inevitably enter. Any effort to exclude it would operate only to distort the intellectual processes of adjudication. This factor in the decision may, of course, render of consequence the choice of forum. Judges in state *B* or in state *C*, having laws similar to *B's*, may not attach the same importance to the limitations on wifely capacity that would be encountered in state *A*. Such differences are inevitable; it is important only that they be frankly encountered. Today, as in the past, their influence may not appear on the surface of opinions, but, if the uncertain course of decision characteristic of most conflicts problems is evidential, such influence had not been wanting. Moreover, a recognition of the necessity for a thorough understanding and appraisal of foreign law should tend to diminish the parochial " affectation of superiority " which now leads the forum so frequently to reject foreign law.

As one's attention becomes focussed upon the problem of what should be the proper result in a case of this sort, as distinguished from the problem of what rule is the proper one to select a jurisdiction whose law should govern it, the irrelevance of a determination where, as a matter of contract law of the forum, this contract was " made " becomes increasingly apparent. Very possibly, in a case in which the time of making was material, the contract would be found to have been made when the lady's order was accepted by the publishing house in state *B*. But the negotiations out of which it arose took place in both states. Most of the dickering probably took place in state *A*. The solution of the occasionally difficult legal question of when the contract would have been created (if any contract were created) would serve only to divert the court from the sufficiently difficult problem of appraising the effect which the various steps in the transaction should have upon the choice of law. Again, a dispute as to the lady's domicil, which might put in issue the nature of her husband's business connection in state *A* or whether he paid taxes there, would at once be seen to "have nothing to do with the case ". Yet the fact of a settled residence, which is also important in the determination of domicil, would be material here. If this lady with intermittent reading proclivities were merely in state *A* on a visit from her home in state *B*, a quite different result might be deemed appropriate.

The necessity for such discriminations can best be appreciated if one considers the new significance with which the suggested approach would invest the " contact ". The contact in the conventional choice-of-law problem is, if I may be indulged in still another conceit, the coin which, when inserted in the doctrinal slot machine, produces the appropriate jurisdiction. Now according to the common understanding which the telephone company shares with the mass of mankind, the only requisite of such a coin is that it fit the slot. So with the conflict of laws contact. One does not have to appraise the significance of the contact in the light of the consequences worked by the law whose application it dictates. The conflicts rule vouches for it; and that rule is the product of efforts, whether theoretical or positive, to allocate legal problems among territorial jurisdictions, not to decide specific cases justly. But if a law is to be chosen with some consideration of the result it effects in a given litigation, then the contact should itself be significant in relation to that result. The fact that legal consequences might in another connection be attached to conduct not in itself important should not alone suffice to render that conduct significant as a contact. The mailing of a letter, for example, may be the act which, in a case where the point was in issue, could be said to " make " a contract, yet the fact that that mailing occurred in a certain place must remain to those not habituated to conflicts doctrine a circumstance of utter triviality.

V

This effort to portray an approach to problems of conflicting laws which would free the courts from the blindfold of a theory which has compelled them to grope for solutions to problems for which perspicacity is peculiarly essential has been argumentative and discursive. At the risk of distorting an idea not susceptible of blackletter statement, I shall hazard this summary:

When a court is faced with a question whether to reject, as inapplicable, the law of the forum and to admit in evidence, as determinative of an issue in a case before it, a rule of law of a foreign jurisdiction, it should

(1) scrutinize the event or transaction giving rise to the issue before it;

(2) compare carefully the proffered rule of law and the result which its application might work in the case at bar with the rule of the forum (or other competing jurisdiction) and its effect therein;

(3) appraise these results in the light of those facts in the event or transaction which, from the standpoint of justice between the litigating individuals or of those broader considerations of social policy which conflicting laws may evoke,

link that event or transaction to one law or the other; recognizing

a) in the use of precedent, that those cases which are distinguishable only in the patterns of domestic laws they present, may for that very reason suggest materially different considerations than the case at bar, and

b) in the evaluation of contacts, that the contact achieves significance in proportion to the significance of the action or circumstance constituting it when related to the controversy and the solutions thereto which the competing laws propound.

The end-product of this process of analysis and evaluation would, of course, be the application to the case at bar of a rule of law, derived either from the municipal law of the forum or that of some foreign state if proof of the latter law were duly made.[35] The choice of that law would not be the result of the automatic operation of a rule or principle of selection but of a search for a just decision in the principal case. But lawyers are a rule-making sect. Would not that decision be the seed from which a rule or principle for the choice of law might spring? And, given sufficient decisions utilizing this approach, would not a commentator in time be able to construct from them a system of rules for choice of law which would certainly be displeasing to other commentators who would in turn construct their own systems? Very probably. The analytical incorporation of the rule chosen into the "local law" would not conceal the all too apparent choice.[36] But the activities of the rule makers are not

[35] There is, of course, the logical alternative that a rule derived from none of the domestic laws in question should be fashioned for the case. Professor Jitta, a vigorous critic of mechanical rules for choice of law, suggests that this be done wherever "a juridical relation may not belong to the active local life of a society but to the active, international or universal life". The law to be applied in such a situation may be "an independent provision which is derived from a consideration of the local public order and the universal public order". 1 JITTA, LA SUBSTANCE DES OBLIGATIONS DANS LE DROIT INTERNATIONAL PRIVÉ (1906) 23, quoted by Lorenzen, *supra* note 18, at 668. Professor Lorenzen dismisses the proposal on the ground that it "leaves the judge practically without any definite guide to go by". *Id.* at 669. Insofar as this comment applies to the concoction of "independent provisions", I am in complete accord. The difficulties incident to the application of the doctrine of Swift v. Tyson leave one skeptical of proposals which might lead to further multiplication of rules of substantive law.

[36] It is possible, of course, to describe the body of legal rules in a given juris-

deplorable *per se*. Convenience demands a degree of order in the classification of judicial decisions; and, in a land where they proliferate so luxuriantly, summarization may be a necessary tool for the practising lawyer and the busy court. The questions on which their evaluation depends are, first, whether in their inception, inquiry into factors otherwise relevant has or has not been trammelled by pre-existing rules creating artificial limitations upon relevancy and, second, whether, in their employment, they stifle or guide inquiry.

Too frequently legal rules are the product of inbreeding. The considerations out of which they are conceived have been restricted in scope by the operation of other legal doctrines whose own relation to the problem at hand escapes inquiry. This is, of course, the burden of those who deplore a deductive methodology whose postulates create artificial barriers to the exploring mind. Yet such limitations may accompany the employment of a "positive" methodology. They may be less patent since they are concealed in the terms of the problem set for examination, in the case of choice-of-law problems, by the requirement of a jurisdiction-selecting rule.[37] The suggested approach, however, places no such limitation upon the range of inquiry other than the requirement that the substantive rule ultimately applied be one found in the domestic rules of the states concerned.

It is equally important that rules, once formulated, do not operate to foreclose inquiry. The mechanical rule radically re-

diction without distributing them between the categories of domestic rules dispositive of local situations and choice-of-law rules directing the court to the dispositive domestic rule of some other state. One may say that a state has one set of dispositive rules for a situation whose facts are wholly local, another for a situation which includes certain foreign facts, and so on. But so long as a court is limited in the framing of its dispositive rules for situations of the latter type to rules which happen to be in force in a foreign state connected with that situation, the actuality of the choice is apparent. It is rendered all the more so by the procedure followed in the proof of foreign law. The absurdity of submitting such proof to the jury should in time lead to the elimination of the practice; but it is open to question whether judicial notice should be substituted for proof of foreign law to the court.

[37] To return again to the problem of contractual capacity, if one seeks by a scrutiny of social and economic factors to determine whether the *lex loci contractus* or the *lex domicilii* should "govern", he has ruled from his inquiry a consideration of the fact that in one case the *lex loci* may restrict that capacity, while in the next, it may not. The inquirer would, of course, be aware of this fact but the goal of the inquiry would render it irrelevant.

stricts the range of facts pertinent to its application,[38] and only as to problems susceptible of mechanical disposition is its employment justified. Where, as in choice-of-law cases, the problem is essentially complex, the rules developed must contain variables to permit some degree of accommodation to those complexities whose precise nature cannot be anticipated.[39] Where those variables comprise the considerations which reach to the nub of a problem — and this result the proposed approach would foster — the rule will have focussed attention on that point toward which inquiry and argument, if they are to be fruitful, must be directed. That there should be disagreement as to the terms which will satisfy those variables is inevitable. To the extent that such disagreement provokes discussion, it may be welcomed, for the critique which discussion affords when properly directed is a tonic with which no legal order can dispense.

Moreover, to him who sees a return to *cadi* justice in the disintegration of rules of the sort that have competed for acceptance in the conflict of laws or even in the gradual development of rules

[38] Virtually all rules have this effect to a greater or less degree; whether any exception should be recognized presents a problem in the definition of "rule". There is, however, one form which legal doctrine may take which operates only to emphasize certain factual considerations appropriate to the decision of a type of case without excluding others which may be relevant in any specific case. An example is furnished by the section of the Torts Restatement dealing with proximate cause wherein various considerations recurring frequently in proximate cause cases are enumerated as guides to judicial inquiry. The enumeration is not exclusive, however. See TORTS RESTATEMENT (Tentative Draft, 1932) § 317. It is difficult to regard such an enumeration as either a "principle" or "standard". Unless a new term is to be adopted to designate such monitions, I feel no hesitancy in classifying them as rules.

[39] It may well be that room would be left for the development of some mechanical rules in the application of which regard for the content of domestic laws would not be necessary. These would probably be negative in character. Our current rules serve a dual function: they indicate a jurisdiction as a source of law, and in so doing, they also exclude from consideration all other jurisdictions. This exclusionary function may survive. A physician may deliberate long before choosing between two courses of treatment for a given condition and yet be justified in dismissing without hesitation a number of others. Thus, in a problem of choice of law, a court may assert that the mere act of mailing a letter of acceptance in a state would not alone suffice to sustain the application of its law, whatever its content. Such a decision might properly serve as a basis of a rule to that effect. Similarly, the Ross case, discussed in note 16, *supra*, may possibly be regarded as establishing that the domicil of the settlor of a trust of personalty will not alone suffice to justify the application of the *lex domicilii*.

which meet the criteria outlined above, a reminder is due. Nothing in the proposed approach is inconsistent with the continuance of the doctrine of *stare decisis*, properly conceived. Indeed, to borrow Professor Oliphant's phrase for use in a context which seems emphatically to justify its employment, that approach would accelerate " the return to *stare decisis*." [40] The conflict of laws emerged in Anglo-American law at a time when the *stare decisis* of the common law was being converted into the *stare dictis* of contemporary jurisprudence, and the older conception of *stare decisis* was alien to its civilian heritage. A return to *stare decisis* with its pragmatic limitations on the scope of precedents in lieu of the present recourse to broad rules would implement, not preclude, the utilization of the judgment of the past; and in those choice-of-law problems wherein the patterns of fact and of substantive domestic laws are constantly reduplicated in experience, there is no reason to anticipate a capricious disregard of the solutions propounded for them in the decisions of courts of last resort.[41]

Furthermore, the creation and fruitful employment of rules of this sort must be attended by the development of standards for the evaluation of the facts which they render significant. This

[40] In *A Return to Stare Decisis* (1928) 14 A. B. A. J. 71, 107, 159, Professor Oliphant deplores " the process of logical elaboration " that has led away from the patient particularization of the judges and scholars of the early law, which, partly through the definitiveness of the older system of writs and pleading, insured a correspondence between the classifications of law and experience that is lacking in the general rules compounded by the legal scholars and encyclopedists of today. This tendency has resulted, he finds, in " a shift from *stare decisis* towards *stare dictis* ", especially in the domain of legal scholarship, a shift which is leading to abstraction and unreality in the law.

[41] The conflict of laws relating to trusts of personalty affords an example of the stabilizing influence which *stare decisis* may exert where stability exists in the underlying situation. Most of the cases in this field have arisen because of the limitations imposed by the peculiar New York rule against perpetuities. Since all the neighboring states adhere to the common-law rule, the patterns of law cannot be greatly varied and the transactions, testamentary and *inter vivos*, which involve them do not present many significant variations. In a period of not over twenty years, the New York courts in which the bulk of the cases arose worked out solutions to the perpetuities problems which are in general quite satisfactory when their results are appraised in the light of the substantive rules of law involved (see Note (1932) 32 COL. L. REV. 680, 684) but which are difficult to rationalize by one employing the conventional logical apparatus of the conflict of laws (see Cavers, *supra* note 26, at 162–68).

is a problem which the exorcisers of legal conceptualism cannot long ignore. In the conflict of laws it presents a peculiar difficulty since the operative facts in choice-of-law cases have heretofore called for no such appraisal. We have looked for the *situs* of the property, the *locus* of the tort, or the place of performance of the contract with an austere unconcern for the consequences of the discovery. Of recent years there have been pressed the subversive suggestions that what constitutes " domicil " in a voting case may not satisfy " domicil " in a divorce case; [42] that the " *situs* " of intangibles in an assignment case may not be the same as their " *situs* " for tax purposes.[43] In yielding to these insinuations, we have been obliged to appraise the facts alleged to comprise " domicil " in, say, a tax case in the light of the purpose of that litigation and of the laws involved therein. Were the suggested approach adopted, the necessity for such appraisals and discriminations would be present not only in these but in all choice-of-law cases. That this places a heavy responsibility upon legal science cannot be denied; but the consideration of how that responsibility can best be met will be deferred until some objections to the proposal have been discussed.

VI

Certain of the objections which may be anticipated are sufficiently formidable as to be deserving of more extended treatment, although they may have been adverted to above. It seems to me that these objections, though they may be advanced separately, are based on a central assumption and may be knitted into a single argument. The assumption and argument may, perhaps, fairly be set forth as follows:

The suggested approach would preclude the attainment of either certainty or uniformity in the conflict of laws because under it the decision of a case involving a choice of law would depend on the content of the conflicting laws and the relative desirability of their application in the light of the facts of the controversy in

---

[42] For an interesting discussion of this view, see (1925) 3 AM. L. INST. PROCEEDINGS 226.

[43] See, *e.g.*, Cavers, *supra* note 26, at 171; *cf.* Lowndes, ***Tendencies in The Taxation of Intangibles*** (1930) 17 VA. L. REV. 146.

litigation. A decision now depends on the essentially mechanical application of a rule for the selection of an appropriate jurisdiction, irrespective of the substance of its relevant rule of law. Certainty, in the sense of predictability, is peculiarly important in this field because of the growing importance of interstate and international commercial and social relations. However certain the domestic laws of two states in a given field may be, the issue of controversies arising out of transactions in that field is unpredictable if those laws differ and if the relevant conflict of laws rules are not predictable. In many instances, therefore, the consequences of the application of either law are not as important as the predictability of its application. Uniformity in rule is equally important. Where conflicts rules are not uniform, certainty is measurably diminished since the selection of the forum then enters as a factor which may not be predictable. Moreover, it is unjust that the selection of a forum should determine the result of litigation since that empowers the party having control over that choice to select the forum most favorable to him. Finally, certainty and uniformity are necessary as a curb on local bias which leads to the application of the *lex fori*, or a law similar thereto, in preference to a different law whose claims for consideration, objectively appraised, are superior.

Of course, the basic assumption may be challenged. We have neither certainty nor uniformity despite the formulation of rules and principles of the conflict of laws without regard for the substance of the law whose application they dictate. Moreover, that the formal certainty and uniformity which the wide acceptance of a general formula imparts is deceptive is an observation whose corroboration in the law is becoming so comprehensive that all broad rules are now suspect. On the other hand, it must be conceded that the suggested approach would give an impetus to the individualization of cases. This would lead for a time to disagreement both as to the extent to which such a tendency might properly be carried and to the propriety of the results reached in specific instances. But the factors of judgment would be exposed to, not concealed from, the tempering process of criticism. Eventually, there would be a tendency toward stability in those fields at least where the factual pattern was relatively stable. The basic assumption is, therefore, by no means axiomatic. There is, however, some risk of augmenting for a time at least the current complaints in this field. But may not these complaints be exaggerated?

One distrusts an argument which proceeds from the persistence of a lack of certainty in a field of law to the exigency of the need for it. Granting, with a reservation,[44] the accelerating increase in interstate and international transactions, nevertheless, the phenomenon is scarcely novel. If the consequences of uncertainty and want of uniformity in the conflict of laws were as intolerable as is often suggested, one would surmise that the problem would have been attacked more vigorously heretofore. One would suppose, for instance, that the first objective of the Commissioners of Uniform State Laws would have been comprehensive legislation enacting statutory rules of the conflict of laws to protect our citizenry during the period that their uniform legislation was being formulated and obtaining acceptance. That this aspect of the problem has been virtually disregarded[45] suggests that while the conduct of business and certain social activities may be embarrassed by a want of uniformity in the laws of the forty-eight states, that embarrassment springs primarily from the cost and difficulty of ascertaining accurately the content of those laws and not from the admitted difficulty of predicting their territorial application.

The willingness, not infrequently encountered in writings on

---

[44] Both the horizontal and vertical integration of industry and commerce tends to reduce the volume of interstate legal transactions. Twenty years ago a large food distributing house located in Washington would enter into contracts with local wholesalers in Virginia, Maryland, West Virginia, and North Carolina. Today it may sell the bulk of its products in Washington to chain store organizations which distribute directly to consumers in all those states. Interstate distribution of those products continues; interstate sales are eliminated. Similarly, a large industrial establishment in Michigan may have iron mines in Minnesota, coal mines in Pennsylvania, and chemical works in Delaware. It can now acquire those materials without resort to interstate contracts.

[45] Very few Uniform Acts affect choice-of-law problems, and these do not relate to problems of commercial importance. Moreover, the Acts dealing with substantive topics do not embody choice-of-law provisions. Even though the goal of the Commissioners were attained by the adoption of their Acts in every state, still such rules would be of value in international situations. Furthermore, although experience has long since instructed the Commissioners that general adoption can seldom be anticipated, yet such knowledge does not seem to have worked any change of policy in this regard.

conflict of laws topics,[46] to concede that certainty in rule is of more significance than the rule's content, is more revelatory as an evaluation of conflicts rules than it is significant as a judgment upon the need for certainty in this field. One conflicts rule may point to one jurisdiction as the source of the appropriate law; a second and competing conflicts rule, to another jurisdiction. What consequence the adoption of either rule will have in a given case will depend not on the rule but on the domestic law of the jurisdiction thereby selected. Until a specific case is considered in which the rules work different results, any estimate of their operation must in a large measure be conjectural. Naturally, in such a situation, the importance of certainty will loom disproportionately large. When, instead, the social value of a painstaking balancing of competing considerations to reach just results in specific cases, which the proposed approach would compel, is weighed against the social value of rules to determine such results mechanically, if predictably, the case for certainty becomes dubious. Even though it were conceded that the decisions in many of these cases would not have significant repercussions upon social and economic behavior, the question would remain open. In how many other branches of the law is such a standard set? This indifference to the disposition of individual cases is atypical in the profession and is strongly suggestive of a defense mechanism born of repeated failures to achieve the certainty and uniformity desired.

A more difficult problem which a want of uniformity in conflict of laws rules poses is, of course, the fact that the choice of forum may thereby become determinative of the results of litigation. If all jurisdictions recognized the same conflict of laws rules and applied them without deviation, then the law of only one jurisdiction would ever be invoked to govern a given case. Should the attainment of this ideal be jeopardized by a quixotic seeking after " just results "? Without indulging the tempting *tu quoque,* one may point out that for want of uniformity to render the power to choose the forum of great value to plaintiff or defendant, the decisions of the potential forums must be predictable. Consequently, at least one of the virtues ascribed to the mechanical

[46] See, *e.g.*, Cook, *supra* note 3, at 488; Lorenzen, *supra* note 4, at 750; CARDOZO, PARADOXES OF LEGAL SCIENCE (1928) 67.

approach will have to have been attained by its alternative before this evil can arise. More important, however, is the consideration that greater individualization of conflicts cases would permit a court to consider whether the result normally reached by it would be equally appropriate in a case where its selection as forum seemed to have been dictated by motives ulterior to the convenience of the parties. With a wholesome disregard for the doctrinal dilemmas and logical subtleties of *renvoi* theory, a court in such a situation might wisely avail itself of *renvoi* procedure.

Still another check on the misuse of the power to determine the forum when different results in conflicts cases may be forecast in different jurisdictions, lies in the development of rules regulating the place of trial. Conceivably, all choice of law problems could be eliminated by the extension of this device and the restriction of the forum to its domestic law. The greater elasticity which makes the method afforded by the procedure now in use much to be preferred should not blind one to the possibilities which a discriminating control of the place of trial may afford.[47]

That parochialism which leads a court to employ its own rule of law where the application of a foreign rule would seem preferable, and to invoke incontinently a " public policy " to reject a foreign law is, of course, a tendency which should be discouraged. But, as has already been pointed out, it represents in no small measure a resistance to the automatic operation of jurisdiction-selecting rules.[48] A mere refusal by commentators to recognize the rôle of public policy in conflicts cases will not suffice to scotch this tendency. On the other hand, an insistence upon the necessity for a full understanding of the reasons for and operation of the foreign rule as part and parcel of the process of selecting an appropriate law in any given case, would tend to diminish the prejudice which feeds on ignorance.[49]

---

[47] These have been persuasively developed in two valuable articles by Professor Foster, *Place of Trial in Civil Actions* (1930) 43 HARV. L. REV. 1217; *Place of Trial — Interstate Application of Intrastate Methods of Adjustment* (1930) 44 HARV. L. REV. 41. Compare the heightened significance of this factor in Roman and Continental law. See WESTLAKE, *op. cit. supra* note 23, c. IX.

[48] See p. 183, *supra*.

[49] The neglect of studies in the field of comparative law, especially in this country, is responsible in a measure for that provincialism which students of the conflict

The only alternative is for the Supreme Court to assume the rôle of policeman. This it has already done on occasion, wielding the " due process " or the " full faith and credit " clause to break down the exaggerated insularity of state courts when that seemed to stand in the way of justice.[50] The Court's tendency has been distinctly selective, and the criterion of selection seems to have been the national character of the interest adversely affected. The rigidity which would be imparted to the process of adjusting controversies involving conflicts of law were the Supreme Court to write into the Constitution in each conflicts case it heard, its then prevailing view as to the proper rule for choice of law renders it important that the Court's intervention in this field should be indulged with circumspection. The reasons leading the Court to intervene might well be set forth more explicitly than has heretofore been the custom. Obviously no rule can be elaborated which could forecast accurately when the Court would apprehend constitutional violations, but for that very reason it becomes important to know the motivation of its action when it does act. It does not suffice to know that a vested right is being preserved from unconstitutional indignities.

Probably the situation wherein the invocation of local policy is least deserving of consideration is that in which the only fact upon which to predicate a conflict of laws is the choice as forum of a jurisdiction other than the one to which all the other facts in the case are related. The problems set by the employment of the forum's procedural machinery are perhaps inevitable here. Again, there may now and then arise a claim whose enforcement would be genuinely repugnant to the moral standards prevailing at the forum. So long as courts are not regarded as machines for the conversion of imported *obligationes* into domestic *fieri facias,* some allowance must be made for judicial scruples. But there seems no reason to suppose that the approach proposed would aggravate judicial sensibility. Surely the acceptance of the " vested rights " theory is not requisite to the realization that a

of laws deplore without realizing the extent to which the limitations of their own theories contribute to it.

[50] For a discussion of the Supreme Court cases in this field, see Dodd, *supra* note 22. The more recent decisions are commented on in Note (1932) 46 HARV. L. REV. 291.

disregard of the *lex loci* in essentially intrastate events or transactions can be justified only by exceptional circumstances.[51]

The argument for certainty and uniformity in the conflict of laws based upon the fear of local bias, has an aspect not generally adverted to. We have imported much of our learning in this field from the Continent where such problems have their origin primarily in international rather than interstate events and transactions. In important controversies the interest of the individual may not easily be dissociated from the interest of the nation. "International private law" may thus bear a resemblance to "international public law" in more than name. The application of mechanical rules of law in such a situation may, accordingly, be regarded as necessary to safeguard the alien litigant from xenophobia. Discretion is a safe tool only in the hands of the disinterested. Such disinterestedness may more readily be credited to courts within the bounds of a federal union.[52] Its exercise by state courts in the United States may be welcomed, not feared, if and when the courts restate not their rules but their problem.

Whether these counter-considerations to the objections based upon a need for certainty and uniformity in the conflict of laws are persuasive must depend ultimately on the temperament of the reader. One cannot marshal data to demonstrate beyond risk of rebuttal in kind the soundness of either position. But the proponent of change has more than the burden of persuasion. There always lurks to strangle his infant idea the serpent suspicion: it is quite academic.

---

[51] *Cf.* Cardozo, J., in Loucks v. Standard Oil Co. of N. Y., 224 N. Y. 99, 113, 120 N. E. 198, 202 (1918).

[52] In Du Bois, *The Significance in Conflict of Laws of the Distinction Between Interstate and International Transactions* (1933) 17 MINN. L. REV. 361, 378–79, the author reaches the conclusion that "it is an exceptional case that the crossing of an international boundary line has given rise to distinctive treatment in conflict of laws." On the question whether the form choice-of-law rules have taken has been dominated by interstate or international considerations, the author observes, "As a rule, the effects of the international organization of society do not appear to have any considerable influence in determining the expediency of adopting a particular conflict rule." *Ibid.* But influences of this sort are not likely to manifest themselves in judicial opinions, and they seem to have been given very limited consideration by the treatise writers.

VII

All too palpably, the insinuation is correct. Dicey has stated of the theoretical method that "it leads the writers who adopt it to treat as being law what they think ought to be law, and to lay down for the guidance of the Courts of every country rules which are not recognised as law in any country whatever." [53] The writer has not, it is true, laid down rules of law "for the guidance of the courts"; but to urge at least the reconsideration, perhaps the abandonment, of all the current rules, and the adoption in their stead of an approach fundamentally different from that which seems generally to have been pursued by the courts, may seem no less presumptuous. Indeed, it would be little short of fatuous to suppose that judges, having these views pressed upon them, would put aside their stock of assorted doctrines to set to probing in that complex of fact and law which is the typical conflicts case.[54] Quite clearly, the proposal is academic.

Fortunately, however, we have academies, and the nurture of ideas which are quite clearly academic is still a responsibility of theirs. If, then, this conception of the problem basic to choice-of-law cases and the mode of attack which it indicates are not themselves to be barren, it will be because they give direction to the study of such cases. In the law schools alone can ideas of this sort take root; once having rooted there, the process of transplanting them to less sheltered fields may be gradual, but it is sure.

The study of the conflict of laws has been focussed upon rules, not upon decisions.[55] We can explain, approve, or condemn a

[53] DICEY, CONFLICT OF LAWS (3d ed. 1922) 18. This charge was withdrawn in the fourth edition, and for it was substituted a statement which, with minor modifications, appears in the fifth edition as follows: "It is not, indeed, open to the objection that it takes no account of laws as they actually exist, for it is normally based upon careful investigation into the rules as to the conflict of laws which in fact prevail in given countries, *e.g.*, France or the United States. But its results are essentially subjective, often diverge widely, and in no case represent faithfully the laws of any given country". DICEY, CONFLICT OF LAWS 13.

[54] This is especially true as to the trial courts which naturally feel the weight of "*stare dictis*" more heavily than appellate tribunals.

[55] There are few, if any, decisions in which a "narrow" as well as a "broad" issue cannot be isolated. Frequently, the explanation of the former is closely in consonance with the explanation of the latter. Ordinarily, in choice-of-law cases,

given rule, but we can seldom say why a given decision should be reached except insofar as we can attribute that decision to a pre-existing rule. We know only to a very limited extent what the courts have actually done in choice-of-law cases.[56] Instead of making a searching inquiry into what has happened in cases of conflicting laws, the commentator's chief concern heretofore has been to ascertain what rules for choice of law the courts have adopted. On each question in this field, a poll of the several states has been taken, their votes for the various rules recorded, and numerous instances of plural voting duly noted. The canvasser, after reporting the customary confusion of authority, takes advantage of the license which this situation confers upon him to become the advocate of the rule he finds most appealing. To support it he spins, if this be his bent, theories of the nature of law and of the state, discovers, in any event, pressing considerations of policy which dictate its recognition, points with dismay to the harsh results worked by competing rules, and extenuates as inevitable and occasional those produced by the one he champions. Of course arguments of the same sort can be and are constructed for other rules. The process has grown stale.[57]

Suppose, however, that one were to disregard for a time those rules for which courts and commentators have contended to so little profit. There would still remain the cases. In each of

only the broad issue — what is the proper rule to select the jurisdiction? — is considered. The narrow issue is seldom recognized, much less discussed. If the thesis of this paper is correct, any consonance between the explanation of its solution and that of the solution of the broad issue, will usually be accidental.

[56] The distinction between what a court "does" in a given case and what it "says" is a difficult one to draw, as discussions of the doctrine of *stare decisis* have made evident. Judicial "doing" might be regarded as confined to the mere rendition of judgments. Obviously the material for the study of cases must be broader than this. The facts of the event or transaction, the conflicting claims of the parties, and their resolution by the courts decision may, very possibly, be isolated with profit from the apologetics which comprise the court's opinion.

[57] In this regard, I am not without sin. In an earlier article, my approach was much as that outlined above. See Cavers, *supra*, note 26. In seeking to formulate a rule of law to "govern" *inter vivos* trusts of personalty which would not be mechanical in operation, I urged the intention-of-the-parties rule without recognizing its character as an escape devise. An interesting, contrasting approach to an important aspect of the trust problem which, although it does not discriminate between trusts *inter vivos* and testamentary, is directed chiefly toward the character of the substantive rule involved is to be found in Note (1932) 32 COL. L. REV. 680, 684.

them, there is reported a sequence of acts and events leading up to a controversy to whose solution there is applied, as a rule for decision, a rule of law of a state to which some of these facts bear relation. One can usually predict the probable consequences of the application of that rule to the case, or at least compare its effect with the result a competing rule might have worked. Here is material enough for study without, for the time, giving heed to the reasons vouchsafed by the court for selecting the state whose law it applied.[58] Let all the cases of this character in a given field, say, contractual capacity, be dissected to determine, *inter alia*, what facts accompany decisions admitting rules establishing incapacity, whether there is any correlation apparent between the existence of this rule at the forum and its application, whether the manner in which the transaction was conducted may have been influential, whether any one form of incapacity or of contract seems to have been singled out for special treatment. Possibly such a quantitative analysis of the capacity cases would not be revealing. Where the reported cases in a given field are not numerous, generalization would have to be cautious. One would be constantly handicapped by the reporting of facts inadequately for this purpose. But an inquiring mind asks for a problem, not for a guarantee of " results ", and here is a field for inquiry which is virtually untouched. After such studies had been undertaken it would become important to include as well a consideration of

[58] An appeal for such an approach to all case material was voiced by Professor Oliphant, *supra* note 40, at 161, in which he said: " Our case material is a gold mine for scientific work. It has not been scientifically exploited. The science of mechanics was built up by experimentation, but geology, for example, has had to rely almost solely upon observation. In law we cannot institute suits to test judicial behavior, as the physicists make experiments to test the behavior of matter. But each case is a record of judicial behavior. And there is a wealth of such records equaling that to which geology, for instance, has had access and the individual records are not more fractional or otherwise imperfect. A sufficient number of recorded experiments, all of whose factors are not known but with the unknown factors varying, may be quite as illuminating as a limited number of controlled experiments. Why has not our study of cases in the past yielded the results now sought? The attempt has been made to show that this is largely due to the fact that we have focused our attention too largely on the *vocal behavior* of judges in deciding cases. A study with more stress on their *non-vocal behavior*, *i.e.*, what the judges actually do when stimulated by the facts of the case before them, is the approach indispensable to exploiting scientifically the wealth of material in the cases."

the relation of the facts and correlations revealed to the rules for choice of law which the courts had invoked and to those discoveries of intent and of public policy which they had made and declared determinative. Here again, the significance of the findings cannot be forecast; one can only affirm the need for search.

Such studies might contribute considerably to a technique for predicting judicial action in this field. But of more importance is the training that they would surely afford in the evaluation of significant facts in conflicts cases, the need for which has already been stressed. The legal scholar has long evaded this responsibility. Within the confines of traditional legal dialectic, its assumption has not been necessary. The work of today has been the breaking-down of those confines. The work of tomorrow must be the utilization of the new freedom. But the scope and needs of law teaching have to so large a measure given direction to research in legal problems that it would be idle to hope for the vigorous prosecution of any line of advanced study tangential to the line of law teaching. It is quite evident, moreover, that the proposed approach is not adapted to the subject matter of current conflict of laws courses. Choice-of-law problems in the conflict of laws constitutes perhaps the minor portion of a course which must include many and varied problems of jurisdiction and of the effect of foreign judgments, yet these choice-of-law questions cut across almost every field of domestic law. Any course which purports to deal with all or even most of them is by the force of circumstance confined to a hasty development of the competing rules for choice of law as illustrated by a handful of cases in each field. To pause for a careful and comprehensive analysis of the cases along the lines suggested sufficient to lead the student to delve for the considerations which may or should have been controlling therein, is patently incompatible with an all-inclusive survey.

The alternative which this conflict suggests is obvious enough. Where intensive cultivation of a field of study alone can promise a real appreciation of its problems, then the abandonment of the attempt at its extensive development is clearly indicated. This should be done in the conflict of laws. If students were thoroughly apprised of the intricacies of choice-of-law problems in one or two branches of the law, it would suffice to acquaint them with the verbal formulæ employed in judicial opinions in the other branches. Thanks to their initiation, they would be put on notice of the superficiality of these formulæ and their susceptibility to manipulation. Faced, subsequently, with a case in such a field, the student thus trained would be far more adept than one who had enjoyed only a necessarily hurried excursion through the case law of conflicts.

The academic implications of this attack on the conventional concept of the choice-of-law problem derive immediacy from the work of the American Law Institute. If we are to elevate certainty and uniformity above all other objectives in this branch of the conflict of laws, it will no longer be fertile soil for scholarship. Study provokes incertitude, poses questions, suggests discriminations, differentiations. What will then be needed is something quite different: agreement on a single set of well-defined rules, to be followed by a period of watchfulness wherein their propounders will be quick to detect and decry deviations therefrom by courts or aberrant scholars. To the extent that the Restatement of the Conflict of Laws in the sections devoted to choice-of-law questions represents such an agreement, it will tend both to foster unanimity in doctrine and to stifle continued inquiry into the sources, use, and consequences of such doctrine.[59] If, on the other hand, those two objectives are to be revalued, their deflation will carry with it the chief arguments on behalf of mechanical rules for choice of law. The opportunity can then be taken to start anew. If, and only if, we are no longer bound to concern ourselves only with rules for the choice of appropriate jurisdictions without regard for the results their choice entails, can we utilize the methodology and the resources which modern scholarship is exploiting in other branches of legal study. A fresh approach will beget new and truer problems.

David F. Cavers.

DUKE UNIVERSITY SCHOOL OF LAW.

[59] Professor Beale remarked in the course of the discussion by the American Law Institute of the rule to select the law governing the validity of a contract, "It is not the purpose of the Restatement, as I understand it, to prevent the evolution of a better rule in the course of future decisions". 6 AM. L. INST. PROCEEDINGS (1928) 458. Unfortunately, the Restatement contains no principle of growth and can give no direction to its development. It is a closed system.

[3]

THE QUALIFICATION, CLASSIFICATION, OR CHARACTERIZATION PROBLEM IN THE CONFLICT OF LAWS

By ERNEST G. LORENZEN†

I.

THE problem in the Conflict of Laws which today is known on the continent as the problem of "qualification" and in recent Anglo-American literature as that of "classification" or "characterization" was brought to the attention of students of the Conflict of Laws fifty years ago. In the very year of the founding of the YALE LAW JOURNAL, Franz Kahn published an article in Jhering's *Jahrbücher*[1] in which he pointed out that even if the rules of the Conflict of Laws in the different countries were the same, identity of results in individual cases would not follow because of latent conflicts inherent in the different systems of law.

Bartin dealt with the same problem in 1897, under the title *De l'impossibilité d'arriver à la suppression définitive des conflits de lois,* apparently unaware of the fact that Kahn had written on the subject before him. Bartin spoke of the problem as one of "qualification," and since that time the problem has been known on the continent by that name.[2]

There is no agreement among the writers concerning the type of questions properly belonging to a discussion of the qualification problem. Some use the term in a very broad sense and others in a narrower sense. I shall deal with the following classes of cases:

(1) The first class is one in which the fact situation is characterized under the law of the forum in a way different from that in which it is characterized under the *lex causae* — the law of the state or country with which it is connected. It may be regarded by one law as presenting a question of contracts and by the other law as a question of torts or property, by one law as a question of matrimonial property and by the other

---

† Edward J. Phelps Professor of Law, Yale Law School.

1. Kahn, *Gesetzeskollisionen: Ein Beitrag zur Lehre des internationalen Privatrechts* (1891) 30 JHERING'S JAHRBÜCHER FÜR DIE DOGMATIK DES HEUTIGEN RÖMISCHEN PRIVATRECHTS 1, reprinted in LENEL & LEWALD, ABHANDLUNGEN ZUM INTERNATIONALEN PRIVATRECHT (1928) 1.

2. 24 Clunet 225. Beckett was the first to suggest that "classification" was linguistically a better term in English than "qualification." *The Question of Classification ("Qualification") in Private International Law* (1934) 15 BRIT. Y. B. INT. L. 46, n. 3. Falconbridge regards the term "characterization" as the most suitable English word. *Characterization In The Conflict of Laws* (1937) 53 L. Q. REV. 235, 239, n. 17. Nussbaum admits that "characterization" is linguistically more correct, but thinks that the internationally accepted technical term "qualification" should be given preference in a discussion of international import. Book Review (1940) 40 COL. L. REV. 1461, n. 2.

law as a question of succession, by one law as a question of succession and by the other law as a question of administration. Because of these divergencies in classification, different rules of the Conflict of Laws may become applicable. The problem is whether the qualification or characterization is to be made on the basis of the law of the forum or on that of the foreign law.

The same problem may also arise in situations in which the law of the forum and that of the foreign country differ as to whether certain property is movable or immovable, or in which they differ on questions of capacity and form. Are these questions to be resolved on the basis of the law of the forum or on the basis of the foreign law?

(2) The second class of cases involves the qualification of the connecting factor. A choice-of-law rule of the forum may determine legal relations by reference to the law of domicile, the law of the place of contracting, the law of the place of performance, or the law of the place where the tort is committed. The terms "domicile," "place of contracting," "place of performance," or "place of the wrong" are here connecting factors. The law of the forum and the foreign law involved may have the same connecting factors in their systems of the Conflict of Laws but different meanings may be attached to them. Here again the question is whether the meaning of these connecting factors should be determined in the light of the law of the forum or of the foreign law.

(3) A third class of cases arises after the applicable foreign law has been selected by the law of the forum. Here again the law of the forum and the foreign law may entertain different views as to whether a provision of the foreign law is to be regarded as substantive or procedural, a decision upon which the applicability of different laws may depend. How is this question to be determined?

It should be noted that in each of the above classes of cases the choice of law depends upon the qualification problem. If the problem is answered on the basis of the law of the forum, one law becomes applicable; if it is answered on the basis of the *lex causae,* another law determines the solution of the case. By limiting this discussion to these three classes, it will be possible to deal with the subject of qualification without running over the entire field of the Conflict of Laws, and to give some sort of unity and cohesion to the treatment.

The assertion has been made that real qualification questions have been presented in only a few cases and that the problem is therefore devoid of practical interest.[3] The enthusiastic discussion which the qualification problem has evoked has been ascribed as due largely to an unrealistic approach to the Conflict of Laws, principally exhibited by the adherents of the "logistic school." This school, it is said, attempts to perpetuate

3. Nussbaum, Book Review (1940) 40 Col. L. Rev. 1461, 1468-1469.

an international point of view in the Conflict of Laws on grounds of pure logic after it has become apparent that the law of nations cannot furnish an adequate basis.[4] It is true that there have been, relatively speaking, only a few decisions in which a court has been clearly confronted with the necessity of choosing between the qualification of the forum and a qualification which would be different under the *lex causae*.[5] As between states and countries belonging to the common law group, the categories in which fact-situations are grouped are generally the same, so that there is usually little occasion for the problem of qualification, although even here cases of this sort have presented themselves. The problem may readily arise, however, where the common law comes into contact with the civil law. It has practical, as well as scientific, importance and for that reason deserves consideration.

Both Kahn and Bartin concluded that no uniform solution could be found which would answer the above problems and that each forum would have to deal with them on the basis of its own internal law. Despagnet attempted to bring about uniformity by suggesting that the questions be referred to the *lex causae*, the law governing the legal transaction in question.[6] Another writer, Gemma, realizing, no doubt, the impossibility of qualifying legal transactions by the *lex causae* (*i.e.*, on the basis of some law which remains yet to be ascertained), proposed to reach uniformity among the different countries by qualifying legal transactions with reference to the requirements of international life.[7]

My own reactions to the problem in the light of the existing Anglo-American decisions were set forth in an article published in 1920, in which I agreed in the main with the conclusions of Kahn and Bartin, that there is generally no escape from applying the internal law of the forum to the qualification of legal transactions.[8] In common with some foreign writers, however, I favored these exceptions: (1) that the qualification of rights affecting tangible property should be made on the

4. *Id.* at 1469, 1470.

5. Nussbaum cites the following: Harral v. Wallis, 37 N. J. Eq. 458 (1883), *aff'd sub nom.* Harral v. Harral, 39 N. J. Eq. 279 (1884) (domicile); Wood & Selick v. Compagnie Générale Transatlantique, 43 F. (2d) 941 (C. C. A. 2d, 1930) (statute of limitations); University of Chicago v. Dater, 277 Mich. 658, 270 N. W. 175 (1936) (contract, *lex loci contractus*); St. Louis-S. F. R. R. v. Fox, 171 Ark. 103, 283 S. W. 31 (1926) (settlement of injury claim rescinded, mode of tender); *cf.* ROBERTSON, CHARACTERIZATION IN THE CONFLICT OF LAWS (1940) 157–222, 235–279 (hereinafter cited as ROBERTSON); New England Mutual Life Ins. Co. v. Spence, 104 F. (2d) 665 (C. C. A. 2d, 1939).

6. *Des conflits de lois relatifs à la qualification des rapports juridiques*, 25 Clunet 253, 261, 262; also PRÉCIS DE DROIT INTERNATIONAL PRIVÉ (1909) 353 *et seq.*

7. PROPEDEUTICA AL DIRITTO INTERNAZIONALE PRIVATO (1899) 91, 111-112.

8. *The Theory of Qualifications and the Conflict of Laws* (1920) 20 COL. L. REV. 247.

basis of the *lex rei sitae,*[9] and (2) that if the forum is interested in a case only insofar as it is the place of trial, the courts of the forum should follow a qualification agreed upon by the foreign states or countries concerned.[10]

Since 1920, the continental literature on the subject has assumed vast proportions.[11] The great majority of writers have been forced to agree with Kahn and Bartin; and Despagnet's view that the *lex causae* should determine the question has found but a very few followers.[12] Gemma's attempt to supplant the use of the internal law both of the *lex fori* and of the *lex causae* with a consideration of the international requirements has led to some important developments in recent years. The most outstanding effort in this direction has been made by Rabel.[13] According to this eminent writer, it is a mistake to assume that the sole background of a choice-of-law rule is the material law of the forum. Each country's rules of private international law are designed, in his view, to bring about international harmony between the law of the forum and that of all other countries, which can be attained only on the basis of more abstract notions than the concrete institutions of any particular country. Notwithstanding great diversities in the legal institutions of civilized countries, Rabel contends, they generally resemble each other sufficiently to permit the creation of more abstract notions which are valid for all national legislations. By way of illustration he takes the subject of "Guardianship" referred to in Article 23 of the Introductory Law of the German Civil Code, which he would understand as an abstract notion of guardianship derived from a comparative study of the institution in the entire civilized world instead of as referring merely to guardianship as understood in German internal law. Rabel admits that the method of comparative law will not resolve the problem of qualification in those cases where the differences between the legislations are so great that it is impossible to set up a compromise between the opposing points of view.

9. See, in general, Falconbridge, *Contract and Conveyance in the Conflict of Laws* (1933) 81 U. OF PA. L. REV. 661, 663-666, 682-683; *Characterization in the Conflict of Laws* (1937) 53 L. Q. REV. 235, 543; *Conflict of Laws: Examples of Characterization* (1937) 15 CAN. B. REV. 215, 234; ROBERTSON 190 *et seq.*

10. *Accord,* ROBERTSON 177. If all the operative facts occurred in a single foreign country the law of that country would, of course, control without regard to whether the question was characterized in one way or another. The only exception to the rule would be for matters which the law of the forum would deem to be procedural.

11. For the bibliography, see ROBERTSON xxv-xxix; for a representation in English of the Italian viewpoint, see Meriggi, *Conflicts of Law — A Theoretical Approach* (1934) 14 B. U. L. REV. 319.

12. *E.g.,* WOLFF, INTERNATIONALES PRIVATRECHT (1933) 37; PACCHIONI, DIRITTO INTERNAZIONALE PRIVATO (2d ed. 1935) 173.

13. *Das Problem der Qualifikation* (1931) 5 ZEITSCHRIFT FÜR AUSLÄNDISCHES UND INTERNATIONALES PRIVATRECHT 241. Republished in revised form in Italian: *Il Problema della Qualificazione* (1932) 2 RIV. INT. DI DIR. PRIVATO E PROCESSUALE 97, and in French: *Le Problème de la Qualification* (1933) 28 REV. DE DR. INT. PRIVÉ 1.

In 1930 Bartin[14] added the following limitation to his original thesis that the *lex fori* governed the qualification of legal transactions: "After the law of the forum, on the basis of its own qualification, has chosen a foreign law as governing a particular legal institution, all subsidiary qualifications arising thereafter and necessary for the decision of the case are determined by the foreign law."

In 1932 Neuner[15] published the first monograph on the subject, in which he rejected all the foregoing conclusions, the problem of qualification having, in his opinion, no right to existence. According to this author, the fundamental error consists in the assumption that there exists in each country a body of choice-of-law rules which are applicable to all situations that may be presented to a court, whereas there are actually only about twenty or thirty such rules, which are entirely inadequate for that purpose. The primary need is, therefore, the working out of additional rules, together with the further elaboration of the existing rules and their application in a manner calculated to bring about reasonable and just results.[16]

Recently, English and American writers also have begun to take interest in the problem of qualification. Beginning with 1934, a series of articles which dealt with the subject appeared. The earliest was by Beckett,[17] who conceived the proper principle to be that the classification should be made on the basis of analytical jurisprudence and comparative law. Like Rabel, he felt that if the rules of Conflicts are to perform the function for which they are designed, they must be applied in a manner suitable for appreciating the character of the rules and institutions of all legal systems. The conception of these rules must, therefore, be of a very general character, which can be derived only from analytical jurisprudence and comparative law.

---

14. 1 PRINCIPES DE DR. INT. PRIVÉ (1930) 235; *La Doctrine des Qualifications et ses rapports avec le caractère national des règles du Conflit des Lois* (1930) ACADÉMIE DE DR. INT., REC. DES COURS I, 565-620. See also Maury, *Règles Générales des Conflits de Lois* (1936) ACADÉMIE DE DR. INT., REC. DES COURS III, 329, 493 *et seq.*

15. DER SINN DER INTERNATIONALPRIVATRECHTLICHEN NORM, EINE KRITIK DER QUALIFIKATIONSTHEORIE (1932).

16. Neuner says that the Conflict of Laws rules are not as general as they are believed to be and as they must be deemed to be if they are to govern all cases. In his view they are only general propositions, the extent and application of which remain to be worked out. The case of Ogden v. Ogden, *infra* p. 755, may serve as an illustration. According to Neuner the English courts never really adopted the broad rule that capacity to marry is governed by the law of domicile but adopted it only with respect to prohibited degrees of relationship. As the law of the place of celebration in all other respects governs marriage in English law, it would therefore also apply to the question of parental consent. Such an interpretation of the English law would, of course, eliminate the qualification problem.

17. *The Question of Classification ("Qualification") in Private International Law* (1934) 15 BRIT. Y. B. INT. L. 46.

Beckett's conclusions were accepted by Cheshire in the first edition of his textbook in 1935.[18] In the second edition in 1938,[19] Cheshire draws a distinction between primary classification, arising before the law applicable to the case is selected, and secondary classification, which arises after the selection of such law.[20] He would determine the former with reference to the *lex fori* and the latter with reference to the *lex causae*. This division corresponds to Bartin's later views.

In 1940 Robertson published a comprehensive monograph on *Characterization in the Conflict of Laws*.[21] As his work contains a detailed examination of the views of all Anglo-American writers, and of the most important continental writers, as well as a discussion of most English and American cases presenting fact situations involving the problem of characterization, our further development of the subject will center its attention upon the conclusions reached by this author.

II.

Falconbridge was the first writer to suggest that the problem of qualification should be considered in connection with each of the different stages presented in the solution of a Conflicts problem.[22] Before a judge can select the choice-of-law rule applicable to a situation presented to him, he must know whether the question relates to contracts, torts, property, succession, or some other field. He will usually be quite sure of the category to which the question belongs. Many differences do exist, however, between the different systems of law in the classification of legal transactions, and the question is what a judge is to do when confronted with a situation treated variantly in different systems. Most writers seem to feel that in the present stage of our law there is no practical alternative to the application of the law of the forum.[23] It is conceded that this is an undesirable state of affairs because different solutions will be reached in different countries having identical Conflicts rules. Vigorous efforts

18. Cheshire, Private International Law (1st ed. 1935) 14.

19. *Id.* (2d ed. 1938) at 24-25.

20. Cheshire, Private International Law (2d ed. 1938) 30, 37. For a discussion of secondary classification, see p. 753 *et seq. infra*.

21. For other articles on the subject by English and American writers, see Falconbridge, *Characterization in the Conflict of Laws* (1937) 53 L. Q. Rev. 235, 537; *Conflict of Laws: Examples of Characterization* (1937) 15 Can. B. Rev. 215; *Renvoi, Characterization and Acquired Rights* (1939) 17 Can. B. Rev. 369; Unger, *The Place of Classification in Private International Law* (1937) 19 Bell Yard 3; Cheatham, *Internal Law Distinctions in the Conflict of Laws* (1936) 21 Corn. L. Q. 570.

22. *Characterization in the Conflict of Laws* (1937) 53 L. Q. Rev. 235, 236.

23. Falconbridge is in accord, but he urges that in order to bring about reasonable economic or social results the process of selecting the proper law be rendered as flexible as possible. He suggests, therefore, that the characterization should be made in the light of all potentially applicable rules of law. *Renvoi, Characterization and Acquired Rights* (1939) 17 Can. B. Rev. 369, 374-375.

have therefore been made to avoid this conclusion, but, except in one or two directions,[24] no practical escapes have been found.

Robertson is in general agreement with the above views but contends that further clarification is necessary concerning the process of qualification by the *lex fori*. He makes particular objection to the statement that the qualification must be on the basis of the "internal" law of the forum.[25] Unger called attention to this point in connection with two English cases.[26] One involved a foreign contract unsupported by consideration. The contract, being governed by the foreign law and valid there, was enforced in England.[27] If the court had applied the strictly internal law, which required that a contract be supported by consideration, the fact-situation presented could not have been characterized as a contract. Unger holds, therefore, that it is sufficient if the case falls within the "analytical framework" of the legal system of the forum. The second case recognized the validity of a Russian marriage in England.[28] As a Russian marriage is terminable at will, it does not correspond to the English notion of marriage. Unger would say that the Russian marriage was rightfully recognized in England because it fell within the English analytical framework concerning marriage. Robertson regards Unger's formulation of the rule as still too narrow because it does not include cases involving foreign institutions entirely unknown to the internal English law. Such a situation was presented to the House of Lords in the case of *DeNicols v. Curlier*.[29] A French couple came to reside in England. At the husband's death, the widow claimed one-half of all the property acquired by the husband during the marriage, including the property acquired in England, basing her claim on the French matrimonial property régime. No such property régime was known to the internal English law. The House of Lords felt that the French law should control and, in so holding, recognized a foreign institution which did not exist in England and so could not fall within the framework of the English internal law. Robertson therefore concludes that, insofar as the characterization of foreign legal situations is determined by the *lex fori*, the term does not mean the strictly internal law of the forum, but a wider concept which needs to be worked out for purposes of the Conflict of Laws.[30] This conclusion clearly seems to be correct.

In my Article dealing with the statute of frauds,[31] published in 1923, I was already aware that qualification in accordance with the internal law

24. See pp. 744–745 *supra*.
25. ROBERTSON 29 *et seq.*
26. Unger, *supra* note 21, at 7.
27. Re Bonacina [1912] 2 Ch. 394 (C.A.).
28. Nachimson v. Nachimson [1930] P. 217.
29. [1900] A. C. 21.
30. ROBERTSON 89.
31. *The Statute of Frauds and the Conflict of Laws* (1923) 32 YALE L. J. 311.

of the forum would not do. In most instances the categories of internal law will also suffice for purposes of the Conflict of Laws but there are situations where they may not. In the Article referred to, I stated that the statute of frauds might well be classified as procedural for purposes of internal law and yet be substantive from the point of view of the Conflict of Laws.[32] The clearest example of such a distinction in Anglo-American law relates to "penal" laws. There have been many American decisions holding that a statute which gives a plaintiff damages in excess of the amount of his loss, or without reference to such amount or the cause of the loss, is a penal statute. The United States Supreme Court[33] and the English Privy Council[34] have held, however, in *Huntington v. Attrill* that, for purposes of the Conflict of Laws, an international test should be adopted, restricting the definition of a penal law to a law punishing a person for the infraction of a public law. Here we have two distinct tests of what constitutes a penal law, one for internal law purposes and the other for questions of the Conflict of Laws. Similarly, as regards the qualification of legal transactions, the classification or characterization may have to be upon a broader or narrower basis than the internal law of the forum if it is to be suitable for the needs of the Conflict of Laws. In certain cases it may suffice, as suggested by Unger, that the transaction fall within the analytical framework of the internal law of the forum. In other cases it may not, so that wider categories may have to be discovered.[35] To this end a knowledge of Comparative Law may be useful.

III.

Let us consider next the characterization of the connecting factor. After having reached the conclusion that the situation presented to the court is one of succession, or one of contracts or torts, the judge will be directed by the choice-of-law rules of the forum to apply the law of the domicile, the *lex loci contractus,* the *lex loci solutionis,* or the *lex loci delicti,* respectively. He may find, however, in a given case that different meanings are attached to such connecting factors. For example, the English courts recognize the reverter doctrine in connection with domicile. Our courts do not. In the English law a married woman cannot acquire

32. *Id.* at 330.

33. Huntington v. Attrill, 146 U. S. 657 (1892).

34. Huntington v. Attrill [1893] A. C. 150 (P.C.).

35. In the cases used by way of illustration above, the characterization of the situation as "contract," "marriage," or "penal" may not have determined the choice of law within the strict meaning of the qualification problem as defined in this article. The question was in fact only whether a wide or a narrow meaning should be given to the terms in connection with the enforcement of the foreign "contract," or "penal" liability, or the recognition of the foreign "marriage." The same reasoning is valid, however, where a choice of law is dependent upon the qualification problem as herein defined.

a separate domicile. Under our law she may. Under our law a contract by correspondence is deemed concluded when the letter of acceptance is posted. On the continent and in Latin-America, the formation of the contract is not infrequently postponed to the time when the answer reaches the offeror. Differences exist also with respect to the place of performance of a contract or the place where a tort is committed. On the continent the qualification of nationality as a connecting factor is of great importance because in many countries the *lex patriae* has been substituted for the *lex domicilii* in the determination of the personal law. As the laws governing the acquisition and loss of nationality vary considerably in the different countries, by what law is the judge to determine the nationality of the parties before him? I dealt with this problem in an earlier Article,[36] and, as it has little practical importance in the Anglo-American system of the Conflict of Laws, it need not be reconsidered here.

Apart from the qualification of "nationality," it may be said that there appears to be general concurrence, at least among Anglo-American courts and writers,[37] that the law of the forum must determine the meaning of the connecting factors. Where a person lives in a single foreign country, it is, of course, quite simple to determine his domicile with reference to such foreign law. Difficulties would arise, however, if he were to live in several foreign countries unless there were agreement between those countries regarding his domicile. So far as the question has been presented to Anglo-American courts, they have determined domicile in accordance with the *lex fori*.[38] Whether they would accept the common characterization of two foreign states to which the factual situation was exclusively related, the law of the forum being interested solely as the place of trial, is not certain.[39] The foreign characterization might well be adopted in this situation in the interest of uniformity, as there is no inescapable necessity for applying the law of the forum. Similarly, with respect to the remaining factors. Thus in a contract case, if the law in a given jurisdiction directs the judge to apply the law of the place of contracting and the contract is deemed concluded by the *lex fori* in the state or country in which the acceptance is mailed and the law of the foreign state regards it as formed when the acceptance reaches the offeror, the law of the forum would necessarily have to control. However, if the law of the forum should have no other relation to the case than as the place of trial, and the laws of the foreign countries between which the negotiations were carried on should agree that a contract is completed at the

36. *The Theory of Qualifications and the Conflict of Laws* (1920) 20 COL. L. REV. 247, 250-252.

37. For a discussion of the English and American cases, see ROBERTSON 224-229.

38. See ROBERTSON 108; Lorenzen, *supra* note 36, at 248-250; RESTATEMENT, CONFLICT OF LAWS (1934) § 10.

39. See RESTATEMENT, CONFLICT OF LAWS (1934) § 10, *caveat*.

place where the acceptance reaches the offeror, uniformity in the Conflict of Laws would be promoted by accepting the foreign characterization.

Where the connecting factor has significance in the internal law of the country as well, it should conform for the purposes of the Conflict of Laws, to the international requirements, instead of being limited to the internal law concept. Our courts have shown an awareness of this fact in connection with domicile when they contrast "municipal" domicile with domicile for purposes of the Conflict of Laws.[40]

Robertson agrees that the connecting factor should generally be determined by the law of the forum. As he is inclined to accept the renvoi doctrine in the Conflict of Laws, he would, insofar as that doctrine applies, allow an exception to the above rule and accept the characterization of the connecting factor by the foreign law.[41] He gives as an illustration the case of an American citizen with a domicile of origin in Iowa who acquires a domicile of choice in England. He then decides to give up his English domicile and return to the United States to end his days. He dies on his way home. An English court is called upon to administer his estate. By English law the decedent died domiciled in Iowa because the domicile of origin automatically reverted upon the abandonment of his English domicile. By Iowa law, the decedent died domiciled in England because his English domicile of choice continued until a new domicile was established in Iowa. If, in the light of *In re Annesley,*[42] the English judge is to decide the case in the same way as the judge sitting in the court of the domicile would do; he will have to follow the reference of Iowa law to English law in the matter of domicile. He would thus have to accept the determination of the connecting factor—domicile—by the Iowa court, instead of reaching a conclusion on the basis of the English law of domicile.

The case of *University of Chicago v. Dater*[43] may be explained on this basis. A married woman in Michigan signed a note, dated and payable in Chicago, and secured by Illinois real estate. According to Michigan law, the contract was deemed concluded in Illinois. But when it was proved that under the Illinois rule as to the formation of contracts the contract was deemed concluded in Michigan, the Michigan court applied its own rule that the married woman was under a disability to enter into the contract. The majority opinion does not disclose any awareness of the problem involved. The dissenting opinion, on the other hand, clearly expresses the usual view toward this question. If, under the

40. "This is an illustration applicable to a change of municipal domicile. But the domicile required by the divorce statute seems to be more analogous to what is termed by Mr. Jacobs, in his work on Domicile, a quasi-national domicile." King v. King, 74 N. J. Eq. 824, 827, 71 Atl. 687, 688 (1908).

41. ROBERTSON 110.

42. [1926] Ch. 692.

43. 277 Mich. 658, 270 N. W. 175 (1936).

Michigan Conflicts rule, the law of the place where the contract was technically made determined the capacity of married women to contract, the Michigan court was obliged, of course, to ascertain where under the circumstances of the case the contract was made. This question the court resolved correctly on the basis of the Michigan decisions. The connecting factor was thereby established and there was no occasion to determine it over again on the basis of Illinois law. Therefore the court should have applied the Illinois law governing the capacity of married women to contract unless it was prepared to accept, with respect to contracts, the renvoi doctrine in the *In re Annesley* sense. Under the *Annesley* rule, the Michigan court should decide the case as the Illinois court would. It would be immaterial how the Illinois court reached its conclusion that Michigan law was applicable: whether it did so because its Conflict of Laws rule regarding capacity to contract was different from that of Michigan (it might determine such capacity with reference to the law of the domicile of the married woman), or whether the Conflicts rule regarding capacity to contract was the same as the Michigan rule but the Illinois court disagreed with the Michigan court's characterization of the connecting factor as the place of contracting.

A word of caution may be in order here. Although a goodly number of decisions and dicta in England seem to accept renvoi, there is no clear-cut decision by a higher court which really establishes the doctrine in English law. It should also be remembered that the English renvoi cases have been almost exclusively concerned with matters of succession where the English rule of domicile came into conflict with the continental rule of nationality. Moreover, even as limited to succession cases, the *In re Annesley* rule is only one of several interpretations which the English lower courts have given to the renvoi doctrine. Uniform results arose in *In re Annesley* from the fact that the French courts did not interpret their renvoi doctrine in the way the English court did. If the interpretation given to the renvoi doctrine by *In re Annesley* is the true one on principle, it must be correct for every other country. If the French courts had interpreted their renvoi doctrine in the same way as *In re Annesley,* they would have had to decide the case in the same manner as an English court, and if an English court had to decide in the same way as a French court, no conclusion could have been reached. As long as some countries apply the renvoi doctrine in the French way, which is the traditional one, uniformity would be reached, with reference to those countries, on the basis of the *In re Annesley* doctrine. Personally, I cannot approve a doctrine which is workable only if the other country rejects it. Apart from that, I do not favor handing over our Conflicts problems to so-called experts on foreign private international law. It is difficult enough to get accurate expert testimony with respect to foreign municipal law, but such testimony is much more unreliable with respect to foreign Conflict of

Laws. For these reasons I should still regard the general acceptance of the renvoi doctrine in our law as most unfortunate.

IV.

We come now to the third step in the solution of a Conflict of Laws problem, which is called by Robertson "The delimitation and application of the proper law."[44] In a case involving the distribution of personal property upon death, an Anglo-American court would find the connecting factor to be the decedent's domicile at the time of death and, characterizing this term on the basis of the *lex fori,* it might conclude that the domicile was in France. In a contract case, let us assume that a court has found it to be the settled law of the state that the law of the place of contracting controls, and, characterizing this connecting factor on the basis of the *lex fori,* let us assume that the court has found that the place of contracting was in France. In both instances the question will then be what is *the* French law that is to be applied? If the French law should have rules of the Conflict of Laws different from those of the forum, applying the national law of the decedent to questions of succession and the intention of the parties as governing the validity of the contract, we should be faced again with the renvoi doctrine, that is, whether the law of the forum should regard its Conflicts rules as referring to the French municipal or internal law (law of succession or contracts), exclusive of its rules of the Conflict of Laws, or the French law in its totality, including its rules of the Conflict of Laws. This assumes, of course, that the question is not regarded by the courts of the forum as one of procedure in the Conflicts sense. If it should be so regarded, the procedural rules of the forum would apply.

This is not the place to go further into the subject of renvoi in general. So far as it bears upon the question of characterization arising in connection with the third step in the solution of a Conflicts problem — the application and delimitation of the foreign law — it operates in the same manner as it operates in dealing with the qualification of the connecting factor. In other words, if the renvoi doctrine in the *In re Annesley* sense is adopted by the law of the forum, the court would have to regard itself in the above cases as sitting in France and decide the case as a French court would decide it.[45] If a question of qualification were involved, it would mean, of course, that the law of the forum would follow the decision of the French court. To the extent, therefore, that the law of the forum accepts the renvoi in the *In re Annesley* sense, any qualification

44. ROBERTSON 17-18.

45. Falconbridge is of the opinion that the renvoi doctrine should be recognized with respect to status, and for that reason he would justify characterization of status on the basis of the foreign law governing such status. *Characterization in the Conflict of Laws* (1937) 53 L. Q. REV. 235, 544-546; *Conflict of Laws: Examples of Characterization* (1937) 15 CAN. B. REV. 215, 244.

arising in the application or delimitation of the French law would actually be determined by the *lex causae.*

As the renvoi doctrine has not been recognized in American law, except for certain purposes, let us consider the characterization problem arising in connection with the third step in the solution of a Conflict of Laws problem (the application and delimitation of the foreign law) on the assumption that the Conflicts rules of the forum apply strictly to the internal law of the foreign country and not to its Conflicts rules. Robertson calls this the problem of secondary classification and argues that secondary classification should be on the basis of the *lex causae* — on principle, and not merely by way of exception, as in the case of primary characterization. He thus accepts Bartin's later generalization,[46] according to which the law of the forum disinterests itself in the case after it has chosen the foreign law and turned the case over to such law, so that any problem of characterization arising in the application of the foreign law will be governed by that law. Cheshire drew the same distinction between questions of characterization arising before and after the foreign law has been chosen by the *lex fori.* We find, however, that these supporters of the secondary classification theory do not agree among themselves as to the types of cases which are subject to secondary characterization. Robertson goes beyond Cheshire, by including in this class the question whether a legal provision relates to capacity or formalities.

The two cases generally discussed in this connection by writers on the qualification problem are a Dutch will case and the English case of *Ogden v. Ogden.*[47] The former involved a holographic will made by a Hollander in France,[48] the Dutch law prohibiting Hollanders from executing their wills in the holographic form either at home or abroad.[49] Bartin originally regarded this situation as one in which no uniformity of decision could be reached, on the assumed ground that from the Dutch point of view the question would be one of capacity while from the standpoint of French law it would be one of formality.[50] The Dutch courts would regard the will as void, whereas the courts of the country in which the will was executed or the courts of third countries might apply the law of the place of execution to matters of formality and so hold the will valid. This viewpoint has had the approval both of courts[51] and

46. Bartin, *La Doctrine des Qualifications et ses rapports avec le caractère national des règles du Conflit des Lois* (1930) Académie de Dr. Int., Rec. des Cours I, 565, 608.

47. [1908] P. 46.

48. A similar question is presented by the prohibition of joint wills, which is regarded by some as appertaining to capacity and by others as appertaining to form.

49. Holland: Civil Code (1921) art. 992.

50. 24 Clunet 225, 229-230.

51. *France:* Cass. (Civ.) Aug. 25, 1847, Dalloz Jurisprudence, 1847 I. 273; *Germany:* Hans. OLG, May 2, 1917, Hans. G.Z., 1917, Beibl., 252.

writers.[52] Cheshire regards the problem as one of primary characterization, to be determined on the basis of the *lex fori*.[53] According to Robertson's theory of secondary characterization, if such a will, disposing of movable property, is executed in England, and the English courts regard the law of domicile as governing capacity to make a will and the law of the place of execution as governing formalities, the courts should inquire of the Dutch law what it understands by capacity and of the English law what it means by formalities.[54] Others have denied the validity of the will anywhere, either because they regarded the Dutch legislation as affecting *capacity* and therefore governed by the testator's personal (Dutch) law[55] or, conceding that the Dutch statute affected *formalities*, because they did not attribute an absolute character to the rule that the law of the place of execution governed formalities, but regarded it, with respect to Dutch nationals, as subject to modification by the national legislation.[56] Bartin seems to have adopted this view in his later years.[57] From the standpoint of the Dutch law, the will would be invalid without any need of characterizing the legislation as relating to capacity or to form.[58] The case presented, therefore, is in reality not at all a problem of differences in qualification.

The facts in *Ogden v. Ogden* were as follows: In 1898 a marriage was celebrated in England between Sarah, a domiciled Englishwoman, and Philip, a domiciled Frenchman, who was 19 years of age. In 1901 this marriage was annulled by a French court on the ground that the consent of Philip's surviving parent had not been obtained as required by French law. Philip subsequently married a French woman in France. Sarah thereupon, in 1903, instituted a suit in England for the dissolution of her marriage with Philip on the ground of his adultery and desertion. This suit was dismissed for want of jurisdiction because Philip was domiciled

52. 1 Arminjon, Précis de Dr. Int. Privé (2d ed. 1927) 135; 6 Staudinger's Kommentar zum Bürgerlichen Gesetzbuche (Raape's 9th ed. 1931), part II, 18. See also Pillet & Niboyet, Manuel de Dr. Int. Privé (1928) 503; Despagnet, Précis de Dr. Int. Privé (5th ed. 1909) 354; Surville, Cours Élémentaire de Dr. Int. Privé (7th ed. 1925) 19, n. 3.

53. Private International Law (2d ed. 1938), 34 *et seq.*

54. Robertson 238, 244-245.

55. In favor of this view: *France:* Dufour v. Dufour, Trib. Seine, Aug. 13, 1903, 31 Clunet 166; *Belgium:* Willemsen v. Brands, Trib. Brussels, July 21, 1886, 14 Clunet 495; Isabaert v. Barbiaux, Trib. Termonde, March 24, 1907, 35 Clunet 885; Froidbise v. Horsten, App. Brussels, Jan. 9, 1937, Pas. 1937, II. 56.

56. *France:* Leeuwn v. Guilbot, Trib. Seine, Feb. 19, 1927, 55 Clunet 707; *Italy:* Ogtrop v. Formica, App. Genoa, Aug. 4, 1891, 20 Clunet 955, *aff'd*, Cass. Turin, Apr. 12, 1892, 21 Clunet 1083. This would be tantamount to the recognition of a new choice-of-law rule with respect to formalities.

57. Bartin, *supra* note 46, at 576.

58. Kosters, Het Internationaal Burgerlijk Recht in Nederland (1917) 643; Amsterdam, Rechtbank, June 19, 1924, 12 Bull. de L'institut Intermédiare International 118.

in France. In 1904 Sarah, describing herself as a widow, married Ogden, a domiciled Englishman, in England. In 1906 Ogden obtained an annulment of the marriage on the ground that at the time of their marriage Sarah was married to Philip. So far as *Ogden v. Ogden* held that the French decree of nullity was not entitled to recognition in England, it is deemed overruled by subsequent English cases. The case is principally of interest because of the problem of qualification involved in it and the decision that the requirement of parental consent to the marriage was to be characterized as a part of the formalities, so that the marriage between Sarah and Philip was validly contracted from the English point of view.

Various solutions of the *Ogden* problem have been suggested. Beckett would give effect to all French provisions, though relating to formalities abroad, for the reason that they are matters of family law and intended for the protection of family interests.[59] Cheshire[60] and Falconbridge[61] insist that the qualification of the French requirement must be according to the *lex fori*. Says Cheshire:

> "In order to reach a decision, he [the English judge] examines the terms in which the rule is expressed, and he considers the construction put upon it by French expert witnesses, but he must ultimately determine its true nature by an application of the canons and principles recognized in England. If the rule reads as follows:
>
> > 'The son who has not reached the age of 25 years cannot contract marriage, without the consent of his father and mother,'
>
> it would seem that it must be classed as affecting the capacity of the parties. . . . If an English judge applies French law merely because a French lawyer would regard the question *sub judice* as one of capacity, though in England it is regarded as one of formal validity, the result is the application of a legal system which in this country is considered inappropriate in the matter at hand."[62]

If the English rule that capacity to contract a marriage is governed by the law of domicile is a general one, its characterization should be on the basis of the *lex fori* and not on that of the *lex causae*. The ultimate question is whether French or English law is to be applied to the matter of consent of parents. The answer to the question depends upon

59. Beckett, *The Question of Classification ("Qualification") In Private International Law* (1934) 15 BRIT. Y. B. INT. L. 46, 78.

60. PRIVATE INTERNATIONAL LAW (2d ed. 1938) 36.

61. *Characterization in the Conflict of Laws* (1937) 53 L. Q. REV. 235, 249 (maintains that parental consent cannot be characterized in the abstract; that it may be a question of formality in one context and capacity in another).

62. PRIVATE INTERNATIONAL LAW (2d ed. 1938) 36, 37. In applying the foreign law selected by the forum, the court should take into consideration all relevant provisions, though they may appear in some other title or division of the Code.

whether the consent of parents is to be characterized as appertaining to capacity or form. This question the law of the forum must decide for itself. If the English judge were to submit to the French view in this situation and regard a French provision as one of capacity when from the English point of view it is a matter of form, he would, as Cheshire points out in the above quotation, apply a law which is considered inappropriate by the law of the forum. He would apply French law because of the French characterization when he should apply English law according to the English characterization. As well might the English judge prefer the French to the English rules for the choice of law, *i.e.*, accept the renvoi doctrine. Robertson appears to favor the renvoi and this no doubt accounts for his suggestion that in the case of multiple qualification (where, for example, capacity is governed by the law of domicile and formalities by the law of the place where the transaction occurs), the characterization should be on the basis of the *lex causae* (*i.e.*, the domiciliary law should characterize capacity and the *lex loci actus* should characterize matters of form). That suggestion is unacceptable.

Both Cheshire and Robertson assume that there is an established rule in the English Conflict of Laws that capacity to marry is governed by the law of domicile and formalities by the law of the place of celebration. If the English rule that the law of domicile controls the capacity to marry were of a more restricted character so as to be limited (as submitted by Neuner and Rheinstein[63]) to degrees of relationship, all other matters being subject to the law of the place of celebration, the marriage in *Ogden v. Ogden* would of course have been valid in England, but no question of characterization would have been presented.

The problem remains whether or not questions of qualification which may arise after the foreign law has been chosen by the *lex fori* should be referred to the foreign law (*lex causae*) as Bartin, Cheshire and Robertson advocate. It goes without saying that if the qualification problem merely involves the application of the foreign internal law, the foreign law should control. The law of state *X*, which has been chosen by the law of the forum as governing a contract or tort, necessarily governs any subsidiary question relating to such contract or tort; for example, whether a particular contract is to be regarded as a loan or deposit, or whether the master is responsible for the torts of his servants, and what is meant by master and servant in that connection. It is also reasonable that if the French Civil Code permits Frenchmen to execute wills in the "authentic" form abroad, the requirement may be deemed satisfied if the nearest equivalent existing in the place of execution is complied with (for example, where a will is executed in England before witnesses).

63. See Neuner, *op. cit. supra* note 15. Compare also Rheinstein, Book Review (1938) 8 BROOKLYN L. REV. 253, 257.

Does it follow that the *lex causae* should likewise determine whether a particular provision of the foreign law relates to substance or procedure? The principal examples of secondary qualification given by Cheshire relate to substance and procedure. Robertson also dwells at length upon this subject in his discussion of secondary characterization. According to these writers, if the law of the forum has decided that a contract or a tort is governed by the law of state *X* and no rules of procedure of the forum are involved, such questions as whether a writing required by the law of state *X* affects the formation and validity of the contract or relates to evidence, whether by the law of state *X* the running of the statute of limitations discharges a contract or merely bars the remedy for its breach, whether the failure to give notice to the wrong-doer required by the law of state *X* will discharge the cause of action or whether it is merely a procedural requirement for the bringing of the suit, should be governed by the law of state *X*. What are the consequences of this view? According to the proponents of the secondary classification theory, if the law of the forum says that the statute of limitations is substantive and the law governing the contract says it is procedural, the action would be maintainable, even though it is not brought within the time prescribed by either law.[64] The statute of limitations of the forum would be applicable only to contracts governed by the law of the forum and the foreign statute of limitations, being procedural, would be disregarded, as the courts do not enforce the procedural laws of another country. The same would be true in the case of the statute of frauds. If the law of the forum says it is substantive and the law governing the contract says it is procedural, the contract would be enforceable upon reasoning similar to that used in connection with the statute of limitations, although neither statute is satisfied.[65] If the law of the forum should have a substantive

64. This is the view taken by Cheshire and Robertson. To the same effect with respect to the Statute of Frauds, see WHARTON, CONFLICT OF LAWS (3d ed. 1905) 1445. If it should be asked why, under the secondary classification theory, the characterization by the foreign law of the Statute of Limitations or of the Statute of Frauds as procedural was not binding upon the courts of the forum so as to make the statute of the forum applicable, the answer is, because the law of the forum, in submitting the matter to the foreign law, has thereby already decided that the question is one of substance. Procedural matters are always subject to the law of the forum.

65. The German Supreme Court took this view in a suit upon a Tennessee contract. The German statute (3 years) did not apply because it was regarded as substantive and thus applicable only to contracts governed by German law. The Tennessee statute (6 years) was found to be procedural from the viewpoint of American law and hence not applicable. There being no statute of limitations applicable to the situation, the action was allowed. German Supreme Court, January 4, 1882, 7 RGZ 21. Later cases have taken the view advocated in this Article: that the foreign statute be qualified on the basis of the law of the forum. After a detailed comparison between the effects of the foreign statute and the German statute of limitations the court found that they were substantially the same. That being the case, it felt that the case could be dealt with on the basis of German law, which had rejected the notion, formerly prevailing, that the statute of

rule requiring notice of the injury suffered by the plaintiff and the law of the place where the injury arose should regard the requirement of notice as a matter of procedure, the action would lie, although no notice was given, that is, neither law was complied with. If the law of the forum should regard the burden of proof as substantive and the law of the state where the wrong was committed should regard it as procedural, there would theoretically be no law applicable to the burden of proof.[66]

Results like these would seem sufficient to prove the unsoundness of the secondary classification theory. If an applicable foreign statute of frauds or statute of limitations has not been satisfied, the plaintiff has no right to damages for the breach of the contract under the law governing the contract. If this is so, there is no reason why the plaintiff should be given greater rights in any other state. The very object of the rules of the Conflict of Laws is to keep the rights of parties the same, regardless of the state or country in which the litigation may take place. If the law of the forum chooses the law of state *X* as governing the contractual rights of the parties, it does so on considerations of fairness and justice. If the law of the foreign state or country says that the plaintiff never had an enforceable right, he should not have an enforceable right anywhere else. An unenforceable right is equivalent for purposes of the Conflict of Laws to no right. The statement that courts should enforce foreign substantive rights but not foreign procedural laws has no justifiable basis if the so-called procedural law would normally affect the outcome of the litigation. If there is any sense in the proposition that the law of state *X* governs the contract — and if there is no sense in that proposition, the entire Conflict of Laws should be scrapped — it must mean that all municipal laws of the state normally affecting the rights of the parties (that is, the recovery of damages), such as the statute of frauds and the statute of limitations, should control.

The parties cannot, of course, expect the courts of the forum to adapt their legal machinery to that of any foreign state or country. So far as the detailed steps and modes of procedure are concerned, courts can operate only in their accustomed manner. A Connecticut court cannot without undue inconvenience try a case in accordance with New York procedure and it would be quite impossible to try a case in accordance with a continental or Latin-American system of procedure. The law of the forum is thus obliged, on grounds of necessity, to apply its own pro-

limitations belongs to the law of procedure. RG, Nov. 21, 1910, Juristische Wochenschrift 1911, 148; July 6, 1934, 145 RGZ 121.

Nussbaum regards the analysis and appraisal of the integration process—the process of determining whether the foreign institution conforms substantially to that of the forum—as constituting the central problem of qualification, which is rarely touched upon by the writers on the subject. Book Review (1940) 40 Col. L. Rev. 1461, 1465; *cf.* Wood & Selick v. Compagnie Générale Transatlantique, 43 F. (2d) 941 (C. C. A. 2d, 1930).

66. In this predicament the court would probably apply the law of the forum.

cedural laws and disregard those of other states. However, foreign statutes of limitations and statutes of frauds do not fall within that category, for they can be proved as readily and without greater inconvenience than any other foreign law that may be applicable under the rules of the Conflict of Laws of the forum.

V.

We have arrived, then, at the following conclusions:

(1) The question whether a situation is to be classified as one of contracts, torts, succession, matrimonial property, and the like, is necessarily to be determined by the law of the forum. The foreign institution need not conform strictly to the internal law of the forum; it should be sufficient if it falls within its analytical framework or within some special concept worked out for purposes of the Conflict of Laws.

(2) The same conclusion applies to the characterization of the connecting factor. However, to the extent that the law of the forum accepts the renvoi doctrine in the *In re Annesley* sense, the characterization of the connecting factor by the foreign law would prevail.

(3) As the law of the forum is chosen in the above classes of cases for want of any other practicable rule, it should be abandoned whenever some other reasonable solution can be found. For that reason the question whether tangible property is movable or immovable should be determined on the basis of the law of the situs. Again, if the fact situation is exclusively connected with foreign states or countries, the law of the forum being interested solely as the place of trial, a common characterization placed upon it by the law of all the foreign states or countries involved should be accepted.

To the extent that the law of the forum understands its Conflicts rules in the renvoi (*In re Annesley*) sense, the adoption of the characterization made by the foreign law would follow.

(4) The suggestion that the *lex causae* should determine all questions of characterization arising after the foreign law has been selected by the *lex fori* — the "secondary characterization" of Cheshire and Robertson — is not to be approved. As in the preceding cases, such questions of characterization should be resolved on the basis of the *lex fori*.

[4]

RENVOI REVISITED *

FORTY years have now passed since the French word " renvoi " first made its appearance in English legal print.[1] That the idea is still a " foreign doctrine "[2] has not been from want of adequate attention on the part of Anglo-American legal writers. Indeed, the paper and ink devoted to the problem had already been so great a number of years ago that one author recorded in despair that " Juristic speculation has been almost infinite ".[3] Into such a field one steps with diffidence and trepidation. Whether the step has been a misstep can only be judged by others.[4]

---

* The title is obviously modelled on Mr. Beale's *Haddock Revisited* (1926) 39 HARV. L. REV. 417. The analogy is not perfect, for this is the first time the author has publicly paid his respects to the renvoi. The allusion is to the numerous visits made by other writers in the past which form the background of this article.

Acknowledgment is made to my colleague, A. H. Feller, and to A. H. Robertson, graduate student in the Harvard Law School, who read the manuscript and furnished many valuable suggestions.

1 Apparently the first allusion to " renvoi " in English is a brief note in (1898) 14 L. Q. REV. 231. See also a Note by Baty in (1899) 25 LAW MAG. & REV. 100.

Dicey had raised the problem a short while before in the first edition of his treatise. DICEY, CONFLICT OF LAWS (1st ed. 1896) 6, 76–78. See also McIlwraith, *The Bourgoise Case in London and Paris* (1890) 6 L. Q. REV. 379, 387n.

2 1 BEALE, CONFLICT OF LAWS (1935) § 5.1.

3 Note, *A Distinction in the Renvoi Doctrine* (1922) 35 HARV. L. REV. 454. " The literature on the subject is immense." CHESHIRE, PRIVATE INTERNATIONAL LAW (2d ed. 1938) 50n.

4 No effort is made in this article to present a review of all the cases, either English or American, which have involved renvoi problems. This has been done repeatedly elsewhere, sometimes with almost painful thoroughness. Discussions of the English cases may be found in BATE, NOTES ON THE DOCTRINE OF RENVOI IN PRIVATE INTERNATIONAL LAW (1904); DICEY, CONFLICT OF LAWS (5th ed. 1932) 863–78; MENDELSSOHN-BARTHOLDY, RENVOI IN MODERN ENGLISH LAW (1937); CHESHIRE, PRIVATE INTERNATIONAL LAW (2d ed. 1938) 45–67. Both the English and the American cases are considered in Abbot, *Is the Renvoi a Part of the Common Law?* (1908) 24 L. Q. REV. 133; Lorenzen, *The Renvoi Theory and the Application of Foreign Law* (1910) 10 COL. L. REV. 190, 327; Lorenzen, *The Renvoi Doctrine in the Conflict of Laws — Meaning of " The Law of a Country "* (1918) 27 YALE L. J. 509; Schreiber, *The Doctrine of the Renvoi in Anglo-American Law* (1918) 31 HARV. L. REV. 523; Bates, *Remission and Transmission in American Conflict of Laws* (1931) 16 CORN. L. Q. 311. Numerous other references to discussions of the renvoi problem are contained in the footnotes which follow.

Neither is any attempt made here to explore the extensive continental literature on the question. The best key to this in English is to be found in Lorenzen's articles referred to above. See also LORENZEN, CASES ON THE CONFLICT OF LAWS (4th ed.

I

At the outset, it will doubtless be desirable to state as clearly as possible the nature of the problem raised. The supposed typical example is usually put as follows: An Englishman dies domiciled in France, and a question arises in an English court as to the distribution of tangible moveable property which he leaves in England.[5] It is of course well-established English law that a decedent's property is distributed on death according to " the law of the country of his domicil ". Let us suppose, however, that the conflict of laws rule applicable in France is that an alien decedent's property is to be distributed according to " the law of the country of his nationality ",[6] which in our case is English. Now the question obviously arises: when the English conflicts rule directs the court to " the law of " France, is the reference (a) simply to the " internal law " of France, that is, the law which a French court would apply to a situation all of whose elements were French, or is it (b) to what may be called the " whole law " of France, including not only the French internal law but also the French rules of conflict of laws?[7] If the latter alternative is correct, then the French law refers back in our case to " the law of " England, and

1937) 52; (1931) 5 TULANE L. REV. 643; 10 LAPRADELLE AND NIBOYET, RÉPERTOIRE DE DROIT INTERNATIONAL (1931) 412–35.

[5] The problem is of course not confined to France and England. The example put is taken simply because it is convenient and readily understood; but it should not be inferred that there is anything " international " or " foreign " about the situation. The basic problem can arise (and does perhaps oftener than is suspected) just as well between states of the United States.

[6] Whether this is or is not in fact the law of France need not concern us now. As to the law of France on this point, see Falconbridge, *Renvoi and Succession to Moveables* (1930) 46 L. Q. REV. 465, 472–74.

[7] It has been pointed out that " the whole law of France " may be an ambiguous phrase; *i.e.*, it might lead to two rules, the one established by French " internal " law, and the other, a possibly different rule, pointed to by the application of French conflict of laws. See Abbot, *Is the Renvoi a Part of the Common Law?* (1908) 24 L. Q. REV. 133, 135–36; HARPER AND TAINTOR, CASES ON CONFLICT OF LAWS (1937) 298n. This seems, however, to call only for more careful definition of terms. The meaning of the phrase is clear when we recall the fact that the question " What law is applicable? " must be disposed of in every case which comes before a court. Even if all the elements are local we have to decide that local law applies, and, though it may be assumed or done unconsciously, this is not an essentially different process from that involved where we decide that some foreign law controls because

the same question arises again. What is the law of England? Is the reference to the "internal" law of England, or to all English law including English conflict of laws? If in each case we refer to all the law, including the conflicts rules, we are apparently on a merry-go-round.[8] How is it possible to get off?

II

The extensive literature shows that in general four possible ways of dealing with the question have been advanced. These may be stated briefly as a basis for further consideration of the problem.

1. We may say, if we choose, that the reference made by the English conflict of laws to "the law of France" is solely to the French internal law, without regard to any conflict of laws rules that might be applied in France. In this way, it is said, we do not have to worry about how to get off the merry-go-round, for we never get on it. This is usually referred to as "rejecting the renvoi", and, as will be pointed out below, has the approval of the writers, both English and American, by a very considerable margin. It results in our case in the disposition of the controversy by applying the "internal law" of France.

2. Another way of handling the problem is to say that the reference is to French law in its entirety, thus including the French rule that distribution in the case supposed is to be by the law of the nationality, which is English. When the English court finds itself referred back to the law of England, it might conclude that the reference to France has not provided a direct solution, that is,

---

there are foreign elements in the situation. Every case in court involves a choice of law. The phrase thus means simply the French "internal" law if the French choice of law rule points to the French internal law, and some other body of law if the French choice of law rule points elsewhere. The two alternatives are mutually exclusive.

[8] This has been referred to as a "game of lawn tennis" [Buzzati, Il Rinvio (1898) 77, quoted in Baty, Polarized Law (1914) 117], a "logical 'cabinet of mirrors' (*Spiegelkabinet*)" [Kahn, in 30 Jhering's Jahrbücher (1891) 23], and as a "*circulus inextrabilis*" [Matter of Tallmadge, 109 Misc. 696, 712, 181 N. Y. Supp. 336, 346 (Surr. Ct. 1919)], or "endless circle" [Bates, *Remission and Transmission in American Conflict of Laws* (1931) 16 Corn. L. Q. 311, 313].

From the logical point of view it is apparently not an instance of circular reasoning, but rather of a regression. See Lewis and Langford, Symbolic Logic (1932) 438–85.

that France has refused to determine the controversy by its internal law. The English court might decide, therefore, to accept the re-reference from France, and to apply its own "internal" law. This possibility is generally known in the literature as "accepting the renvoi", although the terminology is not used with absolute uniformity. Its application in our case would result in the disposition of the controversy in accordance with the "internal law" of England.

3. A third technique reaches the same result as the method just described, but on a rather different theory. According to this view, the English judge, on being referred to the law of France as the law of the domicil, finds that France has no rules of law as to persons domiciled in France, since its law proceeds on a different theory, namely, that of nationality. Because the basis of the French law is nationality, it may be said to claim no authority over Englishmen, or, to put it another way, to make no provision for the disposition of property of Englishmen. The reference to French law having produced no French law applicable to the situation, there is said to be nothing else for the English court to do but apply English law. This is sometimes referred to as the *désistement* theory.[9] It has been chiefly advanced in English by Westlake.[10] Its adoption in the case supposed would result in the application of the "internal law" of England.

4. There is, finally, a fourth method of approach, which, though in some quarters apparently regarded as novel, was the earliest of all to appear in the English cases. The English judge in our case is referred by his conflict of laws rule to the law of France. What is the law of France? According to this view it is the law which a French court would apply to this very case. If a French court would apply French "internal law" (either because it "accepts the renvoi" or for any other reason), then the English court should

[9] See Schreiber, *The Doctrine of the Renvoi in Anglo-American Law* (1918) 31 HARV. L. REV. 523, 529–33.

[10] See WESTLAKE, PRIVATE INTERNATIONAL LAW (5th ed. 1912) 32–34; *id.* (7th ed. by Bentwich 1925) 29–33. See also a Note by Westlake in (1900) 18 ANNUAIRE DE DROIT INTERNATIONAL 35–40, and his discussion reported *id.* 164–68 ("*Mais la loi anglaise ne renvoie pas. Elle ne fait que se désintéresser.*"). This view seems also to have been adopted by von Bar. See 1 THEORIE UND PRAXIS DES INTERNATIONALEN PRIVATRECHTS (2d ed. 1889) 278–81, and (1900) 18 ANNUAIRE DE DROIT INTERNATIONAL 153–57, 174–75.

apply French " internal law ". If the French court would apply English " internal law " (either because it " rejects the renvoi " or for any other reason), then the English court should apply English " internal law ". If the French court would apply Chinese " internal " law, the English court should do the same. This view was apparently expressed nearly a hundred years ago, in a case where the decedent had been domiciled in Belgium, when it was said: " The Court sitting here decides from the evidence of persons skilled in that law, and decides as it would if sitting in Belgium." [11] This view seems likewise to have been the basis of three more recent English decisions.[12] It cannot be said definitely what result the application of this approach would lead to in the case supposed at the beginning of this article; it would be whatever law the French court would apply. If it develops that France adopts any one of the first three views, then the English court is led to a certain result. If, perchance, the French court should itself adopt this fourth view, then there would be trouble; for the English court would decide the case the way the French court would, and the French court would decide the way the English court would, and Alphonse and Gaston would never get through the door unless we could find some other way to help them out.[13]

One further observation should be made before leaving the statement of the problem. In actual practice the reference in the foreign conflict of laws rule may not always be " back ", as in the case supposed. It may instead be to the law of some third state. Thus, suppose that the decedent whom the English court regarded as domiciled in France was a German rather than an Englishman. If the court, following its rule of domicil, refers to the law of France, and understands this to mean " all French law, including French conflict of laws ", it may be referred by the French law to the law of Germany, as the state of nationality of the decedent. This reference " across " rather than " back " is sometimes

[11] Collier v. Rivaz, 2 Curteis 855, 863 (Ecc. Ct. 1841). See also De Bonneval v. De Bonneval, 1 Curteis 856, 869 (Ecc. Ct. 1838): ". . . the Courts of that country are the competent authority to determine the validity of his will and the succession to his personal estate; . . ."

[12] *In re* Annesley, [1926] Ch. 692; *In re* Ross, [1930] 1 Ch. 377; *In re* Askew, [1930] 2 Ch. 259.

[13] *Cf.* CHESHIRE, PRIVATE INTERNATIONAL LAW (2d ed. 1938) 65. See further discussion of this question at pp. 1192–93, *infra*.

designated as "transmission", while the case first mentioned is said to be a case of "remission". This indicates that the problem cannot be wholly stated in terms of "accepting the renvoi" or rejecting it, for there is not always a reference back. We may, however, adopt Schreiber's formulation as stating the problem with substantial accuracy: "*When the conflict-of-laws rule of the forum refers a jural matter to a foreign law for decision, is the reference to the corresponding rule of the conflict of laws of that foreign law, or is the reference to the purely internal rules of law of the foreign system*; i.e., *to the totality of the foreign law, minus its conflict-of-laws rules?*"[14] The adoption of the second or fourth of the possibilities outlined above involves the recognition, and to some extent the application, of the foreign conflict of laws rule, while the third possibility involves at least the recognition of the foreign conflicts rule. The first view alone is that described as "rejecting the renvoi"; that is, the first view alone ignores entirely the existence and the content of the foreign views of conflict laws.

III

The legal writers, though they fall just short of being unanimous, seem overwhelming, both in their number and their certainty, in favor of the conclusion that English and American courts *do* and *should* "reject the renvoi". The earliest general surveys of the cases were made more than thirty years ago. The first, by Bate, is not a little hard to follow; but he does make clear his view that "the Renvoi-theory is inconsistent with" fundamental doctrines of English law.[15] In 1908 the cases were reviewed by Edwin H. Abbot, Jr., and his article concluded with these words: "At present, therefore, the *renvoi* cannot be considered a part of the Common Law, either on principle or on authority."[16] Two years later Professor Lorenzen presented the

[14] Schreiber, *The Doctrine of the Renvoi in Anglo-American Law* (1918) 31 HARV. L. REV. 523, 525. This statement of the problem has also been accepted in GOODRICH, CONFLICT OF LAWS (1927) 24, and 1 BEALE, CONFLICT OF LAWS (1935) § 7.3.

[15] BATE, NOTES ON THE DOCTRINE OF RENVOI IN PRIVATE INTERNATIONAL LAW (1904) 108. See also BATY, POLARIZED LAW (1914) 115–20 ("*renvoi* has still to make its way here").

[16] Abbot, *Is the Renvoi a Part of the Common Law?* (1908) 24 L. Q. REV. 133, 146.

first extended study in an American periodical, and he, too, reached the same conclusion:

> The *renvoi* doctrine is, therefore, no part of the Conflict of Laws of the United States. Its introduction into our law would be most unfortunate on account of the uncertainty and confusion to which it would give rise in the administration of justice and its demoralizing effect upon the future development of the Conflict of Laws.[17]

In a further elaboration of his views eight years later, this conclusion was forcefully adhered to; [18] but there was a brief indication at the end of the article that there might be "certain exceptional cases in which a recognition that the *lex fori* should incorporate the foreign law inclusive of its rules of the conflict of laws may be either necessary or expedient".[19] That Professor Lorenzen, in outlining these possible exceptional situations, did not mean to recant his fundamental opposition to the doctrine was made plain a short time later in a Note, where he wrote that: "A mere statement of the operation of the 'renvoi doctrine' should be sufficient to condemn it." [20] The same conclusion was likewise reached by Schreiber, whose extensive analysis of the problem

[17] Lorenzen, *The Renvoi Theory and the Application of Foreign Law* (1910) 10 COL. L. REV. 190, 327, 344.

[18] Lorenzen, *The Renvoi Doctrine in the Conflict of Laws—Meaning of "The Law of a Country"* (1918) 27 YALE L. J. 509, 528, 529: "A greater state of uncertainty in the law than that which arises from the theory of *renvoi* proper in its wider form is difficult to conceive. The general recognition of the *renvoi* doctrine in either of the forms outlined above would be fatal to the harmonious development of the rules of the conflict of laws in the future. No proper system of the conflict of laws can be built up among the civilized nations as long as this doctrine remains. . . . Whatever strength this doctrine may gain temporarily because of the equivocal meaning of the term 'law of a country' and the natural predisposition on the part of judges to apply their own law, there can be no doubt of its ultimate overthrow. Its days ought to be few after its deceptive character is fully understood."

[19] *Id.* at 529–31.

[20] E. G. L., *Renvoi in Divorce Proceedings based upon Constructive Service* (1921) 31 YALE L. J. 191, 192. The possibility of exceptions was again recognized here; but hearty approval was accorded to the following passage quoted from Matter of Tallmadge, 109 Misc. 696, 181 N. Y. Supp. 336 (Surr. Ct. 1919): "On account of its inconsistency with common-law theories of the conflict of laws, its fundamental unsoundness and the chaos which would result from its application to the conflicts arising between the laws of the states of this country it is my opinion that the 'renvoi' has no place in our jurisprudence." Professor Lorenzen's approval of the Tallmadge decision had been previously expressed in a Note in (1919) 29 YALE L. J. 214, 217, where he said: "The *renvoi* doctrine is not supported by reason. . . .

and of the English and American cases appeared at this period. He referred to "the insidious nature of the renvoi", and "the discordance of that doctrine with common-law conceptions of the conflict of laws", and closed his article with the statement that "An examination into its merits and demerits will, it is believed, require its rejection in all but the most exceptional cases".[21]

During the same period Professor Beale joined the forces battling against the renvoi. The preliminary part of his *Treatise on the Conflict of Laws* appeared in 1916, and disposed of renvoi very briefly:

> We may be the less troubled about the finer points of this discussion because the territorial theory of the conflict of laws, which is accepted by the American courts, has no room for any doctrine of *renvoi*. . . . In no case is the court concerned with the views of any foreign court on a question of the conflict of laws.[22]

In the definitive edition of his *Treatise*, the discussion is somewhat altered but the conclusion remains unchanged. Mr. Beale now states his view that the renvoi "has been rejected or is in course of being rejected", and that this is in accordance with what "is believed to be the sound doctrine in our law".[23] Other recent American writers have also adhered to the same view. Goodrich tells us that: "On common law principles of Conflict of Laws there is no occasion for using the doctrine. . . . Out of harmony as it is with our principles of Conflict of Laws, it seems important to know chiefly to avoid its unconscious acceptance."[24] And

To state accurately the problem involved in regard to *renvoi* would seem almost sufficient to refute the doctrine."

The latest expression of Lorenzen's views is found in a review of Mendelssohn-Bartholdy's book in (1938) 47 YALE L. J. 857, where he recounts the author's insistence that the renvoi should logically be rejected, and concludes (p. 859): "In that he is right."

[21] Schreiber, *The Doctrine of the Renvoi in Anglo-American Law* (1918) 31 HARV. L. REV. 523, 570, 571. Sir Frederick Pollock also expressed his opposition to the renvoi at this time. Pollock, Book Review (1915) 31 L. Q. REV. 106, 107; Pollock, *The 'Renvoi' in New York* (1920) 36 L. Q. REV. 91.

[22] BEALE, TREATISE ON THE CONFLICT OF LAWS (1916) 77.

[23] 1 BEALE, CONFLICT OF LAWS (1935) §§ 5.1, 7.3. The most recent expression of Mr. Beale's view is in his review of Mendelssohn-Bartholdy's book, in (1938) 24 A. B. A. J. 31.

[24] GOODRICH, CONFLICT OF LAWS (1927) 24, 25. See also de Sloovère, *The Local Law Theory and Its Implications in the Conflict of Laws* (1928) 41 HARV. L. REV.

Stumberg, in his recent excellent handbook, joins the verbal chorus.[25]

Current writers in England, too, have taken a strong position against the recognition of foreign rules of conflict of laws. Within the past year Mendelssohn-Bartholdy's little book has appeared.[26] The conclusion is wholly against any doctrine of renvoi and the several English cases which might be thought to have accepted it in some form. The amount of microscopic hairsplitting required along the way to this result, however, might possibly be a basis for some doubt as to its merits. Most recent of all is Dr. Cheshire's treatment of the problem in the second edition of his justly praised *Private International Law*. He examines the English authorities with care, and states his view as follows:

> Despite the three most recent decisions it is submitted in conclusion that upon a right view of the authorities as a whole, English law recognizes neither the doctrine of *renvoi* nor the somewhat analogous doctrine that a reference to a foreign law means a reference to the whole of that law as it would be expounded and administered in its own country.[27]

To complete the current British picture, reference should be made to the articles of Dean Falconbridge and his conclusion that the renvoi is "intrinsically illogical, and unsatisfactory in its results".[28]

It is not surprising that the American Law Institute in its

421, 447; Coudert, *Some Considerations in the Law of Domicil* (1927) 36 YALE L. J. 949, 953: "The renvoi doctrine is a resultant of legal casuistry and over-subtlety. It is a doctrine over-complicated, unsound and revolutionary."

[25] "It seems to be quite generally accepted that 'renvoi' is no part of American law." "Renvoi is not a part of the American law of Conflict of Laws." STUMBERG, CONFLICT OF LAWS (1937) 11n., 203n.

Reference may also be made to the article on Conflict of Laws in (1937) 11 AM. JUR. 287, where it is said (§ 3): "The doctrine of renvoi has generally been repudiated by the American authorities."

[26] MENDELSSOHN-BARTHOLDY, RENVOI IN MODERN ENGLISH LAW (1937); reviewed in (1938) 51 HARV. L. REV. 573, (1938) 1 MODERN L. REV. 332, and (by Lorenzen) in (1938) 47 YALE L. J. 857. In a review by Professor Cook in (1937) 32 ILL. L. REV. 504, 505–06, he states his view that in handling our problem reference to the law of the domicil "ought to signify the purely local or domestic rule of the domicile".

[27] CHESHIRE, PRIVATE INTERNATIONAL LAW (2d ed. 1938) 65. Similar views are presented in Morris, *The Law of the Domicil* (1937) 18 B. Y. I. L. 32.

[28] Falconbridge, *Renvoi and Succession to Moveables* (1930) 46 L. Q. REV. 485, (1931) 47 *id.* 271, 291.

Restatement of Conflict of Laws has adopted a rule in accordance with the conclusions reached by the many writers referred to. It takes a rather cumbrous section to do it; but it is done in Section 7 in these words:

> Except as stated in § 8, when there is a difference in the Conflict of Laws of two states whose laws are involved in a problem, the rule of Conflict of Laws of the forum is applied;
>
> . . . .
>
> (b) where in making the choice of law to govern a certain situation the law of another state is to be applied, since the only Conflict of Laws used in the determination of the case is the Conflict of Laws of the forum, the foreign law to be applied is the law applicable to the matter in hand and not the Conflict of Laws of the foreign state.

The exceptions referred to in Section 8 relate to "title to land" and "the validity of a decree of divorce" which are said to be controlled by the law of the situs of the land, or of the domicil of the parties, respectively, "including the Conflict of Laws rules of that state".[29]

---

[29] These sections had a rather complicated history in the development of the Restatement. In the first published draft [known as Restatement No. 2 (1926)] § 7 was in much simpler form, but to the same effect. The exceptions covered in § 8 related to questions of "status or of title to land". The "Commentaries" on § 7 simply referred to Lorenzen's and Schreiber's articles for the "authorities which are generally in support of the view stated in the text". Commentaries on Conflict of Laws Restatement No. 2 (1926) 5. These sections invoked practically no discussion when they were considered at the Annual Meeting of the Institute on May 1, 1926. As to § 7, Mr. Beale simply stated: "This is rather clumsy, but this is the best way in which we could state our refusal of the so-called 'renvoi' in ordinary cases." 4 PROCEEDINGS OF THE AMERICAN LAW INSTITUTE (1926) app. 260. In the Proposed Final Draft No. 1 (1930) there are verbal changes in § 7, while the exception in § 8 is narrowed to questions of "marital status or of title to land". In the Proposed Final Draft No. 4 (1934), § 7 is shortened somewhat, so that it reads substantially like the first paragraph in the official volume. The exception in § 8 is made applicable to questions of "title to land or of chattels or as to the validity of a decree of divorce". When the official draft made its appearance, § 7 had acquired two explanatory paragraphs, of which paragraph (a) related to the problem of classification, and paragraph (b) was concerned with renvoi. The latter is set out in the text above. The exception in § 8 was recast into two subdivisions, and was narrowed to questions of "title to land" and the "validity of a decree of divorce".

All of this discloses some underlying uncertainty, perhaps, but if anything, a tendency to emphasize the general applicability of the rule and to minimize and restrict the exceptions.

Before leaving the question of the reactions of the academic and other nonjudicial writers on the subject, mention should be made of a few authors who were not so certain that reference to foreign rules of conflict of laws was such a heinous offense. In an early article based on *In re Johnson*,[30] W. Jethro Brown reached the conclusion that the court should have applied the "whole law" of the domicil.[31] A few years later Bentwich presented a careful examination of the decisions, asserting that they gave "a clear and steady support to the doctrine"; [32] and the same author has very recently called attention to further applications of the renvoi notion.[33] Dicey, too, has consistently held to the position that the law of a country as applied by the English cases means "any principle or body of law" which the courts of that country "hold applicable to the particular case".[34] Dicey's editor, Keith, has steadfastly maintained this ground.[35] But both Dicey and Keith disclaim any consideration of the question whether "English Courts act wisely or unwisely, logically or illogically, in accepting the doctrine of the *renvoi*". Occasionally the notion that there may be some merit to the idea that "the law of a country" may include the conflict of laws of that country has raised its head

30 [1903] 1 Ch. 821. A British subject with Maltese domicil of origin acquired a domicil of choice in Baden, and died there, leaving a will in Baden form, which, however, did not dispose of all her property. The question was as to the proper distribution of the moveables which were not covered by the will. Evidence showed that under the law of Baden the distribution would be made in accordance with the decedent's national law. The Court held that the distribution should be made according to the law of Malta, partly on the ground that this was the result which a Baden court would have reached.

The question what is the "national law" of an American citizen or British subject domiciled abroad may of course be a troublesome one to the foreign court. See the note by Frederick Pollock in (1909) 25 L. Q. Rev. 157. [*Cf.* the question of the law applicable in the United States Court for China; (1936) 49 Harv. L. Rev. 793.] The concept of domicil of origin seems a useful analogy here. It seems to be the analogy which the English court in *In re* Johnson held the Baden court would follow. Apparently the same conclusion was reached as to the French law in Matter of Tallmadge, 109 Misc. 696, 181 N. Y. Supp. 336 (Surr. Ct. 1919).

31 Brown, *In re Johnson* (1909) 25 L. Q. Rev. 145, 157.

32 Bentwich, Law of Domicile in its Relation to Succession (1911) 179.

33 Bentwich, *Recent Application of the Renvoi in Matters of Personal Status* (1936) 14 Can. Bar Rev. 379.

34 Dicey, Conflict of Laws (1st ed. 1896) 77. See *id.* (2d ed. 1908) 715–23; *id.* (3d ed. 1922) 771–81.

35 Dicey, Conflict of Laws (4th ed. 1927) 811–25; *id.* (5th ed. 1932) 863–78.

elsewhere. Reference may be made again to the "exceptional cases" tentatively accepted by Professor Lorenzen,[36] and to the exceptions embodied in Section 8 of the *Restatement*. There have been occasional suggestions elsewhere that "rejecting the renvoi" may not be a rule that can be applied all the way down the line.[37] But these have been expressed as exceptions begrudgingly admitted to an otherwise universal rule.

IV

What are the reasons advanced for the conclusion so generally accepted that "the law of a country" in the situation we are considering means its internal law alone, without any regard to its rules of conflict of laws? The most recent advocacy for this view is found in the new edition of Cheshire's *Private International Law*. It is true that Dr. Cheshire does not purport to exhaust the arguments on his side, but it may be convenient to take up first some of the grounds which have led him to eschew the "vagaries" of this "remarkable" doctrine.[38]

First, we are told that any acceptance of renvoi is "illogical".[39] "It is illogical, because it defeats the purpose which a national system of Private International Law is designed to effect, i.e. to indicate the mode in which a conflict of laws must be solved." Even if we accept this as an accurate statement of the purpose of a conflict of laws system, the conclusion derived from it does not seem to follow. Indeed, this argument seems nothing short of a begging of the question. Grant that English conflict of laws exists for the purpose of indicating the mode in which a conflict of laws must be solved. The English method of solving this conflict may be to refer to (a) the internal law of some other country for final disposition, or (b) the whole law of that country as it would be administered by that country's courts. One cannot prove that the

---

[36] Lorenzen, *The Renvoi Doctrine in the Conflict of Laws — Meaning of "The Law of a Country"* (1918) 27 YALE L. J. 509, 529–31.

[37] See Notes, *A Distinction in the Renvoi Doctrine* (1922) 35 HARV. L. REV. 454, *The Renvoi Theory Rejected — Exceptions* (1926) 36 YALE L. J. 114.

[38] CHESHIRE, PRIVATE INTERNATIONAL LAW (2d ed. 1938) 50. Much the same arguments against any form of renvoi are advanced in Morris, *The Law of the Domicil* (1937) 18 B. Y. I. L. 32.

[39] CHESHIRE, *op. cit. supra* note 38, at 57.

English conflicts rule embodies the first of these alternatives by assuming that it does. The English conflicts rule will be just as much a rule for indicating the mode in which a conflict of laws must be solved if the second alternative is adopted. Either is just as "logical" as the other. The choice cannot be made between them on imperative grounds.

It may promptly be conceded that there is no logical basis for choosing between the first and second of the possible views outlined at the beginning of this article.[40] If we get into a situation where there is an endless series of references, there is no logical reason for stopping after the second reference (or "accepting the renvoi"); it would be just as "logical" to stop after the third reference or the seventeenth. But by the same token, it is no more "logical" to stop after the first reference. It may or may not be expedient to stop there for one reason or another, but a solution reached on this ground cannot be accorded the accolade of logic. This is just another way of putting the point made in the preceding paragraph. It does seem sufficient to show, however, that any approach to this problem which purports to be based upon "logic" can only end in a *petitio principii.*

Second, we are told by Dr. Cheshire that any acceptance of a renvoi doctrine is "subversive" and "flouts" the law. "It involves a conscious neglect of the rules that are binding upon the Court."[41] If the English rule directs the judge to the French law for a decision, and the English judge finds that a French court would dispose of the case by applying English internal law, the English judge, says Dr. Cheshire, must nevertheless apply French internal law; "on what possible ground can the English Court justify its action in casting aside its own rule for the choice of law in favor of one that is preferred abroad."[42] To do so is "not only contrary to common sense", but it is "repugnant to the true nature of any system of Private International Law", since it involves "the abandonment of a domestic rule for the choice of law merely because some foreign country prefers a different rule".[43] Apart from the fact that this argument, too, seems to beg the ques-

---

[40] See pp. 1167–69, *supra.*

[41] CHESHIRE, *op. cit. supra* note 38, at 57, 59.

[42] *Id.* at 58.

[43] *Id.* at 65.

tion,[44] it is hard to suppress surprise at finding such an argument advanced in the field of conflict of laws. After all, what is the conflict of laws, unless it is a science for telling a court when it should cast aside its own rule in favor of one that is preferred abroad? If Parliament has made a rule for distributing decedents' property (or of torts or contracts), why should an English court ever bother about the rules of other countries. On this basis, the whole conflict of laws is " subversive ". Of course, England " prefers to consider itself civilized and to act accordingly ".[45] For this purpose, she has developed rules of conflict of laws to point out the cases to which English law, though absolute in form, should not be applied. But these rules of conflict of laws are themselves English law. Whatever their content is, it is that prescribed by English law. And if the content of the English rule is that it refers to the whole of the law of another country, including its conflict of laws, an English judge who follows the rule is not being subversive or false to his oath; he is simply doing his duty. We are back to our fundamental question, what is the proper nature of the reference according to the English rule? [46]

The *third* argument advanced by Dr. Cheshire is that any recognition of foreign conflicts rules will lead to great uncertainties. If the English judge is to do what the foreign judge would do, the English judge will have great difficulties if the foreign judge would have any question of renvoi to decide. We are reminded that " the recognition of *renvoi* by a particular foreign law is seldom a matter of certainty but is generally the subject of acute controversy among the learned ". Furthermore, " In Continental countries the views of the jurists upon the doctrine not only change from year to year but are frequently divergent at any one time, and reliance can scarcely be placed on the decisions of

[44] For the very question is: what is the English choice of law rule? We cannot answer that by assuming that the English rule refers only to the internal law of the country to which it is directed.

[45] See Disconto-Gesellschaft v. United States Steel Corp., 267 U. S. 22, 28 (1925).

[46] The arguments in this paragraph seem also to answer the contention that the reference must be only to the internal law for the reason that the conflict of laws " has spent itself ". Morris, *The Law of the Domicil* (1937) 18 B. Y. I. L. 32, 34. This is a little reminiscent of the statement that the reason the Statute of Uses did not execute a use on a use was because the statute was " exhausted " after executing the first use — an explanation which was more picturesque than accurate. See Ames, *The Origin of Trusts* in Lectures on Legal History (1913) 243.

the Courts, for, owing to the non-recognition of the principle *stare decisis*, what is decided by one Court to-day is disavowed by another to-morrow." [47] Two partial answers may be made to this contention. The reference to what the foreign court will do may not lead to any question of renvoi in the foreign law; and these problems do not always lead us to the Continent. These questions can and frequently do arise among states of the United States. A reason which might be of some weight in a case where Continental law has to be applied ought not to be generalized into an absolute rule against any recognition of foreign conflicts rules in any circumstances whatever.[48]

The answers just given are, however, only partial answers. The fact remains that if the reference to foreign law includes a reference to foreign conflict of laws, it may be difficult to determine what the foreign conflicts rule is. That there is force to this cannot be denied. It does not seem, though, that it ought to be regarded as conclusive. There may be ways and means of finding out what the foreign law is as to the particular case.[49] But even if there are not, mere difficulty of deciding a question has not ordinarily been regarded by common-law courts as a reason for refusing to undertake a decision. Our federal courts do not refrain from deciding a question of state law on the ground that it has not been decided by the state courts [50] or that the state decisions are in hopeless confusion.[51] An argument something like this was advanced by Judge Learned Hand in *Moore v. Mitchell* [52] in holding that one

[47] CHESHIRE, PRIVATE INTERNATIONAL LAW (2d ed. 1938) 62, 65.

[48] Compare the argument that conflict of laws rules in situations involving states of the United States, or other Anglo-American jurisdictions, may well be different from the rules applicable where the reference is to a foreign or non-common-law country. This is best developed in DuBois, *The Significance in Conflict of Laws of the Distinction Between Interstate and International Transactions* (1933) 17 MINN. L. REV. 361.

[49] See pp. 1188–89, *infra*.

[50] See, *e.g.*, Siler v. Louisville & Nashville R. R., 213 U. S. 175, 194 (1909) ("we must proceed in the absence of state adjudication on the subject"); Risty v. Chicago, R. I. & Pac. Ry., 270 U. S. 378, 387 (1926); Railroad Commission v. Los Angeles Ry. Corp., 280 U. S. 145, 152 (1929); Camunas v. New York & P. R. S. S. Co., 260 Fed. 40, 48 (C. C. A. 1st, 1919).

[51] *Cf.* Edward Hines Trustees v. Martin, 268 U. S. 458, 463 (1925); Myrick v. Heard, 31 Fed. 241, 243 (C. C. S. D. Ga. 1887).

[52] 30 F.(2d) 600, 604 (C. C. A. 2d, 1929), *aff'd on other grounds,* 281 U. S. 18 (1930).

state would not enforce another's tax claims. In reply to this it was observed that "About the only answer to this is that courts have undertaken equally difficult judicial problems before now. The fact that a problem is hard has not generally been deemed of itself a sufficient reason for courts refusing to undertake it".[53] And it may be added, now, that the hostility to the extrastate enforcement of tax claims seems to be breaking down.[54]

Reference may again be made in this connection to Professor Lorenzen's conclusions that the recognition of foreign rules of conflict of laws leads to "uncertainty and confusion", and will have a "demoralizing effect on the future development of the Conflict of Laws". This argument seems not a little hard to follow. "Accepting the renvoi" in either the second or the third senses, as we have spelled them out above,[55] leads unerringly to the application of the domestic internal law. There should if anything be less uncertainty in this process than in the application of the French internal law, which is the result of "rejecting the renvoi". Under the fourth view, that which requires the domestic court to decide the case as the foreign court would decide it, it is true that there will or may be difficulties in determining how the foreign court would dispose of the case. But the fact that the task may not be an easy one should not be conclusive, as we have just tried to show.

Indeed, it should be pointed out that "rejecting the renvoi" leads to uncertainty and contradiction in a manner which should give its proponents pause. It seems almost inevitably to result in the very sort of conflict which the conflict of laws is in part designed to prevent. To go back to our original case, if an English court "rejects the renvoi" then it will decide the case according to French internal law. But by the same token, if the same controversy arises before a French court, and it "rejects the renvoi", then it will decide the case according to English internal law. The actual disposition of the rights of the parties will depend on the wholly irrelevant fact of the forum in which the case is brought. The plaintiff who is well advised will win because he has been

[53] Leflar, *Extrastate Enforcement of Penal and Governmental Claims* (1932) 46 HARV. L. REV. 193, 218.

[54] See Milwaukee County v. M. E. White Co., 296 U. S. 268 (1935).

[55] *Supra*, pp. 1167–68.

circumspect in selecting his forum and for no other reason. Indeed the same question might come before both forums and lead to wholly inconsistent decisions of the ultimate point in issue. It hardly seems that this leads to certainty in the law. It might be said, rather, that such a conclusion has a demoralizing, and even stultifying, effect on the future development of the conflict of laws. If there is any way in which such a consequence can be escaped in any considerable number of cases it should certainly be looked upon with sympathetic favor.

Finally, let us consider the arguments advanced by Mr. Beale in opposition to the renvoi. "The vice", he says,[56] "results from the assumption that the foreign law has legal force in a decision of the case; whereas, . . . the only Conflict-of-Laws rule that can possibly be applied is the law of the forum and the foreign law is called in simply for furnishing a factual rule for the succession to the estate. The rule of the foreign law adopted by the law of the forum is the rule of succession, not the Conflict-of-Laws rule." We may agree wholeheartedly with Mr. Beale that "the only Conflict-of-Laws rule that can possibly be applied is the law of the forum". On this both the territorial and the "local law"[57] approaches seem agreed. It is not easy to see how they could differ. But that still leaves us the question of the delimitation of the forum's conflicts rule. We cannot assume that "The rule of the foreign law adopted by the law of the forum is the rule of succession, not the Conflict-of-Laws rule", for that is the very question to which we are directing attention. In short, though we may agree heartily that the forum can only apply directly its own law, it remains necessary to determine what that law is.

V

If the reasons advanced for "rejecting the renvoi" do not seem persuasive, we are still left with the question whether there is a more satisfactory approach. Where Beale and Lorenzen are in agreement, not to mention so many other writers, the presumption

---

[56] 1 BEALE, CONFLICT OF LAWS (1935) § 7.3.

[57] See Cook, *The Logical and Legal Bases of the Conflict of Laws* (1924) 33 YALE L. J. 457, 469: "the forum, when confronted by a case involving foreign elements, always applies its own law to the case."

is clear and strong against any who essays to defend another view. It is nevertheless the thesis of this article that domestic courts referred abroad should not blind themselves to foreign rules of conflict of laws. They should instead, as a matter of course, look first at the "whole law" of the other state, and undertake to dispose of the case as the foreign court would dispose of it; and if the foreign court would in its disposition apply some rule of conflict of laws the domestic court should do the same. There will be a few cases which will not lend themselves to this approach, but it is believed that these will in fact be rare and that they can be handled as and when they arise. The conclusion is in other words that common-law courts should adopt the fourth view outlined at the beginning of this article and should abandon it only if it is clear that it does not lead to a definite and satisfactory disposition of the particular case.

Keith has observed that the word "renvoi" is "rather a misnomer"; [58] and this is particularly true of the phrases "accept the renvoi", and "reject the renvoi". These phrases have been used here only because it seems impossible to consider past discussions of the problem without using them. We have already agreed [59] that there is no more logic in "accepting the renvoi" in the senses of our second and third views than there is in rejecting it. But the question whether there is a better solution still remains.

The thought persists that previous efforts to approach the problem have apparently been obscured because attention was focused so firmly on a tree that the forest went unseen. The problem which we have put at the beginning of this article has been regarded as the typical problem. The question has often been treated as though it grew out of the rule of domicil alone.[60] And then the possibility that in this class of cases an approach which recognizes the foreign conflicts rule may lead to an endless chain of references has been generalized into a universal rule that the foreign conflict of laws must be disregarded. It is true that certain exceptions to this conclusion have been recognized in some

---

[58] Review of RESTATEMENT, CONFLICT OF LAWS in (1935) 21 A. B. A. J. 237.

[59] See p. 1177, *supra*.

[60] For instance, in the first edition of Cheshire's book the discussion of renvoi (pp. 131–41) was in the chapter on Domicil.

of the writings. But these exceptions have been narrowly limited (as, for instance, in the *Restatement*), and have been admitted solely as exceptions. There seems ground to believe that there would be progress towards solution if this whole approach could be reversed. When a court is referred by its own conflicts rule to a foreign law, it should, as a matter of course, look to the entire foreign law as the foreign court would administer it. In most cases, it will find in this process a solution. In a few conceivable situations it will not, and these will remain to be dealt with. But these cases should be treated as the exceptions, not as the general rule. It may be that this is just a change of emphasis, simply an expanding of the exceptions to the rule which is now so generally said to require "rejecting the renvoi" until they eat up the substance of the rule itself. But the point made seems more fundamental than this. It is a wholly different approach. It involves the recognition in each case of the foreign conflicts rule, and the application of that rule as the foreign court would apply it, except in the few cases where this step would lead to the insoluble difficulty of the endless chain.

What is the basis for saying that only a few cases will present this insoluble difficulty? This seems to be the case for at least three reasons: (A) In the "transmission" situation recognition of the foreign conflicts rule will often not lead to any endless chain at all. (B) In other situations we can determine that for one reason or another the foreign conflicts rule in the particular case does in fact refer only to the internal law of the forum or of a third country. (C) And in any event there is no endless chain unless we find that the foreign court would decide the case according to our law and would determine our law by finding out what our courts would decide.[61] This possibility certainly presents a theoretical difficulty[62] but it does not seem a very real one. It

[61] This would be true, too, if the foreign court would decide the case according to the law of a third state, as that state's courts would apply it, and the third state would decide it as the second state's courts would.

[62] *Cf.* Dr. Schoch's review, (1938) 51 Harv. L. Rev. 1310, 1312, where she says that "the author destroys *en passant* one of the arguments put forward by supporters of renvoi, by admitting that renvoi functions as a 'harmonizer' only as long as the different systems of law involved in an actual case are not agreed on its application — certainly not a recommendation for its universal adoption!" See also Yntema, Book Review (1936) 3 U. of Chi. L. Rev. 337, 339.

seems to be a product of a rather Continental mode of thought which considers problems in the abstract rather than as they exist. The world is not a checker board made up of black squares and white squares, each one with its own law and a uniform conflict of laws to govern all the moves. We are not trying to develop a theory for universal application, but rather a sensible way of handling certain very practical questions that come before our courts. If we can discover a feasible way of handling those problems we need not be deterred by the fact that that way would not be so feasible under other circumstances which do not and may never exist.

Part of the difficulty with past treatments of the problem may possibly have come from the rather artificial and mechanical way in which it has sometimes been approached. But Anglo-American courts, as it has been observed, do not ordinarily operate this way. "Their aim has been to render a just decision under the circumstances of the particular case and they have reached their conclusions so far as possible by a consideration of the social interests involved." [63] The question is not: what *must* we do?; but rather: what *ought* we to do? — using "ought" in a sense more practical than ethical. We may well agree with Professor Cook that "that can be answered intelligently only if the question is asked and answered: For what purpose or purposes are we to 'apply' the 'lex' of the domicil? What is the reason which underlies that common-law rule?" [64]

Professor Cook reaches the conclusion that "'lex' . . . ought to signify the purely local or domestic rule of the domicil".[65] But this seems very difficult to follow. Why does English law refer the question of succession to "the law" of the country of the decedent's domicil? It is not, one may say with confidence, because of any love of French law in the example we have taken, nor because of any preference for foreign law in general — nor, finally, because of any distrust of the fairness of English "internal" law. Cheshire's view is that "If X takes up his permanent abode in Italy, and so virtually becomes an Italian, his succession ought in the nature of things, and certainly in our view, to be regulated

[63] Lorenzen, *Territoriality, Public Policy and the Conflict of Laws* (1924) 33 YALE L. J. 736, 750.

[64] Cook, Review of MENDELSSOHN-BARTHOLDY, RENVOI IN MODERN ENGLISH LAW (1937), in (1937) 32 ILL. L. REV. 504, 505.

[65] *Id.* at 505–06.

by exactly the same law that applies to native-born Italians".[66] As to this we may ask: is it true that an Englishman "virtually becomes an Italian" by taking up his "permanent abode" in Italy? Were Byron and the Brownings Italian poets?[67] Again, Cheshire refers to the rule of the domicil as representing "the essentially English view that whenever a man is connected with a country by the tie of domicile his will should be subject to the internal law that applies to the national inhabitants of that country". The last statement seems only to assert the answer to our question. To the extent that a person may properly be regarded as submitting himself or identifying himself with the law of a country in which he is domiciled, is it not the law which is applicable to him? — and that means the whole law and not the so-called internal law alone.

Perhaps there is merit in the suggestion that the purpose underlying the rule of domicil is to achieve uniformity in the succession to the property of a decedent, so that, as far as possible, his estate will be distributed as a unit. The moveable property of a decedent is thought of as an "*universitas*".[68] If there is to be uniformity in its distribution, all the courts before which the question may come must agree to follow the rule which will be applied by some one of them. The English rule of the domicil seems to be an expression of the conclusion that the court which should control is the court at the domicil. Ordinarily that is where most of the decedent's moveable property will be located; where his family will usually reside; where the question is most likely to arise. That, from the English point of view, is the place of primary administration. The courts of other countries act in an ancillary capacity and should achieve a uniform distribution by adjusting their conclusions to accord with those reached by the

[66] CHESHIRE, PRIVATE INTERNATIONAL LAW (2d ed. 1938) 58.

[67] If someone were to undertake to show me that on the facts Byron and the Brownings were not "domiciled" in Italy, I should be inclined to demur. If they are not good illustrations of the point others can be found. Consider, too, the case of the English wife, who is deserted by her husband, and the husband establishes his domicil in Italy. By English law her domicil is in Italy though she never leaves England's shores. Does she "virtually become an Italian"?

[68] Holmes, J., in Blackstone v. Miller, 188 U. S. 189, 204 (1903). Compare the rule that marital property rights in moveables are governed by the law of the matrimonial domicil. 2 BEALE, CONFLICT OF LAWS (1935) § 289.1; CHESHIRE, PRIVATE INTERNATIONAL LAW (2d ed. 1938) 492–94.

courts of the domicil — which have been selected as the primary tribunal by the rule of English law.

Further support for this conclusion may be found in the doctrine which generally favors the enforcement of "vested rights". There is no thought here that courts *must* enforce "vested rights". But it can hardly be denied that in many situations courts have concluded that that was the sound and proper thing to do. Here, too, the conflict of laws serves as an aid in achieving the end of uniformity, for, to the extent that "vested rights" are enforced abroad a man receives substantially the same treatment no matter what court he may come before. Let us take our original case, and suppose that the Englishman who died domiciled in France left an automobile in France. A French court applying whatever rule it would apply would say that *X* succeeded to it, although according to the internal law of France *Y* would become its owner. If, before any French decision, *X* brings the automobile to England, should *Y* be able to invoke an English court's aid to take it away from *X*? The "rejection of the renvoi" would seem to require this result, inept as it may be. And to take care of the situation by an exception is to make it seem that what we are doing is exceptional, when it is not. Without any thought that there is anything inevitable or logically necessary about the process, is it not true that the enforcement here of rights which would be recognized abroad is ordinarily sound conflict of laws? [69] And if we can find in this situation that the courts abroad to whom we (by our law) have referred the problem would recognize and enforce certain rights, should we not recognize and enforce the

[69] Justice Holmes, in speaking of "an *obligatio,* which, like other obligations, follows the person, and may be enforced wherever the person may be found" [Slater v. Mexican National R. R., 194 U. S. 120, 126 (1904)], and Judge Cardozo ["The plaintiff owns something and we help him to get it"; Loucks v. Standard Oil Co., 224 N. Y. 99, 110, 120 N. E. 198, 201 (1918)] were not wholly off base. They were aware that they were not expressing an inexorable rule, but rather a standard which generally yields advantageous results in handling conflicts cases. It is more, it would seem, than a mere "convenient way of stating a result". *Cf.* Cook, *The Logical and Legal Bases of the Conflict of Laws* (1923) 33 YALE L. J. 457, 481. It is rather an expression of the ends of uniformity and certainty which (though some writers sometimes seem to overlook them) are among the goals which a conflict of laws system may well seek to achieve — not because it must, but because on the whole they are desirable and useful ends. "The very conception of law involves ideas of uniformity, regularity, predictability." POUND, LAW AND MORALS (2d ed. 1926) 79.

same rights? It is not a little difficult to understand why the exponents of the " vested rights " point of view in conflict of laws have also been leading opponents of the renvoi in any sense.[70] Cheshire has met the inconsistency by stating that he has abandoned the vested rights approach.[71] But he repeatedly acknowledges the propriety of recognizing and enforcing foreign rights.[72] Conflict of laws could hardly exist without such recognition. It is of course true that we need not recognize the right which the foreign court would recognize and enforce; but ordinarily we will want to recognize it. The difficulty may be with Cheshire's view on renvoi and not with the vested rights approach as a standard to be followed in the absence of some persuasive reason to the contrary.

Finally, it is asserted with some confidence that, quibbling aside, most of the English and American cases (though plainly not all) have proceeded on the basis that a reference to a foreign law means that the local court should reach the conclusion which the foreign court would reach on the same facts.[73]

---

[70] Mr. Beale's argument against renvoi seems very difficult to reconcile with his vested rights approach. " If an American court, having according to the territorial theory to apply its own law to existing rights, finds that a right has, by its law, arisen under another law, it has only to learn the terms of that law and the nature of the right which it created; if, on the other hand, it is a question of a new right, created by the law of the forum, but the latter law in creating the right acts in accordance with the provisions of some foreign law, as for instance the law of a foreign domicil, again it has only to learn the terms of that particular foreign law and apply it. In no case is the court concerned with the views of any foreign court on a question of the conflict of laws." BEALE, TREATISE ON THE CONFLICT OF LAWS (1916) 77, reprinted in 3 BEALE, CONFLICT OF LAWS (1935) 1939. This is difficult to read in harmony with the conception that the conflict of laws " deals with the recognition and enforcement of foreign created rights ". Beale, *Summary of the Conflict of Laws*, in 3 BEALE, CASES ON THE CONFLICT OF LAWS (1902) 501, reprinted in 3 BEALE, CONFLICT OF LAWS (1935) 1968. The same may be said for the position adopted by Schreiber and Goodrich. Dicey alone seems to have been consistent here.

[71] CHESHIRE, PRIVATE INTERNATIONAL LAW (2d ed. 1938) v, 85–91. See also note 148, *infra*.

[72] See, for example: " Whether any particular ceremony constitutes marriage depends solely upon the law of the country where the ceremony took place." *Id.* at 322.

[73] In addition to the cases cited elsewhere, reference may be made to dicta along the lines here indicated in Dupuy v. Wurtz, 53 N. Y. 556, 573 (1873); Harral v. Harral, 39 N. J. Eq. 279 (1884); Maltass v. Maltass, 1 Rob. Eccl. 67, 72 (1844); Crookenden v. Fuller, 1 Swa. & Tr. 441 (Prob. 1859); Laneuville v. Anderson, 2 Swa. & Tr. 24, 38–39 (Prob. 1860); Onslow v. Cannon, 2 Swa. & Tr. 136 (Prob. 1861); In the Goods of Bianchi, 3 Swa. & Tr. 16, 17 (Prob. 1862).

VI

It may be appropriate next to consider how the approach suggested here would work out in practice. Suppose a court does conclude that it should look to the "whole law" of some foreign state, and then decide the case before it just as the foreign court would decide the same case. How can it know what conclusion the foreign court would reach? There seem to be a number of possible suggestions here:

1. The foreign conflicts rule in many cases will in fact be a very simple one; there may be no substantial room for doubt. This is often the case with respect to the "borrowing" statutes which are considered below.[74] Under these statutes the validity of a will or a deed, or the expiration of a limitations period, may be made to depend on the law of some other state. The ascertainment of the existence of such a statute and its application will be far simpler in ordinary cases than the determination of many matters in the foreign internal law.[75]

2. The foreign court may have already decided the very question. If, for instance, the decedent died domiciled in France, the French court may have entered a decision sustaining his will or disposing of his French assets. It should not be an undue burden on the parties to produce proof of this decision in the local court; and on such proof, the local court should not have difficulty in conforming to the decision so made.[76]

3. Even if the foreign court has not yet decided the question, it may be a matter which in due course (as in the case of the administration of an estate) will come before the foreign court. In such a case, the domestic court might well continue the case

---

[74] See pp. 1201–02, *infra*.

[75] This was done, for instance, in Holmes v. Hengen, 41 Misc. 521, 85 N. Y. Supp. 35 (Sup. Ct. 1903), *aff'd mem.*, 94 App. Div. 619, 88 N. Y. Supp. 1104 (1st Dep't 1904), with certainty and without difficulty to the court. See also Ross v. Graham, 122 Misc. 574, 203 N. Y. Supp. 390 (Sup. Ct. 1924).

[76] See Onslow v. Cannon, 2 Swa. & Tr. 136 (Prob. 1861). The situation in *In re* Trufort; Trafford v. Blanc, 36 Ch. D. 600 (1887), was similar, although the decision which was given effect had been made by a court of Switzerland, to whose law France, the country of domicil, referred the case for decision. See also Matter of Marsland, 142 Misc. 230, 231, 254 N. Y. Supp. 293 (Surr. Ct. 1931) ("the admission to probate thereof by the Swiss courts conclusively demonstrates the validity of the document according to their laws").

until the foreign court has entered its decision.[77] This was in fact the procedure followed in *De Bonneval v. De Bonneval*,[78] one of the earliest renvoi cases in the English books. The sentence of the court there was that the courts of France were the proper authority to determine the validity of the will, and —

> the Court suspends the proceedings here, as to the validity of the will, till it is pronounced valid or invalid by the tribunals of France.[79]

4. Even if no proceedings are in fact pending before the foreign court it may be possible to institute such proceedings. If either or both of the parties is unwilling, it may be possible for the local court, through its control over the parties and the cause before it, to coerce the institution of a suit in the foreign court. Such a suit could apparently be maintained in many cases even though there is no *res* or other subject matter before the foreign court. This would seem to be a proper situation for a declaratory judgment or its equivalent, since the parties have an actual dispute and their rights are in fact dependent on the determination of the foreign law.[80]

---

[77] A similar situation is presented where a suit is brought in one state on a judgment of another state, which is still subject to review on appeal. See Paine v. Schenectady Insurance Co., 11 R. I. 411, 416 (1876) (". . . we think the pendency of the appeal in New York may be a good ground for delaying judgment here until the appeal is disposed of").

Compare the practice of the Supreme Court in remanding cases to state courts for the determination of supervening state questions. See Dorchy v. Kansas, 264 U. S. 286 (1924); Cobb Brick Co. v. Lindsay, 275 U. S. 491 (1927), (1928) 41 HARV. L. REV. 400; Liggett Co. v. Lee, 288 U. S. 517, 541 (1933).

See also Hoare v. Bremridge, L. R. 8 Ch. App. 22 (1872), where an equity court stayed proceedings pending the trial of the same issue at law. *Cf.* United States v. Bank of New York, 296 U. S. 463, 480 (1936); Landis v. North American Co., 299 U. S. 248 (1936).

[78] 1 Curteis 856 (Ecc. Ct. 1838).

[79] *Id.* at 870. The French court held the will to be valid, applying English "internal law". De Bonneval c. De Bonneval, Court of Cassation, Feb. 6, 1843, RECUEIL GÉNÉRAL DES LOIS ET DES ARRÊTS (1843) pt. 1, p. 209.

Hare v. Nasmyth, 2 Add. Eccl. 25 (1815), cited in De Bonneval v. De Bonneval, is another case where an English probate court suspended proceedings pending the determination of the validity of a will by the courts of the testator's domicil. See Schreiber, *supra* note 21, at 538–39.

[80] Guaranty Trust Co. v. Hannay & Co., [1915] 2 K. B. 536, [1918] 2 K. B. 623, was substantially such a proceeding. It was a suit for a declaratory judgment brought in order to ascertain the English law, after the Circuit Court of Appeals in Guaranty Trust Co. v. Hannay, 210 Fed. 810 (C. C. A. 2d, 1913), had decided that

But, even with these possible means of ascertaining the foreign law, are we not certain to become entangled in the endless chain in the many cases in which they are not available? It seems that we are far from certain to encounter that difficulty.

1. Recognition of the foreign conflict of laws will not lead us into any endless chain of references if the choice of law rule of the foreign country is the same as the choice of law rule of the country to which it refers.[81] This will be true in many cases of "transmission"; perhaps we can say that it will ordinarily be true. Consider the case of a German who dies domiciled in France, leaving goods in England. Let us suppose that French and German law agree in adopting the rule of nationality as controlling the succession in such cases. If the English court refers to the whole law of France, as the law of the domicil, it will find that the French court would refer the matter to German law, and that Germany in turn would dispose of the case by German internal law. Here then is a situation where a German court would distribute the decedent's German property by German internal law, and a French court would distribute his French property according to German internal law. Is there any reason why an English court should ignore these facts and should nevertheless distribute the English property according to French internal law? There is here no endless chain, no logical or other obstacle to prevent the uniform distribution of this one man's estate — which, as we have contended, is the ultimate purpose of the English conflict of laws rule.

2. Recognition of the foreign conflict of laws rule will not lead us into an endless chain of references if it is clear for any reason that the particular foreign conflicts rule (or any rule along the line of reference) is one which refers to the internal law alone.[82]

the case before it was governed by English law and had remanded the case for a new trial on that basis. See Notes (1919) 32 Harv. L. Rev. 560, 563, n.14, (1918) 27 Yale L. J. 1046.

[81] Perhaps this would be more technically put by saying that an endless chain of references will not occur if at any point along the way we are referred to the law of a country which by its own choice of law rule would apply its own internal law. This is very likely to occur at the second reference, but it might occur at the third as in *In re* Annesley, [1926] Ch. 692; and it might conceivably happen somewhere farther down the line.

[82] This, too, might happen somewhere farther down the line than the second reference, but this would be unusual in practice.

This, of course, is the case if the foreign law is one which "rejects the renvoi",[83] or, indeed, if it "accepts the renvoi".[84] It is also the situation in a large class of other cases. If the statutes of a state provide that a will shall be valid if it has three witnesses or if it meets the requirements of the law of the place where it was executed, it is clear that the latter provision refers to the internal law of the place of execution.[85] Thus let us suppose that a question arises in the courts of Ohio concerning the distribution of goods left in Ohio by a man who died domiciled in Massachusetts leaving a holographic will which he had executed in California. By the internal law of Massachusetts a will must have three witnesses,[86] but a will is also valid if it is executed in accordance with the law of the place of execution.[87] By the internal law of California holographic wills are valid.[88] It is clear, then, that the courts of Massachusetts would uphold the decedent's will. Is there any reason why a court of Ohio should look only to Massachusetts internal law and hold that the decedent had died intestate?[89] The case put is one of transmission, but the same disposition may be open where there is remission — as, for instance, if the question arose in California rather than Ohio. Consider *Frere v. Frere*.[90] There the decedent died domiciled in Malta, leaving a will executed in England and valid by English internal law, but invalid by Maltese internal law, which required five wit-

---

[83] *In re* Ross, [1930] 1 Ch. 377.

[84] *In re* Annesley, [1926] Ch. 692.

[85] The statute should probably be construed to mean that a will would be valid if validly executed *either* by the internal law of the place of execution *or* pursuant to the whole law of the place of execution. This is in substance the decision in In the Goods of Lacroix, 2 P. D. 94 (1877). Despite the assertions of writers (Schreiber, *supra* note 21, at 549; Morris, *supra* note 38, at 42n.), there is nothing inconsistent in this. Certainly it is a conceivable construction of the reference statute.

[86] MASS. GEN. LAWS (1932) c. 191, § 1.

[87] *Id.* § 5.

[88] CAL. PROBATE CODE (Deering 1937) § 53.

[89] Baird's Estate, Orphan's Court of Philadelphia, July 18, 1916, unreported, but stated in Bates, *Remission and Transmission in American Conflict of Laws* (1931) 16 CORN. L. Q. 311, 316, answers this question in the negative. A Pennsylvania citizen domiciled in France (*cf.* note 30, *supra*) made his will in New York in New York form. The Pennsylvania court sustained the will on a showing that the French conflict of laws would have referred the question to New York.

[90] 5 Notes of Cases 593 (1847). Another case to the same effect is In the Goods of Brown-Séquard, 70 L. T. (N.S.) 811 (1894). Ross v. Ross, 25 Can. S. C. 307 (1894), is very similar. See also *In re* Martin, [1900] P. 211.

nesses. It was established by evidence that the Maltese courts would uphold the will "if it be made according to the law of the place in which it was executed". This Maltese rule was apparently not statutory, but this would seem immaterial. The English court followed it, and upheld the will. It has been criticized for doing so on the ground that it apparently was not aware of what it was doing; [91] but the question may again be asked: is there any reason why an English court should refuse to uphold the will of a man domiciled in Malta which would be upheld by the Maltese court itself?

So we see, that by approaching the matter from the abstract and theoretical point of view, the fear of the endless chain has been magnified into a generalization; while the endless chain is in fact and in practice an extremely rare apparition. Doubtless, we cannot leave this discussion without conceding that it may sometime appear. What will we do if we refer a question to the law of some other state and that state in turn refers it back to us and tells us that it will dispose of it as we do? One is tempted to follow the common-law tradition and say that it will be time enough to dispose of that question when it really arises.[92] But in the meantime we can say that one thing is clear. No disposition can be made of the question which is not arbitrary. There is no more reason for "rejecting the renvoi" than for "accepting" it. It would seem that this is simply a hiatus in the operation of our conflicts rule. Our law refers us to a foreign law which does not (except by an arbitrary assumption) furnish a means of disposing of the case. This is not *désistement*; it is rather the recognition of a fact. If anyone prefers to call it "accepting the renvoi", he

[91] MENDELSSOHN-BARTHOLDY, RENVOI IN MODERN ENGLISH LAW (1937) 67–69; Schreiber, *The Doctrine of the Renvoi in Anglo-American Law* (1918) 31 HARV. L. REV. 523, 541–42.

[92] Matter of Tallmadge, 109 Misc. 696, 181 N. Y. Supp. 336 (Surr. Ct. 1919), may possibly be thought to be a case where it did arise. But the charge cannot be admitted. The evidence there was that the French court would apply the "internal law of New York", 109 Misc. at 705, 181 N. Y. Supp. at 342. The New York court therefore was not faced with an endless chain. It could have disposed of the case as the French court would dispose of it by applying New York internal law. There is nothing to indicate whether the same question was in fact involved in any case before the French court, or which might arise in a French court, so that the New York court could await an actual French disposition of the case. Until it was clear that a French court would dispose of the case only as the New York court would decide it, there was no endless chain.

is free to do so. It seems to be open to no more objection than is equally applicable to "rejecting the renvoi"; and it has the positive merit that application of domestic law will ordinarily be an easier and surer task than applying foreign internal law, which the latter expedient requires.

It is somewhat as if our law had referred us to the law of an area which has no law.[93] In such a case there might be reason for disposing of the case according to our own internal law, in default of any other law which will settle the question. This is the solution adopted by the common law in the situation where a conflicts rule refers to the law of a foreign state and there is a failure to prove what that law is.[94] There is here in effect a failure or inability to prove how the foreign court would dispose of the case. The law is full of such arbitrary dispositions where there is no other persuasive basis for settling the issue.[95] Since this is really a case where the conflicts rule is in fact ineffective, the legislature might well provide by statute that the court should dispose of the case by applying its own internal law.[96] In any event, the important thing to bear in mind is that the endless chain is a remote possibility, not the central theme of renvoi, and the possibility of its appearance should not be allowed to distort the law in the many cases where it is not present.

---

[93] *Cf.* the note on *Law Governing Acts done in Uncivilized Countries* in DICEY, CONFLICT OF LAWS (5th ed. 1932) 879–82.

[94] See Savage v. O'Neil, 44 N. Y. 298, 301 (1871) ("and in the absence of proof our own law must of necessity furnish the rule for the guidance of our courts"); 3 BEALE, CONFLICT OF LAWS (1935) §§ 622A.1–623.1; CHESHIRE, PRIVATE INTERNATIONAL LAW (2d ed. 1938) 129 ("The presumption is that foreign law is the same as English law.").

[95] Consider, for example, the distribution of a loss between two persons equally blameless; or the varying methods devised for the case where they were equally blameworthy, letting the loss lie where it fell, dividing it equally, or comparative negligence. *Cf.* POUND, LAW AND MORALS (2d ed. 1926) 77–78.

Another problem in the law which arises in the form of a circle or regression is circuity of lien. For the various expedients adopted to handle this situation, see Campbell, *Protection Against Indirect Attack* in HARVARD LEGAL ESSAYS (1934) 3, 16–20; Benson, *Circuity of Lien — A Problem in Priorities* (1935) 19 MINN. L. REV. 139; White, *A Problem in Priorities* (1926) 25 OHIO L. REPORTER 116.

[96] Or the law of some other state, if the legislature preferred that other law, which would be unlikely.

VII

Let us now consider some cases where Anglo-American courts do refer to the conflicts rule of a foreign state, or at least may be thought to make such a reference. This is not an effort to present an exhaustive survey of Anglo-American cases which may have involved renvoi questions, but rather an attempt to set forth certain situations which seem to support the approach which has been outlined above.

1. It may be suggested as a possibility that the generally stated rule that succession to tangible moveable property follows the law of the domicil is itself an example of renvoi in our sense. Let us suppose that *A* dies domiciled in Massachusetts leaving tangible moveable property in New Hampshire, and an issue depending on the succession to this property arises in New York. The traditional statement is that the succession is governed by the law of the domicil, which in our case is Massachusetts. Is this not in truth a bit of shorthand? May it not be that New York is in fact looking primarily to the law of the situs; [97] but on looking at the "whole law" of New Hampshire, it finds that a New Hampshire court would distribute the property according to the law of the domicil, which is Massachusetts? The latter state agrees [98] and so the New York court is led unerringly to the internal law of Massachusetts for its disposition of the case.[99]

This suggestion may be tested in several ways. In the first place, if *A* had died intestate and without heirs, would the New York court apply Massachusetts "internal" law. By that law the state of Massachusetts would be the successor to the property.

[97] Compare the rule that only the state of the situs can impose a death tax [Frick v. Pennsylvania, 268 U. S. 473 (1925); City Bank Farmers Trust Co. v. Schnader, 293 U. S. 112 (1934)], and that the state of the situs has jurisdiction to administer the property. Iowa v. Slimmer, 248 U. S. 115 (1918).

[98] The Massachusetts rule would be that Massachusetts internal law controls the succession to moveables left outside the state by a Massachusetts decedent if the law of the situs refers to Massachusetts as the law of the domicil. This is simply the converse of the rule suggested in the previous sentence of the text. The two rules together lead to no endless chain.

[99] See GOODRICH, CONFLICT OF LAWS (1927) 368–72.

Cf. CAL. CIV. CODE (Deering, 1937) § 946: "If there is no law to the contrary, in the place where personal property is situated, it is deemed to follow the person of its owner, and is governed by the law of his domicile." The same provision is found in N. D. COMP. LAWS ANN. (1913) § 5444, OKLA. STAT. ANN. (1937) tit. 60, § 311, and in S. D. COMP. LAWS (1929) § 470.

Yet we know that in such a case the state which succeeds to *bona vacantia* is the state of the physical situs of the property.[100] It is not material whether this is " a true right of succession ".[101] The important thing is that it seems to show that the forum looks first to the law of the situs and then on to the law of the domicil only if the whole law of the situs refers it there. The choice of law rule of the situs is that the ownership of property on death is determined by the law of the domicil, *unless* the decedent died intestate and without heirs.[102]

Moreover, the law of the situs need not refer to the law of the domicil at all. There are at least two states in this country which do not follow the traditional choice of law rule of the domicil. In both Illinois [103] and in Mississippi [104] the applicable choice of law

100 *In re* Barnetts' Trusts, [1902] 1 Ch. 847. *Cf.* Estate of Musurus, [1936] 2 All Eng. 1666. This was apparently Story's view as expressed in Harvey v. Richards, 1 Mason 381, 411 (C. C. D. Mass. 1818). See also 2 Beale, Conflict of Laws (1935) § 309.1; Cheshire, Private International Law (2d ed. 1938) 513–14.

101 Cheshire, Private International Law (2d ed. 1938) 513.

102 *Cf.* Sneed v. Ewing, 5 J. J. Marsh, 460 (Ky. 1831), where slaves were left in Kentucky by a decedent domiciled in Indiana. By the law of Indiana, there was no legal property in slaves. But this was held to be in substance merely the " internal law " of Indiana, the court saying (p. 484) that " the interdict is merely social and territorial. It does not operate on an individual citizen of Indiana *as a citizen.* It does not disqualify him from holding, *as a citizen of Indiana*, slaves, wherever slavery is permitted." Applying this then as the " whole law " of Indiana, the Kentucky court distributed the slaves in Kentucky according to the Indiana rule of distribution.

See also Cameron v. Watson, 40 Miss. 191 (1866); Higgins v. Eaton, 202 Fed. 75 (C. C. A. 2d, 1913). The latter case involved property left in New York by a woman domiciled in Michigan. A New York court admitted a codicil to probate, but the Michigan probate court rejected it as improperly executed. The federal court held that the rights in the property were determined by the New York decision.

103 Ill. Rev. Stat. (1937) c. 39, § 1: " That estates, both real and personal, of resident and nonresident proprietors in this state dying intestate, . . . shall descend to and be distributed in manner following, . . ." This provision goes back at least as far as 1829. See Ill. Rev. Code (1829) 205. It was applied in Headen v. Cohn, 292 Ill. 210, 126 N. E. 550 (1920). There, a decedent who was domiciled in California owned some money which was physically located in Illinois. The court held that the distributee according to Illinois law took in preference to the distributee designated by California law.

104 Miss. Code Ann. (1930) § 1401: " All personal property situated in this state shall descend and be distributed according to the laws of this state regulating the descent and distribution of such property, regardless of all marital rights which may have accrued in other states, and notwithstanding the domicile of the deceased may have been in another state, and whether the heirs or persons entitled to distribution be in this state or not; . . ." This apparently first appeared in Miss. Rev. Code (1857) c. 60, art. 110.

rule is that the intestate property of nonresident decedents is distributed according to the local internal law.[105] In Illinois the statute is construed to apply only to tangible property within the state,[106] while in Mississippi it is applied as well to debts owed by Mississippi debtors or shares in Mississippi corporations.[107] Let us suppose that *A* dies domiciled in Wisconsin leaving an automobile in Illinois. By the law of Wisconsin *B* would succeed to it, but under the Illinois statute of descent it goes to *C*. On being advised of this *B* goes to Illinois and quickly drives the car to Indiana, where *C* overtakes him and seeks to recover it. Is it not fairly clear that Indiana *should* look to the Illinois law, including its choice of law rule, and hold that *C* is the owner of the car? It will not look to the law of the domicil unless the "whole law" of the situs refers it there. The answer would seem to be the same even though the question arose in Wisconsin, the state of the domicil.

The point is also illustrated by two old cases. In *McCollum v. Smith*[108] the court in Tennessee was called upon to determine the title to certain slaves located in Louisiana which had been left by a woman who was domiciled in Tennessee. Under the Louisiana Code[109] slaves were "considered as immovable by the operation of law". The court held that this provision made the slaves

[105] This is also the rule as to all moveable property left in Russia; and, conversely, Russia recognizes the law of the situs as to all property left outside of Russia, even though owned by Russian decedents. It has been suggested that this may lead to an endless chain problem in the case of chattels left in England by a person domiciled in Russia. See Dobrin, *The English Doctrine of the Renvoi and the Soviet Law of Succession* (1934) 15 B. Y. I. L. 36. It would seem arguable that the Russian reference is intended to be to the internal law of the situs (*cf.* pp. 1190–91, *supra*), so that, in the case put, the property should be distributed according to the internal law of England.

Cf. CAL. PROBATE CODE (Deering, 1937) § 100: "The interpretation of wills, wherever made, is governed, when relating to property within this state, by the law of this state, . . ."

[106] See Cooper v. Beers, 143 Ill. 25, 33 N. E. 61 (1892); Channel v. Capen, 46 Ill. App. 234 (1892).

[107] See Jahier v. Rascoe, 62 Miss. 699 (1885); Neblett v. Neblett, 112 Miss. 550, 73 So. 575 (1916); Ewing v. Warren, 144 Miss. 233, 109 So. 601 (1926).

[108] Meigs 342 (Tenn. 1838). Jones v. Marable, 6 Humphreys 116 (Tenn. 1845), is substantially similar, except that the slaves were in Arkansas rather than in Louisiana. The court said (p. 118): "And although it is a rule of international law that the succession to personal property is controlled by the law of the domicil, yet it is in the power of any State to change the law in this respect; . . ."

[109] ORLEANS DIG. (1808) bk. 2, c. 2, art. 19.

immovable property so that their ownership passed according to the Louisiana law. This is commonly cited as a decision to the effect that questions of classification are governed by the law of the situs.[110] But may it not as well be said to be a case in which the forum looked to the law of Louisiana as the law of the situs, and in looking to the Louisiana law it was guided by the "whole law" of Louisiana, including the Louisiana choice of law rule — which in this case led to the application of Louisiana internal law.[111] The other early case, *Williamson's Adm'rs v. Smart and Kilbee*,[112] is very similar on its facts. There the question arose in North Carolina as to the ownership of slaves located in Virginia which had been left by a decedent domiciled in North Carolina. By the law of Virginia "negro property was made to descend like land to the heirs at law".[113] The court nevertheless held that the North Carolina next of kin were entitled to the slaves. They reached this conclusion by holding that the Virginia rule was one which Virginia would apply only to the estates of Virginia decedents.[114] On this basis then, the Virginia choice of law rule was that Virginia would apply Virginia internal law to slaves left by Virginia decedents, but would apply the internal law of the domicil to slaves left by non-Virginia decedents. Applying then the "whole law" of Virginia, including this choice of law rule, the North Carolina court was led to the law of North Carolina, which it accordingly applied. In both cases, the court looked to the "whole law" of the state of situs; but the choice of law rule found to be embraced within the "whole law" was different in one case than in the other, thus leading to different results.[115]

---

110 CHESHIRE, PRIVATE INTERNATIONAL LAW (2d ed. 1938) 411.

111 *Cf.* 2 BEALE, CONFLICT OF LAWS (1935) § 208.1: ". . . the law of Louisiana has effect not as affecting the character of the property but as the law of the situs of the property which must determine its devolution."

112 C. & N. 145 (N. C. 1801).

113 *Id.* at 151.

114 ". . . there can be no reason wherefore that state should be concerned about the manner in which strangers hold that sort of property, which they may freely carry away with them. . . . Therefore, if in the state of Virginia this property is cloathed with some of the qualities of real estate . . . the local policy which hath thus distinguished it, must necessarily confine the operation of the laws respecting it to the citizens and inhabitants of that state: . . ." *Id.* at 155.

115 Whether the North Carolina court was correct in its construction of the Virginia choice of law rule is not material for our purposes. In either event, it ought to dispose of the case as it concludes the Virginia court would. If the North

The contention has been made that cases of the sort we have just been considering are not examples of looking at the " whole law " of another state. Instead, it is said:

> The ordinary rule of succession, namely, that moveables pass in accordance with the law of the domicil, is not a doctrine of the Conflict of Laws, strictly speaking, but is a rule of the common law of succession, that is, a part of the law of the state of situs. When that doctrine is changed by statute it is not a statutory change of the Conflict of Laws but a statute of the law of succession of the situs and it is for that reason that the statute can be applied in a case where the domicil of the decedent is outside the state.[116]

This suggestion has also been made elsewhere.[117] To some extent, of course, it is a matter of definition. The result is the same whether the foreign rule applicable to extrastate elements is looked to because it is defined into the " internal law " or because the reference is to the " whole law " of the foreign country. But ordinarily, at least, conflict of laws is thought of as the subject which determines the effect to be given to extrastate elements in any situation.[118] The question involved in our problem is the effect to be given to a foreign element, namely, the foreign domicil of a decedent who formerly owned the property. Any rule of the situs determining the effect of this foreign element would seem to be properly regarded as a choice of law or conflict of laws rule, and this without regard to whether it was so designated in the statute book, or was simply one of the provisions in the general statute of distributions. What would seem to be called for is a greater friendliness to renvoi rather than a revision of our conception of the field of conflict of laws.

Carolina court had concluded that a Virginia court would apply Virginia internal law, then McCollum v. Smith is an authority that the North Carolina court should do the same.

116 1 BEALE, CONFLICT OF LAWS (1935) § 8.2.

117 CHESHIRE, PRIVATE INTERNATIONAL LAW (2d ed. 1938) 53: ". . . a legislature may *in its internal law* have different rules for persons within the jurisdiction according as they are nationals, residents, or visitors." See also the similar statement in MENDELSSOHN-BARTHOLDY, RENVOI IN MODERN ENGLISH LAW (1937) 60, which is called a " startling asscrtion " in the review of the book by Unger in (1938) 1 MODERN L. REV. 332, 333.

118 Cheshire defines conflict of laws as that part of English law which " comes into operation whenever the Court is seised of a suit that contains a foreign element ". CHESHIRE, PRIVATE INTERNATIONAL LAW (2d ed. 1938) 3.

2. It may be possible that the same sort of thing is happening in the law applicable to the validity of marriages. It is sometimes stated that capacity to enter into a marriage is governed by the law of the state where the ceremony is performed,[119] though exceptions are recognized to the generality of the rule.[120] It seems possible that we may have here another situation where the general rule is really a short-hand statement. A more accurate statement may be that capacity to enter into a marriage is governed by the law of the domicil — the "whole law" of the domicil; in many situations the law of the domicil refers the question to the law of the place of contracting (there is our general rule), while in others it does not (the exceptions). But in any event we take our guide from the whole law of the domicil.[121]

An illustration of this approach may be found in the Uniform Marriage Evasion Act.[122] Where there is a statute of this type at the domicil, if a person who is disabled from contracting marriage at the domicil goes into another state and endeavors to contract a marriage, "such marriage shall be null and void for all purposes in this state". Let us suppose that *A* is domiciled in state *X* which has such a statute, and that *A* is prohibited from marriage in *X* because he is under the age of 16. *A* goes into *Y* and enters into a marriage valid by the internal law of *Y*, returning at once to *X* and intending to live in *X*. Should this marriage be recognized in a third state *Z*? It would seem a desirable solution to say that *Z* should look to the "whole law" of *X* including its choice of law rule which directs that the matter be governed by *X's* in-

[119] See 2 BEALE, CONFLICT OF LAWS (1935) § 121.6. *Cf.* RESTATEMENT, CONFLICT OF LAWS (1934) § 121.

[120] RESTATEMENT, CONFLICT OF LAWS § 132.

[121] See Beale, Laughlin, Guthrie and Sandomire, *Marriage and the Domicil* (1931) 44 HARV. L. REV. 501, 529 ("control over the marital status rests with the domicil"); STUMBERG, CONFLICT OF LAWS (1937) 262–65: "If it found that the marriage is one that would be regarded as valid at the domicil, it should give it effect in order to further uniformity. If it found that it is invalid there, for the same reason, it should refuse recognition." *Cf.* CHESHIRE, PRIVATE INTERNATIONAL LAW (2d ed. 1938) 220–22; Graveson, *Matrimonial Domicil and the Contract of Marriage* (1938) 20 J. COMP. LEG. 55.

[122] ILL. REV. STAT. (Cahill, 1933) c. 89, ¶¶ 20–26; LA. GEN. STAT. ANN. (Dart, 1932) §§ 2186–89; MASS. GEN. LAWS (1932) c. 207, §§ 10–12, 50; VT. GEN. LAWS (1917) §§ 3514–15, 3794, *as amended by* Vt. Laws, 1925, p. 60; WIS. STAT. (1935) § 245.04. Similar statutes in force in several other states are cited in CHEATHAM, DOWLING AND GOODRICH, CASES ON CONFLICT OF LAWS (1936) 793n.

ternal law. On this basis the marriage is invalid, and *Z* should so hold. If on the other hand, *X* by its whole law should hold the validity of the marriage to be governed by the law of the place of contracting, then *Z* should follow the reference to the law of *Y* and decide accordingly. This approach is apparently being accepted in an increasing number of cases.[123]

3. Another situation in the law which may be very tentatively advanced as fitting into the approach here suggested is the problem of the law governing the effect of the ratification of an unauthorized contract. It is generally said that where a contract is made without authority in state *X* and the principal subsequently ratifies it in state *Y*, the validity of the contract is governed by the law of *X*, even though the principal was always in *Y*.[124] This is said to be because the principal " submits " himself to the law of *X*.[125] Might there be value in an approach which said that the principal's act was governed by the law of *Y* where he acted, but the " whole law " of *Y* in such a case might well refer to the law of *X*? This could be tested to some extent if *Y* were to adopt a statute (or rule of decision) that no act of ratification done in *Y* should be effective. In the presence of such a statute it seems arguable that the law of *Y* should control, and that the principal should not be regarded as bound on the contract either in *X* or a third state.[126]

---

[123] See Meisenhelder v. Chicago & N. W. Ry., 170 Minn. 317, 213 N. W. 32 (1927); People v. Steere, 184 Mich. 556, 151 N. W. 617 (1915); Hall v. Industrial Commission, 165 Wis. 364, 162 N. W. 312 (1917). *Cf.* Owen v. Owen, 178 Wis. 609, 190 N. W. 363 (1922). See Taintor, *Effect of Extra-State Marriage Ceremonies* (1938) 10 MISS. L. J. 105.

Another case involving marriage where foreign conflicts rules were recognized and followed is Lando v. Lando, 112 Minn. 257, 127 N. W. 1125 (1910). See also Hubbard v. Hubbard, 228 N. Y. 81, 126 N. E. 508 (1920).

[124] 2 BEALE, CONFLICT OF LAWS (1935) § 331.1; RESTATEMENT, CONFLICT OF LAWS (1934) §§ 68, 331.

[125] See Beale, *The Jurisdiction of a Sovereign State* (1923) 36 HARV. L. REV. 241, 258–59.

[126] The whole question of the application of the approach which looks to the " whole law " of a state to the field of contracts is tantalizing, but it is too complex for further discussion here. *Cf.* Schreiber, *The Doctrine of the Renvoi in Anglo-American Law* (1918) 31 HARV. L. REV. 523, 569, discussing Guernsey v. Imperial Bank of Canada, 188 Fed. 300 (C. C. A. 8th, 1911): " The case suggests, however, a fertile field for the application of the renvoi should it ever gain a foothold in our law, that is, in the field of the choice of law governing contractual validity and obligation." See also Gutteridge, *The Unification of the Law of Bills of Exchange* (1931) 12 B. Y. I. L. 13, 22–24.

4. For further illustration, reference may be made again to the "borrowing" statutes. These seem to be chiefly of three types, relating to (a) the validity of wills,[127] (b) the validity of deeds,[128] and (c) the application of the statute of limitations.[129] Statutes of all of these types are widespread.[130] If it be objected that they are irrelevant to our discussion because they are statutes, we may recall that "much of what is ordinarily regarded as 'common law'

[127] The Uniform Wills Act, Foreign Executed, is typical: "A last will and testament, executed without this state in the mode prescribed by the law, either of the place where executed or of the testator's domicile, shall be deemed to be legally executed, and shall be of the same force and effect as if executed in the mode prescribed by the laws of this state, provided, said last will and testament is in writing and subscribed by the testator." This is now in force in thirteen states. See 9 U. L. A. (Supp. 1937) 236. In Bordwell, *The Statute Law of Wills* (1929) 14 IOWA L. REV. 1, 443–46, thirty states are listed as having statutes to substantially this effect. See also Lorenzen, *The Validity of Wills, Deeds and Contracts as Regards Form in the Conflict of Laws* (1911) 20 YALE L. J. 427, 432–37.

Apparently the original of these statutes was Lord Kingsdown's Act, (1861) 24 & 25 VICT. c. 114, which, however, is applicable only to wills of moveables made by British subjects.

[128] See, *e.g.*, OHIO GEN. CODE ANN. (Page, 1926) § 8516: "All deeds, mortgages, powers of attorney, and other instruments of writing for the conveyance or incumbrance of lands, tenements, or hereditaments situate within this state, executed and acknowledged, or proved, in any other state, territory or country, in conformity with the laws of such state, territory or country, or in conformity with the laws of this state, shall be as valid as if executed within this state, in conformity with the foregoing provisions of this chapter."

Such statutes are not as common as in the case of wills. In 1911, they were found in eleven states and in Alaska. See Lorenzen, *supra* note 127, at 433–34.

[129] The most comprehensive of these is NEB. COMP. STAT. (1929) § 20-215: "All actions and causes of action which are barred by laws of any other state, territory or country shall be deemed barred in this state; but no action shall be barred by laws of any other state, territory or country unless the same would have been barred by the provisions of this chapter had the defendant been a resident of this state for the period herein prescribed."

Thirty-three states have statutes referring to the law of other states for limitations periods under certain circumstances. These statutes vary greatly in detail and application. See Legis., *Legislation Governing the Applicability of Foreign Statutes of Limitations* (1935) 35 COL. L. REV. 762, an extensive Note in (1931) 75 A. L. R. 203, and (1938) 51 HARV. L. REV. 1290. For Notes on the New York statutes, see (1932) 9 N. Y. U. L. Q. REV. 480, and (1934) 4 BROOKLYN L. REV. 76. Somewhat similar questions are raised by the "tolling" statutes in force in every state but Louisiana. These are discussed in Legis. (1933) 46 HARV. L. REV. 706.

[130] See also N. J. REV. STAT. (1937) § 2:42–7, providing that a nonresident may not attach the personal property of another nonresident "if such property is exempt from liability for debts by the law of the state of which the debtor and creditor are residents".

finds its source in legislative enactment".[131] If a state to which our law refers has a statute of this type, there seems to be no valid reason for ignoring it.

A will of moveables which is valid by the "whole law" of the domicil should be accepted as valid everywhere to the extent that the law of the domicil is referred to. Similarly, a deed valid by the law of the place of execution should be accepted as valid everywhere if the deed would be valid under a "borrowing" statute of the situs. Similarly, if our statute says that a cause of action is barred here if it is barred in the state where it arose, and it arose in a state which like Nebraska says that it is barred in six years or if it is "barred by laws of any other state, territory or country", then we should apply the "whole law" of the state to which we are referred and hold that the action is barred here if the court of the state to which we are referred would hold it to be barred there.[132] As has been pointed out,[133] the reference in all of these statutes would seem (as a matter of statutory construction) to be in the alternative, that is, the will or deed is valid if it complies with the requirements of either the internal law of the country to which reference is made or its "whole law"; and the same construction seems to be proper with respect to the limitations statutes.

5. Reference may next be made to the exceptional cases recognized by the *Restatement*.[134] The first of these relates to title to land. So far as the validity of wills and deeds to land is concerned, this is largely the same as the question discussed in the previous paragraph. The point which is urged here is that there is nothing exceptional about the reference to the whole law with respect to title to land. It is merely a normal application of the general approach which, it is submitted, should be applied to all cases. It is just as applicable to chattels as it is to land.

A case illustrating this point is *In re Baines*.[135] There an Eng-

[131] Landis, *Statutes and the Sources of Law*, in HARVARD LEGAL ESSAYS (1934) 213, 214. *Cf.* Cook, *The Logical and Legal Bases of the Conflict of Laws* (1924) 33 YALE L. J. 457, 461.

[132] See Holmes v. Hengen, 41 Misc. 521, 85 N. Y. Supp. 35 (Sup. Ct. 1903), *aff'd mem.*, 94 App. Div. 619, 88 N. Y. Supp. 1104 (1st Dep't 1904); Ross v. Graham, 122 Misc. 574, 203 N. Y. Supp. 390 (Sup. Ct. 1924), cited *supra* note 75.

[133] See note 85, *supra*.

[134] See p. 1174, *supra*.

[135] Unreported, stated in DICEY, CONFLICT OF LAWS (5th ed. 1932) 877–78. This is said to be "the only case found in the books in which the title to foreign real estate has been dealt with in this way". 1 BEALE, CONFLICT OF LAWS (1935) § 8.1. *In re* Ross, [1930] 1 Ch. 377, is, however, another such case. Part of the property

lish decedent left land in Egypt. The land was sold and the proceeds were brought to England. The decedent's will was valid by English law, but invalid by the internal law of Egypt. It was shown, however, that by Egyptian law succession to land is governed by the law of nationality, and that an Egyptian court would hold that the succession was governed by the internal law of England. The court accordingly upheld the will under local English law.[136] That this should be treated as an exceptional doctrine seems exceeding strange.

6. The other exception recognized by the *Restatement* relates to the validity of decrees of divorce. These cases, too, seem to be simply straightforward applications of the approach which is advocated in this article. In *Armitage v. Attorney-General*[137] a woman had been domiciled with her husband in New York. Later she went to South Dakota and obtained a divorce there, but without domicil. Her husband appeared in the South Dakota suit. Thereafter the wife married an Englishman, and some question having arisen as to the validity of this latter marriage, she brought a suit in England raising the issue. The evidence showed that the divorce would be recognized as valid in New York, though it was not granted on a ground provided by the internal law of New York. The court held that it should determine the validity of the divorce as a New York court would, and accordingly the subsequent English marriage was held valid. The questions presented in *Ball v. Cross*[138] and *Dean v. Dean*[139] were substantially similar and led to

there involved was land in Italy, and the court said (p. 405) that "the lex situs must . . . be construed in the way the courts of the country where the immoveables are situate would themselves determine". To the same effect is Faris v. Tennant, 194 Ind. 506, 141 N. E. 784 (1923).

[136] *Cf.* the discussion of the case in Schreiber, *The Doctrine of the Renvoi in Anglo-American Law* (1918) 31 HARV. L. REV. 523, 559.

[137] [1906] P. 135. Another case to the same effect is Clark v. Clark, 37 T. L. R. 815 (1921).

[138] 231 N. Y. 329, 332, 132 N. E. 106, 107 (1921): "If the state of which she was then a citizen recognizes such a decree as that obtained in Nevada, and gives it full force and effect, then it is not for us to say that it is void as to her."

[139] 241 N. Y. 240, 149 N. E. 844 (1925). A husband and wife lived in Ontario. The husband then abandoned the wife and went to Pennsylvania where he obtained a divorce. He married again and took up residence in New York. The first wife then sued him for divorce in New York. This was granted on evidence that the Pennsylvania divorce would not be recognized in Ontario. "We find nothing in our public policy to justify a holding that the wife, who remained a wife while she kept her domicile in Ontario, should be deemed to have ceased to be one when she changed her domicile to New York." 241 N. Y. at 245, 149 N. E. at 846. See Notes (1926)

the same result. If the domestic conflicts rule looks to the law of the domicil to determine the validity of a divorce, then the " whole law " of the domicil should be regarded and the question should be determined as a court at the domicil would dispose of it. Again there seems to be no reason why this should be treated as in any way an exceptional doctrine.

Other cases may be mentioned as examples of this approach.[140] But, as has been pointed out, this is not an effort to exhaust the cases, either English or American. The discussion is presented merely in support of the thesis that the recognition of the " whole law " of a foreign country as its courts would apply it is ordinarily feasible and will in general lead to more satisfactory and uniform results than the adoption of a rigid head-in-the-sand rule that salvation is to be found alone in the " internal law ".

VIII

Finally, reference may be made to three cases, one of twenty years ago, and the others recently decided, in all of which hostility to renvoi has played a perhaps unwarranted part. The first is the well known case of *Matter of Tallmadge*.[141] Here French internal law was applied to the estate of an American who died domiciled

---

39 HARV. L. REV. 640, (1926) 35 YALE L. J. 372. See also Powell v. Powell, 211 App. Div. 750, 208 N. Y. Supp. 153 (1st Dep't 1925).

[140] Guernsey v. Imperial Bank of Canada, 188 Fed. 300 (C. C. A. 8th, 1911), contains at least a dictum in favor of our approach. The case involved a promissory note made, delivered and endorsed in Illinois, but payable in Canada. Demand, protest and notice of dishonor were in a form complying with the Canadian law, but were not sufficient to hold the indorser according to Illinois internal law. The court said (p. 301): " If, therefore, as counsel contend, the law of the place where the indorsement was made, the law of Illinois, governs the sufficiency of the notice of dishonor in this case, that notice was good, for it was sufficient under the law of Canada where the note was payable, and the law of Illinois was that in a case of this character the law of the place where the note was payable governed the time and manner of giving the notice of dishonor." *Cf.* Bell v. Riggs, 34 Okla. 834, 127 Pac. 427 (1912), discussed in (1913) 11 MICH. L. REV. 236, which is somewhat to the contrary.

The cases which have sustained a general bequest in a foreign will as an exercise of an English power of appointment have generally proceeded on the ground that that is the result the foreign court would reach. *In re* Price, [1900] 1 Ch. 442, 453; *In re* Simpson, [1916] 1 Ch. 502, 508; *In re* Lewal's Settlement Trusts, [1918] 2 Ch. 391, 397, 398.

[141] 109 Misc. 696, 181 N. Y. Supp. 336 (1919). This was an opinion of a referee in a Surrogate's court. It is a little aggravating to have it referred to as establishing

in France, thus wholly "rejecting the renvoi", to the satisfaction of the critics.[142] Professor Lorenzen's conclusion that "The *renvoi* doctrine is, therefore, no part of the Conflict of Laws of the United States", was quoted, and obviously had a great influence on the author of the opinion. The possibility that the American court should have decided as a French court would was not even considered, though the evidence was stated as showing that a French court would apply New York internal law.[143] There seems room to argue that the most satisfactory result was not reached by wholly ignoring the French conflicts rules as the French court would apply them.

The first of the more recent cases is *Gray v. Gray*,[144] which concerned a husband and wife, domiciled in New Hampshire. While riding in an automobile in Maine, the wife was injured in an accident which was alleged to have been due to the husband's negligence. Suit was brought in New Hampshire, and the defendant put in a plea that by the law of Maine a wife was barred from suing her husband; and the court held that this plea was a sufficient answer to the action brought in New Hampshire. Under the approach suggested in this article the court would have said that although the matter is to be governed by the law of Maine, since the event occurred there, it should be governed by the "whole

"the solution adopted in America". Morris, *The Law of the Domicil* (1937) 18 B. Y. I. L. 32, 33. *Cf.* Scott, Book Review (1935) 48 HARV. L. REV. 535, 537.

142 See Notes (1919) 29 YALE L. J. 214, (1919) 19 COL. L. REV. 496; Pollock, *The Renvoi in New York* (1920) 36 L. Q. REV. 91.

143 See note 92, *supra*.

144 87 N. H. 82, 174 Atl. 508 (1934). There is a comment on the case in (1935) 44 YALE L. J. 1233. *Cf.* Cavers, Book Review (1935) 44 YALE L. J. 1478, 1481n. Similar conclusions were reached in Dawson v. Dawson, 224 Ala. 13, 138 So. 414 (1931); Howard v. Howard, 200 N. C. 574, 158 S. E. 101 (1931), but with less evident influence from the writers on renvoi. Substantially the converse decision was made in Forbes v. Forbes, 277 N. W. 112 (Wis. 1938), where an Illinois wife was allowed to sue her husband in Wisconsin for an injury occurring in Wisconsin, although by the law of Illinois, the domicil, she would have had no cause of action. From our point of view, this amounts to a decision that the "whole law" of Wisconsin is that actions may accrue to wives against husbands in Wisconsin regardless of their domicil. Would Illinois recognize this? *Cf.* Mertz v. Mertz, 271 N. Y. 466, 3 N. E.(2d) 597 (1936).

Pringle v. Gibson, 195 Atl. 695 (Me. 1937), was a suit by an automobile guest against a Maine defendant, arising out of an injury in New Brunswick. A New Brunswick statute providing that the driver of an automobile should not be liable to persons carried in the car was held to prevent any action in Maine. This would seem to be a proper construction of the statute, that is, that it was applicable to all injuries in New Brunswick regardless of the residence of the driver.

law " of Maine, that is, it should be decided the way the Maine court would decide it. This would involve an inquiry into the nature of the Maine rule disabling wives from suing husbands. It might well have been decided that the Maine rule was one of local policy only, which the Maine court would apply only to Maine husbands and wives, on the ground that it was designed to prevent domestic strife in Maine, a matter of concern to Maine alone.[145] As to foreign husbands and wives this policy is not applicable, and whether they could maintain suits in Maine should depend upon the law of their domicil, since the capacity of spouses to sue each other is a matter of concern to the domicil alone. If the New Hampshire court had looked to the " whole law " of Maine, therefore, it might have concluded that a Maine court would hold the capacity to be governed by New Hampshire law and thus allow the suit. And, we may ask, from the pragmatic point of view, is there any reason why a New Hampshire wife should not be allowed to sue a New Hampshire husband in a New Hampshire court merely because a local Maine policy prevents Maine wives from suing Maine husbands in Maine courts? Is there any reason for looking at the " internal law " of Maine alone? There is no endless chain, for the Maine reference to the law of the domicil as governing capacity is obviously a reference to the internal law of the domicil.

The court, indeed, considered this possibility. But it, too, quoted Lorenzen's conclusion that the renvoi " is . . . no part of the Conflict of Laws of the United States ",[146] though it ultimately concluded that it did not have to pass on the question.[147] It does

---

[145] The point is nicely illustrated by the recent case of Proctor v. Frost, 197 Atl. 813 (N. H. 1938). This was a suit to foreclose a mortgage on New Hampshire land executed in Massachusetts by a Massachusetts married woman as security for her husband. N. H. PUB. LAWS (1926) c. 288, § 2, provides that " No contract or conveyance by a married woman, as surety or guarantor for her husband, . . . shall be binding on her, . . ." The court nevertheless held the mortgage valid, saying that the statute was " intended to affect " only the conveyances " of married women made in New Hampshire. . . . Our conclusion, therefore, is that the legislature has not attempted, in the statute under consideration, to affirm or deny the capacity of married women to make contracts or conveyances except when such transactions take place in this state. . . . This is the New Hampshire rule which determines the validity of the mortgage in question."

[146] 87 N. H. at 88, 174 Atl. at 511.

[147] This conclusion was doubtless technically sound for the case arose on a demurrer to a plea which alleged that " Under the laws of said state of Maine, the

not seem clear that a more satisfactory result might not hereafter be reached if the rigid views of writers in this field can be modified so that later courts will feel more free to look to the "whole law" of a state to which they are referred by their primary choice of law rule.[148]

The other recent case is *University of Chicago v. Dater*,[149] where the apprehension as to renvoi appeared in a dissenting opinion. There a note was signed in Michigan by a Michigan married woman. The note was then sent to Illinois where a mortgage on Illinois land securing it was placed on record. After this was done the money was advanced in Illinois by the lender, which had not previously incurred any obligation to lend it. The mortgage was foreclosed in Illinois and suit was then brought in Michigan to recover the balance due on the note. By the internal law of Michigan a wife could not bind herself by signing notes, while by "the law of Illinois a married woman is as free to contract as a man".[150] The majority of the court held that the wife's capacity was governed by the law of the place of contracting, which it held to be

---

plaintiff being the wife of said defendant is barred from maintaining this action". But the court could have granted leave to withdraw the demurrer and file a denial of the plea if it had felt that a different approach should have been taken to the case. See, for example, the action of the same court in allowing an amendment in Brahmey v. Rollins, 87 N. H. 290, 302, 179 Atl. 186, 195 (1935).

[148] The discussion above of Gray v. Gray is in line with comments which have been made with respect to Milliken v. Pratt, 125 Mass. 374 (1878). There a wife in Massachusetts sent an instrument guaranteeing her husband's debts to Maine, where it was accepted by the shipping of goods. By Massachusetts law she had no capacity to guarantee her husband's debts. By the internal law of Maine, Maine wives had such capacity. The court, speaking through Gray, C. J., held that the question was governed by "the law" of the place of contracting, and that the contract was made in Maine. The question whether "the law" of Maine might be ambiguous was not noticed; it was assumed that it meant the internal law of Maine, and accordingly the wife's liability was upheld. It has been pointed out that in doing so the Massachusetts court was not applying the law of Maine to the very facts of this case, but was rather applying the law which a Maine court would apply to another case all of whose elements were in Maine. Cook, *The Logical and Legal Bases of the Conflict of Laws* (1924) 33 YALE L. J. 457, 471–73. To the same effect is STUMBERG, CONFLICT OF LAWS (1937) 9–11, 202–03. Cook uses the case as an example of the impropriety of the vested rights point of view. It may, however, be rather an instance in which the existence of a renvoi problem was overlooked.

[149] 277 Mich. 658, 270 N. W. 175 (1936). There are comments on the case in *Developments in the Law — Conflicts* (1937) 50 HARV. L. REV. 1119, 1159; (1937) 35 MICH. L. REV. 1299; and (1937) 21 MINN. L. REV. 739.

[150] 277 Mich. at 663, 270 N. W. at 177.

Illinois. But it was further found that an Illinois court would hold in such a case that the wife's capacity was governed by the internal law of the place of execution.[151] Accordingly, since an Illinois court would hold the wife not liable, the Michigan court decided likewise. But three members of the court dissented, one of them asserting that to ascertain what the foreign court would hold would result in " hopeless confusion ".[152] It would seem that the majority of the court was correct. Moreover, the observation of a commentator that " having once got on the renvoi merry-go-round, there is no logical reason " why the Michigan court should have stopped at the reference back to Michigan law,[153] seems unsound. The Michigan court never got on a renvoi merry-go-round. It referred to the whole law of Illinois, and having found how the Illinois court would dispose of the case, it did the same. Why should the court have looked only to the internal law of Illinois, and let an Illinois plaintiff succeed in Michigan when it could not have succeeded in Illinois where the contract was made?

Envoi

The renvoi problem is indeed difficult. Previous approaches have shed much light upon it, and the debt of one who writes now to those who have written before is very great. Where there has been disagreement here, it has been in an effort to build upon their work. Reconsideration seems to show, as English and American courts have found, that there are many situations where satisfactory solutions to puzzling problems can be worked out by looking to the " whole law " of a country designated by a local choice of law rule, and then reaching the same result which would be reached by the courts of that country. That there is room in our law for development along this line is the thesis of this article. That the material here presented may serve to answer some of the academic obstacles to this development is its hope.

Erwin N. Griswold.

Harvard Law School.

---

151 This was held to be the result of the decision in Burr v. Beckler, 264 Ill. 230, 106 N. E. 206 (1914).

152 277 Mich. at 667, 270 N. W. at 178.

153 *Developments in the Law — Conflicts* (1937) 50 Harv. L. Rev. 1119, 1159.

[5]

CHOICE IN CHOICE OF LAW†

P. M. North*

I Introduction

It is a truism that there are three fundamental questions which may arise in the course of examining a civil legal issue which has international aspects. First, if the issue were to involve litigation in this country, would our courts have jurisdiction to entertain the proceedings? Second, if the issue has already resulted in litigation in another jurisdiction will the decision of the foreign court be recognised and enforced in this country? Both these questions have an interesting, and narrowing, characteristic. They are concerned with matters which have reached the point of breakdown, *i.e.* of litigation and judicial decision-making. The third issue is really very different. It is concerned with the law to be applied to a civil legal issue whose circumstances involve factors connected with more than one jurisdiction. Of course, if the issue is litigated, the determination of the applicable law will be a necessary part of the process. There are, however, many circumstances, by far the majority, where the determination of the applicable law is made without any prospect of a legal dispute or litigation. Parties from different countries may be planning to get married and wish to know whether they are free to do so. A social security official may be trying to decide whether a woman was validly married abroad to the deceased so as to qualify for benefits as a widow. Companies negotiating an international sales contract need to clarify their mutual obligations in the light of the law to govern it. A middle aged couple, with assets in several countries, are anxious to make a new will or to provide for their children by establishing a trust.

All of these circumstances raise choice of law issues and most of the examples just given involve a degree of concern over the legality or effectiveness of future conduct. One question that is posed thereby is whether, and to what extent, there is a freedom for the parties to choose the law to govern their transnational affairs. It has also to be considered whether any choice can be used to order future events or only to govern the situation when a dispute has arisen and litigation looms.

† This article is the text of the inaugural lecture delivered on 19 March, 1992 in a series of annual lectures at King's College, London, in memory of Professor R. H. Graveson, C.B.E., Q.C.

* C.B.E., M.A., D.C.L., F.B.A., Principal of Jesus College, Oxford.

It is important to be clear from the outset of any examination of these issues that the nature of our rules of private international law is such that there can be two kinds of choice involved in the determination of the relevant rule to be applied to a particular case. The simplest way in which choice is exercised to determine the law to be applied or whether a court is to have jurisdiction is by the parties actually choosing by agreement the governing law or selecting one or more countries before whose courts any litigation is to take place. One part, indeed a major part, of my concerns in this present discussion is to examine the types of case in which choice of that kind, whether express or implied, is to be permitted. It would be wrong, however, to exclude from consideration the element of choice which may be involved indirectly. One form that this may take is where it is not the applicable law which is chosen but rather the factors or elements which go to constitute the connecting factor which our rules of private international law have laid down for determining the applicable law. Another form is seen where the freedom to choose the jurisdiction in which to proceed carries with it a determination of the law to be applied. A further form is where choice is exercised through the rules relating to the pleading of foreign law. All these kinds of indirect choice merit some examination.

II Indirect choice

Indirect choice, both through choice of jurisdiction and of the elements within the appropriate connecting factor, may be exemplified by choice of law rules in the field of family law where no significant place has yet been found, either in the rules as formulated by the courts or in proposals for reform, for the idea of direct choice of the applicable law. Three or four different aspects of indirect choice may be illustrated by the choice of law rules relating to divorce and to marriage. These aspects involve both agreement between the spouses and unilateral choice by one of them.

(a) Divorce

Turning first to divorce, this is an aspect of family law which has engendered very little examination of the choice of law issue.[1] It seems clearly to have been accepted that, if an English court has jurisdiction over a divorce petition, even though both parties are domiciled in another country,[2] then the substantive divorce law to

[1] Though see North [1980] I Hague Recueil 9, 77–88; [1990] I Hague Recueil 9, 112–114.

[2] *E.g.* by reason of the habitual residence in England of one of the spouses: Domicile and Matrimonial Proceedings Act 1973, s.5(2)(b).

be applied is that of the forum, *i.e.* English law. The same is also true of the law to be applied to important ancillary issues such as disputes over children or money. It may be argued that the almost unthinking application of the law of the forum does little to enhance the general choice of law process, but in the present context the selection of English law to be applied is made, in effect, by the decision of one of the spouses, the petitioner, to bring divorce proceedings in England. Two elements of this so-called "choice" should be emphasised. The first is that it is unilateral, not requiring the agreement of the other spouse. The second is that it is not unlimited. English law will only be applied as the law of the forum if a jurisdictional link here can be established, through the fact that one of the parties is domiciled or habitually resident in England. Of course, if there is an alternative jurisdictional link established with another common law jurisdiction, which is also very likely to apply its own divorce law to any petition before its courts, a petitioner has the power to "choose" the law to be applied by reason of the decision to petition there.[3]

(b) Marriage

Marriage choice of law rules provide rather different examples of indirect choice. The most straightforward is that of the law to govern the formal validity of a marriage. There seems to be widespread acceptance that the English (and general common law) choice of law rule here is that matters of formal validity are governed by the law of the place of celebration of the marriage. The selection of the country of celebration is one for the spouses jointly to make, given that they are both going to be present there for the marriage ceremony, at least if one disregards the rare instances of proxy marriages. Here, therefore, the choice by the parties of the place of celebration effectively constitutes a choice of the law to govern formalities.[4] Whilst, in many cases, that choice will be determined by social and domestic factors or even the desire for a package holiday including a wedding on a tropical island, it is not unknown for spouses to choose to marry in a particular country in order to take advantage of the legal rules there in force relating to the validity of a marriage.[5] Whilst, therefore, there is a real and fairly direct element of choice here involved, it has to be remembered that it is a limited choice. The

[3] Contrast Dutch law where, under the International Divorce Act 1981, a wider freedom of choice is permitted: De Boer (1990) 54 RabelsZ 24, 38.

[4] Whether a choice has been freely made may raise issues as to the law governing consent to marry which would seem to be governed by the law applicable to issues of essential, rather than formal, validity.

[5] *E.g. Reed* v. *Reed* (1969) 6 D.L.R. (3d) 617.

law to be applied follows from the choice of the place of celebration. It is not possible, under present English choice of law rules (subject to a narrow exception relating to military marriages), actually to choose a law different from that of the place of celebration to govern matters of formal validity.

When considering choice of law rules to govern essential validity, the position in relation to choice is somewhat more complicated, not least because there is no clear acceptance of what law does govern matters of essential validity or whether the same choice of law rule applies to all such matters. Leaving aside for the moment the varied suggestions that have been made, for example, to introduce separate choice of law rules for different aspects of essential validity or to introduce the concept of "the proper law of the marriage",[6] there are two long-established contenders for acceptance as the connecting factor to decide the law to govern essential validity. The first, associated with John Morris, is the dual domicile test, namely that one applies the law of each party's ante-nuptial domicile to determine their respective capacities to marry. The other test, associated with the name of Geoffrey Cheshire, is that one looks to see if the parties have, or had, an intended matrimonial home. If so, that law is to govern matters of essential validity. If not, reference is to be made to the law of the husband's domicile at the time of the marriage. Much has been written about the respective merits of these two approaches and, though the weight of judicial authority tends to support the dual domicile approach, as the Law Commission has said "there is no decision which prevents the Court of Appeal or the House of Lords from adopting either test."[7] What is of interest in the present context is, however, the extent to which the two approaches reveal elements of "choice" by the parties of the applicable law.

Not unlike the formal validity rule, the first branch of the Cheshire approach, "the intended matrimonial home" test, provides a good instance of the parties making an indirect choice of the governing law, this time by choosing the country where they are to live. It is also to be classed as an agreed choice by both of them because, without that consensual element, there would be no matrimonial home. The choice is legally wide in that the matrimonial home could be anywhere. The constraints are social and economic. On the other hand, the choice is limited in that no law other than that of the intended matrimonial home can be selected. The connecting factor can be freely chosen but then the determination of the applicable law follows automatically. Support

[6] See North [1990] I Hague Recueil 9, 63–74.
[7] Law Commission Working Paper No. 89 (1985), p.60.

for the idea that the Cheshire approach embodies choice also comes, paradoxically, from the opposition that has been expressed to it on the ground that parties ought not to be given the freedom to select the law to govern matters of capacity.[8]

On the other hand, the Morris approach, the dual domicile test, involves a much more limited and more indirect element of choice by the parties. The determination of a person's domicile is governed by rules of law, which by way of aside are both complex and in need of reform.[9] It is not possible expressly to choose a domicile. Expressions of such intent are to be given due consideration but they are not binding on a court and indeed have to be treated with some caution. This means that the way in which choice is exercised is simply by means of selecting those aspects of life, such as residence, citizenship, house purchase or even choice of a burial plot, which then cause a court to decide that the necessary intention and factual connection are present so as to lead to the conclusion that a domicile of choice has been acquired. Although it is undoubtedly the case that in some contexts, most notably taxation, such choices are consciously made in order to affect the conclusion as to the acquisition of a domicile, this seems to be far more improbable in the context of the law to govern the essential validity of a marriage. Were the relevant connecting factor to be habitual residence which is less hedged about with technical rules and which has, indeed, been proposed in Ireland as the major connecting factor for essential validity,[10] then it would be more likely that choice would in fact be exercised through selection of the connections which constitute habitual residence.

It has to be accepted that the element of choice of the applicable law involved in voluntary selection of those factors which lead to the conclusion of the acquisition of a domicile or habitual residence is both limited and indirect. On the other hand, there is considerably more reality of choice involved in the selection of the place of the intended matrimonial home, of the celebration of the marriage and, indeed, of the forum for a divorce petition. What is interesting is that this does not seem to have led on to any suggestion, either judicially or in law reform proposals, that the spouses should have a broader and more direct freedom to choose the law applicable to such matrimonial issues. The main reasons for this seem to be twofold. The first, adverted to already, is that issues of essential validity amount predominantly to issues of capacity and it is often stated that parties should not, by choosing the applicable law, be

---

[8] *E.g. Muhammad* v. *Suna* 1956 S.C. 366, 370; and see Anton, *Private International Law*, 2nd ed. (1990), p.429; North [1990] I Hague Recueil 9, 65–66.

[9] See Law Com. No. 168 (1987).

[10] Irish Law Reform Commission Report (1985) L.R.C. 19.

able to confer capacity on themselves. The second is that marriage is to be regarded as more of a status than a contract with the corollary that "its incidents are determined not by the will of the parties but by the prescriptions of the law."[11] Such a statement is however, in the international context, more impressive than convincing. It assumes that there is a readily identified, obviously correct "law" to be applied, free from determination by the will of the parties. That that is a rash assumption in English private international law is revealed by the lack of certainty as to what law does in fact govern matters of essential validity. The issue has been discussed for well over a century and is still not finally resolved. It is also rash because, as has been seen, the parties may by indirect choice exercise a considerable influence on the determination of the substantive marriage law to be applied. Such indirect choice is seen at its most significant in the U.S.A. where the basic choice of law rule is that essential, as well as formal, validity is to be governed by the law of the place of celebration,[12] which place is, of course, chosen by the parties.

(c) Choice through pleading

Another form of implied choice can be illustrated by the fact that the law reports provide many examples of cases where the foreign elements of a dispute have been ignored, with the result that English law alone has been applied. These examples stem from the common law rules relating to the pleading and proof of foreign law.[13] Foreign law is to be proved as a matter of fact and it is entirely up to one or other of the parties to decide whether or not to plead evidence of foreign law. If neither does so, then the court assumes that the rules of the foreign legal system otherwise applicable are the same as English law, which law is then applied.

There can, in fact, be at least three different types of situation involved. The first is where no attention is drawn to the foreign elements in the case. In these circumstances, the case proceeds as an entirely English case without there even being an assumption that foreign rules are the same as English rules; the case does not get as far as identifying which foreign rules might be applied were they to be proved. The second type of case is where it is apparent, for example from the terms of a contract which has been put in evidence, that the dispute is to be governed by foreign law but neither party chooses to plead it. The third type of case is really a variant on this but one where the parties' decision is express,

[11] Anton, *Private International Law*, 2nd ed. (1990), pp.418–419.

[12] See Scoles and Hay, *Conflict of Laws* (1982) pp.421 *et seq.*

[13] Cheshire and North, *Private International Law*, 12th ed. (1992), ch. 7; and see Kahn-Freund [1974] III Hague Recueil 139, 422–426.

rather than inferred from inactivity, namely where they agree, rightly or wrongly, that the foreign rules are the same as the English rules.[14]

The overall effect of these rules is that, through a procedural device, the parties can by agreement, which is more likely to stem from common inaction than from specific consensus, exercise a choice as to the law to govern their dispute. Admittedly the choice is limited in that failure to plead foreign law always leads to the application of the law of the English forum. The effect of the device is, however, not only to cause English law to be applied to an issue where the application of foreign law has not expressly been raised, but also to act in substance as a variation of a choice of law clause. If the parties agree that New York law is to govern their contract but neither pleads New York law, the effect is a consensual application of English law thus, in essence, varying the choice of law clause.[15]

It may be argued that there is a whole variety of reasons why foreign law is not, in fact, pleaded.[16] This is no doubt true. For example, it may be too complicated or expensive to determine the foreign rules of law;[17] there may be a lack of confidence that the process of proof using conflicting expert witnesses will in fact lead to a correct determination of the foreign law;[18] or it may indeed be the case that lawyers wish to avoid the "uncertainties and ambiguities"[19] which are still to be found in the English choice of law process. Nevertheless, though the reasons for running to the security of the law of the forum may be mixed and may indeed differ as between the parties to the litigation, there seems little doubt that reliance on this pleading device can provide a valid example of freedom of choice, albeit one which is more often implicit than explicit.

III Direct choice

(a) Contract

We tend, today, to regard the law of contract as providing the firmest example of the freedom of the parties directly to choose

[14] *E.g. E Pfeiffer Weinkellerei-Weineinkauf GmbH & Co.* v. *Arbuthnot Factors Ltd.* [1988] 1 W.L.R. 150.

[15] See North in *Multum Non Multa*, Festschrift fur Kurt Lipstein, 205, 214.

[16] Fentiman (1992) 108 L.Q.R. 142, 150–152; and see Schlesinger (1973) 59 Cornell L. Rev. 1, 2–3.

[17] *Muduroglu Ltd.* v. *T. C. Ziraat Bankasi* [1986] Q.B. 1225, at 1246.

[18] It seems clear, for example, in *Sayers* v. *International Drilling Co. N.V.* [1971] 1 W.L.R. 1176 that a crucial mistake was made as to the Dutch law relating to employment contracts; see De Boer, *Beyond Lex Loci Delicti* (1987) pp.185–186.

[19] Fentiman (1992) 108 L.Q.R. 142, 151.

the legal system to govern their rights and obligations.[20] The role of party autonomy has been put beyond doubt by the 1980 Rome Convention on the Law Applicable to Contractual Obligations, given the force of law in this country by the Contracts (Applicable Law) Act 1990.[21] Article 3(1) of the Convention is quite clear on this point, providing that:

> "A contract shall be governed by the law chosen by the parties. The choice must be expressed or demonstrated with reasonable certainty by the terms of the contract or the circumstances of the case."

What is also worth noting is how unfettered is this freedom. At common law, there was debate as to the limits of the freedom of choice. We were told that the choice had to be "bona fide and legal" and not contrary to public policy.[22] There was debate as to how far a law unconnected with the contract could be chosen; though it has been pointed out that commercial men and women are likely to have good reasons, which should be accepted, for such a choice.[23] Under the Convention, there are no real limits on the freedom of choice of the applicable law, as such. However, mandatory rules of the forum will continue to be applied,[24] and rules of the chosen law may be refused application as being contrary to the public policy of the forum.[25] These are likely to be relatively minor limitations in practice and the Convention marks a high point in the acceptance of party autonomy.

Whilst there is no intention to examine closely the detailed rules on freedom of choice in contract, not least because such freedom is generally accepted, it may be of interest to point to reasons why such freedom is accepted here, because such reasons may well inform consideration of whether freedom of choice should be extended to choice of law rules in other contexts. One reason peculiar to contracts is that "contracting parties can best select for themselves the law appropriate to the system of reciprocal obligations they intend to establish".[26] If they voluntarily enter into a contract, then they should be allowed also to choose the applicable law. Other suggested reasons have a wider scope than

[20] For an historical and comparative account of the development of autonomy in contract, see Yntema (1952) 1 Am. Jo. Comp. L. 341.

[21] See Plender, *The European Contracts Convention* (1991), ch. 5.

[22] *Vita Food Products Inc.* v. *Unus Shipping Co. Ltd.* [1939] A.C. 277 at 290.

[23] F. A. Mann (1987) 36 I.C.L.Q. 437, 447.

[24] Art. 7(2). The United Kingdom has exercised the power of reservation, under Art. 22(1)(a), not to apply Art. 7(1); see Contracts (Applicable Law) Act 1990, s.2(2). It is also the case, under Art. 3(3), that choice of the law of one country when all the elements of the contract but for the choice are connected with the law of another country is not to prejudice the application of the mandatory rules of that second country.

[25] Art. 16.

[26] Anton, *Private International Law*, 2nd ed. (1990), p.264.

contract. The parties may wish to secure the application of a system of law or indeed, through a jurisdiction clause, a forum which is "neutral as between them".[27] This interest could, in some circumstances, as we shall see, be relevant elsewhere in the law of obligations, in particular in the law of torts. Furthermore, issues raising matters of private international law can be redolent of uncertainty. Taking an example from the present context, the rules for the determination of the applicable law in contract used, at common law, to depend on finding the country of closest connection; that is still the case under the Rome Convention subject to the application of rebuttable presumptions, not the least of which is that of "characteristic performance".[28] Here lies uncertainty which to the businessman or woman is both inconvenient and expensive. But such uncertainty is not the exclusive prerogative of contract choice of law rules. It can be found wherever the law has failed to develop clear choice of law rules, as is the case in the context of the essential validity of marriage, or where the rule is clear but its application is not, as with any rule which is dependent on the present law of domicile as its operative connecting factor. Freedom of choice in contract can be justified as desirable because the parties need certainty in order to plan their future affairs. They are looking at their legal obligations prospectively rather than retrospectively—what Kahn-Freund has described as the "prophylactic" function of choice of law rules.[29] This need to plan ahead is, as suggested earlier, not restricted to contracts. It can be seen most clearly also in relation to marriage, and to the making of wills and to the creation of trusts. It may have a role to play in the field of torts and in other aspects of property law.

It has been said in favour of freedom of choice in contract that "To allow the parties to choose the localising elements, yet to restrict them in their choice of law, is inconsistent".[30] This argument also has a force beyond contract. It could be taken to support freedom of choice virtually everywhere, in that parties often choose the elements which constitute a specific connecting factor, as has been shown earlier in relation to marriage. More specifically, it would support some freedom of choice where the general choice of law rule is based on the idea of closeness of connection as, for example, some have suggested for some types of marriage issue[31] or has variously been propounded in the field of tort in the form of the proper law of the tort,[32] as a flexible exception to the current

[27] *Ibid.*
[28] Art. 4(2).
[29] [1974] III Hague Recueil 147, 341, 344.
[30] F. A. Mann (1950) 3 I.L.Q. 60, 68.
[31] See North [1990] I Hague Recueil 9, 63–68.
[32] Morris (1951) 64 Harv. L. Rev. 881.

double actionability[33] rules, or as the residual choice of law rule under the Law Commissions' proposals for reform.[34]

(b) Choice of choice of law rules

Before turning, however, to look more directly at choice of law in tort, the wide freedom to choose the applicable law in contract leads on to a different, but related, issue. Though it is an issue theoretically of general application, it has arisen most recently in the context of contract choice of law rules and that is where it is most convenient to examine it. The broad question of whether parties are free to select the substantive law to be applied to a legal issue arising in the trans-national context masks a logically anterior question. This is whether the parties have any freedom to choose the choice of law rules which are to be applied to determine the governing substantive law. What seems generally to have been accepted is that it is the law of the country of the forum, not the parties, which decides on the rules to be applied. Thus choice of law rules have been described as "the rules voluntarily chosen by a given State for the decision of cases which have a foreign complexion".[35] This has the effect for example that, when a court is considering the meaning and extent of a connecting factor such as domicile or habitual residence, it applies the rules laid down in forum law, as part of its rules of private international law, to resolve this issue. Reference is not generally made to rules relating to such issues under a foreign law.

If there seems little doubt of the correctness of the statement that the choice of law rules of a state "are as much part of its own territorial law as those that regulate the conveyance of land in its own country",[36] why, then, is it even worth discussing whether the parties have any freedom to choose the applicable choice of law rules? The answer lies in a recent suggestion by Francis Mann that, at least in the field of contract, such a choice may be available.[37] This suggestion arose in the context of a further,[38] and sadly final, attack by him on the Contracts (Applicable Law) Act 1990 and the (1980) Rome Convention on the Law Applicable to Contractual Obligations to which it gives effect. Francis Mann and I have had very differing views as to the acceptability of the new European Community-wide choice of law rules contained in the Rome

[33] *Boys* v. *Chaplin* [1971] A.C. 356.

[34] Law Com. No. 193 (1990), Draft Tort and Delict (Applicable Law) Bill, clause 2(3), (4).

[35] Baty, *Polarized Law*, p.148.

[36] Cheshire and North, *Private International Law*, 12th ed. (1992), p.39; and see Anton, *Private International Law*, 2nd ed. (1990) pp.2–3.

[37] (1991) 107 L.Q.R. 353.

[38] For an earlier one, see, *e.g.*, (1983) 32 I.C.L.Q. 265, 266.

Convention.[39] This is not the place, however, to examine that broad issue,[40] but rather his suggestion that, in his words, "the unfortunate consequences which are likely to show up in the future"[41] might be avoided by contractual choice of law provisions. Terms suggested by him included choice by the parties of "English law excluding the Act of 1990" or "English law as in force on March 31, 1991", *i.e.* the day before the 1990 Act came into force. His justification for such an approach was that not all law is mandatory and that in contract the parties often have the freedom to exclude statutory provisions, such as those, for example, of the Sale of Goods Act 1979. Furthermore, as the Rome Convention expressly allows the parties freedom to choose the law to govern their contract,[42] it seems reasonable, it was said, for it not to preclude freedom to choose a system of choice of law independent of the Convention.

This suggestion raises a variety of problems. First, it has to be pointed out that the freedom to agree by contract not to apply implied terms in the Sale of Goods Act 1979 is a freedom which is different in kind from the freedom under consideration here. We are concerned with a freedom to agree by contract to determine the law to govern the validity of a contract otherwise than by reference to the choice of law rules laid down by the legislature of the forum for that purpose. There are two types of issue here, one of detail and the other of broad principle. The issue of detail is whether there is anything in the 1990 Act or in the Rome Convention to support the idea that the choice of law rules therein are voluntary, giving the parties freedom to decide whether or not they should operate. This issue has been examined by a more recent commentator who, through analysis of the provisions of the Convention, suggests that its choice of law rules are mandatory.[43] For example, the Convention gives States an express power[44] not to apply certain provisions,[45] and this carries a clear implication that there is no power in a State and, a fortiori, in parties to a particular contract to contract out of other provisions. Reliance is also placed on Article 15 of the Convention which excludes the

[39] See correspondence in *The Times*, December 14 and 19, 1989.

[40] His comment, however, at (1991) 107 L.Q.R. 353, 355, that the 1990 Act was passed without consultation with lawyers and traders cannot be left to go unchallenged. Not only was there extensive consultation during the years of negotiation which led to the conclusion of the Rome Convention, there was also consultation by the Lord Chancellor's Department with judges and others on a range of issues before the Bill which became the 1990 Act was introduced.

[41] (1991) 107 L.Q.R. 353, 355.

[42] See Art. 3.

[43] Hogan (1992) 108 L.Q.R. 12.

[44] Art. 22(1).

[45] Arts. 7(1), 10(1)(e).

operation of renvoi by stating that "The application of the law of any country specified by this Convention means the application of the rules of law in force in that country other than its rules of private international law". It is said, correctly in my view, that choice of the former English choice of law rules would infringe the provisions of Article 15 both because the choice was not of substantive contract law rules and because it was of rules which are no longer "in force" in England. That does not, however, deal with the more fundamental argument that the parties may wish to choose the old common law choice of law rules, thus excluding the Convention rules, including Article 15 itself.

That takes us to the broader issue. There is no doubt that those who drafted the Rome Convention took the view that its choice of law provisions were mandatory, not optional. As is said in the Giuliano and Lagarde Report on the Convention, "the chief aim of the Convention is to introduce into the national laws of the EEC Member States a set of uniform rules on the law applicable to contractual obligations and on certain general points of private international law to the extent that these are linked with those obligations".[46] It was made quite clear that those uniform rules are in substitution for existing national rules of private international law.[47] Furthermore, for such uniform rules to be other than mandatory would be inconsistent with one of the perceived objects of the Convention,[48] namely to act as an adjunct to the (1968) Brussels Convention on jurisdiction and enforcement of judgments in civil and commercial matters so as to ensure that, under the uniform jurisdictional rules, the same law is applied irrespective of the Contracting State in which the case is heard. No-one has yet argued that the rules of the Brussels Convention as implemented by the Civil Jurisdiction and Judgments Act 1982 are optional!

It is suggested, therefore, that there is nothing in the new choice of law legislation on contracts which either does, or should, undermine the basic rule that it is for the forum, and not the parties, to determine what set of choice of law rules is to be applied. That is, of course, without prejudice to the question whether the forum's rules allow choice of the substantive law to be applied. Indeed the weakness in the Mann argument lies in the implied assumption that, even before the 1990 Act, parties could have chosen French rather than English choice of law rules to determine the law applicable to their contract. Of such freedom not only is there no evidence, but there is clear judicial authority

46 O.J.C. 282/8, October 31, 1980.

47 *Ibid*, 282/13.

48 *Ibid*, 282/4–5; and see Plender, *The European Contracts Convention* (1991), p.7.

that an English court had to apply English choice of law rules.[49] The broad freedom to choose the law applicable to contracts does not, therefore, extend to a freedom also to choose the choice of law rules applicable to contractual, or any other, issues.

(c) Tort

As contractual obligations arise, in form at least, from the voluntary agreement of the parties it is not surprising that, as we have seen, private international law rules extend that freedom to choice of the applicable substantive law. If, however, we turn to another major area of the law of obligations, tort, is a similar freedom to be found? It is certainly the case that there is no reported judicial examination in England of whether the parties can choose the law to govern their liability in tort. However, in Europe, for example, there is support in Germany[50] and the Netherlands[51] for some freedom to choose the law to govern tort liability. Moreover, the recent Swiss Law on Private International Law also confers an express but limited freedom of choice on the parties in tort cases;[52] it allows the parties, at any time after the tort was committed, to choose the application of the law of the forum,[53] *i.e.* Swiss law.[54] This is, of course, no wider a choice than parties to English litigation could make procedurally by declining to plead foreign law.[55] There is, however, American authority apparently upholding a wider freedom of choice.[56]

This willingness to give some rein to the parties' choice of the applicable law is also evidenced in the Law Commissions' work on the reform of the tort choice of law rules. In their substantial Working Paper,[57] published in 1984, two main Models for reform

[49] See, *e.g. Banco Atlantico S.A.* v. *The British Bank of the Middle East* [1990] 2 Lloyd's Rep. 504, 506.

[50] See Kahn-Freund [1974] III Hague Recueil 139, 341 n.44.

[51] De Boer, *Beyond Lex Loci Delicti* (1987) pp.66–67, 101. It is interesting to note the discussion, on p.67 n.177, of the further Dutch proceedings in the leading case before the European Court of Justice on jurisdiction over tort claims under Art. 5(3) of the Brussels Convention on jurisdiction and enforcement of judgments: Case 21/76 *Bier B.V.* v. *Mines de Potasse d'Alsace S.A.* [1976] E.C.R. 1735; [1978] Q.B. 708, where a choice of Dutch law was upheld. See also De Boer (1990) 54 RabelsZ 24, 38.

[52] Art. 132. For an English translation, see Simeonides (1989) 38 Am. Jo. Comp. Law 187; and see Samuel (1988) 37 I.C.L.Q. 681.

[53] An earlier draft of the Swiss Law allowed a choice also of the law of the parties' common habitual residence, see McCaffrey (1980) 28 Am. Jo. Comp. L. 235, 280.

[54] The Dutch case referred to in n.51 above also in fact involved a choice of forum law.

[55] Discussed above.

[56] *E.g. Camporese* v. *Port Authority of New York and New Jersey*, 415 N.Y.S. 2d 28 (1979), affd 426 N.Y.S. 2d 977 (1980).

[57] Law Commission Working Paper No. 87 (1984). For comments thereon, see Fawcett (1985) 48 M.L.R. 439.

were proposed for consultation one was essentially the application of the law of the place of the tort, subject to an exception in favour of the law of the country of closest connection, and the other involved the application of the law of the country of closest connection subject to presumptions that that was the place of the tort. What is significant here is that both of those solutions were qualified by the parties' freedom to choose the applicable law. The Commissions provisionally proposed that "it should be possible (before or after a tort or delict occurred) to agree by means of contract what law should govern the parties' mutual liability in tort or delict. Such agreement should be effective whether or not it results in the application of the law of the forum".[58]

This proposal has been welcomed as "long overdue";[59] though there is little doubt that, embodied in legislative form, it would need further elaboration in order to determine whether there were to be any limits on the freedom of choice in terms of the law which might be chosen, such as whether any other connection with the chosen law was required, and to determine the extent to which the public policy or mandatory rules of the forum, English law, would continue to operate despite a choice by the parties.[60] There would be nothing new in all of that. After all it would amount simply to the application in the tort context of details which have been developed for choice of law in contract.[61] When we turn, however, to the Law Commissions' Report on Choice of Law in Tort and Delict[62] not only is there no provision in the draft Tort and Delict (Applicable Law) Bill allowing for freedom of choice, there is no discussion of the issue at all in the body of the Report. The matter has disappeared without trace. It exclusion from any legislation based on the draft Bill would effectively exclude it from English choice of law rules, because the draft Bill itself makes clear that the choice of law rules in tort are to be those laid down in the Bill. In any event, it seems highly improbable that courts would feel free to develop at common law a concept of party autonomy in tort alongside a regime of statutory choice of law rules.[63]

---

58 *Ibid*, p.265, and see para. 4.21.

59 Castel, *Canadian Conflict of Laws*, 2nd ed. (1986), p.621.

60 One strange limitation that has been proposed is that freedom of choice should be allowed only if permitted by the law of the country or countries which would otherwise govern liability; see Kaye, *Private International Law of Tort and Product Liability* (1991), p.63. To adopt such a limitation would defeat much of the purpose of permitting party autonomy in the field of tort law.

61 Contracts (Applicable Law) Act 1990, Sch. 1, Arts. 3, 7, 16.

62 Law Com. No. 193 (1990). For general discussion of the Report, see Kaye, *Private International Law of Tort and Product Liability* (1991), chs. 16–18; Carter (1991) 107 L.Q.R. 405; North (1991) 42 N.I.L.Q. 183, 194–198.

63 See the discussion, above, of the idea that parties could choose not to apply the rules in the Contracts (Applicable Law) Act 1990.

Whether the introduction of some freedom of choice were to be effected by legislation or by judicial development, there remains the question whether it is desirable or realistic for the law to move in that direction. It is obviously the case that responsible people usually neither wish nor plan to commit torts against others. There is not the same degree of forward planning of relationships and obligations as exists in contract. That does not mean that there is no room for the operation of choice before a tort is committed. The *possibility* of being liable in tort is not necessarily far from people's minds. It is always, formally, present in terms of use of a motor vehicle through the need to take out at least third party insurance, coupled with the desirability of extending insurance cover through the Green Card scheme when taking the vehicle abroad. This was put graphically by Kahn-Freund over twenty years ago, when he said: " 'When in Rome do as the Romans do' reads in our world 'when in Rome see that your insurance policy covers the risks against which Romans insure' ".[64] Obviously if I have a traffic accident in Rome in which an Italian is injured, there is little prospect that the victim and I will earlier have agreed what law is to govern his tort claim. The position may well be very different if the accident injures, instead, a passenger in my car who has travelled with me from England to Italy. Other striking examples can be provided by situations where the parties are in a contractual relationship but the plaintiff wishes to formulate a claim in tort, as where an employee injured abroad wishes to sue his employer[65] or a passenger injured on a foreign holiday coach trip wishes to sue the bus company. The contract of employment or of travel might well include a choice of law clause. It would not, it is suggested, be improper for that clause to extend from contractual to tortious liability or indeed for the contract to make separate choice of law provision for each.[66]

Once a tort has been committed, choice of the applicable law ceases to have a prophylactic or prospective planning role to play, but may well be at least as, if not more, significant. In such a case the plaintiff is now identified, as are the substantive tort laws which may have a claim to being applied. Arguments advanced earlier relating to expense, difficulties of proof of foreign law, and the uncertainties of the litigation process come into play. These are strengthened when the generally applicable tort choice of law rules

[64] Kahn-Freund [1968] II Hague Recueil 5, 44.

[65] *E.g. Coupland* v. *Arabian Gulf Oil Co.* [1983] 1 W.L.R. 1136; *cf. Matthews* v. *Kuwait Bechtel Corpn.* [1959] 2 Q.B. 57.

[66] Though in the employment context, the freedom of choice might need to be restricted to the same extent as it is for contractual claims: Contracts (Applicable Law) Act 1990, Sch. 1, Art. 6; and see Morse (1992) 41 I.C.L.Q. 1.

are as unsatisfactory as are the present common law rules,[67] requiring as they do actionability by both the law of the forum and the place of the tort, coupled with an exception thereto of indeterminate range and scope.[68] Parties may well conclude that their dispute must be litigated but may, in some cases, be able to agree on the law to be applied. Subject to the broad public policy safeguards also available to a court when asked to apply foreign law, there seems no reason why the choice of the parties should be restricted, as in Switzerland or under the English pleading device, to the law of the forum. Indeed an obvious law on which to agree might be that of the place where the tort was committed. Certainly, the Law Commissions' reform proposals do not provide so clear an answer in all varied tort cases as to obviate the desirability of rules permitting choice being introduced in any implementing legislation. Such a course would be both prudent and practical.

(d) Property

Turning now to property law, support for party autonomy may be found in both choice of law rules relating to trusts and settlements, and to wills. These will be considered in turn.

(i) Trusts

It seems to have been accepted at common law, in relation both to testamentary[69] and inter vivos trusts,[70] that the settlor might either expressly or impliedly choose the law to govern the validity of the trust. This would appear to have been the case whether the choice was of foreign law by an English domiciled testator or settlor, or of English law by a foreign domiciliary.[71] Such an approach is confirmed by the Recognition of Trusts Act 1987 which gives effect in this country to the (1986) Hague Convention on the Law Applicable to Trusts and on their Recognition. Under Article 6, a trust is to be governed by the law expressly or impliedly chosen. The chosen law is given wide effect in that it governs the validity of the trust (presumably both essential and formal), its construction, effects and administration.[72] Furthermore, express approval is given to the idea that severable aspects of the trust may be governed by different laws.[73] One interesting facet of this general statutory

[67] *Phillips* v. *Eyre* (1870) L.R. 6 Q.B. 1; *Boys* v. *Chaplin* [1971] A.C. 356.

[68] For criticisms, see North [1990] I Hague Recueil 9, 206 *et seq.*

[69] *Re Lord Cable* [1977] 1 W.L.R. 7 at 20; and see *Att.-Gen.* v. *Campbell* (1872) L.R. 5 H.L. 524; *Re Healy's Will* 125 N.Y.S. 2d 486 (1953).

[70] Apart from the decisions on marriage settlements, see *Augustus* v. *Permanent Trustee Co. (Canberra) Ltd.* (1971) 124 C.L.R. 245; and see *Harris Investments Ltd.* v. *Smith* [1934] D.L.R. 748.

[71] *Cf. Canterbury Corpn.* v. *Wyburn and Melbourne Hospital* [1905] A.C. 89.

[72] Art. 8.

[73] Art. 9.

freedom of choice is that it is subject to few limitations. There is no requirement (as hinted at at common law)[74] that the chosen law should be otherwise connected with the trust. However, a choice will be disregarded if the concept of trust is unknown under the law chosen.[75] Notwithstanding the choice, English courts, as being those of the forum, may still disregard the choice of a law whose application would be contrary to public policy[76] and must[77] apply both English mandatory rules[78] and, in certain circumstances, those of the law of a foreign country.[79] These limitations are, however, not substantial and party autonomy is given very free rein.

The Trusts Convention only provides choice of law rules to govern the validity of a trust which has already been validly created. It makes clear in Article 4 that it is not concerned with the law to determine the validity of the instrument of creation, whether it be an inter vivos or a testamentary trust. If there is an inter vivos trust created by a contract then there is little doubt that the validity of the trust-creating contract is governed by the general rules applicable to contracts. There is, however, very little direct authority on whether parties may choose the law to govern the validity of a voluntary settlement effected by deed; though such as there is supports freedom of choice.[80]

It seems fair to conclude that the factors which have justified a wide freedom of choice in contract have similarly led to the conclusion that, both in the instrument creating an inter vivos trust and in relation to all trusts validly created, such freedom is also justified. One powerful argument here is that the dispositions of property which are being established are normally of a voluntary nature. Furthermore, the settlor, trustees and beneficiaries are all likely to be anxious at the outset to know whether the instrument just created is valid and what legal regime is to govern its, possibly long, life.

---

[74] Dicey and Morris, *The Conflict of Laws*, 11th ed. (1987), p.1074.

[75] Art. 5. Also other Contracting States may refuse to recognise a trust which is most closely connected with a country where trusts are unknown but for the choice of the applicable law, the place of administration and the habitual residence of the trustee: Art. 13. The United Kingdom has chosen not to exercise this power in relation to foreign trusts.

[76] Art. 18.

[77] Recognition of Trusts Act 1987, s.1(3).

[78] Art. 16. The United Kingdom has exercised a power of reservation not to apply the mandatory rules of sufficiently closely connected third states under the second paragraph of this Article.

[79] Art. 15.

[80] *Augustus* v. *Permanent Trustee Co. (Canberra) Ltd.* (1971) 124 C.L.R. 245, esp. at 260; and see *Re Pilkington's Will Trusts* [1937] Ch. 574.

(ii) Wills

This then leads on to the question whether similar freedom is to be permitted in the case of wills. If, as the Hague Trusts Convention permits, a testator may by will determine the law to govern the trusts created thereby, may he also by will determine the law to govern its, the will's, validity? Orthodoxy suggests that there is one aspect of the law of wills where effect is certainly to be given to the intentions of the testator and that is in relation to construction of the will.[81]

This seems, however, to be the limit of the freedom afforded to the testator. There is, it appears, no significant place for party autonomy in testate succession. Should this, however, be so? Like making a contract, making a will is a voluntary act. It is not necessary to do so in order to arrange for succession on death. The rules of intestate succession will fill any gap. The disposition of the estate made by the will is also a matter of choice—for example whether assets are left to grandchildren or to charity. Furthermore, the decision whether to establish trusts under the will is again one of choice and, as we have seen, the testator can choose the law to govern those trusts—but not, it appears, to govern the instrument creating them.

It is perfectly understandable that there should be some ways in which the freedom of a testator to dispose of his property as he wishes may be constrained. Obvious examples are the need to protect the financial position of relatives, and some legal systems require a proportion of the estate to be left to a widow or children, to give effect to rules on the remoteness of vesting or rules prohibiting gifts to charities, or to ensure that the law of the situs has ultimate control over land there. It is not, however, self-evident that such concerns should exclude, as opposed to limiting the effect of, freedom of choice.

There is, of course, some limited indirect choice open to a testator in that the essential validity of a will of movables is governed by the law of his domicile on death. However, the testator may have made his will having in mind the law of his domicile at the time of making it, only for his beneficiaries to find the testator's wishes frustrated by a conclusion that his domicile had changed before death. It is, of course, an answer to say that if the testator changed his domicile he should change his will but that is requiring him to do indirectly what free choice would have allowed him to do directly. Furthermore, the complexities of the law of domicile are such that he may not know whether or not it has changed.

[81] See *Philipson-Stow* v. *Inland Revenue Commissioners* [1961] A.C. 727 at 761; and see *Bradford* v. *Young* (1885) 29 Ch.D. 617 at 623, 625.

The voluntary nature of a will and the desirability of determining its incidents and effects when it is made provide strong arguments for party autonomy. As pointed out earlier, if the testator can choose the law to govern the essential validity of the trusts he creates by his will, is it not reasonable that he should have some freedom to choose the law to govern the validity of the legal instrument which creates those trusts?[82] It should not be overlooked that the case for freedom of choice, albeit of a somewhat limited kind, has been accepted in the (1988) Hague Convention on the Law Applicable to Succession to the Estates of Deceased Persons. Whilst this has not, as yet, proved to be a particularly successful Hague Convention,[83] and is one which I believe to be seriously flawed in a number of respects,[84] it has the interesting feature of allowing the deceased to choose the law to govern succession to his estate, whether testate or intestate. Indeed this freedom of choice has been described as a "main characteristic" of the Convention.[85] Choice takes two forms. The deceased may, under Article 5(1), choose the law of his nationality or habitual residence, either at the time of choice or of death, to govern succession to his whole estate. This cautious approach, limiting the range of choices, was thought desirable because party autonomy in succession matters was a new proposition for virtually all states.[86] Freedom of choice is, however, extended in that the deceased may choose other laws, such as the law of the situs, to govern succession to particular assets, though subject to the mandatory rules of the otherwise applicable law.[87] Whilst this two-pronged approach makes for an unnecessarily complex structure of rules, and whilst it may be argued that the general freedom of choice conferred by the Convention is unduly limited, nevertheless the party autonomy provisions of the Convention undoubtedly provide a helpful model on which reform of our succession choice of law rules might build.

---

[82] It is also reasonable to suggest that freedom of choice has effect elsewhere in the law of property. For example, in the case of assignment reference is made either to the contract of assignment or to that under which the original debt arose: Contracts (Applicable Law) Act 1990, Sch. 1, Art. 12. Freedom of choice will apply to both those contracts. A case can also be made for party autonomy when dealing with the transfer of tangible movables, leaving only a residual role for the law of the situs.

[83] It has been signed by only two states and ratified by none.

[84] North [1990] I Hague Recueil 9, 278–282.

[85] Waters, Explanatory Report on the Convention, Actes et Documents de la Seizième Session, Vol. II 526, 535.

[86] Switzerland was an exception; see Lagarde (1989) 78 Rev Crit dr int privé 249, 260, and see the Swiss Statute on Private International Law, 1987, Arts 90–91.

[87] Art. 6.

IV Conclusions

The choice of law process involves, as I have endeavoured to show, a range of ways in which the parties may influence the law to govern the transnational legal issue with which they may be faced. This influence is less obvious where it is exercised through indirect choice of connecting factors, through choice of the forum or through choice of English law by reason of pleading no other. Whilst, however, it may be less obvious than direct choice of the applicable law, it is not a negligible influence. Direct choice of the applicable law, so long regarded as a characteristic of contract but not of other areas of law, is undoubtedly growing in acceptability. It is now established in the law of trusts and also of marriage settlements. It forms part of the law reform debate on choice of law in tort and in succession.

This is, I suggest, a significant and welcome development. Ease of travel and communication mean that the lives of far more people are touched by transnational problems than ever was the case a few decades ago. Wisely, the majority wish to avoid the difficulties which may arise and which private international law rules are designed to resolve. They certainly wish to avoid the cost and anxiety of the litigation process. Choice of law rules should be designed to fulfil this prophylactic role. This is why choice in choice of law is so important.

Forum Law and Foreign Law

[6]

MICHIGAN LAW REVIEW

Vol. 58 MARCH 1960 No. 5

THE LEX FORI — BASIC RULE IN THE CONFLICT OF LAWS

*Albert A. Ehrenzweig**

A. Lex Fori: Exception or Rule?

ONCE a court has taken jurisdiction, it will usually apply its own law, unless the parties' own choice or an important foreign fact, such as a foreign domicile, a foreign situs, or a foreign conduct, appears to require application of another law. Most judges and lawyers will agree with this simple proposition—and yet text books, class notes, the *Restatement,* and even much language of the courts, would have it otherwise: foreign domicile, foreign situs, foreign conduct and other foreign "contacts" are said a priori to require application of a foreign law, unless the court can be persuaded for special reasons to turn to its own law or to the law chosen by the parties. This blatant discrepancy between the actual doing of the courts and "official" theory in the law of conflict of laws has made an awesome mystery or an object of ridicule of this subject in the eyes of many. The time has come for a stock taking and re-evaluation of accepted techniques in the light of practical needs, history and comparison.

* Walter Perry Johnson Professor of Law, University of California, Berkeley.

Note. The following works (treatises and articles) will be referred to herein only by the names of their authors: BATIFFOL, TRAITÉ ÉLÉMENTAIRE DE DROIT INTERNATIONAL PRIVÉ, 2d ed. (1955); BEALE, A TREATISE ON THE CONFLICT OF LAWS OR PRIVATE INTERNATIONAL LAW (1916); CHESHIRE, PRIVATE INTERNATIONAL LAW, 5th ed. (1957); DICEY, CONFLICT OF LAWS, 7th ed. (1958); EHRENZWEIG, CONFLICT OF LAWS (1959); FALCONBRIDGE, ESSAYS ON THE CONFLICT OF LAWS, 2d ed. (1954); GAMILLSCHEG, DER EINFLUSS DUMOULINS AUF DIE ENTWICKLUNG DES KOLLISIONSRECHTS (1955); Gutzwiller, "Le développment historique du droit international privé," 29 RECUEIL DES COURS 289 at 298 (1929). LAINÉ, INTRODUCTION AU DROIT INTERNATIONAL PRIVÉ (1888); Meijers, "L'Histoire des principes fondamentaux au droit international privé à partir du moyen âge," 49 RECUEIL DES COURS 547 (1934); NEUMEYER, DIE GEMEINRECHTLICHE ENTWICKELUNG DES INTERNATIONALEN PRIVAT-UND STRAFRECHTS BIS BARTOLUS (1901, 1916); NIEDERER, EINFÜHRUNG IN DIE ALLEGMEINEN LEHREN DES INTERNATIONALEN PRIVATRECHTS (1954); NUSSBAUM, PRINCIPLES OF PRIVATE INTERNATIONAL LAW (1943); QUADRI, LEZIONI DI DIRITTO INTERNAZIONALE PRIVATO, 2d ed. (1958); STORY, COMMENTARIES ON THE CONFLICT OF LAWS (1834); WOLFF, PRIVATE INTERNATIONAL LAW, 2d ed. (1950).

I am indebted to Professor Rodolfo de Nova for many valuable suggestions offered during the completion of my research at the University of Pavia.—A.A.E.

For several centuries courts have, in varying ways and degrees, recognized foreign contracts or testaments which were valid under the law of their execution, permitted an alleged wrongdoer to show that he acted lawfully under the law of his conduct, or treated the transfer of foreign land in accordance with the law of its situs. Refinements have resulted in longer lists of such exceptions from the basic rule of the law of the forum. But it should not have been forgotten that foreign laws originally assumed these functions only to fill vacua created by superior legal orders or the forum's self-limitation. The Pope could and did prohibit the bishop from enforcing the law of his diocese against foreigners; the feudal creed could and did prevent the court of Paris from applying its own law to land in Lyon; the parties' choice could and did exclude the rules of the forum; the United States Constitution and international treaties can, and do at times, prohibit states from applying their own laws "extraterritorially." In all these cases foreign laws have supplemented, rather than displaced, a law of the forum limited by superior orders. Self-limitations of that law have had the same effect. Sister state customs were admitted in medieval Italy, where city ordinances would in terms limit themselves to citizens. Foreign customs were applied in feudal France, where seignorial courts would grant (and expect) localization of statuta realia. The laws of other sovereigns were extended courtesy in the Dutch provinces whose laws in turn had disclaimed ubiquitous validity. The "civil ley" of the world community of commerce was applied in English courts merchant where the common law had denied itself to foreigners and foreign facts. And foreign laws were permitted to operate by "analogy" where "unilateral" or "spatial" rules of modern codes provided for their application to nationals, domiciliaries or domestic transactions.

These situations in which foreign laws have thus been called upon to fill a vacuum could well have been collected and classified in a catalogue of exceptions from the basic rule of the law of the forum, governed by party autonomy on the one hand, Roman common law, feudal order, natural law, the law merchant and international law, on the other hand. Instead, in a gradual process of academic petrification, which reached its climax after, and perhaps because of, the disappearance or weakening of superior orders and ideologies, doctrine has traded the fertile inconsistencies and intricacies which would have characterized this scheme, for the sterile consistencies and simplicities of dogmatic formulas, which distinguish our current "official" law of conflict of laws.

These formulas have in turn relegated both party autonomy and the basic lex fori to the status of exceptions, and have, in spite or rather because of their consistency and simplicity, brought this branch of the law to the brink of defeat.

Beginning with D'Argentré's nearly all-embracing "statuta realia," through Story's private "international" law, Savigny's "seat" of legal relationships, and the English dogma of foreign-created "obligations," to Holmes' "first principles of legal thinking," Beale's "vested rights," and the *Restatement's* "legislative jurisdiction," forum and foreign laws have been made to "govern" by virtue of postulates which have always required, and now lack, foundation and sanction in a superior order. For, all of these orders have long disappeared with the common law of Rome, the feudal order of the Franks, the natural law of Grotius and Pufendorf, and the "civil ley" of the English law merchant. And the internationalist "creed" of the last century is on the wane.[1] Nevertheless, long obsolete ideologies have continued to serve as the bases of the "official" conceptions and language of conflicts law, and have thus caused much unnecessary difficulty and confusion in American decisions, even in those of our most courageous courts which have achieved justice in spite of the conceptions thus forced on them. In a series of articles I have given many examples for this judicial predicament in the conflicts law of torts and contracts conflicts.[2] Mention of two will suffice at this point.

A California citizen was killed in an automobile accident in Arizona. In a California law suit the California defendant claimed that the plaintiff's cause of action had died under "applicable" Arizona law, although California had long abolished what even a hundred years ago was felt to be a rule contrary to "justice,"[3] and

[1] NUSSBAUM 26. This creed had resulted in "a transmutation of forceful liberal and cosmopolitan tendencies into dogmas through a psychological process also observable elsewhere."

[2] Ehrenzweig: "The Real Estate Broker and the Conflict of Laws," 59 COL. L. REV. 303 (1959); "The Statute of Frauds in the Conflict of Laws," 59 COL. L. REV. 874 (1959); "Contracts in the Conflict of Laws," 50 COL. L. REV. 973, 1171 (1959); "Contractual Capacity of Married Women and Infants in the Conflict of Laws," 43 MINN. L. REV. 899 (1959); "Adhesion Contracts in the Conflict of Laws," 53 COL. L. REV. 1072 (1953); Book Review, 12 J. LEGAL ED. 137 (1959); "The Place of Acting in Intentional Multistate Torts," 36 MINN. L. REV. 1 (1951); "Alternative Actionability in the Conflict of Laws of Enterprise Liability," 63 JURID. REV. 39 (1951); "Guest Statutes in the Conflict of Laws," 69 YALE L. J. 595 (1960); and my forthcoming articles, "Alienation of Affections in the Conflict of Laws," 45 CORN. L. Q. —(1960); "Products Liability in the Conflict of Laws," "Vicarious Liability in the Conflict of Laws," 69 YALE L. J. —— (1960).

[3] Beach v. The Bay State Co., 27 Barb. (N.Y.) 248 (1858).

permitted the survival of tort actions. Nevertheless it took the imaginativeness and scholarship of a progressive court to defeat the defendant's seemingly conclusive insistence on the law of the "place of the wrong" in order to do justice between two California citizens according to California law. And in order to be able to do so, the court had to resort to dogmatic language devised 700 years ago for totally different purposes.[4]

An uncle and his niece, both citizens of the Commonwealth of Massachusetts, were traveling through Italy. Desirous of giving his companion a valuable gift, the uncle handed his niece a sealed envelope which contained shares in a Massachusetts corporation. On his death his administrator claimed the shares, because the validity of the transfer "is to be judged by the law of Italy, and . . . certain formalities required by the law" had not been observed. To the Massachusetts court "plainly that which was done in Italy would have been sufficient, if it had been done in Massachusetts, to effect a transfer of legal title to the shares." But, feeling compelled to concede the plaintiff's argument with regard to the transfer of movables in general, the court, in order to do justice between two Massachusetts citizens according to Massachusetts law, had to develop a special rule for shares of stock[5] that may well become a new source of confusion in future cases.[6]

Decisions of this kind could be multiplied at will: from the Connecticut automobile renting agency which could be held liable in Connecticut under Connecticut strict liability law to a Connecticut citizen for a Massachusetts accident only because the court, while conceding the "place of wrong" adage, was able to transform a tort into a contract;[7] to the contract valid under the law of Alaska, the state of the domicile of both parties, which, having accidentally been concluded in New York (where it was invalid) had to be validated in Alaska by resort to renvoi;[8] to the numberless cases in

[4] Grant v. McAuliffe, 41 Cal. (2d) 859, 264 P. (2d) 944 (1953), per Traynor, J. To the contrary, although conceding that "equity" might require another answer, Allen v. Nessler, 247 Minn. 230 at 242, 76 N.W. (2d) 793 (1956), in unfortunate reliance on the *Restatement*, Beale and Wharton, and authors of annotations.

[5] Morson v. Second Nat. Bank of Boston, 306 Mass. 588, 29 N.E. (2d) 19 (1940), per Qua, J.

[6] As long as four centuries ago, Dumoulin, the great advocate of the principle of autonomy, asked the question whether it would be desirable to apply the purely accidental lex contractus to a sale between two foreigners traveling in Italy, of a house located in their home country. MEIJERS 651.

[7] Levy v. Daniels' U-Drive Auto Renting Co., 108 Conn. 333, 143 A. 163 (1928). See also Graham v. Wilkins, 145 Conn. 34, 138 A. (2d) 705 (1958); Ehrenzweig, "Vicarious Liability in the Conflict of Laws," 69 YALE L.J. —— (1960).

[8] Alaska Airlines v. Stephenson, (9th Cir. 1954) 217 F. (2d) 295.

which American courts, in order to be able to apply their own law to the American property of alien decedents, have had to apply artificial techniques of the most varied kinds to justify their preference for American law.[9]

Less frequent, though more disturbing, are those cases in which less courageous judges, or judges less familiar with the tools at their disposal, have more or less grudgingly acquiesced in what they thought to be compelling precedent, and have done injustice by refusing to apply their own laws. Few will be those to acclaim the Alabama court which denied the injury claim of the Alabama brakeman against the Alabama railroad under Alabama law for negligent conduct committed in Alabama because the injury was inflicted in Mississippi and the "Code of Alabama had no efficiency beyond the lines of Alabama,"[10] or the astounding ruling of an Illinois court which, in 1958, denied recovery to an Illinois citizen against Illinois tavern keepers for an injury sustained in an automobile accident caused by a driver to whom defendants had unlawfully sold liquor in violation of the Illinois Dram Shop Act—because the place of the tort or wrong was Missouri, and its laws determine "whether the act . . . gives rise to a cause of action,"[11] or those cases in which courts have refused to limit liability under their own guest statutes, or insisted on applying foreign statutes of this type notwithstanding the fact that both parties were citizens of the forum state and could not possibly have considered foreign standards for their conduct simply because of crossing into another state.[12] In the field of contracts, cases are rare, but equally regrettable, where courts have seen fit to sacrifice the parties' unambiguous intention to the magic of words.[13]

The dogma which has so often either misled the courts during the past few decades, or has forced them into artificial evasions or reluctant acceptance, is being slowly—too slowly— discredited and

[9] See Yiannopoulos, "Wills of Movables in American International Conflicts Law: A Critique of the Domiciliary 'Rule,'" 46 CALIF. L. REV. 185 (1958).

[10] Alabama Great Southern R. Co. v. Carroll, 97 Ala. 126, 11 S. 803 (1892).

[11] Butler v. Wittland, 18 Ill. App. (2d) 578, 153 N.E. (2d) 106 (1958). *Contra*, Schmidt v. Driscoll Hotel, 249 Minn. 376, 82 N.W. (2d) 365 (1957), distinguished on clearly inadequate grounds. See, in general, note, [1958] ILL. L. FORUM 287. Cf. Waynick v. Chicago's Last Dept. Store, (7th Cir. 1959) 269 F. (2d) 322.

[12] See, e.g., Loranger v. Nadeau, 215 Cal. 362, 10 P. (2d) 63 (1932). See, in general, Ehrenzweig, "Guest Statutes in the Conflict of Laws," 69 YALE L.J 595 (1960).

[13] For examples, see Ehrenzweig, "The Statute of Frauds in the Conflict of Laws," 59 COL. L. REV. 874 (1959); "Contracts in the Conflict of Laws," 59 COL. L. REV. 973, 1171 (1960); "Contractual Capacity of Married Women and Infants in the Conflict of Laws," 43 MINN. L. REV. 899 (1959); "Releases of Concurrent Tortfeasors in the Conflict of Laws," 46 VA. L. REV. —— (1960).

destroyed.[14] This task will be rendered easier if we realize that, by expressly treating traditional conflicts rules as exceptions from a basic law of the forum, we would not abandon valuable achievements of a more refined era, nor return to a regrettable "provincial" attitude, but, on the contrary, promote the actual application of foreign law by improving and refining the rules pertaining to specific typical situations. We would merely restore a highly cultured, world-minded law but recently threatened by a nearly world-wide sweep of a dogmatic conceptualism which has sacrificed reality and the painstakingly and slowly progressing idealistic rationalism of centuries to ideological rather than idealistic formulas, at the risk of losing everything and gaining nothing. We shall continue, through international treaties, constitutional control and determined scholarship, to strive for an ever-closer relation between both the world's and the Union's legal systems. But I believe we shall not be able to do so with any hope of success if we continue to speak the language of an unattainable fantasy. Great scholars everywhere, including the "local law" advocates in this country, have long attacked the various techniques of the false internationalism underlying our recent conflicts law. We shall have to find the courage to retrace our steps to that period of American law in which the imaginative searching of a young society for new answers to new problems was not yet obscured and emasculated by the all-too-easy acquiescence in common-place generalizations, a period in which courts still felt free to treat their own law as primarily entitled to application unless displaced by the parties' reliance on another law or similar compelling considerations.

By this return to earlier periods, the superstructure of the last century need not be entirely lost. An important, though yet little-explored achievement of "classic" conceptualism is the "adjustment" to the concepts of forum law of the concepts of the applicable foreign rule.[15] Moreover, there is merit in the compilation of a catalogue of those principles which, though necessarily inconsistent with each other,[16] like all principles of "justice,"[17] may, if

14 NUSSBAUM 26-32; and, in general, EHRENZWEIG 13.

15 See, e.g., Kegel, "Begriffs-und Interessenjurisprudenz im Internationalen Privatrecht," FESTSCHRIFT FÜR LEWALD 259 at 282 (1953).

16 See Wengler, "Die Allgemeinen Rechtsgrundsätze des Internationalen Privatrechts und ihre Kollisionen," 23 ÖFFENTL. RECHT 473 (1943); Wengler, "Les principles généraux du droit international privé et leurs conflits," 41 REV. CRIT. DE DR. INT. 595 (1952); 42 id. 37 (1953). See also Wengler, "Skizzen sur Lehre vom Statutenwechsel," 23 ZEITSCHRIFT FÜR AUSLÄNDISCHES UND INTERNATIONALES PRIVATRECHT 535 (1958) (hereinafter cited RABELS Z.).

applied consciously and without a priori priorities,[18] assist the judge in his decision: the forum's "political" interest including its conception of its "public policy";[19] the substantive harmony between laws applicable to a unitary set of facts, such as a family,[20] a decedent's estate or a contractual relationship; the reduction of possible conflicts between the decision reached by the forum and that likely to be reached by a foreign court as to the same facts;[21] and perhaps the effectuating of as many party expectations as possible.[22]

Finally, acceptance of the lex fori as a basic rule and relegation of traditional conflicts rules to the status of exceptions keyed to ever narrower fact situations[23] will not substantially alter their scope and contents. Lex situs, lex loci and personal law will be called upon, as they are now, to give better "conflicts justice"[24] than the lex fori. But the judge will not have to rely on qualifications, renvoi or public policy to justify his preference for his own or another proper law,[25] and applicability of the foreign law will in each new situation have to be established to his satisfaction.[26] The following summary of this thesis will show its essential connection with the progressing reform of the law of jurisdiction.[27]

The Thesis

1. American courts have in fact nearly always given preference to their own laws in the decision of conflicts cases, both interstate

[17] BIENENFELD, REDISCOVERY OF JUSTICE (1947). Kegel, "Begriffs-und Interessenjurisprudenz im Internationalen Privatrecht," FESTSCHRIFT FÜR LEWALD 259 at 270 (1953), develops a specific concept of "conflicts" justice.

[18] Kegel, note 17 supra, at 268, against Wengler, "Die Allgemeinen Rechtsgrundsätze des Internationales Privatrechts und ihre Kollisionen," 23 Z. ÖFFENTL. RECHT 473 at 497 (1943).

[19] See, in general, Currie's articles cited in EHRENZWEIG 16.

[20] As to "status," see, e.g., 1 RABEL, CONFLICT OF LAWS, 2d ed., 109 (1958). But cf. EHRENZWEIG 85.

[21] Kegel, note 15 supra, at 269, simplifying a longer catalogue of Wengler, note 16 supra. See also Zweigert, "Die dritte Schule im Internationalen Privatrecht," FESTSCHRIFT FÜR RAAPE 35 (1948); Beitzke, "Betrachtungen zur Methodik im Internationalen Privatrecht," FESTSCHRIFT FÜR SMEND 1 (1952).

[22] See Kegel, note 17 supra, at 271. On the lex validitatis in contracts law, see Ehrenzweig, "Contracts in the Conflict of Laws," 59 COL. L. REV. 973 (1959).

[23] Kegel, note 17 supra, at 279.

[24] See Cavers, "A Critique of the Choice-of-Law Problem," 47 HARV. L. REV. 173, 193 (1933); and, in general, EHRENZWEIG 13.

[25] See text accompanying notes 243-339 infra.

[26] See Traynor, "Law and Social Change in a Democratic Society," [1956] ILL. L. FORUM 230 at 234.

[27] See, in general, EHRENZWEIG 88, 120.

and international, and have usually applied foreign law only in situations where such preference was contrary to the intentions of the parties or would have caused hardship on other grounds. The first exception based on the parties' intention is so firmly established that it may be regarded as the second basic rule.[28] Other propositions as to a priori "applicable" or "governing" law, such as the lex loci delicti or situs, and particularly rules serving the unity of status and estates, should be preserved, but only where, and insofar as, they have sufficiently crystallized in certain specific situations so as to be tenable as other exceptions from a basic lex fori.[29]

2. The converse treatment of the lex fori as an exception from such a priori propositions, far from being based on "logical" postulates or practical exigencies, is the heritage of academic aberrations in the history of conflicts law. The latest of these aberrations, in this country as well as abroad, is an internationalist or universalist ideology which has established a fictitious allocation of "competencies" thought to entitle the several laws to ubiquitous application according to a small number of broad and vague formulas.[30] This ideology has forced American courts to justify the actual application of their own law or the law intended by the parties, by various artificial devices such as arbitrary localizations of allegedly decisive contacts, procedural characterization, renvoi and resort to public policy. The current decline of this ideology will facilitate the abandonment of these academic exercises, which is suggested in the final part of this article, and the return to the lex fori as the basic principle, which alone can remove the prevailing uncertainty and confusion.

3. Conscious recognition of this basic principle would concentrate our effort on a search for a scheme of international and interstate jurisdiction which would secure a lex fori properly applicable in view of a substantial contact of the court with parties or facts. Such an effort would be assisted by the current extension of traditional jurisdictional concepts and their concomitant limitations under what may broadly be called a doctrine of forum conveniens.

4. Once the ascertainment of a convenient forum would thus have become the primary object of the law of conflict of laws,

[28] Note 22 supra.

[29] Note 2 supra.

[30] For a bibliography, see MEILI, GESCHICHTE UND SYSTEM DES INTERNATIONALEN PRIVATRECHTS 8 (1892).

conflicts rules, insofar as they are not established by constitutional limitations[31] or international conventions,[32] would, upon a comparative analysis of forum and foreign policies, come into play primarily in determining whether the defendant would be unfairly dealt with under the law of the forum, and where governmental interests otherwise require displacement of that law.

The third proposition has been extensively discussed in the first part of my book on the Conflict of Laws dealing with "Jurisdiction and Judgments."[32a] Full proof of the fourth proposition will have to await a detailed analysis of all typical situations, a contribution to which I hope to offer in a series of articles and in the second part of my book. In order to establish the first two propositions, a historical and comparative analysis will demonstrate that, besides party autonomy,[33] application of the lex fori has always been the basic principle of conflicts law and was merely temporarily displaced from time to time. So clearly has the lex fori been prevalent all through history that our discipline even lacked a name until the internationalist period of the last century, when the conflicting claims of foreign laws produced both the "Conflict of Laws"[34] and "Private International Law."[35] Insofar as the following analysis is concerned with the doctrine of earlier centuries, it must partly be based on conjecture. This doctrine followed largely scholastic tradition and did not necessarily reflect living law. I believe, however, that the interpretations offered in these pages, have strong support in available authority, and that these interpretations, if found tenable, could go a long way toward destroying the dangerous idols of current dogma and restoring the lex fori to its rightful place. This historical analysis will follow the sequence in which the several countries originally entered upon the world scene of private international law.[36]

31 See Currie, "The Constitution and the Choice of Law," 26 UNIV. CHI. L. REV. 9 (1958). But cf. EHRENZWEIG 29.

32 See, e.g., the Hague resolution of August 30, 1875, INSTITUT DE DROIT INTERNATIONAL, TABLEAU GÉNÉRAL DES RESOLUTIONS (1873-1956) 365 (1957). On the pertinent conventions on specific jurisdictional subjects, see EHRENZWEIG 23.

32a EHRENZWEIG, *passim*. For an excellent foreign analysis, see Neuhaus, "Internationales Zivilprozessrecht und Internationales Privatrecht," 20 RABELS Z. 201 at 247-269 (1955).

33 Note 22 supra.

34 This term is usually ascribed to Huber. See NUSSBAUM 7. But see also note 148 infra.

35 Story is the creator of this phrase. NUSSBAUM 7.

36 Primary sources have been extensively used in this analysis. Since most of these sources are in foreign languages, references are, however, prevailingly to the classic studies by Lainé, Neumeyer, Meijers, and Gutzwiller. See *Note*, p. 637 supra.

B. HISTORY AND COMPARISON

1. *Italy*

The great fulfillment of Roman law as a jus gentium governed the Empire. As the law prevailing in all fora, it excluded conflict.[37] Ambiguously, the beginning of conflicts law is often identified with the general regime of "personal laws" within the several territories of the conquering Germanic tribes.[38] But conflict of laws in our sense can arise only from a competition between a lex fori and foreign laws, and there was no such lex fori to contest the free reign of each litigant's own law.[39] Nor was there such competition when those great "personal" laws, the perfected and later declining "lex" of the Langobards,[40] and the defeated and later rising laws of the Romans,[41] had yielded, as had the King's powers, to the feudal laws, the Frankish capitularia,[42] and the customs and statutes of the city states.[43] All of these, though on different grounds, claimed general "territorial" application to both citizens and foreigners, to the exclusion of all foreign laws; and the lex fori ruled supreme,[44] confirmed in its rule by treaties among the city states.[45] It would be wrong to treat this stage as one of primitive unawareness of inequities thus caused.

[37] See, e.g., Yntema, "The Historic Bases of Private International Law," 2 AM. J. COMP. L. 297 at 300 (1953); BATIFFOL 10; Niederer, "Ceterum quaero de legum Imperii Romani conflictu," FESTSCHRIFT FÜR FRITZSCHE 115 (1952); SCHWIND, GEISTGE UND HISTORISCHE GRUNDLAGEN DES INTERNATIONALEN PRIVATRECHTS (1959).

[38] See, in general, MEIJERS 549; CALISSE, A HISTORY OF ITALIAN LAW 39 (1928). But see QUADRI 32-42.

[39] 1 NEUMEYER 11; BATIFFOL 11; MEIJERS 572. The translation of "Stamm" by "tribe" is misleading since we are dealing with highly organized and advanced communities rather than with primitive hordes. Concerning the fundamental difference between the "personal laws" of that period and that following the regime of an integrated lex fori in the 10th century, see 1 NEUMEYER 14. As to the gradual decline of the old personal laws, through the return of Roman law, the parties' choice, and needs of commercial intercourse, see 1 NEUMEYER 143, 147, 160.

[40] At the time of the Frankish conquest in 774, Lombard law had reached the stage of its highest development as the "best law nearly generally known." 1 NEUMEYER 23, referring to a statement by King Liutprand.

[41] Roman law had persisted and was rejuvenated as both local and universal law. 1 NEUMEYER 44-50. For its co-existence with Lombard law, see id. at 57, 134.

[42] 1 NEUMEYER 29-33; BATIFFOL 13; WOLFF 21. See, in general, BORETIUS, DIE CAPITULARIEN IM LANGOBARDENREICH 14 (1864); ABIGNENTE, STORIA DEL DIRITTO IN ITALIA 186 (1884).

[43] 1 NEUMEYER 39, 59, 65, 70.

[44] 2 NEUMEYER 1, 13; GUTZWILLER 298.

[45] The oldest treaty is that between Pisa and Amalfi assuring the merchants of each party of treatment under the lex fori. 2 NEUMEYER 5. Apparently as a courtesy to the neighboring state, criminal jurisdiction was extended to crimes committed abroad. 2 NEUMEYER 29.

The city judge applied the Roman rules of competency.[46] Since the primary tenet of these rules was the parties' subjection to the court of the defendant's domicile as his "forum generale,"[47] application of this forum's law would neither aggrieve the defendant nor the foreign plaintiff.[48] On the other hand, a foreign defendant could hardly complain if the added competencies of the place of contracting,[49] of the delict,[50] of the thing in issue,[51] made applicable a forum law which had the most significant contacts with the case.[52] Nor was injustice done where a Venetian's will executed abroad was subjected to Venetian law by a Venetian statute.[53]

But the lex fori, after a regime of one hundred years, was rendered inadequate at the beginning of the thirteenth century, when, presumably in part because of the revived influence of Roman law,[54] foreigners were deprived of both the burdens[55] and the privileges of forum law.[56] This development seems to have occurred rather abruptly, although around 1200 Aldricus had opened the first breach in the lex fori when he referred the judge to the "stronger and more useful law."[57] Accursius, as late as 1228, had quite generally permitted the place of litigation to determine the applicable custom.[58] But only a few years later, this great master

[46] 2 NEUMEYER 23. On the early identity between problems of jurisdiction and choice of law, see MEIJERS 572.

[47] 2 NEUMEYER 94.

[48] 2 NEUMEYER 30, 80, 82.

[49] This competency found a counterpart in the cities' revenue interest in the "curatura," a levy on local contracts of foreigners. 2 NEUMEYER 31. On the impact of usury legislation, see id. at 32.

[50] 2 NEUMEYER 31.

[51] On the financial background of this competency, see 2 NEUMEYER 33.

[52] Paulus de Castro (died 1441) limits the Roman principle that the plaintiff must and may follow the defendant in his own forum (actor debet sequi forum rei), to the case of a foreign defendant sued in contract or quasi-contract and about to depart from the forum. 1 LAINÉ 189.

[53] See GUTZWILLER 299.

[54] 2 NEUMEYER 73. See also id. at 23 ("invention of the theoreticians"). On the influence of Byzantine law in Bologna, see Pringsheim, "Beryt and Bologna," FESTSCHRIFT FÜR LENEL 204 (1921).

[55] Thus, a citizen of Pisa defended himself successfully in Pistoja against the charge of having carried arms there unlawfully, by pleading his citizenship. 2 NEUMEYER 75, n. 4. And a statute of the Città de Castello which required an owner seeking to recover stolen goods from a bona fide purchaser to reimburse him for the purchase price, was held inapplicable in that city against a citizen of Arezzo. 2 NEUMEYER 79.

[56] Even against a counteraction the foreigner could not invoke forum law in his favor. Albericus de Rosate, statutis II 9, cited 2 NEUMEYER 78. See also MEIJERS 594.

[57] 2 NEUMEYER 66, 101. For a related canon law doctrine, see 2 NEUMEYER 131.

[58] 2 NEUMEYER 60, 66, 76, 101. See, in general, LANDSBERG, DIE GLOSSE DES ACCURSIUS UND IHRE LEHRE VOM EIGENTUM (1883). Concerning Azo's similar theory, see 2 NEUMEYER 59, n. 1; MEIJERS 594.

of the Gloss made the now famous concession that in Modena the citizen of Bologna must not be adjudged under the laws of Modena.[59]

What, then, was the foreigner's law in Modena? "At first there seemed to present itself an easy solution. Local laws were considered mere modifications of the common law which bound everybody everywhere. What was simpler than to apply this very common law to the foreigner?"[60] But this easy solution could not, in the long run, satisfy new needs. It was at this point that the inventiveness of scholars devised the first casuistic rules of conflict of laws. Indeed, "the groping and uncertain experiments of those scholars constitute the starting points for all theoretical endeavors which our time continues to employ in private international law."[61]

To fill a gap, then, a gap left by the self-limitation of the lex fori and the failure of the common law, the canonists, as well as, independently, secular scholars led by Jacobus Balduini and Ubertus de Bobio, having first found the law of the forum applicable to foreigners as to contracts made in the forum state, began, conversely, to apply foreign laws to foreign contracts.[62] And it was similarly to fill a gap that courts upheld testaments made by citizens abroad not only under the lex fori, but under the foreign law as well.[63] These conflicts rules, without displacing the lex fori, thus had come to its rescue. Wherever the lex fori was willing to operate, it retained its effect,[64] far from conceding to the foreign law a right to "govern" a legal relation;[65] and it is fundamental for the understanding of this origin of all private international law that probably *all* of its early rules were at least explained by

[59] See, e.g., Yntema, "The Historic Bases of Private International Law," 2 AM. J. COMP. L. 297 at 302 (1953); 2 NEUMEYER 76.

[60] 2 NEUMEYER 82.

[61] 2 NEUMEYER 83. The same period also saw the creation of that differentiation between procedural and substantive law which has remained a principal tool of our theory. 2 NEUMEYER 85, 88.

[62] 2 NEUMEYER 84, 102.

[63] 2 NEUMEYER 45; 2 LAINÉ 338; PARRA, LA REGLA "LOCUS REGIT ACTUM" Y LA FORMA DE LOS TESTAMENTOS 30, 34, 52 (1955). As to the relevance of the situs, see PARRA 27, 48, 60. The famous "English question," debated by Bartolus and his contemporaries (Italian estate of Englishman), foreshadows the broadening of the conflicts rule. GUTZWILLER 315. See also MEIJERS 597, 608 on the influence of the school of Orleans.

[64] Where jurisdiction was based on the place of contracting, a Modena court would adjudicate a Modena contract under Modena law even as to a Bologna citizen. 2 NEUMEYER 84. This seems to have been true also where jurisdiction was based on the defendant's domicile (2 NEUMEYER 94) or where the foreigner was not familiar with the lex contractus (2 NEUMEYER 137).

[65] See notes 70, 72 infra.

the "principle of the parties' autonomy,"[66] which later conceptualist dogma was to betray to the lasting detriment of doctrine and practice.

To be sure, the Commentators, following their academic leaning toward generalization and faithful to the persisting idea of an all-embracing law of Rome,[67] were ultimately inclined to grant to foreign law, at least in a few specific situations, the same claims to extraterritorial application which earlier they had granted to the lex fori.[68] Their ever-recurring invocation of the clearly inapplicable imperial decree of *Cunctos Populos* in the very titles of their works makes this more than likely.[69] But, contrary to later misinterpretations, most dramatically exemplified in Professor Beale's mis-translation of Bartolus,[70] the earlier Italian Commentators had, in general, recognized the priority of the lex fori by organizing their analysis around the effectiveness of the lex fori as to either foreigners before the forum or forum citizens abroad.[71] Balduini had merely asked the forum to "inspect" the customs of the place where the contract was located.[72] The same language was still used by Bartolus[73] (1314-1355) and Baldus[74] (1327-1400). Only Salicet may be said to have foreshadowed later dogma which may well have been promoted by the universalist tendencies of a canon law coordinated by the Pope's sovereignty.[75] It seems that in what was probably the most frequent conflicts situation, namely the case involving a foreigner's contract, the court would take jurisdiction over the foreigner as the court of the place of contracting, in the expectation that the judgment would be recognized by the

[66] MEIJERS 633 with primary reference to the writings of Salicet.

[67] MEIJERS 630.

[68] NIEDERER 38.

[69] Codex Justinianus 1.1.1. This technique was used all through history from Accursius to d'Argentré. NIEDERER 39.

[70] BEALE, BARTOLUS ON THE CONFLICT OF LAWS 18 (trans. 1914), consistently translates the word "inspicitur" by "govern." 1 LAINÉ 135 correctly translates: "il faut considérer," and "il faut avoid égard." But see also VAN DE KAMP, BARTOLUS DE SAXOFERRATO 1313-1357 235 (1936) ("geldt het recht").

[71] As to the international criminal law of Bartolus and his successors, see MEILI, BARTOLUS ALS HAUPT DER ERSTEN SCHULE DES INTERNATIONALEN STRAFRECHTS 30, 43 (1908).

[72] 2 NEUMEYER 86 ("inspicitur," "spectatur").

[73] See note 70 supra.

[74] Baldus de Ubaldis (1327-1400), in his COMMENTARIA IN PRIMUM, SECUNDUM ET TERTIUM CODICIS LIBRUM, DE SUMMA TRINITATE, L. 1, no. 57 (ed. Augustae Taurinorum 1576). This work deals almost exclusively with the newly discovered "personal law." Note 40 supra.

[75] Note 91 infra.

foreigner's home state.[76] Although Salicet (died 1412) would insist that also a foreign lex contractus "shall" be applied,[77] he, too, returned to the lex fori where the contract was to be performed in the forum state.[78] Rochus Curtius (died 1495) was perhaps first generally to discuss the applicability of foreign "customs."[79] But court practice even then seems to have largely ignored dogmatic developments,[80] and further generalizations were left to the French statutists.[81]

Passing over less significant writers, such as Chasseneuz (died 1541) and Tiraqueau (died 1558), Dumoulin (1500-1566) may perhaps be considered as the last exponent of the Italian school. He, too, refrains, with certain traditional exceptions, from ascertaining a "governing" law and is satisfied with examining the limits of a lex fori which he supplemented by the ubiquitous applicability of the common law and the test of natural justice.[82] Indeed, to his contemporaries, Dumoulin seems to have been an advocate of the primary rule of the lex fori.[83] It may not be a coincidence that this scholar, who kept himself free of later conceptualistic generalizations, is also often credited with having re-emphasized in the law of conflict of laws the great principle of the autonomy of the parties, and that it was in turn this great principle which has remained the object of contempt and attack by those preferring neat dogma to living law.[84]

Perhaps it was fortunate for Italy's legal history that, for the next two centuries, political upheavals virtually excluded her

[76] See, for early French law, Neumeyer, "Zur Geschichte des internationalen Privatrechts in Frankreich und den Niederlanden," 11 ZEIT. FÜR VÖLKERRECHT 190 at 192, 195 (1920).

[77] BARTHOLOMAEUS A SALICETO, PARS PRIMA IN PRIMUM ET SECUNDUM CODICIS LIBROS, L. cunctos populos, no. 4 ff. (1574), L. 6, tit. 2, lib. XXI, Dig., uses the phrase "caveri oportet."

[78] 1 LAINÉ 180.

[79] ROCHUS CURTIUS, TRACTATUS UTRIUSQUE JURIS, tit. II, 376 (1584) uses in the heading of the second part the phrase "an judex debeat equi."

[80] This observation has been based on such statements as that of Coquille (1523-1603), according to whom the French coûtumes are not to be treated as "local to the same extent as the Docteurs ultramontains have considered their Statutes" (trans). 2 COQUILLE, OEUVRES, LES COUSTUMES DU PAYS ET COMTÉ DE NIVERNOIS 1 (1703). Cf. GAMILLSCHEG 98. See also NIEDERER 37; 1 LAINÉ 300. CALASSO, LEZIONI DI STORIA DEL DIRITTO ITALIANO, rev. ed., 317 (1948), refers to Cujas' criticism of the commentators for being "verbose as to easy matters, silent as to difficult ones, and diffuse in a narrow spot." (trans). Simply to ascribe Coquille's anti-statutism to his resentment of the Lutheran Dumoulin's attack against his uncle Bourgoin, a Catholic, is hardly justifiable. DUPIN, LA COUTUME DE NIVERNAIS 432 (1864).

[81] Note 105 infra.

[82] GAMILLSCHEG 73, 88, 93.

[83] GAMILLSCHEG 33, 98.

[84] See 1 LAINÉ 223; GAMILLSCHEG 110-124.

from the arena of conflicts scholarship which during that period was largely one of dogmatic deviation.[85] Yet it was only two years after Sardinia's defeat in 1851 that Italian scholarship was to set the stage for another great victory when Mancini (1817-1888) in a now famous speech added the political ideas of his country's *resorgimento* to the European concert of internationalist doctrine.[86] Supported by the reforms of the French Code,[87] he urged the nationality principle as the primary basis of a truly international conflicts law. Its force was spent in an unparalleled impact on legislation and literature at home and abroad.[88] In Italy, too, the international dream has yielded to a new "territorial" realism,[89] which may or may not coincide with the peculiarly Italian doctrine of "incorporation" authorizing the judge, in applying his own law, to incorporate foreign laws in that law by a creative act.[90]

2. *The Canon Law*

As in the secular law of the Italian city states, the lex fori governed supreme in early canon law.[91] And as in the secular law of the Italian city states, the lex fori of the canon law at one time met situations which seemed to require its withdrawal. But problem and solution differed substantially in the two laws. While the laws of the Italian cities had denied their own applicability

85 It seems that the treatise by ROCCO, TRATTATO DI DIRITTO CIVILE INTERNAZIONALE (originally published in 1837, ed. 1859), which adopts a natural law ideology, was unable to survive the impact of Mancini's work. See BAR, DAS INTERNATIONALE PRIVAT-UND STRAFRECHT 44 (1862).

86 MANCINI, DELLA NAZIONALITA COME FONDAMENTO DEL DIRITTO DELLE GENTI (1851). See also MANCINI, LA VITA DEI POPOLI NELL' UMANITA (1872). Among others, Mancini relied on the teachings of Savigny (note 155 infra) and Westlake (note 169 infra). See also 1 CLUNET 221 at 230 (1874).

87 See LEREBOURS-PIGEONNIÈRE, DROIT INTERNATIONAL PRIVÉ, 7th ed., 83-88 (1959).

88 The Codice Civile Italiano of 1865 (amended 1942) and the Spanish Civil Code of 1889 relied largely on Mancini. See, in general, NIEDERER 66; LEREBOURS-PIGEONNIÈRE, note 87 supra, at 331.

89 See, e.g., AGO, TEORIA DEL DIRITTO INTERNAZIONALE PRIVATO 59-94 (1934); BALLADORE-PALLIERI, DIRITTO INTERNAZIONALE PRIVATO, 2d ed., 9-11 (1950); De Nova, "Solution du conflit de lois et réglement satisfaisant du rapport international," 37 REV. CRIT. DE DR. INT. 178 (1948); MORELLI, ELEMENTI DI DIRITTO INTERNAZIONALE PRIVATO ITALIANO, 6th ed., 20-23 (1959); PACCHIONI, ELEMENTI DI DIRITTO INTERNAZIONALE PRIVATO 111-122 (1930); QUADRI 168-289. For bibliographies, see, e.g., De Nova, "La jurisprudence italienne en matière de conflits de lois de 1935-1949," 39 REV. CRIT. DE DR. INT. 159-162 (1950); NIEDERER 69; BATIFFOL 258, 278.

90 This theory is often identified with the name of Anzilotti [STUDI CRITICI DI DIRITTO INTERNAZIONALE PRIVATO (1898)]. See, e.g., Ago, "Règles Générales des Conflits de Lois," 58 RECUEIL DES COURS 243 at 303 (1936); Esperson, "Le Droit International Privé dans la législation italienne," 6 CLUNET 329 (1879); 7 id. at 245, 337 (1880). See also NIEDERER 371; 1 RABEL, THE CONFLICT OF LAWS, A COMPARATIVE STUDY, 2d ed., 16, 62 (1958).

91 2 NEUMEYER 126. See also RIGAUD, ACTES DU CONGRÈS DE DROIT CANONIQUE (1950).

to foreigners and foreign facts, the clerical judge found himself unable to apply his law for other reasons. Delegation of judicial authority was the rule and neither the delegating nor the delegated judge seemed entitled to his own law.[92] Moreover, the right to appeal to a judge in another territory raised the question as to the law applicable in the appellate court.[93] Perhaps in part for these reasons the parties were given the right to choose their own judge and their own law long before similar rights were available in secular courts.[94] That, in the absence of such choice, the defendant's law was given preference[95] is additional support for the assumption that the law of the forum, i.e., typically the law of the defendant's domicile, had even then remained the law entitled to primary consideration.[96]

As in the Italian city states more complex fact situations required greater refinement. Here, as there, other laws were permitted to aid the lex fori where it had become deficient. And here, as there, contracts and testaments led the way,[97] with delicts following suit.[98] But canon law, too, even earlier than its secular counterpart, prompted by its coherence under one sovereign, succumbed to dogma. Pope Boniface VIII (1294-1303), in his *Decretale Ut Animarum* (1298), had decreed that the bishop's ordinance threatening excommunication for larceny, did not bind his subjects outside the diocese, because, in the words of the Roman jurist Paulus, "nobody may pronounce law (jus dicere) outside his own territory."[99] Although Paulus' adage referred to judicial rather than to legislative jurisdiction,[100] even a contemporaneous Gloss extended the *Decretale* to restrict the legislative power as such,[101] precluding the forum from applying its own law to foreigners or foreign transactions, or a foreign law to citizens or domestic transactions. It may be regrettable that the final text of the *Codex Juris Canonici* preserved this theorem by presuming every law to be

[92] 2 NEUMEYER 129.

[93] 2 NEUMEYER 129. For analogies in early French feudal law, see Neumeyer, "Zur Geschichte des internationalen Privatrechts in Frankreich und den Niederlanden," 11 ZEIT. FÜR VÖLKERRECHT 190 at 195 (1920).

[94] 2 NEUMEYER 129.

[95] 2 NEUMEYER 113.

[96] 2 NEUMEYER 132. An exception existed where the plaintiff's law was more favorable to the defendant or was more likely to do justice. 2 NEUMEYER 131.

[97] 2 NEUMEYER 131, 135.

[98] 2 NEUMEYER 138.

[99] DIG. 2, 1, 20.

[100] PACELLI, LA PERSONNALITÉ ET LA TERRITORIALITÉ DES LOIS PARTICULIÈREMENT DANS LE DROIT CANON 2 (1945).

[101] Id. at 5.

territorial.[102] To be sure, an earlier draft,[103] conversely favoring a presumption of personality, would have similarly recognized a regime of rigid rules. But the reversal, thus proposed, of an age-old formula might have strengthened those other provisions of the Code which may mark a trend back to the pre-Bonifacian lex fori.[104]

3. *France*

The spouses De Ganey, domiciliaries of Paris, had made each other heirs of all their after-acquired property. In a dispute between the heirs of husband and wife the former claimed a piece of land in Lyon as not having been included in the mutual gift. That gift had been made under the community property law of the Paris Coutume, it was claimed, which lacked extraterritorial validity in Lyon, a city subject to the Roman *droit écrit*. The Bartolist and royalist *Dumoulin* rendered a famous opinion favoring application by the Paris judge of his own law which, through the contract, had been deprived of its local character.[105] Lex fori, then, and party autonomy, even as to foreign land![106]

To d'Argentré[107] this opinion was intolerable. In his all-pervasive desire to support Breton feudalism against the King by giving priority to the lex situs as to Breton land, he felt compelled to oblige the judge equally to apply the lex situs to foreign land.[108] Whatever the rationale of this obligation—and there are almost as many interpretations as authors dealing with this question[109]—the lex fori had found its limitation, one not self-imposed or suggested by the common law, like the limitation of the Italian city laws, nor decreed by the sovereign, like the limitations of the several jurisdictions of the canon law. Rather, the feudalist displacement of the law of the forum was demanded by a political ideology

102 Codex Juris Canonici, Canon 12.

103 Draft 1914, Canon 7, quoted Pacelli, note 100 supra, at IV.

104 Codex Juris Canonici, Canon 14, §1, no. 1.

105 See, e.g., D'ESPINAY, LA FÉODALITÉ ET LE DROIT CIVIL FRANCAIS 343 (1862); GAMILLSCHEG 42.

106 As to French antecedents, see MEIJERS 549. For a different view of the controversy, see NEUMEYER, "Zur Geschichte des internationalen Privatrechts in Frankreich und den Niederlanden, 11 ZEIT. FÜR VÖLKERRECHT 190 at 199 (1920).

107 D'ARGENTRÉ (1519-1590), COMMENTARII IN PATRIAS BRITONUM LEGES SEU CONSUETUDINES GENERALES ANTIQUISSIMI DUCATUS BRITANNIAE, Art. CCVIII, Gloss 6 (ed. Paris 1621).

108 GAMILLSCHEG 103, 202. See also 1 CATELLANI, IL DIRITTO INTERNAZIONALE PRIVATO, 2d ed., 441 (1895), citing De la Lande de Calan's dissertation (1892); NIEDERER 46.

109 See GAMILLSCHEG 104.

to which that law had to yield the power over land,[110] and perhaps by that nascent internationalism[111] which, too, endowed the foreign law with a right to recognition.[112]

If d'Argentré had stopped at this point, he could have retained in his scheme the predominance of the lex fori with the one great exception of the lex situs.[113] But the great scholar, judge and legislator did not stop there. His was the urge for a simplification of the administration of justice in his native Brittany, his a predominant concern for those feudal interests which were just then facing the first stage of their decline. If statuta realia, the laws governing land, were to gain the great standing he desired for them, he may well have wished to restore an at least apparent balance by giving imperative effect, also, to those ancient statuta personalia, which are carried about by everybody "wherever he may go."[114]

The inevitable inconsistency between these two principles has often been pointed out.[115] The all-importance of a "territorialism" purporting to embrace all legal relations as to forum land seems irreconcilable with the forum's duty, though secondary, to recognize as to such land personal laws "created" by another sovereign. D'Argentré, the feudalist, attempted to minimize this inconsistency by reducing, as far as possible, the scope and impact of the foreign personal laws intruding on the forum law of the situs.[116] But neither later scholars nor the courts followed suit.[117] The conflict remained unresolved, and the lex fori continued, openly or in disguise,[118] to determine French law until the eve of the great

[110] GAMILLSCHEG 104.

[111] 1 LAINÉ 270.

[112] For antecedents, see GAMILLSCHEG 105; Neumeyer, "Zur Geschichte des internationalen Privatrechts in Frankreich und den Niederlanden," ZEIT. FÜR VÖLKERRECHT 190 at 193 (1920).

[113] The regime of the lex situs has since been surrounded by something close to a psychological taboo. See in general, EHRENZWEIG 206. For early history, which can be traced back to 1270, see BATIFFOL 261.

[114] D'ARGENTRÉ, note 107 supra, at no. 4. See 2 LAINÉ 320.

[115] 2 LAINÉ 322.

[116] This D'Argentré sought to achieve by subjecting the statuta mixta to the regime of the statuta realia without regard to a possible preponderance of their personal character (which Dumoulin had conceded), and by limiting the effect of personal statutes to those which purport to affect the "general status," to the exclusion of those which "merely create a limited incapacity." D' ARGENTRÉ, note 107 supra, at no. 14. See 2 LAINÉ 324. For criticism of the resulting predominance of the lex fori, see 2 LAINÉ 316; BATIFFOL 267.

[117] 2 LAINÉ 338, 389, 394; DELAUME, LES CONFLITS DE LOIS A LA VEILLE DU CODE CIVIL 333 (1947).

[118] Concerning the continued impact of the lex fori through the process of qualification, the renvoi, and the ordre public, see DELAUME, note 117 supra, at 49, 93, 114.

codification and beyond.[119] In this form, strengthened by Dutch influence,[120] French doctrine, in the writings of Boullenois (1680-1762), Bouhier (1673-1746), Froland (+ 1746), and Merlin,[121] came to play its important role, shared with that of Dutch and German scholars, in the formative process of American conflicts law.[122] This American law was in turn partly responsible for that internationalist affliction which for a considerable period was to hem the natural development of French conflicts law.[123] Foelix, the author of the first French treatise of the 19th century, announced flatly his "complete adoption" of Story's teaching.[124] But it was Savigny whose internationalist idealism probably gave the decisive impulse to that dogmatic deviation which culminated in the work of Pillet, Beale's great French counterpart.[125]

It would seem, however, that in France, too, the restoration of the lex fori is around the corner. Notwithstanding Niboyet's somewhat ambivalent support of Pillet's teaching,[126] Bartin's realism has prevailed[127]—though veiled in a universalist aura of philosophy

[119] See, in general, id. at 86, 336; and Delaume, "The French Civil Code and Conflict of Laws: One Hundred and Fifty Years After," 24 GEO. WASH. L. REV. 499 (1956).

[120] Apparently Boullenois himself had been strongly influenced by the Dutch doctrine. 2 LAINÉ 426.

[121] See 2 LAINÉ 418; GAMILLSCHEG 185; BATIFFOL 271. The main contribution of these authors has been seen in their revival of Dumoulin's autonomy of the parties and their refinement of the law of succession. BATIFFOL 273.

[122] Boullenois' work [TRAITÉ DE LA PERSONNALITÉ ET DE LA RÉALITÉ DE LOIX, COUTUMES, OU STATUTS (1766)] was one of the main sources of Story's *Commentaries*. See also GAMILLSCHEG 247; BEALE 44.

[123] See Louis-Lucas, "Conflits de méthodes en matière de conflits de lois," 83 CLUNET 774 at 780 (1956) (with English translation). For an earlier adherent of the lex fori (based on a rational system of jurisdiction), see GAND, CODE DES ÉTRANGERS OU ÉTAT CIVIL ET POLITIQUE EN FRANCE (1853).

[124] FOELIX, TRAITÉ DE DROIT INTERNATIONAL PRIVÉ 12 (1843). See VAREILLES-SOMMIÈRES, LA SYNTHÈSE DU DROIT INTERNATIONAL PRIVÉ 165 (1897); BATIFFOL 284. On MASSE, LE DROIT COMMERCIAL DANS SES RAPPORTS AVEC LE DROIT DES GENS ET LE DROIT CIVIL (1884), see BAR, DAS INTERNATIONALE STRAF-UND PRIVATRECHT 45 (1862).

[125] See BATIFFOL 280; Louis-Lucas, note 123 supra, at 803.

[126] See, e.g., Niboyet, "Territoriality and Universal Recognition of Rules of Conflict of Laws," 65 HARV. L. REV. 582 (1952). Recognition, at the outset, "that attempts to achieve a universal private international law have failed" is in peculiar contrast to Niboyet's advocacy of unilateral conflicts rules. See also Makarov, "Der allgemeine Teil des internationalen Privatrechts im Entwurfe des neuen französischen Kodifikationswerkes," FESTSCHRIFT FÜR WOLFF 247 at 261 (1952); LOUSSOUARN, "The French Draft on Private International Law and the French Conference on Codification of Private International Law," 5 INT. & COMP. L. Q. 378 (1956).

[127] BATIFFOL 289. See also, e.g., Louis-Lucas, "Existe-t-il une compétence générale du droit français pour le réglement des conflits de lois?" 48 REV. CRIT. DE DR. INT. PRIVÉ 405 (1959); Maury, "Règles générales des conflits de lois," 57 RECUEIL DES COURS 329-563 (1936).

and aesthetics in the great work of Batiffol.[128] Thus, in the law of torts no less an authority than Mazeaud[129] has expressly advocated the outright application of the lex fori.[130]

4. *Netherlands*

What d'Argentré's feudalistic theorem did not achieve in France, it did apparently at first achieve in the Netherlands.[131] There, at the end of the 17th century, it not only gained full acceptance but did so in displacing the last elements of Bartolist theory which had been part of Dutch scholarship for a long time. Where the French resisted the single-minded application of a lex fori et situs, the Dutch welcomed it wholeheartedly in their new spirit of feudal independence. Thus, d'Argentré's teaching was responsible for the famous Perpetual Edict of July 12, 1611 which provided for the application of the lex rei sitae even to such questions as that of testamentary capacity and the form of the execution of wills. Nicholas Burgundus[132] (1586-1649) may be considered the most distinguished and radical representative of that trend. He exercised decisive influence not only on later Dutch writers but in France as well. "Things do not follow the person but attract the persons themselves."[133] It is not surprising that from such premises there could easily arise a conception of a right "created" by the statute of the situs, a conception appearing in the very title of the treatise of Rodenburgh (1618-1668) who, directly and through the work of Boullenois (1680-1762),[134] greatly influenced the theory of Joseph Story.

128 BATIFFOL, ASPECTS PHILOSOPHIQUES DU DROIT INTERNATIONAL PRIVÉ (1956); also Louis-Lucas, note 123, supra, at 805. For a purely philosophical universalist approach, see GOLDSCHMIDT, SISTEMA Y FILOSOFIA DEL DERECHO INTERNACIONAL PRIVADO (1948-1949); Goldschmidt, "Die philosophischen Grundlagen des internationalen Privatrechts," FESTSCHRIFT FÜR WOLFF 203 (1952).

129 Mazeaud, "Conflits de lois et compétence internationale dans le domaine de la responsabilité civile délictuelle et quasi-délictuelle," 29 REV. CRIT. DE DR. PR. 377 at 382, 387, 398 (1934), establishing his thesis *de lege lata* and *de lege ferenda;* 3 MAZEAUD, TRAITÉ THÉORIQUE ET PRATIQUE DE LA RESPONSABILITÉ CIVILE, 4th ed., 339 (1950). On French doctrine in general, see BATIFFOL 50.

130 In the drafting of the new civil code, Niboyet's vested rights (supra note 126) seem to have prevailed. See Commission de Réforme du Code Civil, TRAVAUX 1949-1950, at 618; AVANT-PROJET DE CODE CIVIL 63, 220 (1955).

131 This analysis is based primarily on the sources discussed by 1 LAINÉ 396. See also KOLLEWIJN, HET BEGINSEL DER OPENBARE ORDE IN HET INTERNATIONAAL PRIVAATRECHT (1917).

132 BURGUNDUS, AD CONSUETUDINES FLANDRIAE ALIARUMQUE GENTIUM CONTROVERSIAE (1646). See 1 LAINÉ 401.

133 1 LAINÉ 403, quoting from Burgundus' original Latin.

134 Boullenois' work, discussed notes 120, 122 supra, includes a French translation of Rodenburgh's work.

But the doctrine seems to have ignored much of the living law. Only twenty-three years after the Edict of 1611, its insistence upon the lex situs was "interpreted" out of its language where the situs was not in the forum state. In 1634 the Princes rendered the opinion that the Senate of Milan had not properly invoked this Edict when it had declared void a testament executed in Brussels in compliance with local requirements, on the ground that the testament had failed to satisfy the requirements of the law of Milan, the situs of the property.[185] And Burgundus' teaching was in part refuted by one of his contemporaries, Pierre Stockmans (1608-1671), who, in angry language, castigated the "pragmatists" with their "universal rules."[186] The soil was prepared for the Voets and for Ulricus Huberus who, being averse to both the academic strife of the Bartolists and the feudal preoccupation with the omnipotence of the lex situs, may be credited with having swept aside the dogmatic inroads in the basic character of the lex fori which in fact had probably never ceased to prevail.

Paul Voet (1619-1667) still follows accepted statutist dogma and merely anticipates new things to come by permitting both real and personal statutes to extend abroad if comity so requires. This comity became the basis of the theory of Ulricus Huberus (1647-1694): how may one legislator compel another legislator of equal rank to apply one law rather than the other? With the conclusion that one declared incompetent in Holland cannot rely in that province on a contract concluded by him in Friesland, though he would there be treated as competent,[187] Johannes Voet abandoned the later statutist postulate that questions concerning the same set of facts must be uniformly decided wherever litigated. Although the foreign domiciliary law may be applicable to the transfer of domestic movables on grounds of comity, any sovereign state remains free to apply its own law if it so desires.[188]

Notwithstanding this courageous emancipation from universalist doctrine, the Dutch school started from an unrealistic premise which was to facilitate its conversion into its seeming opposite, the doctrine of vested rights, the premise, namely, which apparently had been inherited from the statutists, that the law of conflict of

185 See 1 LAINÉ 400.

186 1 LAINÉ 406.

187 See GAMILLSCHEG 174, 180.

188 2 JOHANNES VOET, COMMENTARY ON THE PANDECTS (Paris ed. 1829), Gane trans. (1955), Bk. V, tit. 1, §51, p. 64. See GAMILLSCHEG 181, and, in general, see SCHOLTEN, COMITAS 11-78 (1949).

laws is concerned with relations between sovereigns. It is clearly of no concern to any sovereign whether his law is or is not applied in foreign litigation between private parties. But neither Asser's anti-comity approach[139] nor Jitta's "ultranational" order based on a law of humanity[140] have seriously affected the consistent realism of Dutch scholarship,[141] whose only reproach to Huber and the Voets has been that they "did not further develop their fundamental idea."[142] This idea would have required abandonment of the statutist tradition and the search, in each case, for "solutions best suited to serve the real interests of human society and a good administration of justice."[143] As to torts, Netherlands courts have not hesitated to resort to the lex fori where justice so required,[144] and a Dutch scholar has developed a brilliant scheme of dealing with conflicts problems in this field, which would favor a lex fori controlled by rational rules of jurisdiction.[145]

5. *Germany*

Such early German codes as the Sachsenspiegel (1215-1235) and the Schwabenspiegel (1273-1276) were satisfied with the lex fori even where contemporary Italian doctrine would have conceded another solution. Thus, even the law of succession was apparently always that of the forum situs.[146] What was perhaps a Bartolist interlude of nascent conflicts rules was dislodged in the 16th century, as it was in France, by feudal preference for the lex situs. Mynsinger (1514-1588) and Gaill (1526-1587) have been

139 ASSER, ÉLÉMENTS DE DROIT INTERNATIONAL PRIVÉ, Rivier trans. 30 (1884).

140 JITTA, INTERNATIONAAL PRIVAATRECHT (1916). Cf. BEALE 95.

141 For a bibliography, see NIEDERER 371. See also Ofterhaus, "L'Université d'Amsterdam et le Droit International Privé," FESTGABE GUTZWILLER 283-302 (1959); KOLLEWIJN, GESCHIEDENIS VAN DE NEDERLANDSE WETENSCHAP VAN HET INTERNATIONAAL PRIVAATRECHT TOT 1880 (1937).

142 MEIJERS 668.

143 Ibid.

144 De Beer v. de Hondt, Hague App. June 16, 1955, N.J. 1955, no. 615, 3 NED. TIJDSCHR. INT. R. 290 (1956), applying Dutch law to a French automobile accident between nationals. But see for Belgium, Overstraeten v. Sainte, Cour de Cass. Belg. Mai 17, 1957 (Dutch law applied to Dutch accident between Belgians).

145 Drion, "De ratio voor toepassing van vreemd recht in zake de onrechtmatige daad in het buitenland," [1949] RECHTSGELEERD MAGAZIJN THEMIS 3, 64. Cf. De Nova, "Appunti sull'illecito civile in diritto internazionale comparato," 4 COMMUNIC. E STUDI 7 at 18 (1952).

146 Beckmann, "Zum internationalen Privat-und Prozessrecht des Sachsenspiegels," 1 ZEIT. FÜR VÖLKERRECHT 394, 470, 476 (1907); NIEDERER 37.

considered as the most important representatives of this trend, and, among their successors, Hertius (1651-1710) became an outstanding follower of the extreme positions of d'Argentré and Burgundus.[147] Significantly, apparently for the first time in Germany, Hertius refers to the conflict ("collisio") of laws—a terminology which presupposes recognition of a foreign law's claim to application; and Cocceji (1644-1719) was the first German author to base his related theory on an international order closely tied to prevailing natural law conceptions.[148]

These and other "universalists" were strongly criticized by Carl Georg von Wächter,[149] who thus has come to be known as the outstanding advocate of the lex fori. This much is true: Wächter, perhaps for the first time since the 13th century, consciously and expressly put the lex fori into the center of his system.[150] But he, too, of course, recognized the need for cataloguing the situations where the lex fori, to avoid hardship, must yield to foreign laws by limiting its own scope. Wächter's catalogue includes the express or implied choice of law by the parties, certain phases of personal capacity, domestic relations, succession and formalities of legal transactions, always with proper regard for the priority of coercive rules of the forum.[151]

Quite improperly, I believe, Wächter's courageous abandonment of earlier academic deviations is said to have been discredited by the work of Savigny, that other great German scholar,

147 1 LAINE 408; GAMILLISCHEG 163.

148 Earlier treatises merely referred to the extraterritorial validity of laws. See, e.g., STRYCK, DE JURE PRINCIPIS EXTRA TERRITORIUM (1674). TITIUS, JUR. PRIV. ROM. GERM. lib. 1, ch. 10, "De conflictu statutorum eorumque in ceteros valore" (1709), introduced conflicts terminology.

149 Wächter, "Ueber die Collision der Privatrechtsgesetze verschiedener Staaten," 24 ARCH. CIV. PR. 230 (1841); 25 id. 1 (1842).

150 But, in doing so, Wächter can claim a long line of later statutists who began their investigations with the lex fori as the basic law, 25 ARCH. CIV. PR. 1 at 15 (1842) (e.g., Mevius, Stryck, Bohmer). Moreover, Wächter's theory seems to have been preceded by a contemporary controversy. See SCHÄFFNER, ENTWICKLUNG DES INTERNATIONALEN PRIVATRECHTS 31-36 (1841), who had made short shrift of the "adventurous idea" of comity which he had found foreign to actual practice. Id. at 37-38. 1 ZACHARIÄ, HANDBUCH DES FRANZÖSISCHEN CIVILRECHTS, 2d ed., p. XLI (1811) had treated conflicts rules as mere exceptions from the lex fori.

151 For adherents of Wächter, see PFEIFFER, DAS PRINCIP DES INTERNATIONALEN PRIVATRECHTS (1851); MITTERMAIER, GRUNDSATZE DES GEMEINEN DEUTSCHEN PRIVATRECHTS, 7th ed., §30, p. 115 (1847); PUCHTA, PANDEKTEN, 9th ed., §113, p. 171 (1863); PÜTTER, DAS PRAKTISCHE EUROPAISCHE FREMDENRECHT (1845). See also THÖL, EINLEITUNG IN DAS DEUTSCHE PRIVATRECHT 168 (1851); THÖL, 1 HANDELSRECHT §17 ("In the first place the judge shall apply his own laws").

whose writings have acquired considerable reputation in this country—perhaps in part due to the fact that he paid his repeated respects to the work of his contemporary, Joseph Story.[152] But Savigny, like Wächter, rejected clearly and definitively the logical circle of "vested rights,"[153] denied to any foreign law a right to application, and thus recognized the lex fori as the fountainhead of all conflicts law.[154] His great contribution was that he enriched Wächter's catalogue of exceptions by his theory of the "seat of the legal relation," and sought specific solutions for specific problems on grounds of justice and expediency rather than dogma.[155] On the other hand, Savigny is probably also responsible for the internationalist illusion of his successors.[156] To him, the regime of the lex fori was modified by an "international common law of nations."[157] While, in Savigny's work, this modification was still one in fact rather than by necessity, Bar[158] assigned to conflicts law a supra-national power, and Zitelmann treated it outright as a branch of public international law.[159] But universalist ideologies have succumbed in Germany as they have in Italy, France and the Netherlands.[160] Kahn, like Bartin,[161] developed, for a new

152 Cf. 8 SAVIGNY, SYSTEM DES HEUTIGEN RÖMISCHEN RECHTS, BOOK 3, 28 (1840).

153 SAVIGNY, CONFLICT OF LAWS 147 (1849, trans. Guthrie 1880). Credit for this argument should, however, go to Wächter, note 149 supra, at 25 ARCH. CIV. PR. 4 ("petitio principii"), or KORI, ERÖRTERUNGEN PRAKTISCHER RECHTSFRAGEN, III, 3 (1833). Notes 220-223 infra.

154 SAVIGNY, note 153 supra, at 71, 78, 144. In the law of torts, Savigny even gave greater emphasis than Wächter to the lexi fori by refusing to admit defenses under the lex loci. For criticism, see BAR, DAS INTERNATIONALE PRIVAT-UND STRAFRECHT 317 (1862).

155 On Savigny in general, see GUTZWILLER, DER EINFLUSS SAVIGNYS AUF DIE ENTWICKLUNG DES INTERNATIONALPRIVATRECHTS (1923); Gutzwiller, "Le développement historique du droit international privé," 29 RECUEIL DES COURS 289 at 353 (1929); EHRENZWEIG 6, n. 2. See also Maridakis, "Die internationalprivatrechtliche Lehre Savignys im Lichte seiner Rechtsentstehungstheorie," FESTSCHRIFT FÜR LEWALD 309 (1953); Gaudemet, "La théorie des conflits de lois dans l'oeuvre d'Antoine Pillet et la doctrine de Savigny," 1 MÉLANGES PILLET 89 (1929).

156 See NUSSBAUM 21; BATIFFOL 285; BEALE 88. But see also SCHÄFFNER, ENTWICKLUNG DES INTERNATIONALEN PRIVATRECHTS (1841).

157 SAVIGNY, note 153 supra, at 70. See also id. at 145, where he points to the problems which would arise from a general use of the lex fori under our system of concurrent international jurisdiction.

158 BAR, DAS INTERNATIONALE PRIVAT-UND STRAFRECHT (1862). See BEALE 89.

159 ZITELMANN, INTERNATIONALES PRIVATRECHT (1897); ZITELMANN DIE MÖGLICHKEIT EINES WELTRECHTS (1888). See, e.g., BEALE 91; NIEDERER 136; Gutzwiller, "International-Privatrecht," in 1 STAMMLER, DAS GESAMTE DEUTSCHE RECHT 1515 at 1532, 1538, 1552 (1931). For a more recent internationalist system, see FRANKENSTEIN, INTERNATIONALES PRIVATRECHT (Grenzrecht) (1926-1935).

160 Notes 89-90, 127-130, 141-145 supra. Austria had withstood the internationalist interlude owing to its specific code provisions. Thus, DAS ALLGEMEINE BÜRGERLICHE GESETZBUCH (A.B.G.B.) §35ff. make the lex fori almost always applicable to contracts, giving

"positivist" approach, a theory of conflict of laws based on the lex fori.[162] Niemeyer, in his proposals for the codification of private international law,[163] equally rejected universalist dogma. And the German civil code, contrary to earlier drafts, has mostly limited itself to circumscribing the scope of the lex fori. German courts, presumably influenced by the conceptualistic jurisprudence of the beginning of this century, have largely frustrated this conscious choice of the legislature by re-interpreting" unilateral norms" as "bilateral" ones;[164] but contemporary writers like Kegel, Nussbaum, Raape and Wengler have reversed the trend.[165]

6. *England*

In the 17th century England knew valiant attempts at introducing the Roman law, as the law of reason, to govern relations with foreigners.[166] But in merchant courts and admiralty the law of the international community of merchants[167] was available as the lex fori both to and against foreigners, upon both domestic and foreign transactions. Common law courts had no need and, indeed, no inclination to deal with matters foreign. Not until these courts, owing to the decline of first the law merchant and then the courts of admiralty, had begun to take cognizance of such matters under

prevalence to the law of nationality and intention. See, in general, WALKER, INTERNATIONALES PRIVATRECHT 407 (1934).

161 BARTIN, PRINCIPES DE DROIT INTERNATIONAL PRIVÉ (1930).

162 Kahn, "Gesetzkollisionen," 30 IHERINGS JAHRBÜCHER 1, 141 (1890).

163 NIEMEYER, VORSCHLÄGE UND MATERIALIEN ZUR KODIFIKATION DES INTERNATIONALEN PRIVATRECHTS (1895).

164 See text at notes 329-339 infra.

165 Kegel, "Begriffs-und Interessenjurisprudenz im Internationalen Privatrecht," FESTSCHRIFT FÜR LEWALD 259 (1953); NUSSBAUM, DEUTSCHES INTERNATIONALES PRIVATRECHT (1932); RAAPE, INTERNATIONALES PRIVATRECHT, 4th ed. (1955); WENGLER, note 16 supra. But cf. Gutzwiller, "Fünfzig Jahre Internationalprivatrecht," 23 RABELS Z. 403 (1958) who expresses new internationalist hopes in his survey of recent history. See, generally, BALLARINO, PROBLEMI GENERALI DEL DIRITTO INTERNAZIONALE PRIVATO NELLA RECENTE LITTERATURA TEDESCA (1958).

166 See, for a vigorous plea, WISEMAN, THE LAW OF LAWS: OR THE EXCELLENCY OF THE CIVIL LAW, ABOVE ALL OTHER HUMAN LAWS WHATSOEVER 146, 161 (1647).

167 "And this law of Merchants hitherto observed in all countries, ought in regard of commerce to be esteemed and held in reputation as the Law of the twelve Tables amongst the Romans. For herein you shall find everything built upon the foundations of Reason and Justice." Malynes, Consuetudo, vel, Lex Mercatoria (1686) 6. For an attack against "Bartolus, Baldus, Justinian . . . and divers other Doctors and learned of the civil Law," with their "many long discourses and Volumes and Books on the questionable matters . . . ," see id. at 3.

the common law of England did the problem of conflict of laws arise.[168]

At the beginning of this new era, the lex fori was not threatened as the basic rule. Owing to jurisdictional limitations, it could (usually) be applied without hardship to either party.[169] Where foreign contract law interposed itself, as it had in early continental law, it did so as the law presumably intended by the parties,[170] while other exceptions from forum law were dominated by the Dutch theory of comity.[171] But here, as elsewhere, conceptualist dogmatism gradually turned pragmatic exceptions into a scheme of purportedly self-evident conflicts rules precariously hidden in the obsolete statutist terminology.[172]

Westlake's text of 1858 (which saw its last edition as late as the second decade of this century) was as much influenced by continental models as was its precursor, Story's *Commentaries*. But Westlake remained fully conscious of the predominant role of a lex fori whose application seemed justified by the choice of jurisdiction.[173] Westlake, like Phillimore,[174] may thus be considered as Savigny's counterpart. Indeed, both expressed their indebtedness to this great German scholar. Since the American Wharton limited himself to a comparative digest,[175] and Foote to a largely uncritical re-examination of the case law,[176] it was left to Dicey to introduce in Anglo-American law the product of continental conceptualism at its worst, the vested rights theory, although that theory by then had long been discredited in the country of its

168 See, in general, EHRENZWEIG 5. On early Scottish conflicts law, see Gibb, "Le droit international privé en Écosse au XVIe et au XVIIe siècle," 25 REV. DE. DR. INT. PRIVÉ 560 (1930), particularly at 571 on the natural law approach of Lord Stair.

169 See, e.g., WESTLAKE, PRIVATE INTERNATIONAL LAW 53, 91, 102, 153, 156 (1859).

170 See Dungannon v. Hackett, 1 Eq. Ca. Abr. 289, 21 Eng. Rep. 1051 (1702) (rate of interest); Foubert v. Trust, 1 Brown Parl. Cas. 129, 1 Eng. Rep. 464 (1703) (marital agreement). See NUSSBAUM 15.

171 Cf. Robinson v. Bland, 2 Burr. 1077, 97 Eng. Rep. 717 (1760); Holman v. Johnson, 1 Cowp. 341, 98 Eng. Rep. 1120 (1775), per Lord Mansfield.

172 BURGE, COMMENTARIES ON COLONIAL AND FOREIGN LAWS GENERALLY (1838); HENRY, THE JUDGMENT OF THE COURT OF DEMERARA 1, 34 (1823).

173 Note 169 supra.

174 4 PHILLIMORE, COMMENTARIES UPON INTERNATIONAL LAW, 3d ed., Preface, p. XV (1889).

175 WHARTON, CONFLICT OF LAWS OR PRIVATE INTERNATIONAL LAW INCLUDING A COMPARATIVE VIEW OF ANGLO-AMERICAN, ROMAN, GERMAN, AND FRENCH JURISPRUDENCE (1872).

176 FOOTE, PRIVATE INTERNATIONAL LAW BASED ON THE DECISIONS OF THE ENGLISH COURTS (1878).

origin.[177] Dicey's *First Principle* was that "any right which has been duly acquired under the law of any civilized country is recognized and . . . no right which has not been duly acquired is enforced . . . by English courts."[178]

Some English writers continue, at least in part, to approve this meaningless and therefore harmful displacement of the lex fori,[179] but Cheshire[180] and Falconbridge[181] have abandoned this approach. So have the editors of the 7th edition of Dicey who have made the *First Principle* contingent upon "the English rules of the conflict of laws."[182] Regrettably this complete abandonment of Dicey's fundamental assumption is explained in a mere note which may easily be overlooked.[183] Nothing short of an open break would have done justice to the entirely original work of the editors who have, in fact, joined those rejecting all universalist dogma and toiling for a proper delimitation of the lex fori as the basic principle of conflict of laws. The history of the conflicts laws of torts and contracts which I have more fully discussed elsewhere[184] seems best suited to illustrate the hesitant progress of English law.

Notwithstanding unsupported assumptions to the contrary,[185] torts did not become a subject of conflict of laws until the middle of the 19th century. To be sure, civil suits against British Crown officers with regard to their colonial administration raised the question earlier whether such officers could justify themselves by reference to the colonial law.[186] But these questions were raised and answered in close analogy to those of criminal responsibility which had been discussed ever since Bartolus' *Commen-*

177 Note 153 supra and note 221 infra. See also CHESHIRE 32. Holland's jurisprudence had prepared the ground. See Nadelmann, "Some Historical Notes on the Doctrinal Sources of American Conflicts Law," FESTGABE GUTZWILLER 263 at 276-278 (1959).

178 DICEY, A DIGEST OF THE LAW OF ENGLAND WITH REFERENCE TO THE CONFLICT OF LAWS, p. xlii (1896).

179 SCHMITTHOFF, ENGLISH CONFLICT OF LAWS, 3d ed. (1954). GRAVESON, CONFLICT OF LAWS, 3d ed., 30 (1955) seems to take an intermediate position.

180 CHESHIRE 32.

181 FALCONBRIDGE 11.

182 DICEY 9.

183 DICEY 12.

184 See note 2 supra.

185 See Smith, "Torts and the Conflict of Laws," 20 MOD. L. REV. 447 at 450 (1957). Cf. BATIFFOL 260, stressing the analogy to crimes.

186 See Mostyn v. Fabrigas, 1 Cowp. 161, 98 Eng. Rep. 1021 (1774).

taries.[187] Wächter[188] was probably the first author to deal with tort conflicts on a more general scale, and it was he who apparently inspired Willes, J., in his now famous opinion in the leading case of *Phillips v. Eyre.*[189] This opinion announced those rules which are still treated as the basis of English tort conflicts law. To both Wächter and Justice Willes the foreign law was nothing but a defense, while the lex fori governed supreme as the sole basis of liability. In fact, even this function of foreign law seems to have been limited to its use "as an authority or ratification in the particular case, and on the peripheral question of vicarious liability."[190]

More fortunate than the United States, England has seen those dogmatic attempts fail at their inception which would endow the foreign law with the power to "create" a tort liability.[191] Indeed, we may wonder at the "metaphysical attractions of an obligation springing to birth out of the soil at the possibly unsuspecting actor's feet and hanging himself around his neck like an albatross."[192] The feat of turning this nightmare into law was reserved to the American Law Institute's *Restatement of the Law of Conflict of Laws.*[193] But even in England dogmatization of isolated legal rules has created new problems in both the tort and contracts law of conflicts.

To be sure, the English tort rule which requires actionability under both the lex fori and the lex loci is clearly justified as to moral wrongs for which it was devised. But dogmatic generalization is probably responsible for the application of this

187 This persistent connection is well illustrated by Codex Maximilianeus Bavaricus Civilis (1756) Part I, c. 2, §17, which deals with the problem of "different laws, statutes and customs prevailing in loco Judicii, Delicti, Rei sitae, Contractus and Domicilii," and clearly identifies "delict" in this phrase with a crime whose "punishment" is subjected to the "laws of the place where it was committed." On the other hand, Part IV, c. 16 which deals with "crimes and obligations arising therefrom," recognizes, in addition to "penal actions," "persecutory actions" which inter alia include tort actions such as those under the lex Aquilia (§6) or de effuso vel dejecto (§8).

188 Note 149 supra.

189 Phillips v. Eyre, [1870] L.R. 6 Q.B. 1 at 29. See FALCONBRIDGE 809; Yntema, Book Review, 27 CAN. B. REV. 116 (1949).

190 Smith, note 185 supra, at 452. See also DICEY 941, 951. On this ground the much criticized decision in Machado v. Fontes, [1897] 2 Q.B. 231, seems entirely proper, in which liability for a Brazilian libel was found under English law. FALCONBRIDGE 820. Only a vested rights approach could doubt the "logical" accuracy of this decision. Pollock, note 13 L.Q. REV. 233 (1897).

191 See concerning Westlake's theory to this effect, Smith, note 185 supra, at 454.

192 Id. at 457.

193 See text at notes 213-223 infra.

rule to "tort" liabilities which serve modern principles of enterprise risk allocation rather than the sanction of moral wrongs. In such cases the lex loci delicti as such has no claim to application, and other tests must be sought to supply such exceptions from the lex fori[194] as may be required by the policies underlying each specific rule of enterprise liability.[195]

To illustrate: Where an Ontario plaintiff brought a suit in Saskatchewan against his employer, a national railroad, for an injury sustained in Ontario through the negligence of a fellow servant, dismissal could well have been supported on the ground, advanced by the trial court, that the forum should not have taken jurisdiction. But it is unfortunate that the Privy Council preferred to rest its decision against plaintiff on the purely conceptualistic argument that the law of the place of accident had preserved the fellow servant rule which had been abolished by the lex fori.[196] Should the decision have been the same if the plaintiff had been a Saskatchewan resident? Since it was not a "wrong" that had been sued upon, the defendant could not, in its calculations, have relied on an antiquated common-law rule widely abolished. The lex fori must prevail where the forum's selection does not impose hardship on the defendant.

In other fields, the allegory of a foreign law creating rights to be enforced or recognized in the forum has been even more harmful. To be sure, the lex contractus which has left its fatal marks in the American *Restatement*[197] has long yielded in England to a flexible non-rule of "proper law," which is simply an admonition to the court to consider whether a foreign law in the particular case would be more appropriate than the lex fori—to "inspect" that foreign law in the true sense of Bartolus.[198] But there are other problem situations in which the lex fori is being given its due only in the circuitous ways of renvoi, pro-

[194] Wortley, "The General Principles of Private International Law from the English Standpoint," 71 RECUEIL DES COURS 5 at 59 (1947), advocates outright application of the lex fori in tort cases.

[195] See my papers, note 2 supra.

[196] McMillan v. Canadian Northern Ry. Co., [1923] A.C. 120. See also Ehrenzweig, "Alternative Actionability in the Conflict of Laws of Enterprise Liability: An American Comment on M'Elroy's Case," 63 JURID. REV. 39 (1951) and, in general, Ehrenzweig, "Vicarious Liability in the Conflict of Laws," 69 YALE L.J.—(1960).

[197] See, in general, Ehrenzweig, "Contracts in the Conflict of Laws," 59 COL. L. REV. 973, 1171 (1959).

[198] Notes 70-72 supra. See also CHESHIRE 205.

cedural characterization or public policy.[199] England, like the United States, seems entitled to a new start, discounting the dubious achievements of this dogmatic century.

7. *United States*

In order to obtain a proper perspective in history and comparison, there must be excluded at the outset all those problems which, while phrased in terms of choice of law, concern the recognition of judgments or quasi-judgments, i.e., of individual foreign governmental acts directed against individual persons. Recognition of such acts is clearly governed by considerations quite different from those involved in the choice of foreign abstract rules which purportedly are better equipped to decide the case at bar than the lex fori. In the former category we find most of the earliest conflicts questions, such as the recognition of foreign discharges in bankruptcy,[200] or of assessments by foreign administrative officers and the like.[201]

Any attempt at classifying Story's general theory of choice of law would be futile. He was an eclectic, willing to accept the experience of England and Scotland in their mutual dealings with domestic relations, to combine elsewhere the inconsistent theorems of the Dutch supremacy of local law with the French feudalists' wholesale acceptance of the lex situs, and to sanction the internationalist ideology of his own time by endowing it with the new name of "private international law."[202] This much seems certain, however, that Story was far from replacing the lex fori by a set of a priori rules calling for the application of foreign law.[203] Professor Beale thought otherwise. But for his contention of an

[199] See text following note 243 infra.

[200] See, e.g., LIVERMORE, DISSERTATIONS ON THE QUESTIONS WHICH ARISE FROM THE CONTRARIETY OF THE POSITIVE LAWS OF DIFFERENT STATES AND NATIONS 140 (1829); 2 KENT, COMMENTARIES 321 (1827); HENRY, THE JUDGMENT OF THE COURT OF DEMERARA IN THE CASE OF ODWIN v. FORBES ON THE PLEA OF THE ENGLISH CERTIFICATE OF BANKRUPTCY IN BAR, IN A FOREIGN JURISDICTION (1823).

[201] EHRENZWEIG 31.

[202] STORY 100-192, 7-38, 358-390. See Yntema, "Contract and Conflict of Laws: 'Autonomy' in Choice of Law in the United States," 1 N.Y. L. FORUM 47 at 51 (1955) ("derived from a variety of conflicting views"). Cf. Nadelmann, "Some Historical Notes on the Doctrinal Sources of American Conflicts Law," FESTGABE GUTZWILLER 263 at 272-276 (1959). See also IRMER, "COMITY," NEDERLANDSE INVLOED OP HET RECHT DER VERENIGDE STAATEN 28-41 (1948).

[203] Story's chapter on Jurisdiction and Remedies kept the door wide open for applying the lex fori to both contracts and torts.

early vested rights tradition of Anglo-American law[204] he relied on one English[205] and one Massachusetts case,[206] both of which concerned the effect of "quasi-judgments" in bankruptcy[207] not here pertinent. And such dicta in the Massachusetts case as concerned choice of law refute Beale's thesis. The court did not suggest that "an act or obligation valid by the laws of the place where made was valid everywhere."[208] What the court did say was that "as the laws of foreign countries are not admitted ex proprio vigore, but only ex comitate, the judicial power will exercise a discretion with respect to the laws they may be called upon to sanction . . .," and that the lex contractus does not apply to contracts "entered into with a view to the laws of some other State."[209]

When Field prepared his *Outlines of an International Code* in 1872, he was understandably influenced by the internationalist ideology which was then approaching its climax. But, while treating conflicts law as an essential part of international law, he did not hesitate to state the "well settled rule founded on reason and authority . . . [that] the lex fori . . . furnishes in all cases, prima facie, the rule of decision; and if either party wishes the benefit of a different rule or law, as for instance the lex domicilii, lex loci contractus, or lex rei sitae, he must aver and prove it."[210] In 1875 the Supreme Court of Wisconsin felt able to call the principle that a personal injury action was governed by the lex fori, "almost too familiar . . . for discussion or authority."[211] As late as 1879 Rorer's text on *American Inter-State Law*, while conceding certain conflicts principles to be based on "natural rights," the "law of nations," or "universal law" (including personal law and the lex contractus), starts with the proposition that "the rule of comity will not be enforced as against domestic law or the legal rights and interests of *citizens*, or to their injury."[212]

204 BEALE 105.
205 Potter v. Brown, 5 East 124, 102 Eng. Rep. 1016 (1804).
206 Blanchard v. Russell, 13 Mass. 1 (1816).
207 Note 201 supra.
208 BEALE 105.
209 Blanchard v. Russell, 13 Mass. 1 at 4-5 (1816).
210 FIELD, OUTLINES OF AN INTERNATIONAL CODE 439 (1872), relying on Norris v. Harris, 15 Cal. 226 at 253 (1860), per Field, C.J., with earlier authority.
211 Anderson v. Milwaukee & St. Paul R.R., 37 Wis. 321 (1875).
212 RORER, AMERICAN INTER-STATE LAW 5 (1879). Emphasis added.

It was left to Joseph Beale to implant in American law the conceptualist thinking of his continental contemporaries. Dean Griswold has said that "it is very hard to think of any other field of the law which has been so much 'made' by one man."[213] It will take many more to un-make his law, for Beale became the author of the *Restatement*, and the teacher of many judges and scholars who even today continue to speak his language. Un-made this "law" must be, as the frustrated attempt by a great man to make this a better world.

When Professor Beale began to teach conflict of laws in 1893 this subject was not taught at any American law school, and he found no textbook usable for his purpose.[214] His first course was presented as one on "Conflict of Laws and International Law." Notwithstanding his later emphasis upon the distinction between the two subjects, his first casebook would seem to support the conclusion that his thinking which equated interstate and international conflicts was very definitely influenced by an international ideology.[215] Only this ideology can explain his lack of interest in interstate problems for which, indeed, a text would have been available,[216] and his all-pervading theory of "vested rights."

Professor Beale believed this theory, around which he built his *Restatement* and his treatise, to be an "indigenous" creation of the common law, whose earlier appreciation he credited —with "a conceit, strange and . . . inexpedient"[217]—only to Dicey's text with its "crowning quality," its "ability to keep clear of the Continental writers."[218] But Dicey himself had acknowledged his debt to "foreign jurists, such as Savigny, Bar, and Foelix," as well as to Westlake[219] who, in turn, ever since his first

213 Griswold, "Mr. Beale and the Conflict of Laws," 56 HARV. L. REV. 690 (1943).

214 Ibid.

215 1 BEALE, A SELECTION OF CASES ON THE CONFLICT OF LAWS, p. V (1900): ". . . questions of international law, which should properly be decided in every country in the same way."

216 Rorer, note 212 supra, discounted in 1 BEALE, CONFLICT OF LAWS (1935), p. XXX, as of "no independent authority," "a summary statement of the doctrines of the Conflict of Laws *merely* as they apply between the states, together with a considerable body of constitutional law." Emphasis added.

217 Yntema, Foreword to RABEL, THE CONFLICT OF LAWS, A COMPARATIVE STUDY, at XVI (1945).

218 Beale, "Dicey's 'Conflict of Laws'," 10 HARV. L. REV. 168 at 169 (1896).

219 DICEY, A DIGEST OF THE LAW OF ENGLAND WITH REFERENCE TO THE CONFLICT OF LAWS, pp. vi, vii (1896).

edition, had stressed the overwhelming importance of continental writers for the development of English conflicts law.[220] And those continental writers, well-known to Beale,[221] had discarded the theory of vested rights, erroneously praised by him as "indigenous" to the common law, as perhaps the most harmful loan from the internationalist doctrine of the last century.[222] Fortunately, a new generation of judges and writers in this country, too, has begun to discount this aberration.[223]

C. THE BASIC RULE IN DISGUISE

As long as a quarter of a century ago, an outstanding French scholar urged "that the role attributed to the foreign law is too broad and that attributed to the lex fori is too narrow. We have reason to assume that the lex fori has a strong claim to be applied to everybody, even to foreigners, a claim which to promote we have applied considerable coquetry, and which is based on the fact that the lex fori is the law most adequate for the country where the litigation occurs, and perhaps even most adequate for the conflicting private interests."[224] I have tried to show in this paper that this new stress on the predominance of the lex fori is but a return to its historical mission. In a series of articles, I have tried to show the need for a factual and policy analysis of those typical situations in which American conflicts law should continue to refer to foreign laws.[225] This task might take decades to complete. In the meantime, traditional formulas will fill what we may hope will be an ever-diminishing gap. Personal law, lex situs and lex actus will continue to force us to choose between them. But, once relieved of dogmatic pretense, the choice can be narrowed and simplified. In the absence of a different autonomous choice by the parties, the lex fori will yield to foreign laws only for specific reasons which may be more readily analyzed and

220 See, e.g., WESTLAKE, PRIVATE INTERNATIONAL LAW, 5th ed., 23 (1912).

221 BEALE, CONFLICT OF LAWS (1916) added to the author's Treatise as an Appendix. 3 BEALE, CONFLICT OF LAWS 1879 (1935).

222 See notes 153, 177 supra. See also, e.g., NUSSBAUM 27; WICHSER, DER BEGRIFF DES WOHLERWORBENEN RECHTS IM INTERNATIONALEN PRIVATRECHT 7, 22 (1955). 4 PHILLIMORE, COMMENTARIES UPON INTERNATIONAL LAW, 3d ed., Preface, p. XI (1889), still refers to "acquired" rights entitled to recognition according to "reason and the interests of society."

223 See EHRENZWEIG 13.

224 Louis-Lucas, "Remarques sur l'ordre public," 28 REV. DE DR. INT. PR. 393 (1933). See also id. at 442.

225 See note 2 supra.

classified than those now allegedly calling for their a priori application. Suggestions that the lex fori be thus restored as the basic rule of conflict of laws often meet dogmatic criticism as being "provincial," "nationalist," "defeatist," even among those willing to recognize the realities of everyday practice. But, as Justice Traynor has remarked, "The hazard is less of impassioned provincialism than of the lingering ills of a passive formalism."[226]

The lex fori, in many different disguises, is about to regain that position in theory which it has always maintained in effect. In all countries whose legal histories have been retraced in this paper, and elsewhere, the dogmatic interlude is drawing to a close. In Italy, Mancini's postulates based on the law of nationality have yielded to a new emphasis on the internal character of conflicts rules, and, more generally, to a new "territorialism" which, in effect, favors the lex fori.[227] In France, Bartin, Lerebours-Pigeonnière and Batiffol have long overcome Pillet's internationalist flight into fancy.[228] Neither the Netherlands[229] nor the Scandinavian countries since Ørsted's pioneering fight against statutist theory have ever abandoned their realistic preferences for the lex fori and the autonomy of the parties.[230] In Germany, modern writers have long found the way back to a functional analysis of specific fact situations, in disregard of Zitelmann's international dream and the conceptual jurisprudence of the latter statutists.[231] In England, Dicey's "vested rights" have been emasculated by his contemporary editors who have joined Cheshire in assisting the courts in the rebuilding of a modern doctrine.[232] In the United States leading judges and virtually all writers on the subject, outside the American Law Institute, have begun to build again on the "wreckage"[233] left by the destruction of the

226 Traynor, "Is This Conflict Really Necessary?" 37 TEX. L. REV. 657 at 675 (1959).

227 Note 88 supra.

228 Notes 126-130 supra.

229 Note 141 supra.

230 See e.g., MALMSTRÖM, SOME ASPECTS OF CHARACTERIZATION IN PRIVATE INTERNATIONAL LAW: LIBER AMICORUM BAGGE 130, 131 (1956); Hambro, "Autonomy in the International Contract Law of the Nordic States," 6 INT. AND COMP. L.Q. 589 (1957). See also, in general, Korkisch, "Der Anteil der nordischen Länder an den Fragen des internationalen Privatrechts," 23 RABEL Z. 599 at 604 (1958); GJELSVIK, DAS INTERNATIONALE PRIVATRECHT IN NORWEGEN 37 (1935); MICHAELI, INTERNATIONALES PRIVATRECHT 39-45 (1947).

231 Notes 162-165 supra.

232 Note 180 supra.

233 Traynor, "Law and Social Change in a Democratic Society," [1956] UNIV. ILL. L. FORUM 230 at 234. See also Traynor, "Is this Conflict Really Necessary?" 37 TEX. L. REV. 657 (1959).

Restatement's house of cards.[234] And everywhere courts seek to overcome antiquated "rules" and official theory by manipulating these rules or their connecting factors, or by creating "exceptions" such as procedural,[235] "preliminary," [236] and other[237] characterizations of questions or rules, renvoi,[238] fraud on the law,[239] "estoppel,"[240] failure of proof,[241] and above all, public policy.[242] All these exceptions are designed to reach results indirectly which could be reached directly by recognizing the lex fori as the rule primarily to be applied. A brief analysis of some of these techniques will readily show their inadequacy.

1. *"Public Policy" and "Ordre Public"*

"The notion that the rules of Conflict of Laws can be derived from some general formula or theory is responsible for another doctrine—that of 'public policy'—which in turn has caused the utmost confusion."[243] This statement of Professor Lorenzen disposes, for our present purposes, of the controversy between those who think that public policy is "peculiarly English and smacks of the particular genius of the common law,"[244] and those who concede a much greater part to this concept in continental law.[245] In both legal systems the appearance of public policy

234 Note 223 supra.

235 Notes 279-296 infra.

236 Notes 321-328 infra.

237 Classic examples are the contracts characterizations of tort and land cases [see Ehrenzweig, "Contracts in the Conflict of Laws," 59 COL. L. REV. 973, 1171 (1959)]. See also notes 4 and 7 supra.

238 Notes 301-320 infra.

239 This term is not yet fully accepted in the common law. But see, e.g., FRANCESCAKIS, LA THÉORIE DU RENVOI 43 (1958).

240 See 2 MADSEN-MYGDAL, ORDRE PUBLIC OG TERRITORIALITET 822 (1946) (English summary).

241 Notes 297-300 infra.

242 Notes 243-278 infra.

243 Lorenzen, "Territoriality, Public Policy and the Conflict of Laws," 33 YALE L.J. 736 at 746 (1924).

244 PATON, JURISPRUDENCE, 2d ed., 98 (1951). See also Winfield, "Public Policy in the English Common Law," 42 HARV. L. REV. 76 at 98 (1928) ("part of the spirit of the common law").

245 GUTTERIDGE, COMPARATIVE LAW, 2d ed., 98 (1949). See, in general, LLOYD, PUBLIC POLICY 73 (1953); LEREBOURS-PIGEONNIÈRE, PRÉCIS DE DROIT INTERNATIONAL PRIVÉ, 6th ed., 288 (1954); MAURY, L'ÉVICTION DE LA LOI NORMALEMENT COMPÉTENTE 33-36 (1952); KOLLEWIJN, HET BEGINSEL DER OPENBARE ORDE IN HET INTERNATIONAAL PRIVAATRECHT (1917); and particularly Nussbaum, "Public Policy and the Political Crisis in the Conflict of Laws," 49 YALE L. J. 1027 (1940); Kahn-Freund, "Reflections on Public Policy in the English Conflict of Laws," 39 GROT. SOC. 39 (1954); Sperduti, "Ordine pubblico inter-

coincides with the climax of those universalist aspirations which undertook to displace the lex fori by a uniform conflicts law and thus required measures to make such a law as harmless as possible to the law of the forum. Wherever that law continued to need protection, reference to public policy, or the "ordre public" was given an ever-increasing play as an "exception." Traceable to the statuta odiosa of statutist eras[246] (which, however, may originally have merely limited the laws of the forum themselves) and to the cautious and incidental reliance of Huber on the forum's interest[247] (unnecessary under his rationale of mere comity), the ordre public was moved into the center of attention by Mancini[248] and again by Bartin.[249]

A historical study of the origin of the doctrine in Anglo-American conflicts law is lacking.[250] English cases habitually adduced to prove early application are not in point.[251] And it seems clear that there was neither need nor use of the doctrine in this field until the establishment of the vested rights doctrine at the end of the last century.[252] For here, as elsewhere, "public policy" appears where the common law fails to keep "in touch with the needs of the day."[253] The same observation applies to the history of American law.[254] Not until the era of vested rights

nazionale e ordine pubblico interno," 37 RIV. DIR. INT. 82 (1954); LAGARDE, RECHERCHES SUR L'ORDRE PUBLIC EN DROIT INTERNATIONAL PRIVÉ (1959); SCHLESINGER, COMPARATIVE LAW, 2d ed., 465 (1959).

[246] BATIFFOL 263.

[247] BATIFFOL 270.

[248] NUSSBAUM 110.

[249] BARTIN, ÉTUDES DE DROIT INTERNATIONAL PRIVÉ (1899).

[250] Both English and American texts rely indiscriminately on cases decided prior to and after the invasion of vested rights. See, e.g., CHESHIRE 150; 3 BEALE, CONFLICT OF LAWS 1647 (1935). See also Katzenbach, "Conflicts on an Unruly Horse: Reciprocal Claims and Tolerances in Interstate and International Law," 65 YALE L. J. 1087 (1956); note, 33 COL. L. REV. 508 (1933). Paulsen and Sovern, "'Public Policy' in the Conflict of Laws," 56 COL. L. REV. 969 at 972, 980 (1956) helpfully distinguish the "classical concept" from the "choice of law function" of public policy. On the history of public policy in general, see 8 HOLDSWORTH, A HISTORY OF ENGLISH LAW 56 (restraint of trade), 383 (contract) (1926).

[251] Robinson v. Bland, 2 Burr. 1077, 97 Eng. Rep. 717 (1760) (unenforceable contract under law of forum invoked by plaintiff); De Wutz v. Hendricks, 2 Bing. 314, 130 Eng. Rep. 326 (1824) (English contract unenforceable as directed against friendly government); Hope v. Hope, 8 DeG., M. & G. 731, 44 Eng. Rep. 572 (1857) (unenforceable contract bearing on family relations); Santos v. Illidge, 8 C.B. (n.s.) 861, 141 Eng. Rep. 1404 (1860) (interpretation of statute in terms applicable to foreign transaction); Grell v. Levy, 16 C.B. (n.s.) 73, 143 Eng. Rep. 1052 (1864) (contracts to be performed in England).

[252] For recent authority, see CHESHIRE 150.

[253] 8 HOLDSWORTH, A HISTORY OF ENGLISH LAW 56 (1926).

[254] See Lorenzen, "Territoriality, Public Policy and the Conflict of Laws," 33 YALE L.J. 736 (1924); Paulsen and Sovern, "'Public Policy' in the Conflict of Laws," 56 COL. L. REV. 969 at 981 (1956).

which reached its climax in Beale's *Restatement* did public policy become an essential part of American conflicts law and an additional source of its confusion.[255]

In 1827 the Louisiana court remarked "that in the conflict of laws, it must often be a matter of doubt, which should prevail; and that whenever a doubt does exist, the court, which decides, will prefer the law of its own country to that of the stranger."[256] Story found "great truth" in this statement and returned to its message in virtually every chapter of his analysis without having to resort to an exception of public policy.[257] Only where past centuries had produced a semblance of rules "by which nations are morally or politically bound,"[258] was there room in his work for such an exception.[259] Legislation at first failed to alter this situation as long as judicial distrust left undisturbed the regime of the common law of the lex fori where dealing with foreign facts. The history of wrongful death statutes offers an example for both this early lack of conflicts law and its later functioning by rule and exception. Such statutes[260] began to spread through the United States after the enactment of Lord Campbell's Act in England in 1846.[261] Presumably owing to judicial preference for the common law, forum statutes were treated as local and limited to domestic causes of action, notwithstanding early claims that these statutes should equally be applied to foreign accidents, having removed a procedural limitation[262] or a defect in the common law.[263] No wonder then that conversely the common law of the forum was preferred to

[255] CONFLICT OF LAWS RESTATEMENT §612 (1934).

[256] Saul v. His Creditors, (La. 1827) 5 Martin R. (n.s.) 569 at 595.

[257] See, e.g., STORY 29.

[258] STORY 71.

[259] "Generally speaking, the validity of a contract is to be decided by the law of the place, where it is made." STORY 201. But the lex fori re-enters as to contracts "against good morals, or religion, or public rights." Id. at 213. The same rule and exception apply to the "favored contract" (id. at 100) of marriage. Id. at 104. Limitations on the parties' autonomy were rare. Paulsen and Sovern, "'Public Policy' in the Conflict of Laws," 56 COL. L. REV. 969 at 972 (1956).

[260] EHRENZWEIG 4.

[261] For abortive colonial legislation, see, e.g., CHARTER AND GENERAL LAWS OF THE COLONY AND PROVINCE OF MASSACHUSETTS BAY, c. 8, 43 (1759), COLONIAL LAWS OF MASSACHUSETTS, 1660-1672 (Whitmore's Reprint 1889) 126; Conn. Acts and Laws (1750) 17; Conn. Pub. Stat. (1808) 120. See, in general, Rose, "Foreign Enforcement of Actions for Wrongful Death," 33 MICH. L. REV. 545 at 552 (1935): ". . . the body of the present law is blemished by early preconceptions."

[262] Stat. 9 & 10 Vict., c. 93.

[263] This argument was made in Whitford v. Panama R.R., 23 N.Y. 465 (1861) by the dissenting judge.

foreign statutes.[264] But the universalist illusion of "governing" conflicts rules had progressed far enough to compel, almost from the very beginning, dogmatic rationalizations of this practice. As early as 1857 we find the New York court refusing to apply its wrongful death statute to a Connecticut accident because "whether an act or omission affords a right of action depends on the law of the place where it is done or omitted."[265] And this rationalization gained a life of its own when in 1880 the Supreme Court announced the ubiquitous applicability of the wrongful death statute of any state in which "a right of action has become fixed and a legal liability incurred."[266]

It was then, and only then, that courts had to seek to control an over-generalized "rule." The first "exception," which permitted the foreign statute to be enforced only if substantially similar to that of the forum,[267] promised preservation of the lex fori as the basic law. But this principle was not acceptable to Holmes[268] and Cardozo,[269] judges steeped in the universalist illusion of their time, who were about to lay the groundwork for the grand scheme adopted in the *Restatement*, according to which rights lawfully vested shall be everywhere maintained.[270] All that seemed left of the lex fori in that scheme was the possible exception, recognized with apparent reluctance by both these judges and the *Restatement*, that the foreign law is to be ignored

[264] Campbell v. Rogers, 2 Handy 110, 12 Ohio Dec. 355 (1855).

[265] Richardson v. New York Central R. Co., 98 Mass. 85 (1867). See also Anderson v. Milwaukee & St. Paul Ry. Co., 37 Wis. 321 at 322 (1875), refusing to apply an Iowa statute that had abolished the fellow servant rule: "The action here is a personal action, for personal injury, governed by the *lex fori*. This is almost too familiar a principle for discussion or authority." See also Vandeventer v. The New York and New Haven R.R., 27 Barb. (N.Y.) 244 (1857); Whitford v. Panama R.R., 23 N.Y. 465 (1861).

[266] Dennick v. Railroad Co., 103 U.S. 11 at 18 (1880). This was new doctrine. Three of the cases relied on by the Court did not concern torts. In the fourth case, Great Western Ry. Co. v. Miller, 19 Mich. 305 (1869), a judgment based on a Canadian statute, was reversed on what amounted to a theory of forum non conveniens. And N. & C. R.R. v. Sprayberry, 8 Bax. (67 Tenn.) 341 (1874), upheld a foreign tort claim for the death of wife and children without facing the problem.

[267] Wooden v. Western N.Y. & P. R.R. Co., 126 N.Y. 10, 26 N.E. 1050 (1891). The oldest case seems to be Leonard v. Columbia Steam Navigation Co., 84 N.Y. 48 (1881). Texas and Maryland seem still to adhere to this test. See Paulsen, "Foreign Law in Texas Courts," 33 TEX. L. REV. 437 (1955); Paulsen and Sovern, "'Public Policy' in the Conflict of Laws," 56 COL. L. REV. 969 at 975 (1956).

[268] Walsh v. New York and New England R.R., 160 Mass. 571, 36 N.E. 584 (1894).

[269] Loucks v. Standard Oil Co., 224 N.Y. 99, 120 N.E. 198 (1918).

[270] In contrast to the draftsman, Professor Beale [A TREATISE ON THE CONFLICT OF LAWS 105-107 (1916)] the *Restatement* has abandoned the language, though not the concept, of vested rights. See, in general, EHRENZWEIG 9-10.

where it "outrages the public policy" of the forum.[271] But this would not do. Only a few years later Chief Judge Lehmann found it necessary to broaden the applicability of the lex fori by, inter alia, excluding a foreign law as being "contrary to the law of this state."[272] This broad test would, of course, exclude generally the application of foreign laws. It is as unworkable as its counterpart, Justice Cardozo's vested right. But both Lehmann and Cardozo could have reached the desired result by abandoning both "rule" and "exception," in favor of an outright application of the lex fori.[273]

Similar difficulties in international conflicts cases have prompted international conferences to recommend to the several countries the classification and enumeration of those specific situations in which the public policy exception seems indispensable.[274] But these recommendations remained unheeded and had to be abandoned.[275] Even such more definite categories as have been developed both internationally and nationally as the alleged "unenforceability" of "penal" and "revenue" laws are in the process of disintegration.[276] This fact "ought to have been a warning that there was something the matter with the reasoning upon which the rules to which it is the exception were supposed to be based,"[277] and renewed analysis of these rules should have become the primary objective of scholarship. But "the principal vice of the public policy concepts is that they provide a substitute for analysis. The concepts stand in the way of careful

271 Loucks v. Standard Oil Co., 224 N.Y. 99 at 111, 120 N.E. 198 (1918). See also Goodrich, "Foreign Facts and Local Fancies," 25 VA. L. REV. 26 at 33 (1938).

272 Mertz v. Mertz, 271 N.Y. 466, 3 N.E. (2d) 597 (1936). Remedial characterization was used as another ground of the decisions. See also Paulsen and Sovern, " 'Public Policy' in the Conflict of Laws," 56 COL. L. REV. 969 at 995 (1956).

273 For a pragmatic analysis of the problem involved in both Loucks v. Standard Oil Co., note 269 supra and Mertz v. Mertz, note 272 supra, see Ford, "Interspousal Liability for Automobile Accidents in the Conflict of Laws," 15 UNIV. PITT. L. REV. 397 (1954). See also Ehrenzweig, "Parental Immunity in the Conflict of Laws," 23 UNIV. CHI. L. REV. 474 (1956). For the role of public policy in the contracts field, see Ehrenzweig, "Contracts in the Conflict of Laws," 59 COL. L. REV. 973, 1171 (1959). See also Ehrenzweig, "Guest Statutes in the Conflict of Laws," 69 YALE L.J. 595 (1960).

274 Institut de Droit International, Tableau Général des Résolutions (1873-1956), Resolution of March 30, 1910, p. 277.

275 BATIFFOL 378. MADSEN-MYGDAL, ORDRE PUBLIC OG TERRITORIALITET (1946) has made a valuable attempt at saving both the rules and the concept by detailed classifications. See id. at 813, 818 (English summary).

276 See EHRENZWEIG 131, 201.

277 Lorenzen, "Territoriality, Public Policy and the Conflict of Laws," 33 YALE L. J. 736 at 747 (1924).

thought, of discriminating distinctions, and of true policy development in the conflict of laws."[278]

2. *"Procedure"*

American doctrine started with the assumption "universally admitted and established" that "the forms of remedies, and the modes of proceeding . . . are to be regulated solely and exclusively by the laws of the place where the action is instituted."[279] This principle goes back to the time when certain foreign laws were first said to be entitled to "inspection."[280] Thus, when Balduini formulated the "remedy" rule he merely confirmed the continuation of the regime of the lex fori as against these new exceptions.[281] The rule was broadly interpreted, therefore, and presented few problems.[282] Only when the internationalist dogmatization of conflicts law by the latter-day statutists began to require the application of foreign law did procedural characterization assume its modern function as the basis for exceptional applications of the lex fori. In the common-law orbit this function is traceable to Dutch doctrine.[283] But it did not become significant until the victory of the doctrine of vested rights, against which the lex fori asserted itself as requiring its own procedures,[284] "machinery,"[285] or "remedy."[286]

[278] Paulsen and Sovern, "'Public Policy' in the Conflict of Laws," 56 COL. L. REV. 969 at 1016 (1956).

[279] STORY 468. For a history of the distinction, see Ailes, "Substance and Procedure in the Conflict of Laws," 39 MICH. L. REV. 392 at 396 (1941).

[280] Note 72 supra.

[281] MEIJERS 595, with additional sources. See also Ailes, "Substance and Procedure in the Conflict of Laws," 39 MICH. L. REV. 392 at 396 (1941).

[282] The laws of evidence, execution, default, statutes of limitations, and arbitration were included. MEIJERS 615, 616.

[283] Cf. STORY 472, quoting Johannes Voet.

[284] Concerning the logical inconsistency between this doctrine and its "procedural" exceptions, see, e.g., Yntema, "The Hornbook Method and the Conflict of Laws," 37 YALE L. J. 468 at 478 (1928). In contract cases the forum's remedies had always been withdrawn from the parties' autonomy. Melan v. Duke de Fitzjames, 1 Bos. & Pul. 138, 126 Eng. Rep. 822 (1797). See, in general, Ailes, "Substance and Procedure in the Conflict of Laws," 39 MICH. L. REV. 392 at 393 (1941).

[285] Slater v. Mexican National R. Co., 194 U.S. 120 (1904) is probably the outstanding case using this technique. In that case the Court, speaking through Justice Holmes, denied a tort claim for periodical payments under Mexican law because the Texas court had "no power to make a decree of this kind contemplated by the Mexican statutes." Id. at 128.

[286] See, e.g., note 272 supra.

That the dichotomy is analytically meaningless has now been generally recognized.[287] But it seems equally clear that solution of the resulting practical problems cannot now be sought in the abolition of a distinction so well established in the language of the courts.[288] There remains the real need for a technique enabling the courts to restore to the lex fori some of the ground which it has lost through the dogmatic generalizations of the last decades. Thus, nothing would be gained by the discovery that statutes of limitations, whether part of the right or "remedial," are really substantive because they affect the cause of action,[289] that survival statutes must not be characterized as procedural as was recently done by a leading court,[290] or that statutes of frauds,[291] the standing to sue or be sued,[292] or damages[293] cannot in any proper sense be treated as procedural to assure application of the lex fori. But, like public policy, procedural characterization should be used only as a makeshift device until the law of the forum can again be recognized as the basic rule subject to displacement by foreign laws only under well-established exceptions grounded on reason and policy. Then, and only then, will it have become unnecessary to salvage the lex fori by such devices.[294]

When Chief Judge Lehmann refused to apply Connecticut law over the forum's prohibition of inter-spousal suits, he proved too much when he claimed that "no other state can, outside its own territorial limits, . . . provide by its law a remedy avail-

287 NUSSBAUM 187; Cook, "'Substance' and 'Procedure' in the Conflict of Laws," 42 YALE L. J. 333 (1933); LORENZEN, SELECTED ARTICLES ON THE CONFLICT OF LAWS 336 (1947); FALCONBRIDGE 301.

288 Ailes, "Substance, and Procedure in the Conflict of Laws," 39 MICH. L. REV. 392 at 413 (1941).

289 See EHRENZWEIG 128. Continental jurisprudence which favors substantive characterization has hardly progressed further. See id. at 129, n. 1.

290 Grant v. McAuliffe, 41 Cal. (2d) 859, 264 P. (2d) 944 (1953). Compare Currie, "Survival of Actions: Adjudication Versus Automation in the Conflict of Laws," 10 STAN. L. REV. 205 (1958); Traynor, "Is This Conflict Really Necessary?" 37 TEX. L. REV. 657 at 670, n. 34 (1959).

291 See Ehrenzweig, "The Statute of Frauds in the Conflict of Laws," 59 COL. L. REV. 874 (1959).

292 EHRENZWEIG 37.

293 See Ehrenzweig, "Contracts in the Conflict of Laws," 59 COL. L. REV. 973, 1171 (1959); and, in general, WOLFF 233, 238, 242.

294 Cook, "'Substance' and 'Procedure' in the Conflict of Laws," 42 YALE L. J. 333 (1933) would have the court apply foreign law wherever it can do so "without unduly hindering or inconveniencing itself." See also note, 47 HARV. L. REV. 315 (1933); Comment, 10 LA. L. REV. 365 (1950) (contributory negligence).

able in our courts which our law denies to other suitors."[295] Of course, Connecticut cannot, in the New York court, "provide" a new remedy. But New York may, under Connecticut law, grant a remedy for Connecticut accidents. That it may choose not to do so in order not to discriminate against those suing on New York accidents is a question to be settled by re-formulating the New York conflicts rule so as to extend the New York disability to foreign accidents.[296] Only such unworkable "rules" as that of the *Restatement* which purports to require ubiquitous application of the lex loci have compelled such unworkable exceptions as that purporting to require general application of the lex fori to all "remedies." Nothing less will do but a rethinking of those conflicts rules as exceptions from the lex fori.

3. *Failure to Prove the Foreign Law*

Notwithstanding any foreign laws allegedly "governing" the case, American courts have, in literally hundreds and perhaps thousands of decisions, applied their own law, in reliance on the often obviously unrealistic principle that the foreign law not properly pleaded or proved may be presumed to be identical with the law of the forum.[297] Only rarely have courts assumed an independent conflicts rule calling in such cases for the application of that law as such.[298]

The indispensability of such a rule is demonstrated by those few but unluckily highly authoritative decisions in which suits have been dismissed on the ground that the "governing" law had not been established.[299] When it is recognized, and only when it is recognized, that the law of the forum as the Basic Rule is entitled to application at the outset unless displaced by

295 Mertz v. Mertz, 271 N.Y. 466, 3 N.E. (2d) 597 (1936).

296 For an attempt to reconcile the case law with a view to the parties' domicile, see Ford, "Interspousal Liability for Automobile Accidents in the Conflict of Laws," 15 UNIV. PITT. L. REV. 397 (1954); Haumschild v. Continental Cas. Co., 7 Wis. (2d) 130, 95 N.W. (2d) 814 (1959.)

297 Currie, "On the Displacement of the Law of the Forum," 58 COL. L. REV. 964 (1958); Nussbaum, "The Problem of Proving Foreign Law," 50 YALE L. J. 1018 (1941). On judicial notice of foreign laws, see also, e.g., Stern, "Foreign Law in the Courts: Judicial Notice and Proof," 45 CALIF. L. REV. 23 (1957); 23 A.L.R. (2d) 1437 (1952).

298 See, e.g., Leary v. Gledhill, 8 N.J. 260, 84 A. (2d) 725 (1951).

299 Walton v. Arabian American Oil Co., (2d Cir. 1956) 233 F. (2d) 541, cert. den. 352 U.S. 872 (1956), relying on Cuba Railroad v. Crosby, 222 U.S. 473 (1912). As to the English doctrine to the contrary, see Currie, "On the Displacement of the Law of the Forum," 58 COL. L. REV. 964 at 967 (1958).

a more appropriate law invoked by either party can the authority of such unfortunate decisions permanently be discounted.[300]

4. *Renvoi*

English and American law have long resisted that peculiar device by which a forum, having found itself obligated to apply a foreign law, returns to its own law by invoking that foreign law's own directives. And, indeed, until such an obligation to apply the foreign law began to dispace confidence in a primary lex fori, there was no need for this technique.

A significant illustration for this genesis of renvoi may be found in a 14th century proposal of Ubertus de Bobio who, having with apparent reluctance accepted Balduini's advocacy for the lex contractus,[301] suggests that the lex fori may still remain applicable where the lex contractus itself does not wish to be applied to foreigners.[302] Once the conflicts rule for contracts was firmly established on the basis of the presumed intention of the parties,[303] this rationale excluded, of course, the idea of renvoi.[304] It is clearly absurd to argue that where the parties intended a foreign law to be applied they also intended that part of that law to apply which denies its applicability by referring to another law. Such reasoning denies the very intention it invokes. Conversely, where the lex contractus is not, or should not be, referred to by the law of conflicts, in the absence of an intention to this effect, the lex fori should be applied without the need for legalistic subterfuge. Not until irrational dogma had displaced party autonomy and the lex fori as basic rules could renvoi gain entry in the law of conflict of laws.[305]

In 1882, the French court in the *Forgo* case applied the French law of succession to the French estate of a Bavarian domiciliary

300 Where the court invoked lacks a contact with the case justifying application of its own law, the suit might be dismissed as brought in a forum non conveniens. See EHRENZWEIG 119.

301 Note 62 supra.

302 2 NEUMEYER 84. For other instances of early judicial decisions erroneously considered the "first manifestations of the renvoi doctrine," see Lewald, "La théorie du renvoi," 29 RECUEIL DES COURS 519 at 533 (1929).

303 Note 84 supra.

304 NUSSBAUM 95. But see, e.g., Mason v. Rose, (2d Cir. 1949) 176 F. (2d) 486.

305 For references to the enormous literature, see, e.g., 1 RABEL, THE CONFLICT OF LAWS, 2d ed., 75-76 (1958); BATIFFOL 350; FRANCESCAKIS, LA THÉORIE DU RENVOI 275-289 (1958).

who had, in fact, lived and died in France.[306] If at that time the lex fori had not been replaced by an iron-clad internationalist doctrine, allegedly compelling the application of Bavarian law as the law of the decedent's legal domicile, the French court would have been free to apply its own law in the absence of any reason for another solution, and would not have felt impelled to introduce into conflicts law a concept which has been called "heretic," "puerile," "paradoxical," and "burlesque," and has been accused of "denaturing, falsifying and annihilating Private International Law."[307]

There is little more to be said in favor of those well-known decisions which have, belatedly and yet too early, introduced renvoi in English and American law.[308] Were it not for dogmatic "compulsion" to apply a foreign law by virtue of an allegedly self-evident international allocation of competencies, the English court would have had no difficulty in upholding under its own law the will of an Englishman domiciled in Malta who had made his will in England according to English law. To avoid the alleged "rule" that the law of domicile always "governed" the form of making a will, the court had to resort to renvoi, and probably incorrect renvoi at that.[309] And when, on the other hand, the court in a leading case invalidated the French will of an Englishwoman domiciled in France (according to English, though not French, conceptions) as violating a French rule favoring her children, it could have done so by simply interpreting the English conflicts rule as referring to the law of the domicile determined by English law, instead of sitting as a French court which in that case would have accepted renvoi.[310]

[306] Cour de Cassation, Civ. June 24, 1878, D.P. 79.1.156, S. 78.1.429.

[307] NUSSBAUM 92, n. 9, quoting from Lainé, "De l'application des Lois Etrangères en France," 23 CLUNET 241 at 257, 260 (1896), and Pillet, "Contre la Doctrine due Renvoi," REV. DE DR. INT. PR. 5 at 9, 10, 13 (1913). See, in general, BATIFFOL 253.

[308] For a history of this concept in English law, see Griswold, "Renvoi Revisited," 51 HARV. L. REV. 1165 (1938). See also De Nova, "Considerazioni sul rinvio in diritto inglese," 30 RIV. DIR. INT. 308 (1938).

[309] Frere v. Frere, 5 NOTES OF CASES IN THE ECCLESIASTICAL AND MARITIME COURTS 593 (1847). Cf. CHESHIRE 76, also discussing other cases most of which are reconcilable as documenting a favor testamenti. For criticism, see MENDELSSOHN-BARTHOLDY, RENVOI IN MODERN ENGLISH LAW 67 (1937); Schreiber, "The Doctrine of the Renvoi in Anglo-American Law," 31 HARV. L. REV. 523 at 541 (1918); DICEY 80. For a defense, see Griswold, "Renvoi Revisited," 51 HARV. L. REV. 1165 at 1192 (1938).

[310] In re Annesley, [1926] Ch. 692. For a criticism of that case as well as of the most recent announcement of the Privy Council in Kotia v. Nahas, [1941] A.C. 403, see CHESHIRE 76, 81. But see, for a defense of renvoi, Inglis, "The Judicial Process in the Conflict of Laws," 74 L. Q. REV. 493 (1958).

In the now famous, or should we say, infamous, case of *In re Schneider's Estate*,[311] the New York court applied the lex fori in denying forced heirship under Swiss law in favor of the estate of an American citizen against a New York will leaving the entire property to an English devisee. The court could have done so on the simple ground that the New York conflicts rule did not require displacement of the New York law by mere virtue of the fact that the New York funds were derived from Swiss real estate. But it chose to establish this conclusion by a process of multiple renvoi which was not only improper under New York law but required misinterpretation of Swiss law in several respects.[312]

It cannot be a mere coincidence that the cases referred to by Dean Griswold in defense of the renvoi doctrine[313] are all explainable by a reformulation of the conflicts rule allegedly applied;[314] and those cases criticized by him as improperly rejecting the doctrine[315] could have been satisfactorily decided by the same technique.[316] Indeed, "the result is the same whether the

[311] In re Schneider's Estate, 96 N.Y.S. (2d) 652 (1950), 100 N.Y.S. (2d) 371 (1950). The facts appear from In re Schneider's Will, 298 N.Y. 532, 80 N.E. (2d) 667 (1948). See also In re Duke of Wellington, [1947] Ch. 506, affd. [1948] Ch. 118 (situs of real property for légitime). For other American cases, see FALCONBRIDGE 246. Cf. De Nova, note, 11 GIUR. COMP. DIR. INT. PR. 120-121 (1954).

[312] See, e.g., FALCONBRIDGE 233, 246.

[313] Griswold, "Renvoi Revisited," 51 HARV. L. REV. 1165 at 1186 (1938). Cases involving transmission to a third law are not included in the present analysis. See id. at 1188. These cases are often explainable by formulating an exception from the primary conflicts rule. See id. at 1194, 1199, 1203 (lex situs rather than domiciliary law in succession cases).

[314] If X, the presumable owner of an automobile devolving to him under English law from the French estate of an Englishman dying domiciled in France, takes the automobile to England, he should of course not be defeated in an English court by Y's claim that French internal law, referred to by the English conflicts rule, would allocate the automobile to him. Interpretation of the English conflicts rule as calling for the application of English internal law to the English estate of an Englishman dying in a country which does not apply its own law to foreign citizens, would suffice to justify this result without resort to an acceptance of French renvoi. But see Griswold, "Renvoi Revisited," 51 HARV. L. REV. 1165 at 1186 (1938). See also University of Chicago v. Dater, 277 Mich. 658, 270 N.W. 175 (1936), id. at 1207; and the hypothetical case, id. at 1191. The same observation applies to the *Restatement's* renvoi as to title to land and validity of divorce. See id. at 1203. For similar criticism, see COOK, THE LOGICAL AND LEGAL BASES OF CONFLICT OF LAWS 246 (1949).

[315] Griswold, "Renvoi Revisited," 51 HARV. L. REV. 1165 at 1204 (1938).

[316] In Gray v. Gray, 87 N.H. 82, 174 A. 508 (1934), a New Hampshire court denied under the law of Maine a wife's claim against her husband for injuries sustained in a Maine automobile accident. In order to reach the lex fori, it would not have been necessary to resort to renvoi. Instead of weighing the policy of Maine as to the applicability of its law to foreign domiciliaries, which Dean Griswold (note 315 supra, at 1205) suggests, the New Hampshire court could and should have found its own law applicable because the

foreign rule applicable to extrastate elements is looked to because it is defined into the 'internal law' or because the reference is to the 'whole law' of the foreign country."[317] But increasing recognition of the futility of accepted generalizations of "applicable" conflicts rules seems to require their progressive specification as exceptions from the lex fori rather than their correction by the artificial process of renvoi, which would thus lose its last justification as an "exception" from a non-existing international order,[318] together with such tottering superstructures over a tottering structure as the theory of désistement which seeks to defeat renvoi by an unwilling law, instead of refusing to invoke that law in preference to the lex fori.[319]

Two examples may explain this thesis and its possible exceptions. In a series of articles I have tried to show that the application of foreign enterprise liabilities is determined by a principle of reasonable insurability rather than by a reference to the fortuitous place of the wrong. Once a court has decided that the policy of its tort rule is primarily designed to serve the distribution of inevitable loss, and that liability under a foreign legal system, being foreseeable and insurable, is a burden properly distributable by the enterprise, a conflicts rule of that legal system is, ordinarily, irrelevant from the standpoint of the policies which have initially caused resort to the liability rule of that system.

Occasionally, however, particularly in the law of domestic relations, the application of a foreign rule may be required by deference to a foreign governmental interest, as, e.g., where the

lex loci delicti was not pertinent at the outset. Modern courts have so held. See Ehrenzweig, "Parental Immunity in the Conflict of Laws: Law and Reason Versus the Restatement," 23 UNIV. CHI. L. REV. 474 (1956). See also note 273 supra; COOK, note 314 supra, at 248. For a forthright rejection of the renvoi doctrine in a case involving interspousal immunity, see Haumschild v. Continental Cas. Co., 7 Wis. (2d) 130, 95 N.W. (2d) 814 (1959).

[317] Griswold, note 315 supra, at 1198. Dean Griswold's analogy, id. at 1193, between the renvoi problem and that arising where the alleged conflicts rule refers to "no law," is perfect. But in both cases the lex fori remains applicable.

[318] See Lewald, "La théorie du renvoi," 29 RECUEIL DES COURS 519 at 615 (1929); WOLFF 186; and, in general, FRANCESCAKIS, LA THEORIE DU RENVOI (1958). For the last author's own views which reject the doctrine almost completely, see particularly id. at 150, 189, 260. Cf. Ehrenzweig, Book Review, 8 AM. J. COMP. L. 233 (1959). But see also Maury, Book Review, 48 REV. CRIT. DE DR. INT. PR. 602 (1959).

[319] WOLFF 198. Concerning the general rejection of renvoi by Scandinavian courts and writers, see Korkisch, "Der Anteil der nordischen Länder an den Fragen des Internationalen Privatrechts," 23 RABELS Z. 599 at 614 (1958). For a similar attitude of Italian law, see Migliazza, note, "Critiche sul problema del rinvio," 4 STUDI MESSINEO 209-264 (1959). On Westlake's early use of the doctrine, see FALCONBRIDGE 21.

conflicts rule of the forum determines capacity to marry under the law of the parties' nationality or domicile. Assuming respect for that law to be the prevailing rationale of this conflicts rule, it would be senseless to apply that rule also in cases where the foreign law in turn is willing to defer to the law of the forum either as such or as the law of celebration. This simply means that the conflicts rule initially applied must be rephrased to read that capacity is determined by the law of nationality or domicile provided it purports to be thus applicable. Here, as always, the concept of renvoi is dispensable and must be discarded as "a classic example of violently prejudiced literature confronting naïvely consistent practice."[320]

5. *The "Preliminary Question"*

Had the lex fori been restored to its proper function a few decades ago, we would have been spared another miscreant of a conceptualism gone rampant in private international law. The "preliminary question" would never have reached even that modest standing it now enjoys in the literature of the subject. To be sure not a single decision by a Commonwealth or American court has yet applied this new concept, but enough scholarly investigations continue to appear on this subject[321] to tempt a court to use it as a much needed tool for the evasion of obsolete conflicts law—unless we render this evasion unnecessary.

Succession to movables is generally said to be "governed" by the law of the decedent's domicile.[322] In a contest in California

320 1 RABEL, THE CONFLICT OF LAWS, 2d ed., 75-76 (1958). Where courts have been compelled to make renvoi an essential part of their practice as they have in Japan, such practice indicates a fundamental flaw in the primary rules. See Ehrenzweig, Ikehara and Jensen, "American-Japanese Private International Law" (forthcoming); Ehrenzweig, "Torts in the Horei," EGAWA FESTSCHRIFT (forthcoming).

321 See NUSSBAUM 104; Gotlieb, "The Incidental Question in Anglo-American Conflict of Laws," 33 CAN. B. REV. 523 at 535 (1955); ROBERTSON, CHARACTERIZATION IN THE CONFLICT OF LAWS 137 (1940); Maury, "Règles générales des conflits de lois," 57 RECUEIL DES COURS 329, 558 (1936); Cormack, "Renvoi, Characterization, Localization and Preliminary Question in the Conflict of Laws," 14 SO. CAL. L. REV. 221 (1941); DICEY 57; RAAPE, INTERNATIONALES PRIVATRECHT, 4th ed., 113 (1955); WOLFF 206; MELCHIOR, DIE GRUNDLAGEN DES DEUTSCHEN INTERNATIONALEN PRIVATRECHTS 245 (1932); Wengler, "Die Vorfrage im Kollisionsrecht," 8 RABELS Z. 148 (1934); RIGAUX, LA THÉORIE DES QUALIFICATIONS EN DROIT INTERNATIONAL PRIVÉ 444 (1956); Venturini, "Le questioni pregiudiziali nel diritto internazionale privato," 11 GIUR. COMP. DIR. INT. PR. 184 (1954); Migliazza, "Le questioni pregiudiziali in diritto internazionale privato," 26 TEMI 477 (1950); Bentivoglio, note, 12 GIUR. COMP. DIR. INT. PR. 104 (1956); Lopez, "La cuestion incidental en derecho internacional privado" 9 REV. ESP. DIR. INT. 125 (1956).

322 But see Yiannopoulos, "Wills of Movables in American International Conflicts Law: A Critique of the Domiciliary 'Rule,'" 46 CALIF. L. REV. 185 (1958).

between the widow and an alleged illegitimate child of a foreign domiciliary concerning movable property located in California, the decedent's domiciliary law will therefore be applied to determine the relative ranking of the two claimants. The widow asserts that an illegitimate child is not entitled to inherit under the decedent's domiciliary law which determines this question as "preliminary" to the principal question of succession. On the other hand, the son relies on the more favorable California law as the law of his own domicile governing his status.

There exists one good argument for the widow's contention, namely that application of a law other than that governing the principal question could distort the intended effect of that law since that law's provisions are interdependent. In other words, the decedent's law, the widow will argue, had it been faced with the possibility of inheritance claims of illegitimate children—which it was not since it has excluded such children from the legal definition of children in general—would have specifically excluded them from the right to inherit. On the other hand, the son's theory would treat his status alike for all purposes, so that a ruling on this status under one law for one purpose would preclude its redetermination under another law for another purpose. Usually, preliminary questions are discussed in relation to the even more complex problem whether, once it is conceded that foreign law applies to such questions, that law includes its conflicts rules or whether recourse is to be had to the conflicts rules of the forum.

No generally satisfactory solution has been suggested. Nevertheless one need not go so far as to see "as many problems as there are cases in which incidental questions may arise."[323] Nor need we be satisfied with announcing a system of friendly "co-existence" of conflicts rules.[324] The issue will lend itself to a more definite analysis once the lex fori is restored to its proper place as the basic rule. Where the lex fori has yielded to a foreign law chosen by the parties to a contract, it has done so in order to give effect to the parties' intention. Since this intention is quite generally directed to the application of foreign domestic

[323] DICEY 62, quoting Gotlieb, note 321 supra.

[324] RAAPE, INTERNATIONALES PRIVATRECHT, 4th ed., 116 (1955).

law, the problem of renvoi cannot arise.[325] Similarly, the applicability of foreign law to incidental questions is but a matter of intention. The same principle must apply where the lex fori has been displaced on other grounds. The policy calling for this displacement must equally determine its scope. Thus, if the forum refers to the decedent's domiciliary law to determine succession to forum property, it presumably does so to give effect to the decedent's likely intention. In the above example he may be assumed to have chosen not to make a will in reliance on the fact that only his legitimate children would take under the law of his domicile. Construction of the word "child" under the law of each situs or status would be contrary to this presumed motivation.

On the other hand—to take a situation raised in connection with a related though not dispositive Minnesota case[326]—should the status of an Illinois widow for the purpose of her wrongful death claim brought in Minnesota against an Illinois defendant be determined under the conflicts rule of the forum (which would validate the marriage between first cousins under the Kentucky law of celebration), or under the law of Illinois as the place of wrong (which would invalidate the marriage of residents as violating her Uniform Marriage Evasion Act)? Suppose that the "place of wrong" rule is established in Minnesota in the determination of a widow's standing to sue.[327] If the defunct vested rights rationale is properly ignored, Minnesota law has yielded in this case presumably on the ground that a potential accident victim has a right to rely on his own law in planning his financial protection by insurance and otherwise. Under this rationale he was certainly entitled to rely on the law of his domicile also concerning the status of his dependents. In other words, Minnesota should apply Illinois law as the law of the victim's domicile whether or not Illinois was the place of accident. The preliminary question of the widow's status remains in this sense subject to the conflicts rule of the forum.[328]

325 Note 304 supra.

326 A hypothetical case, discussed by Harper, "Torts, Contracts, Property, Status, Characterization, and the Conflict of Laws," 59 COL. L. REV. 440 at 455 (1959), with reference to Meisenhelder v. Chicago & N. W. Ry., 170 Minn. 317, 213, N.W. 32 (1927), involving the Federal Employers Liability Act.

327 See EHRENZWEIG 46.

328 See Kegel, Commentary to Articles 1-31 of the Introductory Law to the German Civil Code, SOERGEL, BÜRGERLICHES GESETZBUCH, vol. 4, 8th ed., 16 (1955). The problem has arisen with particular frequency concerning the right of a foreign-adopted child to

6. *"Unilateral" and "Spatial" Self-Limitation*

One of the most significant phases of last century's struggle between dogma and reality may be found in the controversy between the adherents of "unilateral" and universal conflicts rules. This controversy is clearly reflected in the history of the German Civil Code of 1896.[329] At the time of its preparation the internationalist ideologies had probably reached their climax. Nevertheless, for reasons never fully ascertained, Parliament rejected almost all those universal rules of earlier drafts which, following these ideologies, had purported to distribute international legislative competencies.[330] Instead, it enacted so-called "unilateral" rules which merely limited the applicability of German law in the presence of certain foreign contacts. Thus, in lieu of providing that marriage is "governed" by the law of the place of celebration, the Code provides that "the personal relations between German spouses are subject to German law."[331] This change, while probably induced by political considerations, was in accord with the position taken by commentators, who considered universal rules as encroachments upon foreign sovereignties,[332] as inconsistent with the essentially procedural character of conflicts law,[333] or as potentially contrary to public international law.[334]

If taken literally, "unilateral" statutory provisions leave a vacuum in many cases such as those concerning foreign nationals engaged in foreign transactions. Assuming a distribution of competencies by international agreement or uniform conflicts

succeed to forum property. It is the forum law that must determine whether a foreign adoption is of the kind that would create succession rights under forum law. See De Nova, "Considerazioni comparative sull' adozione in diritto internazionale privato," FESTGABE FÜR MAKAROV 730 at 739-763 (1958).

329 See NIEMEYER, ZUR VORGESCHICHTE DES INTERNATIONALEN PRIVATRECHTS IM DEUTSCHEN BURGERLICHEN GESETZBUCH (1915). As to similar statutes, see NIEDERER 122; WOLFF 84. Cf. particularly French Civil Code, Art. 3.

330 See, e.g., NIEDERER 116; RAAPE, INTERNATIONALES PRIVATRECHT, 4th ed., 19 (1955).

331 Introductory Law to German Civil Code, art. 14. See also, e.g., id., art. 12 which disposes of tort conflicts law with the provision that claims against Germans on foreign torts are limited to damages allowable under German law; and in general Schnell, Über die Zuständigkeit zum Erlass von gesetzlichen Vorschriften über die räumliche Herrschaft der Rechtsnormen," 5 ZEIT. FÜR INTERNATIONALES RECHT 337 (1895).

332 NIEDNER, DAS EINFÜHRUNGSGESETZ VOM 18 August 1896 (Commentary), 2d ed. (1901).

333 Concerning Zitelmann's and Frankenstein's theories, see WIETHÖLTER, EINSEITIGE KOLLISIONSNORMEN ALS GRUNDLAGE DES INTERNATIONALEN PRIVATRECHTS 9 (1956).

334 See, in general, KEGEL, note 328 supra, at 8, 10.

laws, these cases could be simply excluded from domestic jurisdiction after ascertainment of an available foreign forum. In the absence of such agreements and uniformity, German courts, like English courts since Lord Mansfield, have had to find a solution in rules of choice of law. For this purpose they have by the use of analogy applied unilateral rules as general. But this analogy, far from being "almost self-evident,"[335] is improper. Considerations which lead to the application of the law of the forum to foreign transactions do not necessarily support application of a foreign law to corresponding domestic transactions. Article 7 (1) of the German Introductory Law, which makes German law applicable to German spouses abroad, cannot "by analogy" be said to imply that relations between foreign spouses in Germany must be treated under their national law. Only a pseudo-internationalist-conceptualistic attitude could justify this simple equation.

This has been often recognized and whole new theoretical systems have been aimed at a more accurate interpretation of unilateral conflicts rules. Pilenko in France[336] and Sohn in the United States[337] may be taken as typical representatives of this "school."[338] Both advise the judge inter alia to fill the vacuum by applying that foreign law, and only that foreign law, which claims applicability in the particular case.[339] This approach seems objectionable on the ground that it concedes to foreign conflicts law a decisive role which may or may not coincide with the policy of the forum. The forum may prefer to apply foreign or forum law notwithstanding foreign conflicts rules to the contrary. Both Pilenko and Sohn, as well as all other "unilateralists," notwithstanding their antagonism to internationalism in conflicts law,

335 NIEDERER 122. See also WOLFF 94; LEWALD, RÈGLES GÉNÉRALES 17 (1941); RAAPE INTERNATIONALES PRIVATRECHT, 4th ed., 33 (1955).

336 Pilenko, "Le droit spatial et le droit international privé dans le projet du nouveau Code Civil français," 6 REV. HÉLLÉNIQUE DR. INT. 319 (1953); Pilenko, "Droit spatial et le droit international privé," 6 IUS GENTIUM 34 (1954); See De Nova-Pilenko, "Uno Corrispondenza," 13 DIR. INT. 198 (1959).

337 Sohn, "New Bases for Solution of Conflict of Laws Problems," 55 HARV. L. REV. 978 (1942).

338 See also Vivier, "Le caractère bilateral des règles de conflit de lois," 42 REV. CRIT. DE DR. INT. PR. 655 (1953), 43 id. 73 (1954); and, in general, WIETHÖLTER, EINSEITIGE KOLLISIONSNORMEN ALS GRUNDLAGE DES INTERNATIONALEN PRIVATRECHT (1956); QUADRI 271-275, 289; De Nova, "I conflitti di legge e le norme con apposita delimitazione della sfera di efficacia," 13 DIR. INT. 13 (1959). On the counterpart of this "introvert" doctrine, Ago's insistence on the purely foreign-directed function of conflicts law, see De Nova, supra, at 14.

339 Refinements vary, particularly as to the solution of two competing foreign laws. See WIETHÖLTER, note 338 supra, at 33.

are themselves internationalists in that they deny the forum law's predominant position by permitting the foreign law to "govern." But the lex fori is the rule rather than the exception.

The thesis of this paper endeavors to preserve the traditional precepts of conflicts law, now threatened by their failure as independent "rules," by reinterpreting them as exceptions from the lex fori. But this thesis can be fully established only through a study which would re-examine the entire case law bearing on each specific factual situation. In the second part of my treatise on the *Conflict of Laws* I hope to complete a series of studies which I have submitted as bearing on some of the more important conflicts problems of every-day legal life in the United States.

[7]

REJECTION OF FOREIGN LAW: SOME PRIVATE INTERNATIONAL LAW INHIBITIONS*

By P. B. CARTER[1]

THE corpus of private international law is traditionally presented in three major divisions. These divisions are respectively designated jurisdiction, choice of law and foreign judgments. The first of these divisions, jurisdiction, relates to the limitations placed upon the competence of a national court which may result from the circumstance that in a private international law case the fact situation contains one or more foreign elements or bears an international complexion. The second division, choice of law, relates to the process and techniques to which a jurisdictionally competent court will resort in order to identify the *lex causae*, that is to say, the pattern of legal rules by reference to which the issues presented to it are to be determined. The third division of the subject, loosely labelled foreign judgments, denotes something rather different, namely consideration of the circumstances in which recognition will be accorded to the efficacy of a judgment of a foreign court, and the circumstances in which the present *forum* will sometimes go further and take authoritative steps with a view to enforcing such a judgment. This traditional arrangement of private international law does not, however, constitute simply a method of presentation, or a way of expounding the subject in an orderly fashion. Nor does it merely represent a well-tested way of promoting thought about the subject within a logical and readily comprehensible framework. It is an arrangement which rests upon certain fundamental assumptions, to query or doubt the validity of which would smack, or at least until recently would have smacked, of heresy.

Orthodoxy posits that the choice of law process is an essential element in any sophisticated system of private international law. There is here a basic assumption that it would not be acceptable to confine private international law to questions of jurisdiction—to the delimitation of the competence of a national *forum*, and to the delimitation, for recognition purposes, of the competence of foreign courts, when dealing with transnational fact situations—the corollary of such a confinement being that a jurisdictionally competent court would then always apply its own domestic law, although, of course, that law might itself include special rules for application in particular international situations. It may, however, be

 Adapted from a paper read to the British Branch of the International Law Association at Oxford in May 1983.

[1] Barrister and Honorary Bencher of the Middle Temple; Fellow of Wadham College, Oxford.

noted in passing that the EEC Convention on Jurisdiction and the Enforcement of Judgments in Civil and Commercial Matters, to be incorporated into English private international law by the Civil Jurisdiction and Judgments Act 1982, does represent, in the limited area of its operation, retreat from choice of law.

A related fundamental assumption of orthodox private international law is that a choice of law process must be directed towards the identification of a legal system by reference to which the rights of the parties to a dispute must automatically be determined, rather than towards the identification of a particular foreign rule apt for that determination. This is sometimes (rather infelicitously) referred to as a choice of jurisdiction approach as distinct from a choice of rule approach. It might be more aptly described as a choice of legal system approach. The validity of this assumption has been challenged in recent decades in the United States; but it remains firmly embedded in English private international law doctrine.

This article is written on the basis of acceptance of the validity of these two fundamental assumptions—that is to say, acceptance of the proposition that choice of law is a desirable, and often virtually an essential, ingredient of many branches of private international law, and acceptance of the proposition that choice of law involves choice of legal system not choice of specific rule. However, the risk involved in acceptance of these propositions is that unwavering and inflexible adherence to them is liable in practice to lead to palpable injustice in particular cases. That risk could be reduced by the careful and detailed formulation of a large number of choice of law rules, each tailored to cover a fairly precisely defined, and often relatively narrow, range of situations. In fact, however, private international law has been bedevilled by the generality of many of its choice of law rules. In any event there are limits on what could be achieved by way of rectifying this. Even if a high degree of refinement and detail is achieved in the formulation of choice of law rules, there will always remain *some* cases in which the application of an orthodox type of choice of law technique is liable to lead to an unjust result. There must therefore be instances in which refusal to apply the otherwise applicable *lex causae* is justifiable. In the interests of certainty and predictability of decision it is desirable that, so far as is practicable, these instances be classified, and be put into readily identifiable categories. This, in considerable measure, has been done in English private international law. An object of this article is consideration of the nature of, and justification for, some of these categories. The acceptance of the notion of choice of law, that is the acceptance of rules which require jurisdictionally competent courts to apply laws other than their own, coupled with the acceptance of the orthodoxy that choice of law denotes choice of legal system, has given rise to a need for escape routes. Rules permitting or requiring rejection of the *lex causae* in particular circumstances mark out these escape routes. It is obvious that in some respects access to these routes has to be easier than would be the case if the aforementioned orthodoxies were to be abandoned—but in the author's view this price, although high, is not too high to pay for avoidance of the consequences of their abandonment. The escape routes must be well marked and clearly signposted. But, at the same time, the categories of permitted exclusion of foreign law must not themselves be too rigidly defined, or they will be in danger of being self-defeating. Unavoidably implicit in the interaction of choice of law and exclusion of foreign law is the familiar dilemma posed by the conflicting *desiderata* of on the one hand certainty and predictability of result, and on the other hand sufficient flexibility to accommodate what would otherwise be hard cases.

Basic English doctrine concerning the recognition and enforcement of foreign judgments is in one important respect more rigid and restrictive than is basic choice of law doctrine. Regarding foreign judgments the basic doctrine is that, provided the foreign court was jurisdictionally competent according to certain criteria, an English court will not enquire into the merits of the judgment, this meaning that it will not consider even the foreign court's choice of law. In these circumstances it is not surprising that in this branch of private international law some escape routes are well established and have been well trodden. They mostly take the form of defences to common law actions on unsatisfied foreign judgments *in personam*, and of reasons for refusing to register, or for setting aside registration, under respectively the Administration of Justice Act 1920 and the Foreign Judgments (Reciprocal Enforcement) Act 1933. The defence of fraud (the definition of fraud for this purpose being idiosyncratically wide) represents a long established escape route in common law cases of indirect enforcement, and equivalent provisions are made in the 1920 and 1933 Acts. In the nature of things no analogous need for this particular escape route arises in the context of choice of law in an English *forum*. However, generally speaking and fraud apart, the circumstances and the situations in which there is liable to be a need to escape in English proceedings from the automatic application of the *lex causae* (that is from the law indicated by the relevant choice of law rule) have a more or less marked correspondence with the circumstances and situations in which there is a need to escape from the automatic impact of the general rule that the judgment of a jurisdictionally competent foreign court be recognized, and, where appropriate, enforced.

The nature of these escape routes, or categories of exclusion of foreign law, reflect *forum* inhibitions about applying, or sometimes even recognizing the application of, particular species of foreign law. In English private international law a classification of these categories has emerged which is generally accepted both in the choice of law context and in the context of recognition of foreign judgments. The categories cannot be regarded as entirely mutually exclusive. Moreover, some categories are themselves more precisely defined than are others.

114 REJECTION OF FOREIGN LAW

First, an English court will not itself apply a foreign penal law. Nor will it enforce a foreign penal judgment. The dogma is that an English court will not lend its aid either directly or indirectly to the enforcement of a foreign penal law. Whether a law is penal depends primarily upon its purpose. The principal criterion is as to whether the main thrust of the law is the infliction of punishment at the instance of, or on behalf of, the State, or is the award of compensation.[2] The imposition of a penalty is said to reflect the exercise by a State of its sovereign power, and this can have no effect in the territory of another State. This is scarcely adequate either as an analytical, or as a practical, explanation of the rule. The ultimate explanation is probably to be found in more mundane considerations of policy and of practicality. The hard core of the rule can be expressed in the aphorism that there is no private international law of crime. States do not enforce each other's criminal laws. This is partly for reasons of policy; the content of criminal law, its sanctions, and the fact and methods of its enforcement are regarded as essentially and exclusively national or domestic matters. At the same time the rule is partly a consequence of the wide variety and often controversial nature of criminal penalties. Attitudes are not in all respects absolute as is evidenced by the growing proliferation of extradition treaties; but acceptance of the *forum* inhibitions reflected by this category of exclusion of foreign law is consonant with the present international order.

Secondly, but it is submitted much more controversially, it has been generally accepted since the time of Lord Mansfield, although the actual authority until 1955 was very meagre,[3] that an English court will not enforce either directly or indirectly a foreign revenue law. England, it would seem, should be a haven for foreign tax evaders and defaulters. In 1955 the *imprimatur* of the House of Lords was placed upon the rule in *Government of India* v. *Taylor*.[4] There an English company had carried on business in India, where it became liable for Indian capital gains tax on the sale of its business. The company was subsequently wound up in England, and the Indian revenue authorities lodged a claim in the liquidation proceedings in respect of that unpaid tax. The House of Lords held that the liquidator had been correct in rejecting this claim because only liabilities which could have been enforced against the company in England were properly receivable, and the liability, being a liability to pay tax imposed by a foreign government, could not have been enforced in England. It is to be noted that the Indian law was not a penal law. It is to be noted, too, that

[2] There is some authority for the view that a law may also be treated as penal if its purpose is the prevention of the commission of a crime. See *Schemmer* v. *Property Resources Ltd.*, [1975] Ch. 273, where Goulding J said (p. 288): 'In my judgment, and in the absence of specific legislation founded on treaties, preventive criminal justice is no more a proper subject of international enforcement than retributive criminal justice.'

[3] It seems to have consisted almost exclusively of two decisions at first instance: *Municipal Council of Sydney* v. *Bull*, [1909] 1 KB 7, and *Re Visser*, [1928] Ch. 877.

[4] [1955] AC 491.

it was far from being a law of a type unknown to the domestic law of the *forum*.

An English *forum* will not lend its aid to even the indirect enforcement of a foreign revenue law. Thus in *Rossano* v. *Manufacturers' Life Insurance Co.*[5] in an action on a debt, the debt being situated in Egypt, defendants in English proceedings were not allowed to rely upon garnishee orders served upon them in Egypt by the Egyptian revenue authorities in respect of tax allegedly unpaid by the plaintiffs. The defendants contended that payment to the plaintiffs would not absolve them from the obligation to comply with the orders as well. McNair J nevertheless held that the orders could not be recognized: '. . . I have reached the conclusion that the fundamental objection to the recognition of these orders is that their recognition would offend against the well-established principle that the English court will not recognise or enforce directly or indirectly a foreign revenue law or claim. . . .'[6] The defendants could not in effect contend that they would pay the plaintiffs' foreign tax instead of paying them.[7] McNair J's reference to recognition as distinct from enforcement could, however, be misleading. Lord Mansfield did say in a series of cases[8] that 'no country ever takes notice of the revenue laws of another', but it is now accepted that this is too wide. A distinction is to be drawn between indirect enforcement and recognition. In *Re Emery's Investment Trusts*[9] the equitable presumption of advancement raised by a husband's registration of securities in his wife's name could not be rebutted by evidence that his real purpose was to evade foreign income tax. Equity would not grant relief in respect of a transaction carried out in contravention of law, albeit a foreign revenue law. Note was taken of the foreign revenue law, but the effect of this was not to facilitate payment of the foreign tax.

Forum inhibitions concerning foreign revenue laws are similarly manifest in the approach taken to the recognition and enforcement of foreign judgments. In *United States of America* v. *Harden*[10] the Supreme Court of Canada upheld the refusal of the British Columbia Court of Appeal to allow an action on an unsatisfied Californian tax judgment. To have allowed it would have constituted indirect enforcement of a Californian revenue law. The Supreme Court also rejected the argument that an agreement by way of compromise for valuable consideration to pay a sum of money in satisfaction of a foreign tax claim could be enforced as a contract. Of this argument Cartwright J, delivering the judgment of the Court, said: 'We are concerned not with form but with substance, and, if it can properly be said that the respondent made an agreement, it was simply

[5] [1963] 2 QB 352.

[6] *Per* McNair J at p. 376.

[7] On the withholding of indirect enforcement see, too, *Brokaw* v. *Seatrain UK Ltd.*, [1971] 2 QB 476, below.

[8] *Planché* v. *Fletcher* (1779), 1 Doug. 251, 253; *Holman* v. *Johnson* (1775), 1 Cowp. 341, 343; *Lever* v. *Fletcher*, unrep.

[9] [1959] 1 Ch. 410.

[10] [1963] SCR 366; (1964) 41 DLR (2d) 721.

an agreement to pay taxes which by the laws of the foreign state she was obligated to pay.'[11]

The general rule relating to foreign revenue laws is now firmly established, and its implications have been somewhat relentlessly worked out, but two basic questions still remain. What is meant by a revenue law? And why should such a law not be enforced?

Characterization or categorization of a law as revenue or otherwise is, of course, a matter for the *forum*. For example, in the Scottish case of *Metal Industries (Salvage) Ltd.* v. *Owners of ST 'Harle'*[12] it was held that a claim on behalf of the French Government, in respect of arrears of compulsory employer's contributions to a French State health insurance and family benefits scheme for seamen, was not enforceable in Scotland, although by French law it might not be regarded as a revenue law. But what is the criterion to be applied in an English or Scottish *forum*? Dicey and Morris state that 'A "revenue law" has not been defined, but seems to be a rule requiring a non-contractual payment of money or kind in favour of a central or local government'.[13] Some examples are given of laws that have been characterized as revenue laws: rules imposing income tax,[14] customs duty,[15] stamp duty,[16] succession duty,[17] municipal rates,[18] capital gains tax,[19] and a profits levy.[20] On the other hand, *moratorium* laws[21] and rules abrogating gold clauses,[22] which do not provide for the collection of money but rather for the protection of its value, have not been so classified. The courts have adopted an ambivalent attitude towards foreign currency and exchange control regulations. These have been said by the House of Lords not to be revenue laws: *Frankman* v. *Prague Credit Bank*[23] and *Kahler* v. *Midland Bank*;[24] but reservations as to whether this is so for all purposes were expressed by Slade J in 1977 in *Re Lord Cable*.[25] It is to be noted, too, that, whereas in the *Metal Industries (Salvage)* case[26] a rule imposing compulsory contributions to a State insurance scheme was held to be a rule of revenue law, rules under which a State can recover social security payments have been held in Canada not to be rules of revenue law,[27] and in

[11] [1963] SCR 366, 371; (1964) 41 DLR (2d) 721, 725.

[12] [1962] Scots LT 114.

[13] Dicey and Morris, *The Conflict of Laws* (10th edn., 1980), p. 92.

[14] *Indian and General Investment Trust Co. Ltd.* v. *Borax Consolidated Ltd.*, [1920] 1 KB 539, 550. See, too, *United States of America* v. *Harden*, above.

[15] *Holman* v. *Johnson* (1775), 1 Cowp. 341, 343; *Attorney-General for Canada* v. *Schulze* (1901), 9 SLT 4.

[16] *James* v. *Catherwood* (1823), 3 Dow. & Ry. (KB) 190, 191.

[17] *Cotton* v. *R*, [1914] AC 176, 195; *Re Visser*, [1928] Ch. 877; *Re Lord Cable*, [1977] 1 WLR 7, 13.

[18] *Municipal Council of Sydney* v. *Bull*, [1909] 1 KB 7, 12.

[19] *Government of India* v. *Taylor*, above.

[20] *Peter Buchanan Ltd.* v. *McVey*, [1954] IR 89; [1955] AC 516 n.

[21] *Re Helbert Wagg & Co. Ltd.'s Claim*, [1956] Ch. 323.

[22] *R* v. *International Trustee for the Protection of Bondholders*, [1937] AC 500.

[23] [1948] 1 KB 730, 746.

[24] [1950] AC 24, 26-7.

[25] [1977] 1 WLR 7, 13.

[26] Above. But cf. *The Acrux*, [1965] P 391.

[27] See alternative *ratio* (or *dictum*) in the Manitoba case of *Weir* v. *Lohr* (1967), 65 DLR (2d) 717.

New Zealand rules for the obtaining of legal aid contributions have been held not to be rules of revenue law.[28] These doubts and apparent inconsistencies must reinforce curiosity as to the purpose and rationale of the rule that courts will not enforce either directly or indirectly foreign revenue laws.

Why should a rule of foreign law be accorded markedly less respect than would otherwise be the case *simply* because it is a rule of 'revenue' law? In *Taylor*'s case Lord Somervell said: 'Tax gathering is not a matter of contract but of authority and administration as between the State and those within its jurisdiction.'[29] This, with all respect, to the extent that it is not simply a restatement of the rule in the form of a principle, smacks of excessive formalism. If there is any justification for discriminating against foreign revenue laws, it must be found in more practical considerations. Moreover, account must be taken of a strong countervailing consideration. This latter derives from the fact that in modern times the State, and organs of the State, have become involved in a wide and diverse range of day-to-day commercial, quasi-commercial, and social activities—from the fact that, for example, State or local authority provision of services in return for direct or semi-direct payment has become commonplace.

Of course, if a foreign revenue law is penal in nature, it will not in any event be enforced. Again, if, as will be pointed out below, it is expropriatory in nature it will sometimes for that reason be denied even recognition. Or again, as is also discussed below, if the content of a foreign rule is unacceptably repugnant it will be rejected on grounds of public policy: a court will, for example, have severe reservations about enforcing a foreign law which discriminates on the basis of race, colour or creed quite regardless of whether the law is a revenue law. The question under consideration now is as to whether the mere fact that a foreign law is a revenue law should *in itself* constitute an absolute bar to its enforcement in another *forum*. What policy requires that, whereas the use of the courts as instruments for the enforcement of locally imposed obligations to pay taxes is legitimate and desirable, their use as instruments for the enforcement of similar validly imposed foreign obligations is in no circumstances to be countenanced? As a distinguished Canadian writer on private international law has written: 'Why is it unlawful in Canada to evade local taxes and yet perfectly legitimate to refuse to pay foreign taxes? How can the public policy of Canada be invoked to protect foreign tax dodgers when our own legislative bodies impose similar taxes?'[30] Consideration of specific cases only emphasizes the difficulty in answering these general questions. For example, is there some overriding justification for a national court's refusal to enforce a foreign rating authority's claim for the payment of general rates lawfully imposed upon the authority's local

[28] *Connor* v. *Connor*, [1974] 1 NZLR 632.
[29] [1955] AC 491, 514.
[30] Castel, *Canadian Conflict of Laws* (1975), vol. 1, p. 64.

residents? Should it make any difference if the rate is one imposed for a particular purpose such as a water rate? In such a case should this depend upon the extent to which the amount is calculated by reference to the quantity of water consumed? If a service such as electricity is supplied by a local authority, does policy require that foreign courts discriminate between claims for unpaid electricity bills where the obligation to pay is contractual and claims where it is statutory? Or again, should a *forum* discriminate in this regard between claims by local authority suppliers and claims by private suppliers? If so, on which side of such a line should the position of a foreign equivalent of a Crown corporation fall?

If there be some policy which requires that a national *forum* never enforce a foreign revenue law, it is perhaps permissible to conjecture why this policy does not reach out to cases in which all that is at issue is bare recognition. A *dictum* of Lord Denning MR in *Brokaw* v. *Seatrain UK Ltd.*[31] is illuminating in this connection. In that case goods were shipped in a United States ship from Baltimore, in the State of Maryland, to London via Southampton. While the ship was on the high seas the United States Treasury served on the shipowners in the United States a notice of levy in respect of unpaid tax demanding surrender of any property in their possession belonging to two United States taxpayers. When the ship docked at Southampton the United States Government claimed possession of the goods by virtue of the notice of the levy. The plaintiffs, who were the ultimate consignees of the goods, brought an action in detinue in England against the defendant shipowners for the return of the goods and damages for their detention. On the shipowners' interpleader summons, bringing in the Government of the United States as claimants, the Master ordered that they be barred. The claimant government unsuccessfully appealed from the Master's Order to the Court of Appeal. Lord Denning MR, delivering the judgment of the Court, held that the claim of the Government of the United States was a claim to enforce, albeit indirectly, part of its revenue law and must, accordingly, fail. This is clearly in accord with the principles laid down by the House of Lords in the *Taylor*[32] case, and more specifically follows the decision in *Rossano* v. *Manufacturers Life Insurance Company*.[33]

What is of wider interest is that Lord Denning MR did go out of his way to point out that

> If this notice of levy had been effective to reduce the goods into the possession of the United States Government, it would, I think, have been enforced by these courts, because we would then be enforcing an actual possessory title. There would be no need for the United States Government to have recourse to their revenue law.... If the United States Government had taken these goods into their actual possession, say in a warehouse in Baltimore, or maybe by attornment of the master to an officer of the United States Government, that might have been

[31] [1971] 2 QB 476. [32] [1955] AC 491, above. [33] [1963] 2 QB 352, above.

sufficient to enable them to claim the goods. But there is nothing of that kind here. The United States Government simply rely on this notice of levy given to the shipowners, and that is not, in my view, sufficient to reduce the goods into their possession.[34]

The technical distinction adverted to by the Master of the Rolls is, of course, clear. On the other hand, that the outcome of the proceedings should turn upon such a distinction is indicative. If a foreign government seeks to enforce indirectly a tax law by seeking the surrender of a defaulting taxpayer's goods, it will fail. If, on the other hand, the seizure has already taken place, this seizure may well be respected. Comment is scarcely necessary.

It is perhaps salutary for an English lawyer to reflect upon how he would be disposed to regard the attitude of a foreign court which *mutatis mutandis* declined to enforce a British governmental or local authority's claim against a defaulting taxpayer or ratepayer who had taken refuge in the foreign haven.

It must of course be conceded that the reversal of the rule in *Government of India* v. *Taylor* would have certain important consequences. It would give rise to a need for the formulation of rules to govern jurisdiction, and of choice of law rules to be applied, in revenue matters. Hitherto the need for such rules specifically tailored so as to accommodate such matters has been largely obviated by the blanket refusal to enforce foreign revenue laws or foreign revenue judgments. The lifting of that blanket might properly provoke *de novo* consideration of the appropriateness in this area of the general rules of English private international law relating both to the jurisdiction of English courts, and to the jurisdiction of foreign courts in the context of recognition and enforcement of their judgments. The formulation of relevant choice of law rules would also demand careful thought. Moreover, it would be necessary to ensure that the new pattern of the law could accommodate the various types of double taxation agreement entered into between States. Satisfaction of all these needs might well be a formidable task of considerable complexity. Total refusal to enforce foreign revenue laws has, it must be readily conceded, one undoubted attraction—that of simplicity. This is a quality which it shares with many arbitrary and irrational phenomena.

Exclusion of a third category of foreign law is sometimes said to derive from the proposition that a national court will not give extraterritorial effect to foreign expropriatory laws. In England, whereas by virtue of the doctrine of *Luther* v. *Sagor*[35] such a law will be accorded recognition to the extent that it affects property which was situated at the time of the expropriation within the territory of the expropriating State, it will not be treated as affecting property situated in England at that time.[36] In *Luther*

[34] [1971] 2 QB 476, 482–3.

[35] [1921] 3 KB 532.

[36] *Bank voor Handel en Scheepvaart* v. *Slatford*, [1953] 1 QB 248. Although Devlin J there declined

v. *Sagor* a Russian timber merchant failed to obtain a declaration that he was still owner of timber which had belonged to him before title to it had been vested in the Soviet State under a Soviet decree. The timber, although subsequently brought to England and still in England at the time of the English proceedings, had been situated in Russia at the time of the expropriatory decree. If the operative principle here is simply that the *lex situs* governs, no departure from otherwise applicable private international law is involved, and a separate category of exclusion of foreign law is not constituted. It is, however, to be noted that on this basis if, for example, in *Luther* v. *Sagor* the timber had been situated in a third country at the time of the Soviet decree, an English court would have determined its effect upon the claimant's title to it in the way in which that issue would have been determined in the courts of that third country—even though this could involve the English court in giving extraterritorial effect to the decree. This, it is submitted, is the correct approach. That public international law does not generally require that a State give extraterritorial effect to such decrees is no reason for denying a State the right to do so in what it deems to be appropriate cases through the application of its own rules of private international law. In proprietary matters the doctrine of the *lex situs* is well established in the private international law of most States, and departure from it calls for strong and specific justification. If a foreign expropriatory law is penal, or if its content is so unacceptably repulsive that it will be rejected on grounds of public policy, effect will not be given to that law. This is, however, not to say that *any* expropriatory law—this broad category covering cases of nationalization and requisition as well as confiscation—should automatically be accorded a respect less than that required by general rules of private international law.

Fourthly, there is some authority for the view that an English court will not enforce the 'public laws' of another State. There is here a threshold problem—that of definition. It might be said that a public law is generally a law which by its nature cannot be directly enforced in the country of its enactment or promulgation by an individual as distinct from the State or an instrumentality of the State. This, like any definition of public law, is open to criticism, but the important issue is more fundamental than mere agreement upon an acceptable verbal formulation. As a distinguished United States scholar has written in a rather different context, the distinction between public and private law

> postulates a day when private property, private wrongful conduct, and private contract were indeed separated intellectually, legally, sociologically, and, in many ways, economically and politically, from the activities of the state. That day is long

to follow the earlier case of *Lorentzen* v. *Lydden & Co.*, [1942] 2 KB 202, and *Slatford*'s case was itself reversed on other grounds on appeal ([1954] AC 584), it is generally accepted as representing English law. See, too, to the same effect the Scottish case of *Government of the Republic of Spain* v. *National Bank of Scotland*, [1939] SC 413.

gone. Only in rarefied legal conceptions, in political polemics, and in the romance of nostalgia does this distinction still operate. It may in some legal systems be a handy part of a table of contents, but it is little more than that. . . . We live in a day when multinational and other huge agglomerations of so-called private power are tightly intermeshed at all levels with more traditional sovereigns. To try to distinguish between public and private law in such circumstances as a basis for determining a court's jurisdiction is most unwise.[37]

The House of Lords has recently confirmed in *Buttes Gas and Oil Co.* v. *Hammer* (*Nos. 2 and 3*)[38] that there exists in English law a general principle that the courts will not adjudicate upon the transactions of foreign sovereign States. Lord Wilberforce (with whose judgment the other Lords of Appeal concurred) saw the doctrine as being one of judicial restraint or abstention,[39] but he emphasized that 'This principle is not one of discretion, but is inherent in the very nature of the judicial process'.[40] The principle is a general one, but it is a principle that is essentially concerned with judicial restraint or abstention in relation to what may be described as 'inter-state issues and/or issues of international law'.[41] It in no way indicates judicial unwillingness to apply foreign 'public' laws generally. On the present state of English authorities, laws falling into this latter category can realistically only be seen as constituting a somewhat miscellaneous group of unenforceable foreign laws. Dicey and Morris describe them as 'all those rules (other than penal and revenue laws) which are enforced as an assertion of the authority of central or local government. It is a residual category which will include such topics as import and export regulations, trading with the enemy legislation, price control regulations and anti-trust legislation.'[42] The learned authors also suggest that, although the authority is very slight, even a title to property validly acquired by way of a recognized foreign expropriatory law (recognized because the property was situated in the country of expropriation at the relevant time) will not be enforced, as distinct from merely recognized, in England if the property has not already been reduced into the possession of the foreign expropriatory State or its agent.

It is submitted that the case for withholding or limiting the effect to be given to each of these miscellaneous types of foreign 'public' law should be assessed on its individual merits. In the case of some of them, not least the last mentioned,[43] the merits may not be great. Be this as it may, their existence certainly does not warrant any general assertion that a court will

[37] Macneil, *Canadian Business Law Journal*, 7 (1982–3), pp. 432–3. For a full comparative treatment of public law in private international law see Mann, *Recueil des cours*, 132 (1971–I), pp. 107 ff.

[38] [1982] AC 888. [39] Ibid. 931. [40] Ibid. 932. [41] Ibid. 938.

[42] Dicey and Morris, *The Conflict of Laws* (10th edn., 1980), pp. 93–4.

[43] The only justification offered in *Dicey and Morris* for the suggestion that an expropriatory title validly acquired under the *lex situs* should be regarded in England as a 'valid but unenforceable title' unless the property has already been 'reduced into the possession of the foreign State' (although, it would appear, perhaps is no longer in that possession), is the dogma that 'the courts have no jurisdiction to countenance a claim by a foreign State based upon an exercise of its sovereign power'

not apply foreign public laws—an assertion of uncertain meaning and of possibly dangerous width.

Fifthly and finally, sometimes an English court will refuse on grounds of public policy to apply a particular rule of foreign law which would otherwise fall to be applied. Equally a foreign judgment may be denied recognition on the ground that the foreign court did apply such a rule. Overt resort to public policy in English private international law is, however, relatively rare, or at least considerably more rare than has been resort to corresponding doctrines in the private international law of many countries of continental Europe. Public policy should not be invoked in private international law merely because it could be invoked in the *forum* if the same facts had been presented in a purely domestic context—unless, of course, the domestic law of the *forum* is the *lex causae*. Courts should heed the famous words of Cardozo J in *Loucks* v. *Standard Oil Co.*:[44]

> The courts are not free to enforce a foreign right at the pleasure of the judges, to suit the individual notion of expediency or fairness. They do not close their doors unless help would violate some fundamental principle of justice, some prevalent conception of good morals, some deep-rooted tradition of the commonweal.

In the nineteenth century and in the early years of the present century resort was, it is true, occasionally had more freely to public policy so as to avoid the application of an unfamiliar foreign law; however, subsequently greater restraint was exercised. It is instructive to contrast, for example, the approach of the Court of Appeal in 1904 in *Kaufman* v. *Gerson*[45] with that taken half a century later by Streatfield J in *Addison* v. *Brown*.[46] In the former case the plaintiff, a domiciled male French national, had coerced the defendant, a domiciled female French national, into signing a contract in France by threatening that if she refused he would prosecute her husband. The defendant's husband had misappropriated money entrusted to him by the plaintiff, and by the contract the defendant undertook to repay the plaintiff by instalments the full amount misappropriated. The contract was seemingly valid by French law, but the English Court of Appeal refused to enforce a contract entered into under duress because to do so would 'contravene what by the law of this country is deemed an essential moral interest'.[47] '[I]t is a universal principle of the courts of this country that they will not enforce any contract which has

(Dicey and Morris, op. cit., p. 94). It is not easy to discern the policy underlying a rule which would deny the claim of a foreign State to property to which it is acknowledged to be entitled unless the property has at some stage already been 'reduced into its possession'—especially as 'reduction into possession' can itself in some circumstances be a process of dubious attraction.

[44] 224 NY 99, 111; 120 NE 198, 202 (1918).

[45] [1904] 1 KB 591; recently referred to as 'a very extraordinary case': *Israel Discount Bank* v. *Hadjipateras*, [1984] 1 WLR 137, *per* O'Connor LJ at p. 146.

[46] [1954] 1 WLR 779.

[47] [1904] 1 KB 591, 599–600.

been brought about by coercion.'[48] In *Addison* v. *Brown* a wife sued a husband to recover arrears of maintenance due under a contract governed by Californian law. This contract contained a clause ousting the jurisdiction of the Californian courts. It was argued that such an agreement would be contrary to public policy under English domestic law. Streatfield J rejected the contention that for this reason the action could not be heard.

The fact that overt resort to public policy became, and in spite of recent developments to be considered below still is, relatively rare in English private international law cannot, however, be seen as a symptom of an 'internationalist' attitude. Indeed, it is in a sense an indication of the contrary, for it in part results from the *forum*-orientated bias built into many English choice of law rules themselves. English domestic law is applied in many cases of family law, e.g. divorce, separation, guardianship, custody, adoption and maintenance, in which under many foreign systems a law other than that of the *forum* might fall to be applied. So in these spheres of law in England the opportunities are fewer, and the pressure is the less, for resort to public policy in order to avoid the application of a rule of a foreign *lex causae*, than is often the situation elsewhere. Similarly there may be little scope for the doctrine of public policy in English tort actions if it is still the law that no such action will lie at all unless *inter alia* the wrong complained of would be actionable under English domestic law. Indeed it is perhaps significant that it is in the private international law relating to commercial contracts—an area in which English choice of law rules are markedly 'internationalist'—that public policy has been most frequently successfully invoked in England.

It would be both difficult and undesirable to attempt anything approaching a catalogue of types of case in which public policy does, or should, operate. Even a general classification has its hazards. But two formal patterns of the operation of the doctrine are discernible.

First, the doctrine may be invoked if the nature or content of the foreign rule is so unacceptably repugnant that it could never be applied in England, nor could its application elsewhere necessarily be recognized in England. A contract for the sale of slaves would not be enforced in England, nor would an action on a foreign judgment enforcing such a contract be entertained.[49] The case of a foreign prostitute suing for her unpaid honorarium is probably in the same category. As Lord Cross (with whom Lords Hailsham, Hodson and Salmon agreed) said in *Oppenheimer* v. *Cattermole*[50] of a German law depriving German Jews living abroad of

[48] It may be noted, however, that in the very recent case of *Israel Discount Bank* v. *Hadjipateras*, [1984] 1 WLR 137, at least one member of the Court of Appeal would have been willing, had it been necessary, to apply the principle 'that an agreement obtained by undue influence, like an agreement obtained by duress or coercion, may [*sic*] be treated by our courts as invalidating a foreign judgment based upon the agreement, or as a ground for not enforcing it as contrary to the distinctive public policy of this country' (*per* Stephenson LJ at p. 143).

[49] Although this was not always the case; see *Santos* v. *Illidge* (1860), 8 CB (NS) 861. See, too, *Harris* v. *Cooper* (1871), 31 Upper Canada QB 182.

[50] [1976] AC 249.

German nationality and of their property without compensation: 'To my mind a law of this sort constitutes so grave an infringement of human rights that the courts of this country ought to refuse to recognise it as a law at all.'[51] So, too, a foreign status or incapacity based upon purely religious or racial discrimination might well not be recognized. It is to be emphasized that, as Stephenson LJ has recently observed,[52] in this type of case it has been 'only because the law or practice of the foreign country . . . differed from that policy [i.e. the distinctive public policy of the *forum*] that the question . . . was raised'. At the same time it is to be remembered that unfamiliarity with the type of foreign law in question is obviously not in itself a ground for denial of recognition. Foreign legitimations by subsequent marriage were recognized in England long before legitimation was possible under English domestic law. And polygamous marriages are now recognized in England for almost all purposes. Moreover, the mere fact of unfamiliarity ought usually to carry little, if any, weight in assessing unacceptable repugnance.

It is to be noticed that in this framework within which resort to public policy operates there is implicit something of an 'all or nothing' attitude. If a foreign law is unacceptable, it is totally unacceptable regardless of the context. This lack of sophistication can lead to difficulty. Consider for example the case of a person wishing to marry in England who lacks capacity by the law of his or her domicil on the ground of race or colour. That incapacity would rightly be disregarded for reasons of public policy. Should it necessarily follow that an English court should also regard as valid a marriage celebrated in the country of the domicil between two local domiciliaries, that marriage being according to the law of that country, although valid in point of form, void on the ground of this incapacity? Has not the time come perhaps to recognize openly that there is a separate category of foreign laws for which a *forum* may have a marked distaste—not sufficiently strong for it to reject them altogether—but sufficiently strong to warrant denying them efficacy unless the facts are in effect entirely domestic to the foreign country in question. There would, of course, still remain some types of law to be rejected absolutely.

The other framework within which public policy may be seen to operate is one in which the focus is not so much upon the nature or content of a foreign rule, but rather upon the undesirability of a British court being seen to act in a particular way. The main thrust of public policy here is not to achieve the rejection of an intrinsically repugnant foreign rule, but rather to protect the public or national interest or image of the United Kingdom. Thus public policy may require that a court should not enforce, or even recognize the enforcement of, an otherwise valid transaction if the fact of such enforcement or recognition would be liable to jeopardize good relations existing at a national, or even political, level between the United Kingdom and a foreign State. For example, a contract of loan for the

[51] At p. 278. [52] *Israel Discount Bank* v. *Hadjipateras*, [1984] 1 WLR 137, 144.

purpose of financing a revolt in a friendly foreign country would not be enforced in England although valid by its proper law. Two cases may be mentioned: *Foster* v. *Driscoll*[53] which was concerned with a contract for the introduction of liquor into the United States during the prohibition era; and *Regazzoni* v. *Sethia*[54] which was concerned with a contract to circumvent an Indian law prohibiting the export of certain commodities from India to South Africa. In neither case was the contract enforced. It is true that in each case the *lex causae* was English, but it can be assumed that enforcement would have been refused even if it had been the law of a third country. The overriding principle is that an English court will decline to take action which would be liable to be significantly detrimental to the national or international interests of the United Kingdom, and this is so regardless of the identity of the *lex causae*

In some cases these two recognized patterns of public policy invocation may seem to overlap or coalesce; the case of a contract to bribe a foreign customs officer might be seen as exemplifying this.

To be distinguished from the invocation of public policy is the refusal of an English court to recognize a foreign judgment on the ground that it was obtained in circumstances amounting to a denial of natural justice. Denial of natural justice denotes procedural unfairness. A typical instance is one in which a defendant was not given notice, or was given inadequate notice, of the foreign proceedings; or one in which he was not given an opportunity to present his case. In practice the English courts have shown themselves somewhat loath to deny recognition to a foreign judgment solely on this ground. When recognition has actually been withheld there has usually been present some additional factor such as fraud.

The extent to which public policy may properly be invoked even within these two general frameworks inevitably allows for considerable variation; and, indeed, as social attitudes change, so variations are warranted with the passage of time. Nevertheless it is trite learning that public policy is an unruly horse, and courts should heed the words of a distinguished American writer on the conflict of laws, Professor George Stumberg, words uttered nearly fifty years ago: 'The real difficulty with public policy as a limitation is that it is incapable of measurement. All law is an expression of policy, and whether a particular foreign rule falls under the ban is a matter of opinion which can easily become a matter of whim.'[55] In private international law there is superimposed an additional factor making for unruliness in the horse. This stems from a natural, if often subconscious, 'homing instinct' on the part of judges. There is the temptation to apply standards which may be apt in a domestic factual context but which are not apt universally, for public policy ever beckons as the easy escape route to the familiar comforts of the *lex fori*. However, as has already been suggested,[56] English judges, at least by comparison with

[53] [1929] 1 KB 470.

[54] [1958] AC 301.

[55] Stumberg, *Conflict of Laws* (1937), p. 179.

[56] p. 122, above.

continental counterparts and at least since the early years of the present century, have for one reason or another been largely able to withstand these dangers,[57] both when deciding whether the content of a foreign law is so intrinsically repugnant that it can never be applied, nor can its application in a foreign court ever be recognized, in an English *forum*; and also when deciding whether the fact of enforcement by a British court of a particular rule or transaction, English or foreign, would be unacceptably detrimental to the national interest.

However, a purpose of this present article is to draw attention to something different—namely, that in recent years there have been various and ominous indications of a judicial willingness to see public policy in private international law as operating outside these two frameworks, and indeed in effect as operating outside any framework at all. This wide-ranging operation of the doctrine is markedly reminiscent of the hazy notion that English courts have an inherent residual 'last-ditch' discretion (sometimes put in terms of doing 'substantial justice' between particular parties in particular cases) to which resort has occasionally been had in the past—mostly in certain family law contexts. A relatively early example was provided by the Court of Appeal case of *Gray* (*orse. Formosa*) v. *Formosa*.[58] There a Maltese nullity decree was denied recognition on the ground that recognition would offend against English notions of 'substantial justice'. At least one member of the Court conceded that the Maltese court was jurisdictionally competent, the parties being domiciled there. No Maltese procedural inadequacy or unfairness was found. The Maltese court had annulled the marriage because by Maltese law the man, who was a Maltese Catholic domiciled in Malta, had no capacity to marry except in accordance with the rites of the Catholic Church. The marriage had in fact taken place in an English register office. The Court of Appeal did not assert that the rule of substantive law applied by the Maltese court was so intrinsically objectionable that its application could never be countenanced in an English *forum*, or indeed that its application should be confined to purely Maltese fact situations. The Court instead held in effect that the recognition of its application *on the facts of the instant case* would cause substantial injustice. The focus is not on the content of the foreign rule, but upon the consequences of recognition in the particular circumstances of an instant case. That the Court decided in

[57] In the recent case of *Empresa Exportadora de Azucar* v. *Industria Azucarera Nacional SA* (*The Playa Larga*), [1983] 2 Ll.R.171 (see vol. 54 of this *Year Book*, pp. 297 ff.), the Court of Appeal declined to disregard a Cuban law freezing all property wholly or partly owned by Chilean official agencies or by juridical persons in which the Chilean State had an interest. The law was seen as a legitimate means of achieving compensation for damage to Cuban property resulting from a political coup in Chile. The court distinguished the words of Lord Cross in *Oppenheimer* v. *Cattermole*, [1976] AC 249, 278, cited above, and also referred to the possibility of jeopardizing friendly relations at the national level. Ackner LJ, speaking for the Court of Appeal, said (at p. 190): 'A judge should, of course, be very slow to refuse to give effect to legislation of a foreign state in any sphere in which, according to accepted principles of international law, the foreign state has jurisdiction.'

[58] [1963] P 259.

terms of doing 'substantial justice' rather than in terms of public policy is itself perhaps indicative of a judicial consciousness of the novelty in the approach.[59]

This new and ill-defined enhanced scope for public policy has been manifested in a statutory context by the loose interpretation that has been placed upon the wording of section 8 (2) (b) of the Recognition of Divorces and Legal Separations Act 1971. It provides that recognition of a foreign divorce or legal separation shall be withheld if 'recognition would manifestly[60] be contrary to public policy'. In *Kendall* v. *Kendall*[61] Hollings J refused on grounds of public policy to recognize a Bolivian divorce, even though the actual ground upon which the divorce had been granted by the Bolivian court was physical cruelty—a ground obviously in no way in itself repugnant to English public policy. There had in a very real sense been a gross denial of natural justice in the Bolivian proceedings, but the learned judge, construing section 8 (2) (a) (which deals with non-recognition on that ground) very narrowly, declined to withhold recognition on this basis. Instead he clearly took the view that section 8 (2) (b) empowered him to refuse recognition on 'public policy' grounds if to grant it would in the circumstances of the particular case lead to an unfair result. Again, in *Joyce* v. *Joyce and O'Hare*[62] Lane J gave the same sort of twist to traditional public policy doctrine in English private international law. She first declined to recognize a Quebec divorce on the ground that there had been a denial of natural justice in the Quebec proceedings, the respondent wife there not having been given a reasonable opportunity to participate. Lane J then gave in five lines, as an alternative ratio for her decision, a finding that recognition would 'manifestly be contrary to public policy' within the meaning of section 8 (2) (b)—even though the Quebec divorce had seemingly been pronounced on the ground of mental cruelty. English courts have often recognized decrees granted on this ground without the spectre of public policy being raised. What is most remarkable, however, is that Lane J did not refer to the content of the Quebec law, but merely indicated that the factors, which she thought it proper to take into account when considering whether the wife had in fact had an adequate opportunity to participate in the Quebec proceedings, in themselves also justified her in invoking the doctrine of public policy. This alternative ratio was in effect that the wife had had a rather raw deal.

The Recognition of Divorces and Legal Separations Act 1971 was largely based upon an international convention. This provokes the

[59] In *Gray* (*orse. Formosa*) v. *Formosa* it would seem that what may be described as substantial justice was only achieved by virtue of the combination of refusal to recognize the Maltese nullity decree with the immediately subsequent granting of a divorce. But for the availability of that divorce it would appear that departure from the normal recognition rules could well have actually caused substantial injustice. See vol. 38 of this *Year Book*, pp. 497 ff.

[60] The use of the word 'manifestly' is curious. If contravention of public policy were to be serious but insidious, could it be said to be manifest?

[61] [1977] Fam. 208.

[62] [1979] Fam. 93.

conjecture that, in order to achieve international agreement on the terms of such conventions, there may be a temptation to introduce a loose 'public policy' type escape clause, which is liable to be variously utilized by different countries subscribing to the convention. In this way a spurious appearance of uniformity may be achieved, but uncertainty is introduced into national laws.

In a recent House of Lords case not involving statutory interpretation, approval appears to have been bestowed upon this new unstructured role for public policy in English private international law. In *Vervaeke* v. *Smith*[63] three of the Lords of Appeal (Lord Hailsham of St Marylebone LC, Lord Simon of Glaisdale and Lord Brandon of Oakbrook)[64] invoked public policy as an alternative reason for withholding recognition from a Belgian nullity decree. This case constituted what one may suppose was the final stage in litigation which had spread over more than a decade. The facts giving rise to, and the course of, the litigation in so far as they were relevant to the decision were as follows. In 1954 the petitioner, a woman domiciled in Belgium, went through a ceremony of marriage in England with a domiciled Englishman named Smith. The sole purpose of this marriage was to enable the petitioner to acquire British nationality and thus to be able to practise her profession of prostitute without running the risk of deportation. The parties to the marriage had no intention of living together and did not do so. Eleven years later the petitioner, having taken early retirement from prostitution, went to Italy to live with a man, E. Messina. In 1970 Messina went through a ceremony of marriage in Italy with the petitioner, but he died a few hours later. Messina died leaving a considerable amount of immovable property situated in England, and the petitioner wished to claim this as his widow. In June 1970 she obtained a declaration of nullity in respect of her prior marriage to Smith on the ground of lack of consent on her part. However, before this decree was made absolute, S. Messina (E. Messina's brother) and the Queen's Proctor having intervened, Ormrod J set aside the decree nisi and declared the marriage valid.[65] Subsequently the petitioner sought and obtained a decree of nullity in Belgium. The Belgian courts held that the petitioner had never intended to contract a genuine or real marriage with Smith and that such a fake or sham marriage could not be treated as valid. The Court of Appeal in Ghent held that capacity to marry is governed by the personal law of each party, which in the case of the petitioner was Belgian law as the law of her nationality. By that law she lacked capacity. The marriage was therefore void *ab initio*.[66] The petitioner then proceeded to petition the

[63] [1983] 1 AC 145.

[64] Lord Diplock (with whom the fifth Lord of Appeal, Lord Keith of Kinkel, agreed), although confining his judgment to other grounds, did expressly disclaim any expression of opinion that Lord Hailsham's reasoning in relation to public policy was incorrect.

[65] *Messina (formerly Smith orse. Vervaeke)* v. *Smith (Messina intervening)*, [1971] P 311.

[66] See translation of excerpts from the Belgian judgment quoted by Waterhouse J in his judgment at the High Court hearing in the present proceedings: [1981] Fam. 77 at p. 88.

English High Court for a declaration that the Belgian decree was entitled to recognition. A further petition was later filed praying for a declaration that the marriage to Messina was valid. Waterhouse J dismissed both petitions, and the Court of Appeal dismissed the petitioner's appeal.[67] The House of Lords dismissed her further appeal for reasons which involved invoking the doctrine of *res judicata* and reliance upon public policy. The House was unanimous in holding that the proceedings came within the doctrine of estoppel *per res judicatam* and that the earlier judgment of Ormrod J had concluded the matter so far as English courts are concerned. But it is the alternative resort to public policy, explicitly relied upon by three members of the House, that has direct bearing upon the matters now under discussion, for the circumstances of *Vervaeke* v. *Smith* would not appear to fit easily, or indeed at all, into either of the frameworks within which public policy has traditionally operated. It would be hard to contend that the Belgian court in refusing to give validity to a 'sham' marriage was applying a rule so intrinsically repugnant that it could in no circumstances be applied or recognized in England. Again, any suggestion that recognition of the Belgian judgment would have tended to jeopardize good relations between the United Kingdom and either Belgium or Italy (where the judgment would apparently be recognized) would be palpably insupportable. Indeed it could be plausibly argued that the reverse is so. Non-recognition of the decree of a jurisdictionally competent court sitting in a friendly country would, if anything, be more, not less, likely to jeopardize the United Kingdom's relations with that country than would recognition.

The somewhat diffuse reasons which underlay the invocation of the doctrine of public policy in *Vervaeke* v. *Smith* were expounded in the judgments of the Lord Chancellor and of Lord Simon. In each judgment focus is largely directed not to the content, as such, of the rule or rules of law applied in the Belgian courts, but primarily to the impact of their application (as seen from the point of view of an English *forum*) in the circumstances of the instant case. In this context one of the factors which clearly influenced their Lordships was the behaviour of the appellant at earlier stages of the litigation. Lord Hailsham said:

> Contrary to the view of the Court of Appeal and Waterhouse J, although I agree with them in seeing nothing offensive or unjust as between the parties in the doctrine of public policy propounded by the Belgian courts, I am of the opinion that the law of England . . . at least in the present case takes the case outside the rules for the recognition of foreign, and, in particular, Belgian, decrees, that is at least as regards a marriage celebrated in England between a British national and an alien for an extraneous purpose of the kind contemplated by the parties in the present case, viz. using the marriage as a vehicle for conferring British nationality on the alien partner so as to save her from deportation after conviction for criminal offences.[68]

[67] [1981] Fam. 77, 118 ff.

[68] [1983] 1 AC 145, 156–7.

It is the present writer's submission with all respect that if one goes beyond consideration of the intrinsic nature of a suspect rule of law and considers, in addition or instead, the effect of its application or recognition in an instant fact situation, in order to justify its exclusion on the grounds of public policy—although one may mask what one is doing by re-defining the rule narrowly so as precisely and deliberately to produce a desired result in the instant case—one is in substance embarking upon the exercise of an unstructured discretion.[69]

It has been suggested earlier that the role of public policy in private international law might be more satisfactorily defined if it were to be acknowledged that there is a separate category of foreign laws which a *forum* may regard with a degree of distaste that warrants, not total rejection, but simply limitation upon their acceptance to cases in which the facts are in all significant respects purely domestic to the foreign country in question. Such a relaxation would, of course, not only in principle but also in practice be quite different from an approach which permits avoidance of a foreign law on public policy grounds, even though that law is not regarded as being intrinsically even marginally distasteful, and even though the fact of its recognition or enforcement would not be detrimental to national interests. This latter approach could allow *forum* notions of public policy even greater scope in the international sphere than is allowed to it in the domestic sphere. Resort to public policy involves refusal to apply an otherwise applicable rule of law. There is a danger that a feeling may be engendered that departure from a *forum*'s own choice of law or recognition rule is in some way less radical (and therefore more acceptable) than is departure from a rule of the *forum*'s domestic law. Whereas, of course, the contrary should be the case: a *forum* should be more, not less, reluctant to impose its own national policy attitudes and criteria in a factually international context than it is in a factually national context.

Once it is accepted that a rule of private international law, a rule of the *lex causae*, or a decision reached by a jurisdictionally competent foreign court can be discarded as a matter of 'public policy' simply in order to achieve what by *forum* criteria appears to be a just result in a particular case, the gate is opened wide through which the proverbial unruly (but locally bred) horse can pass so as to wreak havoc in international pastures. In English private international law most of the manifestations of this

[69] It is perhaps sobering to reflect that not only did the unanimous holding of their Lordships on the *res judicata* point render reference to public policy unnecessary, but *Vervaeke* v. *Smith* could also, it is submitted, have been decided on a different ground, had the opportunity been taken to clarify an aspect of the general law relating to the recognition of foreign nullity decrees. In *Vervaeke* v. *Smith* the marriage to Smith was valid at its inception in accordance with English private international law criteria. In these circumstances to hold that it was subsequently annulled by a foreign court of competent jurisdiction ought not to have involved holding, too, that the court's decree had retroactive effect—even if it purported to do so. It is one thing for a *forum* to accept that such a decree can terminate a valid marriage, but it would be quite another to hold that the *forum* must also accept the negativing of its own choice of law rules governing the original validity of marriage. Shorn of retroactive effect the Belgian decree would not have validated the marriage to Messina.

relatively recent tendency to inflate the role of public policy and to see it as sometimes little more than a vehicle for the exercise of an ill-defined or undefined discretion have so far been in the area of family law.[70] An outbreak of insular palm tree justice is, however, not to be viewed with equanimity in any branch of private international law. The ultimate remedy must largely lie in a combination of judicial restraint with a constant striving to bring about marked improvement in the detail and the sophistication of the rules of private international law themselves.

[70] But see *dicta* of Slade J in *Winkworth* v. *Christie, Manson and Woods*, [1980] Ch. 496, a case concerned with the *inter vivos* transfer of movable property.

See, too, the Foreign Limitation Periods Act 1984, which provides that in English private international law all matters of limitation of actions and prescription shall usually be determined by reference to the *lex causae*. Section 2 (1) introduces a general public policy reservation, but section 2 (2) goes on to prescribe specifically that the application of the *lex causae* 'shall [*sic*] conflict with public policy to the extent that its application would cause undue hardship to a person who is, or might be, a party to the action or proceedings'.

[8]

CORNELL LAW REVIEW

Volume 59 November 1973 Number 1

A RECURRENT PROBLEM IN TRANSNATIONAL LITIGATION: THE EFFECT OF FAILURE TO INVOKE OR PROVE THE APPLICABLE FOREIGN LAW*

Rudolf B. Schlesinger†

I

Introduction: The Elements of Complexity

When, under the forum's choice of law rules, some or all of the substantive issues in a case are governed by the law of another country, but the parties fail to give timely notice of the foreign law or to show what it is, how is the court to arrive at a decision? This question presents itself with considerable frequency.[1] The courts and legal writers have paid a great deal of attention to the matter;[2] but the

* The substance of this Article was originally presented at Columbia University Law School on the occasion of the 1973 Parker School Conference "On Interaction of Foreign and Domestic Law in Settlement of Disputes in the United States." In the present version, the text of the original talk has been revised only slightly; but the footnotes have been considerably augmented. In doing this, the author received valuable assistance from Richard D. Avil, Jr., a member of the Cornell Law School Class of 1974. This help is gratefully acknowledged.

As a member of the U.S. Government's Advisory Committee on International Rules of Judicial Procedure (*see* Act of September 2, 1958, Pub. L. No. 85-906, 72 Stat. 1743), the author was one of the draftsmen of Rule 44.1 of the Federal Rules of Civil Procedure. It goes without saying, however, that the views expressed herein are those of the author and do not necessarily reflect the thinking of any of the other individuals or groups that had a hand in formulating and promulgating Rule 44.1.

† William Nelson Cromwell Professor of International and Comparative Law, Cornell University. Dr. Jur. 1933, University of Munich; LL.B. 1942, Columbia University.

[1] *See, e.g.*, Lady Nelson, Ltd. v. Creole Petroleum Corp., 286 F.2d 684 (2d Cir. 1961); Philp v. Macri, 261 F.2d 945 (9th Cir. 1958); Fitzgerald v. Fitzgerald, 66 N.J. Super. 277, 168 A.2d 851 (Ch. 1961); Sonnesen v. Panama Transp. Co., 298 N.Y. 262, 82 N.E.2d 569 (1948), *reargument denied*, 298 N.Y. 856, 84 N.E.2d 324, *cert. denied*, 337 U.S. 919 (1949). *See also* cases collected in Annot., 75 A.L.R.2d 529 (1961); notes 3-128 *infra*.

[2] *See, e.g.*, R.B. Schlesinger, Comparative Law 148-84 (3d ed. 1970); Keeffe, Landis &

voices of those who have treated the problem are not in harmony, and by virtue of the remarkable discordance of some of the suggested approaches the whole subject has acquired the reputation of being controversial and confused. It may be useful, therefore, as a first step to analyze the elements of the existing confusion. At least three such elements can be discerned.

A. *Simplistic "Single Rule" Response to Diverse Problems*

The basic problem is invariably defined in abstract language such as "failure to invoke or prove the applicable foreign law."[3] This abstraction may be useful for some purposes; but it tends to make us forget that, like many other abstract expressions, it covers a great deal of ground. In fact, it applies to a variety of situations which in functional and practical terms, and in terms of simple justice, do not necessarily call for uniform treatment.

A litigant's failure to give notice and to provide information as to the applicable foreign law may be due to many diverse reasons. Perhaps his lawyer is incompetent, and hence does not realize that a case involving foreign elements cannot be handled like an ordinary domestic case. Or maybe the lawyer has recognized that there is a possible foreign law problem, but has wrongly assumed that the court either would apply the forum's own domestic law, or would place the burden of invoking and proving the foreign law on his opponent. In other cases, the lawyer failing to plead and prove the foreign law may be a tricky type. Perhaps he has looked at the foreign law and has found it less favorable to his client than the internal law of the forum. Thus, regardless of the rules on choice of law and burden of proof, he speculates that he might be able to trick his less sophisticated opponent into handling the case as a domestic one until it becomes too late for either party to invoke the foreign law. Sometimes the lawyers on both sides—each analyzing the forum's internal law, the choice of law rule and the burden of proof in a different manner—try to outsmart each other in this way. In still other cases, an attorney, without being

Shaad, *Sense and Nonsense About Judicial Notice,* 2 STAN. L. REV. 664 (1950); Miller, *Federal Rule 44.1 and the "Fact" Approach to Determining Foreign Law: Death Knell for a Die-Hard Doctrine,* 65 MICH. L. REV. 613 (1967); Nussbaum, *Proof of Foreign Law in New York: A Proposed Amendment,* 57 COLUM. L. REV. 348 (1957); Nussbaum, *The Problem of Proving Foreign Law,* 50 YALE L.J. 1018 (1941); Stern, *Foreign Law in the Courts: Judicial Notice and Proof,* 45 CALIF. L. REV. 23 (1957); Annot., 75 A.L.R.2d 529 (1961).

[3] *See* Leary v. Gledhill, 8 N.J. 260, 267, 84 A.2d 725, 728 (1951): "Thus the failure to plead and prove the foreign law has not generally been considered as fatal." *See also* N.J. STAT. ANN. § 2A:82-27 (Supp. 1973): "In the absence of . . . pleading or notice [of the law of another country], it shall be presumed that the common law of such State is the same as the common law as interpreted by the courts of this State."

either incompetent or tricky, may soundly conclude that to prove the foreign law, or to submit materials relating to it, is simply too expensive for his client. The assumption that a single and simple rule will do justice to all of these motley situations surely is one of the causes of the existing confusion.

B. *Antithetical Theories*

The second element of confusion results from the scholars' inability, thus far, to develop a viable theory for dealing with our problem. In every legal system it has long been the habit of courts and scholars to pose the problem in the form of the question whether foreign law should be treated as fact or law.[4] This is most unfortunate, because either of these theoretical characterizations, if consistently applied, leads to absurd results. The ultimate absurdity reached under the "fact" theory[5] is that issues of foreign law have to be determined by the jury.[6] It is no less faulty, however, indiscriminately to equate foreign law with domestic "law." Since the ascertainment and interpretation of foreign law require skills which the court simply does not possess, the procedural treatment of a foreign law question cannot be quite the same as that of a question of domestic law.[7] The soundest approach would be to give up all attempts to characterize foreign law as either "fact" or "law" and to start writing a new theory on a clean slate. But in the United States, at least, this

[4] *See* Kegel, *Zur Organisation der Ermittlung Ausländischen Privatrechts,* 1 FESTSCHRIFT FÜR NIPPERDEY 453 (1965); Sass, *Foreign Law in Civil Litigation: A Comparative Survey,* 16 AM. J. COMP. L. 332 (1968); Zajtay, *The Application of Foreign Law,* in 3 INTERNATIONAL ENCYCLOPEDIA OF COMPARATIVE LAW 14-1 (1972); Zajtay, *Le traitement du droit étranger dans le procès civil–Étude de droit comparé,* 4 RIVISTA DI DIRITTO INTERNAZIONALE PRIVATO E PROCESSUALE 233 (1968).

[5] Under the "fact" theory, a court is not expected to know the applicable foreign law in the same way that it is presumed to know the law of its own jurisdiction. Rather, the foreign law must be brought to the court, through pleading and evidence, in the same manner that any other fact must be shown. *See* Liechti v. Roche, 198 F.2d 174, 176 (5th Cir. 1952).

[6] For a discussion of this point, see Fitzpatrick v. International Ry., 252 N.Y. 127, 136-41, 169 N.E. 112, 116-17 (1929). In most common-law jurisdictions, legislative action was required in order to overcome the effect of this logical but absurd deduction from the "fact" theory. *See* R.B. SCHLESINGER, *supra* note 2, at 69, 72.

[7] In Diaz v. Gonzalez, 261 U.S. 102, 106 (1923), Mr. Justice Holmes commented on the plight of an American court faced with a civil law problem:

> When we contemplate such a system from the outside it seems like a wall of stone, every part even with all the others, except so far as our own local education may lead us to see subordinations to which we are accustomed. But to one brought up within it, varying emphasis, tacit assumptions, unwritten practices, a thousand influences gained only from life, may give to the different parts wholly new values that logic and grammar never could have got from the books.

Moreover, a court may not have access to libraries with sufficient foreign law materials to allow it to find and verify the applicable rules of foreign law.

seems almost impossible. American common-law doctrines,[8] and in large part the pertinent statutes,[9] are so clearly based on the fact theory that in dealing with existing law we cannot afford completely to dismiss that unsound theory from our minds.

The difficulties flowing from the use of the fact-law dichotomy are intertwined with, and compounded by, the well-known and tedious battle between two contending conflict of laws theories. The vested rights theory, as preached by Holmes[10] and Beale,[11] had, until recently, a strong impact on the case law in this area.[12] According to the apostles of that theory, it is axiomatic that a foreign cause of action is an *obligatio* created by the command of a particular foreign sovereign.[13] The cause of action does not exist apart from the foreign law which creates and defines it. If one accepts this premise, and combines it with the "fact" theory, it follows with logical necessity that a plaintiff who alleges a cause of action governed by foreign law, but fails to allege and prove the relevant command of the foreign sovereign, has failed to show one of the material "facts" of his case and thus must lose.[14] The same fate befalls a defendant who fails to allege

[8] *See* notes 24-78 and accompanying text *infra*.

[9] *See* R.B. SCHLESINGER, *supra* note 2, at 67-69.

One should not overestimate the significance of statutory provisions such as the last sentence of Federal Rule of Civil Procedure 44.1, which provides that the court's determination of the foreign law (if such determination is made) "shall be treated as a ruling on a question of law." This does not mean that a question of foreign law shall for all purposes be treated as a question of law. The effect of this provision is merely to make it clear that an issue of foreign law is to be determined by the court, and not by the jury, and that for purposes of appellate review the trial court's determination shall be treated as a ruling on a question of law. Plainly, it was not the intention of the draftsmen of Rule 44.1 to equate foreign law and domestic law in all respects. If that had been the intention, the responsibility for ascertaining the foreign law would have been thrown wholly upon the court, and the court would have been instructed to ascertain the foreign law regardless of the assistance or lack of assistance offered by the parties. The most cursory glance at the second sentence of Rule 44.1 shows that such was not the intent of the draftsmen. That sentence leaves it to the discretion of the court whether judicial notice should be taken of the foreign law. It is a well-known fact that in the exercise of that discretion the courts tend not to conduct independent research concerning alien law when they have received no aid from counsel. Thus, it is crystal clear that foreign law is not treated like domestic law, which under all circumstances, and regardless of party presentation, must always be ascertained and determined by the court. *See* Sass, *supra* note 4, at 342-47.

[10] *See* Cuba R.R. v. Crosby, 222 U.S. 473 (1912); Slater v. Mexican Nat'l R.R., 194 U.S. 120 (1904).

[11] 3 J. BEALE, A TREATISE ON THE CONFLICT OF LAWS 1968-69 (1935).

[12] *See, e.g.*, Philp v. Macri, 261 F.2d 945 (9th Cir. 1958); Cosulich Societa Triestina Di Navigazione v. Elting, 66 F.2d 534 (2d Cir. 1933); Industrial Export & Import Corp. v. Hongkong & Shanghai Banking Corp., 302 N.Y. 342, 98 N.E.2d 466 (1951); Riley v. Pierce Oil Corp., 245 N.Y. 152, 156 N.E. 647 (1927).

[13] *See* Slater v. Mexican Nat'l R.R., 194 U.S. 120, 126 (1904).

[14] We repeat that the only justification for allowing a party to recover when the cause of action arose in another civilized jurisdiction is a well founded belief that it was a

and prove the foreign law on which an affirmative defense is based.[15]

The local-law theory, on the other hand, postulates that the internal law of the forum governs all aspects of a case unless a sufficient justification is shown for displacing it; and according to at least some of the modern anti-Bealeans, such as Professor Ehrenzweig and the late Professor Currie, the law of the forum is never effectively displaced unless the applicable foreign law has been invoked in proper and timely fashion.[16] Thus, if the parties fail to invoke the pertinent foreign law, the court will look to its own domestic law as the rule of decision.[17]

Among the scholars, the antithetical nature of these two theories has engendered a continuing controversy conducted with the earnestness and reckless abandon of a Holy War.

To make things worse, the violent disagreement between the contending scholarly camps concerns not only the solution of the problem, but even its nature and curricular allocation. The "fact" theory, with its emphasis on establishing the foreign law by formal proof or by certain presumptions, had the effect of largely allocating the whole problem to the field of Evidence.[18] Those scholars, however, who prefer to formulate the problem in terms of "displacement of the law of the forum," claim that it constitutes an important and indeed basic Conflict of Laws issue.[19] This debate about the proper allocation of the problem, which at first blush appears to be mere academic infighting, is not without practical significance; in the federal courts, the *Erie* doctrine and the terms of the Enabling Act[20] make it necessary to determine whether the problem is procedural or substantive.

> cause of action in that place. The right to recover stands upon that as its necessary foundation. It is part of the plaintiff's case, and if there is reason for doubt he must allege and prove it.

Cuba R.R. v. Crosby, 222 U.S. 473, 479 (1912). *See* cases cited in note 15 *infra*.

[15] *See* Tidewater Oil Co. v. Waller, 302 F.2d 638 (10th Cir. 1962); Eisler v. Soskin, 272 App. Div. 894, 71 N.Y.S.2d 682 (1st Dep't 1947), *aff'd*, 297 N.Y. 841, 78 N.E.2d 862 (1948). *See also* note 40 *infra*.

[16] *See* B. CURRIE, SELECTED ESSAYS ON THE CONFLICT OF LAWS 3-76 (1963), *reprinted from* Currie, *On the Displacement of the Law of the Forum*, 58 COLUM. L. REV. 964 (1958); A. EHRENZWEIG, A TREATISE ON THE CONFLICT OF LAWS 360 (1962); Ehrenzweig & Westen, *Fraudulent Conveyances in the Conflict of Laws*, 66 MICH. L. REV. 1679, 1685-90 (1968).

[17] *See, e.g.*, Michael v. S.S. Thanasis, 311 F. Supp. 170, 176 n.10, 177 (N.D. Cal. 1970). *See also* 1700 Ocean Ave. Corp. v. GBR Associates, 354 F.2d 993 (9th Cir. 1965); Leary v. Gledhill, 8 N.J. 260, 84 A.2d 725 (1951). For further references, see note 50 *infra*.

[18] *See, e.g.*, MCCORMICK, HANDBOOK OF THE LAW OF EVIDENCE § 335, at 779 (2d ed. 1972).

[19] *See, e.g.*, Ehrenzweig, *The Lex Fori–Basic Rule in the Conflict of Laws*, 58 MICH. L. REV. 637, 678-79 (1960).

[20] *See* 28 U.S.C. § 2072 (1970).

C. *The Complex Structure of the Pertinent Legal Rules*

In every American jurisdiction, there has been a considerable growth of common-law rules concerning the consequences of a failure to plead or prove the applicable foreign law.[21] In almost half of the jurisdictions—including all of those which have a considerable volume of foreign law litigation—we also find judicial notice statutes that have been superimposed upon the common-law rules.[22]

The complexity arising from this interaction of judge-made and statutory law is further enhanced by the fact that all of the rules specifically dealing with the problem of invoking or proving the applicable foreign law have to be read against the backdrop of other, more general rules of procedure. Especially important are those procedural rules which determine when and how a foreign law issue has to be raised in order to be considered by the trial judge and to be preserved for appellate review.[23]

In order to chart a path through this complex maze of legal rules—judge-made and statutory, specific and general—the discussion which follows will initially separate (*1*) the common-law background, (*2*) the judicial notice statutes, and (*3*) the relevant procedural rules of a more general nature. Only on the basis established by such separate analysis, can we examine the interaction of the three sets of rules.

II

Survey of Existing Law

A. *The Common Law*

1. *Conventional Analysis: Split Among Conflicting "Rules"*

The common-law rules are presented by most of the commentators as reflecting a basic split, and a superficial examination seems to lend some credence to the conclusion that the courts are divided. On the one hand, there are decisions influenced by the vested rights theory and thus leaning toward the rule that a cause of action or a defense based on foreign law is lost if the party asserting it fails to plead and prove the applicable foreign law.[24] The classical example is the infamous case of *Crosby v. Cuba Railroad Co.*,[25] in which the

[21] *See* notes 24-78 and accompanying text *infra*.

[22] *See* notes 79-106 and accompanying text *infra*.

[23] *See, e.g.*, Fed. R. Civ. P. 51; N.Y. Civ. Prac. Law §§ 4017, 5501(a)(3) (McKinney 1963); *id.* § 4110-b (McKinney Supp. 1973).

[24] *See* cases cited in note 12 *supra*.

[25] 222 U.S. 473 (1912).

opinion was written by the most fanatical of vested rights fanatics, Mr. Justice Holmes himself.[26] In the *Crosby* case, the plaintiff became aware of a defect in his employer's machinery. He reported this dangerous situation and was promised that it would be quickly rectified. In the meantime, the plaintiff was instructed to continue with his work.[27] An accident caused by the defective machinery ensued, and the plaintiff lost a hand. Although the accident had taken place in Cuba, and no evidence was introduced concerning the applicable Cuban law, the trial judge allowed the jury's verdict for the plaintiff to stand.[28] Both he[29] and a majority of the court of appeals[30] placed on the defendant the burden of proving that the foreign law was different from the law of the forum. Under the forum's law the plaintiff was entitled to recover. In reversing and remanding for a new trial, the Supreme Court, per Mr. Justice Holmes, disagreed with the rationale of the lower courts. According to Justice Holmes, the plaintiff had the burden of pleading and proving the specific Cuban law which defined his right of recovery.[31] The plaintiff's failure to meet this burden brought about his defeat.

The courts, however, have always recognized important exceptions to the orthodox rule applied[32] in the *Crosby* case. Under the exceptions, the internal law of the forum will be applied whenever it is reasonably probable that the foreign law in question is similar to domestic law. Such likelihood of similarity exists (*1*) when the foreign country belongs to the common-law orbit,[33] and (*2*) in any event,

---

[26] Eight years before the *Crosby* case, Holmes had delineated his theory of "vested rights" in Slater v. Mexican Nat'l R.R., 194 U.S. 120 (1904). He posited:

> The theory of the foreign suit is that although the act complained of was subject to no law having force in the forum, it gave rise to an obligation, an *obligatio*, which, like other obligations, follows the person, and may be enforced wherever the person may be found. . . . But as the only source of this obligation is the law of the place of the act, it follows that that law determines not merely the existence of the obligation, . . . but equally determines its extent.

Id. at 126 (citations omitted).

[27] 222 U.S. at 477.

[28] *Id.* at 477.

[29] On a motion, after trial, to set aside the jury verdict, the judge emphatically stated:

> He [the plaintiff] had the right to set forth a cause of action, which, according to the law of the forum, would be complete, and, in the event of a conflict between the lex loci and the lex fori, the defendant ought to have shown by a proper plea that, under the lex loci, the plaintiff acquired no right of action.

Crosby v. Cuba R.R., 158 F. 144, 147 (C.C.D.N.J. 1908).

[30] *See* Cuba R.R. v. Crosby, 170 F. 369 (3d Cir. 1909).

[31] *See* note 14 *supra*.

[32] Perhaps misapplied would be more accurate. *See* text accompanying notes 36-40 *infra*.

[33] Judge Learned Hand has stated:

> The extent of our right to make any assumptions about the law of another country depends upon the country and the question involved; in common-law countries we may go further than in civil law; in civilized, than in backward or barbarous.

E. Gerli & Co. v. Cunard S.S. Co., 48 F.2d 115, 117 (2d Cir. 1931).

whenever the point at issue is so fundamental that even a country outside of the common-law orbit may reasonably be presumed to have adopted a solution similar to our own.[34]

In spite of these wide-ranging exceptions, the orthodox rule has been criticized as harsh.[35] *Quaere,* however, whether the occasional harshness of judicial decisions using the orthodox approach stems from the rule itself or from its misapplication. If a case like *Crosby* came up today in the federal courts, the orthodox common-law approach would not lead to a harsh result. Today, the defendant would be prevented by Rule 44.1[36] and by several other provisions of the Federal Rules of Civil Procedure[37] from raising the Cuban law point on appeal. Thus, the plaintiff would win. Even in 1912, the plaintiff would have won if Justice Holmes had realized that "assumption of the risk" is an affirmative defense and that the burden of proving the Cuban law supporting this affirmative defense was on the defendant.[38] This was a case in which the plaintiff had a so-called fundamental cause of action—one presumed to be recognized in all civilized legal systems—while the affirmative defense was nonfundamental[39] and thus dependent on a proper showing of the applicable foreign law.[40] It follows that correct application of the

[34] *See, e.g.,* Parrot v. Mexican Cent. Ry., 207 Mass. 184, 93 N.E. 590 (1911). Further references are collected in Arams v. Arams, 182 Misc. 328, 45 N.Y.S.2d 251 (Sup. Ct. 1943).

[35] Professor Ehrenzweig has called application of the orthodox rule a "miscarriage of justice." A. EHRENZWEIG, *supra* note 16, at 360.

[36] *See* notes 37 & 87-93 and accompanying text *infra.*

[37] The defendant in the *Crosby* case raised the foreign law point for the first time after trial, in a motion for judgment notwithstanding the verdict. If the case came up today, it would be arguable that, regardless of the merits of the foreign law point, the defendant had waived its objection concerning that point, and that the intermediate appellate court was authorized and indeed compelled by Federal Rules of Civil Procedure 12(h)(2) and 51 to affirm the judgment for the plaintiff. *Cf.* Black, Sivalls & Bryson, Inc. v. Shondell, 174 F.2d 587 (8th Cir. 1949).

[38] *See* James, *Assumption of Risk: Unhappy Reincarnation,* 78 YALE L.J. 185, 195-96 (1968) and authorities cited therein.

[39] Clearly, it cannot be taken for granted that assumption of risk as a complete defense is universally recognized by civilized legal systems. In our own country, the defense has been abolished, by statute or judicial decision, in a number of jurisdictions. *See* W. PROSSER, LAW OF TORTS 454-57 (4th ed. 1971). Even in states where the defense still exists, it would be unlikely to prevail in a case in which, as here, the defendant employer promised to repair the defective machinery and requested the employee to continue its use in the meantime. *See id.* at 452.

[40] *See* cases cited in note 15 *supra.*

On the other hand, when the plaintiff's cause of action and defendant's affirmative defense both were based on "fundamental" principles, and the plaintiff sought to counter the defense by a reply not borne out by such principles, the burden of proving the foreign law (*i.e.,* the foreign law supporting the reply) was held to be on the plaintiff. *See* E. Gerli & Co. v. Cunard S.S. Co., 48 F.2d 115 (2d Cir. 1931); Mangrelli v. Italian Line, 208 Misc. 685, 144 N.Y.S.2d 570 (Sup. Ct. 1955).

orthodox rule and its recognized exceptions would have led to the correct result: affirmance of the judgment for the plaintiff.

Another famous case often cited by the critics of the orthodox approach is *Walton v. Arabian American Oil Co.*[41] Walton was an American citizen who was temporarily in Saudi Arabia. While there, he suffered serious injuries in an automobile accident[42] when his car collided with one of the defendant's trucks. Neither the plaintiff nor the defendant, an American corporation, attempted to prove the applicable law of Saudi Arabia. Under the New York conflict of laws rules as they stood at the time of the *Walton* case, the substantive law of the place where the tort occurred was controlling.[43] Thus, the burden was thought to be on the plaintiff to prove the applicable Saudi Arabian law. Because he did not do so, the trial judge dismissed the action. This judgment was upheld reluctantly by the court of appeals.[44] The result in *Walton* was not quite as revolting as that in *Crosby,* because in the *Walton* case the plaintiff's counsel had been warned repeatedly by the trial judge that the plaintiff would lose if he did not prove the law of Saudi Arabia.[45] Whatever harshness remained was, perhaps, the result of the rigid choice of law rule prevailing at that time, and not of the orthodox approach to the consequences of failure to prove the foreign law. In 1971, the United States District Court for the Southern District of Texas had to deal with a case the facts of which were virtually identical with those of *Walton,* except that the accident occurred in Libya rather than in Saudi Arabia.[46] In that case, the problem of invoking and proving Libyan

---

[41] 233 F.2d 541 (2d Cir.), *cert. denied,* 352 U.S. 872 (1956).

[42] *Id.* at 542.

[43] *Id.* Prior to Babcock v. Jackson, 12 N.Y.2d 473, 191 N.E.2d 279, 240 N.Y.S.2d 743 (1963), New York generally applied the rule of lex loci delicti to all substantive issues arising in a tort case.

[44] The only opinion in the case was written by Judge Frank, who, in part, dissented from the majority holding. *See* note 126 and accompanying text *infra.* In that opinion, which undertook to express both the views of the majority and the reasons for his own dissent, Judge Frank stated:

> This conclusion [that dismissal of the action should be affirmed] seems unjust for this reason: Both the parties are Americans. The plaintiff was but a transient in Saudi Arabia when the accident occurred and has not been there since that time. The defendant company engages in extensive business operations there, and is therefore in a far better position to obtain information concerning the "law" of that country. But, under the New York decisions which we must follow, plaintiff had the burden. As he did not discharge it, a majority of the court holds that the judge correctly gave judgment for the defendant.

233 F.2d at 545 (footnotes omitted).

[45] *See id.* at 545-46.

[46] Couch v. Mobil Oil Corp., 327 F. Supp. 897 (S.D. Tex. 1971).

law was avoided because the court, focusing on the parties' common nationality and domicile, decided that Texas was the state of the most significant relationship,[47] and hence applied the substantive law of Texas.[48] Thus, by adopting a more flexible choice of law rule, the court was able to hold in favor of the plaintiff and to obviate repetition of the *Walton* scenario.[49]

We must now turn to a different line of cases which, to the superficial observer, seems irreconcilable with *Crosby* and its offspring. In these cases, which are quite numerous,[50] failure to invoke or to prove the otherwise applicable foreign law led the courts to apply the domestic law of the forum.[51] Sometimes, as in the late Chief Justice Vanderbilt's well-known opinion in *Leary v. Gledhill,*[52] this result is explained in terms of the parties' acquiescence.[53] On other occasions, it has been said that domestic law should be applied because it is the only law the court knows; or the case was decided in accordance with the forum's internal law without any explanation at all.[54] Those who follow the teachings of Professor Ehrenzweig or of

[47] *Cf.* RESTATEMENT (SECOND) OF CONFLICT OF LAWS §§ 6, 145, 146 (1971).

[48] 327 F. Supp. at 905.

[49] Even if, as a matter of choice of law, the court had held that some of the relevant substantive issues in the case were governed by the law of Libya (which remained unproved), a satisfactory result—more satisfactory than the result in *Walton*—could have been reached under the modern approach explained below. In light of the fact that the defendant had much easier access to the sources of the applicable foreign law than the plaintiff, a modern court might well place the burden of proving such law on the defendant, with the understanding that the substantive law of the forum will be applied if that burden is not met. *See* note 73 and accompanying text *infra*. In other words, tinkering with choice of law rules is not the only method by which a court today could avoid the harshness of the *Walton* result.

[50] *See* cases collected in §§ 3-6 of Annot., 75 A.L.R.2d 529 (1961), and in RESTATEMENT, *supra* note 47, at § 136, Reporter's Note on comment *h* (1971) (with references concerning rule in England).

[51] This approach might be called the forum-law approach, as distinguished from the orthodox approach exemplified by *Crosby*.

[52] 8 N.J. 260, 84 A.2d 725 (1951).

[53] Chief Judge Vanderbilt stated:

> The presumption that in the absence of proof the parties acquiesce in the application of the law of the forum, be it statutory law or common law . . . , may be universally applied regardless of the nature of the controversy. . . . We are of the opinion, therefore, that in the instant case the rights of the parties are to be determined by the law of New Jersey which unquestionably permits recovery on the facts proven.

Id. at 269-70, 84 A.2d at 730.

[54]
> We agree . . . that the general, if not universal, rule is that the rights of succession of a husband to personal property of his wife is [*sic*] governed by the law of the domicile of the owner at death. . . . [I]n the instant case, there was no pleading or proof as to what, if any, marital rights Wackwitz would have, or what conduct, if any, on his part would forfeit such rights under the laws of his wife's domicile. We cannot judicially notice the law of Germany. . . . In the absence of proof of such law we must apply the law of Missouri.

Lane v. St. Louis Union Trust Co., 356 Mo. 76, 82, 201 S.W.2d 288, 291 (1947); *see* Savage v. O'Neil, 44 N.Y. 298, 300-01 (1871).

the late Professor Currie will, of course, explain all these decisions on the ground that, as a matter of choice of law doctrine, the forum's internal law remains the rule of decision unless it is displaced by a properly invoked foreign law.[55]

This approach, too, contains some seeds of unfairness. Suppose the plaintiff has cleverly chosen a forum that has little connection with the transaction, but whose domestic law favors the plaintiff's side. If the court is willing to substitute its own law for the properly applicable but unproved foreign law, then the plaintiff by this maneuver has successfully relieved himself of the burden and expense of proving the foreign law, and has thrown that burden on the defendant.

Again, it is important to recognize that even those courts which pay unqualified lip service to the forum-law rule, do not apply it in all cases. There are situations in which it would be patently absurd to substitute domestic law for the applicable foreign law. Suppose, for instance, that the plaintiff sues for breach of contract, and the defendant seeks to excuse his nonperformance by asserting that performance on his part became impossible due to an embargo imposed by the government of Ruritania. If in this case the defendant fails to prove the Ruritanian statute or decree imposing the embargo, he will lose. It would be unjustifiable to let him substitute the law of the forum on this point. Even Currie and Ehrenzweig do not contend otherwise; in their opinion, the explanation is that in such a case the Ruritanian embargo provisions do not constitute the rule of decision, but a mere "datum."[56] However, since the borderline between a "datum" and a rule of decision has never been staked out with any precision, this is not an explanation, but merely a statement of the result. The significant fact is that in the view of all courts and all scholars there are *some* cases in which it is inappropriate to substitute domestic law for the otherwise applicable foreign law.[57]

---

[55] *See* notes 16 & 19 *supra*.

[56] It has been claimed that there are "situations in which application of the foreign law is required under all circumstances." But these situations are limited to those where knowledge of a foreign law is required as a datum for the application of the domestic rule. To determine whether defendant was negligent per se (under forum law) because of having exceeded a speed limit prevailing at the foreign place of accident, that speed limit must of course be established to make the complaint conclusive.

A. EHRENZWEIG, *supra* note 16, at 362; *see* Currie, *supra* note 50, at 1012-14 (1958); Traynor, *Conflict of Laws: Professor Currie's Restrained and Enlightened Forum*, 49 CALIF. L. REV. 845, 873-75 (1961). It should be pointed out, however, that Professor Ehrenzweig more recently has modified his view that except in the "datum" situations the court should always follow the forum-law approach. *See* note 72 *infra*.

[57] The following hypothetical situation, inspired by the facts of an actual case, may serve as a further illustration. Suppose Mr. and Mrs. Meyer, natives and nationals of Austria, were domiciled in that country until early 1972, when they immigrated into the United States and

It follows that the orthodox rule and the forum-law rule are not as irreconcilable as appears at first blush. When the two allegedly conflicting "rules" *and their "exceptions"* are compared, it becomes clear that almost all of the relevant decisions, in spite of their differences in articulation, can be reconciled in terms of the results reached.

2. *Suggested Analysis: A Multi-Factor Approach*

In contract cases, it will sometimes be arguable that the parties' failure to invoke the foreign law amounts to conscious and genuine acquiescence in the application of domestic law. This may be regarded as a contractual choice of the applicable law, and today such a choice will normally be honored by American courts;[58] it certainly must be honored in a case governed by the Uniform Commercial Code, provided there is some reasonable relation between the transaction and the forum state.[59]

At the opposite extreme, there are situations in which it would violate basic dictates of fairness and common sense to apply domestic law to legal phenomena wholly and ineradicably rooted in a foreign legal system.[60] In these latter situations, application of domestic law may well be unconstitutional under *Home Insurance Co. v. Dick*;[61] thus,

became domiciliaries of New York. Their marriage was celebrated in Austria in 1971, a short time before their emigration. In 1973, Mr. Meyer brings an annulment action against Mrs. Meyer, in a New York court, on the alleged ground that she induced him to marry her by fraudulent misrepresentations concerning her willingness to bear children. The facts alleged by the plaintiff—facts which under New York law would make the marriage voidable—are proved at the trial to the satisfaction of the court. But neither party presents any evidence or materials concerning the pertinent provisions of Austrian law, and the court is unwilling (and perhaps unable) independently to investigate the relevant Austrian sources and authorities. Clearly, the annulment action must fail. It would be ridiculous to judge the validity of this Austrian marriage by the substantive standards of New York law. Even an express stipulation of the parties calling for application of New York law would not be honored by a New York court in a matrimonial case. *See, e.g.*, Fraioli v. Fraioli, 1 App. Div. 2d 967, 150 N.Y.S.2d 665 (2d Dep't 1956). Thus, the plaintiff must lose because he has failed to prove one of the essential elements of his cause of action.

In this hypothetical, it seems rather doubtful whether the Austrian law can be called a mere "datum." Concerning the issue of the validity of the marriage, Austrian law appears to be the rule of decision. But that is only an unimportant semantic quibble. What is important is to recognize that substitution of forum law for the uninvoked or unproved foreign law does not solve all of the cases, just as we have seen that the orthodox approach of deciding against the party who has the burden of proof does not always lead to sound results.

[58] *See* RESTATEMENT (SECOND) OF CONFLICT OF LAWS § 187 (1971).

[59] *See* UNIFORM COMMERCIAL CODE § 1-105.

[60] *See* notes 56 & 57 and accompanying text *supra*.

[61] 281 U.S. 397 (1930).

In the *Home Insurance* case, a Mexican fire insurance company contracted with Dick to insure the latter's tug. Dick, although technically perhaps a citizen of Texas, was living in Mexico at the time. The Mexican company reinsured a part of its liability with two other insurance

a court would have no choice but to follow the orthodox approach and to make the outcome of the case depend on the burden of proof.

Between these extremes, however, there is a large middle field, where the consequences of the parties' failure to invoke or prove the foreign law cannot and should not be treated by way of a simple, definite rule. The older cases, whether they favored or opposed *Crosby,* often attempted to formulate rigid rules,[62] and most of the text writers still follow this obsolete method.[63] In the more modern cases, however, an entirely different trend is discernible. Flexibility is the new watchword. In a 1968 case, the Supreme Court of Vermont announced that substitution of domestic law for the uninvoked foreign law "is justified so long as it is reasonable and does not impose oppressive consequences."[64] Judge Wisdom, speaking for the United States Court of Appeals for the Fifth Circuit, put it even more bluntly: "In the interest of arriving at a just adjudication, the trial judge should have discretion in determining whether the law of the forum, with or without the disguise of a presumption, should prevail."[65] The New York Court of Appeals, which previously had vacillated between the forum-law rule and the *Crosby* rule,[66] finally adopted a similarly flexible approach in *Watts v. Swiss Bank Corporation.*[67]

Flexibility, of course, does not leave the courts without

companies in New York. More than one year after the boat had been destroyed by fire, Dick sued the New York companies in Texas. Their defense was that under the terms of the insurance policy the insured's claim had to be filed within one year. Dick sought to counter this defense by attempting to have the Texas court apply its own substantive law, which would invalidate the contractual one-year time limit. The trial court held for Dick, and the state appellate courts affirmed. However, the Supreme Court, reversing, stated:

> All acts relating to the making of the policy were done in Mexico. All in relation to the making of the contracts of re-insurance were done there or in New York. And, likewise, all things in regard to performance were to be done outside of Texas. Neither the Texas laws nor the Texas courts were invoked for any purpose, except by Dick in the bringing of this suit.... Texas was, therefore, without power to affect the terms of contracts so made. Its attempt to impose a greater obligation than that agreed upon and to seize property in payment of the imposed obligation violates the guaranty against deprivation of property without due process of law.

Id. at 408.

The holding of the Supreme Court apparently was to the effect that since Texas had no substantial relation with the contract or the parties, it was a violation of due process to subject the contract to the substantive law of Texas.

[62] *Compare* Western Union Tel. Co. v. Brown, 234 U.S. 542 (1914), *with* McLoughlin v. Shaw, 95 Conn. 102, 111 A. 62 (1920).

[63] *See generally* 9 J. Wigmore, Evidence § 2536 (3d ed. 1940).

[64] Pioneer Credit Corp. v. Carden, 127 Vt. 229, 234, 245 A.2d 891, 894 (1968).

[65] Seguros Tepeyac S.A., Compania Mexicana de Seguros Generales v. Bostrom, 347 F.2d 168, 175 (5th Cir. 1965).

[66] The vacillating course of the earlier New York decisions is traced in Justice Walter's scholarly opinion in Arams v. Arams, 182 Misc. 328, 45 N.Y.S.2d 251 (Sup. Ct. 1943).

[67] 27 N.Y.2d 270, 265 N.E.2d 739, 317 N.Y.S.2d 315 (1970).

guideposts. In determining whether to apply domestic law or to decide the case against the party bearing the burden of proof, the courts are aided by a number of identifiable factors such as the following:[68]

(a) *The degree to which a strong public interest is involved in the parties' dispute.* If there is no such public interest, the forum-law approach normally is preferable.[69] This is true not only in contract cases (in which the parties' acquiescence in the application of forum law may amount to a choice of law agreement),[70] but equally in noncontract actions, provided the dispute touches nobody's interests except the private concerns of the parties.[71] When, on the other hand, there is a strong public interest, as in matrimonial or criminal cases, it is clear that the parties should not have the power by their action or inaction to determine the applicable law. In cases of the latter kind, therefore, little or no weight should be accorded to the fact that the parties have "acquiesced" in the application of domestic law.[72]

(b) *The parties' access to foreign law materials.* In some cases, especially when exotic legal systems are involved, the court should give some consideration to the parties' relative ability to procure information concerning the foreign law (*e.g.*, the law of Saudi Arabia).[73]

(c) *Forum shopping.* The forum chosen by the plaintiff may be highly artificial as well as inconvenient to the defendant. If this does not lead to a discretionary dismissal under the doctrine of forum non conveniens, it should in any event be treated as a factor which strongly militates against rewarding the forum-shopping plaintiff by the application of domestic law.[74]

---

[68] The enumeration which follows in the text is a slightly rearranged and updated version of the similar list of factors previously submitted by the author in R.B. SCHLESINGER, *supra* note 2, at 168-69.

[69] *See* Kalyvakis v. T.S.S. Olympia, 181 F. Supp. 32, 36 (S.D.N.Y. 1960).

[70] *See* notes 58 & 59 *supra*.

[71] A caveat should be noted: The criterion stated in the text may prove difficult to apply in some types of cases, especially tort cases. At first blush, most tort actions perhaps appear to be purely private disputes; but the public interest may enter, *e.g.*, when a breadwinner has been killed or incapacitated, and a tort recovery is the only way to keep his dependents off the welfare rolls. It is hard to deny, also, that the public interest becomes involved in a tort case when the defendant invokes the protection of a workmen's compensation statute. *Cf.* Tidewater Oil Co. v. Waller, 302 F.2d 638 (10th Cir. 1962).

It is submitted that in cases which straddle the fence between purely private litigation and the public interest, one must look primarily to the other factors, to be listed in the text *infra* under (b), (c), and (d).

[72] *See* A. EHRENZWEIG, PRIVATE INTERNATIONAL LAW 182-83 (1967); Nussbaum, *supra* note 2, at 1040-42. *See also* note 57 *supra*.

[73] *Cf.* Walton v. Arabian Am. Oil Co., 233 F.2d 541, 545, *cert. denied*, 352 U.S. 872 (1956); note 44 *supra*.

[74] If the forum lacks a substantial connection with the transaction or the parties, applica-

(d) *The nature of the foreign legal system and of the issue involved in the case.* Finally, and perhaps most important, a judge's readiness to substitute forum law for the otherwise applicable foreign law will be enhanced if he can rationally assume that with respect to the point at issue the two laws do not radically differ from each other. Such an assumption may be based on the fact that the foreign legal system in question belongs to the common-law orbit.[75] Sometimes an assumption of similarity may be warranted even though the foreign system in question is part of an alien world, *e.g.*, that of the civil law. To the extent that the issue at hand appears to be governed by a "fundamental principle," forum law may be applied on the theory that, unless the contrary is shown, the law of the foreign country in question, and perhaps the laws of all civilized nations, can be expected to be in harmony with the forum's law on that issue.[76]

In connection with the last point, a judicial notice statute can play an important role. Formerly, courts had to rely on an uninformed judicial hunch when they assumed (or refused to assume) that a particular cause of action or defense was based on fundamental principles of law presumably recognized by the foreign legal system in question or indeed by all civilized nations. Under a judicial notice statute, however, a court may undertake what Judge Breitel has referred to as "cursory independent research" concerning the foreign law.[77] Such cursory research perhaps will not enable the court exhaustively to resolve the foreign law issue; but if it discloses that on the point in question there is no real clash between domestic law and the governing foreign law, this will constitute a potent factor against using the *Crosby* approach and in favor of relying on forum law as the rule of decision.[78]

It is submitted that if these variables are kept in mind, the actual results reached (although perhaps not the language used) in most of the reported cases can be reconciled. Thus, in the place of two allegedly conflicting "rules," there emerges a flexible but unified

tion of its own substantive law may be unconstitutional. *See* note 61 *supra*. It should be noted, however, that cases may arise in which the forum chosen by the plaintiff is not so completely contactless as to bring this rule of constitutional law into play, but in which the forum nevertheless is a highly artificial one, selected by a shrewd lawyer with a keen eye for unfair advantages to be gained by forum shopping. In such a case, the artificiality of the forum should at least constitute a *factor* militating not only against the forum's exercise of jurisdiction, but also against application of its own internal substantive law.

[75] *See* note 33 *supra*.

[76] *See* authorities cited in note 34 *supra*.

[77] *See* Watts v. Swiss Bank Corp., 27 N.Y.2d 270, 275, 265 N.E.2d 739, 742, 317 N.Y.S.2d 315, 319 (1970).

[78] *See id.*

approach. In the hands of present-day courts, this approach probably will lead to the application of forum law in the majority of cases. It should not be assumed, however, that forum law automatically can be substituted in every case in which there has been a failure to invoke or ascertain the applicable foreign law. Although perhaps not overly numerous, there are situations—especially those which involve marriage and family or are characterized by blatant forum shopping—in which, despite the parties' "acquiescence," the factors listed above may point away from the forum-law solution.

B. *Judicial Notice Statutes*

Almost half of the states, including all of those in which transnational litigation occurs with some frequency, have enacted statutes or rules either providing for "judicial notice" of foreign-country law or in other ways authorizing the court, in determining foreign law, to consider any relevant material or source, regardless of admissibility under technical rules of evidence, and regardless also of whether or not such material was submitted by a party.[79] These judicial notice statutes, it should be emphasized at the outset, have not displaced the common-law doctrines discussed above. The statutes are merely superimposed on the common-law doctrines, which thus retain their vitality in the many situations in which the statutory provisions do not lead to actual notice being taken of the foreign law.

1. *Interaction of Judicial Notice Statutes and Decisional Law*

Even in a jurisdiction which has a judicial notice statute, the statute is not a solvent for every foreign law case. Most of the statutes are permissive only, so that the court's determination, whether or not to take judicial notice of the foreign law, is a discretionary one.[80] In exercising this discretion, courts naturally are disinclined to engage in independent research concerning a strange legal system if they receive no help from counsel. Even when the statute is drafted in mandatory terms, the result is not very different.[81]

---

[79] For a brief survey of these statutes, see R.B. SCHLESINGER, *supra* note 2, at 67-69.

As applied to the ascertainment of foreign law, the term "judicial notice" may well be inappropriate. A few of the pertinent enactments, such as Federal Rule of Civil Procedure 44.1, have been deliberately drafted so as to avoid that term. For good or for ill, however, most of the relevant statutes in fact speak of "judicial notice."

Courts and legal writers generally refer to all of the relevant enactments, whether or not the term "judicial notice" is used therein, as judicial notice statutes. For the sake of brevity and convenience, the same usage will be followed in this Article.

[80] *See* note 79 *supra*. *See also* Sass, *supra* note 4, at 343-47.

[81] *See* Cannistraro v. Cannistraro, 352 Mass. 65, 70, 223 N.E.2d 692, 695 (1967) (Cutter, J.,

Some of the more sophisticated statutes provide that in general it is discretionary with the court whether to take judicial notice of foreign-country law, but that judicial notice becomes mandatory if one of the parties has given timely notice of his intention to rely on the foreign law and has supplied the court with sufficient information concerning such law. The idea of such bifurcation between permissive and mandatory judicial notice, which first emerged in the Uniform Rules of Evidence,[82] has been adopted, *inter alia*, in California[83] and New York.[84] It is clear, however, that such a bifurcated rule is in essence permissive, because it is left to the court to determine whether the information submitted to it is "sufficient." It follows that, no matter how the statute is formulated, cases of a discretionary refusal to take judicial notice of the foreign law will arise with some frequency.

A few of the statutes, moreover, use pleading or notice requirements as a restriction on judicial notice. In California,[85] and arguably in New York,[86] the parties' failure to invoke the foreign law merely has the effect of making judicial notice of foreign law permissible rather than mandatory. But in other jurisdictions,[87] and notably under Federal Rule 44.1,[88] the notice requirement may have stronger teeth. In *Ruff v. St. Paul Mercury Insurance Co.*,[89] the Second Circuit held that unless reasonable written notice of the foreign law issue has been given in the district court, the appellate court cannot look at the foreign law. The result reached in the *Ruff* case was a harsh one, as the court admitted;[90] but the judges of the Second Circuit probably felt

concurring). *See also* Strout v. Burgess, 144 Me. 263, 274-76, 68 A.2d 241, 249-50 (1949) and cases cited therein.

[82] Uniform Rules of Evidence 9-10.

[83] Cal. Evid. Code §§ 310-11, 452-53 (West 1966).

[84] N.Y. Civ. Prac. Law R. 4511 (McKinney 1963).

[85] *See* note 83 *supra*.

[86] New York has a pleading requirement with respect to foreign law. *See* N.Y. Civ. Prac. Law R. 3016(e) (McKinney 1963). It is nevertheless arguable, although not certain, that the court may, and under appropriate circumstances should, take judicial notice of an unpleaded proposition of foreign law. This result is based on the theory that an unpleaded allegation, although it may not be proved over the opponent's objection, may yet be judicially noticed. *See* R.B. Schlesinger, *supra* note 2, at 76.

[87] *See* R.B. Schlesinger, *supra* note 2, at 68.

[88] Fed. R. Civ. P. 44.1 provides:

> A party who intends to raise an issue concerning the law of a foreign country shall give notice in his pleadings or other reasonable written notice. The court, in determining foreign law, may consider any relevant material or source, including testimony, whether or not submitted by a party or admissible under Rule 43. The court's determination shall be treated as a ruling on a question of law.

[89] 393 F.2d 500, 502 (2d Cir. 1968).

[90] Ruff, a Pennsylvania citizen, was teaching law at the Arthur Grimes School of Law of the

that to hold otherwise would render the notice requirement toothless.[91] *Quaere,* however, whether the provision really would lose all of its teeth if it were construed differently, *e.g.*, as meaning that nonobservance of the notice requirement should make the court *reluctant* to take judicial notice, but would not completely destroy its *power* to do so.

Whether or not it was correctly decided, the *Ruff* case serves as a reminder that even in jurisdictions where a judicial notice statute is in existence, situations frequently arise in which the court either lacks the power to take judicial notice, or as a matter of discretion will refuse to do so.[92] In every case of this sort, the judicial notice statute in effect becomes inoperative; and just as in the old common-law days, the court is then faced with the question of how it should react to the parties' failure to invoke or prove the foreign law. Most of the statutes are silent on this point.[93] To find an answer, the court must turn to decisional rules—the same rules which would govern in the absence of a judicial notice statute.[94] It follows that these decisional rules continue to play an important role even in those jurisdictions which have adopted a modern statute.

In California and New Jersey, the judicial notice statute itself contains an express direction, telling the court what to do in case the foreign law is neither proved nor judicially noticed.[95] The New Jersey statute, as recently amended, favors application of domestic law in

---

University of Liberia when he contracted poliomyelitis, an endemic disease. Ruff sued upon an insurance policy issued to his employer. The district court dismissed the action on the ground that endemic diseases were expressly exempted from the coverage of the policy. On appeal, Ruff for the first time brought up the point that under Liberian law the exemption was ineffective. The court of appeals, however, held the point to be precluded by the first sentence of Rule 44.1. In reluctantly affirming the dismissal of the action, the appellate court stated: "While the result is not one which we like to reach, we cannot rewrite the policy because of our sympathy for Ruff." 393 F.2d at 502.

[91] Alternatively, the court held that even if it were to take judicial notice of the Liberian law, plaintiff would still lose in this action against the insurance company, because Liberian law, although it might enlarge the liability of the employer, could not change the effect of an insurance policy issued by an American insurance company to an American insured (*i.e.*, Ruff's employer). *See* 393 F.2d at 502.

The combined effect of the court's two alternative holdings seems to be that the plaintiff might have won his case if (*1*) he had sued his employer rather than the insurance company, and if (*2*) he had given timely notice of his intention to raise an issue concerning Liberian law.

[92] *See* O. SOMMERICH & B. BUSCH, FOREIGN LAW—A GUIDE TO PLEADING AND PROOF 64-74 (1959) and cases cited therein.

[93] California and New Jersey, however, provide for this contingency in their judicial notice statutes. *See* notes 95-100 and accompanying text *infra*.

[94] *See* notes 24-78 and accompanying text *supra*.

[95] CAL. EVID. CODE § 311 (West 1966); N.J. STAT. ANN. § 2A:84A-16 R. 9(3) (Supp. 1973).

such a case,[96] while the much more sophisticated California provision, by vesting the court with a great deal of discretion,[97] arrives at a result similar to that which has been reached by the most recent judicial decisions.[98] Although essentially declaratory of decisional law, the California statute has two original and valuable features. It warns the court of the constitutional doubts which may be created by imposing domestic law on a legal relationship which lacks any reasonable contact with the forum;[99] and it provides that when an action is dismissed because of the plaintiff's failure to prove the pertinent foreign law, the dismissal should be without prejudice.[100]

2. *Unproved and Unnoticed Foreign Law in the Federal Courts*

A special problem confronted the draftsmen of Federal Rule 44.1. It was realized that it would be conducive to clarity if the Rule spelled out the consequences that ensue when the foreign law is neither proved nor judicially noticed. But there was a hitch. Although the provision authorizing a court to take judicial notice can be viewed as a rule of adjective law, and thus covered by the Enabling Act, a rule spelling out the consequences of failure to take judicial notice is more difficult to characterize. A rule of the latter kind might be thought to be a choice of law rule and thus beyond the scope of the Supreme Court's rule-making power.[101] Because of this doubt, the draftsmen refrained from determining, in the Rule itself, the consequences

---

[96] "In the absence of an adequate basis for taking judicial notice of the law of any jurisdiction other than this State, and the United States, the judge shall apply the law of this State." N.J. STAT. ANN. § 2A:84A-16 R. 9(3) (Supp. 1973).

[97]
> If the law of . . . a foreign nation . . . or a public entity in a foreign nation . . . is applicable and such law cannot be determined, the court may, as the ends of justice require, either:
>
> (a) Apply the law of this state if the court can do so consistently with the Constitution of the United States and the Constitution of this state; or
>
> (b) Dismiss the action without prejudice or, in the case of a reviewing court, remand the case to the trial court with directions to dismiss the action without prejudice.

CAL. EVID. CODE § 311 (West 1966).

[98] *See* notes 64-67 and accompanying text *supra*.

[99] CAL. EVID. CODE § 311(a) (West 1966). *See* Home Ins. Co. v. Dick, 281 U.S. 397 (1930); notes 61, 97 *supra*.

[100] CAL. EVID. CODE § 311(b) (West 1966); *see* note 97 *supra*. Even in the absence of a statutory direction, a wise trial judge normally will dismiss "without prejudice" in such a case. *See* R.B. SCHLESINGER, *supra* note 2, at 155 and authorities cited therein. Nevertheless, since some trial judges perhaps are not as wise and experienced as others, the statutory reminder is valuable.

[101] Under 28 U.S.C. § 2072 (1970), the Supreme Court may promulgate *procedural* rules but may not use its rule-making power to "abridge, enlarge or modify any substantive right."

which follow when the foreign law is neither proved nor judicially noticed. This left a gaping hole in the Rule. According to the prevailing view, this hole must be filled, at least in a diversity case, by reference to state law.[102] However, Professor Arthur Miller, in his well-known "Death-Knell" article, developed plausible arguments in support of the position that federal decisional law rather than state law should determine the matter in the federal courts.[103] What influence Professor Miller's position will have on the courts remains to be seen. If his argument should prevail, the federal courts would have to fashion their own rule in diversity as well as nondiversity cases; and if past experience in nondiversity cases is a guide, there would then be some danger that lower federal courts would feel bound by the only Supreme Court decision directly in point: the somewhat sinister holding of *Crosby*.[104]

3. *Judicial Notice of Uninvoked Foreign Law*

In those cases in which the court actually utilizes its statutory power to take judicial notice of foreign law, the problem of the consequences of the parties' failure to invoke and prove that law becomes moot. True, when the foreign law in question belongs to an alien system, and the parties have given the court no aid in ascertaining it, the court normally will decline to ascertain the foreign law by its own independent efforts; but unless the point is precluded on grounds of lateness, this is completely a matter of discretion. Most of the statutes make it quite clear that the parties' failure to invoke the foreign law does not prevent the court from judicially noticing it, and that the court, even though totally unaided by the parties, has the *power* to undertake its own research.[105] Even the late Professor Currie, who strongly opposed the utilization of uninvoked foreign law, and who for this reason criticized the sweeping language usually found in judicial notice statutes, made it quite clear that his criticism was presented *de lege ferenda.*[106]

Although under most judicial notice statutes the court thus has the power independently to dig up foreign law points never invoked

[102] *See* Krasnow v. National Airlines, 228 F.2d 326 (2d Cir. 1955), *relying on* Klaxon Co. v. Stentor Elec. Mfg. Co., 313 U.S. 487 (1941).

[103] Miller, *supra* note 2, at 702-15, 723-31, 746-48.

[104] This danger is illustrated by Ozanic v. United States, 165 F.2d 738, 744 (2d Cir. 1948). *But see* note 65 *supra*.

[105] *See, e.g.*, N.Y. CIV. PRAC. LAW R. 4511(b) (McKinney 1963). "Every court may take judicial notice without request of . . . the laws of foreign countries or their political subdivisions."

[106] Currie, *On Displacement of the Law of the Forum*, *supra* note 16, at 981.

by a party, the question remains whether the court may and should decide the case without having given the parties an opportunity to respond to the results of the court's own foreign law research. This question will be taken up below (under III).

C. *Other Pertinent Procedural Rules*

In many cases, of course, the initiative in finding and presenting the foreign law will be taken by the parties, and not by the court. When the parties make an intelligible presentation of the relevant sources and materials, the court in general will be inclined to make use of the powers conferred by the judicial notice statute. But frequently it happens that the parties and the court neglect a decisive foreign law point until after the trial. Perhaps the point is raised by the parties, or discovered by the court, for the first time in connection with a post-trial motion, such as a motion for judgment n.o.v. or for a new trial.[107] Or—and this is not infrequent—the foreign law point turns up for the first time on appeal.[108] Is the point now waived or precluded by lateness?

The answer to this question depends, in the first place, on whether the statute contains a notice requirement, and whether the courts have added teeth (or perhaps dentures) to that requirement. In this respect, the judicial notice statutes differ among each other. On the one hand, there is Federal Rule 44.1, with its express notice requirement, which, at least in the Second Circuit, has been taken so seriously that the foreign law point is dead unless introduced in good time.[109] On the other hand, most of the state statutes (except those patterned after Federal Rule 44.1) either have no notice requirement at all, or provide that the parties' failure to give timely notice does not preclude the court from looking into the foreign law.[110]

This, however, is not a complete answer to the question of preclusion. Even when, as in California and New York and a number of other states, the judicial notice statute itself contains no preclusionary rule, belated resort to the foreign law may be precluded by general principles of procedure. Suppose, for instance, that in a jury case the judge has instructed the jury in accordance with domestic law, and the

[107] *See, e.g.*, Frummer v. Hilton Hotels Int'l, Inc., 60 Misc. 2d 840, 304 N.Y.S.2d 335 (1969). *See also* note 86 *supra*.

[108] *See, e.g.*, Ruff v. St. Paul Mercury Ins. Co., 393 F.2d 500 (2d Cir. 1968); Sonnesen v. Panama Transp. Co., 298 N.Y. 262, 82 N.E.2d 569 (1948), *reargument denied*, 298 N.Y. 856, 84 N.E.2d 324, *cert. denied*, 337 U.S. 919 (1949).

[109] Ruff v. St. Paul Mercury Ins. Co., 393 F.2d 500, 502 (2d Cir. 1968).

[110] *See* notes 79-86 and accompanying text *supra*.

parties have failed to raise the foreign law issue by timely requests or exceptions. In such a case, it might well be too late to argue on appeal that the judge committed error by charging the jury in accordance with the law of the forum.[111]

Even in a nonjury case, a foreign law issue may be similarly precluded if raised too late. Suppose, for instance, that in an action brought in a state court the complaint alleges invasion of privacy. Although the allegedly tortious acts occurred in Ruritania, where the plaintiff lived at the time, the case is tried on the assumption that it is governed by the law of the forum. After a trial without a jury, the court holds for the plaintiff. On appeal, the defendant for the first time claims that the law of Ruritania controls, and he submits ample materials demonstrating that under the law of that country an invasion of privacy such as shown in this case is not actionable. Even though the forum state's judicial notice statute contains no notice requirement, the point may be precluded. It is true, of course, that pursuant to the classical rule the defendant may at any time, and even for the first time on appeal, point to the legal insufficiency of the complaint.[112] But the classical rule has been changed in a number of states.[113] Under the influence of Federal Rule 12 (h),[114] several states now provide that after the end of the trial a defendant may no longer attack the sufficiency of the complaint unless he has previously raised the objection.[115]

These preclusionary rules are technical and refined. Suppose that in the hypothetical invasion of privacy case the trial court, although applying domestic law, for some reason had dismissed the complaint, and the plaintiff had appealed. In that event, it might be possible for the defendant, *as appellee*, to urge affirmance on the basis of Ruritanian law. Some cases, at least, seem to suggest this distinction in favor of the appellee.[116]

---

[111] *See, e.g.*, FED. R. CIV. P. 51; N.Y. CIV. PRAC. LAW §§ 4017, 5501(1)(3) (McKinney 1963); *id.* § 4110-b (McKinney Supp. 1973).

[112] *See* F. JAMES, CIVIL PROCEDURE 135 (1965).

[113] *See, e.g.*, ARIZ. R. CIV. P. 12(i); N.C.R. CIV. P. 12(h); VT. R. CIV. P. 12(h).

[114] FED. R. CIV. P. 12(h); *see* Black, Sivalls & Bryson, Inc. v. Shondell, 174 F.2d 587 (8th Cir. 1949).

[115] *See, e.g.*, Dale v. Lattimore, 12 N.C. App. 348, 183 S.E.2d 417 (1971).

In a jurisdiction in which foreign law does not have to be pleaded, or failure to plead it is not fatal, the objection may be thought to go to the sufficiency of the evidence rather than to the sufficiency of the complaint. Even so, however, the objection may be precluded by the defendant's failure, at the time when he moved for dismissal at the end of the plaintiff's case or at the end of the whole case, to specify the foreign law point as a ground for such motion. *See, e.g.*, J. WEINSTEIN, H. KORN & A. MILLER, NEW YORK CIVIL PRACTICE ¶ 4401.09 (1963).

[116] *See* Southard v. Southard, 305 F.2d 730 (2d Cir. 1962); Archer v. United States, 217 F.2d 548 (9th Cir. 1954), *cert. denied*, 348 U.S. 953 (1955).

In many jurisdictions, moreover, there is a more general rule that prohibits the parties, or at least the appellant, from raising new points of any kind for the first time on appeal.[117] True, this rule is applied with considerable flexibility, and it is generally thought that an appellate court, in its discretion, can disregard the rule whenever its strict application would lead to injustice.[118] In spite of its flexibility, however, the rule lurks in the appellate practice of most jurisdictions. A lawyer devising litigation strategy in a foreign law case thus should keep in mind that even under the most liberal judicial notice statute, it may be dangerous to hold a foreign law point in reserve for an eventual appeal.

In any event, in order properly to appraise the consequences of a failure to invoke or prove the applicable foreign law, one must realize that the pertinent common-law rules[119] interact not only with judicial notice statutes but also with other, more general rules of trial and appellate procedure, and that under rules of the latter kind a foreign law point may be precluded unless seasonably raised.[120]

III

Some Modest Suggestions

The conclusion that emerges from the foregoing survey is only mildly encouraging. Once one discerns all the facets of the problem, and recognizes the complex interaction among the pertinent rules of decisional and statutory law, it becomes apparent that these rules are rational and consistent, and that on the whole they lead to workable solutions. Many of these solutions, however, are based on overly complex reasoning, and some of them may not be entirely fair.

Our aim, in foreign law cases as much as in other types of litigation, is not merely to develop rational rules and to devise workable solutions, but "to secure the just, speedy, and inexpensive determination of every action."[121] Few will argue that in the area under discussion we have reached, or even approached, that lofty objective.

---

[117] *See, e.g.*, 14 Cyclopedia of Federal Procedure § 67.09 (3d ed. 1965); R. Stern & E. Gressman, Supreme Court Practice 297 (4th ed. 1969).

[118] *See* Jannenga v. Nationwide Life Ins. Co., 288 F.2d 169 (D.C. Cir. 1961), *noted in* 14 Stan. L. Rev. 162 (1961). *See also* H. Cohen & A. Karger, The Powers of the New York Court of Appeals §§ 161-69 (1952); 14 Cyclopedia of Federal Procedure, *supra* note 117, at § 67.09; 11 Carmody-Wait 2d: Cyclopedia of New York Practice §§ 71:116-17 (1966).

[119] *See* notes 24-78 and accompanying text *supra*.

[120] The procedural consequences that ensue when the foreign law point is raised too late, are discussed somewhat more extensively in R.B. Schlesinger, *supra* note 2, at 182-83.

[121] *See* Fed. R. Civ. P. 1 (second sentence).

But some progress toward that objective, it is submitted, could be achieved by adopting the relatively modest proposals that follow.

The first suggestion is simple and not at all novel; indeed, its adoption may be constitutionally mandated. It is to the effect that no trial or appellate court should ever decide a case on the basis of its own discoveries concerning the foreign law, without having given the parties an opportunity to present arguments and materials on what the court thinks the foreign law to be. The California statute so provides.[122] The Advisory Committee Notes on Rule 44.1 express a similar thought, but present it as if it were merely a matter of good practice.[123] This author, on the other hand, earnestly submits that the requirement is one of due process, and that this result is supported by authority as well as by considerations of fundamental fairness.[124]

A second suggestion is similar in spirit, but goes somewhat further. The time has come to recognize how far the actual practice in these matters has strayed from the mythological common-law model of a purely adversary procedure. By the enactment of statutes which authorize a court, in determining foreign law, to consider any relevant material or source, whether or not admissible under rules of evidence, and whether or not submitted by a party, our legislators have taken a long step away from the common-law tradition of treating the court as a passive umpire. Our judicial notice statutes do not go as far as the German Code of Civil Procedure, which, at least in theory, places the entire responsibility for ascertaining the foreign law upon the court.[125] Clearly, however, in those American jurisdictions which have adopted judicial notice statutes, we have instituted a system under which that responsibility is shared by court and counsel. By way of allocating their respective functions, we have given to the court the important power to decide whether it will consider foreign law materials submitted without evidentiary formalities, and, even more important, whether and to what extent it will conduct its own research on points not covered, or insufficiently covered, by adversary presentation.

---

[122] CAL. EVID. CODE §§ 455(a), 459(c), (d) (West 1966).

[123] There is no requirement that the court give formal notice to the parties of its intention to engage in its own research on an issue of foreign law which has been raised by them, or of its intention to raise and determine independently an issue not raised by them. Ordinarily the court should inform the parties of material it has found diverging substantially from the material which they have presented; and in general the court should give the parties an opportunity to analyze and counter new points upon which it proposes to rely.

NOTES OF ADVISORY COMMITTEE ON RULES, FED. R. CIV. P. 44.1.

[124] *See* Arams v. Arams, 182 Misc. 328, 330-31, 45 N.Y.S.2d 251, 253 (Sup. Ct. 1943); *cf.* Saunders v. Shaw, 244 U.S. 317 (1917). The point is also discussed in the broader context of the constitutionality of judicial notice statutes, in R.B. SCHLESINGER, *supra* note 2, at 172.

[125] *See* R.B. SCHLESINGER, *supra* note 2, at 185-87.

Such tremendous discretionary power naturally engenders responsibility. Thus, a court operating under a judicial notice statute is under a duty to inform the parties whether, to what extent, and under what circumstances it will take judicial notice of the foreign law. Failure to give this vital information to the parties, and to supply it in time to be acted upon, should be treated as reversible error. This was the point of the late Judge Jerome Frank's somewhat cryptic but trailblazing dissent in the *Walton* case[126]—a point the soundness of which has become even more apparent since the enactment of Rule 44.1.

When it comes to foreign law issues, it will no longer do to say that under the common-law tradition the issues are always formed by the parties. With respect to the procedural treatment of foreign law, we have largely abandoned the common-law tradition. It follows that in performing the tasks of identifying, researching, and resolving foreign law issues, responsibility must be shared by court and counsel. For this reason, foreign law issues should always be brought up for discussion at the pretrial hearing. When this is done, the judge has an opportunity to admonish the parties to state whether and to what extent they intend to rely on foreign law, and what, if anything, they propose to do in order to assist the court in ascertaining it. If it turns out, as it often does, that each party wishes to place the burden of invoking and proving the foreign law on his opponent, the court can end this game of musical chairs by an immediate ruling—ultimately reviewable on appeal—concerning the burden of proof.[127] These simple steps, designed to neutralize ignorance as well as trickiness on the part of counsel, should be taken by every trial court faced with a foreign law case, and it should be reversible error not to take them.[128]

This does not place too heavy a burden on the court. The fact that a case involves foreign elements, and that the law of a foreign country might be relevant to some of the issues, usually can be

---

[126] The writer of the opinion thinks we should remand for this reason: Apparently neither the trial judge nor the parties were aware of New York Civil Practice Act, § 344-a [New York's judicial notice statute at that time]; consequently, in the interests of justice, we should remand with directions to permit the parties, if they so desire, to present material which may assist the trial judge to ascertain the applicable "law" of Saudi-Arabia.

Walton v. Arabian Am. Oil Co., 233 F.2d 541, 546 (2d Cir. 1956) (footnotes omitted).

[127] At the same time, the court should inform the parties whether the burden has to be met by the introduction of formal evidence, or whether (and under what conditions) judicial notice will be taken of the foreign law.

[128] Experienced trial judges have long followed the practice suggested in the text. *See* Sommerich, *Comment*, 4 AM. J. COMP. L. 473 (1955). For instance, in Walton v. Arabian Am. Oil Co., 233 F.2d 541 (2d Cir. 1956), the trial judge had repeatedly informed counsel that in his opinion the burden of proving Saudi Arabian law was on the plaintiff, and that failure to sustain that burden would lead to dismissal of the action.

gathered by a cursory glance at the pleadings. Upon finding that a foreign law question potentially lurks in the case, the court clearly has the power—under Federal Rule 16[129] and its counterparts in state court practice—to demand that the parties clarify their positions as to what law applies and how any applicable foreign law should be ascertained.

In general, it is true that a court's powers under Rule 16 are discretionary; but when dealing with foreign law issues—that is, issues no longer covered by the ancient principle of purely adversary litigation—a judicial duty to seek clarification must go along with the power.[130] Once all of our trial courts recognize this duty, or are forced by appellate decisions to do so, we shall be rid of many of the complex subtleties which today, at least occasionally, still breed sharp practices and inequitable results in this area of the law.

[129] FED R. CIV. P. 16. Under this Rule, the district court has the power, in its discretion, to order a pretrial conference. During such a conference, the court may seek clarification and limitation of the issues to be litigated. Moreover—and this may be of special significance in a case involving issues of foreign law—the attorneys for the parties may be directed to consider "the possibility of obtaining admissions of fact and of documents which will avoid unnecessary proof" and "the limitation of the number of expert witnesses." The court, in addition, may bring up for discussion "such other matters as may aid in the disposition of the action."

[130] Perhaps it would be useful, by way of amending Rule 16 and its counterparts in state practice, to spell out the procedural consequences flowing from the enhanced responsibility which the court bears in foreign law cases.

Foreign Proceedings

[9]

FRIEDRICH K. JUENGER

The Recognition of Money Judgments in Civil and Commercial Matters

I. INTRODUCTION

A. *The National Reports*

In preparing this general report on judgments recognition for the Twelfth International Congress of Comparative law, I benefited from the research of scholars and practitioners from four continents who prepared the twenty-one reports on which I was able to draw.[1] These national reports cover a wide variety of legal systems. In addition to jurisdictions with a distinctive common law or civil law

---

FRIEDRICH K. JUENGER is a Member, Board of Editors.

1.

Argentina:	Grigera Naón, "The Recognition of Money Judgments in Civil and Commercial Matters," in: *Asociación Argentina de Derecho Comparado, National Reports to the International Congress of Comparative Law* 54 (1986)
Australia:	Pryles
Brazil:	Valladão
Canada (Common Law Provinces):	Sharpe, "The Enforcement of Foreign Judgments," in: *Debtor-Creditor Law: Practice and Doctrine* 641 (Springman & Gertner eds. 1985).
Canada (Quebec):	Talpis & Goldstein
Czechoslovakia:	Steiner, "The Recognition of Money Judgments in Civil and Commercial Matters," in: 7 *Travaux de droit comparé* 99 (1986)
Finland:	Möller
France:	Gaudemet-Tallon, "La reconnaissance des jugements étrangers portant sur une somme d'argent en matière civile et commerciale," in: *Etudes de droit contemporain*, 38 *Revue internationale de droit comparé* 487 (1986)
Germany (Democratic Republic):	Strohbach, "The Recognition of Money Judgments in Civil and Commercial Matters," in: *National Committee for Legal Science of the German Democratic Republic, National Reports for the XIIth International Congress of Comparative Law* 49 (1986)

heritage, mixed systems—Israel, the Philippines and the Canadian province of Quebec—are represented, as well as nations which, like Finland and Sweden, have a legal tradition that sets them apart from the two major legal cultures. Four national reports come from socialist countries (Czechoslovakia, German Democratic Republic, Poland and Romania).

Several of the nations for which reports were submitted have a federal form of government (Argentina, Australia, Brazil, Canada, Czechoslovakia, Switzerland, the United States and Venezuela). While in some of these nations private law and civil procedure are unitary,[2] in others the laws of the constituent states or provinces are controlling,[3] which poses the problem of interstate judgments recognition. With the exception of Canada,[4] in these non-unitary systems that problem is governed by federal constitutional and statutory pro-

---

Germany (Federal Republic):	Martiny, "Recognition and Enforcement of Foreign Money Judgments in the Federal Republic of Germany," in: 35 *Am. J. Comp. L.* 721 (1987)
Israel:	Shapira, "Recognition and Enforcement of Foreign Money Judgments in Civil and Commercial Matters," in: *Israeli Reports to the XII International Congress of Comparative Law* 132 (1986)
Japan:	Takakuwa
The Netherlands:	Kokkini-Iatridou & Verheul, "Recognition and Enforcement of Foreign Judgments in Civil and Commercial Matters," in: *Netherlands Reports to the Twelfth International Congress of Comparative Law* 189 (1987)
Philippines:	Azcuna
Poland:	Tomaszewski, "Recognition of Foreign Judgements in Civil and Commercial Law," in: *Rapports Polonais présentés au douzième Congrès International de Droit Comparé* 107 (1986)
Romania:	Filipescu
Sweden:	Bogdan, "The Recognition in Sweden of Money Judgments in Civil and Commercial Matters," in 1985 *Nordisk Tidsskrift for International Ret* 85
Switzerland:	Dubler
Turkey:	Özsunay
United States of America:	Joiner, "The Recognition of Foreign Country Money Judgments by American Courts," 34 *Am. J. Comp. L.* 193 (Special Supp. 1986)
Venezuela:	Rouvier

2. Brazil, Czechoslovakia and Venezuela.

3. Argentina, Australia, Canada, Switzerland and the United States.

4. See Sharpe at 641 & n. 1 (judgments from other Canadian provinces treated in the same fashion as foreign country judgments). But see Talpis & Goldstein at 27, 141 (*révision au fond* of foreign country judgments, whereas the merits of judgments from Canadian provinces are reviewed only in exceptional circumstances).

visions,[5] whereas the recognition of foreign country judgments, absent a treaty, depends primarily on state or provincial law.[6]

The reports from member states of the European Communities (France, Federal Republic of Germany, the Netherlands) also discuss the quasi-federal recognition practices prevailing within the Common Market pursuant to the Brussels Convention,[7] and the two reports from Scandinavia (Finland and Sweden) address the Nordic Convention on the Recognition and Enforcement of Judgments in Civil and Commercial Matters of 1977 as well as implementing legislation. Similarly, the Argentinian and Venezuelan national reports refer to the Inter-American Convention on Extraterritorial Validity of Foreign Judgments and Arbitral Awards of 1975.

Regrettably, no report was received from the United Kingdom, whose recognition practices have influenced those of other common law nations and, in many ways, can serve as a model for international cooperation.

B. The Recognition Problem

Judge Learned Hand once said, "I must say that, as a litigant, I should dread a lawsuit beyond almost anything else short of sickness and death."[8] If one lawsuit is bad, two are worse. Within each legal system, the salutary principle of *res judicata* avoids the expense and inconvenience of having to try the same dispute more than once. But while that principle is universal, state and national borders diminish its efficacy. A case conclusively determined in one state may have to be relitigated in another because foreign adjudications are not entitled to automatic respect. The credit they receive depends on the vagaries of each recognition state's rules and practices, and

5. See Dubler at 8; Grigera Naón at 54-55 (Argentina); Joiner at 198-201 (U.S.); Pryles at 1 (Australia).

6. See Dubler at 9-17, 26 (Switzerland); Joiner at 198 (U.S.); Pryles at 1-2 (Australia). In Argentina, it is doubtful whether state or provincial law controls. See Grigera Naón at 56-57. In Switzerland, status judgments are currently controlled by federal law, while the recognition of money judgments is governed by cantonal law. The enforcement procedures, however, are federal. The entire body of law dealing with foreign country judgments will be federalized if—as is expected—the draft Federal Act on Private International Law is enacted by the Swiss Parliament. See Dubler at 9-17, 23, 26-29, 53.

7. Convention on Jurisdiction and the Recognition of Judgments in Civil and Commercial Matters of 7 September 1968, 15 O.J. Eur. Comm. (No. L 299) 32 (31 December 19, 1972), as amended, 25 O.J. Eur. Comm. (No. L 388) 1 (1982). The Convention leaves untouched the member states' practices concerning the recognition of judgments rendered outside the European Communities. See Juenger, "La Convention de Bruxelles du 27 septembre 1968 et la courtoisie internationale," 72 *Rev. crit. d.i.p.* 37 (1983). But cf. Dubler at 53 (Swiss negotiations with the European Communities for a treaty paralleling the Brussels Convention).

8. Quoted in Frank, *Courts on Trial* 40 (1950).

legal systems are reluctant to accord the same deference to foreign judgments as to foreign law. As Nussbaum observed:

> International comity in recognizing and enforcing foreign judgments is subject to much stronger inhibitions than in applying foreign law. The result is deplorable. The impossibility of having monetary judgments enforced abroad hampers international credit and commerce. . . .[9]

Although current practice shows some improvement, the overall picture, as documented by the national reports, remains checkered at best. A few jurisdictions, notably South Australia, follow liberal, common-sensical policies. But in all too many others juridical ethnocentricity, distrust, ingrained dogma, inexperience and insufficient attention by reformers contribute to the preservation of a *status quo* that is far from satisfactory. Especially those states that confer upon local courts broad if not exorbitant jurisdiction over foreign parties and transactions tend to be quite illiberal when it comes to respecting the powers of foreign courts. Also, many legal systems that readily honor arbitral awards, irrespective of where they were rendered, refuse to give the same credence to judgments handed down abroad. Thus, paradoxically, decisions of "regular and duly organized agencies" receive less credit than those of "informal and in a sense irregular tribunals"[10] composed of private arbitrators.

The consequences of a narrow-minded attitude toward recognition are deplorable. To retry cases that have been authoritatively decided violates fundamental tenets of judicial economy. Moreover, it is presumptuous for the courts of one country to review the judgments of another, especially if the underlying transaction has but a slight connection with the jurisdiction in which the judgment creditor seeks enforcement. And yet, there are reported decisions of cases fully tried—and even appealed—in the courts of one country, which then had to wind their way through the entire judicial hierarchy of another, remote from the situs of the facts that gave rise to the dispute, for the disappointing determination that the foreign adjudication was not binding after all.[11] Such duplication is not only wasteful; it punishes private litigants and exacts a toll from international commerce. To protect their interests, parties engaged in multinational transactions must either resort to arbitration or insist on advance payments or guarantees, which increases the transaction costs of doing business abroad.

---

9. In Cheatham, Dowling, Goodrich & Griswold, *Cases and Materials on Conflict of Laws* 272, 274 (1936).

10. Meacham v. Jamestown, F. & C. R.R., 211 N.Y. 346, 353, 105 N.E. 653, 655 (1914) (Cardozo, J., concurring).

11. See infra nn. 17, 150-53, 158-59 and accompanying text.

C. *Scope*

Recognition problems are not limited to money judgments. The repercussions of a refusal to recognize a foreign divorce, for instance, can be dire indeed. Yet, to allow for a sufficiently focused discussion, I requested the national reporters to confine themselves to unsatisfied ("executory") money judgments in civil and commercial matters. To include other forms of adjudications—such as declaratory judgments, decrees for specific performance and decrees in matters relating to status or support—would merely complicate comparison. Nor does the general report purport to deal with actual enforcement, although the added delay, cost and inconvenience a judgment creditor may encounter, even if the judgment is recognized, can seriously impede the free movability of judgments. Finally, such issues as limitation periods, finality, scope of *res judicata* (e.g., issue preclusion and effect on third parties), and the defensive use of foreign judgments are excluded, as are problems relating to governmental or diplomatic immunity and the recognition of penal, tax and administrative decisions.[12] Even within these narrow confines, a large number of problems remains, and the practices of the various states and nations in dealing with them vary widely.

II. Differences in Approaches to Judgments Recognition

To "recognize" a foreign judgment means to respect the foreign court's decision as *res judicata*. There are three basic approaches to the question whether judgments rendered abroad should be given effect locally: (1) the forum may simply disregard foreign decisions; (2) it may recognize only those rendered in states that honor the forum's judgments; (3) it may recognize any foreign judgment that meets certain procedural and substantive standards. Historically, civil law countries have favored the first two approaches, whereas common law jurisdictions have tended to opt for the third. Since choices made centuries ago still influence today's recognition practices, it seems useful briefly to sketch the evolution of the law of judgments recognition in the two principal legal cultures.

A. *The Civil Law Evolution*

1. The Notion of Sovereignty

Once upon a time, the principle *res judicata pro veritate accipitur*[13] prevailed on the European continent. The medieval revival of

12. Also happily beyond the purview of this report are such peculiar enactments as the British and Australian nonenforcement and "clawback" provisions directed against American multiple-damages judgments in competition matters.
13. Dig. Just. 1.5.25.

Roman law and the idea of a Holy Roman Empire favored recognition, because a judgment handed down abroad was not perceived as emanating from a "foreign" legal system. A different perspective, however, emerged once the concept of territorial sovereignty began to spread. At that point, judgments came to be regarded as governmental acts whose compulsory effect was limited to the sovereign's territory. This notion became so ingrained that even within political systems that were subject to a common government recognition was no longer taken for granted. Thus, after the Dutch provinces were united in 1579 pursuant to the Union of Utrecht, it was considered necessary to issue a decree ordaining that judgments rendered in one province had to be enforced in others where the judgment debtor had assets.[14] Similarly, in France article 120 of the 1629 Ordinance commonly called "*Code Michaut*" directed the *parlements* to enforce each other's judgments without fee, re-examination of the merits, or a hearing.[15]

2. The Principle of Nonrecognition

As these examples show, once judgments are perceived as an emanation of governmental authority—rather than merely as resolutions of private disputes—their extraterritorial efficacy becomes problematic. If even the mutual enforcement by coordinate courts within a unified system required specific legislation, the status of truly foreign judgments was all the more precarious. Thus article 121 of the *Code Michaut* provided:

> Judgments rendered . . . in foreign kingdoms and sovereignties . . . shall have no lien or execution in our kingdom . . . and notwithstanding such judgments, our subjects against whom they have been rendered may contest their rights anew before our judges.[16]

Although it implicitly recognizes that foreign judgments can bind

14. See Nadelmann, "Non-Recognition of American Money Judgments Abroad and What to do About It," 42 *Iowa L. Rev.* 236, 237-38 (1957).

In his correspondence with the General Reporter Professor Verheul, Netherlands National Reporter, has questioned Nadelmann's conclusions. Verheul points out that the decree to which Nadelmann refers was promulgated by the Province of Holland to unify *intra-provincial* law, and that the provision on enforcement "should be seen as confirming existing customary law." Verheul adds that "the procedure of letters requisitorial was applied, as a matter of course, between courts of different provinces and even of different countries." He also surmises that French practice was similar. Letter from J.P. Verheul (22 Sep. 1987) to Friedrich K. Juenger.

15. See Nadelmann, supra n.14 at 238. See also 2 Batiffol & Lagarde, *Droit international privé* 548-49 (7th ed. 1983).

16. Translated from the French text quoted in Weiss, *Traité élémentaire de droit international privé* 826-27 (2d ed. 1890).

aliens, with respect to French judgment debtors this provision repealed the principle *res judicata pro veritate accipitur*.

In the early part of the nineteenth century, the *Cour de cassation* extended the pre-revolutionary rule to foreign judgment debtors. Although it could have read article 2123 of the Civil Code and article 546 of the Civil Procedure Code (which provided for the enforcement of foreign judgments through a summary *exequatur* proceeding) to imply a legislative policy favoring recognition, the court decided otherwise. In one of the first cases to come along, it construed these provisions to allow the re-examination of the merits of a judgment rendered by a Massachusetts federal court against an American citizen.[17] For almost a century and a half, the highest French court adhered to the parochial view that judges are not bound by foreign judgments, but can review errors of fact and law. In 1964, the famous *Munzer* case[18] finally abolished this discretionary *révision au fond*. By then, however, the example set by the *Cour de cassation* had already influenced the practice of other nations, and to this day a number of countries still adhere to the principle that foreign judgments are not conclusive.[19]

3. Reciprocity

To disregard the binding effect of foreign court decisions is a rather drastic way of vindicating sovereign concerns. Such assertiveness not only punishes private litigants, it is ultimately self-defeating: tempting other states to retaliate, it undercuts the efficacy of domestic judgments.[20] A somewhat more enlightened manner of pursuing perceived national self-interests is suggested by the notion of comity. The term "*comitas*," which 17th century Dutch authors introduced into the vocabulary of private international law, reflects the idea that deference to foreign law promotes the mutual concerns of sovereigns. Transposing this idea to the realm of judicial decisions, whatever sacrifice of sovereignty recognition might entail could be justified as the price to be paid for inducing foreign courts to give extraterritorial effect to the forum's judgments. Or, put neg-

17. Holker v. Parker, decision of 19 Apr. 1819, Cass. civ., 1819 S. Jur. I 288. The rule established by this case differed in some respects from the provision in the *Code Michaut*. See infra text accompanying nn. 146, 155.

18. Decision of 7 Jan. 1964, Cass. civ. lre, 1964 J.C.P. II 13590. See Gaudemet-Tallon at 490, 497-98 (with further references). With respect to status judgments, the *Cour de cassation* had abandoned *révision au fond* much earlier. See decision of 9 May 1900, Cass. civ., 1905 D.P. I 101 (*de Wrède*); Gaudemet-Tallon at 488, 497.

19. See Bogdan at 85 (Sweden); Kokkini-Iatridou & Verheul at 190 (The Netherlands); Möller at 1 (Finland); Talpis & Goldstein at 141 (Quebec).

20. Legal systems that require reciprocity will obviously refuse to recognize judgments rendered in a jurisdiction that allows relitigation. See Mayer, *Droit international privé* 289 & n. 5 (2d ed. 1983); Bogdan at 87; Martiny at 27; Tomaszewski at 110-11; infra nn. 152-53, 159, 169 and accompanying text.

atively, by insisting on reciprocity courts and legislatures could retaliate against those foreign states whose recognition practices were overly restrictive.

To condition recognition on reciprocity must have seemed logical once nations began to enter into treaties for the mutual enforcement of judgments. At that point, it became apparent that what a formal international compact might do could also be accomplished by means of a unilateral policy to honor judgments from states that were prepared to enforce those of the forum. Whatever the explanation, during the nineteenth century the *quid-pro-quo* approach to judgments recognition enjoyed considerable popularity. Although it originated in continental Europe, the notion of reciprocity also spread to common law countries. The U.S. Supreme Court adopted it, before the turn of the century, in *Hilton v. Guyot*.[21] It also made a more modest appearance in the United Kingdom's Foreign Judgments (Reciprocal Enforcement) Act of 1933 and similar statutes passed in other Commonwealth countries.[22]

4. The Role of Treaties and Conventions

To alleviate the rigors of unduly parochial recognition practices, many nations have found it necessary to resort to international negotiations, leaving to diplomats the resolution of difficulties domestic courts and legislatures had created. As a result, countries that allow a *révision au fond*—as France did—[23] and those that require reciprocity—as Germany still does[24]—entered into numerous bilateral arrangements for the mutual enforcement of judgments. Thus the desire to protect litigants and international commerce from the untoward consequences of an unreasoning insistence on juridical sovereignty spawned entire networks of treaties.

Bargaining for recognition may have the virtue of fostering cooperation among nations. Bilateralism is not, however, an unmixed blessing. The vagaries of negotiation processes are apt to produce disparate recognition standards for judgments from different countries. Once treaties proliferate, inconsistencies and complexities are unavoidable; only multilateral conventions can assure uniformity. Especially within a setting like the Common Market, multilateralism is indeed a feasible alternative, as the Brussels Convention dem-

21. 159 U.S. 113 (1895). Israel, a mixed legal system, adopted the reciprocity requirement by statute. See Shapira at 142.

22. This statute does not require reciprocity as a condition for recognition; it merely facilitates enforcement by providing for the registration of judgments from countries that are prepared to accord similar summary enforcement to United Kingdom judgments. Australia has borrowed this legislation. See Pryles at 6.

23. See Gaudemet-Tallon at 489.

24. See Martiny at 749-52.

onstrates. Yet, such regional schemes can be faulted for discriminating against outsiders.[25] Moreover, the reliance on international accords to correct deficiencies in domestic law can engender a "conflict of conventions," which one national reporter called a "nightmare for lawyers in international litigation."[26] Perhaps the most beneficial effects of treaty arrangements are indirect: they allow courts to gather expertise in dealing with foreign judgments, and they set standards for the liberalization of domestic recognition practices.[27]

B. The Common Law Evolution

1. Early English Law

In marked contrast to the civilians' insistence on domestic juridical prerogatives, the common law tradition has been singularly urbane. The liberal tendency that characterizes this legal culture has its roots in early English practice. Given the nature of their business and their belief in a *ius gentium*,[28] it must have seemed natural to English maritime and mercantile tribunals to honor decisions rendered outside the realm. For a rather peculiar reason, the common law courts—whose outlook was rather more parochial—were equally generous in dealing with foreign judgments. Originally, they could not try cases involving transactions that took place in another country, because the jury had to be drawn from the vicinage where the operative facts had happened.[29] Unless admiralty and mercantile courts took jurisdiction, parties to a foreign contract or tort were therefore compelled to sue abroad. The refusal then to recognize the judgment there obtained would have left the plaintiff without any recourse in England. The desire to avoid such a denial of justice offers a plausible explanation for the common law courts' readiness to acknowledge the binding effect of foreign adjudications.[30]

2. The Basis of Judgments Recognition

The concept of sovereignty, however, did prompt English judges, like the civilians, to ponder why foreign judgments should be able to claim effect within the realm. Several seventeenth century cases espoused the view that the law of nations required courts of different countries to aid one another in the administration of jus-

---

25. See Juenger, supra n. 7 at 41-43.
26. Martiny at 727. See also Dubler at 17-18, 19.
27. Cf. Martiny, in *3 Handbuch des Internationalen Zivilverfahrensrechts* 93 (pt. 1) (1984). See also Dubler at 17-18.
28. See Juenger, "A Page of History," *32 Mercer L. Rev.* 419, 437 (1984).
29. See Sack, "Conflicts of Laws in the History of the English Law," in 3 *Law: A Century of Progress* 344-49 (1937).
30. Id. at 381-85.

tice.[31] Later on, judges occasionally referred to comity[32] and argued that recognition serves as an inducement for foreign courts to honor English judgments.[33] Yet, unlike the U.S. Supreme Court in *Hilton v. Guyot*, the English courts never interpreted comity to require reciprocity, and they ultimately premised recognition on an entirely different rationale. In *Russell v. Smyth*,[34] decided in 1842, Baron Parke analogized foreign judgments to foreign law: they create "obligations,"[35] which—like those arising from a contract made abroad—can be enforced in England by an action of debt. That "debt," however, could not be controverted; it was conclusively established by the judgment, which "merged" the underlying cause of action. In consequence, the foreign decision was considered to preclude relitigation; English judges refused to re-examine its merits, even if, for instance, the foreign court misapplied English law.

The later case of *Schibsby v. Westenholz*,[36] which reiterated that ingenious doctrine,[37] definitively disavowed comity as the basis for judgments recognition.[38] Apart from its implicit rejection of the reciprocity requirement, this doctrinal reorientation had important practical and doctrinal repercussions. Treating foreign judgments like obligations implied that both should be enforced in the same manner.[39] Hence arose the need for an action on the foreign judg-

31. See, e.g., Cottington's case, 36 Eng. Rep. 640 (H.L. 1678); Wier's case, 1 Rolle, Abridgment 530 (K.B. 1607).

32. See Alves v. Bunbury, 171 Eng. Rep. 10 (Nisi Prius 1814) (Lord Ellenborough); Geyer v. Aguilar, 101 Eng. Rep. 1196 (K.B. 1798).

33. Hughs v. Cornelius, 83 Eng. Rep. 247 (K.B. 1683).

34. 152 Eng. Rep. 323 (Exch. 1842).

35. "Where the Court of a foreign country imposes a duty to pay a sum certain, there arises an obligation to pay, which may be enforced in this country." Id. at 347.

36. 6 L.R.-Q.B. 155 (1870).

37. "[T]he judgment of a court of competent jurisdiction over the defendant imposes a duty or obligation on the defendant to pay the sum for which judgment is given, which the courts in this country are bound to enforce . . . ." Id. at 159. But cf. Carl Zeiss Stiftung v. Rayner & Keeler Ltd. (No. 2), (1967) 1 A.C. 853, 967 (Lord Wilberforce) ("considerations of public interest in limiting relitigation").

38. 36 L.R.-Q.B. 159. See also Godard v. Gray, 6 L.R.-Q.B. 139, 152 (1870).

39. The parity of foreign judgments and obligations might, in turn, explain why the judgment creditor may bring an action on the underlying cause of action, rather than suing on the foreign judgment. See *Restatement (Second) of Conflict of Laws* § 95, comment c 1 (1971) (whereas sister-state judgments "merge" the underlying cause of action, foreign country judgments do not preclude an action *de novo*); Pryles at 7; Sharpe at 659. See also Shapira at 136 (Israel following English practice); cf. Azcuna at 12 (Philippines). The technical explanation for this option is that foreign judgments, unlike local ones, do not "merge" the cause of action. A more practical consideration would be to protect the judgment creditor, in cases where recognition is doubtful, against adverse effects of nonrecognition, e.g., the running of a statute of limitations.

Perhaps for the same reason, some civil law countries likewise permit a judgment creditor to bring a new action, instead of petitioning for an exequatur. See, e.g., Dubler at 4 (Switzerland); Gaudemet-Tallon at 496-97 (France); Grigera Naón at 76 (Argentina); Martiny at 757-58 (Federal Republic of Germany); Özsunay at 18

ment (as contrasted with the mere judicial confirmation by an *exequatur* proceeding, which is customary in most civil law countries[40]). At the same time, the notion of an obligation that must be enforced by a new suit directed attention to the fundamental distinction between recognition and enforcement. Finally, the common law approach brought into sharper focus the specific grounds for nonrecognition.

C. Common Requirements

However liberal a state's attitude to foreign judgments may be, some scrutiny for possible defects is indispensable. Although nations differ widely on the basic approach to recognition, there is a remarkable measure of agreement on the minimum requirements a foreign decision must meet to qualify. These preconditions may be less readily discernible in legal systems that do not accord conclusive effect to foreign adjudications. Thus, as long as France allowed a *révision au fond* there was no pressing need to delineate specific grounds for nonrecognition, whereas English judges had to spell out why a particular foreign judgment ought not to be enforced. Still, even before the *Munzer* case enumerated the grounds on which an *exequatur* should be denied, French courts did state reasons for exercising their discretion in favor of a retrial, and these reasons closely parallel those their English counterparts gave for denying recognition.[41]

A tribunal in which a foreign judgment is presented is bound to ask whether the court that rendered it had the necessary authority to decide the case. Second, the recognition forum will want to know whether the losing party was sufficiently apprised of the foreign litigation and had a realistic opportunity to defend. Finally, a court is unlikely to honor foreign judgments that violate fundamental tenets of justice or were procured in a fraudulent manner. Thus, while recognition practices differ widely, it is possible to discern much common ground. All legal systems distinguish between foreign and

---

(Turkey). But see Filipescu at 55 (Romania); Strohbach at 57 (German Democratic Republic); Takakuwa at 4 (Japan); cf. Steiner at 131-32 (Czechoslovakia).

Where judgments recognition rests on a firm treaty basis, judgment creditors usually do not have this option. See, e.g., Brussels Convention arts. 26-29; De Wolf v. Cox (Case No. 42/76), 1976 E. Comm. Ct. J. Rep. 1759; Möller at 4 (Nordic Judgments Act).

40. See, e.g., Dubler at 27 (Switzerland); Gaudemet-Tallon at 495-96 (France); Martiny at 756 (German *Vollstreckungsklage*); Takakuwa at 1, 2 (Japan); Tomaszewski at 117-18. But see Steiner at 107-08 (except in status matters, Czechoslovakia provides no special proceeding for the execution of foreign judgments). Venezuela requires an exequatur not only for the enforcement but also for the recognition of foreign judgments. Rouvier at 3-5. Quebec, a mixed jurisdiction, follows the common law practice of an action on the foreign judgment. Talpis & Goldstein at 2.

41. See Weiss, supra n. 16 at 823-24.

domestic judgments; none accords automatic recognition, sight unseen, to foreign adjudications. Beyond that, there is a universal consensus—in spite of numerous variations in detail—on certain minimum procedural and substantive standards a foreign judgment has to meet to claim efficacy locally: it must have been rendered by a competent court after due notice to the defendant, and it may not offend the recognition forum's public policy.[42]

D. *The Causes of Disparity*

While all agree on the need for certain minimum standards, beyond this basic consensus the national reports reveal considerable divergencies. Although it is difficult to compile a general report that adequately reflects the entire range of responses, it is possible to pin down the reason underlying this diversity. A judgment has a dual aspect. On the one hand, it is a determination of a private dispute; on the other, it is an exercise of state power. A legal system's approach to recognition depends on where the emphasis is put. The common law, as noted earlier, came to view foreign judgments much like foreign legal rules, i.e., as an authoritative pronouncement of private rights and duties. This perspective suggests that a decision rendered abroad is binding as long as the foreign proceeding was regular and fair. Civilians, in contrast, have historically been preoccupied with the notion of juridical sovereignty.

That difference in viewpoint explains why recognition practices vary as much as they do. Mere compliance with basic tenets of justice and procedural decency will not satisfy those who believe that deference to a foreign adjudication amounts to an encroachment on the forum's prerogatives. To anyone who shares this belief it must appear entirely proper either to insist on the power to review the foreign judgment's merits, or to use sovereignty as a bargaining chip, exacting reciprocity as a precondition to recognition. Indeed, if recognition is considered to entail a surrender of forum sovereignty, the temptation looms large to impose any number of additional conditions for such a sacrifice, e.g., requirements that are designed to protect forum citizens or to control the foreign court's choice of law.

In consequence, there is a basic split between legal systems that emphasize their juridical autonomy, and those that stress the litigants' interests and the policy of *res judicata*. It is therefore possible to group impediments to judgment recognition under two distinct headings. The first comprises prerequisites that are considered essential by all states; the second those on which there is no

42. In addition, the foreign decision must qualify as a "judgment" and be "final." This report does not discuss the variations in the meaning of these terms in different legal systems.

general agreement. In the following, I shall attempt to offer a critical assessment of the particular impediments found under either of these headings in the light of trends discernible in judicial opinions and scholarly discourse. No effort will be made to distinguish between prerequisites and defenses. Although classifying a particular impediment under one or the other of these categories may have important practical consequences, it seems more useful to discuss each requirement on its merits, irrespective of how legal systems allocate the burden between the parties claiming and resisting recognition.

III. Universal Requirements

A. *Jurisdiction*

With the notable exception of the State of South Australia, all legal systems for which national reports were submitted exercise some form of review of the rendition state's jurisdiction.[43] The need for such control arises from the fact that the bases for adjudication vary from state to state. Some of these heads of jurisdiction, such as the universally accepted maxim *actor sequitur forum rei* and the defendants' consent, or general appearance, are unobjectionable. Others, however, are obviously exorbitant. That is true, for instance, of the common law's "transient rule,"[44] which subjects those temporarily present to the forum's authority, of the privilege ac-

43. This is usually true even among member states of a federal union. See Dubler at 8 (Switzerland); Grigera Naón at 54-55 (Argentina); Sharpe at 641 & n. 1, 642-43, 645-47 (Canada); Talpis & Goldstein at 14, 89-97 (Quebec). But see Pryles at 1 (no jurisdictional challenge to sister-state judgments in Australia); cf. Brussels Convention art. 28(1).

In the United States, jurisdiction is considered to be a matter of due process, so that a judgment rendered by a court which lacks the necessary "minimum contacts" is invalid even in the state of rendition. See Joiner at 203-04.

The South Australian rule is uniquely liberal: courts can order the registration of a foreign country judgment, irrespective of whether the foreign court had "international jurisdiction," if it is, "in the opinion of the Court, just and equitable that the judgment be enforced." Pryles at 2.

44. Ehrenzweig, *A Treatise on the Conflict of Laws* 103 (1962). The term refers to the traditional common law practice of basing jurisdiction on the service of process within the forum state. See id. at 88, 104-07; Juenger, "Judicial Jurisdiction in the United States and in the European Communities: A Comparison," *82 Mich. L. Rev.* 1195, 1196 (1984). Common lawyers tend not to view this jurisdictional assertion as exorbitant. See Pryles at 4 ("long-arm jurisdiction" rather than "transient jurisdiction" considered exorbitant); cf. Azcuna at 3-4 (Philippines); Shapira at 145-46 (Israel). But cf. Sharpe at 644, 645, 647-48 ("physical presence" defined in terms of residence); Uniform Foreign Money-Judgments Recognition Act § 4(b)(6), 13 U.L.A. 417 (1980) (discretionary nonrecognition of judgment rendered on this basis by a "seriously inconvenient forum"). In the United States, however, the constitutionality of premising jurisdiction on the mere fact of service within the rendition forum has become doubtful. See Shaffer v. Heitner, 433 U.S. 186 (1977); Juenger, supra at 1201 and n. 49.

corded French plaintiffs by article 14 of the French Civil Code,[45] and of the asset-based jurisdiction pursuant to section 23 of the West German Code of Civil Procedure.[46]

Thus, the word "jurisdiction" lacks a single meaning; it covers a wide variety of assertions, some of which are reasonable and some of which are not. Unless some higher law—such as the constitution of a federal system, a treaty or a convention—establishes rules binding on both the rendition and the recognition state,[47] each legal system is free to determine which jurisdictional bases are acceptable for recognition purposes. But before reaching this point, a distinct, though related, question arises: what law should the recognition forum consult in determining whether the foreign court had "jurisdiction"? As the national reports show, there is no consensus on whether that characterization is governed by the jurisdictional rules of the recognition forum or the rendition forum, or by an entirely separate set of principles.

1. Characterization

a. Rendition State Law

Because exorbitant assertions abound, few legal systems consider it sufficient that the rendition court could claim jurisdiction pursuant to its own law. Those that do, e.g., the German Democratic Republic, Romania and Turkey, exercise some measure of control by withholding recognition from judgments rendered abroad in disputes over which their own courts claim exclusive jurisdiction.[48] Brazil and Poland follow a similar rule, but, in addition, permit nonrecognition if the foreign court lacked a "sufficiently strong and real connection" with the controversy.[49] The Nordic Judgments Act takes a somewhat different approach: it precludes inquiries into the rendition court's jurisdiction, except if it is based on the mere presence of assets or the defendant's temporary presence.[50]

45. See Gaudemet-Tallon at 490-91. See also Kokkini-Iatridou & Verheul at 194 (plaintiff's domicile confers jurisdiction pursuant to the law of The Netherlands).

46. See Martiny at 739-40. See also Bogdan at 87 (Swedish law); Dubler at 34 (Swiss *forum arresti*); Kokkini-Iatridou & Verheul at 194 (Netherlands pre-judgment attachment).

47. See Gaudemet-Tallon at 502-03 (Brussels Convention); Joiner at 203-04 (due process clauses of the fifth and fourteenth amendments of the U.S. Constitution).

48. See Filipescu at 13-15; Özsunay at 8, 10; Strohbach at 51-52. See also Gaudemet-Tallon at 490 (French minority view).

49. See Tomaszewski at 111; Valladão at 2.

50. See Möller at 2, 3-5. That Act also permits nonrecognition in cases where the recognition forum claims exclusive jurisdiction. Id. at 3.

On the use of this technique ("*System der Negativliste*") in bilateral treaties see generally 1 Geimer & Schütze, *Internationale Urteilsanerkennung* (part 2) 1508-10 (1984). See also Martiny at 735 (two German bilateral treaties have adopted this approach).

b. Recognition State Law

The largest single group of reporting countries measures the foreign court's jurisdiction by reference to the bases found in their own laws.[51] At first blush, the "mirror-image principle"[52] appears eminently fair. What could be more reasonable than to concede as much jurisdiction to the rendition state as the recognition state claims for itself? In reality, however, this version of the Golden Rule is at once too narrow and too broad. It is too narrow because the forum's rules may be unduly restrictive, which jeopardizes the recognition of judgments that rest on an otherwise unobjectionable basis. Conversely, the mirror-image principle projects into the foreign legal system all of the recognition state's jurisdictional assertions, however extravagent they may be.[53] In effect, it endorses foreign exorbitance by honoring judgments of courts that lack a reasonably close relationship to the dispute.

No doubt, the objective of the mirror-image principle, i.e., the congruence of "indirect" and "direct" jurisdiction,[54] has a certain visceral appeal. But the adoption of a single standard for adjudication and recognition makes sense only if that standard is finely tuned. To work well, the jurisdictional bases used must be, on the one hand, sufficiently broad and, on the other, subject to constraints that effectively curtail excessive assertions. Mechanisms to achieve fine-tuning exist only in federal nations such as the United States, whose Supreme Court exercises constitutional control over state court jurisdiction,[55] and in quasi-federal systems such as the European Communities, where the Brussels Convention establishes jurisdictional rules that are binding on the member states and whose interpretation is supervised by the Communities' Court of Justice.

c. "Jurisdiction in the International Sense"

Recognizing the problems of measuring jurisdiction, for recognition purposes, by recourse to domestic or rendition state rules, the

51. See Azcuna at 3 (Philippines); Dubler at 30-34(Switzerland); Grigera Naón at 57, 61-62 (Argentina); Joiner at 203-04 (U.S.); Martiny at 734-35 (Federal Republic of Germany); Rouvier at 8 (Venezuela); Steiner at 109-10 (Czechoslovakia); Takakuwa at 12-13 (Japan); cf. Gaudemet-Tallon at 491 (French jurisdictional bases except for those that are exorbitant).

52. Martiny at 734. See also Dubler at 32-34.

53. See Martiny at 739-40 (West German assets jurisdiction); Steiner at 120 (Czechoslovakian assets jurisdiction). But cf. Gaudemet-Tallon at 491 (exorbitant bases excluded from "mirror-image principle").

54. This useful pair of concepts serves to distinguish adjudicatory jurisdiction from jurisdiction for recognition purposes. Originally developed in France, it is now widely used in civil law countries. See, e.g., Dubler at 30-32; Martiny at 734; Steiner at 109.

55. See supra n. 43.

English courts have long taken the position that the efficacy of a foreign judgment ought not to depend on the internal law of either. Instead, they seek to ascertain whether the foreign court had "jurisdiction in the international sense."[56] This concept reflects the belief in internationally acceptable jurisdictional bases that may differ from those found in the *lex fori*. Similarly, the French courts, proceeding from the felicitous notion of "*compétence indirecte*,"[57] have begun to develop special jurisdictional rules that do not necessarily mirror those controlling their own power to adjudicate.[58]

The application of different rules for adjudication and recognition originally served the negative purpose of justifying the refusal to enforce a judgment despite the fact that the jurisdiction claimed by the foreign court had a parallel in forum law.[59] In other words, courts created a double standard that was less favorable than the mirror-image principle. However, notions such as "jurisdiction in the international sense" and "*compétence indirecte*" also have an innate propensity to liberalize recognition practices. They can be used to justify the enforcement of a foreign judgment that is premised on some reasonable jurisdictional basis, even if that basis has no counterpart in domestic law.[60] As several national reports suggest, there may indeed be a trend toward international criteria of reasonableness.[61] The elaboration of such criteria would not be unduly burdensome, for international treaties furnish sufficient guidance to distinguish between acceptable and exorbitant jurisdictional bases.[62]

2. Relevance of the Rendition Forum's Rules on Jurisdiction and Competence

Whatever criteria the recognition forum may choose to deter-

56. See Pemberton v. Hughes, (1899) 1 Ch. 781, 792; Cheshire & North, *Private International Law* 341 (11th ed. 1987).

The phrase "jurisdiction in the international sense" is also used in other common law countries. See Pryles at 2, 3-4 (Australia); Sharpe at 645-48 (Canada). There, however, it has taken on a curiously provincial connotation, i.e., jurisdiction premised on the service of process within the rendition forum. See supra n. 44. See also Talpis & Goldstein at 91 (Quebec). But cf. Shapira at 144-46 (Israel).

57. See supra n. 54.

58. See Gaudemet-Tallon at 491.

59. See Schibsby v. Westenholz, 6 L.R.-Q.B. 155 (1870); Gaudemet-Tallon at 491.

60. For recent French developments in this direction see Gaudemet-Tallon at 491-92. But see Pryles at 2, 3, 4 (restrictive meaning accorded to the phrase "jurisdiction in the international sense"); Sharpe at 645-48 (same).

61. See Kokkini-Iatridou & Verheul at 194; Takakuwa at 13 (minority view in Japan); cf. Uniform Foreign Money-Judgments Recognition Act § 5 (enumeration of jurisdictional bases); Grigera Naón at 64-65 (foreign jurisdiction premised on necessity). This more liberal view coalesces, up to a point, with the practices of those nations that determine jurisdiction by reference to the rendition forum's law. See supra nn. 48-50 and accompanying text. For the even broader rule that prevails in South Australia see supra n. 43.

62. Cf. Martiny, supra n. 27 at 93.

mine indirect jurisdiction, the jurisdictional basis on which the rendition court relied should be of no concern. Rather, it would seem to suffice that the foreign tribunal had, in fact, a close enough nexus with the parties or the transaction.[63] For example, if a French court assumed jurisdiction on the ground that the plaintiff was French—an obviously exorbitant basis—its judgment can nevertheless be recognized by an American court as long as the defendant was "doing business" in France. In other words, whether a proper basis for indirect jurisdiction did exist is a question which the recognition court ought to resolve by applying its own standards to the facts of the case. (In the interest of facilitating recognition, the pertinent findings by the rendition court ought to be accepted as binding, at least if the foreign proceeding was contested.[64])

It would likewise seem irrelevant whether the foreign court correctly applied its own jurisdictional rules, as long as the judgment meets the recognition state's criteria for indirect jurisdiction. Yet, according to several national reports, the judgment debtor is allowed to argue that the rendition court lacked "jurisdiction" because it misapplied its own law.[65] In other words, to qualify for recognition a judgment must comply with both the foreign provisions on direct jurisdiction and the forum's standards of indirect jurisdiction. Such a dual test needlessly complicates the enforcement of foreign judgments.

At first blush, it may appear reasonable to require conformity with at least those foreign jurisdictional rules whose violations would entail invalidity pursuant to the foreign law,[66] because a judg-

63. See, e.g., Kokkini-Iatridou & Verheul at 194-95; Pryles at 4; Strohbach at 51-52, 53.

64. Compare Brussels Convention art. 28(2) and Möller at 2 with Azcuna at 4, Kokkini-Iatridou & Verheul at 195 (unless a treaty provides otherwise) and Martiny at 737 (same).

65. See Azcuna at 3-4 (Philippines); Filipescu at 11, 25 (Romania); Rouvier at 8 (Venezuela). This argument can also be raised in legal systems that provide for *révision au fond*. See Talpis & Goldstein at 82-83 (Quebec).

The problem rarely arises in United States interstate recognition practice, where jurisdiction is determined by reference to standards laid down by the Supreme Court acting under the due process clause. See supra n. 43. Still, there is Supreme Court authority which suggests that the recognition state may refuse to honor the judgment of a sister-state court that lacked "jurisdiction," not under constitutional standards but solely pursuant to its own law. See Treinies v. Sunshine Mining Co., 308 U.S. 66 (1939).

In contrast, the recognition of foreign country judgments is governed by state law. See supra n. 6 and accompanying text. Those American states that have adopted the Uniform Foreign Money-Judgments Recognition Act will presumably not review the rendition court's adherence to its own rules because art. 5, which enumerates various jurisdictional bases, provides that if a judgment complies with any of them, it "shall not be refused recognition for lack of . . . jurisdiction."

66. In the United States, for instance, a court that adjudicates without jurisdiction is considered to violate due process, so that the resulting judgment is unconstitutional and therefore void. See supra n. 43.

ment should not be entitled to greater efficacy at home than abroad.[67] However, few legal systems take the position that jurisdictional defects invalidate a final judgment. Even where such a rule prevails (as, for instance, in the United States) a collateral attack on the judgment in the rendition forum may be barred, on grounds of *res judicata*, if the defendant participated in the suit.[68] Instead of burdening the recognition court with the task of delving into the intricacies of foreign law concerning the consequences of noncompliance with jurisdictional rules, it seems preferable to have the judgment debtor pursue his challenge in the forum where the judgment was rendered.[69]

The same rationale applies, *a fortiori*, if the rendition court's competence (i.e., its "subject matter jurisdiction" as opposed to "personal jurisdiction") is at issue.[70] Requiring the recognition court to wrestle with highly technical rules of foreign law on the allocation of judicial power serves no useful purpose. Nevertheless, U.S. Supreme Court cases suggest that the judgment of a sister-state court which lacked competence pursuant to its own law is not entitled to full faith and credit.[71] Section 4(a)(3) of the Uniform Foreign Money-Judgment Recognition Act extends this dubious rule to foreign country judgments, providing for mandatory nonrecognition in the event that the rendition court "did not have jurisdiction over the subject matter."[72]

3. Exclusive Jurisdiction

Even if a foreign judgment rests on a universally accepted jurisdictional basis, recognition may be precluded because the forum claims "exclusive jurisdiction" over the particular controversy. Such claims are quite common in civil law countries,[73] many of which pur-

67. See Dubler at 21; *Restatement (Second) of Conflict of Laws* § 92 comments c and e; cf. Shapira at 148 (competence); Sharpe at 670 (same).

68. See Baldwin v. Iowa State Traveling Men's Ass'n, 283 U.S. 522 (1931); Joiner at 204-05. This rule applies even if the defendant merely entered a special appearance or moved to dismiss for lack of jurisdiction.

In other legal systems, the defendant's participation in the foreign proceeding can cure jurisdictional defects, but not if he merely contested jurisdiction. See Martiny at 738; Pryles at 4-5; Sharpe at 656. But see Özsunay at 9.

69. Cf. Sharpe at 670 (competence).

70. Sharpe at 670-72; cf. Dubler at 32 (venue).

71. Treinies v. Sunshine Mining Co., 308 U.S. 66 (1939); Thompson v. Whitman, 85 U.S. (18 Wall.) 457 (1874); see *Restatement (Second) of Conflict of Laws* § 105 (1971).

72. See Joiner at 203. Similar views prevail in other nations. See Azcuna at 6 (Philippines); Filipescu at 11 (Romania); Pryles at 5 (Australian dicta); cf. Grigera Naón at 65 ("manifest" lack of foreign court's competence may amount to a violation of the Argentinian constitution's due process clause); Sharpe at 671 ("complete" lack of competence).

73. Common lawyers do not use the phrase "exclusive jurisdiction" in the civil-

port to reserve the adjudication of certain matters to domestic courts, as, for instance, litigation concerning local real estate and rights recorded in local registers, actions relating to the existence or non-existence of domestic corporations, and family law disputes affecting citizens.[74] Moreover, various treaties[75] and international conventions[76] expressly recognize the signatories' exclusive jurisdiction over specific groups of cases.

While the idea of exclusivity still enjoys considerable support,[77] permitting each state unilaterally to reserve the adjudication of certain disputes to its own tribunals invites abuses. A striking illustration is the case law of the *Cour de cassation*, which construed articles 14 and 15 of the French Civil Code to confer exclusive jurisdiction upon domestic courts in all cases where one of the litigants is French.[78] Even apart from this extreme example, it is probably true that "exclusive jurisdictional bases are rarely justified because, as a rule, they unduly impede the pursuit of justice."[79]

3. Forum-Selection and Arbitration Clauses

A somewhat different problem arises when a court fails to honor the parties' contractual choice of a judicial or arbitral forum. Several legal systems enforce forum-selection clauses indirectly by refusing to recognize judgments rendered in disregard of such provisions, at least where the parties conferred exclusive jurisdiction on the forum in which recognition is sought.[80] This practice seems unobjectionable. Forum-selection and arbitration clauses, provided

ian sense, but the concept is not unknown, witness the hoary rules that the state of domicile alone has jurisdiction in matters concerning status, and that only the courts at the situs can adjudicate rights in immovables. See Cheshire & North, supra n. 56, at 622, 777.

74. See Filipescu at 13 (Rumania; status and capacity, immovables, inheritance rights to movables of domiciliaries, legal entities, bankruptcy); Grigera Naón at 58-60 (actions to which Argentina is a party); Martiny at 736-37 (Federal Republic of Germany; immovables and certain actions to which consumers are parties; Öszunay at 6, 8 (Turkey; immovables); Rouvier at 11-12 (Venezuela; immovables); Steiner at 119, 122 (Czechoslovakia; immovables, invalidation of documents with legal effects in Czechoslovakia, declaration of death and probate matters of citizens); cf. Gaudemet-Tallon at 490-91 and infra nn. 156-57 (protection of French nationals); Grigera Naón at 63-64 (Argentine "laws of immediate application"); Talpis & Goldstein at 102-04 (immovables and "laws of immediate application"). The Swiss draft of a Federal Act on Private International Law reduces the importance of exclusive jurisdiction with respect to money judgments. See Dubler at 34-35.

75. See, e.g., Dubler at 35 & n. 123 (Swiss treaties with Belgium, Italy and Liechtenstein); Filipescu at 13 (Romanian treaties with France and Greece).

76. See, e.g., Brussels Convention art. 16; Nordic Judgments Act § 6, par. 5.

77. Indeed, some legal systems go as far as to protect the exclusive jurisdiction of third states. See Martiny at 737; Steiner at 120; Tomaszewski at 111.

78. See Gaudemet-Tallon at 490-91; infra nn. 156, 157 and accompanying text.

79. Kropholler, in *1 Handbuch des Internationalen Zivilverfahrensrechts* 256 (1982).

80. See, e.g., Pryles at 5; Steiner at 120; Uniform Foreign Money-Judgments Rec-

that they neither are the product of overreaching nor conflict with strongly held policies,[81] serve a useful and important role in international transactions. For the same reason, recognition state claims to exclusive jurisdiction should not, as a rule, entail the nonrecognition of a judgment rendered by the *forum prorogatum*.

B. *Notice and Opportunity to be Heard*

1. Notice

The right to be heard is a fundamental tenet, and its exercise presupposes notice sufficient to apprise the defendant of the fact that an action is pending. It is therefore a universally accepted principle that a judgment rendered against a party who was not properly notified of the proceeding, e.g., in the case of service by mere publication,[82] will not be recognized. As far as the implementation of this principle is concerned, however, the practices of various states vary.[83]

There is a split of opinion, for instance, on the question whether failure to notify, or inadequate notification, can be cured by the defendant's actual notice.[84] In addition, differing views prevail concerning the form of notice that is sufficient for recognition purposes,[85] and the language to be used.[86] Also, some nations insist on more stringent notice requirements for their own citizens than

ognition Act § 4(b)(5) (discretionary nonrecognition). But cf. Azcuna at 6-7; Dubler at 34-35; Möller at 2-3; Talpis & Goldstein at 104-05.

81. See Kokkini-Iatridou & Verheul at 196; cf. Martiny at 738. See also Grigera Naón at 65-67.

82. See, e.g., Sharpe at 678-79; Steiner at 111. But cf. Sharpe at 679 (*in rem* proceedings).

83. Moreover, some common law countries fail clearly to distinguish between jurisdiction and notice. The reason for this confusion is that service of process within the forum state was traditionally considered a jurisdictional fact, see supra n. 44, rather than merely a formal notice of the pendency of a lawsuit. See Pryles at 4; Sharpe at 644, 645, 648, 678-79; cf. Shapira at 145-46. But see Mullane v. Hanover Bank & Trust Co., 339 U.S. 306 (1950).

84. Compare Kokkini-Iatridou & Verheul at 196 (irregular service not fatal) and Martiny at 742 (actual notice can cure defects) with Filipescu at 19 (notice must comply with both recognition state and defendant's home state requirements) and Rouvier at 15 (notice must comply with both rendition state and service state requirements). See also Azcuna at 4-5 (noncompliance with technical requirements harmless unless they are "jurisdictional"); Dubler at 41 (written notice of pendency of suit indispensable).

85. Even service effected in full compliance with the rendition state's requirements, and calculated to convey actual notice, may not come to the defendant's attention. Whether such service suffices to entitle the judgment to recognition is doubtful. Compare Sharpe at 679 with Steiner at 111, 121 (Czechoslovakian law requires personal service) and Takakuwa at 15 (service that does not comply with Japanese law is ineffectual); cf. Gaudemet-Tallon at 506 (Brussels Convention).

86. See Joiner at 206-07.

those applicable to foreign judgment debtors.[87] The widespread adoption of the Hague Convention on the Service Abroad of Judicial and Extrajudicial Documents in Civil or Commercial Matters can be expected to eliminate some of these disparities. Moreover, it should be borne in mind that the issue of lack of notice can only arise in the case of default judgments, for a defendant who actually participated in the foreign action is precluded from raising the notice issue at the recognition stage.[88]

2. Opportunity to be Heard

Notice is but a means to an end; its ultimate purpose is to enable a party effectively to contest a lawsuit. Mere service of process does not necessarily safeguard the right of defense. The rendition state's internal law may fall short of providing a full and fair hearing, depriving the defendant of a realistic opportunity to litigate, and thereby violate the maxim *auditur et altera pars*.[89] At the very least, the defendant must be adequately informed of the nature of the proceeding in sufficient time[90] to enable him to protect his rights. If, however, the defendant's inability to participate in the foreign proceeding is a consequence of his own misconduct, the judgment may be recognized.[91]

C. *Public Policy*

Even though the rendition court's jurisdiction is beyond doubt and the judgment debtor had the opportunity to be heard, the foreign judgment may still be unjust. With virtual unanimity, legal systems will refuse recognition in the event that a judgment, for one reason or another, violates their public policy. Not merely domestic law but most recognition treaties[92] and conventions[93] recognize this reservation, even though international compacts often attempt (at

87. See Martiny at 740 (Federal Republic of Germany until 1986); Takakuwa at 14 (Japan).

88. See, e.g., Filipescu at 23; Gaudemet-Tallon at 505 (Brussels Convention).

89. See, e.g., Kokkini-Iatridou & Verheul at 197 (failure to notify defendant of documentary evidence or expert opinion), 11 (failure to notify defendant of criminal proceedings whose findings are conclusive in subsequent civil action); Rouvier at 8 (judgment of Danish "court of dealing"). See also Sharpe at 683.

90. See, e.g., Özsunay at 9-10, 16; Tomaszewski at 112-13.

91. See Martiny at 749 (English judgment rendered against contumacious defendant recognized in the Federal Republic of Germany).

92. See, e.g., Bogdan at 86 (Swedish-Swiss recognition treaty); Rouvier at 7 (Venezuelan-Bolivian recognition treaty). On the question whether a public policy reservation contained in a treaty or convention must be construed "autonomously," see Dubler at 44.

93. See, e.g., Brussels Convention art. 27(1); Código Bustamante art. 423 No. 3; Inter-American Convention on Extraterritorial Validity of Foreign Judgments and Arbitral Awards art. 2(h); Nordic Judgments Act § 6(6).

least verbally[94]) to limit its scope. Apparently, that safeguard of last resort against potential injustice is dispensable only among the constituent political subdivisions of a federal system.[95]

The recognition state's public policy may be offended either by procedural irregularities, such as the lack of a fair hearing,[96] or by substantive deficiencies, such as the violation of fundamental tenets of equal protection.[97] In its broadest sense, this reservation encompasses practically all impediments to recognition, including, for instance, the lack of due notice and fraud. Even if its meaning is more narrowly confined, public policy remains an amorphous concept, and there is no general agreement on its precise scope.

Negatively, the mere fact that a foreign judgment is not accompanied by an opinion,[98] or that it is at odds with the recognition state's substantive, procedural or conflicts law,[99] does not suffice to establish a public policy violation. This is true, generally, even in the event of a conflict with those forum rules that are "mandatory" in the sense that they displace, in choice-of-law cases, the otherwise applicable foreign law.[100] In other words, a foreign decision can be recognized despite the fact that the law on which it is based clashes with important forum policies, so long as the result the foreign court reached is not repugnant to the recognition forum's fundamental notions of justice. As Batiffol put it, in the context of judgments recognition public policy has but an "attenuated effect."[101]

Any attempt to enumerate the instances in which the public

94. A term often used to underscore the exceptional nature of nonrecognition on public policy grounds is "manifestly." See, e.g., Inter-American Convention art. 2(h); Nordic Judgments Act § 6(6). The Brussels Convention contains no such qualifying adjective; but it does limit the sway of public policy by specifying that the reservation may not be used to test the rendition court's jurisdiction. Art. 28(3).

95. See Fauntleroy v. Lum, 210 U.S. 230 (1908); Ehrenzweig, supra n. 44 at 203; Grigera Naón at 54-55 (Argentina); cf. Pryles & Hanks, *Federal Conflict of Laws* 98-99 (1974) (Australia).

96. See, e.g., Dubler at 39 (*"indépendance du tribunal ou le droit d'être entendu"*); Gaudemet-Tallon at 494 (*"droits de la défense"*); Özsunay at 12.

97. See, e.g., Martiny at 723-24 (constitutional rights under Federal Republic's Basic Law); Shapira at 141 (Israel); Tomaszewski (Polish constitutional principles).

98. See, e.g., Filipescu at 29-30, 34; Gaudemet-Tallon at 494; Pryles at 5; Strohbach at 53. But see Azcuna at 6 (violation of Philippine constitution); Grigera Naón at 68 (violation of Argentine constitution); Özsunay at 11 (violation of Turkish constitution).

99. See, e.g., Filipescu at 33; Martiny at 746; Takakuwa at 16.

100. Tomaszewski at 114. But cf. infra nn. 208-11, 215 ("laws of immediate application"); Grigera Naón at 63-65, 71-72; Rouvier at 15 (Venezuelan "public law" and "prohibitive laws"). Quebec law on this point is unsettled. Talpis & Goldstein at 125, 135.

101. Batiffol, "Note," 53 *Rev. crit. d.i.p.* 346, 348 (1964); see Dubler at 39, 43; Gaudemet-Tallon at 493; Martiny at 745. In other words, the public policy reservation does not have the same stringency in judgments recognition as in choice of law. But see art. 17, par. 3, of the Philippine Civil Code, quoted in Azcuna at 7, which deals with foreign laws and judgments in the same breath.

policy reservation can be legitimately invoked would be futile. Nor does it seem advisable to hamper the recognition state's discretion by requiring greater specificity. The national reports suggest that courts do not employ this safety valve in an unduly expansive manner,[102] and that judges can be trusted to determine, on a case-by-case basis, whether a foreign decision is sufficiently aberrational to warrant rejection. To be sure, there are differences of opinion. For example, it is doubtful whether judgments ordering the payment of a gambling debt[103] or treble damages for an antitrust violation[104] ought to be recognized. On the whole, however, it seems that few courts are inclined to listen sympathetically to a judgment debtor's contention that the foreign decision was so grossly unjust that it should be disregarded. Since reasonably developed legal systems afford sufficient opportunities for review, that challenge will usually founder at the recognition stage because errors could have been corrected in the course of the original proceeding.[105] As in domestic law, the defendant's failure to take appropriate steps while the matter was still pending ought to preclude a later attack.

D. *Fraud*

Often treated as a subspecies of the public policy exception,[106] fraud is yet another universally acknowledged reason for denying recognition. The term "fraud" covers misrepresentations addressed to the court or the other party. For instance, there are cases of plaintiffs who pretended to retract a suit for the purpose of inducing the defendant to default,[107] or who failed to disclose the defendant's whereabouts to the court.[108] In common law countries, where service of process on the defendant within the forum state has traditionally been sufficient to confer jurisdiction,[109] some courts have refused to recognize judgments rendered on this basis if the defend-

102. Thus Pryles at 5 notes that few Australian and English cases have denied recognition on public policy grounds. According to Joiner at 210, the "public policy defense is an extremely narrow one, and for all practical purposes is unavailable in strictly commercial cases." See also Dubler at 39, 43 (Switzerland); Shapira at 141 (Israel); Takakuwa at 16 (Japan); Tomaszewski at 114 (Poland).

103. Compare Azcuna at 7, Joiner at 210 n. 95 and Kokkini-Iatridou & Verheul at 197 (futures contract) with Filipescu at 33, Martiny at 745, Möller at 2 (Nordic Judgments Act) and Strohbach at 54 (except where state-licensed gambling).

104. See Martiny at 747-48; cf. U.K. Protection of Trading Interests Act 1980, ch. 11.

105. See Pryles at 6 (English court's refusal to deny enforcement of New York judgment because defendant should have raised the argument of undue influence in the New York proceeding); cf. Tomaszewski at 115.

106. See Filipescu at 35; Grigera Naón at 71; Kokkini-Iatridou & Verheul at 198; Martiny at 748; cf. Sharpe at 676; Talpis & Goldstein at 126.

107. Levin v. Gladstein, 142 N.C. 482, 55 S.E. 371 (1906).

108. See Sharpe at 682. See also Gaudemet-Tallon at 493.

109. See supra nn. 44, 83.

ant was lured into a foreign forum by false representations made by the plaintiff or third parties.[110]

As is true of the public policy defense, the allegation that a foreign proceeding was tainted by fraud is not assured of a favorable judicial response. Like other violations of elementary tenets of fairness, fraudulent machinations are subject to judicial scrutiny, and it is up to the defendant to raise the issue in the original suit.[111] His failure to do so, even though he had a reasonable opportunity to protect his interests, will usually preclude a party from raising the matter after the fact.[112] Even if the judgment creditor's misconduct was such that the judgment should not be allowed to stand, or if it was discovered only after the foreign proceedings terminated,[113] the recognition court might still require the judgment debtor first to exhaust whatever remedies the rendition state may provide.[114]

Civilians sometimes use the term "fraud" in a sense quite different from its ordinary meaning. Thus the *Munzer* case and later French decisions mention "fraud on the law"[115] as one of the impediments to recognition.[116] In reality, however, the problem they address is evasion[117] rather than misrepresentation. That problem largely arises because of forum shopping,[118] especially in divorce cases,[119] and a better way to deal with it is to inquire into the foreign court's jurisdiction.[120] Hence, fraud on the law as a separate defense to recognition—assuming that it does apply to ordinary money judgments—is needed only in those legal systems that lack appropriate safeguards to control indirect jurisdiction.[121] Even there, however, the public policy reservation suffices to combat truly abusive forum

110. See, e.g., Wyman v. Newhouse, 93 F.2d 313 (2d Cir. 1937); Klaiber v. Frank, 9 N.J. 1, 86 A.2d 679 (1952); cf. Blandin v. Ostrander, 239 F. 700 (2d Cir. 1917).

111. See Azcuna at 8; Steiner at 124. For this reason, some common law systems distinguish between "extrinsic" and "intrinsic" fraud. Only the former, which prevents a party from presenting his case or relates to the manner in which the judgment was procured, is said to be a valid defense to judgment recognition. See Joiner at 209.

112. See Grigera Naón at 71; Sharpe at 674, 675-76; Strohbach at 54. But see Pryles at 6.

113. See Sharpe at 673, 675.

114. Strohbach at 54. But see Filipescu at 35; Shapira at 148; Sharpe at 682-83.

115. See, e.g., Filipescu at 35; Grigera Naón at 71-72; Talpis & Goldstein at 129-30.

116. See Gaudemet-Tallon at 493.

117. Steiner at 113-14.

118. Dubler at 47; Grigera Naón at 66, 74; cf. Steiner at 114.

119. Steiner at 16-19.

120. Cf. Grigera Naón at 74; Steiner at 114, 125.

121. See Mayer, supra n. 20 at 318. Except for claims to "exclusive jurisdiction," the national reports do not mention recognition rules specifically designed to curtail forum shopping. See Pryles at 7; Steiner at 127; cf. Martiny at 739. The only statutory rule on point seems to be art. 4(b)(6) of the Uniform Foreign Money-Judgments Recognition Act, which permits the nonrecognition of judgments based on "transient jurisdiction," see supra n. 44, that were rendered in a "seriously inconvenient forum." See Joiner at 214 n. 122. While the American *forum non conveniens* doctrine

shopping;[122] the notion of "fraud on the law," conceived as an independent impediment to judgment recognition, seems dispensable.

E. *Inconsistent Judgments*

As a general proposition, a foreign judgment will not be recognized if it conflicts with a prior adjudication in the recognition state. In the United States, however, a different rule may apply. The Supreme Court has held, in the context of interstate recognition, that a later sister-state judgment is entitled to full faith and credit notwithstanding the fact that it conflicts with an earlier forum judgment.[123] It is doubtful whether this last-in-time rule also applies if the second judgment was rendered abroad. The Uniform Foreign Money-Judgments Recognition Act is silent on this point; article 4(b)(4) merely provides for discretionary nonrecognition in the event of a conflict with "another" judgment.

The national reports indicate the lack of a general agreement on the question of which of two conflicting foreign judgments, i.e., the first[124] or the last[125] should be honored. The first-in-time rule would seem preferable because it deters post-judgment forum shopping.[126] But what does "first in time" mean? The priority among conflicting judgments can be determined in various ways. Possible criteria are the time of filing, service, rendition or finality; and there is no consensus on which of these events should control. Arguably, to discourage multiple lawsuits between the same parties the date of filing or service, rather than rendition or finality, ought to govern. That, at least, is the rule in countries such as the Federal Republic of Germany, which consider the pendency of a foreign proceeding as a bar to local litigation.[127] Whatever the appropriate rule on priority

allows a dismissal to protect defendants against forum shopping, courts have been reluctant to invoke that doctrine to deny recognition. See Joiner at 214-15.

122. See Pryles at 7; Strohbach at 20.

123. Treinies v. Sunshine Mining Co., 308 U.S. 66 (1939); see *Restatement (Second) of Conflict of Laws* § 114 (1971).

124. To that effect, see, e.g., Pryles at 5; Takakuwa at 16-17; Strohbach at 53.

125. In the United States, the law is unclear. While the *Treinies* case and the Second Conflicts Restatement would suggest that the last judgment should prevail, section 4(b)(3) of the Uniform Foreign Money-Judgments Recognition Act, as noted in the text, leaves the question open. The point is also unsettled in Argentina, see Grigera Naón at 68-70, and in Rumania, see Filipescu at 31-32. Özsunay at 11 argues that a Turkish court ought to withhold recognition from both of the two conflicting judgments.

126. Cf. Martiny at 743-44. See also id. at 758 (West German Code of Civil Procedure § 328, par. 1, No. 3 (as revised in 1986) (conflicting foreign country judgments).

127. Martiny at 744. See also Möller at 3 (Nordic Judgments Act); Rouvier at 17 (*de lege ferenda*); cf. Shapira at 18 (prior suit pending in Israel); Strohbach at 53 (no recognition while East German proceedings are pending). Contra Grigera Naón at 68 (foreign judgment recognized despite pendency of litigation in Argentina); Takakuwa at 16-17 (Japanese judgment precludes recognition even though foreign action was instituted before the Japanese suit). But see id. at 28.

may be, it ought to apply equally to foreign and domestic judgments. To prefer forum determinations irrespective of when they were rendered, as some nations do,[128] serves neither comity nor judicial economy.

IV. Other Impediments

Although foreign judgments do deserve respect, a worldwide consensus confirms the appropriateness of submitting them to a minimum of scrutiny. The foregoing discussion shows that most legal systems, in spite of numerous differences in detail, agree on certain fundamental safeguards. But the national reports also list a variety of additional barriers to recognition, ranging from the outright disregard of foreign judgments to the refusal to recognize those that conflict with particular domestic laws. Unlike the prerequisites discussed in Part III of this report, these impediments are not designed to test the foreign court's authority or the fairness of its decision. Rather, they were conceived to vindicate the recognition forum's sovereignty. As elsewhere in the conflict of laws, that notion introduces conceptual difficulties and practical obstacles to the free flow of multistate transactions.

A. *Nonrecognition*

The most drastic way of asserting the forum's prerogative against perceived encroachments from abroad is to disregard foreign judgments altogether.[129] Several legal systems explicitly endorse this approach. Thus article 431 of the Netherlands Code of Civil Procedure states:

> 1. Except for the provisions of articles 985 to 994 [which deal with recognition pursuant to treaties and international conventions], judgments of a foreign court may not be executed within the Netherlands.
> 2. The disputes may be litigated before, and decided by, a Dutch court anew.[130]

The bark of this article is, however, worse than its bite. Although Dutch courts initially construed article 431 literally to deny any relevance to foreign adjudications, they have progressively retreated from this xenophobic position. The Netherlands Supreme

128. See, e.g., Azcuna at 6 (Philippines); Martiny at 744 (West Germany); Özsunay at 12 (Turkey). But cf. Azcuna at 8-9 (Philippine decisions honoring later foreign judgment).

129. With respect to money judgments, an alternative to nonrecognition is the refusal to grant enforcement by exequatur or otherwise. Thus, except for support decrees, Poland does not enforce foreign judgments absent a treaty. Tomaszewski at 1, 14.

130. Translation by Kokkini-Iatridou & Verheul at 190.

Court first recognized the binding effect of judgments rendered abroad pursuant to a forum-selection clause.[131] It then barred a Dutch plaintiff from relitigating a suit he had brought in England.[132] Lower courts increasingly deduced an "implied submission"—i.e., a fictive prorogation—from the fact that the judgment debtor participated in a foreign proceeding, even if he merely contested the foreign court's jurisdiction.[133] Stretching the notion of submission even further, the bare jurisdictional fact of defendant's domicile has been held sufficient to make the foreign judgment binding.[134]

In this fashion, the Dutch courts effectively substituted their own views for the civil procedure code's anti-recognition policy. Although there is no "recognition" in a formal sense, they do permit an action on the foreign judgment. In that proceeding, neither the merits of the foreign decision nor the foreign court's choice-of-law determination are reviewed, nor is reciprocity a precondition for enforcement.[135] Thus, current Netherlands practice parallels that established earlier by English courts.[136] In some respects, e.g., as regards the review of the foreign court's jurisdiction, it may be even more liberal.[137]

The situation is similar in Sweden where, in theory, recognition requires specific statutory provisions or a treaty.[138] Although they are free to re-examine the merits, in practice the Swedish courts do accord binding effect to foreign judgments under the guise of treating them as "evidence" of the facts found and the law applied.[139] At least as long as the rendition court followed Swedish choice-of-law rules the judgment is presumed to be correct, and the burden of showing the contrary is shifted to the judgment debtor.[140] If the foreign judgment was based on an exclusive forum-selection clause, a review of the merits is precluded altogether if the foreign proceedings were fair and the decision does not violate Swedish public policy.[141]

---

131. Id.

132. Id.

133. Id. at 190-91.

134. Id. at 191.

135. Id.

136. See supra nn. 39-40 and accompanying text. Occasionally, however, the Dutch courts take a more narrow-minded position. See Kokkini-Iatridou & Verheul at 191 (nonrecognition of Canadian judgment by Dutch intermediate appellate court).

137. See Kokkini-Iatridou & Verheul at 191, 195 (recognition of Liechtenstein judgment that was arguably premised on an exorbitant jurisdictional basis). See also id. at 194 ("jurisdiction in the international sense").

138. Bogdan at 85. Pertinent statutes and treaties are rare. See id. at 85-86.

139. Id. at 86-87.

140. Id. at 86.

141. Id. at 87.

In contrast to the Swedish courts, those of Finland take the rule that (absent a treaty or statute) foreign judgments are not recognized quite seriously.[142] In that country, a retrial can apparently be avoided only if the foreign action was brought pursuant to a forum-selection clause or if it concerned foreign immovables.[143] One cannot but agree with the Finnish national reporter who characterizes this approach to recognition as "clearly too restrictive."[144]

The experience of these three countries shows that the logical consequence of insisting on juridical sovereignty—i.e., the total disregard of foreign judgments—is bound to prove unsatisfactory. A draconian policy that necessitates the retrial of issues already adjudicated, especially in cases that have little or no connection with the recognition forum, rubs with practical exigencies and offends common sense. It also prompts exorbitant assertions of jurisdiction, which are necessary lest the judgment creditor is left without a remedy.[145] In the long run, considerations of expediency and justice must clash with the unreasoning insistence on domestic prerogatives. As the Dutch example demonstrates, even explicit statutory provisions may have to yield to the realization that it is unseemly to reopen disputes decided by a competent court, domestic or foreign.

B. *Révision au fond*

Révision au fond is a less offensive way of asserting the forum's juridical prerogative than outright nonrecognition. While it leaves courts free to review the foreign tribunal's findings of fact and conclusions of law, they may choose instead to honor the foreign judgment as it stands. In France, where this practice originated, the courts took the position that their discretion was limited to either granting an *exequatur*, which effectively converts the foreign adjudication into a domestic judgment, or refusing enforcement. They did not, however, feel entitled to alter the foreign decision, and would rarely retry a case that had been decided abroad without good reasons.[146]

Although it can work reasonably well in practice, *révision au fond* is not a satisfactory approach. French writers criticized it[147] and lower courts occasionally rebelled against the principle that the *Cour de cassation* had introduced.[148] Long before 1964, when the

142. Möller at 1, 2.
143. Id. at 1.
144. Id. at 4. For a similar conclusion, as regards Swedish law, see Bogdan at 87 ("far too negative").
145. See Bogdan at 87.
146. Gaudemet-Tallon at 497.
147. See id.; Weiss, supra n. 16 at 828-29.
148. See Weiss, supra n. 16 at 829 n. 1; Gaudemet-Tallon at 497-98.

Munzer case finally abolished that impediment,[149] its deficiencies had become abundantly clear. An early nineteenth century case cogently illustrates the untoward results of disregarding foreign judgments. In *Holker v. Parker*,[150] the general partner of a failed American venture absconded to France after accumulating large debts in the United States. Holker, one of his partners, sued him. After protracted litigation, which had reached the U.S. Supreme Court,[151] a federal court in Massachusetts entered judgment against Parker. The attempt to enforce it in France proved nugatory when the *Cour de cassation*, invoking "the French government's right of sovereignty," refused to give it conclusive effect. Thus the hapless judgment creditor was forced to proceed *de novo* in the French courts, far from the situs of the controversy.

Whatever considerations may support the principle of *révision au fond*, expedition and fairness are not among them. Moreover, the practice invites retaliation.[152] In *Hilton v. Guyot*, the U.S. Supreme Court declined to recognize a French judgment which a French firm had recovered against an American partnership, citing the French decision in *Holker v. Parker*.[153] Considering its obvious defects, it is not surprising that, as the national reports show, most legal systems do not permit a *révision au fond*. The practice has become a historical relic, and it appears unlikely that a modern court or legislature would adopt it.[154]

C. Protection of Nationals

Holker v. Parker was an odd decision, considering that both parties were American and their dealings centered in the United States. In fact, the *Cour de cassation* cited article 121 of the *Code Michaut*, which expressly authorized the recognition of judgments against aliens,[155] but it read the pertinent post-revolutionary legislation to imply that foreign judgments are reviewable irrespective of the parties' nationality. Some ten years later, however, the court chose to revive the idea that citizenship does matter. It construed articles 14 and 15 of the Civil Code not merely to grant citizens the privilege of

149. See supra n. 18 and accompanying text.

150. Decision of 19 Apr. 1819, Cass. civ., 1819 S. Jur. I 288.

151. See Holker v. Parker, 11 U.S. (7 Cranch) 436 (1813).

152. See supra n. 20 and accompanying text.

153. Hilton v. Guyot, 159 U.S. 113, 217 (1895).

154. But see Sharpe at 658 n. 65, 659-61 (Manitoba statute authorizing review of foreign country judgments as well as judgments rendered in other Canadian provinces).

While *révision au fond* seems completely out of place in a federal system, in Quebec it is available not only with respect to foreign country judgments but also, in certain limited circumstances, as against Canadian judgments. Talpis & Goldstein at 27, 141, 165.

155. See supra n. 16 and accompanying text.

suing and defending in French courts, but also to protect them against foreign judgments. By claiming exclusive jurisdiction over suits involving French parties,[156] the *Cour de cassation* added to the sword of jurisdictional exorbitance a shield for recalcitrant French judgment debtors.[157]

Other countries, too, discriminate against aliens. The reciprocity rule[158] which the U.S. Supreme Court adopted in *Hilton v. Guyot* was limited to nationals of countries that fail to honor American judgments and only applied to judgments they had obtained against Americans.[159] The Czechoslovakian reciprocity requirement likewise distinguishes between domestic and foreign judgment creditors.[160] Japan bars recognition of a default judgment based on defective service only if the losing party is a Japanese national.[161] Differential treatment based on a party's domicile, rather than nationality, also tends to favor citizens. Thus, the jurisdictional privilege which the Swiss Constitution accords domiciliaries helps protect Swiss judgment debtors.[162]

Dissatisfaction with such favoritism seems to be growing. In France, for example, courts are increasingly inclined to find a waiver of the jurisdictional privileges conferred by articles 14 and 15 of the Civil Code.[163] In West Germany, the recent amendment of section 328, par. 1, No. 2, of the Civil Procedure Code[164] abolished the review of a foreign court's choice-of-law determinations affecting the status of German nationals.[165] The same amendment repealed a provision according to which only citizens could raise the defense of lack of due notice.[166] While that rule still prevails in Japan (which had copied it from Germany), it seems that Japanese courts will permit alien judgment debtors who were not duly notified of the foreign proceeding to invoke the public policy reservation.[167] In the United States, case law and legislation, most notably the Uniform

156. See supra n. 78 and accompanying text.

157. See decision of 17 March 1830, 1830 S. Jur. I 95; Gaudemet-Tallon at 490-91.

158. According to *Hilton v. Guyot*, reciprocity is not required for the recognition of *in rem* or *quasi in rem* judgments and status adjudications. It only applies to executory money judgments, i.e., those that have not already been discharged by payment or otherwise. See 159 U.S. at 167-68.

159. Reciprocity is not required for judgments between foreign citizens or those in favor of an American judgment creditor. Id. at 170.

160. See Steiner at 126.

161. Takakuwa at 14.

162. See Dubler at 13.

163. Martiny, supra n. 27 at 255-57, 301-02.

164. See Gesetz zur Neuregelung des Internationalen Privatrechts of July 25, 1986, art. 4, par. 1, 1986 BGBl I 1142 (English translation in 17 *Ga. J. Intl. & Comp. L.* 237-59 (1987)).

165. See Martiny at 743.

166. See id. at 741.

167. See Takakuwa at 15.

Foreign Money-Judgments Recognition Act, have largely eliminated the reciprocity rule laid down in *Hilton v. Guyot* together with its discriminatory features.[168]

D. Reciprocity

Reciprocity, a more finely calibrated device to vindicate sovereign concerns, is less offensive to one's sense of justice than an across-the-board disregard of foreign judgments or the discriminatory treatment of aliens. Ostensibly, this requirement pays tribute to the idea that states should act *ex comitate ob reciprocam utilitate.*[169] Certainly, using sovereignty as a bargaining chip seems preferable to invoking it as an absolute barrier to recognition. Perhaps for this reason, reciprocity has proved more durable than *révision au fond.*[170]

The manner in which courts and legislatures employ this requirement varies.[171] It can be applied broadly to all foreign decisions—including, e.g., status matters—or it can be restricted to executory money judgments. Some legal systems deny efficacy to any judgment rendered in a state that disregards the forum's decisions,[172] others retaliate against judgment creditors who are nationals of the offending state.[173] Reciprocity, usually a precondition to recognition, can also play a role in the context of enforcement.[174] Nor is there any consensus on what reciprocity really means and how it should be established.[175] To be sure, an official declaration by the foreign state or a showing that it does in fact honor forum

168. See Joiner at 212-14.

169. But see Hilton v. Guyot, 159 U.S. 113, 234 (1895) (Fuller, J., dissenting) ("retorsion").

170. Almost half of the legal systems for which national reports were submitted adhere to the reciprocity requirement. See Dubler at 51 (Swiss cantons); Filipescu at 3, 9, 37 (Romania); Martiny at 749 (Federal Republic of Germany); Özsunay at 5-7, 13-14 (Turkey); Rouvier at 5-6 (Venezuela); Shapira at 142 (Israel); Steiner at 112, 125-26 (Czechoslovakia); Strohbach at 51, 54 (German Democratic Republic); Takakuwa at 17-18 (Japan); Tomaszewski at 109-10 (Poland, which, even if reciprocity is assured, does not enforce foreign judgments absent a treaty).

171. See Lagarde, "La réciprocité en droit international privé," 154 *Rec. des Cours* 103, 141-45 (1977-I). On the evolution of the reciprocity doctrine, see Lenhoff, "Reciprocity and the Law of Foreign Judgments—Critical Analysis," 16 *La. L. Rev.* 465 (1956).

172. See, e.g., Filipescu at 37 (Romania); Rouvier at 6 (Venezuela).

173. See Hilton v. Guyot, 159 U.S. 113 (1895) (foreign judgment creditors; American judgment debtor); Steiner at 126 (reciprocity required only if judgment was rendered against Czechoslovakian party).

174. See Özsunay at 6, 14 (Turkey). Pursuant to the Foreign Judgments (Reciprocal Enforcement) Act 1933 and kindred legislation in other Commonwealth countries, reciprocity entitles a foreign judgment to preferential enforcement by means of registration.

175. Statutes that establish this requirement usually do not define it. See, e.g., Martiny at 750; Shapira at 142.

judgments is usually not required; "de facto recognition"—i.e., some assurance that the rendition state can be expected to recognize forum judgments—will suffice.[176] But who should be required to make such a showing? Rumania puts the onus on the party who raises the issue (i.e., presumably the judgment creditor[177]), while most legal systems do not purport to allocate the burden to one side or the other.[178] Some nations provide for binding decisions by a governmental agency,[179] but whether bureaucracies are better able to make the necessary findings of foreign law, which may well exceed even the judiciary's competence and resources,[180] is another question.

The rigors and complexities of this requirement can be alleviated in a number of ways. Solomonically, the Venezuelan Supreme Court has held that reciprocity is deemed to exist as long as the rendition forum does not review the merits of Venezuelan judgments, and that a certificate signed by two attorneys practicing in the foreign jurisdiction suffices to establish that fact.[181] In Israel, the Attorney General is empowered to request enforcement of a judgment from a state that fails to accord reciprocity.[182] Poland does not require reciprocity in cases involving the inheritance by Polish domiciliaries of assets situated in the rendition state, or if the foreign court had exclusive jurisdiction pursuant to Polish law.[183]

Reciprocity has the purpose of inducing other nations to improve their recognition practices. But even if the specter of retaliation should in fact serve to liberalize judgments recognition, that end hardly justifies the means.[184] It seems unfair to penalize private litigants—who are neither to blame nor in a position to change matters—for the rendition state's lack of comity. This is true especially if the judgment creditor is a national of the recognition state. Nonetheless, some legal systems use "blind" reciprocity requirements[185] that fail to distinguish between alien and domestic judgment credi-

176. See, e.g., Filipescu at 37; Özsunay at 13-14.

177. See Filipescu at 37.

178. See, e.g., Strohbach at 55 (German Democratic Republic); Takakuwa at 18 (Japan).

179. See Filipescu at 37 (Romania); Steiner at 26-27 (Czechoslovakia); Strohbach at 54-55 (German Democratic Republic); Tomaszewski at 111 (Poland).

180. [T]here is often confusion about the actual state of the law; the statements on foreign law are sometimes incorrect, changes in foreign legislation remain unknown and many lists of countries are outdated.

Martiny at 752. See also Takakuwa at 27.

181. See Rouvier at 10-11, 16, 18.

182. Shapira at 142. Some Swiss cantons leave it up to the judge's discretion whether to recognize judgments from a foreign country that fails to honor Swiss judgments. Dubler at 51.

183. See Tomaszewski at 110.

184. See, e.g., Lagarde, supra n. 171 at 146-47; Martiny at 749.

185. Lagarde, supra n. 171 at 142.

tors, and thus punish their own citizens for the defects of foreign law. Effectively to nullify a judgment won abroad seems particularly irrational if a forum-selection clause required the domestic party to sue abroad, or if the foreign court had exclusive jurisdiction by the recognition forum's standards.

The limited reciprocity rule which the U.S. Supreme Court adopted in *Hilton v. Guyot* avoids such absurd results. That rule, however, heaps discrimination upon an already questionable practice. As the dissent in *Hilton* noted,[186] it seems wrong on principle to cast courts of law in the role of instruments of retaliation. Moreover, reciprocity is at odds with fundamental procedural objectives, i.e., the just, speedy and inexpensive determination of disputes. It neither guarantees the intrinsic quality of those judgments that are recognized, nor does it assure a better decision in cases that must be relitigated. Courts and counsel are forced to waste time and money on divining the attitude of foreign legal systems toward the forum's judgments. Because such forays into alien legal systems will often yield inconclusive results, uncertainty is yet another cost imposed by this dysfunctional requirement.

Today, reciprocity no longer enjoys the popularity it did in the nationalistic nineteenth century. Increasingly, courts and legislatures reject this impediment. In the United States, for example, the rule in *Hilton v. Guyot*, which has been condemned by legal writers,[187] is becoming obsolete. Although one would expect a federal system to speak with one voice in matters of international import,[188] disenchantment with the Supreme Court's ruling in that case has prompted state courts and legislatures to abolish reciprocity on their own.[189] The Uniform Foreign Money-Judgments Recognition Act, which has been adopted by a number of important states, omits that requirement.[190] Even where reciprocity persists, courts find ways to ameliorate it. West Germany's *Bundesgerichtshof*, for instance, has retreated from the former *Reichsgericht*'s extreme insistence on a showing that identical recognition practices prevail abroad.[191] Over the years, the Federal Republic's highest court in civil matters has liberalized the recognition of foreign judgments in sundry ways,[192]

186. 159 U.S. at 234.

187. Joiner at 212.

188. See Leflar, McDougal & Felix, *American Conflicts Law* 253 (4th ed. 1986).

189. Joiner at 212-13. Conversely, the Swiss draft Act on Private International Law, which abolishes reciprocity, would preempt the law of those cantons that have retained the requirement. See Dubler at 51.

190. Id. at 21. Some states, however, have incorporated a reciprocity requirement into their version of the Uniform Act. Joiner at 200 n. 36, 213.

191. See Nadelmann, supra n. 14 at 252-54.

192. See Martiny at 750-51. In spite of strong criticism by legal writers, the recent West German conflicts statute has retained the reciprocity requirement. See Martiny at 749-50.

and a similar trend is discernible in the case law of other nations.[193]

E. Control of Choice of Law

A minority of legal systems provide for some form of review of the rendition court's choice-of-law determination.[194] Apparently, the adoption of this impediment was prompted by the desire to prevent evasive divorces in haven jurisdictions.[195] That objective has, of course, become an anachronism. Most nations now have fairly liberal divorce laws so that, as a practical matter, evasion no longer plays the role it once did. Nonetheless, the practice of looking at the law the foreign court applied lingers on in some legal systems, not only in status matters but even with respect to money judgments.[196]

On principle, the review of the foreign court's choice-of-law decision, which amounts to a limited *révision au fond*,[197] has little to commend it.[198] While the recent Turkish conflicts statute adopted this impediment as regards judgments that affect the status of Turkish citizens,[199] it is losing ground elsewhere.[200] Obviously, it is presumptuous for a legal system to dictate its choice-of-law rules and approaches to the world, especially at a time when the conflict of laws is very much in flux. Also, if a foreign court's choice of law should be so grossly erroneous or capricious as to amount to a miscarriage of justice, the public policy reservation offers a sufficient remedy.[201]

193. See Filipescu at 37 (Rumania); Steiner at 126 (Czechoslovakia); Strohbach at 54 (German Democratic Republic); supra n. 181-83 and accompanying text.

194. See Azcuna at 8 (failure to apply the law invoked by Philippine choice-of-law rules potentially violates public policy); Filipescu at 39-40 ("mandatory" Rumanian choice-of-law rules); Gaudemet-Tallon at 492 (France); Tomaszewski at 114 (if, according to Polish conflicts rules, Polish substantive law applies); cf. Talpis & Goldstein at 137-40 (Quebec) (minority view). The misapplication of Japanese law by a foreign court arguably violates Japanese public policy. See Takakuwa at 16. While the Swiss cantons do not provide for a review of the foreign court's choice-of-law decision, some Swiss recognition treaties do. Dubler at 43.

195. In Turkey choice-of-law control is limited to matters affecting the status of nationals. See Özsunay at 6-7, 13, 14; cf. Brussels Convention art. 27, par. 4. It has been argued that the same limitation should apply in France. See Gaudemet-Tallon at 492. See also Filipescu at 39 (status and capacity of Romanian citizens; Romanian immovables).

196. See Tomaszewski at 114. For a peculiar constitutional provision, which could be interpreted to deprive foreign courts of the power to apply Argentine federal law, see Grigera Naón at 58-60.

197. Shapira at 147-48.

198. But see Grigera Naón at 71.

199. See Özsunay at 6-7, 13, 14.

200. The new West German conflicts statute has repealed this impediment. See Martiny at 743. For escape devices used by French courts see Gaudemet-Tallon at 492-93 ("substantial equivalence" and *renvoi*).

201. Azcuna at 8.

F. Protective Legislation

145 years ago, Wächter argued that a foreign judgment should not be recognized if it conflicts with the recognition forum's "mandatory" legislation.[202] The notion that there exists a peculiar class of statutes which is immune to normal conflicts rules has also surfaced in the choice-of-law context. It appears in Savigny's treatise,[203] as well as in the work of various other European authors, notably Mancini[204] and Pillet.[205] This same idea has recently been revived under the name of "laws of immediate application,"[206] or "*lois de police*," i.e., rules of decision that determine—expressly or by implication—the sphere in which they claim effect. Although it is unclear what statutes belong to this category, those that arguably do are imbued with some important societal policy; in Francescakis' words, they are laws which "safeguard the political, social or economic organization of the state."[207]

Several of the national reports allude to these peculiar laws,[208] and the Argentine reporter mentions among the impediments to recognition the foreign court's noncompliance with the recognition forum's *lois de police*.[209] This proposition raises a number of problems. First of all, the category of laws of immediate application is ill-defined. Depending on whether the criterion suggested by Francescakis is interpreted broadly[210] or narrowly, it encompasses a

202. Wächter, "Über die Collision der Privatrechtsgesetze verschiedener Staaten" (pt. 4), 25 *Archiv für die civilistische Praxis* 361, 419 (1842). Similarly, David Dudley Field's draft of an international code provided for the nonrecognition of foreign judgments that conflict with "express provisions" of the recognition forum's law. See Field, *Outlines of an International Code* art. 669 (2d ed. 1876).

203. See 8 F. von Savigny, *System des heutigen Römischen Rechts* 32-37 (1849).

204. See Mancini, "De l'utilité de rendre obligatoires pour tous les Etats, sous la forme d'un ou plusiers traités internationaux, un certain nombre de règles générales du Droit international privé pour assurer la décision uniforme des conflits entre les différents législations civiles et criminelles (pt. 2)," 1 *Journal de droit international* 285, 296-97 (1874).

205. See Pillet, *Principes de droit international privé* 290-99; 371-425 (1903).

206. See generally Francescakis, "Quelques précisions sur les'lois d'application immédiate'et leurs rapports avec les règles de conflits de lois," 55 *Rev. crit. d.i.p.* 1 (1966).

207. Francescakis, "Conflits de lois (principes généraux)," in 1 *Répertoire de droit international* 470, 480 (1968).

208. See Azcuna at 7 (reference to "prohibitive laws" in Philippine Civil Code); Martiny at 747 ("internal mandatory rules"); Steiner at 113 ("directly regulating substantial rules"); Talpis & Goldstein at 102-03 ("*lois d'application nécessaire du for*").

209. Grigera Naón at 63-64, 72. Grigera Naón further maintains that Argentine courts have exclusive jurisdiction to apply such "*lois de police*." Id. at 63-64.

210. As potential sources for rules of this nature Grigera Naón at 63-64 lists statutes dealing with foreign investment, banking and financing, consumer protection, antitrust, promotion of industry, exchange controls and certain aspects of company law. Although only a few rules contained in each of these statutes may qualify as "mandatory," the range of pertinent legislation would open a wide field for judg-

large number or only very few statutes.[211] For practical purposes, it is impossible to know which particular statutes qualify until the recognition forum's highest court authoritatively determines the question. Thus, this impediment introduces an element of considerable uncertainty and delay into recognition practice. Moreover, one may question the propriety of transposing a concept developed in the choice-of-law context to that of judgments.[212]

If it is true that the notion of laws of immediate application serves the purpose of protecting important substantive values, which traditional multilateral choice-of-law rules all too often fail to safeguard,[213] that concept seems out of place in the field of recognition. In that context justice is usually best served by the free movement of judgments. If, on the other hand, a foreign adjudication is in fact unfair, the public policy reservation is ample enough to prevent a possible perpetuation of iniquities by the recognition state.[214] At best, as is true of public policy,[215] in judgments recognition the *lois de police* should have but an "attenuated effect." The contention that a foreign decision conflicts with a local statute that arguably claims immediate application would furnish judgment debtors with all too handy a pretext for delaying or frustrating execution.

G. *Judgments from Substandard Legal Systems*

Section 4(a)(1) of the Uniform Foreign Money-Judgments Recognition Act states that a foreign judgment need not be recognized if it

> was rendered under a system which does not provide impartial tribunals or procedures compatible with the requirements of due process of law.

This rule can be traced to a dictum in *Hilton v. Guyot*,[216] which refers to foreign proceedings "according to the course of civilized juris-

---

ment debtors to search for provisions that arguably deprive the foreign judgment of its binding effect.

211. The term would clearly encompass constitutional rules, especially those that protect fundamental rights. See Grigera Naón at 58. See also Martiny at 724 (explicit reference to constitutional rights in the new West German conflicts statute); Steiner at 122-23 (incorporation of constitutional tenets into the Czechoslovakian public policy provision).

212. But cf. art. 17, par. 3, of the Philippine Civil Code, quoted in Azcuna at 7, which explicitly provides that "prohibitive laws" shall "not be rendered ineffective by *laws or judgments* promulgated . . . in a foreign country" [emphasis added].

213. See Juenger, "General Course on Private International Law," 193 *Recueil des Cours* 205-06, 253-54, 277-79, 283 (1985-IV).

214. Cf. Grigera Naón at 58, 70; Martiny at 747. But see 1 Geimer & Schütze, supra n. 50 at 1583-88.

215. See supra n. 101 and accompanying text.

216. See Uniform Foreign Money-Judgments Recognition Act § 4, Commissioners' comment.

prudence."[217] The provision of the Uniform Act has a counterpart in section 4(c) of the International Law Association's Model Act,[218] which provides for the nonrecognition of judgments that violate "natural justice" because they were "not rendered by an impartial tribunal or under a procedural system compatible with the requirements of due process."

This impediment is expendable. It does not appear in the laws of any legal system, other than the United States, for which a national report has been submitted. No reported American cases have denied recognition on this ground, and a court will rarely reach the conclusion that the administration of justice in a given country falls so far short of commonly accepted standards that all judgments emanating from it must be deemed tainted.[219] Such a wholesale condemnation of another legal system is as unusual as it is unnecessary. If a foreign state should in fact fail to provide adequate procedural safeguards, the public policy reservation suffices to block the enforcement of any judgment that is the product of irregular proceedings.

V. Conclusions

A glance at the list of possible obstacles to judgments recognition suggests that it is by far too long. The fact that few legal systems require a judgment debtor to jump all of these hurdles suggests that some of these impediments simply serve no useful purpose. Most of the prerequisites and defenses enumerated in Part IV of this report are but historical relics rooted in outdated notions of sovereignty. Their preservation is largely due to inertia rather than a rational assessment of the needs of international commerce. In practice, these impediments complicate the administration of justice, deny a remedy for a judicially established right, and encourage judgment debtors to shirk their obligations.

In contrast, the national reports demonstrate a broad consensus on the need for the prerequisites and defenses listed in Part III, which are concerned less with sovereignty than with practicability and fairness. Sound as these impediments are in principle, however, some refinements seem desirable. For instance, while it appears reasonable to scrutinize the rendition forum's jurisdiction,[220] the wisdom of measuring jurisdictional propriety by recourse to the rec-

217. 159 U.S. at 205.

218. International Law Association, Model Act Respecting the Recognition and Enforcement of Foreign Money-Judgments, Report of the Fifty-First (Tokyo) Conference xxii (1964).

219. But cf. Islamic Republic of Iran v. Pahlavi, 94 A.D.2d 374, 464 N.Y.S.2d 487 (1983), aff'd, 62 N.Y.2d 474, 467 N.E.2d 245, 478 N.Y.S.2d 597 (1984).

220. But see supra n. 43 and accompanying text (South Australia).

ognition forum's internal standards is questionable. Similarly, it makes little sense to review the rendition court's competence or venue. Such an inquiry forces the recognition court to wrestle, for no good reason, with intricate points of foreign procedure.

Today, the potential for a consensus on recognition rules that are responsive to international exigencies is within reach. The notion of sovereignty no longer casts the spell it once did, and an ever-increasing flow of multinational transactions calls for workable solutions to problems that, by their very nature, cannot be confined to a particular territory. Trends in domestic laws and treaty practice, as well as the standards set by federal and quasi-federal systems, make it possible to discern the outlines of emerging international norms.

To be sure, the New York Court of Appeals' dated dictum that American judges should not accord greater respect to foreign country judgments than to those of a sister state[221] is still echoed abroad seventy years later.[222] But one may question why a New York court should ever have given greater credit to an Alabama than an Ontario decree, or why a French court ought to prefer Italian to Swiss judgments. In fact, it appears that the experience gained within a system that exacts mutual deference enhances the regard for all foreign adjudications. Thus the routine enforcement of judgments required by the Brussels Convention helps explain the recent evolution of recognition practices in France and the Netherlands. These two European countries have advanced from a narrow, ethnocentric position to one of considerable liberality toward judgments rendered outside the Common Market,[223] just as in the United States the experience gathered under the full faith and credit clause provided a model for comity recognition.

If the law on judgments recognition needs further improvement it is not for lack of comparative information or insight. Rather, apart from sheer inertia, the two principal obstacles to law reform may be the peculiar nature of this field and an erroneous perception of the recognition state's best interests. As to the first, the subject matter is situated in a no-man's land between the conflict of laws and civil procedure. That unfortunate location may inhibit analysis; witness the fact that as sophisticated a legal system as the French has only recently begun to come to grips with the fundamental distinction between recognition and enforcement[224] and that French legal terminology still lacks an expression for the concept of "money

221. Grubel v. Nassauer, 210 N.Y. 149, 150, 103 N.E. 1113, 1114 (1913).

222. According to Gaudemet-Tallon at 509, it "is obviously impossible to extend to all foreign judgments the very liberal scheme of the Brussels Convention."

223. See Kokkini-Iatridou & Verheul at 190-91; cf. Gaudemet-Tallon at 509.

224. See Gaudemet-Tallon at 487-88, 496, 498-502, 507-09.

judgment."[225] The second obstacle is rooted in the dubious notion that inhibiting recognition will somehow profit local judgment debtors and, indirectly, the recognition state. But, as Weiss wrote—almost a century ago—the then prevailing French practice of *révision au fond* was

> quite prejudicial to the Frenchman, by putting foreigners on guard against him, ruining his credit with them, sometimes even provoking retaliatory measures by foreign courts.[226]

225. See id. at 488.
226. Weiss, supra n. 16 at 829.

[10]

TREVOR C. HARTLEY

Comity and the Use of Antisuit Injunctions in International Litigation

Injunctions requiring a party not to commence, or not to continue, proceedings in a foreign court, or to discontinue them (henceforth "antisuit injunctions") are coming to play an increasingly important role in international litigation. They are also giving rise to increasing friction between courts in different countries: recently a district court judge accused an English court of interfering in an American lawsuit "without appropriate regard to principles of comity" when it issued an antisuit injunction to prevent a British company from pursuing an antitrust action in the United States.[1] The purpose of this paper is to examine the use of such injunctions and to consider whether they involve a breach of comity or a threat to good relations with foreign countries.

The nature of the problem is apparent from the *Laker Airways*[2] case. Laker Airways, a small British airline hitherto restricted to charter operations, tried to break into the North Atlantic air transportation market by undercutting the established airlines. At first it succeeded, carrying one in seven of all transatlantic passengers at the high-point of its operations. But then things began to go wrong, and it was eventually forced into liquidation when a re-financing deal fell through at the last moment. In 1982 Laker Airways (now

---

TREVOR C. HARTLEY is Reader in Law, London School of Economics. This article owes its origin to talks given at the Boalt School of Law of the University of California, Berkeley, the Institute of Advanced Legal Studies, London, and a meeting of the British Branch of the International Law Association. I have benefited from research assistance from Peter J.C. Young and Katherine M. Jones, both graduates of the University of Michigan Law School, and Joseph P. Horn, a graduate of the University of Texas. I have received advice from Lawrence Collins, Sir Jack Jacob, Professor David W. Robertson and Professor Michael Zander.

1. Laker Airways v. Pan Am World Airways 559 F. Supp. 1124, 1138 (D.D.C. 1983), aff'd, 731 F.2d 909 (D.C. Cir. 1984).

2. This case was litigated on both sides of the Atlantic. England: British Airways Bd. v. Laker Airways [1985] A.C. 58, reversing [1984] Q.B. 169 (C.A.), reversing [1984] Q.B. 142. America: Laker Airways v. Sabena, Belgian World Airlines, 731 F.2d 909 (D.C. Cir. 1984); Laker Airways v. Pan Am. World Airways, 596 F. Supp. 202 (D.D.C. 1984); Laker Airways v. Pan Am. World Airways, 577 F. Supp. 348 (D.D.C. 1983); Laker Airways v. Pan Am. World Airways, 568 F. Supp. 811 (D.D.C. 1983); Laker Airways v. Pan Am. World Airways, 568 F. Supp. 811 (D.D.C. 1983); Laker Airways v. Pan Am. World Airways, 559 F. Supp. 1124 (D.D.C. 1983) aff'd 731 F.2d 909 (D.C. Cir. 1984).

in liquidation) brought antitrust suits against a number of airlines which fly the Atlantic route, as well as against Laker's aircraft supplier, McDonnell Douglas, and the latter's financial affiliate, McDonnell Douglas Finance Corporation. The airlines included American, British and Continental European operators. In essence, the allegations were two-fold: first, that the airlines had engaged in predatory pricing to drive Laker out of business and, secondly, that they pressured McDonnell Douglas and Laker's bank, Midland Bank, to withdraw from the planned financial rescue operation. The action was filed in the Federal District Court in Washington D.C. and treble damages of over $1 billion were claimed.

The first response came from the Midland Bank, which was not yet a party to the action. It applied for, and obtained, an antisuit injunction in the English High Court, preventing Laker from adding it to the American proceedings.

Perhaps this gave the airlines the idea. In any event some of the airlines, led by British Airways, then applied in the English High Court, first, for a declaration that they had not engaged in any unlawful conspiracy; secondly, for an antisuit injunction to stop the American proceedings against them; and, thirdly, for an injunction precluding Laker from obtaining an antisuit injunction in the United States to block the English proceedings. This last remedy was something of an innovation, but it is the obvious answer to an imminent antisuit injunction. Henceforth it will be called a "counter-antisuit injunction". Laker then hastily applied to the American court and obtained a counter-antisuit injunction to preclude the remaining defendants from obtaining antisuit injunctions or counter-antisuit injunctions in England.[3] At this time the injunctions on both sides of the Atlantic were on a temporary basis only. In May 1983 the application by British Airways for a permanent injunction was heard. This was dismissed by the High Court,[4] granted by the Court of Appeal[5] (after the British Secretary of State for Trade and Industry had issued an order under the British "blocking statute"[6] prohibiting the handing over of documents or information to the United States authorities) and finally rescinded by the House of Lords.[7]

In the United States, meanwhile, the counter-antisuit injunctions were upheld on appeal[8] and some thought was given to what should be done if the English courts definitively confirmed their an-

3. See 559 F. Supp. 1124 (D.D.C. 1983).
4. See [1984] Q.B. 142.
5. See [1984] Q.B. 169.
6. The Protection of Trading Interests Act 1980.
7. See [1985] A.C. 58.
8. See 731 F.2d 909 (D.C. Cir. 1984).

tisuit injunctions.[9] The possibility was mooted of appointing a trustee or receiver to continue the action on Laker's behalf. Such a person, being outside the jurisdiction of the English courts, would be immune from antisuit injunctions. This, of course, proved unnecessary in the end. However, the Midland Bank, whose antisuit injunction was lifted after the House of Lords decision, succeeded in getting it re-imposed by the English Court of Appeal in July 1985.[10] The reasons for this will be explained later.[11] The effect of the lifting of the antisuit injunctions against the defendants in the United States action[12] was to make it possible for that suit to go ahead. The airlines then moved quickly to settle:[13] the injunction battle had proved decisive.

A similar battle could well take place again and the outcome would depend both on the facts—the House of Lords lifted the antisuit injunctions only because they decided that in the circumstances the American action did not involve the extraterritorial application of United States law—and on the speed of action of the lawyers involved. The final result might well depend on which court was the first to grant an injunction.

History

The origins of antisuit injunctions lie in England and are closely linked to the rise of equity and its struggle with the courts of common law. The prototype of the modern antisuit injunction was the so-called "common injunction". Developed in the fifteenth century, this remedy was granted by the Chancellor to stop a party bringing an action in the courts of common law in situations in which this was considered to be against good conscience. Unlike the common-law writ of prohibition, the equitable injunction was not directed against the court but against the plaintiff personally. From the beginning, however, these injunctions caused conflict with the common law courts. This discord was a portent of things to come.[14]

Once the Court of Chancery had established its power to issue

9. See 577 F. Supp. 348 (D.D.C. 1983), where an amicus curiae was appointed. For the report of the amicus curiae, see 23 *Int'l Leg. Mat.* 594 (1984).

10. See [1986] 1 All E.R. 526 (C.A.).

11. See infra text at 495.

12. The Midland Bank was never made a defendant.

13. The terms being considered, though not yet fully public, are far below the $1 billion asked. It is also of interest that, shortly before a visit from Mrs. Thatcher, President Reagan announced that a grand jury investigation of the affair would be terminated for foreign policy reasons.

14. The "common injunction" was abolished by sec. 24(5) of the Judicature Act of 1873 and now no injunction will issue to restrain actions in other Divisions of the English High Court. The power still appears to exist with regard to proceedings in other courts in England, but in practice it is used only with regard to foreign courts.

antisuit injunctions against other English courts, it was only a small extension of this power to start issuing them against foreign courts. The first step was to grant injunctions to stop proceedings in Scotland, Ireland, and the British colonies;[15] then it was an easy matter to issue them with regard to proceedings in foreign countries.[16] Today the power to grant antisuit injunctions is established beyond doubt. The question is simply one of determining when it should be used.

PRESENT-DAY ENGLISH LAW

In the *Laker* case, Lord Diplock drew a sharp distinction between the normal grounds for granting an antisuit injunction, applicable where there are two or more potential forums (one of which is England), and the special grounds, which can apply even if the foreign country is the only possible forum where the action can be heard.

Normal Grounds for Granting an Injunction

The general principles governing antisuit injunctions in England have undergone several changes recently. To understand these, it is necessary to know something about the parallel development of the doctrine of *forum non conveniens*, since the same principles were, for a time, applicable to both.

Though originating in Scotland,[17] *forum non conveniens* was accepted in England only recently. Prior to 1974, it was generally accepted that the dismissal or, more usually, the stay of English proceedings could be obtained only on grounds of vexation or op-

15. See, e.g., Lord Portarlington v. Soulby (1834) 3 My & K. 104, 40 Eng. Rep. 40. Lord Portarlington lost £1,000 gambling and gave a bill of exchange for this sum. The bill of exchange came into the hands of Soulby, who evidently knew of its origin. Soulby sued in Ireland and Lord Portarlington successfully obtained an antisuit injunction in England. The fact that Ireland had its own courts of equity, which could have issued the injunction, was regarded as immaterial. For earlier cases, see Wharton v. May (1799) 5 Ves. 71, 31 Eng. Rep. 454; Kennedy v. Earl of Cassilis (1818) 2 Swans. 313, 36 Eng. Rep. 635; Bushby v. Munday (1821) 5 Madd. 297, 56 Eng. Rep. 908; Hanison v. Gurney (1821) 5 Jac. & W. 563, 37 Eng. Rep. 743; Beauchamp v. Marquis of Huntley (1822) Jac. 546, 37 Eng. Rep. 956; Beckford v. Kemble (1822) 1 Sim. & St. 7, 57 Eng. Rep. 3; Booth v. Leycester (1837) 1 Keen 579, 48 Eng. Rep. 430; Bunbury v. Bunbury (1839) 1 Beav. 38, 48 Eng. Rep. 963; The Carron Iron Co. v. Maclaren (1855) 5 H.L.C. 416 and the unreported case of Campbell v. Houlditch (1820), referred to in Lord Portarlington v. Soulby at p.107. An injunction concerning proceedings in Italy was refused in Love v. Baker (1665) 1 Ch.Ca. 67, 22 Eng. Rep. 698.

16. See e.g. Hope v. Carnegie (1866) 1 Ch.App. 320; Armstrong v. Armstrong [1892] P.98; Moore v. Moore (1896) 12 T.L.R. 221; Pena Copper Mines v. Rio Tinto Co. [1911-1913] All E.R. Reprint 209 (C.A.).

17. See Sim v. Robinow 19 R. (Ct. of Sess.) 665 at 668 (1892); see further Braucher, "The Inconvenient Federal Forum," 60 *Harv. L. Rev.* 908 at 909-910 (1947).

pression. In *The Atlantic Star*,[18] however, the House of Lords re-interpreted this test so as to make it less strict and in *MacShannon v. Rockware Glass Ltd.*[19] it reformulated the doctrine in terms of a two-prong test, under which the defendant had to show, first, that justice could be done in the foreign country at substantially less inconvenience and expense than in England; and, secondly,[20] that the stay would not deprive the plaintiff of a "legitimate personal or juridical advantage".

In 1981, in *Castanho v. Root & Brown*,[21] the House of Lords extended this test to antisuit injunctions. The result was that if, in a normal two-forum case, it could be established that England was the more convenient forum, an injunction would be granted, provided this would not deprive the plaintiff in the foreign court of a legitimate advantage. If, under the same test, the foreign court was the more appropriate forum, the English action would be stayed. This meant, in effect, that the English courts took upon themselves the task of deciding where the action should be heard.

It will be noticed that the *MacShannon* test was a fairly strict version of the *forum non conveniens* doctrine. The way it operated with regard to antisuit injunctions is illustrated by *Castanho*, which was a personal injury suit begun in England where the accident occurred. The defendants were two subsidiaries, one British and one Panamanian, of Jackson Marine, a Texas-incorporated company. Later, after getting an admission of liability and an interim payment, the plaintiff decided to abandon the English action and bring proceedings in Texas where he hoped to recover damages at a very much higher level. The defendants asked the English court for an antisuit injunction. This was granted by the trial judge but lifted by Court of Appeal in a decision upheld by the House of Lords. The House of Lords said that the higher damage awards in America were

18. [1974] A.C. 436.

19. [1978] A.C. 795.

20. It was not entirely clear where the burden of proof lay. The person requesting the stay or injunction had to establish that the first requirement was satisfied, but in certain situations the burden may have been on the other party to show that the stay or injunction would deprive him of a legitimate advantage: see The Atlantic Star [1974] A.C. 436, 454 (Lord Reid); MacShannon v. Rockware Glass Ltd. [1978] A.C. 795, 812 and 815 (Lord Diplock), 820 (Lord Salmon); The Abidin Daver [1984] A.C. 398, 411-412 (Lord Diplock), 416 (Lord Keith); Metall und Rohstoff A.G. v. ACLI Metals (London) Ltd. [1984] 1 Lloyd's L. Rep. 598, 602 (C.A.). This appears to be the law today: Spiliada Maritime Corp. v. Cansulex Ltd. [1986] 3 W.L.R. 972, 985-986; [1986] 3 All E.R. 843, 854-855 (H.L.). The position is, however, different where the proceedings are begun by service of a writ outside England under Order 11 of the Rules of the Supreme Court (equivalent to an American long-arm statute). In this case the plaintiff must obtain leave of court to serve the writ, and this will not be given unless he can show that England is the appropriate forum: Spiliada Maritime Corp. v. Cansulex Ltd. [1986] 3 W.L.R. 972, 987-991; [1986] 3 All E.R. 843, 856-859.

21. [1981] A.C. 557.

a legitimate advantage.[22] This is an important ruling in view of the fact that damage awards are almost invariably higher in the United States than in England, especially in personal injury and products liability cases.[23]

In 1986, however, the English doctrine of *forum non conveniens* underwent yet another change. This occurred in the decision of the House of Lords in *Spiliada Maritime Corp. v. Cansulex Ltd.*,[24] in which the *MacShannon* test was "re-interpreted" in a fairly fundamental way. The first prong now covers not only convenience but all factors relevant to determining the "natural forum", defined as the forum "with which the action has the most real and substantial connection".[25] Additional factors include the residence or place of business of the parties and the governing law. The second prong of the parties and the governing law. The second prong of the *MacShannon* test was also completely re-cast. It is no longer sufficient for the plaintiff to show that his chosen forum provides him with a legitimate advantage, since an advantage to the plaintiff must now be balanced against any corresponding disadvantage to the defendant. Instead, the second prong of the test is now concerned only with the question of substantial justice: the action may be brought in a court other than the natural forum only if justice so demands.[26] This new version of the doctrine appears to give almost complete discretion to the trial judge.

---

22. In the later case of Smith, Kline & French Laboratories v. Bloch [1983] 1 W.L.R. 730, 738 (C.A.), Lord Denning M.R. said that the prospect of higher damages was *not* a legitimate advantage. The other two members of the court held, on the basis of expert evidence (from a professor at the University of Pennsylvania Law School) that, in the circumstances of the case, damages would not be higher in the alternative forum (Pennsylvania) because a court there would apply English law to decide the measure of damages. Lord Denning also said (id.) that the American contingent-fee system was not a legitimate advantage, but in Bank of Tokyo v. Karoon, [1986] 3 W.L.R. 414, 422, [1986] 3 All E.R. 468, 477, Ackner L.J. stated that this is true only where the proceedings are vexatious; otherwise it can be a legitimate advantage. For further discussion of Smith, Kline & French Laboratories v. Bloch, see infra text at 507-08.

23. American courts have taken a different attitude to this question. Piper Aircraft Co. v. Reyno, 454 U.S. 235 (1981), concerned a similar situation to that in Castanho: a wrongful-death action was brought against an American aircraft manufacturer in the United States following an airplane accident in Scotland. The Federal District Court dismissed the action on the ground of *forum non conveniens*; the Third Circuit reversed, at least partly on the ground that dismissal is barred where the law of the alternative forum (here, Scotland) is less favorable than that of the forum chosen by the plaintiff; but the Supreme Court rejected this proposition and ruled that the District Court had not abused its discretion. See also Cheng v. Boeing Co., 708 F.2d 1406 (9th Cir. 1983) cert. denied, 464 U.S. 1017.

24. [1986] 3 W.L.R. 972; [1986] 3 All E.R. 843. A hint of the new approach is to be found in the House of Lord's earlier decision in The Abidin Daver [1984] A.C. 398.

25. [1986] 3 W.L.R. at 987; [1986] 3 All E.R. at 856. This definition was first formulated by Lord Keith in The Abidin Daver, [1984] A.C. 398 at 415.

26. See [1986] 3 W.L.R. at 991-993; [1986] 3 All E.R. at 859-861.

It is fairly obvious that if the *Spiliada* formula were applied to antisuit injunctions, the result would be an even greater willingness on the part of the English courts to interfere with foreign actions. To prevent this, the Privy Council[27] decided, in May 1987, to sever the link between antisuit injunctions and *forum non conveniens*. This was done in the *S.N.I.A.S.* case,[28] where it was said that an injunction will not normally be granted unless it is shown both that England is the natural forum (as defined in *Spiliada*)— and that the injunction will not deprive the plaintiff of an advantage in the foreign forum of which it would be unjust to deprive him. Normally (though not always), vexation or oppression will haveto be shown.

Whether this new formulation will make English courts less willing to grant antisuit injunctions, remains to be seen. The actual decision in *S.N.I.A.S.* make one sceptical. The case arose from a helicopter crash in Brunei in which a wealthy Brunei businessman was killed. The helicopter was manufactured by a French company (S.N.I.A.S.) and operated by a Malaysian company (Bristow) under contract to a Sarawak company (Sarawak Shell). Wrongful death actions were brought in both Brunei and Texas, where S.N.I.A.S. did business. Settlements were reached with Bristow and Shell, leaving S.N.I.A.S. to fight alone. After failing to obtain a *forum non conveniens* dismissal of the action in Texas, it asked the Brunei court for an antisuit injunction. This was refused at first instance and on appeal in Brunei on the basis of the *MacShannon* formula as applied to antisuit injunctions in *Castanho*. The Brunei courts also thought that Texas was, or had become, the natural forum. The Privy Council reversed. They decided that Brunei was the natural forum. They also held that the Texas action would cause injustice to S.N.I.A.S. because it would probably not be able to have Bristow and Shell joined as defendants there, so as to be able to claim a contribution form them if it were held liable. An injunction was therefore granted.

Special Grounds for Granting an Injunction[29]

In addition to the normal grounds (which presuppose the exist-

27. The Privy Council hears appeals from those Commonwealth countries which still allow it, now a dwindling group. Technically a court of the country from which the appeal has come (in the S.N.I.A.S. case, Brunei), the Privy Council is largely made up of the same judges as sit in the House of Lords, and its judgments, though in theory not binding on the English courts, in practice enjoy the same authority as those of the House of Lords. In S.N.I.A.S. the Privy Council was applying the law of Brunei, but it expressly stated that the position was the same under English law.

28. Société Nationale Industrielle Aerospatiale v. Lee Kui Jak, *The Times*, 1 June 1987. The judgment of the Privy Council was written by Lord Goff, who also wrote the leading opinion in *Spiliada*.

29. See Laker Airways v. British Airways [1985] A.C. 58, 80-81.

ence of an alternative forum) there are certain special grounds for issuing an injunction which can apply even if the foreign court is the only possible forum where the action could be brought. In such a case, the effect of the injunction is to deprive the plaintiff of any remedy; nevertheless the English courts can still grant an injunction as long as they have jurisdiction over the party against whom it will operate.[30]

The first such ground is that the plaintiff has entered into a contract with the defendant under which he is obligated not to bring an action in the foreign country.[31] An example of this is an arbitration clause under which the parties agree not to bring legal action until after arbitration has taken place.[32] Another example is a forum-selection clause giving exclusive jurisdiction to some court other than that in which suit was later brought. In neither of these cases is the plaintiff deprived of a remedy.

The second ground does involve depriving the plaintiff of a remedy. It applies where some special defense, usually equitable, is available under English law and concerns situations in which it would be unconscionable for the plaintiff to sue. Examples are estoppel in pais, promissory estoppel, election, waiver, standing by, laches and "blowing hot and cold".

The decision of the Court of Appeal in the *Midland Bank*[33] case

30. The English courts have never squarely faced the question of jurisdiction to grant an antisuit injunction. Is it simply a matter of applying the ordinary principles of *in personam* jurisdiction or is something more needed? According to Lord Scarman in Castanho v. Root & Brown [1981] A.C. 557, 573-574, it is "a question of fact to be determined in the light of the particular circumstances of the case" whether the person concerned has sufficient connection with England to justify the granting of an injunction. As that case makes clear, he need not be resident in England nor need he be a British citizen (though residence in England would certainly be sufficient to give the court jurisdiction). In Castanho the English court had jurisdiction because Castanho was the plaintiff in the English proceedings. Jurisdiction would also exist if the person concerned had agree to an English arbitration clause: see, e.g., Pena Copper Mines v. Rio Tinto Co. [1911-1913] All E.R. Rep. 209 (C.A.); Tracomin S.A. v. Sudan Oil Seeds (No. 2) [1983] 1 W.L.R. 1026 (C.A.). The same would no doubt be true if there was a forum-selection clause in favor of England. In The Tropaioforos (No. 2) [1962] 1 Lloyd's Rep. 410, a Panamanian company, the owner of a ship which had been lost at sea, brought action in England against one of a number of co-insurers of the ship. The owner agreed with the other co-insurers that they would all be bound by the action but, when the action was decided against the owner, it sued the other co-insurers in Greece. The English court granted an antisuit injunction, even though the first action was no longer before the court. It held that it had jurisdiction because the Greek suit was a violation of a contract which had been made in England and was governed by English law. This gave the English court jurisdiction under Order 11 of the Rules of the Supreme Court. The decision in The Tropaioforos was approved in Castanho [1981] A.C. at 574.

31. The Tropaioforos (No. 2) [1962] 1 Lloyd's Rep. 410; cf. Lett v. Lett [1906] 1 Irish Rep. 618.

32. Pena Copper Mines v. Rio Tinto Co. [1911-1913] All E.R. Rep. 209 (C.A.); Tracomin S.A. v. Sudan Oil Seeds (No.2) [1983] 1 W.L.R. 1026 (C.A.).

33. Midland Bank v. Laker Airways [1986] 1 All E.R. 526.

(decided after the House of Lords' decision in *Laker*) throws further light on the grant of antisuit injunctions in single-forum cases. It will be remembered that the Midland Bank was never a party to the American proceedings: it obtained an antisuit injunction before it could be joined.[34] In the English proceedings, it issued a writ claiming, first, a declaration that it was not liable under either English or American law for the collapse of Laker; and, secondly, an antisuit injunction. It obtained an interlocutory antisuit injunction in 1982. After the House of Lords' decision in *Laker*, Leggatt J. discharged the antisuit injunction and struck out the application for a declaration of non-liability under American law.[35] On appeal, the antisuit injunction was reinstated, though the claim for a declaration of non-liability under English law was also struck out.[36] The Court of Appeal's reason for granting the antisuit injunction was that Midland was in a different position from the airlines. The latter had chosen to do business in the United States and the action arose out of their activities there. Midland itself had not done any business there at the time (except on the international interbank market) and its American subsidiaries had done only business which was in no way relevant to the action. Midland subsequently opened up a New York branch, and this presence gave the American courts *in personam* jurisdiction over it, but subject-matter jurisdiction (prescriptive jurisdiction) was lacking. In other words, the Court of Appeal considered that the American action would involve the extraterritorial application of American law; therefore, in the Court of Appeal's view, it was unconscionable for Laker to sue. This was the argument which was unsuccessfully advanced by the airlines in the *Laker* case in the House of Lords. It was rejected because the House of Lords considered that application of American law to *them* would not be extraterritorial.

The *Midland Bank* case therefore adds another ground on which an antisuit injunction will be granted even in a single-forum case: that the foreign proceedings would involve the extraterritorial application of foreign law. As is well known, resistance to what is regarded as the extraterritorial application of American law is a well-established feature of United Kingdom policy.[37] It is probable that antisuit injunctions will also be invoked where other strong policy interests are at stake.

34. See text, supra at 487-89.

35. This was because the House of Lords held in *Laker* that the English courts have no jurisdiction to decide any question of liability under American antitrust law.

36. This left the injunction hanging in mid-air, so to speak, without any substantive cause of action at all.

37. See the Protection of Trading Interests Act 1980; see also British Nylon Spinners v. Imperial Chem. Indus. [1953] 1 Ch. 19 (C.A.), [1955] 1 Ch. 37; In re Westinghouse Uranium Contract [1978] A.C. 547.

THE AMERICAN APPROACH

The Laker Case

The American approach to antisuit injunctions was discussed by the U.S. Court of Appeals for the District of Columbia Circuit in the *Laker* case.[38] Under this approach, as described by Judge Wilkey, an injunction is far less likely to be issued. In fact, he said that he regarded the use of an antisuit injunction as proper in only three cases: first, where it is necessary to protect the forum's jurisdiction (a counter-antisuit injunction will always fall into this category);[39] secondly, to prevent evasion of an important policy of the forum (he said that if a foreign judgment would not be recognized in the United States on public policy grounds, it would be justifiable to issue an antisuit injunction to prevent the case getting as far as judgment);[40] and thirdly, in cases of concurrent proceedings, if the forum court gives judgment before the foreign action is commenced (though he thought that, in addition, a showing of vexation, oppression or other equitable circumstances should normally be required).[41] This was as far as Judge Wilkey was prepared to go. He excluded *forum non conveniens* considerations as a valid ground for granting an antisuit injunction.[42]

To what extent does this represent American law? Judge Wilkey admitted that not all the cases supported his approach. Is there in fact such a big difference between England and America?

Concurrent Proceedings

In contrast to England, it is generally accepted in America that an antisuit injunction cannot be considered unless the same issues are also being litigated between the same parties in an American court, and the disposition of the American action would also resolve the foreign dispute.[43] This requisite is well illustrated by the cases involving patents and trade marks. If X sues Y in the United States for infringement of X's American patent, and if X's German subsidiary sues Y's German subsidiary in Germany for infringement of the

38. Laker Airways v. Sabena, Belgian World Airlines, 731 F.2d 909 (D.C. Cir. 1984).

39. 731 F.2d at 929-931.

40. 731 F.2d at 931-933.

41. 731 F.2d at 928.

42. 731 F.2d at 926-929.

43. See Stein Assoc. v. Heat & Control, Inc., 748 F.2d 653, 658 (Fed. Cir. 1984); American Home Assurance Co. v. Insurance Corp. of Ireland, 603 F. Supp. 636, 643 (S.D.N.Y. 1984); Garpeg, Ltd. v. United States, 583 F. Supp. 789, 798 (S.D.N.Y. 1984); Cargill, Inc. v. Hartford Accident and Indem. Co., 531 F. Supp. 710, 715 (D. Minn. 1982); Medtronic, Inc. v. Catalyst Research Corp., 518 F. Supp. 946, 955 (D. Minn. 1981), aff'd 664 F.2d 660 (8th Cir. 1981); Western Electric Co. v. Milgo Electronic Corp., 450 F. Supp. 835, 837 (S.D. Fla. 1978), aff'd 568 F.2d 1203 (5th Cir. 1978).

equivalent German patent, an antisuit injunction will not be given because the two actions are separate: a ruling on the validity or infringement of the American patent will not dispose of the German dispute because the American and the foreign patents are separate items of industrial property.[44]

Assuming, therefore, that there are concurrent proceedings (actual or potential), in what circumstances will an antisuit injunction be granted? Many of the cases fall into one of three categories in which there is a special reason for granting the injunction. The first category consists of cases in which action is necessary in order to protect forum policies.

Protecting Forum Policies

This issue arises when an important policy of the forum is embodied in a legal provision, usually a statute, and there is reason to believe that the foreign court will not apply it. Antitrust is the best example, and the *Laker* case is a prime instance in which an antisuit injunction was necessary to protect American policy: as was made clear by the House of Lords, the English courts could not, and would not, enforce American antitrust legislation; consequently, if the American courts were prevented from exercising jurisdiction in the case, American antitrust laws, and the policies embodied in them, would have been nullified. This, of course, was the whole basis of the defendants' strategy in bringing the proceedings in England.

A similar case, which, surprisingly, was not expressly decided on this ground, was *Seattle Totems Hockey Club v. National Hockey League*.[45] Here X brought a private antitrust action against Y in an American court and also asked that an agreement between the parties be declared void, presumably because it violated American antitrust law. Some time later, Y sued X in Canada for damages for breach of the agreement, which had been made in Canada and which contained a choice-of-law clause in favor of the law of British Columbia. Since the Canadian court might not have had regard to American antitrust law in determining the validity of the contract, American policy would have been undermined if the Canadian action had been allowed to go ahead. It is hardly surprising that the

44. See Western Electric Co. v. Milgo Electronic Corp. 450 F. Supp. 835 (S.D. Fla. 1978), aff'd 568 F.2d 1203 (5th Cir. 1978); Sperry Rand Corp. v. Sunbeam Corp., 285 F.2d 542 (7th Cir. 1960); Canadian Filters Ltd. v. Lear-Siegler Inc., 412 F.2d 577 (1st Cir. 1969). A different result was reached in Medtronic, Inc. v. Catalyst Research Corp., 518 F. Supp. 946 (D. Minn. 1981), aff'd 664 F.2d 660 (8th Cir. 1981), but here the claim in the American action was that the patent-holder had agreed by contract not to prevent the other party's manufacture of the product. The antisuit injunction was only to prevent the obtaining of an injunction in the foreign proceedings; it did not prevent an action for damages.

45. 652 F.2d 852 (9th Cir. 1981), cert. denied, 457 U.S. 1105 (1982).

court granted an antisuit injunction, but it *is* surprising that it did so on the general ground that duplication of proceedings was wasteful of resources,[46] and not because of the threat to forum policy.

An interstate case falling into this general category is *Cole v. Cunningham*.[47] In essence, the facts were that X, a citizen of Massachusetts, was unable to pay his debts, though he was owed money by Z in New York. One of X's creditors, Y, another Massachusetts citizen, sued X in New York and attached Z's debt.[48] X's assignees in insolvency then applied to the Massachusetts court for an injunction to prevent Y from continuing the New York action, which was designed to give Y preference over the other creditors. The antisuit injunction was granted. The constitutionality of this came before the U.S. Supreme Court which upheld the antisuit injunction as not violating either the Full Faith and Credit Clause or the Privileges and Immunities Clause of the Constitution. In this case, the policy of Massachusetts law was to ensure that all creditors were treated equally, and Y was trying to undermine this goal. The antisuit injunction was the only way the Massachusetts court could protect its policy.

Protection of Forum Jurisdiction

The second general category of consists of cases in which an antisuit injunction is necessary to protect the jurisdiction of the forum and to ensure the efficacy of its orders. All cases involving counter-antisuit injunctions, such as *Laker*, fall into this category. Another example is *Omnium Lyonnais D'Etancheite et Revetement Asphalte v. Dow Chemical Co.*[49] In this case an American defendant was sued in the United States by French plaintiffs. In discovery proceedings the defendant produced various documents, but the court expressly ordered that these documents should not be used in parallel actions in France. In violation of this order, the plaintiffs used them in the French actions and obtained judgment in their favor. The American court then issued an injunction precluding the plaintiffs from enforcing the French judgment until the conclusion of the American action.

Another case which falls within this category, but in which no injunction was issued, is *Garpeg Ltd. v. United States*.[50] Here the Internal Revenue Service took out a summons requiring the Chase

46. See text infra at 500-01.

47. 133 U.S. 107 (1890). For similar cases in England, see Re North Carolina Estate Co., 5 Times L. Rep. 328 (1889); Re Distin, ex parte Ormiston, 24 L. Times 197 (1871); cf. Graham v. Maxwell, 1 Mac. & G. 71, 47 E.R. 1403 (1849).

48. It was a *quasi-in-rem* action.

49. 441 F. Supp. 1385 (C.D. Cal. 1977).

50. 583 F. Supp. 789 (S.D.N.Y. 1984).

Manhattan Bank to disclose documents in its Hong Kong branch relating to Garpeg. Both Garpeg and Chase moved to have the summons quashed; in the alternative, Chase asked for an antisuit injunction requiring Garpeg to discontinue proceedings brought against Chase in Hong Kong to prevent disclosure. The American court refused to quash the summons but also refused to grant the antisuit injunction. It pointed out that the issues were not the same in the two actions and doubted whether it even had power to enforce any rights which Garpeg might have had under Hong Kong banking law.[51] In this case, the efficacy of the American court's order to Chase to produce the documents was threatened by the proceedings brought by Garpeg in Hong Kong. Yet the court refrained, in the interests of comity, from issuing the injunction.

Vexation and Oppression

Vexation is often mentioned as a ground for granting an antisuit injunction, but the concept is rarely defined, perhaps because it is incapable of definition. One situation in which vexation would clearly occur is where the plaintiff brings an action in a foreign court, not because he genuinely thinks that is the best way to settle the dispute, but because he wants to cause difficulties for the defendant, perhaps in the hope of obtaining a favorable settlement. Examples would be where the defendant could not afford to defend the action in a foreign country,[52] where he would be unable to plead a defense available in an American court,[53] where evidence available in the United States could not be used, or where he would otherwise be at an unfair procedural disadvantage.

This sort of situation if often referred to, but there are few international cases in which it actually occurs. The best example is probably *Bethell v. Peace*.[54] In this case Peace, a Florida real estate broker, persuaded six of the seven co-owners of land in the Bahamas to agree to sell the land to her. The six were Florida residents and the agreement was signed in Florida. Peace sued in the Bahamas for specific performance. After this action had been commenced, the successor in title to one of the six sued in Florida for a declaration that the agreement was invalid, for damages and for an antisuit injunction. The injunction was granted by the federal district court and affirmed on appeal. The reason given was that the agreement was invalid on its face; therefore an injunction was justified in order

51. See Garpeg Ltd. v. United States, 583 F. Supp. 789 (S.D.N.Y. 1984).
52. See, e.g., Gage v. Riverside Trust Co., 86 F. 984, 995 (C.C.S.D. Cal. 1898).
53. See, e.g., Hyafill v. Buffalo Marine Constr. Co., 266 F. 553 (W.D.N.Y. 1919).
54. 441 F.2d 495 (5th Cir. 1971).

to relieve the plaintiff of the expense and vexation of having to litigate in a foreign court.

Other Cases

When all the cases where there are special considerations are put to one side, there still remains a hard core of cases in which the existence of concurrent foreign proceedings seems in itself to be the ground for the antisuit injunction. There is a line of cases, beginning with the *Seattle Totems* case,[55] in which it is said that an antisuit injunction will be granted where the existence of separate actions is likely to result in unnecessary delay and substantial inconvenience to the parties and witnesses. The risk of inconsistent rulings or a race to judgment are additional factors for granting the injunction. Now, there can be no doubt that these drawbacks are almost inevitably present wherever there are concurrent proceedings on the same issue in different countries; therefore this line of reasoning leads to the conclusion that in all cases of concurrent proceedings, the forum should either stay or dismiss the action before it—normally on grounds of *forum non conveniens*—or issue an antisuit injunction.

Two insurance cases may be cited as examples. In the first, *Cargill v. Hartford Accident & Indemnity Co.*,[56] the plaintiff took out two insurance policies from the defendant insurance companies covering loss resulting from the dishonesty of its employees and those of certain other companies. Subsequently it made a claim as a result of the dishonesty of the employees of its English subsidiary. The dishonesty and resulting loss occurred in England. On the same day that the American proceedings were filed, one of the insurance companies began an action in England for a declaration that they were not liable. The connections with the United States were probably stronger than those with England—the parties were American and the policies were issued in the United States—but England could not be said to have been a totally unreasonable forum. Nevertheless, the American court issued an antisuit injunction to stop the proceedings.[57] The English action seems, however, to have been a "pre-emptive strike" by the insurance company and this fact, though not emphasized by the American court, might be regarded as justifying the injunction.

The second case was a complicated dispute in which American

55. See supra n. 45.

56. 531 F. Supp. 710 (D. Minn. 1982).

57. It first considered whether it should dismiss the American proceedings on grounds of *forum non conveniens*; once it had decided not to do so, it had little hesitation in granting the antisuit injunction.

insurance companies, which had taken out reinsurance with foreign companies, were claiming reimbursement for claims paid in the United States.[58] There were concurrent proceedings in England. Again, the foreign parties asked for dismissal of the American proceedings on grounds of *forum non conveniens*. This was refused on the ground that, where the plaintiffs are United States citizens, dismissal for this reason is proper only where the bringing of the proceedings in the United States is "unjust, vexatious or oppressive and not merely inconvenient to the defendant".[59] Given this stringent test, it is hardly surprising that the defendants were unable to obtain a dismissal of the American action. Once this had been decided, it was almost inevitable, given the "unnecessary delay" formula, that an antisuit injunction would be granted to halt the English proceedings. Under this analysis it would seem that, if the plaintiffs in the American action are Americans, an antisuit injunction is almost a foregone conclusion—even though the plaintiffs in the foreign action may be citizens of that country (as was the case here).[60]

Conclusions

There is some evidence to suggest that, though American courts are on the whole less ready than English courts to issue antisuit injunctions, the difference is not as great as might be suggested by comparing the judgments in the *Laker Airways* case of Lord Diplock[61] and Judge Wilkey.[62] In particular, the basic English approach exemplified in cases such as *S.N.I.A.S.* is to some extent mirrored by the approach of those American courts applying the "unnecessary delay" formula. Moreover, cases such as *American Home Assurance*[63] seem to go even further than the English decisions, since the test applied appears to be weighted in favor of the American proceedings. However, this formula has not yet been generally accepted in America and has been rejected in some cases.[64] It

58. American Home Assurance Co. v. Insurance Corp. of Ireland, 603 F. Supp. 636 (S.D.N.Y. 1984).

59. 603 F. Supp. at 640.

60. See also In re Unterweser Reederei, 428 F.2d 888 (5th Cir. 1970), vacated on other grounds sub. nom. Bremen v. Zapata Off-Shore Co., 407 U.S. 1 (1972).

61. British Airways Bd. v. Laker Airways [1985] A.C. 58.

62. Laker Airways v. Sabena, Belgian World Airlines, 731 F.2d 909 (D.C. Cir. 1984).

63. 603 F. Supp. 636 (S.D.N.Y. 1984).

64. See, e.g., Compagnie des Bauxites de Guinea v. Insurance Co. of N. Am., 651 F.2d 877, 887 (3rd Cir. 1981), cert. denied, 457 U.S. 1105 (1982). Another case in which an American court showed exemplary restraint was Chase Manhattan Bank v. State of Iran, 484 F. Supp. 832 (S.D.N.Y. 1980). Here a very important policy was at stake (sanctions against Iran during the hostage crisis) and it was by no means certain that the foreign (English) court would give effect to it; yet an injunction was refused since it was recognized that it was reasonable for the Iranian bank to seek to

must also be remembered that American courts (unlike English courts) do not grant injunctions where the substantive issue can be decided only by the foreign forum.

PROCEDURAL DIFFERENCES BETWEEN ENGLAND AND THE UNITED STATES

In England the issue of antisuit injunctions has recently come into prominence; the reasons for this development are almost entirely concerned with the United States. In particular, differences in civil procedure in the two countries have both encouraged British litigants to sue in America and given rise to allegations of vexation and oppression.

On the surface, civil procedure may seem similar in England and the United States, but in fact there are deep-seated differences of attitude and policy. One of these differences is that, to a far greater extent than in the United States, the policy of English law is to regard a lawsuit such as an action for damages[65] as a last-resort method of dispute resolution which should be avoided whenever possible: litigation is discouraged; negotiated settlements are favored.

Discovery is one area in which this policy is applied. In England a party is not expected to embark on litigation unless he already has a clear concept of his cause of action. There is strong disapproval of "fishing expeditions", by which is meant the practice of using discovery for the purpose of finding out whether a cause of action exists. For this reason there is, in general, no right to discovery until the pleadings are closed: the plaintiff must define his case with a fair degree of precision[66] before he can ask for discovery.[67]

Discovery is much more restricted in scope than in the United States. Although relevant documents may be obtained from the other party,[68] there is in general no way of obtaining documentary, or other, evidence from a non-party before trial.[69] Depositions

have the controversy determined in England, where the accounts were located. It is not certain, however, that any injunction granted could have been enforced.

65. Different considerations apply in other types of proceedings, such as divorce.

66. English pleadings are required to be much more precise and specific than their American counterparts.

67. See South Carolina Insurance Co. v. Assurantie Maatschappij "De Zeven Provincien" N.V. [1986] 3 W.L.R. 398, 403-405, [1986] 3 All E.R. 487, 492-493 (H.L.). There are some exceptions to this rule but these exceptions are never permitted merely to allow a party to "fish out" a case: see, e.g., Gale v. Denman Picture Houses [1930] 1 K.B. 588.

68. See Rules of the Supreme Court, Order 24. English law, however, has an entirely different—and immensely more restrictive—concept of when a document is "relevant" for this purpose.

69. There are two exceptions to this rule. The first is that if a person becomes involved in the tortious acts of others and, however innocently, facilitates their

before trial are unknown: a party or witness cannot be required to submit to oral examination before the trial; a party (but not a non-party) can be required to answer written interrogatories, but the procedure for this is cumbersome and it is little used.[70]

There is also a different policy regarding costs. As in the United States, the winning party is routinely awarded costs; but, unlike in the United States, these include attorney's fees.[71] Moreover, contingent-fee agreements are illegal[72]—on the theory that if the lawyer has a financial stake in the outcome of the case, he might be tempted to act dishonestly.[73] The combined effect of these rules is to provide a formidable disincentive to sue unless the plaintiff is confident of success: if he brings an action and does not win he will have to pay both his own attorney's fees and also those of his opponent.

Compared to his English counterpart, the American plaintiff is

---

wrongdoing, he may be required to furnish information (orally or in documentary form) to assist the person who has been harmed: see Norwich Pharmacal Co. v. Customs & Excise Comm'rs [1974] A.C. 133 (in which the British customs administration were required to disclose the identity of a person importing a product in violation of Norwich Pharmacal's patent rights); Bankers Trust Co. v. Shapira [1980] 1 W.L.R. 1274 (C.A.) (in which a London bank was required to assist a New York bank in tracing money obtained from the latter through fraud). The second exception, which is laid down by sec. 32(1) of the Administration of Justice Act 1970, allows the discovery of documents from a non-party in personal-injury and wrongful-death actions. The principal, though not the only, use of this power is to obtain hospital records. In the case of both exceptions, a court order must first be obtained. Though important, these exceptions are limited and there are still many situations in which a plaintiff with an undoubted case will be unable to sue for lack of information. Two examples were given by Lord Reid in Norwich Pharmacal: "A person injured in a road accident might know that a bystander had taken the number of the car which ran him down and have no other means of tracing the driver. Or a person might know that a particular person is in possession of a libellous letter which he has good reason to believe defames him but the author of which he cannot discover . . . it would not be proper in either case to order discovery in order that the person who has suffered damage might be able to find and sue the wrongdoer." [1974] A.C. at 168.

70. See Rules of the Supreme Court, Order 26. A court order must first be obtained. Answers have to be on oath, generally by affidavit.

71. See Rules of the Supreme Court, Order 62. Order 62, rule 28(2) now permits the recovery of all costs "reasonably incurred". Until April 1986, the Rules permitted the recovery of only such costs as were "necessary or proper", which in practice usually covered only about two-thirds to three-quarters of the actual lawyers' bill; the new provision should normally cover almost the whole of it.

72. See Solicitors Act 1974, sect. 59(2)(b); see also Wallersteiner v. Moir (No. 2) [1975] Q.B. 373 (C.A.).

73. See Wallersteiner v. Moir, id at 402. Low-income plaintiffs may qualify for legal aid under the Legal Aid Act 1974. If this is granted, their lawyer's fees will be paid out of public funds (though in some cases they may have to make a contribution). Legal aid is granted, however, only if a legal aid committee considers that the plaintiff is justified in bringing the action. The test is broadly whether, on similar facts, the committee (which consists of lawyers in private practice) would advise a privately-funded litigant to sue: Zander, *Cases and Materials on the English Legal System* 460 (4th ed., 1984).

in an enviable position. In an action for damages his attorney will often be acting on the basis of a contingent-fee agreement: if he loses he will then be required to pay neither his own attorney's fee nor that of his opponent. In such circumstances he might feel justified in taking a gamble on what at the outset appears to be a doubtful case in the hope that discovery will reveal a hitherto-unsuspected cause of action.[74]

Moreover, not only are the risks of litigation greater in England, but the rewards are considerably less. Jury trials have been virtually eliminated in civil actions (except for libel and slander),[75] punitive damages in tort actions are very rare,[76] negligence must be proved in product-liability suits,[77] and there are no private antitrust suits.[78]

These differences add up to a very different view regarding the function of civil litigation. In the United States, civil actions can have important public functions, for example in promoting product safety and maintaining an effective system of competition between business enterprises. Treble damage awards in antitrust suits and punitive damages in product-liability cases may be justified on these grounds. In England these public objectives are attained by other means; private litigation is seen as almost exclusively concerned with private objectives. The function of damages is limited almost entirely to compensation.

In view of these differences, it is hardly surprising that English lawyers find some aspects of American civil procedure hard to ac-

74. But see Rule 11 Fed. R. Civ. P.

75. Other exceptions include fraud, malicious prosecution and wrongful imprisonment. Even in these cases the court can refuse a jury trial if it considers that "the trial requires prolonged examination of documents or accounts or any scientific or local investigation which cannot conveniently be made with a jury": Supreme Court Act 1981, sec. 69(1). In fact, there are not more than two dozen civil jury trials each year in the whole of England: Zander, supra n. 73 at 384.

76. Usually known in England as "exemplary" damages, they are (except where expressly provided for by statute) awarded only in two situations: first, where government officials have acted oppressively, arbitrarily or unconstitutionally; secondly, where an act known to be tortious was committed in the belief that the material advantages to be gained from it would outweigh any compensatory damages likely to be awarded. See Rookes v. Barnard [1964] A.C. 1129; Cassell & Co. v. Broome [1972] A.C. 1027. For a case in which the greater likelihood of obtaining punitive damages in America was regarded as a factor weighing against the granting of an antisuit injunction, see Metall und Rohstoff A.G. v. ACLI Metals (London) [1984] 1 Lloyd's L. Rep. 598 (C.A.).

77. This will change when E.E.C. Directive 85/374, Official Journal of the European Communities, 1985 L. 210/29, (Products Liability Directive) is implemented. See the Consumer Protection Bill 1987.

78. Such actions are possible under E.E.C. law but have not yet become significant: see, e.g., Garden Cottage Foods v. Milk Mkt'ing Bd. [1984] A.C. 130; see generally Davidson, "Actions for Damages in the English Courts for Breach of E.E.C. Competition Law," 34 *Int'l & Comp. L.Q.* 178 (1985).

cept: damage awards which are seen as beyond the bounds of reason, pre-trial discovery which seems to be so onerous that a defendant may decide to settle rather than fight a case he thinks he can win, and actions begun on what to English lawyers seem wholly insufficient grounds.[79] In such cases, an English lawyer might regard the proceedings as vexatious and oppressive, though an American lawyer would consider that nothing out of the ordinary had happened. This is the explanation of the criticism of American procedure which is to be found in some English judgments, criticism which is a factor in the willingness of English courts to grant injunctions to restrain a plaintiff from suing in America.[80]

Even when no question of vexation arises, procedural differences between England and the United States can play a decisive role in balancing advantages against disadvantages. This is illustrated by *Metall und Rohstoff A.G. v. ACLI Metals (London) Ltd.*[81] In this case, a Swiss subsidiary of a New York corporation sued an English company[82] in England. The claim related to disputed transactions on the London Metal Exchange. The English company counterclaimed; a few weeks later it brought an action in a federal court in New York against the New York corporation. This action mirrored the English counterclaim, both being based on allegations of fraud on a massive scale orchestrated by the New York corporation. The latter responded to the New York action by moving for dismissal on grounds of *forum non conveniens* but, before judgment could be given on the motion, it applied to the English court for a declaration of non-liability and for an antisuit injunction. The injunction was granted by the trial court but lifted on appeal.[83] The reasons given were instructive. The Court of Appeal accepted that the advantages to the plaintiff of a New York action included the wider scope of pre-trial discovery under the Federal Rules of Civil Procedure and the greater likelihood of punitive damages. The greater expense and delay of a jury trial in New York were regarded as disadvantages to the defendant. The trial judge had concluded that the English action would almost certainly be decided first and the judgment could then be pled as *res judicata* in New York. On appeal,

79. An American lawyer might feel equally shocked at the obstacles faced by an English litigant.

80. See Midland Bank v. Laker Airways, [1986] 1 All E.R. 526, 536; British Airways v. Laker Airways [1985] A.C. 58, 78; Smith, Kline & French Laboratories Ltd. v. Bloch [1983] 1 W.L.R. 730 (C.A.).

81. [1984] 1 Lloyd's L. Rep. 598 (C.A.).

82. The English company was itself the subsidiary of another New York corporation.

83. The trial court also granted an injunction to prevent suit being brought against the subsidiary; this was not contested on appeal.

the English company agreed to forgo a jury trial in New York,[84] and this agreement was the main reason why the injunction was lifted: the Court of Appeal considered that the New York action would then be decided at about the same time as the English action.[85]

COMITY

In theory, an antisuit injunction does not interfere with the foreign court because it operates *in personam*: it is an order addressed to the litigant, not to the court. But this argument is sophistry. The foreign court cannot decide the case unless the parties take the requisite procedural steps. By barring a party from doing this, a court is in reality deciding whether the foreign court will hear the case.[86] This *is* an interference with the foreign court which by its very nature runs counter to the idea of comity.[87]

This much is generally recognized, but it is thought that in some circumstances the need for an injunction is so overwhelming that comity must give way. There is no doubt that in cases of concurrent proceedings, vexation and oppression, and where the bringing of the action is a breach of contract or otherwise unconscionable, there is a strong case for stopping the proceedings; but the basic objection to antisuit injunctions is that the natural forum to decide such a ques-

84. They also agreed to delete from their defense and counterclaim in England all allegations against the New York corporation.

85. A lesser reason was the trial judge's mistaken assumption that there as a good chance of obtaining punitive (exemplary) damages in England.

86. Over a hundred years ago, an English judge said that an antisuit injunction was "how the proceedings in a foreign court may in effect be stayed": The Christiansborg (1885) 10 P.D. 141, 152-153 (Baggallay L.J.). American courts have also held that "there is no difference between addressing an injunction to the parties and addressing it to the foreign court itself". Compagnie des Bauxites de Guinea v. Insurance Co. of N.Am. 651 F.2d 877 (3rd Cir. 1981), cert. denied, 457 U.S. 1105 (1982). See also, Donovan v. Dallas, 377 U.S. 408, 413 (1964); Central National Bank v. Stevens, 169 U.S. 432, 460 (1898); Peck v. Jenness, 48 U.S. 612, 625 (1849); Laker Airways v. Sabena, Belgian World Airlines, 731 F.2d 909, 927 (D.C. Cir. 1984); O'Hare Int'l Bank v. Lambert, 459 F.2d 328, 331 (10th Cir. 1972); Russell v. Detrick, 23 F.2d 175, 178 (9th Cir. 1927); Lowther v. New York Life Ins. Co., 278 F. 405, 408 (3rd Cir. 1922); Essanay Film Mfg. Co. v. Kane, 264 F. 959 (3rd Cir. 1920). But see, In re Unterweser Reederei, 428 F.2d 888, 892 (5th Cir. 1970), vacated on other grounds sub. nom. Bremen v. Zapata Off-Shore Co., 407 U.S. 1 (1972).

87. In the case of injunctions granted by English courts there is an additional argument, namely that an antisuit injunction violates the principle of territoriality, which is so assiduously protected in other areas. For example, if an American court orders an American bank to produce documents situated at its London branch, the English courts will regard this order as extraterritorial and, if so requested by the customer of the bank, issue an injunction ordering the bank not to comply with the disclosure order: see X AG v. A bank [1983] 2 All E.R. 464. Yet if it is improper for an American court to order an American bank to do something in England, how can it be right for an English court to order a litigant to do (or not to do) something in the United States?

tion is the court where the proceedings are taking place.[88]

Take the case where a court issues an injunction to avoid duplication of proceedings and considers that it, rather than the foreign court, is the more appropriate forum to hear the case. This has happened on a number of occasions in England (with regard to American proceedings) and in America (with regard to English proceedings).[89] However, both England (somewhat belatedly)[90] and America apply the doctrine of *forum non conveniens*. If the foreign court has not yet considered the question, it is hard to see the justification for pre-empting its decision with an injunction.[91] If it has already considered and rejected an application to dismiss, it is hard to see why a court in another country should overrule this decision.[92] If each court believes that *it* is the most appropriate forum, why not allow both actions to proceed?

The position is similar where there is a question of vexation. This was an issue (though not a fully acknowledged one) in the English case of *Smith, Kline & French Laboratories v. Bloch*.[93] Here, an English research scientist entered into a consultancy contract with the English subsidiary of an American pharmaceutical company. He felt the subsidiary had not carried out its side of the agreement, and he decided to sue. Instead of bringing the action in England, however, he commenced proceedings against both the American parent and the English subsidiary in Pennsylvania, the State where the parent corporation had its head office. He gave various reasons for this choice including the American contingent-fee system and the possibility of a jury trial and of punitive damages. The company re-

88. See Metall und Rohstoff A.G. v. ACLI Metals (London) Ltd. [1984] 1 Lloyd's L. Rep. 598, 609 (C.A.); Bank of Tokyo v. Karoon [1986] 3 W.L.R. 414, 431, [1986] 3 All E.R. 468, 486 (C.A.).

89. See supra text at 500-01.

90. See supra text at 491 ff.

91. In Metall und Rohstoff A.G. v. ACLI Metals (London) Ltd. [1984] 1 Lloyd's L. Rep. 598, the English High Court granted an injunction to terminate the American proceedings when the American judge had already considered a motion to dismiss the complaint on the ground of *forum non conveniens* but had not yet delivered judgment. Although this was expected in a matter of days, the English judge refused to delay granting the injunction.

92. In the S.N.I.A.S. case, the Privy Council issued an injunction to stop proceedings in Texas on the ground that not all the defendants could be brought before the Texas court. They considered that this would be unfair to the remaining defendant. However, there is no reason to believe that the Texas court would have been any less willing than the Privy Council to give due weight to this consideration. If the point was not raised before the Texas court (where a motion to dismiss on *forum non conveniens* grounds had been unsuccessful) was it right to allow it to be raised before the Privy Council? If the point was raised, but had been rejected by the Texas court (perhaps on the ground that it was outweighed by other considerations), was it right for the Privy Council in effect to overrule the Texas court?

93. [1983] 1 W.L.R. 730 (C.A.). Another example is the American case of Bethell v. Peace, supra n. 54.

sponded by applying to the English court for an antisuit injunction, and this was granted. The English court thought that England was the natural and convenient forum and that the American parent had been brought into the proceedings only to provide a justification for invoking the jurisdiction of the American courts. There were also grounds for suspecting that the plaintiffs chose to sue in America in order to harass the defendants into a settlement.[94] If the proceedings were vexatious, however, the American court could no doubt have provided a remedy. The company had in fact made an application to the American court for the dismissal of the action but this was rejected. The company then came to the English court[95] to ask for the remedy which the American court had refused. It is hard to see the justification for the English court's' decision to grant it.

Similar arguments apply where the plaintiff is contractually bound not to sue. In *Ellerman Lines v. Read*[96] a British ship's captain entered into a salvage agreement with the captain of another ship. The agreement provided that the salvaged ship would not be arrested if the salvage was successful, and that the salvor's remuneration would, in the absence of agreement, be determined by arbitration. The salvage was successful and the ship was brought to Turkey for repairs. There she was arrested by the salvor who brought a salvage suit in the Turkish courts. The defendant asked for the ship's release on the ground of the salvage agreement and the fact that the salvor had accepted security in London. The salvor swore that he had not accepted security and the Turkish court refused to release the ship. The defendant then withdrew from the proceedings and the plaintiff obtained a judgment. The defendant subsequently went to the English court and obtained an injunction to prevent the plaintiff from enforcing the Turkish judgment. Two reasons were given for the granting of the injunction: first that the bringing of the proceedings was contrary to the salvage agreement; secondly, that the plaintiff's denial that he had accepted security was a deliberate lie. On the facts before the English court the salvor was indeed guilty of unconscionable conduct. Nevertheless, the Turkish courts had jurisdiction over the case, and the defendants

94. The theory was that the company would pay out rather than incur the heavy costs of fighting the case to the finish. This was expressly stated in Lord Denning's judgment and hinted at in the other judgments; see also Laker Airways [1985] A.C. 58, 86; Bank of Tokyo v. Karoon [1986] 3 W.L.R. 414, 422, [1986] 3 All E.R. 468, 477 (C.A.).

95. The English action appears actually to have been brought by the English subsidiary: the American parent was subject to a counter-antisuit injunction granted by the Pennsylvania court preventing it from applying to the English court for an injunction. It was apparently added as a party at the request of Bloch.

96. [1928] 2 K.B. 144 (C.A.). See also The Tropaioforos (No. 2) [1962] 1 Lloyd's Rep. 410.

could have argued their case there (and, if necessary, taken it on appeal).

CONCLUSIONS

It is suggested that an antisuit injunction should not be granted on any ground on which the foreign court could on a proper showing be expected itself to stay or dismiss the proceedings before it.[97] This rule should be subject to two conditions: first, the relevant law and policy of the foreign court must be substantially similar to that of the forum; and, secondly, there must be no reason to believe that the party requesting the stay or dismissal would not get a fair hearing in the foreign court.[98] If this approach were adopted, antisuit injunctions between courts in England and America (as well as most other common law jurisdictions) would not, except in rare cases, be granted on grounds of duplicity of proceedings or vexation, because of an arbitration agreement or forum-selection clause, or on the basis of estoppel or other equitable principles.

This would cover the majority of cases in which antisuit injunctions have been given in England and the United States. There would, however, remain a number of situations (including some of the most controversial, such as *Laker*) in which injunctions would continue to be issued. The most important of these are cases of alleged extraterritoriality, cases where mandatory legislation of the forum would not be applied by the foreign court and cases where the jurisdiction of the forum is under threat.

Extraterritoriality

It was implicit in the judgment of the House of Lords in the *Laker*[99] case and explicit in the judgment of the English Court of Appeal in the *Midland Bank* case[100] that an antisuit injunction is justified if it is necessary to prevent the exercise of exorbitant prescriptive (legislative) jurisdiction by a foreign court.[101] The granting

97. English courts are beginning to accept this: see Metall und Rohstoff A.G. v. ACLI Metals (London) Ltd. [1984] 1 Lloyd's L. Rep. 598, 609 (C.A.); Bank of Tokyo v. Karoon [1986] 3 W.L.R. 414, 431, [1986] 3 All E.R. 468, 486 (C.A.).

98. For example, where the foreign court was biased or corrupt. The House of Lords has, however, said that if a plaintiff wishes to base his case on this ground, he must assert it candidly and support his allegations with positive and cogent evidence: see The Abidin Daver [1984] A.C. 398, 411. In practice this will be very hard to do; but for a case in which a plaintiff was successful in such an argument, see Carvalho v. Hull, Blyth (Angola) Ltd. [1979] 1 W.L.R. 1228 (C.A.). For a contrary example, see Mudurogulu v. T.C. Zirkaat Bankasi [1986] 3 W.L.R. 606; [1986] 3 All E.R. 682 (C.A.).

99. See text supra at 487-89.

100. See text supra at 495.

101. In theory the same might apply in the case of adjudicatory jurisdiction, but this is unlikely to arise between England and the United States.

of injunctions in such circumstances is, of course, highly controversial. Nevertheless, in view of the acute difference of opinion on the subject of extraterritoriality, especially between lawyers in England and America, it would be unrealistic—in the absence of an agreed dispute-resolution procedure—to expect English courts not to grant injunctions on this ground.

Non-Application of Forum Law

The second situation in which the continued use of injunctions is inevitable is where mandatory legislation of the forum, expressly or impliedly applicable to the case in question, would not be applied by the foreign court if it decided the case. Here too there would be no point in asking the foreign court to stay or dismiss the proceedings before it: an antisuit injunction is the only way in which forum policies can be protected.[102]

Protecting Forum Jurisdiction

Special considerations apply where there is a threat to the forum's own jurisdiction or to its ability to control the proceedings before it. In such circumstances it will often be unreasonable to expect the forum to rely solely on the good will of the foreign court: an antisuit injunction, or a counter-antisuit injunction, may be the only answer. American cases of this kind have already been discussed.[103] English cases are less common but the recent decision of the Court of Appeal in *Bank of Tokyo v. Karoon*[104] provides an example. In this case, the Bank of Tokyo was involved in litigation in England with one of its customers, Karoon. In order to obtain evidence needed for the English proceedings, it asked its New York subsidiary, where Karoon also had an account, to supply information concerning that account. The information was provided and put before the English court. Karoon responded by bringing an action in New York against both the Bank of Tokyo and the subsidiary, claiming that the release of the information was contrary to New York law. He argued that the disclosure was a breach of the subsidiary's contractual duty of confidence and a violation of his right to privacy;

102. This ground is generally accepted by American courts (see supra text at 497-99) but has not so far been applied in England (unless one regards it as overlapping with the previous ground). However, there is no reason to doubt that it would be accepted by English courts if the situation arose. For a case in which an English court refused, specifically on this ground, to stay an action before it, in spite of a forum-selection clause in favor of another court, see The Hollandia, [1983] 1 A.C. 565; cf. Union Ins. Soc. of Canton, Ltd. v. S.S. Elikon, 642 F.2d 721 (1981).

103. See supra text at 498-500.

104. [1986] 3 W.L.R. 414, [1986] 3 All E.R. 468; see also Armstrong v. Armstrong, [1892] P. 98.

he also alleged that the parent and subsidiary had entered into a conspiracy to injure him.

The effect of this was that a party to proceedings in England was being sued in a foreign country by another party as a result of evidence obtained in that country for use in the English proceedings. The English court apparently felt that this interfered with its right to control the proceedings before it, and ordered Karoon not to continue the New York action in so far as the Bank of Tokyo was concerned. Views may differ as to the correctness of this decision,[105] but it is significant that the court did not prevent Karoon from continuing the New York action against the subsidiary.[106]

Another case of this kind, where, however, the final outcome was the lifting of the injunction, is *South Carolina Insurance Co. v. Assurantie Maatschappij "De Zeven Provincien" N.V.*[107] Here, one party to an English action applied to a federal district court for judicial assistance under 28 U.S.C. sect. 1782 to obtain evidence for use in the English suit. As this application had been made without its consent, the English court issued an injunction preventing any further steps in the American proceedings. This was done because the English court felt that the application for judicial assistance threatened its control of the proceedings before it. The injunction was upheld by the Court of Appeal, but rescinded by the House of Lords on the ground that the application did not constitute an interference with the English action: Lord Brandon, who gave the leading judgment, pointed out that in civil proceedings the court does not in general exercise control over the manner in which a party obtains evidence. It may, or may not, assist him, but it does not place restrictions on the means used, provided they are not contrary to the law of the country where the evidence is obtained.[108] This case, therefore, while upholding the principle that an injunction may be granted to protect the forum's jurisdiction, illustrates yet again that the House of Lords often adopts a more internationalist approach than some of the lower courts in England.

105. Compare the decision of the English High Court in X A.G. v. A Bank, [1983] 2 All E.R. 464, discussed supra n. 83.

106. That this did not appreciably hamper Karoon's ability to carry on the New York suit is suggested by the fact that Karoon did not appeal against the order; the Bank of Tokyo, on the other hand, appealed (unsuccessfully) against the refusal to extend the order to cover the subsidiary.

107. [1986[3 W.L.R. 398, [1986] 3 All E.R. 487 (H.L.), rev'g, [1985] 3 W.L.R. 739, [1985] 2 All E.R. 1046 (C.A.).

108. Lord Brandon stressed that the reason why English law does not allow pre-trial discovery against non-parties is to protect the latter, not to protect the other party to the action.

Part II
Common Law Traditions in Choice of Law

The Theoretical Tradition in America

[11]

THE
UNIVERSITY OF CHICAGO LAW REVIEW

VOLUME 25 WINTER 1958 NUMBER 2

MARRIED WOMEN'S CONTRACTS: A STUDY IN CONFLICT-OF-LAWS METHOD

BRAINERD CURRIE*

I

THE PROBLEM of *Milliken v. Pratt*[1] has been a featured subject of analysis in two of the most provocative writings in modern times on the conflict of laws.[2] This fact alone, to say nothing of other studies of the same problem, nor of the fact that the casebooks have made the decision familiar to the point of triteness, makes it seem almost presumptuous to offer further discussion. The practical importance of the specific problem is no doubt approaching the vanishing point as a result of the progressive removal of restrictions on the capacity of married women to contract. A number of factors, however, have nurtured the temerity necessary to prompt further comment in such circumstances. In the first place, Cook and Cavers, after all, did not advance solutions of the problem in the papers cited,[3] but only methods of approach to a solution. Cook has been severely criticized for the "destructive" character of his analysis,[4] and Cavers seems to have resigned himself to disillusionment.[5]

* Professor of Law, The Law School, The University of Chicago. Fellow, Center for Advanced Study in the Behavioral Sciences, 1957–1958.

[1] 125 Mass. 374 (1878).

[2] Cook, The Logical and Legal Bases of the Conflict of Laws, 33 Yale L. J. 457 (1924), reprinted in Cook, The Logical and Legal Bases of the Conflict of Laws, c. I (1942), and in Association of American Law Schools, Selected Readings on Conflict of Laws 71 (1956); Cavers, A Critique of the Choice-of-Law Problem, 47 Harv. L. Rev. 173 (1933), reprinted in Association of American Law Schools, Selected Readings on Conflict of Laws 101 (1956). Hereafter, the Association's collection will be cited "AALS Readings."

[3] At a later time, Cook suggested that a somewhat flexible version of the rule referring to domicile would be preferable to the place-of-making rule. Cook, The Logical and Legal Bases of the Conflict of Laws, c. XVI (1942).

[4] Yntema, The Historic Bases of Private International Law, 2 Am. J. Comp. L. 297, 314 (1953) (AALS Readings, at 30, 43).

[5] Cavers, Review of Cook, The Logical and Legal Bases of the Conflict of Laws, 56 Harv. L. Rev. 1170, 1173 (1943). More recently Cavers has returned to the attack with a vigor which considerably discounts the pessimism he expressed in 1943. Cavers, The Two "Local Law" Theories, 63 Harv. L. Rev. 822 (1950) (AALS Readings, at 124).

In the second place, those of us who teach the subject have to treat the case anew each year, no matter how trite or how limited in current "practical" importance it may be; and one harbors a sense of guilt at not having committed one's treatment of it to paper, and hence, perhaps, not having thought it through. As for the diminishing practical importance of the specific problem, that is a circumstance which should not discourage inquiry, at least so long as there is any possibility that the results may have a somewhat broader application. Indeed, I am inclined to think that the fact that a problem is familiar, is limited in scope, and can be viewed in detachment from live controversy over the values involved in the conflicting laws, actually commends the problem for selection as the focus of a study of the methods of conflict of laws.

No further apology is needed for restating the problem, since each year brings another contingent of law students who are unfamiliar with it:

In 1870 Mrs. Pratt, at her home in Massachusetts, executed a guaranty of her husband's credit in favor of a partnership doing business in Portland, Maine. She delivered the instrument to her husband, who mailed it to the firm in Maine. In reliance on the guaranty, and in response to orders placed by Mr. Pratt, the partnership delivered goods to Mr. Pratt, either in person or by common carrier "for him," Mr. Pratt paying the shipping charges. Upon default, the partners sued Mrs. Pratt in Massachusetts on the guaranty. According to a Maine statute enacted in 1866, a married woman was competent to bind herself by contract as if she were unmarried. According to the law of Massachusetts at the time of the transaction, a married woman could not bind herself by contract as surety or for the accommodation of her husband or of any third person.

Reversing a judgment for the defendant, Mr. Justice Gray, for the Supreme Judicial Court of Massachusetts, announced that "[t]he general rule is that the validity of a contract is to be determined by the law of the state in which it is made. . . ." Treating the instrument executed by Mrs. Pratt as an offer for a unilateral contract, and concluding that the offer was accepted when and where the offeree delivered goods to the buyer or to a carrier for him, which was in Maine, the court concluded that Maine law governed and gave the contract validity. The court specifically rejected, on pragmatic grounds, the suggestion that such a question of capacity to contract should be decided in accordance with the law of the domicile. Finally, having determined that the contract was valid according to the applicable foreign law, it declined to take advantage of a second line of defense for Mrs. Pratt, which was available in the doctrine of local public policy. In this it was fortified by the fact that, after the transaction but before the action had been filed, Massachusetts law had been changed so as to remove the incapacity of married women.

Cook's initial interest in the case was limited; he analyzed it only to support his local law theory.[6] Noting that the Massachusetts court applied the rule

[6] Cook, op. cit., supra note 2, at 470 et seq. (AALS Readings, at 82 et seq.). For Cook's later view, see note 3 supra.

which Maine would have applied to a purely domestic case, and did not inquire into the conflicts rules which would have indicated how Maine would have decided this particular case, with its mixed factors, he dealt a heavy blow to the theories according to which courts in conflicts cases are said to apply foreign law and to enforce foreign-created rights. ". . . [I]t follows that we must say that [the Massachusetts court] neither applied Maine 'law' nor 'recognized and enforced a Maine-created right,' as such, and that what it did do was to apply to the case before it the Massachusetts law and so to enforce a Massachusetts-created right."[7]

Cavers did not refer to *Milliken v. Pratt* specifically, but he constructed a hypothetical case which presented the same problem. His analysis, too, was advanced in support of a thesis—which, oversimplified, was "that considerations of justice and social expediency should be . . . the dominant determinants of problems in this field."[8] His principal points in connection with the *Pratt* problem were: (1) that traditional conflicts method wrongly ignores the content of the competing rules of law; (2) that a rule referring to the source of the applicable law without regard to the content of that law will produce anomalous results when the patterns of content are reversed; (3) that the traditional "contacts" which courts seek out in order to relate the case to one state or another are too meager, and too mechanically applied, and that a much wider range of facts should be taken into account; and (4) that the place where the contract is made, determined in accordance with rules of contract law for determining *when* the contract is made, is irrelevant to the selection of the rule which should govern.

This is not, of course, a full statement of the Cavers thesis. It is simply a résumé of the points developed in discussion of the *Pratt* problem, to be woven into the thesis—which, to oversimplify again, was that "[t]he choice of . . . law [sh]ould not be the result of the automatic operation of a rule or principle of selection but of a search for a just decision in the principal case."[9]

Before we begin our discussion of *Milliken v. Pratt,* I should like to change one of the facts. It is evident from the opinion of the court, and the fact has been duly noted,[10] that the change in the Massachusetts law between the time of the transaction and the filing of the suit had a material influence on the decision. But for that fact, it is possible that the Massachusetts court might have held that the applicable law was that of the married woman's domicile,[11] although that seems doubtful in view of Mr. Justice Gray's clear appreciation of the practical inconvenience of such a rule. More likely, the court, while professing adherence to the principle that the law of the place of making governs,

[7] Cook, op. cit. supra note 2, at 473 (AALS Readings, at 84–85).

[8] Cavers, op. cit. supra note 2, at 178 (AALS Readings, at 105).

[9] Id., at 193 (AALS Readings, at 114).

[10] Cook, op. cit. supra note 2, at 473 n. 49 (AALS Readings, at 84 n. 49). See also Union Trust Co. v. Grosman, 245 U.S. 412, 417 (1918).

[11] Cook, op. cit. supra note 2.

would have invoked local public policy as its justification for not applying the "applicable" law. At any rate, the change in the domestic law of Massachusetts destroyed any conflict of interest between Massachusetts and Maine, and so any real problem of conflict of laws.[12] If we are to proceed with this discussion we must have a problem. I therefore suggest that we delete from our consideration the fact that the Massachusetts law was changed. Indeed, I suggest that we go one step farther. We are not a great deal better off if all we know about the position of Massachusetts is that it retained a rule disabling married women to assume the obligations of suretyship. One of the reasons why we can tolerate a mechanical, deductive system of conflict of laws and the anomalies it produces is that frequently—and this is especially true of common-law rules—the purpose and policy of the rule is obscured by the mists of antiquity, or is obsolete, or simply inconsequential. There still may be no discernible conflict of interest. I should therefore like to assume that, shortly prior to 1870, a bill was introduced in the Massachusetts General Assembly for the enactment of a law similar to that enacted in Maine in 1866, removing the contractual disabilities of married women; that the issue was fully debated; that the proposal was defeated by a decisive though by no means overwhelming majority; and that the explicit reason for its defeat was the only one even remotely intelligible in modern times: that (in the judgment of the majority of the General Assembly) married women as a class are a peculiarly susceptible lot, prone to make improvident promises, especially under the influence of their husbands. We thus assume that by its negative action the General Assembly in effect gave deliberate approval to the existing rule: that no contract whereby any married woman might undertake to assume liability as a surety should subject her to judgment in any court.

II

Lawgivers, legislative and judicial, are accustomed to speak in terms of unqualified generality. Apart from the imperatives, the words most inevitably found in rules of law are words like "all," "every," "no," "any," and "whoever." In part, perhaps, this propensity is traceable to the fact that there lurks in all of us some vestige of the superstition that laws have an inherent quality of universality, derived from their association with Justice and Right Reason.[13] This, however, must not be taken too seriously, because in a great many cases

[12] Cf. Cavers, The Two "Local Law" Theories, 63 Harv. L. Rev. 822, 828 (1950) (AALS Readings, at 128). It is interesting to note that, when the rationale is in terms of "local public policy," the outcome of a case can legitimately be affected by a change of law or of circumstances occurring *after* the event. Would such a result become objectionable if the conflict-of-laws rules themselves were stated in terms of policy? Cf. Vanderbilt v. Vanderbilt, 354 U.S. 416, 433–35 (1957) (dissenting opinion); Yarborough v. Yarborough, 290 U.S. 202, 213 (1933) (dissenting opinion).

[13] Possibly this kind of thinking is responsible for such preposterous decisions as that in Ulman, &tc. Woolen Co. v. Magill, 155 Ga. 555, 117 S.E. 657 (1923).

it is quite obvious that the lawgivers do not mean all that they say. Suppose, for example, that we could buttonhole in the statehouse corridor the personification of the Massachusetts General Assembly and ask, "Now, really, do you mean to say that, if a married woman living in Maine should execute in Maine a guaranty of her husband's obligation to a Maine creditor, a Maine court could not or should not enter judgment on the guaranty against her?" There is no doubt at all what the startled, condescending reply would be: "Certainly not. What Maine courts do in actions between Maine parties arising out of Maine transactions is no affair of mine. Massachusetts problems are more than enough to keep me busy, thank you."

The important reason why lawgivers speak in such extravagantly general terms is that they ordinarily give no thought to the phenomena which would suggest the need for qualification. When the Massachusetts legislature addresses itself to the problem of married women as sureties, the undeveloped image in its mind is that of Massachusetts married women, husbands, creditors, transactions, courts, and judgments. In the history of Anglo-American law the domestic case has been normal, the conflict-of-laws case marginal. Probably this is still true, despite the much-publicized mobility of modern society. At least it is true in the thinking of lawyers. Nor is this a circumstance to be altogether deplored; presumptions of normality spare us, personally and professionally, a good deal of unnecessary worry and trouble.

Marginal or not, however, the conflict-of-laws case must be dealt with when it arises, if not before; and between the wholly domestic case visualized by the Massachusetts legislature and the wholly foreign case posed by our impertinent question lies an unimagined range of mixed configurations, each of them, however rare in actual occurrence, a conflict-of-laws case by definition. It may be interesting and even instructive to enumerate these cases in detail, if only because that is rarely, if ever, done. The enumeration will suggest something of the scope and difficulty of the conflict-of-laws problem which the legislature has left to the courts, and may prove an aid to analysis. Within reasonable limits, such an enumeration is possible. At first thought it may seem that, given a multiplicity of possibly significant factors and possibly interested states, the number of possible conflicts cases might verge on the astronomical. By being only a little arbitrary, however, we can keep the problem of enumeration within manageable limits.

Let us stipulate, therefore, that in a case like *Milliken v. Pratt* there are just four factors which may be significant for our purposes:

1. The domicile, or nationality, or residence, or place of business of the creditor;

2. The domicile, or nationality, or residence of the married woman;

3. The place of the transaction, i.e., the place where the contract is made, or possibly the place where it is to be performed;

4. The place where the action is brought.[14]

It is by no means a matter of indifference which of the alternative concepts mentioned in the first three factors is ultimately settled upon as the significant one; but for our immediate purposes it is not necessary to make this choice, and, for the sake of simplicity, we may assume that the facts would satisfy any of the alternatives, and lump each set of alternative concepts together.

There are two additional conditions to be observed: (a) For the time being, we are not interested in the content of the foreign rule (the content of the domestic [Massachusetts] rule is, of course, known); and (b) for present purposes we shall assume that only one foreign state is involved.

In such a case as *Milliken v. Pratt*, then, there are four factors of possible significance for the conflict of laws, each of which may be either domestic or foreign (to Massachusetts).[15] There are therefore sixteen possible combinations —sixteen different cases which may arise. One of these is the purely domestic case, and one is purely foreign. That leaves fourteen conflict-of-laws cases. By oversimplifying the problem and making certain rather arbitrary assumptions we have been able to reduce the possibilities to this relatively small range. Even so, the fourteen different conflict-of-laws cases are difficult to visualize. It may be useful to present the whole array (Table 1).

If we were to place this array before our personification of the Massachusetts General Assembly, asking that he point out just which of the fourteen mixed cases the Massachusetts rule is intended to govern, and why, we should almost certainly meet with impatience and rebuff. Most likely, the reply would be that such questions belong to the realm of conflict of laws, and are for the courts to determine.[16] This does not mean that legislatures, when they are disposed to

[14] Cf. Savigny, Private International Law, A Treatise on the Conflict of Laws and the Limits of Their Operation in Respect of Place and Time 140 (2d Eng. ed., 1880); see Yntema, op. cit. supra note 4, at 310 (AALS Readings, at 40). I am not unmindful of Cavers' admonition that "[t]he problem of defining in a phrase the fact situations presenting conflict-of-laws problems is insuperable, since what the operative facts are depend on the rules for choice of law adopted. Until these rules are definitely ascertained, who can be sure that a given case is wholly 'domestic'?" Cavers, op. cit. supra note 2, at 176 n. 10 (AALS Readings, at 103 n. 10). But one cannot very well begin a chess game with a stalemate. In the end we may find a way out of this dilemma. If we can state conflict-of-laws rules in terms of the factors which bring the policy of a state into play, the "operative facts" are not dependent upon the rules. The dilemma is presented only if we conceive of conflict-of-laws rules as being necessarily universal choice-of-law rules of the traditional type.

[15] The experimentally minded reader may wish to stop at this point and make the enumeration for himself. Unless he is a bit of a mathematician, he is likely to find the process unexpectedly difficult (as I did). Such an experience helps one to understand why legislatures ordinarily do not undertake to specify how laws shall apply to mixed cases.

[16] Cf. Cheatham, Sources of Rules for Conflict of Laws, 89 U. of Pa. L. Rev. 430, 449–50 (1941) (AALS Readings, at 133, 140): "Most statutes are formulated with regard to only the ordinary or internal situations and on the problems of Conflict of Laws they are silent. Their sphere of application or use is to be determined through the principles of Conflict of Laws." See also Cook, "Contracts" and the Conflict of Laws: "Intention" of the Parties, 32 Ill. L. Rev. 899, 908 (1938) (AALS Readings, at 639, 648).

specify how their laws shall apply to cases involving foreign factors, refrain from doing so out of deference to the courts. It simply means, in this case, that the legislature has not thought about the matter, and does not want to think about it.

Left thus to our own devices, we may inquire what policy can reasonably be attributed to the legislature, and how it can best be effectuated by the courts in their handling of mixed cases. At the outset, it is well to recognize that the legislature can effectively control the result of litigation only in its own courts, so that strictly speaking we might concern ourselves here with only half of the

TABLE 1

Case Number	Factors* 1 RC	2 RMW	3 K	4 F		
1	D	D	D	D	All factors domestic	(1)
2	F	D	D	D		
3	D	F	D	D	One foreign factor	(4)
4	D	D	F	D		
5	D	D	D	F		
6	F	F	D	D		
7	D	F	F	D		
8	D	D	F	F	Two foreign factors	(6)
9	F	D	D	F		
10	F	D	F	D		
11	D	F	D	F		
12	F	F	F	D		
13	F	F	D	F	Three foreign factors	(4)
14	F	D	F	F		
15	D	F	F	F		
16	F	F	F	F	All factors foreign	(1)

* 1. Residence of the creditor.
2. Residence of the married woman.
3. Place of contracting.
4. Forum.

cases. We shall not so confine ourselves, however, because the legislature may desire to control the event of litigation in foreign courts, and the foreign court may, for one reason or another, defer to that desire.

It is surely not a difficult matter to formulate the legislative policy in this case. We have in effect already done so in the act of artificial respiration performed on the moribund body of the law concerning the contractual capacity of married women. Massachusetts, in common with all other American states and many foreign countries, believes in freedom of contract, in the security of commercial transactions, in vindicating the reasonable expectations of promisees. It also believes, however, that married women constitute a class requiring special protection. It has therefore subordinated its policy of security of transactions to its policy of protecting married women. More specifically, it has subordinated the interests of creditors to the interests of this particular, favored class of debtors. It has felt the influence of pressure groups—banking and commercial interests, feminists, liberals, traditionalists, conservatives. It has weighed competing considerations. Many of the legislators have been persuaded that there should be a change. Yet, although the decision runs counter to the interests of powerful constituents, the legislature decides in favor of protecting married women.

What married women? Why, those with whose welfare Massachusetts is concerned, of course—*i.e.*, Massachusetts married women. In 1866 Maine emancipated (its) married women. Is Massachusetts declaring that decision erroneous, attempting to alter its effect? Certainly not. Given a slightly different configuration of the little causes that determine the outcome of the legislative process, Massachusetts might have decided the same way. Who can say that Maine, or Massachusetts for that matter,[17] was wrong? All that happened was that in each state the legislature weighed competing considerations, with different results. Well, each to his own. Let Maine go feminist and modern; as for Massachusetts, it will stick to the old ways—for Massachusetts women. Never mind, for the time being, exactly what we mean by "Massachusetts" married women—whether citizens, domiciliaries, residents. For the sake of convenience, until we must decide that question, let us say that it is *residence* in Massachusetts which defines the ambit of the state's protective policy.

The margin, narrow or substantial, by which the proposed change in Massachusetts law failed of enactment will soon be forgotten; when legislation is passed (or not passed) the vote, being immaterial, is not reported in the statute books. The result stands in all its emphatic generality, the word of the legislature, unweakened by expressions of dissent. This is The Law, this is the Just Rule—this, it is all too easy to infer, is Right Reason, all else being error, all else being rejected. But any such inference is a far cry from the realities of the legislative process. The legislature knew very well that it was not discovering the "true" rule, rejecting error. The legislature was not abnegating the principle of security of commercial transactions. Massachusetts had, and still has, *two* interests: security of transactions, and protection of Massachusetts married women. The first has been subordinated; it has not been destroyed. Perhaps the converse is not quite true for Maine. True, for many years prior to 1866 that state had subordinated its interest in the security of transactions to a policy of protecting its married women, and the change in the law may even have come about through a very close vote. Yet it seems far-fetched to say that Maine retains a subordinate interest in the protection of its married women. Security of transactions is, for both states, the basic policy, and the incapacitation of classes

[17] Of course, from the vantage point of 1958, we can make an objective and pragmatic judgment in favor of Maine's policy. The point, however, is that such questions are for legislatures to determine in the light of their advices at the time, and that no higher principles of reason were violated by the legislature of either state. There was no inconsistency in the two laws since, at least in the purely domestic context, each had its impact on a different group of married women.

of persons the exception. It seems more realistic to say that Maine has completely abandoned the policy of treating married women as a favored—or disfavored—class; and that its interest in protecting the weak and susceptible is implemented, with respect to married women, just as it is with respect to other persons generally—*i.e.*, through the more discriminating defenses of duress, fraud, mistake, want of mental capacity, and so on.

So far, nothing that we have said provides any basis for a suggestion that the place where the contract is made has anything whatever to do with the policy of the Massachusetts legislature. Yet Mr. Justice Gray tells us that "[t]he general rule is that the validity of a contract is to be determined by the law of the state in which it is made. . . ." Unless we have been very much mistaken in the foregoing formulation of the Massachusetts policy, the legislature was concerned with *people*—primarily Massachusetts married women—and the effects of their being induced to sign certain documents. What possible difference can it make where the document is signed? What effect will such a general rule have upon the Massachusetts policy?[18]

Before we examine that effect in detail, some preliminary observations are important. First of all, it would be remarkable if a rule, developed in the domestic law of contracts to determine *when* a contract is made, should prove serviceable in determining *where* a contract is made—assuming that the place of making has any relevance at all to such questions in the conflict of laws.[19] For all the conceptual language that went into its development, that rule is best understood and evaluated as an allocation, between parties negotiating by correspondence, of the risks of uncertainty, delay, non-delivery, and so on. The more the rule is shaped consciously to this practical end, the more apparent becomes its irrelevance to the problems of conflict of laws. This is easily demonstrated by the familiar classroom parade of hypothetical cases. If Deering, Milliken & Co. had delivered the goods to Mr. Pratt in Massachusetts using their own wagons, the contract would have been "made in Massachusetts," and Mrs. Pratt presumably would have escaped liability—though the mode of conveyance would seem to be totally irrelevant to any discernible Massachusetts policy.[20] The bilateral contract emerging from a long series of counter-offers, the contract made by telephone, the bargain concluded on board an airplane, all lend themselves to the same demonstration.

Secondly, there is no reason whatever to suppose that any alternate rule, even

[18] The analysis in terms of state interests which is employed here has been most explicitly suggested by Freund, Chief Justice Stone and the Conflict of Laws, 59 Harv. L. Rev. 1210, 1216, 1223 (1946). See also Hancock, Choice-of-Law Policies in Multiple Contract Cases, 5 U. of Toronto L. J. 132, 136–37, 142–43 (1943).

[19] It will be recognized that here, as in much of the argument to follow, I am using ideas advanced by Cavers and Cook. The repetition seems desirable in the interest of development of the argument, and there may perhaps be a somewhat different emphasis.

[20] Cf. Cheatham, Goodrich, Griswold & Reese, Cases and Materials on Conflict of Laws 488 (4th ed., 1957).

one devised expressly to determine *where* a contract is made for the purposes of conflict of laws, as distinguished from one designed to determine *when* it is made for purposes of allocating risks, would serve any useful purpose. I suppose a case can be stated in which there is no conceivable doubt as to *where* the contract is made—and to be performed. The parties meet in person, accompanied by their counsel, in the center of a stadium. The document is read aloud. With solemn, ceremonial flourish the document is signed, sealed, witnessed, and delivered. The parties shake hands. The document provides that when payment—the only performance called for—is due, the parties will meet again in the same place to make and receive it. To devise a rule which would admit the statement that the contract was made in any other place would challenge the ingenuity of a Lewis Carroll.[21] If the scene is enacted in Massachusetts, the immanent law of that state, which droppeth as the gentle rain from heaven, pervades the contract, rendering it, if it is the promise of a married woman to answer for the debt of her husband, wet and void.[22] If, then, as persons seeking shelter from the rain, the parties move their solemn charade across a state line, and act out their parts in a congenially dry climate, what possible difference can that make in terms of anything that Massachusetts or any other interested state may be trying to accomplish through its laws? We may invent doctrines of local public policy[23] and fraud on the law,[24] and resort to other devices to contain the absurdities spawned by sanctification of the place of making; but, as we shall see, they have not been effectively contained. Why not face the fact that the place of making is quite irrelevant; why not summon public policy from the reserves and place it in the front line where it belongs?[25]

But perhaps we move too fast. The way to judge the rule is to see how it operates. The first thing to notice is that, by adoption of the rule that the law of the place of making governs, Massachusetts renounces any claim that its

[21] But cf. California Law Revision Commission, Recommendation and Study Relating to Choice of Law Governing Survival of Actions J-18 (1957): "If legislation were enacted providing that the survival of a tort action is to be controlled by the place of the wrong, this would still leave considerable discretion in the court. Where is the place of the wrong? . . . Further assume that the parties were residents of the same state. . . . Could not the state of residence be reasonably considered the state with the primary interests and hence the place of the wrong?"

[22] "Those laws pervade all transactions which take place where they prevail, and give them their color and legal effect." Bradley, J., in The Scotland, 105 U.S. 24, 29 (1881).

[23] See Union Trust Co. v. Grosman, 245 U.S. 412 (1918).

[24] See Cheatham, Goodrich, Griswold & Reese, Cases and Materials on Conflict of Laws 519–20 (4th ed., 1957).

[25] Five articles are generally helpful in this connection: Nussbaum, Public Policy and the Political Crisis in the Conflict of Laws, 49 Yale L. J. 1027 (1940) (AALS Readings, at 220); Paulsen & Sovern, "Public Policy" in the Conflict of Laws, 56 Col. L. Rev. 969 (1956); Katzenbach, Conflicts on an Unruly Horse: Reciprocal Claims and Tolerances in Interstate and International Law, 65 Yale L. J. 1087 (1956); Neuner, Policy Considerations in the Conflict of Laws, 20 Can. Bar Rev. 479 (1942); Yntema, The Objectives of Private International Law, 35 Can. Bar Rev. 721 (1957).

law should control the result in exactly half of the mixed cases; for in seven of the possible cases the third factor, the place of making, which is all-important, is foreign. Furthermore, of the seven remaining cases, in which the applicability of Massachusetts law is asserted because the place of making is domestic, Massachusetts can be sure of effecting the result it purports to desire in only three, because Massachusetts can directly control the result only in its own courts, and there are only three cases (Nos. 2, 3, and 6) in which the third and fourth factors (place of making and forum) are both domestic. On the face of it, this is an extraordinarily diffident attitude for a "sovereign" state to assume. This rule, this product of the General Assembly's most careful deliberation, is to govern only seven of the fourteen possible cases? And is to govern four of those seven only by the grace and deference of a foreign court?[26]

Assume for the moment a different attitude, carried to an extreme. Assume a quite selfish state, concerned only with promoting its own interests; a state, if you please, blind to consequences, and interested only in short-run "gains." Such a state might be expected to apply its law disabling married women, or to desire its application: (1) to every case in which both parties reside in the state (Nos. 4, 5, and 8), since it has decided to subordinate the interests of domestic creditors to the interests of domestic married women; and, a fortiori, (2) to all cases in which the married woman is domestic and the creditor foreign (Nos. 2, 9, 10, and 14)—in short, to all cases in which the married woman is a local resident, regardless of the creditor's residence. Such a state would not be expected to apply its law to any case in which the creditor is a local resident and the married woman a foreigner (Nos. 3, 7, 11, and 15). It would be indifferent, and would cheerfully apply the foreign law, to the cases in which neither party is a local resident (Nos. 6, 12, and 13). The question is not, for the moment, whether such an attitude would be shocking, or unwise, or unjust, or unconstitutional. The question is whether it would be rational; and the answer is that it *would*—in the sense that, in the short run, without considering how other states or higher authority might react, the state would in this manner be doing all it could to maximize its own interests.

It will be understood, I hope, that to recognize the rationality of such an attitude is not necessarily to commend it. But a statement of what a state would do, acting solely in its own interests, may serve as a gauge to measure the extent to which states do not so act, and thus provide a basis for discussing the phenomenon of their failure to do so.

With these considerations in mind, let us examine the cases which Massachusetts, by embracing the rule that the law of the place of making governs, has (1) determined to control, (2) asserted, somewhat wishfully, an interest in controlling, and (3) disclaimed an interest in controlling.

The cases in the first class are shown in Table 2.

[26] Possibly, of course, by virtue of the full-faith-and-credit clause of the federal Constitution, Article IV, Section 1. But that is a consideration to be reserved for the time being.

In Case No. 2, application of the domestic law makes good sense. It protects Massachusetts married women, and that without expense to Massachusetts creditors. If the foreign state is Maine, Maine's interest in the security of transactions is defeated. But if one state's policy must yield, should not the court prefer the policy of its own state?

In Case No. 3, despite the fact that three of the four factors are domestic, application of the domestic law makes no sense whatever. In the context with which we are concerned, it is abundantly clear that there is at stake no policy of Massachusetts relating to the administration of her courts. Sometimes such a policy is involved, and legitimately, as when the state believes that certain types of claims consume the time of courts without adequate social justification, or tend to the corruption of judicial processes.[27] No such considerations are involved here; no one suggests that the Massachusetts rule as to a married woman's capacity is "procedural." The only policies apparently at stake are

TABLE 2

Case Number	Factors 1 R C	2 R M W	3 K	4 F
2	F	D	D	D
3	D	F	D	D
6	F	F	D	D

those which have been suggested. And how does the application of the domestic law in Case No. 3 accord with those policies? (1) It does not advance the interest of Massachusetts in protecting Massachusetts married women, for the defendant is not a resident of Massachusetts. (2) It subverts the interest of Massachusetts in the security of transactions, to the detriment of a Massachusetts creditor. This interest, it should be remembered, was not renounced by the legislative action, but only subordinated to another interest, which is not present in this case. Moreover, suppose that at this point we inquire into the identity of the foreign state, and into the content of its law. The foreign state proves to be Maine, which has emancipated its married women. In that event, application of the Massachusetts law (3) does not advance any interest of Maine in protecting married women and (4) conflicts with Maine's general policy of security of transactions, although that policy is not directly involved, since the creditor is a Massachusetts resident. In short, application of the domestic rule advances no interest of either state, and clearly subverts an important interest of Massachusetts itself. That is to say, it advances no interest which has yet become apparent. Whether there are higher interests which warrant such apparently irrational behavior remains to be seen.

[27] See N.Y. Civ. Prac. Act § 61-a (1941); N.Y. L. Rev. Comm'n Rep. 243 (1947); id., at 200 (1935); Paulsen & Sovern, op. cit. supra note 24, at 1002.

In Case No. 6, application of the domestic law makes no sense either. Both parties are nonresidents. Massachusetts has no interest in the married woman, and no apparent justification for upsetting the creditor's reasonable expectations. Massachusetts is merely meddling. In so doing, it subverts Maine's legitimate interest in the security of transactions where Maine creditors are concerned, without advancing any state's interest in protecting married women.

In short, of the three cases which Massachusetts has determined to control, and which she can effectively control, the application of Massachusetts law makes sense, in terms of Massachusetts policy, in only one. In the other two, the application of that law advances the interests of neither state, and subverts an interest of one state or the other. This is, indeed, peculiar behavior.

The cases in which Massachusetts had said that Massachusetts law ought to apply, but in which a foreign court will make the decision, are shown in Table 3.

In Case No. 5 it is reasonable enough for Massachusetts to express the hope that other states will apply Massachusetts law. That is what Massachusetts

TABLE 3

Case Number	Factors 1 R C	2 R M W	3 K	4 F
5..........	D	D	D	F
9..........	F	D	D	F
11..........	D	F	D	F
13..........	F	F	D	F

would do if the case were in her courts (Case No. 1). No other state appears to have any legitimate interest in the matter.

In Case No. 9, also, it is reasonable for Massachusetts to hope that foreign courts will apply Massachusetts law. This is the foreign creditor against the domestic married woman. If the case were in the Massachusetts courts, Massachusetts would rationally apply domestic law (Case No. 2, discussed above). This may be asking a good deal of the foreign state, since now the power factor is reversed and Maine is in position to give preference to its own policy. But Massachusetts has done what it can.

In Case No. 11, the creditor is a resident of Massachusetts and the married woman is a nonresident. If the foreign state is Maine, it is simply irrational for Massachusetts to express the hope that Massachusetts law will be applied. True, if the case were in a Massachusetts court, Massachusetts would so decide (Case No. 3, discussed above); but that decision would be irrational, and this is so for the same reasons.

In Case No. 13, the Massachusetts hope that the foreign court will apply Massachusetts law is presumptuous and downright laughable. Massachusetts has nothing whatever to do with the case except that the contract was "made" there. If the foreign state is Maine, Massachusetts is asking that state to subvert its own policy, which gives primacy to the security of transactions, even where Maine interests alone are involved. True, if the case were in a Massachusetts court, Massachusetts would so decide (Case No. 6, discussed above); but if such a result would be indefensible in a Massachusetts court, it would be more painfully so in a court of Maine.

In short, the expression by Massachusetts of hope that foreign courts will apply Massachusetts law makes sense, in terms of Massachusetts interests, in only two of the four cases. In the other two, realization of the hope would advance the policy of neither state, and would defeat the policy of one state or the other.

Of the seven cases which Massachusetts has disclaimed an interest in controlling, four are cases which it has de facto power to control, since they are in Massachusetts courts, as shown in Table 4.

In Case No. 4, the position taken by Massachusetts seems incredibly perverse. No state other than Massachusetts has any interest in the matter. Yet

TABLE 4

Case Number	Factors 1 R C	2 R M W	3 K	4 F
4	D	D	F	D
7	D	F	F	D
10	F	D	F	D
12	F	F	F	D

Massachusetts goes to the trouble of ascertaining and applying foreign law. To what end? The result, if the foreign state is Maine, is to defeat Massachusetts' own preferred policy of protecting its married women, without advancing any policy whatever.

In Case No. 7, where the creditor is domestic and the married woman a nonresident, the application of foreign law, if the foreign state is Maine, results in the furtherance of Massachusetts' subsidiary interest in security of transactions for local creditors without impairing any interest of either state in the protection of married women.

In Case No. 10, application of the law of Maine results in furthering Maine's legitimate interest in security of transactions at the expense of Massachusetts' legitimate interest in the protection of its married women. Let us not condemn such a result hastily. Where the interest of the foreign state is substantial and legitimate, as here, there may well be, among civilized states, reasons for relaxing the uncompromising attitude of selfishness and requiring legitimate local policy to yield.[28] Inquiry into the possible existence of such reasons is

[28] "In saying all this it is not meant to suggest that there are not situations in which a married woman from another state should be held to have the same contractual capacity as married women domiciled in the state in which she acts." Cook, The Logical and Legal Bases of the Conflict of Laws 440 (1942).

deferred for the time being. We should note now, however, that Massachusetts' position in this case is quite inconsistent with its position in Case No. 2, discussed above, where, faced with the identical conflict of interests, Massachusetts reached the conclusion that the foreign policy must yield.[29] If Massachusetts in Case No. 10 is acting upon altruistic or far-sighted considerations which we have not yet discovered, she does not do so consistently.

In Case No. 12, the result of applying foreign law is eminently satisfactory. Maine alone is concerned. Maine would decide the same way if the case were in a Maine court (Case No. 16). Massachusetts has no reason to desire a different result. Maine policy is furthered without impairment of any policy of Massachusetts.

In short, in these four cases where Massachusetts has disclaimed interest and willingly applied foreign law though it had de facto power to do otherwise with less trouble, the result clearly makes sense in terms of Massachusetts' interests in only two cases. In one case Massachusetts' interests are made to yield to

TABLE 5

	Factors			
	1	2	3	4
	R	R	K	F
Case	C	M		
Number		W		
8..........	D	D	F	F
14..........	F	D	F	F
15..........	D	F	F	F

those of the foreign state. In the remaining case, Massachusetts' interests are subverted without advancing any foreign interest.

Finally, Table 5 shows the three cases which Massachusetts has disclaimed an interest in controlling, and which it cannot effectively control since they are in foreign courts.

In Case No. 8, Massachusetts invites Maine to apply Maine law although Maine has no interest in doing so, and although the result is to subvert Massachusetts policy with no advantage to Maine.

In Case No. 14, Massachusetts invites Maine to apply Maine law, preferring the interest of Maine and its creditors to that of Massachusetts and its married women. (Compare Cases Nos. 2 and 10, discussed above.)

In Case No. 15, Massachusetts invites Maine to apply Maine law with the result that Massachusetts' subsidiary interest in security of transactions is advanced without prejudice to any policy for the protection of married women.

In short, the result of the application of foreign law is subversive of Massachusetts' interests in two cases, in neither of which is any interest of the foreign state advanced. In one case the policy of Massachusetts is advanced without detriment to any state's policy.

[29] The positions are inconsistent, that is, unless the fact that the place of making differs in the two cases is ground for distinction, which of course it is not.

Summarizing the entire series, we find that application of the law of the place of making has the results shown in Table 6, if we assume (1) that the foreign law is different and (2) that Massachusetts' wishes will be respected by the foreign state.

A startling fact shown by this table is that the *largest* group of cases (group VI) consists of those in which application of the rule subverts domestic interest without advancing any interest of the foreign state. Add to this the group in which foreign interests are subverted with no advancement of domestic policy (group V), and we have a total of six of the fourteen cases in which the operation of the rule seems purely perverse. Against this result, note that application of the rule advances domestic interests in only five cases (groups I and III), and in two of these does so at the expense of foreign interests. Note also that the re-

TABLE 6

I	Domestic interest advanced without detriment to foreign interests	Case No. 5 (D D D F)	(3)
		Case No. 7 (D F F D)	
		Case No. 15 (D F F F)	
II	Foreign interest advanced without detriment to domestic interests	Case No. 12 (F F F D)	(1)
III	Domestic interest advanced at expense of foreign interests	Case No. 2 (F D D D)	(2)
		Case No. 9 (F D D F)	
IV	Foreign interest advanced at expense of domestic interests	Case No. 10 (F D F D)	(2)
		Case No. 14 (F D F F)	
V	Foreign interest subverted with no advancement of domestic interests	Case No. 6 (F F D D)	(2)
		Case No. 13 (F F D F)	
VI	Domestic interest subverted without advancement of foreign interests	Case No. 3 (D F D D)	(4)
		Case No. 11 (D F D F)	
		Case No. 4 (D D F D)	
		Case No. 8 (D D F F)	

sult in the two cases last mentioned is exactly counterbalanced by the fact that in two cases, apparently indistinguishable (group IV), domestic interests are subordinated to foreign. The deference to foreign interests appears to have a certain rhythm, but is without rhyme or reason.

From the point of view of Maine (*i.e.*, of a state which has emancipated its married women), the array of possible cases is, of course, a mirror image of that presented in Table 1, as shown in Table 1a.

Maine has asserted the primacy of its interest in the security of transactions. In the selfish pursuit of this interest, Maine should logically desire the application of its own law (1) to all cases in which both parties reside in the state (Nos. 6, 12, and 13), and also to all cases in which the creditor is a local resident and the married woman foreign (Nos. 2, 9, 10 and 14)—in short, to all cases in which the creditor is a local resident, regardless of the married woman's residence. When the married woman is a resident and the creditor a nonresident (Nos. 3, 7, 11, and 15), Maine, by applying its own law, can advance the foreign

—the common—interest in security of transactions without impairing any interest of its own. (Maine is not assumed to be so selfish as to want to advance the interests of Maine debtors where it has adopted no relevant protective policy.) It would be indifferent, and would cheerfully apply the foreign law, to the cases in which neither party is a local resident (Nos. 4, 5, and 8).

TABLE 1a

Case Number	Factors 1 R C	2 R M W	3 K	4 F		
1	F	F	F	F	All Factors Foreign	(1)
2	D	F	F	F	Three Foreign Factors	(4)
3	F	D	F	F		
4	F	F	D	F		
5	F	F	F	D		
6	D	D	F	F	Two Foreign Factors	(6)
7	F	D	D	F		
8	F	F	D	D		
9	D	F	F	D		
10	D	F	D	F		
11	F	D	F	D		
12	D	D	D	F	One Foreign Factor	(4)
13	D	D	F	D		
14	D	F	D	D		
15	F	D	D	D		
16	D	D	D	D	All Factors Domestic	(1)

By a repetition of the process previously employed to appraise the results of application of the law of the place of making in terms of the interests of the states concerned (the details need not be repeated here) we can arrive at the results shown in Table 6a, which is, of course, correlative to Table 6.

TABLE 6a

I. Domestic interest advanced without detriment to foreign interests	Case No. 12 (D D D F)	(1)
II. Foreign interest advanced without detriment to domestic interests	Case No. 15 (F D D D)	(3)
	Case No. 7 (F D D F)	
	Case No. 5 (F F F D)	
III. Domestic interest advanced at expense of foreign interests	Case No. 14 (D F D D)	(2)
	Case No. 10 (D F D F)	
IV. Foreign interest advanced at expense of domestic interests	Case No. 9 (D F F D)	(2)
	Case No. 2 (D F F F)	
V. Foreign interest subverted with no advancement of domestic interests	Case No. 8 (F F D D)	(4)
	Case No. 4 (F F D F)	
	Case No. 11 (F D F D)	
	Case No. 3 (F D F F)	
VI. Domestic interest subverted without advancement of foreign interests	Case No. 13 (D D F D)	(2)
	Case No. 6 (D D F F)	

Table 7 compares, for the fourteen conflict-of-laws cases, the results which would be reached in the advancement of the selfish interests of Massachusetts (Column 1), in the advancement of Maine's selfish interests (Column 2), and by the uniform application of the law of the place of making (Column 3). (The plus sign [+] indicates that the contract would be held valid; the zero [0] that it would be held invalid.) This merely confirms what we have already observed, *viz.*, that in six of the fourteen cases the result of the uniform application of the law of the place of making is contrary to that dictated by the interests of both states (Nos. 3, 4, 6, 8, 11, and 13), while in only four (Nos. 5, 7, 12, and 15) does the result conform to that indicated by the interests of both states. In the remaining four cases (Nos. 2, 9, 10, and 14) the result is contrary to the interest of one state or the other.

TABLE 7

Case Number	Law Applied and Result 1		2		3	
2........	Mass	0	Me	+	Mass	0
3........	Me	+	Me	+	Mass	0
4........	Mass	0	Mass	0	Me	+
5........	Mass	0	Mass	0	Mass	0
6........	Me	+	Me	+	Mass	0
7........	Me	+	Me	+	Me	+
8........	Mass	0	Mass	0	Me	+
9........	Mass	0	Me	+	Mass	0
10........	Mass	0	Me	+	Me	+
11........	Me	+	Me	+	Mass	0
12........	Me	+	Me	+	Me	+
13........	Me	+	Me	+	Mass	0
14........	Mass	0	Me	+	Me	+
15........	Me	+	Me	+	Me	+

III

The utility of a rule which operates so capriciously must certainly be suspect. That such a rule should have been announced and followed at all seems almost incredible.[30] In fact, as everyone knows, it has not been followed consistently. When the indicated result is absurd and is perceived to be so, there are means of escaping it. The connecting factor—the place of contracting—is not always intractable, and re-examination of the facts may lead to its relocation.[31] In the cases falling into Group IV (Table 6), applicability of the foreign law may be conceded and the result avoided by invoking "local public policy"; in a case like No. 4 (Table 1) (D D F D) the same idea can be expressed and the same result reached through the expletive "fraud on the law." Alternative choice-of-law rules are available (law of the place of performance, law intended by the parties, law giving validity to the contract, law of the place having the most sub-

[30] Neuner, op. cit. supra note 25, at 498, offers the most charitable explanation.

[31] Compare Mutual Life Ins. Co. v. Liebing, 259 U.S. 209 (1922), with New York Life Ins. Co. v. Dodge, 246 U.S. 357 (1918). See Cavers, A Critique of the Choice-of-Law Problem, 47 Harv. L. Rev. 173, 182 (1933) (AALS Readings, at 107 et seq.).

stantial connection). Fortified with knowledge of the availability of these devices, an uninitiated reader might well ask whether any court would actually reach such results as are indicated in Groups V and VI (Tables 6 and 6a).

It may be doubted that Mr. Justice Gray would have done so. Like an Alpinist ascending an unknown slope, he left inconspicuous little handholds to facilitate his retreat if the route should lead to danger.[32] Let there be no doubt, however, that courts actually do reach the results which seem so indefensible. Bad law makes hard cases. The hypnotic power of the ideas of territorial jurisdiction and vested rights is not to be underestimated. It must not be forgotten that only a few years ago the United States Supreme Court was able to hold that an attempt by a state other than that where the contract was made to control the incidents of a contract was so presumptuous an intermeddling with matters beyond the state's legitimate sphere of governmental function as to amount to a denial of due process of law—and this although the state in question had a substantial practical basis for its asserted interest.[33] In what appears to be the same spirit of conceptualism, the courts have announced capricious results in cases involving married women's contracts. In *Greenlee v. Hardin*[34] a married woman domiciled in Mississippi executed a promissory note dated and payable in Florida to a Florida corporation. Action was brought in Mississippi. By the law of Florida married women lacked capacity to make a valid promissory note; by the law of Mississippi there was no such incapacity. This is precisely Case No. 11 (F D F D) from Tables 1a and 6a. The Mississippi court, relying primarily on the place-of-making rule and secondarily on the place-of-performance rule, held that Florida law governed and the note was invalid. In so doing, the Mississippi court, at some inconvenience to itself, subverted Florida's subsidiary interest in the security of transactions without advancing any interest of either state in the protection of married women. And in *Burr v. Beckler*[35] a married woman who was a resident of Illinois executed a note for the

[32] He stated that the rule was the "general" rule, implying the possibility of exceptions. He stated that a contract valid by the law of the place of making was valid everywhere, but did not state the converse proposition. He noted that the contract was not only made but to be performed in Maine. He also left open the possibility that some significance might be attached to the fact that the guaranty bore "date of Portland." Cf. Chemical National Bank v. Kellogg, 183 N.Y. 92, 75 N.E. 1103 (1905).

[33] New York Life Ins. Co. v. Dodge, 246 U.S. 357 (1918). See also Allgeyer v. Louisiana, 165 U.S. 578 (1897).

[34] 157 Miss. 229, 127 So. 777 (1930).

[35] 264 Ill. 230, 106 N.E. 206 (1914). It may be thought that this decision was influenced by the elements of fraud in the case. If so, we may substitute a similar decision in which there is no indication of such an explanation: Nichols & Shepard Co. v. Marshall, 108 Iowa 518, 79 N.W. 282 (1899). The married woman, domiciled in Iowa, signed the note while temporarily visiting in Indiana. The residence of the creditor does not appear. The Iowa court applied Indiana law to invalidate the note. This is either Case No. 11 or Case No. 13 from Tables 1a and 6a. Whatever the creditor's residence, the decision frustrated one state's interest without advancing any interest of the other.

accommodation of her husband while she was "temporarily sojourning" in Florida. The creditor interests were associated only with Illinois, by whose law married women were competent to make such contracts. Action was brought in Illinois. By the law of Florida, such contracts were invalid. The Illinois court, finding that the place of making was Florida, inexorably applied the Florida rule and held the contract invalid. This is precisely Case No. 13 (D D F D) from Tables 1a and 6a. The decision of the Illinois court, which was not reached without some inconvenience in the ascertainment of foreign law, frustrated Illinois' own interest in the security of transactions without advancing the interest of any state in the protection of married women.

We need not pause to inquire *why* courts behave in such strange ways. The history of conflict-of-laws theory makes that plain enough. The question is whether there is any rational justification for their continuing to do so, now that the infirmities of the traditional method are so well understood.

The most forceful affirmative defense that can be made for the traditional method is that it leads to uniformity of result, regardless of the state in which the action is brought. This, given the assumptions of the method, is undeniably true. It is also undeniably true that uniformity of result should be one of the primary objectives of a rational system of conflict of laws. According to the rule that the law of the place of making governs, any given case is decided in the same way irrespective of the state in which the action is brought. That is to say, this is the result if both states (1) characterize the problem in the same way, as one involving the validity of a contract, and (2) apply the rule that the law of the place of making governs (rather than some alternative rule), and (3) locate the connecting factor (the place of making) in the same way, and (4) do not invoke any second-line defenses, such as local public policy. This is a long list of "ifs," and we are well aware that the discipline of the system is not always sufficient to maintain adherence to all of the necessary conditions when the result is perceived to be anomalous.[36] The ideal uniformity of result is, therefore, to some extent illusory. But assume that the necessary conditions are all observed, and the ideal uniformity results. Is the achievement worth the cost at which it was attained? The cost, be it remembered, is that in six of the fourteen possible cases the interests of one state are defeated without advancement of the interests of the other, and that in two additional cases the interests of the forum are made to yield to foreign interests. In only four cases are the interests of one state advanced without impairment of a foreign interest. In two cases the interests of the forum are given preference over foreign interests. This seems an extravagant price to pay for uniformity of result—the more so since the attainment of that goal is in fact problematical. We are moved to recognize again that uniformity of result, while it is a basic and ever-present desideratum in conflict-of-laws cases, is one which should at times be made to yield to stronger con-

[36] See Cavers, op. cit. supra note 31; Paulsen & Sovern, op. cit. supra note 25.

siderations.[37] And it may be added that, in the only two cases in which uniformity can be said to be without question an imperative objective (Nos. 5 and 12, in which all factors except the place of action are associated with the same state), uniformity would be attained if the respective states did no more than consult their own legitimate interests.

Another argument that may be made for adherence to the system might be called the "dragnet" defense. Sometimes a court may be shrewdly aware that a given choice-of-law rule will sometimes subvert its own state's interest, but will nevertheless adopt the rule in the equally shrewd belief that it will operate in the vast majority of cases in such a way as to advance that interest.[38] So far, in this paper, we have treated each of the fourteen conflict-of-laws cases as equally probable—as if the combinations of factors were determined by pure chance. That, of course, is not always the case. For example, a Massachusetts court committed to the advancement of local interests might reason that the overwhelming majority of all conflict-of-laws cases involving contracts of Massachusetts married women must be brought in Massachusetts, since that is the only state in which it is likely that process may be validly served. It might then, if it could plausibly do so, characterize the Massachusetts rule as one of procedure, to be applied to all actions in Massachusetts courts. In this way it would approximate the implementation of Massachusetts policy, although in rare cases the logic of the system would result in a Massachusetts married woman's being held liable in a foreign court and in a foreign married woman's escaping liability in a Massachusetts court. The device has the virtue of simplicity, since it avoids embroilment in all the variations which have preoccupied us in the discussion so far; it may also avoid, or seem to avoid, troublesome questions of constitutionality. No such manipulation of the system seems possible, however, with respect to the rule that the law of the place of making governs, in its application to the contracts of married women. There is no a priori or other reason for supposing that more such contracts are made at home than abroad. This is a factor, so far as appears, which is in fact determined by pure chance. The result is that the rule cannot be defended on the ground that, in addition to being simple, it will effectuate Massachusetts policy in the bulk of the cases. It will do so in only half.

The last excuse for adhering to the capricious rule which exalts the law of the place of making is that no acceptable substitute has been found. Though purely negative, this defense is a formidable one and doubtless constitutes, at least in modern times, an important reason for the endurance of the system.

[37] Cf. Rheinstein, The Place of Wrong: A Study in the Method of Case Law, 19 Tul. L. Rev. 4, 29–30 (1944); Katzenbach, op. cit. supra note 25, at 1097–1101; Harper, Policy Bases of the Conflict of Laws: Reflections on Rereading Professor Lorenzen's Essays, 56 Yale L. J, 1155, 1159 (1947); Freund, op. cit. supra note 18, at 1211, 1236.

[38] Cf. Emery v. Burbank, 163 Mass. 326, 39 N.E. 1026 (1895); Bullington v. Angel, 220 N.C. 18, 16 S.E.2d 411 (1941).

The available alternative rules for choice of law are not satisfactory substitutes. The place of performance would be quite as irrelevant in the context of the *Pratt* problem as the place of making. This is not to say that the place of performance is always irrelevant; a contract to dance naked in the streets of Rome can hardly be considered without reference to Roman law. It is difficult to perceive any connection, however, between the law of the place where payment is to be made and the capacity of a married woman to contract. The rule that the law intended by the parties shall govern (in so far as it is not a pure fiction, totally incapable of explaining the choice) accords to the incapacitated party the power to contract out of her disability—a privilege she may be assumed not to enjoy in a purely domestic case; and the result is pro tanto the subversion of the interest of the state to which she belongs. Similarly, a rule permitting the selection of the law of any state having a connection (in terms of the given factors) with the case, so long as that law gives validity to the contract, must to some extent impair the apparent interest of a state which has, and has asserted, an interest in protecting the incapacitated party.[39] The rule that points to the law of the state having the most real or substantial connection with the case seems an amorphous substitute for the analysis which must go into any satisfactory handling of this difficult problem.[40]

It is obvious that in this paper considerable emphasis has been placed upon the relationship of the parties to the states involved—*i.e.*, to their residence, or domicile, or nationality. That emphasis is indispensable in any consideration of the respective policies involved; yet a return to the rule, rejected by Mr. Justice Gray, that the contractual capacity of a person is governed by the law of his domicile, is not a satisfactory solution. It is true that, since this rule turns upon a factor which is relevant to the policies involved instead of one which is irrelevant, the results would lack the sheer perversity of those produced by the place-of-making rule. The fact remains that domicile is an intolerably elusive factor in commercial transactions; and, even if this objection could be largely met by substituting a factual concept of "settled residence,"[41] a choice-of-law

[39] See generally Cheatham, Goodrich, Griswold & Reese, Cases and Materials on Conflict of Laws 502–505 (4th ed., 1957), and materials cited. However, the English doctrine of the "proper" law of the contract seems, at least on the basis of some interpretations, to permit something like the analysis of interests here suggested. See Morris, The Proper Law of a Tort, 64 Harv. L. Rev. 881 (1951) (AALS Readings, at 575); and cf. Cook, op cit. supra note 16, at 907–910, 917–20 (AALS Readings, at 648–49, 656–58).

[40] Cf. Jones v. Metropolitan Life Ins. Co., 158 Misc. 466, 286 N.Y.Supp. 4 (S.Ct., 1936).

[41] Cavers, op. cit. supra note 31, at 191 (AALS Readings, at 113), suggests not only the relevance but the workability of the concept of "settled residence." I do not underestimate the difficulties involved in defining and using such a concept, but I think they are overestimated in Reese & Green, That Elusive Word, "Residence," 6 Vand. L. Rev. 561 (1953) (AALS Readings, at 483). Likewise, I think Messrs. Reese and Green overestimate the virtues of the concept of domicile. In part they are able to do this by maintaining, in the teeth of abundant showings to the contrary, that "at least for the same purpose, no one can have more than one domicil at a time." Id., at 563 (AALS Readings, at 484). But cf. Reese, Does Domicil Bear A Single

rule based on such a factor would still be open to objections, which can be most conveniently considered in the section to follow.

The final alternative, or set of alternatives, is offered by the high-minded, transcendent, and form-free counsels of those who tell us that the choice should be of "the more effective and more useful law,"[42] or of the law that fulfills the demands of justice in the particular situation,[43] or of the law which fulfills the "needs and interests of the community,"[44] or of the law which produces acceptable results "in the light of these facts in the event or transaction which, from the standpoint of justice between the litigating individuals or of those broader considerations of social policy which conflicting laws may evoke, link that event or transaction to one law or the other."[45] I have not the slightest wish to imply any derision of such counsels; they represent the finest fruits of critical attempts to deal with the problem. The inescapable fact remains that they have proved ineffective, as their authors would freely concede. This cardinal disappointment is due in part to the intractable character of the problem itself. It is due in part to the fact that the proffered solutions undoubtedly beg the question; for the original question, at least—*i.e.*, the question as it stood prior to the erection by the territorialists of a structure of false questions—was precisely: What is the just result? It is due in part to the fact that the approach attributes to courts a freedom and a competence which they do not possess; for courts are committed to the administration of justice under law, and the constraint of that commitment is not lightly to be thrown off simply because the law in question may seem to the court old-fashioned, unwise, unjust, or misguided.

To my mind the clearest clue to the meaning of the Cavers method—and by the same token one of the best explanations of its ineffectiveness—is contained not in his studied formulation of principle[46] but in a pleasantry dropped by the way in the course of a discussion of the *Pratt* problem. "If the problem is to find a rule to determine the law of what state governs capacity to contract," he

Meaning?, 55 Col. L. Rev. 589, 590–91 (1955). It must be conceded that any analysis which attaches importance to either the residence or the domicile of the married woman will run into complications because either factor may be associated with more than one state. See Neuner, op. cit. supra note 25, at 496–97.

[42] This expression is attributed to Aldricus (c. 1200) by Yntema, op. cit. supra note 4, at 301–302. Lorenzen, Cases on Conflict of Laws 3 (6th ed., 1951), gives fuller information, and refers the reader to 2 Neumeyer, Die gemeinrechtliche Entwicklung des Internationalen Privat- und Strafrechts bis Bartolus 2 et seq. (1916). Lorenzen translates the quoted phrase as the "more powerful and useful" law.

[43] Lorenzen, Territoriality, Public Policy and the Conflict of Laws, 33 Yale L. J. 736, 748 (1924).

[44] Cook, op. cit. supra note 16, at 919 (AALS Readings, at 658).

[45] Cavers, op. cit. supra note 31, at 192 (AALS Readings, at 114).

[46] Id., at 192 (AALS Readings, at 113).

says, "the fact that the law of state A is reminiscent of those days when husband and wife were one is no more material than the fact that the law of state B mirrors the latest views of the National Woman's Party on sex equality before the law.[47] Since the content of the foreign law and the result which its application would work are of basic importance in the Cavers thesis, these two facts presumably would become material if his method were employed. In what way would they be material? The reference to "those days when husband and wife were one" suggests a host of disparaging connotations—not omitting Mr. Bumble's classic characterization of the law as "a ass, a idiot." On the other hand, the reference to "the latest views . . . on sex equality before the law," despite its tongue-in-cheek reservation of the right to belittle the National Woman's Party's pretensions, suggests modernism, enlightenment, sophistication, egalitarianism, and humaneness. In short, this is a subliminal statement of a proposition which cannot with comfort be stated baldly. Baldly stated, the proposition is: In a domestic case, a judge has little choice but to apply the law of his state, no matter how silly or misguided he may think it is or how regrettable the results it produces. In a conflicts case, on the other hand, there is such a great deal of looseness in the joints of the apparatus and such a lack of any clear mandate as to how to proceed that there is available to the judge for the taking a freedom which he should employ with a will, in order to frustrate, in this limited but satisfying area of opportunity, all that is archaic and foolish in the law.[48]

I think it is clear that we cannot accept any conflict-of-laws method which proceeds on such premises. In the context of the contractual capacity of married women the suggestion seems innocuous and almost palatable, since practically everyone will agree, nowadays, that the law imposing incapacity did more harm than good. Transferred to the context of live issues of policy, however, the suggestion is an alarming one. It is simply not the business of courts to substitute their judgment for that of the legislature. The content of the law to be applied must be inquired into, to be sure, and one of the grievous faults of the traditional system is its treatment of that content as immaterial. But the inquiry should be in aid of a determination of the scope of legislative policy and of the ways in which that policy is to be implemented, and not an instrument for undermining that policy. In a conflict-of-laws case a court should have just that degree of freedom to escape the compulsion of a disagreeable law that it has in a purely domestic case, and no more.[49] One thing seems reasonably sure: If the courts

[47] Id., at 180 (AALS Readings, at 105–6).

[48] Cf. Lorenzen, Tort Liability and the Conflict of Laws, 47 L. Q. Rev. 483, 490 (1931): "What is wanted are decisions that appeal to one's sense of justice." See Neuner, op. cit. supra note 25, at 489.

[49] Both the attractiveness and the danger of the suggestion that a court should apply what seems to it the better law are recognized in Freund, op. cit. supra note 18, at 1216: "If one of the competing laws is archaic and isolated in the context of the laws of the federal union, it

were to embark upon such a free-wheeling approach to the conflict of laws, in cases in which really important policies were embodied in the laws in question, they would be brought to heel in due course by legislative mandates that local law be applied.

We have succeeded, somewhat laboriously, in arriving at a point which represents the current condition of conflict-of-laws method—that is to say, at an impasse. For want of an alternative which can convincingly be said to produce rational results with the requisite degree of simplicity and objectivity, we adhere to the discredited method of the recent past, averting our eyes from the spectacle of the unfulfilled promises and the indiscriminately destructive results of that method. In the remaining sections of this paper, an effort will be made to determine whether there is any way of escape from this unhappy situation—not for conflict of laws in general, nor for the whole vexed problem of contracts in the conflict of laws, nor for all questions of validity, but only for this one, small, trite, and not very practical problem concerning married women's contracts.

IV

The fourteen possible conflict-of-laws cases which have been enumerated fall into two classes. The ten cases in the larger class present *no real conflicts problem.* The four cases in the smaller class present real problems, but they are problems which *cannot be solved* by any science or method of conflict-of-laws. Recognition of these blunt facts provides a basis—so far as I can see, the only basis—for progress toward a more satisfactory method of dealing with the cases.

The cases in the first class are Nos. 3, 4, 5, 6, 7, 8, 11, 12, 13, and 15. These are "conflict-of-laws cases" according to a useful definition, which I have no disposition to disturb. That is, each is a case in which potentially (or conventionally) significant factors are associated with more than one state. They do

may not unreasonably have to yield to the more prevalent and progressive law, other factors of choice being roughly equal. A married woman's disability to make a contract, imbedded in the law of one state, may be carried away by the current if contact is made with the main stream in another state. Perhaps one of the functions of conflict-of-laws decisions is to serve as growing pains for the law of a state, at all events in a federation such as our own." See also id., at 1214–15, 1223. In my judgment, if a court is sufficiently convinced that a law of the forum is so obsolete that it should not be applied in a mixed case, the courage of its convictions should lead it to abrogate the law for domestic purposes as well. The holding in Thompson v. Taylor, 66 N.J.L. 253, 49 Atl. 544 (1901), that the New Jersey law disabling a married woman from contracting with her husband was a moribund relic, seems to leave no justification whatever for the continued domestic application of that rule, especially in the light of the preference given to foreign over domestic creditors if the progressive decision is confined to mixed cases. When it is a foreign law that seems archaic, the court at the forum is not justified in nullifying that law where interests of the foreign state alone are affected. When there is a real clash between the interests of the two states, the court is thoroughly justified in applying its own law, according to the argument infra, without reference to whether the law of the forum is the more desirable on the merits.

not, however, present real problems, because they do not involve conflicting interests of the respective states. It is perfectly clear what the result should be in each. Either state, though approaching the case with no other purpose than to advance its own interests, would reach that result. This point will be clarified by a reference to Table 7, supplemented by reference to Tables 6 and 6a. In each of these cases, the result which Massachusetts would reach if it ignored conventional choice-of-law rules and simply consulted its own interest coincides with that which Maine would reach if it adopted the same attitude. These are the cases in which application of the law of the place of making advances the interest of one state without impairing any interest of the other (in which the result is clearly satisfactory) plus the cases in which the interest of one state is defeated without advancing any interest of the other (in which the result is clearly unsatisfactory).

The cases in the smaller class (Nos. 2, 9, 10, and 14) are the cases in which advancement of the interest of one state results in subordination or impairment

TABLE 8

Case Number	Factors 1 R C	Factors 2 R M W
1	D	D
2	D	F
3	F	D
4	F	F

of the interest of the other. Each state has a policy, expressed in its law, and each state has a legitimate interest, because of its relationship to one of the parties, in applying its law and policy to the determination of the case.

Another way of stating this conclusion will serve to simplify the discussion. In the course of our inquiry into the policies embodied in the respective laws we came to the conclusion that two of the presumptively significant factors—the place of contracting and the place where the action is brought—are not, in fact, significant. With only two significant factors left, the number of possible combinations is reduced to four, as shown by Table 8. Each of these cases was repeated three or four times in the previous array, the four being multiplied into fourteen by the inclusion of variations based upon the additional, immaterial factors.

Taking Table 8 to represent the standpoint of Massachusetts, and following the previous analysis, it seems reasonable to say that Massachusetts, in the advancement of its own interests, would apply its own law, or desire its application, in Cases Nos. 1 and 3. It would have no interest in applying its law to Nos. 2 and 4.

Table 8a presents the same cases, viewed from the standpoint of Maine.

Maine should desire the application of its own law in Nos. 2, 3, and 4. It would have no interest in applying its law to No. 1.

Table 9, constructed along the lines of Table 7, indicates, for each of the four cases, the result indicated by Massachusetts interests (Column 1), the result indicated by Maine interests (Column 2), and the clearly satisfactory result (Column 3).

The result in No. 1 is satisfactory because it advances Massachusetts' interests without impairment of any interest of Maine. The result in No. 2 is satisfactory for the same reason. The result is No. 4 is satisfactory for the converse reason, that it advances Maine's interests without impairment of any interest of Massachusetts. (Incidentally, it may be noted that this method leads to uni-

TABLE 8a

Case Number	Factors 1 R C	2 R M W
1.	F	F
2.	F	D
3.	D	F
4.	D	D

TABLE 9

Case Number	Factors 1 R C	2 R M W	Law Applied and Result 1		2		3	
1.	Mass.	Mass.	Mass.	0	Mass.	0	Mass.	0
2.	Mass.	Me.	Me.	+	Me.	+	Me.	+
3.	Me.	Mass.	Mass.	0	Me.	+	?	?
4.	Me.	Me.	Me.	+	Me.	+	Me.	+

formity of result in three-fourths of the possible cases.) In No. 3, however, no satisfactory result, in terms of the conflicting interests involved, is possible. Whichever way the case is decided, one of two interests, each of equal dignity, must be subordinated. To apply the law of the place of making would be to make the result in each case depend upon an irrelevant factor, determined by chance.

The plain truth is that the apparatus designed for the handling of real problems of conflict of laws generates problems where none existed before, and more often than not disposes of those false problems unsatisfactorily; at the same time, it provides no more than the illusion of a solution for the real problems. Where the legitimate interests of two states are in genuine conflict, the system does not reconcile them, nor determine which is more important, nor even permit the state in position to do so to pursue its own interest. It simply strikes down the one interest or the other, indiscriminately, arbitrarily, on the basis of fortuitous and irrelevant circumstances. Ultimately, the survival of such a system can be attributed only to the fact that few people care very much whether such matters are handled intelligently or not, so long as they are more or less expeditiously disposed of.

If this analysis is sound, the situation could be improved at least to the extent of eliminating the false problems which constitute the greater part of the array, together with the unfortunate results which follow in a majority of them. A legitimate question at this point is whether the conclusion—that the bulk of the cases do not present real problems, and can easily be handled to the satisfaction of all states concerned—can be translated into a workable and defensible method. It may be noted that we have proposed nothing in the nature of a traditional choice-of-law rule as a guide to the disposition of these cases, but have spoken only in terms of policies and interests—a terminology which is not congenial to the legal mind, with its insistence on precision and certainty and predictability. It is well, also, at this stage to recall the assumptions on which the analysis has been based. In the beginning, in order to free ourselves to imagine the course which a state would follow in the single-minded pursuit of its own interests, we put aside all the questions of fairness, prudence, and even constitutionality which might be raised by such a course. Is the conclusion, then, a realistic one? Can a workable guide for the courts be formulated? And are the results defensible in terms of the Constitution and of common fairness to the litigants?

There is a short reply to such questions. The mere substitution of a different traditional choice-of-law rule—that the law of the domicile of the married woman governs capacity to contract—would eliminate all the unfortunate results in the false-problem cases. But since, as has been indicated, that rule would not provide a very satisfactory method of dealing with the whole array of cases, let us approach an answer to the questions in another way.

Let us first attempt the formulation of a statement of interest and intention which may reasonably be attributed to a state legislature wishing to confirm its policy of protecting married women and to clarify the applicability of its law on that subject in conflict-of-laws cases. For added realism, let us assume that the Massachusetts legislature, having defeated the attempt to change the existing rule, is contemplating the enactment of a statute which will reaffirm the disability and clarify the applicability of the law, and has asked us, as legislative consultants, to draft the conflict-of-laws section.

We should be on safe ground in adopting, as the first principle to be incorporated in the final draft, the following:

"1. The provisions of this act shall be applied by the courts of this state, and should be applied by the courts of other states, to all cases in which both parties to the contract are residents of this state."

Nor is the second principle very controversial:

"2. The provisions of this act shall not be applied by the courts of this state to any case in which both parties to the contract are residents of another state.

In such cases, the courts of this state shall apply the law of the common residence of the parties."

Since we are concerned for the moment only with the false problems, we may omit the formulation of a principle to cover the case of the foreign creditor and the domestic married woman (which is the case involving a real problem) and proceed to the last principle necessary for present purposes:

"3. The provisions of this act shall not be applied by the courts of this state, and should not be applied by other courts, to any case in which the creditor is a resident of this state and the married woman a nonresident."

This will not do at all. It denies to foreign married women an immunity enjoyed by local married women, for no reason except that they are foreign. Not only does such discrimination offend the sense of fairness; in all probability it is unconstitutional, applied to citizens of other states of the Union, as an infringement of the privileges-and-immunities clause of Article IV, Section 2. Let us concede this without quibbling. Let us not seek refuge in the cases which uphold a distinction drawn between "residents" and "nonresidents" as opposed to one between local "citizens" and "citizens" of other states. In those cases, the fact of residence has some significance, apart from the largely coincident fact of citizenship, tending to make the classification a reasonable one.[60] In the absence of any such significance, a discrimination between residents and nonresidents amounts, in practical effect, to a discrimination merely because of citizenship, and, where citizens of other states are concerned, is forbidden by the Constitution.[61] We may concede that there is no such redeeming significance in the circumstance of residence in the case we are discussing. In fact, "residence" is only one of a set of alternatives in our scheme of discussion; at some other time, we might even be disposed to substitute citizenship for residence as the determinant of the scope of the state's protective policy.[62] The truth is that the only justification for the third principle, as we have formulated it, is that we are seeking advancement of the selfish interests of Massachusetts without regard to other considerations. Since this is carrying that objective to impermissible lengths, we should give limits to that objective here and now.

While we are about it, we may just as well adopt an attitude of fairness toward all nonresident married women, whether they are within the protection of the privileges-and-immunities clause or not. There is no particular point in exploring here the lengths to which the ultimately selfish state might constitutionally go. A discrimination against nonresident aliens might stand,

[60] Douglas v. New York, N.H. & H. R. Co., 279 U.S. 377 (1929); La Tourette v. McMaster, 248 U.S. 465 (1919).

[61] Blake v. McClung, 172 U.S. 239 (1898); Toomer v. Witsell, 334 U.S. 385, 395 (1948); Travis v. Yale & Towne Mfg. Co., 252 U.S. 60 (1920); Mullaney v. Anderson, 342 U.S. 415 (1952).

[62] That, however, would involve difficulties under the equal protection clause. See Truax v. Raich, 239 U.S. 33 (1915); Takahashi v. Fish and Game Comm'n, 334 U.S. 410 (1948).

though other constitutional provisions would present obstacles.[53] The game might not be worth the candle, however. Such an attitude would arouse resentment; it might lead to unpleasant reprisals; we might even be charged, with some justification, with intruding into the sphere of foreign relations, where federal policy should control.[54] As reponsible draftsmen we would do well to counsel moderation at this point.

Does the constitutional difficulty we have encountered vitiate the analysis which proceeds on the basis of the interests of the respective states? By no means. In the immediate discussion we have been proceeding, in traditional fashion, without inquiring into the content of the law of the foreign state. We have only to remove the blindfold to discover a way out of the difficulty. The essential objective, as we have seen, is not graspingly to promote the interests of local creditors at the expense of foreign debtors. It is simply to avoid the anomaly of defeating the reasonable expectations of local creditors without advancing any interest of the foreign state. This objective can be attained if the immunity conferred by the act is extended to the nonresident married woman who enjoys a similar immunity under the law of the state of her residence, but withheld from those who have been emancipated by their home states. Where the nonresident married woman is protected by her home law, the result will be to sacrifice the interest of the local creditor and the subsidiary interest of Massachusetts in security of transactions; but the sacrifice is in favor of an interest to which Massachusetts has given primacy in its own domestic polity. We may therefore redraft the third principle as follows:

"3. The provisions of this act shall not be applied by the courts of this state, and should not be applied by other courts, to any case in which the creditor is a resident of this state and the married woman a nonresident, unless similar immunity is conferred by the law of the state of her residence."

This is clearly not a denial of the privileges and immunities of citizenship. All

[53] As to aliens resident in other states or federal territory, see 16 Stat. 140, 144 (1870), 42 U.S.C.A. § 1981 (1957); Takahashi v. Fish and Game Comm'n, 334 U.S. 410, 419–20 (1948). But as to aliens abroad, see Disconto Gesellschaft v. Umbreit, 208 U.S. 570 (1908); United States v. Pink, 315 U.S. 203 (1942). As to resident aliens, see note 52 supra. As to foreign corporations, compare Kentucky Finance Corp. v. Paramount Auto Exchange Corp., 262 U.S. 544 (1923), with Blake v. McClung, 172 U.S. 239 (1898). Generally, even where constitutional principles may not be controlling, American tradition has shunned discrimination against aliens. See 2 Story, Commentaries on the Constitution of the United States § 1109 (4th ed., 1873); Mulhall v. Fallon, 176 Mass. 266, 57 N.E. 386 (1900); Janusis v. Long, 284 Mass. 403, 188 N.E. 228 (1933), noted in 29 Ill. L. Rev. 101 (1934); Nadelmann, Creditor Equality in Inter-State Bankruptcies, 98 U. of Pa. L. Rev. 41 (1949); Nadelmann, Legal Treatment of Foreign and Domestic Creditors, 11 Law & Contemp. Prob. 696 (1946).

[54] In the absence of international agreement (as to which see Bayitch, Conflict Law in United States Treaties, 8 Miami L. Q. 501, 516 [1954]) this is perhaps a radical suggestion. See Cheatham, Federal Control of Conflict of Laws, 6 Vand. L. Rev. 581 (1953) (AALS Readings, at 255); Clark v. Allen, 331 U.S. 503 (1947); Cheatham, Goodrich, Griswold & Reese, Cases and Materials on Conflict of Laws 616–17 (4th ed., 1957); Ehrenzweig, Interstate and International Conflicts Law: A Plea for Segregation, 41 Minn. L. Rev. 717, 719, 729 (1957).

married women are divided into two classes on a reasonable basis: those who are protected by the laws of their home states, and those who are not. There is no more a forbidden discrimination here than in any choice-of-law rule referring to the law of the domicile. In fact, the practical effect of the principle is exactly the same, in this context, as that of a rule referring to the law of the domicile. Moreover, there is clear precedent for framing conflict-of-laws rules in this fashion.[55]

The three principles may be combined in one brief statement: "The provisions of this act shall be applied in all cases in which the married woman is a resident of this state, or of another state whose laws provide similar immunity."[56] The hope that other states will respect this mandate is implied.

Drafting a similar conflict-of-laws section for the Maine statute removing the common-law disability, we would begin with the elementary principles that the law is to be applied in all cases in which both parties are residents of Maine, and not to cases in which neither party is a resident. Passing the real problem which arises when the creditor is a resident of Maine and the debtor a (protected) nonresident, we come to the case in which the married woman is a resident of Maine and the creditor a nonresident. Since this is the most difficult of the

[55] Dean v. Dean, 241 N.Y. 240, 149 N.E. 844 (1925). It is regrettable that this fascinating case has been dropped from the casebooks merely because the precise problem involved became moot with the end of the era of Haddock v. Haddock, 201 U.S. 562 (1906). A few brief comments may suggest its continuing interest as a subject of analysis: (1) I do not understand why the commentators regarded the decision as an application of the renvoi. Renvoi in Divorce Jurisdiction, 39 Harv. L. Rev. 640 (1926); The Conflict of Laws as to Foreign Divorce, 74 U. of Pa. L. Rev. 738 (1926); Divorce—Recognition of Foreign Decrees in New York, 35 Yale L. J. 372 (1926); Cook, Logical and Legal Bases of the Conflict of Laws 250 n. 24 (1942); Griswold, Renvoi Revisited, 51 Harv. L. Rev. 1165 (1938) (AALS Readings, at 185). It seems to me that the New York rule was simply a conflict-of-laws rule of the kind under discussion in the text, referring simply to the law of another state. In effect, the New York court said: Given freedom to recognize or to refuse to recognize the foreign ex parte decree, we elect not to recognize it in cases in which the defendant spouse is domiciled at the time of the decree in New York or in another state having a similar protective policy. This simply says that the matter will be determined by reference to the law of the domicile. (2) But the New York court did not in fact decide the case as Ontario would have decided it. On the basis of American law the court decided that the wife was domiciled in Ontario, and on the basis of an Ontario case that was not in point it decided that Ontario would refuse recognition to the decree. But as Ontario law stood at the time, the wife could not maintain a domicile separate from that of her husband. Ontario therefore would have recognized the decree to which New York refused recognition on Ontario's behalf. (3) The decision therefore did not deserve the praise it received for promoting uniformity of result. (4) The precise result reached—vindicating the wife's right to support—was years ahead of its time, and coincides with the result which would be reached today by a quite different route. Estin v. Estin, 334 U.S. 541 (1948); Vanderbilt v. Vanderbilt, 354 U.S. 416 (1957). It is especially interesting that Mrs. Dean changed her domicile to New York *after* the divorce decree. Cf. note 12 supra.

[56] Originally, I included the terminal clause, "and in no other cases." This might do no harm in the present context, but it would set a bad precedent for the drafting of such conflicts rules generally. There are cases in which the interests of a state do not require the application of its law, and in which the application of foreign law would serve no useful purpose. In such cases, the courts should be left free to apply local law.

false-problem cases, we may re-examine carefully at this point the analysis which has been employed. Conceivably, our first impulse might be to protect the local married woman against foreign creditors, even though the protective policy has been abandoned where domestic creditors are concerned. That, however, would be to deny to nonresident creditors rights which are given to residents, and would encounter the constitutional and other difficulties which have already been discussed. But, it may be asked, why should not Maine distinguish, as Massachusetts has done, between nonresidents who are favored by the law of their home states and those who are not? Why should we not say, "The provisions of this act shall not apply in any case in which the married woman is a resident of this state and the creditor a nonresident, unless the state of the creditor's residence has similarly removed the incapacity of married women?" The suggested principle has a certain plausibility which, however, seems superficial and largely supported by the dim notion that the development of the Maine policy should be symmetrical with that of Massachusetts. It is at least questionable whether the classification would suffice to meet the objection based on the privileges-and-immunities clause. The classification lacks the clear reasonableness that supports the distinction drawn by Massachusetts. It seems far-fetched to say that Maine is willing to "protect" foreign creditors to the extent that the laws of their own states "protect" them. The domiciliary law may be much less relevant to the rights of persons sui juris than it is to those of persons belonging to protected classes—which is a way of saying that domiciliary law has a relevance to questions of status, or capacity, which it may not have to other questions; and there is no question about the status of the creditor. The suggested principle seems to be not so much a distinction drawn in good faith between persons treated differently by the laws of their own states as it is a simple attempt to discriminate against as many foreigners as possible. As we said before, the most reasonable estimate of Maine policy is that it has not retained the protection of married women as a subsidiary policy, but has abandoned that policy and declared that its married women are sui juris and in no need of such blanket protection. If this is so, to withhold application of the Maine law in such cases would be to defeat the common policy favoring security of transactions without advancing any policy of either state for the protection of married women. If this estimate is erroneous, we shall have to classify this case as one raising a true problem of conflict of interests and treat it accordingly; but we are not forced to that position at this time.

We can summarize the three principles for incorporation in the Maine statute as follows: "The provisions of this act shall be applied in all cases in which Maine is the residence of either or both parties."

If we are right in believing that these conflict-of-laws provisions for the Massachusetts and Maine statutes fairly reflect the moderate self-interest of the respective states, then it is clear that the three cases under discussion present no real conflict of interests, and that the cases would in the normal course be decided in the same way by both states, without the aid of any system of choice of law. The results are those shown by Table 9 with the exception that we have not so far dealt with Case No. 3, the true conflicts case.

The rules which we have proposed for incorporation into the laws of the respective states are not choice-of-law rules in the traditional sense. They have at least as much precision, but they lack that semblance of universal truth which would facilitate their incorporation into a system aimed at achieving uniformity. They do not say directly what law shall govern. They simply say that a particular law is intended to govern in certain cases.[57] It seems to me that there are advantages in this way of stating conflict-of-laws rules. It may very well avoid, or minimize the difficulties of, some of the major ambiguities inherent in the traditional form of rules for choice of law. If courts were to cultivate the practice of stating their common-law conflict-of-laws rules in this fashion, some interesting results might follow. For one thing, the courts would find themselves in step with a movement which may contribute materially to the development of intelligent modes of dealing with conflict-of-laws problems. This is the growing tendency of legislators to specify how their enactments are intended to affect mixed cases.[58] The task of drafting such provisions forces attention to the interests and objectives involved. A legislature is not likely to append to any statute dealing with a specific problem any such rule as that the law of the place where the contract is made shall control. It is much more likely to specify in realistic terms the cases to which its enactment is intended to apply. For another thing, a court which has forsworn reliance on choice-of-law rules of the traditional sort, and therefore deprived itself of the facile syllogisms of the *Restatement*, would find it quite difficult, I think, to make any such statement as: "This law, considered in the light of the moderate interests of the enacting state, is clearly intended to apply to all contracts made within the state, and to no others." As in many other instances, form exacts thought.[59] One might even risk the prediction that this is the form in which the conflict-of-laws rules of the future will be cast.

Turning now to Case No. 3 (Tables 8, 8a and 9), which involves a true conflict of interest, I can only repeat that no satisfactory solution can possibly be evolved by means of the resources of conflict-of-laws law. This does not mean that the problem cannot be solved. It cannot be solved by any effort, judicial or legislative, however brilliant in its conception, on the part of a single state

[57] See Currie, Survival of Actions: Adjudication versus Automation in the Conflict of Laws, 10 Stan. L. Rev. 205 (1958).

[58] Such specifications must, of course, be drafted with wisdom and restraint, and with careful regard to the moderate interests of the state. The fact that sometimes they have been drafted with imperialistic lack of restraint (see Rheinstein, note 37 supra) is not a persuasive reason why the technique should not be encouraged.

[59] "Exigencies of rime and meter
May leave the rude idea neater. . . ."
Bevington, Dr. Johnson's Waterfall 3 (1946).

acting alone; and conflict-of-laws law, strictly speaking, is found only in the laws of individual states. It cannot be solved by the concurrent adoption by all states of the same rule for choice of law, even if the chosen rule is consistently and uniformly applied. A choice-of-law rule, designed to be applied by all states concurrently so that all courts will decide the same case in the same way, and justified in terms of "jurisdiction," is merely a device for preferring one state's policy to that of another, consistently or haphazardly, without facing the difficulties involved in such a choice. It is possible, however, that the conflict may be resolved by agreement between the states concerned, and it is clear that it can be resolved by higher governmental authority.

Paradoxically, the problem is insoluble with the resources of conflict-of-laws law precisely because it is a true problem of conflict of interests, which is presumably the type of problem for which the system of conflict of laws was devised. Maine is committed to a policy of security of transactions, and has a legitimate interest in enforcing that policy where Maine creditors are concerned. Massachusetts is committed to a policy of protecting married women, and has a legitimate interest in enforcing that policy where Massachusetts married women are concerned. The policies are here in direct conflict. Who is to say which is the more important, or the more deserving, or the more enlightened? Not even the United States Supreme Court is in position to do so.[60] Certainly it is not for the courts of one state to sacrifice local policy because they feel that it is relatively old-fashioned or misguided. The legislature might do so; it might conceivably direct that its protective law should not apply to cases in which the local married woman is sued by a foreign creditor; but in such apparent favoritism to foreign as distinguished from domestic creditors it would be destroying the problem, not solving it. In the process it might better remove the disability altogether.[61]

A Massachusetts court, lacking legislative guidance, might tentatively take a similar position with some justification. It might reason: Certainly our law expresses a policy for the protection of married women, and there is no doubt that that policy is to be enforced in the domestic situation. But how far is it to be carried? When a local creditor deals with a local married woman, he is "presumed to know the law," or at least he cannot be heard to assert that he did not know it. But how is it when a Massachusetts woman deals with a businessman in another state, where the law imposes no such disability, who is accustomed to dealing with married women as persons sui juris? Isn't it a bit unfair to "presume" that he knows our law, or to impose on him the burden of ascertaining it? Are we really so deeply concerned about our married women as

[60] Watson v. Employers Liability Ins. Corp., 348 U.S. 66 (1954); Pacific Employers Ins. Co. v. Industrial Comm'n, 306 U.S. 493 (1939); Alaska Packers Ass'n v. Industrial Accident Comm'n, 294 U.S. 532 (1935). See generally Cheatham, op. cit. supra note 54; Jackson, Full Faith and Credit—The Lawyer's Clause of the Constitution, 45 Col. L. Rev. 1 (1945) (AALS Readings, at 229).

[61] See note 49 supra.

to want the protective policy pushed that far? Perhaps it should be applied only where both parties are local residents.[62]

This would be a rational position. It is a recognition of the fact that local policy is relatively weak, and suitable only for home consumption. It is a solution—but, again, one for a case which does not present a true problem of conflicting interests. It will not serve when local policy is strong, or is thought to be strong. The legislature, if it disagrees with the court's estimate of the force of the policy, can direct that its law be applied where the married woman is a local resident and the creditor a nonresident, and we will be back where we started.

There is no conceivable choice-of-law rule which will solve the problem, even though both states adopt it and consistently apply it. The rule that the law of the place of making governs (which ought to be discarded, in the first place, because of the bad results it produces in the majority of the false-problem cases), will advance domestic policy at the expense of foreign in just half of the cases, since the place where a contract is made appears to be a matter of pure chance; in the other half, it will advance foreign policy at the expense of domestic. The rule that the law of the married woman's domicile governs (which eliminates the bad results in the false-problem cases) will always advance the protective interest at the expense of the common interest in security of transactions. There is no apparent warrant for such an arbitrary preference of the one policy over the other; indeed, the result would be quite reactionary in terms of the modern consensus as to the unwisdom of such protective policies. Since most actions against married women may be assumed to be brought in the states where they reside, the application of that rule might not create much excitement, since the court would in those cases be advancing local policy. If the same rule were applied in an action brought at the creditor's residence, however, the preference for foreign policy over domestic should lead to some raised eyebrows in the local law reviews, at least.

The sensible and clearly constitutional thing for any court to do, confronted with a true conflict of interests, is to apply its own law. In this way it can be sure at least that it is consistently advancing the policy of its own state. It should apply its own law, not because of any notion or pretense that the problem is one relating to procedure, but simply because a court should never apply any other law except when there is a good reason for doing so.[63] That so doing will promote the interests of a foreign state at the expense of the interests of the forum

[62] Cf. Thompson v. Taylor, 66 N.J.L. 253, 49 Atl. 544 (1901) (holding that removal of most disabilities of married women constituted an abandonment of protective policy, residual disabilities being mere "regulations"); Bowles v. Field, 78 Fed. 742 (C.C. Ind., 1897). "This court, except as restrained by principle and the great weight of authority, is free to take its own stand, to declare for this state what shall be, in the particular situation, its public policy, till the source for written law shall have acted in the matter." International Harvester Co. v. McAdam, 142 Wis. 114, 125, 124 N.W. 1042, 1046 (1910) (a case, however, in which all contacts at the time of the transaction were associated with the foreign state under whose law the contract was valid).

[63] Cf. Griswold, op. cit. supra note 55, at 1192 (AALS Readings, at 198).

state is not a good reason. Nor is the fact that such deference may lead to a conjectural uniformity of results among the different forums a good reason, when the price for that uniformity is either the indiscriminate impairment of local policy in half of the cases or the consistent yielding of local policy to the policy of a foreign state.

Returning, then, to our legislative drafting project, it is clear that in Case No. 3, where the creditor is a resident of Maine and the married woman a resident of Massachusetts, we should adopt for each state the principle that its own law will be applied. As it happens, the form in which we have summarized the principles in each case already embodies this principle. For Massachusetts' protective statute the conflicts section will be: "The provisions of this act shall be applied in all cases in which the married woman is a resident of this state, or of another state whose laws provide similar immunity." For Maine's emancipation statute the section will be: "The provisions of this act shall be applied in all cases in which Maine is the residence of either or both parties." The results are those indicated in Table 9. There is still no "clearly satisfactory result" in Case No. 3. The result, unhappily for the quest for uniformity, will depend upon the forum. That is not a satisfactory result, but, the ideal being unattainable, it is the one that makes the best sense; it is better than chasing rainbows.

By adding a dimension to our problem we may bring ourselves to confront the ultimate futility of the attempt to solve such problems by conflict-of-laws methods. So long as we confine the case to two states, we can fall back on the sensible and fairly comfortable expedient of applying the law of the forum in cases where the policies are in conflict. But what if, in Case No. 3, the action is brought in a third state? There is no conceivable reason why the forum should prefer the policy of Maine to that of Massachusetts, or vice versa. The forum has no interest in applying its own law, since neither party is within the reach of the forum's governmental concern.[64] Conceivably, the forum might decide to apply the foreign law which coincides with its own—although the connection of the forum with the matter is so slight that it would not justify the application of the law of the forum if both parties were residents of the same foreign state. Application of the law of the place of making means that the disinterested third state would casually defeat now the one and now the other policy, depending upon a purely fortuitous circumstance. One is almost tempted to suggest that it would be better to flip a coin, since that procedure would produce the same results more economically.

[64] In some cases, though not in all, a broadened doctrine of forum non conveniens would provide a handy solution for the third state's difficulty. In the federal courts, the grounds for transfer under § 1404(a) of the Judicial Code are sufficiently broad to include such a case. Norwood v. Kirkpatrick, 349 U.S. 29 (1955). If the action were brought in a federal court in the third state, the question of what law should be applied upon transfer to Maine or Massachusetts would be one of considerable difficulty. See Currie, Change of Venue and the Conflict of Laws, 22 U. of Chi. L. Rev. 405 (1955).

It will be said that this is a "give-it-up" philosophy. Of course it is. A give-it-up attitude is constructive when it appears that the task is impossible of accomplishment with the resources which are available. It would have been constructive if geometricians had given up long before they did the effort to square the circle by means of straight-edge and compass. "The application of analysis to geometry saves effort by showing the direct way to success for soluble problems, and no less by showing certain others to be insoluble. . . . The classic example is the squaring of the circle by an Euclidean construction. For centuries, geometers were convinced that only a little more skill or luck was wanted for success, and no one was then in a position to assert that every conceivable attempt must fail. By the aid of analysis, that assertion is now proved."[65] It would be constructive if legal scholars were to give up the attempt to construct systems for choice of law—an attempt which cannot result in the satisfactory resolution of true conflicts of interest between states, and which is very likely to result in the creation of problems which do not otherwise exist, and which are badly resolved by the system. It would be constructive if the energies thus released were directed to the solution of the true problems by other means, for by the use of other means they may be solved. Let us examine briefly what those other means are.

V

We have suggested that a true conflict of interests between states may perhaps be resolved by agreement between the states concerned, or by competent higher authority. The agreement would probably have to be a negotiated one; mere reciprocity would seem to have no application in the case under discussion. Suppose the objective, in Case No. 3, is to have the protective policy of Massachusetts yield to the common interest in security of transactions. The Massachusetts courts will defer to Maine policy, and apply Maine law, if Maine will—do what? There seems no sensible way to complete the sentence in terms of reciprocity. The concession which Maine will make in return apparently must relate to some interest other than the specific one involved in the conflicts problem at hand. Obviously, the considerations are political, and thus beyond the competence of courts—though not necessarily beyond the competence of lawyers and legal scholars.

The concurrent adoption of uniform laws, while highly commendable because it diminishes the number of conflicts, does just that; it treats the problem by destroying, not by solving, it. For that reason it is not a method which is available for dealing with deeply rooted conflicts.

Even the negotiated agreement, especially when it is conceived as bilateral, turns out on closer inspection to be a less promising device than might at first appear. It is not a comfortable thought that the protection which Massachusetts feels is necessary for its married women might be traded away in exchange for

[65] 1 Encyclopaedia Britannica 869 (1955).

some collateral concession by Maine to other Massachusetts interest groups. Nor is it a comfortable thought that Case No. 3 might be decided differently in the Massachusetts courts if the creditor were from a state other than Maine, the party to the bilateral agreement, even though the law and policy of the state of the creditor's residence were exactly the same as Maine's.[66] In the field of international private law, fairness to the litigants ought to be the primary consideration. That the application of the law of the place of making flagrantly disregards that principle does not justify its disregard in treaties. It is at least questionable whether that principle can be reconciled with the political considerations which apparently must determine the bilateral agreement between states.

The multilateral agreement may be a more useful device. Conceivably, at a world congress of nations at Geneva, the weight of enlightened opinion might induce a fair number of backward countries to adhere to the principle that the common policy of security of transactions should prevail over obsolete protective policies. One may guess, however, that the resulting preferential treatment of foreign creditors by signatories which retained the protective policy for domestic cases would soon lead to abandonment of the policy at home. The inference is that the multilateral agreement, like the uniform law, may not promise very much where conflicting policies are deeply rooted.[67]

It may be that the chief utility of the interstate agreement is not in resolving true conflicts of interest, but in controlling those cases in which a state asserts an unsubstantial, or collateral, or predatory interest.[68] Such agreements may perform the minimal function which is performed by the privileges-and-immunities, full-faith-and-credit, and due-process clauses of our federal constitution, proscribing rank discrimination and the provincial approach to matters with which the state has no legitimate concern. If so, they are not needed by our states, though they may be indispensable among nations. By the same token, since the international agreement is the only method available to independent, sovereign states for the resolution of true conflicts of interest, the limitations of that method may help to explain why continental legal systems have adhered so persistently to the ill-fated effort to find a metaphysical system for resolving those conflicts. There is no reason, however, why we in this coun-

[66] Cf. Ehrenzweig, Interstate and International Conflicts Law: A Plea for Segregation, 41 Minn. L. Rev. 717, 723 n. 31 and related text (1957).

[67] On the extent to which conflict-of-laws matters have been covered by treaties negotiated by the United States, see Bayitch, Conflict Law in the United States Treaties, 8 Miami L. Q. 501 (1954); 9 id. 9 (1954); 9 id. 125 (1955). Further references on the utility ot the international agreement in matters of conflict of laws are given in Cheatham, Goodrich, Griswold & Reese, Cases and Materials on Conflict of Laws 615 n. 2 (4th ed., 1957). See also Jitta, The Development of Private International Law through Conventions, 29 Yale L. J. 497 (1920).

[68] Cf. 38 Stat. 1164, 1165 (1915), as amended, 46 U.S.C.A. § 597 (1944); Strathearn S.S. Co. v. Dillon, 252 U.S. 348 (1920); Zeis, American Shipping Policy 70 (1938). See also Nadelmann, Creditor Equality in Inter-State Bankruptcies: A Requisite of Uniformity in the Regulation of Bankruptcy, 98 U. of Pa. L. Rev. 41 (1949).

try should persist in following these influences, since we have in the federal Union a governmental authority which can deal with such conflicts between the states forthrightly and effectively.

The power of the states of the Union to make agreements among themselves is, of course, limited by the compacts clause of the Constitution.[69] We need not pause to inquire into the extent to which that clause would impede the making of agreements of the sort here contemplated. Bilateral agreements, to the extent that they seem to offer any contribution at all, are unnecessary. No agreement would be very useful unless substantially all of the states were parties to it, and the mechanics of achieving such a many-sided agreement would be prohibitively cumbersome in comparison with available and better ways of attaining the same end.

Turning, then, to the possibilities of employing federal authority in the resolution of true conflicts of interest between states, we first put aside the use of federal legislative power under Article I to regulate the transaction in question. This power is, of course, a mighty weapon for dealing with conflicts between states. Rather than resolving the conflict, however, it displaces the conflicting laws and policies by an overriding national law and policy, applicable in all cases, whether the "factors" are associated with one state or many. Thus the enactment of the Federal Employers' Liability Act destroyed interstate choice-of-law problems, theretofore rife,[70] involving injuries to employees of interstate railroads. Congress has not yet seen fit to regulate the subject of injuries to passengers on interstate railroads, though it could presumably do so. But congressional regulation of the subject under Article I is not the only, nor even necessarily the most desirable, federal approach to dealing with interstate conflicts; and there are many such conflicts (as, for example, those relating to grounds for divorce) which cannot be reached by the exercise of Article I powers.

We should put aside, also, any primary reliance on federal judicial power. This means, first of all, that we should not expect the United States Supreme Court, in reviewing decisions of state courts, to resolve conflicts such as these. We have already made allowance for the restraining influence of the privileges-and-immunities and equal-protection clauses. The due-process clause and the unimplemented full-faith-and-credit clause are appropriately employed not to resolve true conflicts of interest, but only to restrain the assertion of unsubstantial or frivolous interests.[71] The considerations involved in a resolution of truly conflicting interests of different states are, to repeat, not merely "economic and sociological" (which might lead us in these days to contemplate their evaluation by the courts), but political (which should make us realize at once that the courts should have nothing to do with them).

[69] Art. I, Sec. 10, cl. 3.

[70] See, *e.g.*, Alabama G. S. R. Co. v. Carroll, 97 Ala. 126, 11 So. 803 (1892).

[71] See note 59 supra.

We have no choice but to put aside one judicial device which was employed, in some instances, for almost a century: the application in the federal courts of a general federal common law, superseding conflicting state laws in the federal courts much as congressional legislation under Article I supersedes them in all courts.[72] It is a plausible view that, to the framers of the Constitution, "controversies . . . between citizens of different states" may have seemed a reasonably accurate and comprehensive description of conflict-of-laws cases, and that the intention may have been to provide a federal forum and a federal common law for their determination.[73] For the time being, however, that issue is settled; and, in any event, if it were settled otherwise, a general federal common law to be applied in the federal courts could not resolve conflicts encountered in the state courts. And, of course, the experience of a century under federal common law was not exactly that which would be considered the ideal product of a system of conflict of laws.

I have previously expressed the hope that the extension of the *Erie* doctrine which requires federal courts in diversity cases to apply state conflict-of-laws rules[74] may be modified.[75] I retain that hope, since modification would solve some thorny problems in connection with change of venue and, in addition, would permit the federal courts to reach sensible results in the false-problem cases without doing violence to the policy of any state. I do not think that modification would contribute materially to solution of the problem of truly conflicting interest. A federal court is in no better position than a state court to make the political judgments which must enter into any decision that the legitimate interests of one state must yield to the legitimate interest of another.[76] In addition, the development of independent choice-of-law rules by the federal courts can contribute only indirectly to the development of conflict of laws in the state courts, except where the Constitution is involved.

Plenary power is given to Congress to resolve such conflicts by the second sentence of the full-faith-and-credit clause: "And the Congress may by general laws prescribe the manner in which such acts, records, and proceedings shall be proved, and the effect thereof."[77] The power had not been used since 1790

[72] Swift v. Tyson, 16 Pet. (U.S.) 1 (1842), overruled in Erie R.R. Co. v. Tompkins, 304 U.S. 64 (1938).

[73] 1 Crosskey, Politics and the Constitution in the History of the United States 642 et seq. But cf. Hart, The Relations between State and Federal Law, 54 Col. L. Rev. 489, 500 et seq. (1954); Kurland, Mr. Justice Frankfurter, The Supreme Court and the Erie Doctrine in Diversity Cases, 67 Yale L. J. 187, 195 et seq. (1957).

[74] Klaxon Co. v. Stentor Electr. Mfg. Co., 313 U.S. 487 (1941).

[75] See Currie, op. cit. supra note 64, at 502–3.

[76] But cf. Hart, op. cit. supra note 73, at 513–15.

[77] Cook, The Powers of Congress under the Full Faith and Credit Clause, 28 Yale L. J. 421 (1919), reprinted in Cook, The Logical and Legal Bases of the Conflict of Laws c. IV (1942); Jackson, Full Faith and Credit—The Lawyer's Clause of the Constitution, 45 Col. L.

when Cook rediscovered it in 1919; nor has any further use been made of it since that time, despite Cook's clear demonstration of its availability and utility in the treatment of conflict-of-laws problems. This is not the place for a full-dress review of the constitutional question involved; it should be sufficient to note that Cook's interpretation of the clause has not been shaken, and to add that Professor Crosskey's researches[78] may provide a further basis for a holding that the power of Congress is not limited to prescribing the effect of state statutes, as Cook supposed, but extends also to state common law. Those who may regard with apprehension the prospect of federal laws which, on a rational basis, require the policy of one state to yield to that of another are welcome to such comfort as they can find in the present metaphysical system, whereby state policies are frustrated irrationally and at random.[79]

It would be naïve to expect that Congress, which has not used its powers under the full-faith-and-credit clause since 1790, will use those powers now to resolve the conflict of interests in cases of married women's contracts. There must, however, be problems of sufficient importance to justify congressional action; and the expectation of such action might become realistic if legal and other scholars would devote their energies to direct study of the legal, social, economic, and political factors which bear upon the choice of policies in specific conflict situations. I should suppose, for example, that the present conflict-of-laws situation with respect to workmen's compensation[80] gives rise to industrial difficulties of substantial magnitude, and that a supportable legislative program for resolving the conflicting interests involved might well merit some congressional attention. An act resolving conflicting interests between states in this situation would, by the way, bring order into an area which is largely within the scope of federal legislative power under the commerce clause—but without substituting national for state policy.

Even in areas where there is critical need for resolution of conflicting governmental interests, it is unlikely that congressional action will be forthcoming, or that it will be soundly formulated if it is forthcoming, unless the energies which

---

Rev. 1, 21 (1945) (AALS Readings, at 229, 244); Cavers, Review of Cook, supra, 56 Harv. L. Rev. 1170 (1943); Yarborough v. Yarborough, 290 U.S. 202, 215 n. 2 (1933) (dissenting opinion); 1 Crosskey, op. cit. infra note 78, at 553–54.

78 1 Crosskey, Politics and the Constitution in the History of the United States 545–47 (1953). See also Jackson, op. cit. supra note 77, at 11–12 (AALS Readings, at 237–38); Paulsen & Sovern, "Public Policy" in the Conflict of Laws, 56 Col. L. Rev. 969, 1012 (1956); Cheatham, Federal Control of Conflict of Laws, 6 Vand. L. Rev. 581, 602–3 (1953) (AALS Readings, at 255, 272–73).

79 "[T]he states have less to fear from a strong federalist influence in dealing with this than with most other constitutional provisions. The Federal Government stands to gain little at the expense of the states through any application of it." Jackson, op. cit. supra note 77, at 33 (AALS Readings, at 254).

80 See Cheatham, Goodrich, Griswold & Reese, Cases and Materials on the Conflict of Laws, c. 9 (4th ed., 1957).

are now consumed by the metaphysics and the frustrations of conflict of laws are diverted to the formulation and justification of specific legislative programs. Here is challenge enough. Here is the "grand objective"[81] in an attainable, or at least approachable, form. Here is a means of bringing the full capability of the mind to bear upon the problem of "integration of the diversity of laws."[82] In America at least, conflict of laws, that "much maligned branch of the law,"[83] will richly deserve its disrepute so long as we leave the instrument for intelligent resolution of conflicting policies to rust in desuetude, while we waste our energies in the futile search for an *elixir vitae* that will relieve us from the necessity of facing the real problem and from the pain that must ensue when the policy of one state is made to yield to that of another.[84]

[81] Yntema, op. cit. supra note 4, at 312 (AALS Readings, at 42).

[82] Id., at 297 (AALS Readings, at 31).

[83] Id., at 300 (AALS Readings, at 32).

[84] "But the full faith and credit clause is the foundation of any hope we may have for a truly national system of justice, based on the preservation but better integration of the local jurisdictions we have. If I have any message to the legal profession . . . it is this: that you must not suffer this lawyer's clause to become the orphan clause of the Constitution." Jackson, op. cit. supra note 77, at 34 (AALS Readings, at 254).

[12]

CONFLICT OF LAWS AND THE RESTATEMENT SECOND

WILLIS L. M. REESE*

INTRODUCTION

Conflict of laws is in a state of flux. This is particularly true of that most difficult area of the subject, which is frequently referred to as choice of law. Many fundamental rules in this area, that once were generally accepted, have been proved wrong by recent experience.[1] Some of the remaining rules are being subjected to increasing criticism and doubt. More disconcerting is the fact that wide differences presently exist with respect to underlying objectives and values. The suggestion has even been made that all choice-of-law rules should be abandoned.[2] This surely is a time for soul-searching and re-evaluation.

Conflict of laws was one of the first subjects to which the American Law Institute gave its attention. Work on the original *Restatement* was commenced in 1923. At this time the teachings of Professor Joseph H. Beale, the Reporter, were at their heyday. The vested rights theory, of which he was the principal exponent, was widely accepted, and it was generally believed that the entire field could be covered by a relatively small number of simple rules, as that the validity of a contract is governed by the law of the place of contracting and that rights and liabilities in tort are determined by the law of the place of injury.[3] Little wonder as a consequence that the field was deemed ripe for restatement.

The situation had changed by the time the original *Restatement* was published in final form in 1934. The vested rights theory, the foundation on which the *Restatement* was constructed, was beginning to come under devastating attack from Professor Walter Wheeler Cook[4] and others.[5] This increasing turmoil and doubt had some effect upon the *Restatement* itself. Judge Goodrich once told the writer that the reason why the original comments are so terse and laconic is that the Advisers frequently disagreed with the reasons advanced by Professor Beale for his rules although they did not object to the rules themselves. As a result, proposed comments prepared by Professor Beale stating his reasons for the rules were fre-

* B.A. 1935, LL.B. 1938, Yale University. Charles Evans Hughes Professor of Law and Director, Parker School of Foreign and Comparative Law, Columbia University; Reporter, RESTATEMENT (SECOND), CONFLICT OF LAWS.

[1] See generally Cavers, *Change in Choice-of-Law Thinking and Its Bearing on the Klaxon Problem*, AMERICAN LAW INSTITUTE, STUDY OF THE DIVISION OF JURISDICTION BETWEEN STATE AND FEDERAL COURTS 154 (Tent. Draft No. 1, 1963).

[2] Currie, *Notes on Methods and Objectives in the Conflict of Laws*, 1959 DUKE L.J. 171, 177.

[3] For a discussion of the vested rights theory, see Cheatham, *American Theories of Conflict of Laws: Their Role and Utility*, 58 HARV. L. REV. 361 (1945).

[4] Many of Professor Cook's articles are reprinted in WALTER WHEELER COOK, LOGICAL AND LEGAL BASES OF THE CONFLICT OF LAWS (1942).

[5] See, *e.g.*, Lorenzen, *Territoriality, Public Policy and the Conflict of Laws*, 33 YALE L.J. 736 (1924).

quently rejected while the rules themselves were usually allowed to stand. With the exception of chapter eleven, which deals with the Administration of Estates, of which Judge Goodrich was the Reporter, the rules of the original *Restatement* in any event are simple, relatively few in number, and dogmatic. They are consistent with the vested rights theory and they give little indication of the fluidity and of the complexities and uncertainties of the subject.

It now seems evident, in the light of hindsight, that conflict of laws was not ripe for restatement in the 1920's and 1930's, at least in the usual way. The subject was then largely unexplored. This, rather than the Reporter's adherence to the vested rights theory, is believed to be the principal reason for what is now recognized to be the dogmatic and over-simplified character of the original *Restatement*. For it is in the nature of men to seek certainty and simplicity in the law. They will wish to regulate a field by a few simple rules if rules of this nature can be devised to handle adequately the problems involved. And if a few simple rules will handle adequately all, or at least the great majority, of problems that have arisen in a given field, men will be tempted to believe that the same rules can satisfactorily be applied to handle all other problems with which they may thereafter be faced. They will be loath to attempt to conjure up problems that may arise in the future and that could not adequately be handled by the suggested rules. In addition, Professor Beale had a great sense of order and of logic. He had an instinctive liking for simple, dogmatic rules and for theories that would lead to the adoption of such rules. Professor Beale was by no means alone in this regard. His views were shared by such learned and influential judges as Holmes[6] and Cardozo,[7] and, it seems safe to say, by the great majority of lawyers and law teachers of his time.

Following the appearance of the original *Restatement* in 1934, choice-of-law questions came before the courts with increasing frequency. It soon became apparent that many of the rules stated in this *Restatement* are wrong or at least so over-simplified as to be misleading. There was need for a complete revision, and work on such a revision was commenced in 1952. The Reporter of the *Restatement Second* and his Advisers have essentially two advantages over Professor Beale. They can profit from the criticisms that were directed at his work, and they can seek guidance from the large number of cases that have been decided, from the legislation that has been enacted, and from the books and articles that have been written since the appearance of the original *Restatement*. The Reporter and his Advisers, in short, have the opportunity of being more learned simply because there is now more to know.

On the other hand, revision of the *Restatement* at this time poses many difficulties. More, perhaps much more, is known about choice of law than when Professor Beale wrote. But this additional knowledge has not brought certainty and definiteness in its wake. Instead it has brought disagreement, a renewed search for fundamental

[6] See, *e.g.*, Justice Holmes's opinion in Slater v. Mexican National R.R., 194 U.S. 120 (1904).

[7] See, *e.g.*, BENJAMIN N. CARDOZO, THE PARADOXES OF LEGAL SCIENCE 67-68 (1928).

values, and perhaps more uncertainty than ever before. What we do know now with fair certainty is that choice of law is too vast and complicated an area to be governed by a relatively small number of simple rules of general application. What is needed instead is a large number of relatively narrow rules that will be applicable only in precisely defined situations.[8] But, with rare exceptions, experience to date is not sufficient to enable us to construct such rules or to identify all, or even most, of the situations to which such rules will be applicable. Choice of law, even now, is not ripe for restatement in the sense that it is rarely possible to state hard and fast rules with the reasonable assurance based on precedent and the resources of human reasoning and imagination that these rules will work well in all situations to which they literally can be applied.

In these circumstances, one obvious goal of the *Restatement Second* must be not to mislead. Care must be taken not to state rules that will prove wrong when applied to new problems, for if this were to be done with any frequency the *Restatement* would prove to be a hindrance, rather than an aid, in the further development of the subject. Hence, as a general proposition, it is probably better to err on the side of a rule that may be too fluid and uncertain in application than to take one's chances with a precise and hard-and-fast rule that may be proved wrong in the future. To be sure, a rule should not be stated so broadly that it would be consistent with almost any result that a court might reach. Such a rule would in effect be no rule at all. On the other hand, rules cannot bring certainty and predictability to a subject in which these values do not exist. Of necessity, many conflicts rules must be fluid in operation and leave much to be worked out by the courts. A *Restatement*, of course, must provide whatever guidance is possible. Hence the *Restatement Second* should state precise and definite rules in those few areas where this can be done. Elsewhere, broad, flexible rules must suffice. Such rules can be helpful, particularly if accompanied by a statement in the comments of the various policies that should guide the courts in applying them.

All rules of law, and choice-of-law rules are no exception, are the product of policies. A rule is constructed initially to further what the law-maker conceives to be the basic policies involved. And the ultimate success of a rule will depend upon how effective it is in furthering these policies. During the early stages of a rule's development, reference should constantly be made to the underlying policies to determine whether the rule is in need of amendment and whether it should be given a broad or narrow application. Only when the rule has become well established can it safely be applied without conscious reference to the policies involved. What has just been said is particularly applicable to choice-of-law rules. Few are well established and many are in their early stages of development. A court in applying these rules should have constant regard for the relevant policies. And the *Restatement Second* should state rules which in so far as possible will further them.

Some ten years ago Professor Cheatham and the writer published an article

[8] See Cavers, *supra* note 1, at 165.

setting forth some of the policies which in their opinion should guide the courts in deciding choice-of-law questions and in formulating rules for choice of law.[9] Time has not convinced the writer of the error of the views there set forth. It is proposed here to review briefly these policies and to consider the extent to which they are reflected in the rules set forth in the *Restatement Second.*

I

THE POLICIES

The policies described in the article in the order of their mention are:

(1) *The court must follow the dictates of its own legislature, provided these dictates are constitutional.*

If there is any convincing indication, on the face of a statute or otherwise, of the desires of the enacting legislature with respect to the statute's range of application in space, it is the duty of the courts, subject to constitutional restrictions, to give the statute its intended application. Rarely, however, can this policy be applied in practice, because legislatures normally do not give thought to what should be the extraterritorial range of a statute but legislate only with the intrastate situation in mind.

(2) *Choice-of-law rules should be designed to make the international and interstate systems work well.*[10]

On occasion, this basic policy comes to the surface and we find the courts openly seeking to effectuate it. In the United States, this policy is most clearly evident in some opinions of the Supreme Court. Perhaps the opinions dealing with the statutory successor furnish the best example.[11] An insolvent estate can be handled efficiently only by means of a unitary administration. Such an administration cannot be afforded a multistate corporation by a chancery receiver who can sue to collect assets and otherwise act in states not of his appointment only by the grace of those states. To remedy this situation, the Supreme Court seized upon the concept of the statutory successor and held in a series of decisions that such a successor must be permitted under full faith and credit to sue in sister states to collect stockholder assessments as well as other assets of the corporation.[12] Another example of the policy openly at work is *Hughes v. Fetter,*[13] where the Supreme Court was guided by "the strong unifying principle embodied in the full faith and credit clause looking toward maximum enforcement in each state of the obligations or rights

[9] Cheatham & Reese, *Choice of the Applicable Law*, 52 COLUM. L. REV. 959 (1952).

[10] "It [the forum] must temper its freedom to declare local policy and its scope with a sense for harmonious interstate relations as well as for the justifiable expectations of the parties." Traynor, *Is This Conflict Really Necessary?*, 37 TEXAS L. REV. 657, 675, (1959).

[11] See, *e.g.*, Broderick v. Rosner, 294 U.S. 629 (1935); Clark v. Williard, 292 U.S. 112 (1934); Converse v. Hamilton, 224 U.S. 243 (1912); Cheatham, *Note, The Statutory Successor, the Receiver and the Executor in Conflict of Laws*, 44 COLUM. L. REV. 549 (1944).

[12] See authorities cited in note 11 *supra*.

[13] 341 U.S. 609 (1951).

created or recognized by the statutes of sister states"[14] in determining that Wisconsin was required by full faith and credit to entertain suit in its courts to recover for a wrongful death that occurred in Illinois.

This policy is also thought to support the rule that, with rare exceptions, the law of the state of incorporation governs the rights and liabilities of stockholders as well as matters relating to a corporation's internal structure and administration.[15] Particularly in this country, where stockholders of a single corporation are often scattered among several states, it would be inconvenient indeed if stockholder rights and liabilities were not governed by a single law. Likewise in this country, where a corporation is likely to do business in many states, it would be almost intolerable if the law of each of these states were to be applied to determine such matters as the legality of a stock issue or of a dividend. There is need in such matters for the application of a single law, and this need is met by the rule that the law of the state of incorporation governs.[16]

Frequently, of course, it will be impossible to tell whether the needs of the international and interstate systems would best be served by the resolution of a given dispute one way or the other. In such instances, resort must be had to the other policies mentioned below.

(3) *The court should apply its own local law unless there is good reason for not doing so.*

A court should not assume the burden of ascertaining and applying the law of another state without good reason. So a court should apply its own law to matters that are not likely to affect the ultimate result of the case, such as rules of evidence and methods of service. As to still other matters, a court should also apply its own law unless it is required to do otherwise by one or more of the other policies mentioned here.

(4) *The court should consider the purpose of its relevant local law rule in determining whether to apply its own law or the law of another state.*

Every rule of law, whether embodied in a statute or in a common-law rule, was formulated in order to achieve one or more purposes. A court should have regard for these purposes in determining whether to apply its own rule or the law of another state to the matter at hand. If the purposes sought to be achieved by a local statute or common-law rule would be furthered by its application to an out-of-state occurrence, this is a weighty reason why such application should be made. It is only to be expected that a court will favor its own local policies over those of other states. For this reason primarily, a court will be inclined to give its own statutes and rules

[14] *Id.* at 612.

[15] RESTATEMENT (SECOND), CONFLICT OF LAWS §§ 166a, 182-186c (Tent. Draft No. 7, 1963); Reese & Kaufman, *The Law Governing Corporate Affairs: Choice of Law and the Scope of Full Faith and Credit*, 58 COLUM. L. REV. 1118 (1958); Coleman, *Corporate Dividends and the Conflict of Laws*, 63 HARV. L. REV. 433 (1950).

[16] See authorities cited in note 15 *supra*.

a wider range of extraterritorial application than it will give to the statutes and rules of other states.

It must be remembered that, in contrast to the situation dealt with in connection with Policy No. 1, we are here dealing with the usual case where the statute or common-law rule was formulated solely with the intrastate situation in mind and without thought to its possible extraterritorial application.[17] Here the court acts as a free agent and has the pain of deciding whether the policies underlying a local statute or rule should be furthered at the expense of other choice-of-law policies and of the policies of the other interested states. The court must decide this question, since it was not decided by the legislature which enacted the statute or by the court which originally formulated the common-law rule.

There are two ways in which the court can approach the matter. Both will lead the court to the same ultimate result and, in essence, involve only verbalistic differences. Discussion of the two approaches will be clearer if made to revolve around the facts of a particular case. *Bernkrant v. Fowler*[18] has been chosen for this purpose. In that case, the decedent had orally promised the plaintiffs that if they would pay in advance of the due date a substantial part of the indebtedness they owed him, he would provide by will that any part of the debt that remained unpaid at his death should be cancelled. Relying upon this promise, the plaintiffs prepaid a sufficient amount of the debt to meet the defendant's terms. About $6,000 of the debt remained unpaid at the time of the decedent's death but his will made no provision for its cancellation. Accordingly, the plaintiffs brought suit in California against the decedent's executor to enforce the oral agreement. It appeared that the oral contract had been made in Nevada and that at all relevant times the plaintiffs were domiciled in that state. The decedent died domiciled in California. It was uncertain whether he had been domiciled in California or in Nevada at the time when the contract was made. The oral contract was found to be valid under Nevada law. On the other hand, a California statute provided that an agreement to make any provision by will is "invalid unless the same . . . is in writing. . . ."[19]

Since the forum was a California court, it would be bound to follow, subject to constitutional restrictions, any directions of the California legislature as to the statute's range of application. The statute, however, contained no provision in this regard and, presumably, had been enacted only with the intrastate situation in mind. Almost surely, the enacting legislature had not given thought to the question whether the statute should be applied to invalidate an oral contract made in Nevada with Nevada domiciliaries. This being so, the first task of the court, since it was of California, would be to ascertain the purpose, or purposes, that were sought to be achieved by the statute. Almost certainly, the principal purpose of this statute was to protect the estates of California decedents againts false claims. Perhaps it was also

[17] "In the main, local judges as well as legislators make law with the local scene only in mind. . . ." Traynor, *supra* note 10, at 671.

[18] 55 Cal.2d 588, 360 P.2d 906 (1961).

[19] CAL. CIV. CODE § 1624(6).

designed to protect the California courts against perjured testimony. In either event, the purpose, or purposes, underlying the statute would be furthered by having the statute applied to invalidate the Nevada contract. This, however, would not be the end of the matter. Since the legislature had not spoken on the point, the court, as stated above, would have to decide for itself what range of application the statute should have. The court would have to determine whether application of the statute in order to further its underlying purposes was worth the price that would be entailed.

One of the two ways in which the court could approach the question would be to admit frankly that it has the power of decision and then to inquire whether the value of furthering the purposes sought to be achieved by the statute is outweighed in the particular case by other choice-of-law policies and by the policies of other states. This was the approach taken by Justice Traynor. He stated at the outset that California had an interest in having its statute applied but that

> the Legislature, however, is ordinarily concerned with enacting laws to govern purely local transactions, and it has not spelled out the extent to which [this] statute . . . is to apply to a contract having substantial contacts with another state. Accordingly, we must determine its scope in the light of applicable principles of the law of conflict of laws.[20]

Justice Traynor continued by saying that it was possible that the decedent had been domiciled in Nevada at the time when the contract was made. If so,

> the basic policy of upholding the expectations of the parties by enforcing contracts valid under the only law apparently applicable would preclude an interpretation of our statute of frauds that would make it apply to and thus invalidate the contract because Granrud [the decedent] moved to California and died here.[21]

The same result would follow even if the decedent had been domiciled at all relevant times in California. Nevada had a "substantial interest" in having its law applied, since the plaintiffs were domiciled in that state, the contract was made there and was performed there by the plaintiffs and "involved the refinancing of obligations arising from the sale of Nevada land and secured by interests therein."[22] California also would have an obvious interest; and the problem facing the court, as Justice Traynor saw it, was to weigh "the policy to protect the reasonable expectations of the parties" against the policy represented by the California Statute of Frauds.[23] He held that the latter policy must give way because the plaintiffs at the time they made the contract would have no way of knowing whether the decedent would die domiciled in California or in some other state. "Unless they could rely on their own law, they would have to look to the laws of all jurisdictions to which Granrud [the decedent] might move regardless of where he was domiciled when the contract was made."[24] In effect, therefore, Justice Traynor held that the

[20] 55 Cal.2d at 594, 360 P.2d at 909.
[21] *Id.* at 594-95, 360 P.2d at 909.
[22] *Id.* at 595, 360 P.2d at 910.
[23] *Id.* at 596, 360 P.2d at 910.
[24] *Ibid.*

policies underlying the California Statute of Frauds must bow before the choice-of-law policies (a) of protecting the justified expectations of the parties; (b) of applying the law of the state of dominant interest; and (c) of upholding the fundamental policy underlying the local law field involved which, in the case of contracts, is to uphold contractual obligations assumed in good faith.

The other way for a court to approach the question is to pretend that its only task is one of statutory interpretation or, in other words, that it need only inquire whether the legislature did or did not intend to have the statute applied to the particular state of facts. If, as stated above, the legislature did express an intention on the subject, it is the duty of the courts to follow it, subject always to constitutional restrictions. But in the situation now under consideration, the legislature never thought about the matter at all. Hence a court following this approach must inquire what the legislature would have intended, or should have intended, had it thought about the problem. Since the court will naturally assume that the legislature was composed of reasonable men, it will almost inevitably suppose that the legislature would have been moved by the same considerations as would have moved the court. Hence if the court believes that the statute should not be applied because of such choice-of-law policies as protecting the justified expectations of the parties or attaining uniformity of result, it will assume that this must likewise have been the intention of the legislature. So, for example, we find Justice Traynor saying in *Bernkrant v. Fowler* that, because of the policy of upholding the expectations of the parties, "the California statute of frauds, in the absence of a plain legislative directive to the contrary, could not reasonably be interpreted as applying to the contract."[25]

Both approaches involve the same considerations and will lead to the same result. In both, it is the court that decides whether or not to apply the local statute to the foreign state of facts. The only difference is that a court following the first approach will frankly state that it is making the decision, while a court that adheres to the second approach will pretend to be effectuating the intentions of the legislature.

(5) ***Choice of law rules should seek to achieve certainty, predictability, and uniformity of result.***

These are basic values throughout all areas of the law. They can, however, be purchased at too great a price. In a rapidly developing area, such as choice of law, it is often more important that there should be experimentation with new rules than that certainty and predictability of result should be assured through continued adherence to existing rules as to whose essential correctness there is legitimate doubt. Certainty and predictability are of particular importance in areas where the parties are likely to give advance thought to the legal consequences of their transactions. This is recognized, within limits at least, by existing rules of choice of law. So we find the courts virtually agreed that the validity of a will in so far as it concerns movables is governed by the law of the decedent's domicile at the time of

[25] *Id.* at 595, 360 P.2d at 909.

death[26] and by the law of the situs in so far as it concerns land.[27] The courts likewise seek to apply a law that will sustain the validity of either a testamentary or an inter vivos trust.[28] And in the area of contracts, where choice-of-law rules are uncertain, some measure of predictability and certainty is achieved by allowing the parties, within broad limits, to select the law to govern the validity and effect of their contract.[29]

Uniformity of result is of pre-eminent importance when the transfer of an aggregate of movables, situated in two or more states, is involved. Here we find the courts, with considerable unanimity, adopting choice-of-law rules that permit such transfers to be governed by a single law. So, as stated above, the law of the decedent's domicile at the time of death is applied to determine the validity of his will in so far as it deals with movables;[30] the same law is likewise applied to determine the distribution of movables upon intestacy.[31] Also, with some exceptions, the law of the transferor's domicile is applied to determine the validity of an assignment of movables for the benefit of creditors.[32] Uniformity of result is equally important in the case of marital property. For this reason, in part, the law of the spouses' domicile is applied to determine marital interests in movables, irrespective of where these may have been acquired.[33]

Uniformity of result, or the application by all states of the same choice-of-law rule, is also desirable in order to avoid forum shopping. It is not to be expected, however, that differences in choice-of-law rules can ever be entirely eradicated. Likewise, freedom from forum shopping is not the most important value of all and should not be purchased at the sacrifice of all other relevant policies and at the risk of hindering the development of better rules of choice of law.

(6) *The court should seek to protect the justified expectations of the parties.*

This policy has already been seen at work in Justice Traynor's opinion in *Bernkrant v. Fowler*.[34] It can only be operative in those situations where the parties give thought in advance to the legal consequences of their transactions. It is in part because of this policy that the parties are free, within broad limits, to choose the law to govern the validity of their contract,[35] that the courts seek to apply a law that will sustain the validity of a trust of movables,[36] and within narrower limits,

[26] Restatement (Second), Conflict of Laws § 306 (Tent. Draft No. 5, 1959).

[27] *Id.* § 249.

[28] See, *e.g.*, Shannon v. Irving Trust Co., 275 N.Y. 95, 9 N.E.2d 792 (1937); Walter W. Land, Trusts in the Conflict of Laws 116 (1940); Cavers, *Trusts Inter Vivos and the Conflict of Laws*, 44 Harv. L. Rev. 161 (1930).

[29] See, *e.g.*, Siegelman v. Cunard White Star, Ltd., 221 F.2d 189 (2d Cir. 1955); Restatement (Second), Conflict of Laws § 332a (Tent. Draft No. 6, 1960).

[30] Restatement (Second), Conflict of Laws § 306 (Tent. Draft No. 5, 1959).

[31] *Id.* § 303.

[32] *Id.* § 263.

[33] *Id.* § 290.

[34] See discussion at notes 18-25 *supra*.

[35] See note 29 *supra*.

[36] See note 28 *supra*.

the validity of a contract,[37] and that the law of the last domicile is almost invariably applied to govern transfers of movables upon death.[38] To some extent, this policy of protecting justified expectations is but another way of expressing the policy discussed immediately above. A person's expectations are likely to be disappointed if choice-of-law rules do not lead to uniformity, certainty, and predictability of result.

It must be remembered that the policy of protecting the parties' expectations is but one choice-of-law policy and will, on occasion, be outweighed by other policies. This may occur when the court is faced with the problem of deciding whether or not to apply the law of a state which is frankly designed to defeat expectations, as is true of the Statute of Frauds,[39] of the Rule Against Perpetuities,[40] and of rules designed to protect persons against exploitation, as in the case of usury laws[41] and of small-loan legislation.[42]

(7) *The court should seek to apply the law of the state of dominant interest.*

In general, it is fitting that the state whose interests are most deeply affected should have its law applied. Partly for this reason, the law of the situs is applied to determine the validity and effect of a conveyance of land,[43] and the law of the spouses' common domicile is applied to determine the validity of their marriage[44] and their respective interests in movables acquired during coverture.[45] Which is the state of dominant interest may depend upon the issue involved. So if a husband injures his wife in a state other than that of their domicile, it may be that the state of conduct and injury has the greatest interest in determining such questions as whether the husband's conduct was negligent or otherwise tortious and whether the wife was contributorily negligent. On the other hand, the state of the spouses' domicile is the state of dominant interest when it comes to the question whether the husband should be held immune from tort liability to his wife.[46] It should be for this state to determine whether marital harmony is preserved by making spouses immune from tort liability to each other and, if so, whether granting such immunity is worth the price.

Similarly, suppose that a driver and a guest passenger, who are both domiciled in state *X*, start upon a motor trip which is intended to take them from *X* to a point in state *Y* and then back to *X*, and that the guest sustains injury in an accident in state *Y*. Whether the driver was negligent, and the guest contributorily negligent,

[37] See, *e.g.*, Pritchard v. Norton, 106 U.S. 124 (1882); Ehrenzweig, *Contracts in the Conflict of Laws*, 59 COLUM. L. REV. 973, 1171 (1959); RESTATEMENT (SECOND), CONFLICT OF LAWS § 322b, comment *b* (Tent. Draft No. 6, 1960).

[38] RESTATEMENT (SECOND), CONFLICT OF LAWS §§ 303, 306 (Tent. Draft No. 5, 1959).

[39] See Emery v. Burbank, 163 Mass. 326, 39 N.E. 1026 (1895); Rubin v. Irving Trust Co., 305 N.Y. 288, 113 N.E.2d 424 (1953); *but cf.* Bernkrant v. Fowler, 55 Cal.2d 588, 360 P.2d 906 (1961).

[40] See authorities cited in note 28 *supra.*

[41] RESTATEMENT (SECOND), CONFLICT OF LAWS § 334d (Tent. Draft No. 6 (1960).

[42] See, *e.g.*, Kinney Loan and Finance Co. v. Sumner, 159 Neb. 57, 65 N.W.2d 240 (1954).

[43] RESTATEMENT (SECOND), CONFLICT OF LAWS § 215 (Tent. Draft No. 5, 1959).

[44] RESTATEMENT (SECOND), CONFLICT OF LAWS §§ 121, 122, 132 (Tent. Draft No. 4, 1957).

[45] RESTATEMENT (SECOND), CONFLICT OF LAWS § 290 (Tent. Draft No. 5, 1959).

[46] See, *e.g.*, Haumschild v. Continental Casualty Co., 7 Wis.2d 130, 95 N.W.2d 814 (1959); RESTATEMENT (SECOND), CONFLICT OF LAWS § 390g (Tent. Draft No. 8, 1963).

should, normally at least, be determined by the law of *Y*, which is in the state both of conduct and injury. On the other hand, *X* law should be applied to determine the circumstances, if any, under which a guest passenger can recover damages from the driver for injuries caused by the latter's negligence. This is an issue with which *Y* has little concern and with respect to which *X* is clearly the state of dominant interest.[47]

Sometimes two or more states will have nearly equal interests in the decision of a case. If so, the policy under consideration can afford little assistance in the determination of the choice-of-law issue. It should also be stated that this is but one policy, which on occasion will be outweighed by others.

(8) *Choice-of-law rules should be simple and easy to apply.*

The importance of this policy should not be overemphasized. Pushed to its logical conclusion, it would lead to a rule that all cases should be decided according to the local law of the forum. The policy does, however, have some significance. It furnishes perhaps the principal support for the often stated rule that liability in tort is determined by the law of the state where defendant's conduct first resulted in injury.

(9) *The court should seek to further the fundamental policy underlying the local law field involved.*

Situations sometimes arise in which the policies of the interested states are largely the same but in which there nevertheless are minor differences between their relevant local law rules. In such instances, there is good reason for the court to apply the law of that state which will best achieve the fundamental policy underlying the local law field involved.

The usury cases provide an excellent example.[48] Usury laws are designed to protect borrowers against excessive interest rates. Most states have laws of this sort, and these laws differ only slightly among themselves with respect to the maximum rate of interest that can legally be charged. In these circumstances, most courts will sustain a contract against the charge of usury if it is valid under the law of any state having a substantial contact with the transaction. This is done in order to give effect to the fundamental policy underlying the field of contracts, which is that promises should be performed. The rule seems a desirable one since the policies of the interested states are essentially the same, and hence the interests of one state cannot seriously be infringed by the application of another's law.

Another example of the policy at work can be found in the field of trusts, where the courts will go to considerable lengths to apply a law that will uphold the validity of a trust against the charge that it violates the Rule Against Perpetuities.[49] The policy of all states on the subject of perpetuities is essentially the same and their laws differ only as to the length of time during which the power of alienation can

[47] Babcock v. Jackson, 12 N.Y.2d 473, 191 N.E.2d 279 (1963).

[48] RESTATEMENT (SECOND), CONFLICT OF LAWS § 334d (Tent. Draft No. 6, 1960).

[49] See note 28 *supra*.

be suspended, as lives in being, or lives in being plus twenty-one years. Here again the courts feel it more important to further the fundamental policy of trusts, which is to carry out the wishes of the settlor, than to apply the Rule Against Perpetuities of any particular state.

This policy is of less compelling force when there are significant differences in the relevant rules of the interested states. Finally, it can be of no assistance when several policies, none more fundamental than the rest, underlie the given legal field. An example is the law of torts, which, among other things, is designed to compensate the injured party, to deter tortious conduct, and to establish standards of rightful behavior.[50]

(10) *The court should seek to attain justice in the individual case.*

Usually, it will be difficult to tell where true justice lies. Also justice in the individual case, if it were given the most significant role, would be totally disruptive of all legal rules. Nevertheless, no judge will willingly reach a result which he deems to be unjust. And to some undefined extent, judges undoubtedly manipulate choice-of-law rules to permit them to apply the law of the state which to their mind will lead to the best result.

It is believed that this policy is most likely to carry the day in situations in which normal choice-of-law rules would lead to the application of the law of a state which adopts a minority view that is out of tune with the times.[51] Here it is only to be expected that the court will search for a choice-of-law rule that would lead to the application of the law of some other state. *Kilberg v. Northeast Airlines, Inc.*[52] is a case in point. There the court resorted to choice-of-law rules of dubious merit for the frankly avowed purpose of avoiding application of the provision limiting the amount of recovery contained in the wrongful death statute of Massachusetts, the state where the injury occurred and presumably the negligent conduct as well.

II

COMMENT ON THE POLICIES

With one exception, none of the policies described above is of such paramount importance as to outweigh all of the rest. The exception is Policy No. 1, which requires a court to follow the dictates of its legislature provided that these dictates are constitutional. As previously stated, however, this policy can rarely be applied in practice, because legislatures normally legislate only with the intrastate situation in mind and do not give thought to the extent, if any, to which a statute should be applied to situations involving foreign facts.[53]

Decision of a choice-of-law question is easy when all, or most, of the policies point in a single direction. Decision becomes difficult when this is not the case.

[50] ELLIOTT E. CHEATHAM, HERBERT F. GOODRICH, ERVIN N. GRISWOLD & WILLIS L. M. REESE, CASES AND MATERIALS ON CONFLICT OF LAWS 440-41 (4th ed. 1957).

[51] See, *e.g.*, Siegmann v. Meyer, 100 F.2d 367 (2d Cir. 1938).

[52] 9 N.Y.2d 34, 172 N.E.2d 526 (1961).

[53] See text at note 17 *supra*.

What is needed in this latter situation is the development of choice-of-law rules that will give effect to what are the most important policies, or policy, for the precise purpose at hand. Life would, of course, be easier if one policy always stood out from among the rest. But this simply is not true. The relative importance of the policies varies from situation to situation, and choice-of-law rules must recognize this fact.

Let us take in this connection Policy No. 4, which is that a court should consider the purpose sought to be achieved by its relevant local law rule in determining whether to apply this rule, or the law of another state, in the decision of a particular case. The extent to which application of the local law rule would result in the sacrifice of other choice-of-law policies, and the relative importance of these policies, will naturally vary from situation to situation. These variables will be considered by the courts in arriving at a choice-of-law decision.

For example, courts in this country, in the absence of an express legislative directive to the contrary, will apply the law of a decedent's domicile at the time of death to determine either the validity of his will with respect to movables or how these movables should be distributed in the event of an intestacy.[54] The courts will apply this law to local movables even though their own rules are different and even though application of these latter rules would benefit local beneficiaries. The law of the last domicile is applied in this situation because of the obvious desirability of having the distribution of an estate of movables governed by a single law. The interests of all states would suffer if this were not the case. Likewise, and again in the absence of express legislative direction to the contrary, a court will usually not apply its own recording statutes to subordinate in favor of a local purchaser a security interest in a chattel that was brought into the state without the knowledge or consent of the security holder.[55] This rule is designed to encourage the free movement of goods from state to state. It is deemed to be in the interest of all states that security interest should be protected in this instance. On the other hand, in situations in which uniformity of result is not so important and where other significant choice-of-law policies do not stand in the way, there is greater justification for a court's applying its own local rule in order to further the purposes sought to be achieved by the rule. An example is *Kilberg v. Northeast Airlines, Inc.*[56] where the New York Court of Appeals authorized application of the New York rule of damages in a suit to recover for the wrongful death of a New York domiciliary that occurred in Massachusetts. Uniformity of result is not of transcendent importance in tort and wrongful death cases for the reason, among others, that persons are unlikely to act on the assumption that in the event of an accident their rights and liabilities in tort will be governed by the law of a particular state.

[54] RESTATEMENT (SECOND), CONFLICT OF LAWS § 306 (Tent. Draft No. 5, 1959); Griswold, *Renvoi Revisited*, 51 HARV. L. REV. 1165, 1195 (1938).

[55] See, *e.g.*, Metro-Plan, Inc. v. Kotcher-Turner, Inc., 296 Mich. 400, 296 N.W. 304 (1941); RESTATEMENT (SECOND), CONFLICT OF LAWS §§ 268, 275 (Tent. Draft No. 5, 1959).

[56] 9 N.Y.2d 34, 172 N.E.2d 526 (1961).

Partial justification, at least, for the *Kilberg* decision can be found in this fact. A somewhat similar situation exists in the area of contracts. Here choice-of-law rules, in the absence of an express provision on the subject in the contract, are uncertain in the extreme. Because of this uncertainty, uniformity of result is not easily attainable and the parties are unlikely to have had clear expectations with respect to the governing law. These considerations provide the court of an interested state with some justification for applying its own local law to a contract in order to further a local policy. On the other hand, as *Bernkrant v. Fowler*[57] teaches us, the parties will naturally expect that the obligations of a contract will be fulfilled. This fact should make a court hesitate to apply its own local rule to strike down a contract which has its most significant relationship with another state.

It is also to be expected that the need of applying a local rule to foreign facts in order to further the purpose of the rule will vary from case to case. The intensity of this need is another factor that the court should consider in determining whether or not to apply its local rule.

To reiterate, no one policy, except the first, is of such paramount importance that it should always be given effect. Not only will the relative importance of these policies vary from one legal category to another, but each individual case is likely to present a different grouping of policies. Choice-of-law rules must eventually be developed that in so far as possible will take account of these variations. No single approach, no constant obeisance to a single policy will do. We must have narrower and more numerous choice-of-law rules.[58] The task of constructing such rules will not be easy and, in many instances, must be based on greater experience than we presently have. Such difficulties are only to be expected in an area that presents so many complexities as does choice of law.

III

THE RESTATEMENT SECOND

Two things should be stated by way of introduction to a discussion of the extent to which the policies described above are reflected in the rules of the *Restatement Second*. The first is that the *Restatement* states rules rather than policies. The policies are mentioned with some frequency in the Comments in order to explain and to justify the black-letter rules; they are not, however, referred to in the rules themselves.

The second is that the *Restatement* is written from the viewpoint of a neutral forum which has no interest of its own to protect and is seeking only to apply the most appropriate law. This approach is taken for the reason among others that some of the considerations that will induce a court to apply its own local law rather than that of another state are many and varied and are not susceptible to restatement. It can, of course, be said in criticism that cases rarely arise in truly neutral

[57] 55 Cal.2d 588, 360 P.2d 906 (1961).

[58] See Cavers, *supra* note 1, at 165.

forums. This may well be true. Yet the fact remains that the approach adopted appears to be the only practicable one. Also even an interested forum will usually be guided by what it conceives to be correct rules of choice of law. Somewhere it will be made clear in the final version of the *Restatement* that the court of an interested state will depart from the rules stated in obedience to an express legislative mandate and on occasion, in the absence of such a mandate, in order to further an important local policy.

Since the *Restatement* is written from the viewpoint of a neutral forum, Policies No. 1 and No. 4 are often irrelevant. These policies are (a) that a court should follow the dictates of its own legislature and (b) that a court should give consideration to the purpose sought to be achieved by its relevant local law rule in determining whether to apply the rule in a case involving out-of-state facts. These policies have a bearing on the rules of the *Restatement* only when the forum is directed to apply the renvoi doctrine, that is, to refer both to the local and the conflicts law of the state of the governing law in order to decide the case in exactly the same way as a court of the latter state would have done. In these situations, the forum must determine whether a court of the state of the governing law would have been led by Policies No. 1 and No. 4, or by still other considerations, to apply its own local law to the decision of the case. Questions to which the *Restatement* directs application of the renvoi doctrine include (a) the validity of a marriage, governed by the whole (local and conflicts) law of the spouses' common domicile,[59] (b) the transfer of land or of a chattel, governed by the whole law of the situs,[60] (c) marital interests in movables, governed by the whole law of the spouses' domicile at the time of their acquisition,[61] (d) the distribution upon death of land, governed by the whole law of the situs,[62] and (e) the distribution upon death of movables governed by the whole law of the decedent's last domicile.[63]

The *Restatement* makes clear that a court of the state of the governing law would give effect to Policy No. 1, that is to say, would follow the express commands of its legislature in determining whether to apply its own law or the law of another state in the decision of the case. So it is said, for example, that a court of the state of the governing law, if directed to do so by statute, would sustain the validity of a will with respect to formalities by application of the law of the state where the will was executed.[64] Little is said about Policy No. 4, on the other hand, because the considerations that will induce a court, in the absence of a legislative mandate, to apply its local rule in furtherance of a local policy are not susceptible to restatement. Mention is made, however, of situations in which a court will not apply its local law in deference to one or more choice-of-law policies. Examples already mentioned are that (a) courts will not, in the absence of an express legislative

[59] RESTATEMENT (SECOND), CONFLICT OF LAWS §§ 121, 122, 132 (Tent. Draft No. 4, 1957).
[60] RESTATEMENT (SECOND), CONFLICT OF LAWS §§ 215, 254a (Tent. Draft No. 5, 1959).
[61] *Id.* § 290.
[62] *Id.* §§ 245-254.
[63] *Id.* §§ 303-309.
[64] *Id.* § 249, comment *b*.

directive to the contrary, apply their local recording acts to the prejudice of a security interest in the chattel which has been brought into the state without the knowledge or consent of the security holder,[65] (b) the courts of the state of a chattel's situs, again in the absence of an express legislative directive to the contrary, will look to the law of the owner's last domicile to determine inheritance rights in the chattel,[66] and (c) courts will go to considerable lengths to apply a law that will sustain the validity of a trust against the charge that it violates the Rule against Perpetuities.[67] Still another example is to be found in the reluctance of the courts of the state of the spouses' common domicile to apply a local rule to invalidate a marriage good under the law of the state of celebration.[68]

It is said in the *Restatement* that the renvoi doctrine should not be applied to contracts[69] and torts.[70] Hence Policies No. 1 and No. 4 have no application to the *Restatement* rules directed to these two areas, which in all probability present the most difficult choice-of-law problems.

Choice-of-law rules are to be found in those chapters of the *Restatement* which are directed to status, principally marriage and legitimation (chapter 5), agency and partnerships (chapter 5a), corporations (chapter 6), property (chapter 7), contracts (chapter 8), torts (chapter 9), and substance-procedure (chapter 12). Work on chapter twelve has not yet been commenced; hence this area will not here be discussed. By and large, fairly definite choice-of-law rules are stated with respect to status, corporations, and property. This is because the courts are generally agreed on what choice-of-law policies are entitled to the greatest weight in these areas.

According to the *Restatement,* the state of the spouses' common domicile has the ultimate voice in determining the validity of their marriage.[71] This is because this state has the dominant interest in the marital status of its domiciliaries (Policy No. 7). For this reason, the renvoi doctrine is applicable and the courts of other states will seek to decide the case in exactly the same way as would have been done by the courts of the state of the common domicile. On the other hand, the courts of the common domicile will usually uphold the validity of a marriage that is good under the law of the state of celebration. This is done in order to protect the expectations of the parties (Policies No. 5 and No. 6), and because of the general policy in favor of upholding the validity of marriage (Policy No. 9). Questions of legitimation are said by the *Restatement* to be governed by the law of the domicile of the parent against whom the child claims legitimacy.[72] This state will normally at least have as great an interest in the matter as any other (Policy No. 7). Likewise, application of its law may often be required by considerations of

[65] *Id.* §§ 268, 275.
[66] *Id.* §§ 303, 306.
[67] *Id.* § 294, comment *e*; § 295, comment *d*.
[68] RESTATEMENT (SECOND), CONFLICT OF LAWS §§ 121, 132 (Tent. Draft No. 4, 1957).
[69] RESTATEMENT (SECOND), CONFLICT OF LAWS § 332, comment *e* (Tent. Draft No. 6, 1960).
[70] RESTATEMENT (SECOND), CONFLICT OF LAWS § 379, comment *e* (Tent. Draft No. 8, 1963).
[71] RESTATEMENT (SECOND), CONFLICT OF LAWS §§ 121, 132 (Tent. Draft No. 4, 1957).
[72] *Id.* §§ 137-140.

justice to the parent involved (compare Policy No. 10). The renvoi doctrine is also said to apply in this situation. If the courts of the state of the parent's domicile would determine the question of legitimation by reference to the law of another state, the forum will probably do likewise.

Questions involving the internal affairs of corporations are said, with one possible exception, to be governed by the law of the state of incorporation.[73] Such questions include the rights and liabilities of stockholders, the liability of directors and officers to the corporation and its stockholders, stockholders' and directors' meetings, the election of directors, and the validity of stock issues and of dividend payments. Frequently, the state of incorporation will be the state of dominant interest. But the rule is also applicable in situations where the corporation's contacts with the incorporating state are relatively slight and where its principal place of business is elsewhere. Explanation for the rule can be found in the needs of the situation, namely that it is of the utmost importance that matters involving a corporation's internal affairs should be governed by a single law and the state of incorporation is not only easily ascertainable but is also the one that the parties would presumably expect to have applied. A further reason for the rule is that choice-of-law rules should here be definite and clear because this is an area where the parties and their lawyers will normally give deep consideration to possible consequences of proposed conduct before they embark upon it. Hence it would appear that choice-of-law rules are here the product of Policies No. 2 (needs of the interstate system), No. 5 (certainty, predictability and uniformity of result), No. 6 (expectations of the parties), and No. 8 (ease of application). These policies likewise dictate that questions of this sort should be decided in accordance with the local law of the state of incorporation.

Turning now to property, transfers of land are said to be governed by the law of the situs.[74] This is the state of dominant interest (Policy No. 7), and the rule leads to certainty and uniformity of result (Policy No. 5) and is easy to apply (Policy No. 8). Usually, the courts of this state would apply their own local law in deciding the case. In the rare situations in which they would look to the law of another state, as where they are directed by statute to sustain the validity of a will as to formalities if it meets the requirements of some other state, the forum will do likewise.

Chattels present more difficult problems. Because chattels can be moved from state to state, no state is likely to have the same degree of interest in a chattel that it has in local land.[75] Nevertheless, the *Restatement* provides that the law of the situs governs. The clearest situation is that in which, after a security interest, as a conditional sale or chattel mortgage, has been created in the chattel in one state, the chattel is removed to a second state and there is the subject of a second transaction, as a sale to a bona fide purchaser. Here the law of the second state is applied to

[73] Restatement (Second), Conflict of Laws § 166a (Tent. Draft No. 7, 1963).

[74] Restatement (Second), Conflict of Laws § 215 (Tent. Draft No. 5, 1959).

[75] *Id.* § 254a.

determine the effect of the later transaction upon the prior security interest.[76] If the chattel was brought into the state without the knowledge or consent of the security holder, the courts of the second state, in the absence of an express legislative directive to the contrary, will not, as stated above, apply their local recording act to subordinate the interests of the security holder to those of the bona fide purchaser.[77] The forum, in any event, is directed by the *Restatement* to apply whichever law would have been applied by the courts of the second state in deciding the case. These rules rest in part upon the interest of the state of the situs (Policy No. 7). To a greater extent they stem from the policy of protecting the expectations of the parties (Policy No. 6), since one who deals with a chattel would naturally expect that the law of the state where the chattel is situated at the time would be applied to determine the interests that he acquires. On the other hand, he would also realize that the chattel might be moved to another state and that in this event the law of the other state might be applied to determine the nature of the interests acquired by one who there dealt with the chattel. Also, of course, the rule is easy to apply (Policy No. 7) and leads to certainty, uniformity, and predictability of result (Policy No. 5).

The problem becomes more difficult when the controversy with respect to the chattel is between parties to a single transaction, as when the issue is whether a given transaction resulted in the outright sale of the chattel or in a chattel mortgage or whether the security holder has sold the chattel in violation of the debtor's rights of redemption.[78] Here the question is whether the governing law should be that of the chattel's situs at the time of the transaction or the law which governs the contractual relationship between the parties. This would be the law of the state which has the most significant relationship with the parties and the transaction.[79] Much can be said in favor of the latter solution. It provides desirable flexibility and would appear to be in line with the policy that looks towards application of the law of the state of dominant interest (Policy No. 7). On the other hand, application of the law of the situs would find support in the policies of certainty, uniformity, and predictability of result (Policy No. 5) and ease of application (Policy No. 8). The *Restatement* presently provides that the law of the situs governs, but says that the courts of this state might apply the law that governs the parties' agreement in determining their interests in the chattel.[80] In this event, the forum is directed to do likewise. The authorities are uncertain in this area,[81] and it may be the *Restatement* will be amended in its final form to make solely applicable the law that governs the parties' agreement.

The situation is different when the transfer of an aggregate of movables situated

[76] *Id.* §§ 268-271, 274-278.

[77] See text at note 65 *supra*.

[78] RESTATEMENT (SECOND), CONFLICT OF LAWS § 254a, comment *b* (Tent. Draft No. 5, 1959).

[79] RESTATEMENT (SECOND), CONFLICT OF LAWS §§ 332-332b (Tent. Draft No. 6, 1960).

[80] RESTATEMENT (SECOND), CONFLICT OF LAWS § 254a, comment *b* (Tent. Draft No. 5, 1959).

[81] See Cavers, *The Conditional Seller's Remedies and the Choice-of-Law Process*, 35 N.Y.U.L. REV. 1126 (1960).

in two or more states is involved. Here it is obviously desirable that the transfer should be governed by a single law. So, the *Restatement* provides that the validity and effect of a will of movables and the distribution of movables upon intestacy are governed by the law of the decedent's domicile at the time of death,[82] marital interests in movables acquired during coverture are governed by the law of the spouses' domicile at the time of acquisition,[83] and an assignment of chattels for the benefit of creditors is governed by the law of the transferor's domicile at the time.[84] Likewise, the validity and administration of a trust of movables situated in two or more states are said to be governed by a single law.[85] These rules are clearly in line with the policy of making the international and interstate systems work well (Policy No. 2) and of the policy in favor of uniformity of result (Policy No. 5).

Nothing will here be said about the *Restatement* rules on agency and partnerships.[86] These rules are based in large part upon choice-of-law rules relating to contracts and torts. These latter rules will now be discussed.

Contracts is an area in which the parties are likely to give advance thought to the legal consequences of their conduct. There is real need here for choice-of-law rules that will bring certainty, predictability, and uniformity of result (Policy No. 5) and that will protect the parties' expectations (Policy No. 6). These values are achieved in some degree by the *Restatement* rule that, subject to certain limitations, the parties may choose the law to govern the validity and effect of their contract.[87] Where the parties have not made such a choice, the *Restatement* provides that the governing law is that of the state which has the most significant relationship with the contract.[88] The effort is made in the case of particular contracts to state what contact, as the situs of land in contracts dealing with land, will be considered most important by the courts in determining the state of most significant relationship.[89] The rule of most significant relationship is undoubtedly too vague to offer firm guidance in situations where the important contacts are divided more or less equally among two or more states. It is believed, however, that no more definite rule can be stated in view of the relatively unexplored state of the field and the existing confusion among the authorities. A more definite rule would almost surely be proved wrong in the course of time and might actually impede constructive progress.

There are many different kinds of contracts and a vastly greater multitude of issues relating to contracts. The laws of the various states also differ markedly as to the requirements that these contracts must fulfill in order to be valid and entitled to legal effect. Also the contacts which a contract may have with two or more states are likely to differ markedly from case to case. Experience has shown that

[82] RESTATEMENT (SECOND), CONFLICT OF LAWS §§ 303, 306 (Tent. Draft No. 5, 1959).
[83] *Id.* § 290.
[84] *Id.* § 263.
[85] *Id.* §§ 294-298.
[86] RESTATEMENT (SECOND), CONFLICT OF LAWS §§ 151a-151e (Tent. Draft No. 7, 1963).
[87] RESTATEMENT (SECOND), CONFLICT OF LAWS § 332a (Tent. Draft No. 6, 1960).
[88] *Id.* § 332b.
[89] *Id.* §§ 364e-364n.

this large and complicated area cannot adequately be handled by a few single rules. What is needed instead is a large number of rules that are each directed to a relatively narrow situation. Experience to date is not sufficient to permit the formulation of many such rules at the present time. The task of doing so must be left to the future. These rules will have to be developed on a case-to-case basis in the light of all of the policies outlined above. It would, of course, be far easier if it were possible to say that consideration need be given to only one of these policies, as that a court should apply its own law when to do so would further a local interest or, in order to protect the expectations of the parties, should apply a law which will validate the contract.[90] Such a view, however, would vastly oversimplify the problem and would probably prove to be as incorrect as the equally simple, and much criticized, rule of the original *Restatement* that the validity of a contract is governed by the law of the place of contracting.

A rule of validation, for example, would have much superficial attraction and could marshal considerable authority in its support. Undoubtedly, courts on many occasions have sought to uphold a contract by application of a favorable law.[91] But it must be remembered that there are many kinds of contracts and that some of them may be deemed socially undesirable or at least less desirable than others. Likewise, all states have laws which, largely for the purpose of protecting the weak against the strong, limit the parties' freedom to contract by invalidating certain kinds of contractual provisions. Whether a court will seek to apply a validating law in a given case will depend upon the kind of contract or contractual provision involved and also upon the degree of interest which the state of the validating law has in the parties and the transaction.

A rule of validation would also be impossible to apply in the familiar situation where a party claims that he has been relieved of his contractual obligation through the operation of a particular provision in the contract, as that he shall not be held liable in the event of a particular occurrence, or that no suit shall be brought later than a specified time after the occurrence of a loss or injury.[92] Here if the court validates the provision it must perforce hold the obligation ineffective. In order to uphold the obligation, the court must invalidate the provision. In either case, the court must both validate and invalidate. No principle of validation can furnish it with an effective guide.

There is no easy short cut. In each case, all of the policies must be considered and a choice-of-law rule developed that will give effect to what are the most important policies for the precise purpose at hand. It is felt as a result that the *Restatement* cannot usually do more in the case of contracts which contain no choice-of-law provision than to state the general principle of state of most significant relationship in the black letter rule and then to mention in the comments the more important considerations that should motivate the courts in arriving at a decision

[90] See Ehrenzweig, *supra* note 37.

[91] See, *e.g.*, Pritchard v. Norton, 106 U.S. 124 (1882).

[92] Auten v. Auten, 308 N.Y. 155, 124 N.E.2d. 99 (1954), provides another example.

and in general to give whatever guidance is possible. At the very least, such black letter rules and comments will not mislead an unwary court or litigant into believing that the area is governed by well-settled rules.

Torts present different considerations. Rarely do parties contemplate the consequences of tortious conduct, and rarely if at all will they give thought to the question of what law would be applied to govern their conduct if it were to result in injury. In other words, uniformity, certainty, and predictability of result are not as important values in this area as they are in contracts. Until recently, the courts with rare unanimity applied the law of the place of injury to determine rights and liabilities in tort.[93] Recently, however, several important courts have either expressed dissatisfaction with the rule or else have reached results that are inconsistent with it.[94] This trend will probably continue and it is thought that the rule will become eroded, at least in part, in the course of time. As a result, the *Restatement* has adopted in this area also the rule of most significant relationship.[95] The effort is also made, as in the case of contracts, to state with respect to particular torts what contact, as the principal location of the defendant's conduct in the case of alienation of affections, will be considered most important by the courts in determining the state of most significant relationship.[96]

This rule of most significant relationship, at the very least, will not stand in the way of progress. It should aid in inducing the courts to depart from the place of injury rule in situations where this is desirable. And it should make clear to the lawyer and litigant that it can no longer be expected that the place of injury rule will always be applied.

CONCLUSION

It is hoped that the policies outlined in the first part of this paper are correctly reflected in the rules of the *Restatement Second*. Fairly precise rules have in general been stated in the case of status, corporations, and property, since, on the basis of present knowledge, it is deemed possible to identify and to give effect to the most important policies in these areas. Present experience, on the other hand, with respect to contracts and torts does not permit the formulation of definite rules with any reasonable assurance that these rules would give appropriate effect to what are here the most significant policies. Hence the more general and more flexible formulation of "state of most significant relationship" has been resorted to. Presumably more definite and precise rules can be stated after more experience has accumulated. That will be the task of future *Restatements*.

[93] See generally MOFFATT HANCOCK, TORTS IN THE CONFLICT OF LAWS (1942).

[94] See, *e.g.*, Grant v. McAuliffe, 41 Cal.2d 859, 264 P.2d 944 (1953); Schmidt v. Driscoll Hotels, 249 Minn. 376, 82 N.W.2d 365 (1957); Babcock v. Jackson, 12 N.Y.2d 473, 191 N.E.2d 279 (1963); Kilberg v. Northeast Airlines, 9 N.Y.2d 34, 172 N.E.2d 526 (1961).

[95] RESTATEMENT (SECOND), CONFLICT OF LAWS § 379 (Tent. Draft No. 8, 1963).

[96] *Id.* §§ 379a-379k.

[13]

CHOICE-INFLUENCING CONSIDERATIONS IN CONFLICTS LAW

ROBERT A. LEFLAR

I

INTRODUCTION

THERE is a tendency to say that the proper way to deal with choice-of-law problems is to wipe the slate clean of all the old rules and theories, and start afresh. This tendency assumes that the old ideas were based on such mistaken assumptions and unachievable objectives as to make them substantially useless in the light of today's better understanding and scholarship. That there is better understanding and scholarship today is certain. That the past can or should be disregarded is another matter.

The major considerations that should influence choice of law have always been present and operative in the cases. They have not always been identified clearly, nor has the weight given to one or another among them always been logical or sensible. That, however, is a criticism that can be, and is, directed at today's choice-of-law decisions as well as at those handed down a half-century or a century ago. It is also a criticism that today's commentators can and do direct at each other. The process of identifying the choice-influencing considerations and of attaching appropriate significance to each of them is one that will have to continue indefinitely, with little prospect of complete agreement.

This process is by its nature the basic one in choice-of-law analysis. Story dwelt on the various choice-influencing considerations, as he understood them, throughout his treatise.[1] So did Wharton[2] and Minor.[3] Beale thought that mechanical simplicity of rule, with assumed predictability of results as a corollary, was of first importance, though he often mentioned other considerations too and foresaw greater weight to be given them.[4] When his

---

Robert A. Leflar is Professor of Law, New York University School of Law and Distinguished Professor of Law, University of Arkansas.

1. Story's main emphasis was on the virtues of "comity," but throughout his work he pointed out "principles of public policy" which he thought favored his various conclusions. Story, Commentaries on the Conflict of Laws (8th ed. 1883). See Lorenzen, Story's Commentaries on the Conflict of Laws—One Hundred Years After, 48 Harv. L. Rev. 15 (1934).

2. Wharton, Conflict of Laws (3d ed. 1905). This was primarily a source book for case authority, but it repeated the policy evaluations that appeared in the language of the cases.

3. Minor, Conflict of Laws (1901). This book was over-formalistic, but was based on a thoughtful reexamination of reasons and not merely of rules.

4. See Beale, Social Justice and Business Costs—A Study in the Legal History of Today, 49 Harv. L. Rev. 593 (1936). Written in Beale's later years, this short

detractors showed that his assumed predictabilty was often a mirage, and argued that mechanical simplicity of rules was not so important as Beale thought it was in comparison with other values,[5] they too were engaged primarily in identifying and evaluating the relevant considerations.

Emphasis by "local law" theorists on the sovereignty of the forum,[6] basic to the now settled rejection of Beale's super-law of "vested rights," indicated only a new starting point, not the end or even a guide in choice of law. Acceptance of a "local law" theory establishes which state's law of choice of law is to be applied in a given case. It shows that State *F* as forum is free to make its own choice-of-law rules, either legislatively or judicially, for whatever reasons appeal to it, except as the discovered content of the federal constitution puts limits on its freedom.[7] But it does not tell what the choice of law should be.

Different courts have expectably differed as to what choice-influencing considerations are most important. Many for a time accepted the urge for mechanical simplicity which motivated Beale and the first Restatement. Blind regard for supposedly controlling precedent was usually a part of the reason for these holdings. At the opposite extreme were those whose ideal was the just result in the individual case,[8] an ideal sometimes stated openly[9] but more often concealed by manipulative devices such as characterization or multiple-choice conflict rules.

An article by Cheatham and Reese[10] in 1952 was the first thorough effort to catalogue all the choice-influencing considerations. The American Law Institute's Restatement (Second), especially in its comments, makes frequent reference to the Cheatham-Reese list of nine considerations, called "policies," as explanations of rules announced,[11] but the Restatement

article was not a particularly penetrating study of social values in choice of law but it did indicate his recognition of the relevance of those values.

5. See Arnold, Institute Priests and Yale Observers—A Reply to Dean Goodrich, 84 U. Pa. L. Rev. 811 (1936); Heilman, Judicial Method and Economic Objectives in Conflict of Laws, 43 Yale L.J. 1082 (1934); Lorenzen, Territoriality, Public Policy and the Conflict of Laws, 33 Yale L.J. 736 (1924); Yntema, The Hornbook Method and the Conflict of Laws, 37 Yale L.J. 468 (1928).

6. Cook, The Logical and Legal Bases of the Conflict of Laws 1-46 (1942). Cf. Cavers, The Two "Local Law" Theories, 63 Harv. L. Rev. 822 (1950).

7. See Home Ins. Co. v. Dick, 281 U.S. 397, 410-11 (1930); note 20 infra.

8. Cavers, A Critique of the Choice-of-Law Problem, 47 Harv. L. Rev. 173 (1933), is usually cited, fairly or unfairly, to illustrate this position.

9. "I grant that, in this context, I am stressing the need to do justice in particular instances. I do so unashamedly." Siegelman v. Cunard White Star Ltd., 221 F.2d 189, 206 (2d Cir. 1955) (Frank, J., dissenting).

10. Cheatham & Reese, Choice of the Applicable Law, 52 Colum. L. Rev. 959 (1952).

11. See Reese, Conflict of Laws and the Restatement Second, 28 Law & Contemp. Prob. 679, 692-99 (1963).

necessity for producing a mechanically operative rule for each categorized group of fact situations lessens the opportunity to make maximum use of the nine "policies" in determining results for specific sets of facts. The Restatement's "center of gravity" rule for tort[12] and contract[13] cases, for example, undertakes to correlate "dominant contacts" with the distilled essence of the nine policies, but it is evident that a weighing of "significance" in contacts, let alone a "counting" of them,[14] is far from an analysis based on such legitimate considerations as the Cheatham-Reese list of nine policies. The English "proper law" advocates[15] have employed about the same technique as is used in Restatement (Second), except that they have not had occasion to go into as much detail.

Professor Ehrenzweig's principal affirmative contribution to choice-of-law theory (as distinguished from his very real negative one of telling us what the law is *not*) is his analysis of the choice-influencing considerations as *he* identifies and weighs them, differently from other commentators, in the wide variety of fact situations with which he has dealt.[16] He has seen considerations that had not appeared to the eyes of others, and he has been willing to apply them in more detail to a wider variety of fact situations than have others. This has produced fewer hard and fast rules, and greater possibilites for flexibility and individualization, than under the Restatement. At the same time it has produced potent criticisms of the soundness of some of his evaluations.[17]

The point of view in Professor Brainerd Currie's writings[18]

---

12. Restatement (Second), Conflict of Laws § 379 (Tent. Draft No. 9, 1964).

13. Restatement (Second), Conflict of Laws § 332 (Tent. Draft No. 6, 1960).

14. Haag v. Barnes, 9 N.Y.2d 554, 175 N.E.2d 441, 216 N.Y.S.2d 65 (1961), discussed in Ehrenzweig, The "Bastard" in the Conflict of Laws—A National Disgrace, 29 U. Chi. L. Rev. 498-99 (1962).

15. Childres, Toward the Proper Law of the Tort, 40 Texas L. Rev. 336 (1962); Morris, The Proper Law of a Tort, 64 Harv. L. Rev. 881 (1951); Morris & Cheshire, The Proper Law of a Contract in the Conflict of Laws, 56 L.Q. Rev. 320 (1940).

16. This is not only in his treatise, Ehrenzweig, Conflict of Laws (1962), but also in the literally dozens of studies, usually including the words "Law and Reason Versus the Restatement" in their titles, which he has written on choice-of-law topics.

17. E.g., Morris, Enterprise Liability and the Actuarial Process—The Insignificance of Foresight, 70 Yale L.J. 554 (1961).

18. Most of these, except the latest ones, appear in his Selected Essays on the Conflict of Laws 285, 476-77, 580 n.213, 614, 700 (1963). The most succinct summary of Currie's views, prepared by him for use by law students, is in Cheatham, Griswold, Reese & Rosenberg, Cases on Conflict of Laws 477-78 (5th ed. 1964).

is directly opposite to that in Ehrenzweig's. Currie deliberately narrowed and thinned out the list of choice-influencing considerations.[19] Currie of course was not dominated by the same considerations that principally influenced Beale, but there was considerable similarity in their attitudes. Simplicity of rule and ease of judicial administration are prime considerations underlying both their systems, though for different reasons. Beale would have recognized the validity of almost every choice-influencing consideration that may reasonably be urged today, but would have concluded (did conclude) that the virtues supporting his conceptually logical rules were the most worthy ones. Contrariwise, Currie in effect said that many of the considerations that are asserted today ought not to be taken into account at all in the judicial formulation of choice-of-law rules or decisions. He regarded these considerations as matters of "policy" or "politics" that are outside the proper ken of courts, that should be left for legislatures to pass upon. In the absence of legislatively promulgated choice-of-law rules he would have the courts undertake, in "restrained and enlightened" fashion, a process of expanded statutory construction to discover the territorial scope ("governmental interest" territorially allocated) of each state's rule from the sense and context of the rule itself. A forum preference would solve such cases as were otherwise insoluble. Inappropriate judicial legislation would thus presumptively be avoided. The overt weighing of choice-influencing considerations would be kept to a minimum, though in the nature of things such considerations would necessarily have a part in the quasi-interpretative rule-construing process by means of which "governmental interests" would be territorially assigned.

Before choice-influencing considerations are analyzed, it is important that the controlling power of forum law be emphasized, and that this emphasis be appropriately confined. The law of forum *F*, on choice of law, is the law that the courts of forum *F* will follow. This may include a renvoi reference to the conflicts law of some other state, or it may not. It may include any basis for decision, any reference or nonreference to another state's law, any broad-based rule or any free-wheeling choice in individual cases unguided by rule or principle that the forum's law-

19. This does not refer to the "false conflicts" cases, as to which Currie, along with a few other perceptive scholars, performed the tremendous service of pointing out that there are no real choice-of-law problems in them. See M. Traynor, Conflict of Laws: Professor Currie's Restrained and Enlightened Forum, 49 Calif. L. Rev. 845, 846-47 (1961). Though there is no agreement on exactly how far the "false conflicts" category is to be extended, it is intended that the present discussion relate to "true conflicts" cases only, whatever these may be.

making agencies conjure up, provided only that it does not contradict the "law of the land."

Purported forum law that does contradict the "law of the land" is not forum law at all,[20] and we are not further concerned with it. There are areas in which a state court cannot yet know what the law of the land is, either because the Supreme Court has not answered all the questions that will in due time be raised under the relevant constitutional clauses, because the Congress has not enacted all the implementing statutes these clauses authorize, because new treaties are yet to be ratified and old ones yet to be interpreted, or because the subjects of exclusive federal power have not all been identified and defined. On some fronts the permissible variety of state conflicts law is increasing, as the Supreme Court makes clear that it does not propose to make the whole law of choice of law into a branch of constitutional law.[21] On other fronts the functions of state law will decrease as the exercise of federal power inevitably expands. That is not the topic of this article. The discussion here is limited to state choice-of-law decision that does not conflict with federal law. Accepting that limitation as fundamental in State *F*'s law (assuming *F* to be an American state) the conflicts law of *F* is what *F* says it is. No other state or nation can tell *F* what its choice of law shall be.

II

Statutes as the Basis of Choice of Law

It is taken for granted that the primary law-making agency in an American state is the legislature.[22] If the *F* legislature enacts a choice-of-law statute it can be assumed that the *F* courts will follow it. The courts may first, however, have to figure out, or at least go through the form of figuring out, what the statute means. The legislatures of America have in general been neither

20. This refers not only to limitations imposed by or read into the conflicts provisions in the Constitution, such as the full faith and credit, privileges and immunities, and equal protection clauses, but also to the many other provisions dealing with due process of law, the war power, treaties, interstate and foreign commerce, bankruptcy, coinage, and the like which limit state action to varying extents. It also precludes state control in areas where a unitary national law is deemed essential to adequate performance of federal functions, as with international affairs and under the so-called Clearfield rule. See note 65 infra; Leflar, Constitutional Limits on Free Choice of Law, 28 Law & Contemp. Prob. 706, 709, 725-26 (1963); Mishkin, The Variousness of "Federal Law": Competence and Discretion in the Choice of National and State Rules for Decision, 105 U. Pa. L. Rev. 797 (1957).

21. Leflar, States' Rights in Conflict of Laws, 19 Ark. L. Rev. 142 (1965). Compare Ross, Has the Conflict of Laws Become a Branch of Constitutional Law?, 15 Minn. L. Rev. 161 (1931).

22. State constitutions must of course be taken into account, but they seldom have much bearing on choice-of-law problems.

perceptive nor specific in their choice-of-law enactments. Apart from provisions in some carefully drafted uniform acts, and a few others, American choice-of-law statutes have tended to ambiguous generality.[23]

The workmen's compensation acts offer a glaring example. Most of them contain choice-of-law provisions, though it is typical of these, especially in the earlier enactments, that they require extensive judicial implementation. Some statutes do no more than indicate that the act could have some out-of-state applicability in unstated circumstances.[24] The whole choice-of-law problem is left to the commissions and the courts. Amendments to several of the acts have made them a little more explicit as to their coverage in two-state or multi-state situations,[25] but the mass of choice-of-law problems that might arise is left untouched. The strange fact is that in the appellate courts, and even in the commentaries, the conflicts cases from all the states are cited almost interchangeably, from Alabama to Wyoming and California to Maine, as though all the workmen's compensation statutes were worded similarly with reference to territorial applicability, though their language in fact differs considerably. The courts seem to assume that the statutes are as meaninglessly irrelevant as they almost are.

The insurance field is another in which legislatures have at times undertaken to control choice of governing law, usually with a view to assuring the application of the enacting state's own law. Typical statutes have been identified by Professor Carnahan[26] with the phrasings (1) "All contracts of insurance, the application for which is taken within the state shall be deemed to have been made within the state, and subject to the laws thereof,"[27] and (2) "No insurance company transacting

---

23. See Danson, Territorially Limited Statutes and the Choice-of-law Process, 1 Harv. J. Legis. 115 (1964).

24. The Arkansas act is typical. It was one of the last to be enacted (in 1939) and was modeled on the forty-six earlier ones. Its only conflict of laws language appears in two sections. Section 23 provides that "the hearing shall be held in the county where the accident occurred, if the same occurred in this State . . . . If the accident occurred without the State of Arkansas, and is one for which compensation is payable under this act . . . ," other venues are prescribed. The procedure for appeal "if the accident occurred outside the State" is set out in § 25. Ark. Stat. Ann. §§ 81-1323, -1325 (1960). There is no statement in the act as to *what* out-of-state accidents are covered by it.

25. See 2 Larson, Workmen's Compensation §§ 87.00-.14 (1961), for an analysis of the territorial operation of the statutes of many of the states.

26. Carnahan, Conflict of Laws and Life Insurance Contracts § 26, at 124-26 (2d ed. 1958).

27. Alabama, Minnesota, Mississippi, North Carolina, Tennessee, Texas, and Utah are listed as having this form of statute. Id. at 125 n.34. Such statutes some-

business in this state shall hereafter make, issue or deliver herein, any policy or contract of insurance containing any condition, stipulation or agreement requiring such contract of insurance to be construed according to the laws of any other state or country."[28] Other statutes contain exactly contrary provisions, authorizing application of the law of either of two states, presumably with a view to sustaining policy provisions if they are valid by the law of either state.[29] Carnahan cites some states as having both types of enactments.[30] When both are enacted, legislative ambiguity again requires judicial unraveling. Statutes of the first type literally invite unconstitutional application.[31]

Statutes phrased in terms of choice-of-law theory have on the whole been equally poor. The confusion produced by borrowing statutes in the limitations field is classic in its messiness.[32] It is difficult to conceive how the problem could have been handled worse than by the legislatures that have dealt with it. The Georgia statute which declared that

> The validity, form, and effect of all writings or contracts are determined by the laws of the place where executed. When such writings or contracts are intended to have effect in this State, they must be executed in conformity to the laws of this State . . . .[33]

---

times apply also to "all contracts of insurance on property, lives or interests in this state."

28. Arizona, Massachusetts, Nebraska, New York, Texas, Washington, and Wisconsin are listed. Id. at 125 n.35.

29. For the list of states, see id. at 126 n.37. It may be assumed that these statutes were promoted in the legislatures by groups interested in advancement of the insurance business, whereas the restrictive enactments were sponsored by groups which distrusted the insurance companies.

30. Carnahan, supra note 26, at 126 n.37 (listing Arizona, Massachusetts, Tennessee, and Texas).

31. The Mississippi statute which was held unconstitutional in Hartford Acc. & Indem. Co. v. Delta & Pine Land Co., 292 U.S. 143 (1934), when applied to an insurance contract made in Tennessee, provided that "all contracts of insurance on property, lives or interests in this state shall be deemed to be made therein." Id. at 148. See also the statutory phrasing in Aetna Life Ins. Co. v. Dunken, 266 U.S. 389, 390-91 (1924).

32. See Ester, Borrowing Statutes of Limitation and Conflict of Laws, 15 U. Fla. L. Rev. 33 (1962); Nordstrom, Ohio's Borrowing Statute of Limitations—A Quaking Quagmire in a Dismal Swamp, 16 Ohio St. L.J. 183 (1955); Vernon, Statutes of Limitation in the Conflict of Laws: Borrowing Statutes, 32 Rocky Mt. L. Rev. 287 (1960). Even the act promulgated by the National Conference of Commissioners on Uniform State Laws is designed to achieve no virtue beyond a minimum of simplicity in administration. Uniform Statute of Limitations on Foreign Claims Act §§ 2-4.

33. Ga. Code Ann. tit. 102, § 108 (1955). Upon adoption of the Uniform Commercial Code in 1962 matters dealt with therein were supposedly deleted from the old Georgia law by the legislature, and the cited section was amended to read: "When writings or contracts are intended to have effect in this State, they must be executed in conformity to the laws of this State . . . ." Ga. Code Ann. tit. 102, § 108 (Supp. 1965).

had for practical reasons to be reinterpreted until it became hardly recognizable.[34] Academic drafts proposed elsewhere but not enacted[35] have sometimes been as bad, or worse.

The Federal Tort Claims Act, though drafted only after long public discussion of governmental liability, prescribed a completely inept and inappropriate choice-of-law rule which eventually had to be given a new meaning by the courts. The wording of the act was that the federal government should be liable in tort "where the United States, if a private person, would be liable to the claimant in accordance with the law of the place where the *act or omission occurred*."[36] Judge Goodrich attempted to discover why the rule was written in this odd fashion, but only learned that the draftsmen apparently thought this was the standard rule.[37] The United States Supreme Court finally solved the problem by reading a quasi-renvoi gimmick into the enactment, making of it a reference to the "whole law" (including the choice-of-law rule) of the state "where the act or omission occurred."[38] Thus the misshapen abnormality was taken out of its statutory cast and made as flexible as the conflicts rule in the specified state.

Even choice-of-law enactments that were framed in terms of specifically desired socio-economic results have not always worked out, sometimes because of inept phrasing and sometimes because socio-economic standards can change faster than disinterested legislators repeal old and "minor" legislation. Thus, the pre-Confederacy statutes, which classified slaves as "immovables," though honestly designed to further the ends of a plantation economy, created special problems by reason of the inherent contradictoriness of the word used.[39] And the Uniform Marriage Evasion Act,[40] withdrawn by its sponsors after thirty years because its original framers had misjudged societal standards,[41] still remains

34. See Budget Rent-a-Car Corp. of America v. Fein, 342 F.2d 509 (5th Cir. 1965).

35. See Stimson, Simplifying the Conflict of Laws: A Bill Proposed for Enactment by the Congress, 36 A.B.A.J. 1003, 1005-06 (1950) (federal statute to control choice of law); Sumner, Choice of Law Governing Survival of Actions, 9 Hastings L.J. 128, 143 (1958) (statute listing what is "substantive" and "procedural" for choice-of-law purposes).

36. 28 U.S.C. § 1346(b) (1964). (Emphasis added.)

37. Goodrich, Yielding Place to New: Rest Versus Motion in the Conflict of Laws, 50 Colum. L. Rev. 881, 894-95 (1950).

38. Richards v. United States, 369 U.S. 1, 11 (1962).

39. McCollum v. Smith, 19 Tenn. 342 (1838). See Williamson's Adm'rs v. Smart, 1 N.C. 355 (1801).

40. Uniform Marriage Evasion Act (1912).

41. The act was declared "obsolete" in 1943. See 9 Uniform Laws Ann. xxi (1957).

disturbingly on the books of the five states[42] that had in the meantime enacted it. Our experience with choice-of-law statutes has often been an unfortunate one.

In contrast, some choice-of-law statutes have been intelligently framed, with deliberate and foresighted planning of anticipated consequences. Section 1-105(1) of the Uniform Commercial Code is an example. It reads:

> Except as provided hereafter in this section, when a transaction bears a reasonable relation to this state and also to another state or nation the parties may agree that the law either of this state or of such other state or nation shall govern their rights and duties. Failing such agreement this Act applies to transactions bearing an appropriate relation to this state.

Then five areas of the new law are excepted, and more specific choices of law are laid down for them. The two ideas that are basic to the main part of this enactment are (1) parties should be free to plan their transactions with reference to what law is to govern them, and (2) if they have not so planned a given transaction, the "better law" (which has an appropriate relation to the transaction) should govern it. The Uniform Commercial Code constitutes the best and most carefully formulated body of commercial law available anywhere, and this fact by itself is good reason for selecting it as the governing law.[43]

The Uniform Securities Act has detailed choice-of-law sections,[44] of a character quite different from Section 1-105 of the Uniform Commercial Code. The Uniform Securities Act is specific in selecting the places of particular events as providing the governing law for particular issues. This approach is desirable for the types of transactions controlled by this act, as to which it is urgent that the exact legal consequences of acts done be knowable at once. The practical reasons that justify mechanical rules here are similar to those that justify comparable rules in some of the five exceptions to the Uniform Commercial Code's general choice-of-law provision. Good choice-of-law statutes, cleanly and wisely drafted, may employ many different approaches. Their common feature is that they are designed realistically to give practical policy-oriented answers to choice-of-law problems. They

42. Illinois, Louisiana, Massachusetts, Vermont, and Wisconsin.

43. "[A] conflict-of-laws decision refusing to apply a purely local statute or rule of law to a particular multi-state transaction may not be valid precedent for refusal to apply the Code in an analogous situation. Application of the Code . . . may be justified by its comprehensiveness, by the policy of uniformity, and by the fact that it is in large part a reformulation and restatement of the law merchant and of the understanding of a business community which transcends state and even national boundaries."
Uniform Commercial Code § 1-105, comment 3.

44. Uniform Securities Act § 414.

are drafted to help serve the socio-economic functions of the law of which they are a part.

Statutes governing the validity of wills, often copied from the Model Execution of Wills Act,[45] have been drafted with a deliberate purpose of securing the desirable result of sustaining wills if they satisfy *any* law that might reasonably be supposed to control them. The old common-law rule determined the validity of wills of land by the law of the situs and wills of movables by the law of the testator's domicile at death. That rule was unnecessarily narrow and inflexible. Modern statutes, now in thirty-two states,[46] sustain wills, sometimes of land, sometimes of movables, and sometimes of both, if the will would be valid by the law of the situs, of the place where the will was executed, of the testator's domicile at the time it was executed, or of his domicile at death. By this approach the choice-of-law rule is made to serve an identifiable and worthwhile social purpose. It is no longer a mechanical rule of thumb serving only the administrative purpose of enabling a court to decide a case easily.

When statutes deal expressly with choice of law, the function of the courts is an interpretative one, whether the statutory rule be clear or ambiguous, mechanical or policy-oriented, wise or unwise. Reference to the statute is not only proper but necessary. There are some statutes in which the territorial scope of the enactment appears by necessary or logical implication. Traffic laws are of this sort, as are licensing laws, laws prescribing qualifications for public officials, laws setting out procedural rules for courts, and the like. In such enactments the words "in this state" are to be read into the law as surely as if they were written there. A necessary or reasonable implication of extrastate application, as where the statute deals with "all persons domiciled in this state," is possible too, though less frequent. In all such cases a choice-of-law rule can be found in the law itself.

But most law, common and statutory, is promulgated without territorial directives, express or implied. Suggestions have been made that a kind of statutory construction will yield choice-of-law conclusions even for this bulk of law. The pseudo-interpretative process thus called for would be an analysis of the particular law's objectives in territorial terms, which would be an effort to deduce the presence and the weight of state "governmental in-

45. This act was promulgated in 1940 to supersede the Uniform Wills Act, Foreign Executed (1910).

46. See Rees, American Wills Statutes: II, 46 Va. L. Rev. 856, 905-07 (1960). See also Ester & Scoles, Estate Planning and Conflict of Laws, 24 Ohio St. L.J. 270, 274-81 (1963).

terests" relevant to choice of law by a straight-faced (not tongue-in-cheek) search for unexpressed legislative intention.[47]

This process of pretended construction is usually an application of standard choice-of-law considerations, relevant under the common law, to the problem at hand, with the label "statutory interpretation" attached. In such cases the cover-up usually does no real harm except to clarity of expression and resultant understanding. Sometimes, however, common-law choice-of-law considerations may not be employed, or may be incompletely employed, on the theory that they are not essential to the construction of a local statute. That is when harm can be done, because these considerations, or some of them, are almost certain to be relevant. A state's "governmental interests" as they apply to a two-state or multi-state set of facts will seldom be the same as those which apply to an altogether intrastate set of facts. A state's "interests" and policies as applied to purely local facts may be quite insular, or otherwise limited and restricted. The Brandeis idea of each of the states as a sort of socio-legal laboratory, complete unto itself, has most merit when applied to purely intrastate transactions. Not only the extrastate origin of part of the facts, but also the other state's laws as facts in the forum state's litigation, may affect the forum's total "interests" and policies. It is unfortunately true that a legislature sometimes inadequately considers the relevant choice-influencing considerations when it enacts an express choice-of-law rule; the chances of its having considered them sub silentio when there is no express enactment are all the more dim. Solution of choice-of-law problems calls for a high order of deliberate judgment, whether legislative or judicial. If the judgment has actually been exercised by a legislature or legislative draftsman, well and good. If it has not, then the exercise of it is up to the courts, and little but obfuscation is accomplished by pretending to conceal the judicial function behind a false front of deference to legislation.

The frequently static nature of legislation has some bearing on this. Relevant choice-of-law considerations, whether reflected in "governmental interests" or in factors otherwise described, should be discovered as of the time when the case is being de-

47. Cf. Currie, The Distinterested Third State, 28 Law & Contemp. Prob. 754, 761-62 (1963). The idea is that the court finds the territorial choice within the substantive statute itself, so that the court will not have to decide the choice-of-law problem as such. The legislature is deemed to have decided it. "Resolution of a conflict between the interests of coordinate states is a function of a high political order, which courts are not equipped to perform." Id. at 758. Compare Hancock, "In the Parish of *St. Mary le Bow*, in the Ward of *Cheap*," 16 Stan. L. Rev. 561 (1964).

cided,[48] even though the subtantive law of one or another of the states involved may have been enacted in 1935 or 1885. The fact that a statute is still on the books today does not mean that the enacting state's policies and interests with reference to it are the same as when it was enacted. They *may* be the same, or even more potent in its favor, but it is also possible that they are less potent.[49] To the extent that these policies have to be ascertained from other than the statute's words, the job of ascertainment is for the courts, and the franker the courts are in identifying the post-enactment socio-economic changes that affect state policy the more realistic their opinions will be. In the choice-of-law area, this frankness will be achieved by express reference to the considerations that should affect choice of law as such.

Distrust of the judicial process is understandable, though no more understandable than distrust of all the processes of government. Judical restraint and deference to the legislative branch serve useful purposes when they (a) encourage legislatures to act in areas for which they have special competence or (b) give effect to real legislative policies consciously laid down and currently operative. As to (a) in the choice-of-law field, almost no one believes that it would be wise for a legislature, state or national, today or in the near future, to enact a conflicts code, or that such a code would or even could be well drafted. The prospect of enacting wise choice-of-law statutes in little pieces, for the scores and hundreds of areas in which the cases arise, is so faint that it is meaningless. Even if it were attempted, the

48. "A court obviously must decide if the alleged policy of the state is in fact an existing one." Kramer, Interests and Policy Clashes in Conflict of Laws, 13 Rutgers L. Rev. 523, 545 (1959). Nearly everyone agrees that there are some narrow areas in the law—of torts, for example—in which legislative modernization is wholly improbable despite the clear fact that the old rule is a "drag on the coat tails of civilization." Cheatham & Reese, Choice of the Applicable Law, 52 Colum. L. Rev. 959, 980 (1952). Judicial updating of the law is standard for such areas. See James, Tort Law in Midstream: Its Challenge to the Judicial Process, 8 Buffalo L. Rev. 315 (1959); Keeton, Creative Continuity in the Law of Torts, 75 Harv. L. Rev. 463 (1962); Peck, The Role of the Courts and Legislatures in the Reform of Tort Law, 48 Minn. L. Rev. 265 (1963). The possibility that, for any given rule of law, such judicial updating may be just around the corner has clear bearing upon realistic determination of the policies or interests of a state whose last prior adjudication still followed the old rule unaltered.

49. The automobile guest statutes afford an illustration of changing social attitudes toward a statute which in the states that enacted it is still on the books. Such statutes are in general less rigorously applied today than when they were first enacted, and are subjected to increasing criticism. See Pedrick, Taken for a Ride: The Automobile Guest and Assumption of Risk, 22 La. L. Rev. 90 (1961); Comment, The Ohio Guest Statute, 22 Ohio St. L.J. 629 (1961). To illustrate changing judicial attitudes toward the matter, see Cohen v. Kaminetsky, 36 N.J. 276, 176 A.2d 483 (1961); McConville v. State Farm Mut. Auto Ins. Co., 15 Wis. 2d 374, 113 N.W.2d 14 (1962).

likelihood of getting wise rules would be poor, except for a few that might be drafted by agencies such as the National Conference of Commissioners on Uniform State Laws. Specific choice-of-law legislation can be good, but it is not today a realistic approach to framing the body of law in the field. Nor is (b). If a choice-of-law statute, wise or unwise, has been enacted, the courts go on from there. But few have been enacted. To pretend to find choice-of-law guidance in a statute whose framers did not consciously put any such guidance into it is false construction. The fact that courts have for centuries employed the technique of false construction in other areas does not make them any the less false. Identification of the considerations that are genuinely relevant to a decision, which properly underlie the decision whether they are expressed in it or not, should be our aim.

III

The Choice-Influencing Considerations

The Cheatham-Reese summary of nine policy factors affecting choice-of-law rules and results, already mentioned, is the basic study from which any analysis of choice-influencing considerations must commence. A mere listing, without the explanation that accompanied them, reveals their significances only partially, but it is still useful as a preliminary to further inquiry. They are, in the order of importance assigned to them by Cheatham and Reese:

(1) The needs of the interstate and international systems;
(2) A court should apply its own local law unless there is good reason for not doing so;
(3) A court should seek to effectuate the purpose of its relevant local law rule in determining a question of choice of law;
(4) Certainty, predictability, uniformity of result;
(5) Protection of justified expectations;
(6) Application of the law of the state of dominant interest;
(7) Ease in determination of applicable law, convenience of the court;
(8) The fundamental policy underlying the broad local law field involved;
(9) Justice in the individual case.[50]

50. Cheatham & Reese, Choice of the Applicable Law, 52 Colum. L. Rev. 959 (1952). Professor Reese in a 1963 article rephrased the policies slightly, and added a tenth: "The court must follow the dictates of its own legislature, provided these dictates are constitutional." Reese, Conflict of Laws and the Restatement Second, 28 Law & Contemp. Prob. 679, 682 (1963). The added item was set out as a preliminary assumption in the 1952 study, and appears out of

Professor Hessel E. Yntema, covering the same ground, listed seventeen policy considerations that have been said to be relevant in the choice-of-law process, and then reduced them to two main heads:

> [T]he objectives that have been proposed are somewhat heterogeneous and in part artificial. They include, for example: uniformity of legal consequences, minimization of conflicts of laws, predictability of legal consequences, the reasonable expectations of the parties, uniformity of social and economic consequences, validation of transactions, relative significance of contacts, recognition of the "stronger" law, co-operation among states, respect for interests of other states, justice of the end results, respect for policies of domestic law, internal harmony of the substantive rules to be applied, location or nature of the transaction, private utility, homogeneity of national law, ultimate recourse to the *lex fori,* and the like. The last of these, the common idea that the local law should be preferred in case of doubt, is essentially a corollary of the local policy doctrine; it is evidently a counsel of despair, which should be ignored in formulating the policies of conflicts law. It is obvious that many of the remaining conceptions overlap, some are of subordinate significance, and some beg the question or perpetuate superannuated jurisdictional modes of analysis. . . . [I]t is suggested that the essential policy considerations peculiar to conflicts law can be subsumed under two heads: *security*, which is the first principle of utility in Bentham's and most other schemes of legislation, and *comparative justice* of the end result, namely, its consonance with the results of comparative research, an objective that derives from the basically equitable purpose of conflicts law to individualize the treatment of foreign cases.[51]

Under "security" Yntema included such values as that "a given situation should have equal legal treatment everywhere," that there should be an effort "to maximize uniformity in defining the legal and socio-economic consequences of transactions and events," that of "deference to the effective law, namely, that of the state which is in position to control," and that of enabling people "to anticipate the consequences of their conduct, so that they can plan their affairs accordingly," which includes the principle of "validation of transactions."[52] "Comparative justice," under

place in a list of policies. It is basic in our governmental system of separated powers that controlling statutes, if there are any, must be followed.

51. Yntema, The Objectives of Private International Law, 35 Can. B. Rev. 721, 734-35 (1957). Ehrenzweig quotes this list of policy considerations though he by typographical error omits two of them. Ehrenzweig, Conflict of Laws § 122, at 349 (1962). He then adds: "These catalogues are virtually meaningless in view of their generality, comprehensiveness and inevitable inconsistency. In order to derive concrete solutions from them it would be necessary to limit their scope severely and to establish standards of relative effectiveness." Ibid.

52. Yntema, The Objectives of Private International Law, 35 Can. B. Rev. 721, 735-36 (1957).

Yntema's analysis, serves partially as a corrective to over-emphasis on "security," by limiting protection of the expectations of parties to "reasonable" expectations, by evaluating results in terms of justice, and by deliberately choosing between competing laws on the basis of their superiority as law as well as or apart from their territoriality.[53]

Professor David F. Cavers has elaborated the same idea in his recent Cooley Lectures.[54] He has carried the process of evaluating the various policy factors (that Cheatham, Reese, Yntema and others have described) to the extent of formulating for some fact situations a few fairly specific rules, or almost-rules, which he derives from his evaluations. He does not call them rules, however, but "principles of preference," and would have the courts use them not as controls but rather as guides to choice-of-law decision. Whether the Cavers approach is or is not accepted by the courts, it illustrates cogently the possibility of using the policy evaluating process as a means of getting away from broad generalizations and arriving at specific results, or guides to results.

The present writer's approach does not carry him as far as Cavers goes. It is my belief that these choice-of-law policies, which I call choice-influencing considerations, can and should be restated and defined with sufficient particularity that they themselves can be used as a practical (though not a mechanical) test of the rightness of choice-of-law rules and decisions. This involves reducing the considerations to manageable number and identity. Some of the policy factors listed by Cheatham and Reese, by Yntema, and by others will appear in or affect more than one of the ultimate considerations, but there should be a minimum of overlapping among them. There must be frank recognition of some contradiction among them, because all of the opposing values must be included in the restated list of considerations. Testing of rules or decisions under such a set of standards will be a qualitative process of evaluation, and there will be clear room for difference of opinion in it. That is inherent in the nature

53. For a narrower field, Profesor I. F. Baxter of Osgoode Hall, Toronto, has suggested three criteria for recognition of statutes in family law: "(A) the simplicity and efficiency with which the rules produce solutions; (B) the extent to which the rules are consistent with a balance of fairness and justice between the parties; (C) the operation of public policy to prevent solutions which are grossly out of harmony with the beliefs and way of life of the community of the forum, or which provide means of easy evasion of other desirable law within that community." Baxter, Recognition of Status in Family Law: A Proposal for Simplification, 39 Can. B. Rev. 301, 348 (1961). It is notable that these criteria relate almost exclusively to the quality of legal rules and not to their territorial location.

54. Cavers, The Choice-of-Law Process 139-203 (1965).

of conflicts problems; solutions to them should usually not be mechanical, but the relevant considerations should include an indication of when mechanical rules are appropriate.

Testing in these terms will commonly justify choice-of-law rules that apply to categories of cases, so that reexamination of the considerations will not be required for every case that comes along, though oftentimes uniqueness or divergencies of fact or law will make standardized generalizations inappropriate. Such inexactness is not new in conflicts law, and any effort to eliminate it would today be a step backward toward mechanical jurisprudence. The societal function of each area of law in which a conflict arises,[55] as well as the locally conceived functions of the specific rules between which conflict exists, ought to be tied into the choice-of-law process. Identification of choice-influencing considerations will aid in achieving predictability for some types of transactions, but different values will be promoted for other types of transactions. In any event, it seems that an effort to identify and clarify the choice-influencing considerations is worthwhile. The present effort can make no claim to originality nor much to new insight. It merely undertakes to restate the considerations that have, expressly or impliedly, always underlain common-law choice-of-law decisions, as others have from time to time identified them. The result is a list of five, which seem to incorporate all that are in the longer lists:

A. Predictability of results;
B. Maintenance of interstate and international order;
C. Simplification of the judicial task;
D. Advancement of the forum's governmental interests;
E. Application of the better rule of law.

No priority among the considerations is intended from the order of listing. Their relative importance varies according to the area of the law involved, and all should be considered regardless of area. A brief summary of the content of each will be attempted.

A. Predictability of Results

Predictability of results includes the ideal that the decision in the litigation on a given set of facts should be the same regardless of where the litigation occurs, so that "forum shopping" will bene-

55. The function of tort law, or parts of it, might be thought of in terms either of punishment for fault or of distribution of losses. In a tort case, the prevailing attitude toward these opposing philosophies might well affect choice of law through one or another of the identifiable choice-influencing considerations. See Cheatham, Griswold, Reese & Rosenberg, Cases on Conflict of Laws 487-88 (5th ed. 1964) (bases of choice of law in tort actions).

fit neither party. It also includes the companion ideal that parties to a consensual transaction should be able to know at the time they engage upon it that it will produce, by way of legal consequences, the same set of socio-economic consequences (usually but not necessarily based upon the assumed validity of the transaction) regardless of where disputes occur. They should be able to plan their transaction as one with predictable results. At least this is an ideal for some kinds of transactions.[56]

Protection of the justified expectations of parties to a transaction is achieved to the extent that the results are reasonably predictable in advance. A rule that permits parties to select at the time of their transaction the state whose law is to govern it serves this purpose,[57] but we are concerned with serving the purpose even when parties do not know enough about the laws of the two or more states involved to make an advance choice between them, and even when the parties do not think about choice of law at all. Many courts discover a "presumed intent" of the parties, for such cases, to have as governing the law that would sustain their transaction as otherwise planned. When this is done, the court is making a choice of law itself, protecting justified expectations in terms of substantive results by basing its choice on the content of the law more than on territorial reasons. This is true also of Ehrenzweig's closely related "basic rule of validity,"[58] applied in favor of most but not all contracts, trusts, wills,

---

56. "[R]ules cannot bring certainty and predictability to a subject in which these values do not exist. Of necessity, many conflicts rules must be fluid in operation and leave much to be worked out by the courts." Reese, supra note 50, at 681. Reese lists as matters in which predictability is most important the validity of wills, distributions on intestacy, trusts, contracts, conveyances of almost every kind, marital property interests, and transfers of aggregates of movables. Id. at 686-87. The existence of a familial status probably belongs in the list. It is obvious that considerations other than predictability are also relevant in most of the areas named.

57. More than one scholar has suggested that a state may also facilitate commercial transactions having no significant public repercussions and at the same time preclude conflict, by recognizing the autonomy of parties of roughly equal bargaining power in a contract with multistate aspects. When more than one state has substantial contacts with the transaction, it seems reasonable that equal parties should be free to designate the law of one of the states as controlling the validity and effect of their contract, since reasonable certainty is of the utmost importance to the parties and needless uncertainty serves neither private nor state interests.

R. Traynor, Is This Conflict Really Necessary?, 37 Texas L. Rev. 657, 674 (1959).

58. See Ehrenzweig, Conflict of Laws § 139 (marriage), § 141, at 391-92 (legitimacy), § 175, at 465 (contracts), § 232, at 609, § 233, at 613 (land transactions), § 236, at 620-21, § 237, at 623 (chattel transactions), § 244, at 642-44 (trusts), § 247, at 660, § 248, at 666-67 (wills) (1962). Social policy favoring validation is said to be especially strong where negotiable documents and marriages are concerned. Harper, Policy Bases of the Conflict of Laws: Reflections on Rereading Professor Lorenzen's Essays, 56 Yale L.J. 1155, 1168-70 (1947).

commercial instruments, marriages, legitimations, and other socially favored legal arrangements. Under either approach predictability is furthered by making what Professor Cavers has called a choice between laws as distinguished from a choice between jurisdictions.[59] An overt "choice between laws" gives a forum court the opportunity to weigh its decision in terms both of socio-economic results anticipated by the parties and of whatever governmental interests may be present. Most of the other considerations that are relevant in choice-of-law cases can also be furthered by the same choice-between-laws approach.

The eighth item in the Cheatham-Reese list of choice-of-law policies is "the fundamental policy underlying the broad local law field involved." This has to do not with specific rules of forum law but with the broad policy of the society and its law, and it is recognized that this broad policy may even be opposed to some specific local rules, such as those dealing with usurious contracts,[60] or the Rule Against Perpetuities, or accumulations on charitable trusts.[61] For some types of transactions, the forum state's "fundamental policy underlying the broad local law field involved" may well, for multistate cases, be one favoring predictability of socio-economic consequences by sustaining transactions entered into by parties acting in good faith.

A comprehensive element in the predictability consideration is "security," the first of the two policy heads to which Yntema reduced his analysis.[62] Predictability gives security, and without predictability security is appreciably lessened. Lack of security under the law is generally produced by the same opposing con-

---

59. [T]he new approach recognizes that the problem confronting the court is a choice between two particular rules of law to govern the issue before the court; it is not a problem of choosing between two legal systems in their entirety and accepting in advance whatever might, on inspection, prove to be the relevant rules in these two systems. Only if the court is choosing between particular rules can it identify the respective policies embodied in those rules and decide whether they present a true conflict, and, if so, which law appears to have the better claim to application in the light of the facts of the case, including the expectations of the parties.

Cavers, Change in Choice-of-Law Thinking and Its Bearing on the Klaxon Problem, in ALI Study of the Division of Jurisdiction Between State and Federal Courts 154, 164-65 (Tent. Draft No. 1, 1963). This suggestion was introduced in Cavers, A Critique of the Choice-of-Law Problem, 47 Harv. L. Rev. 173, 183, 201 (1933), and repeated in Cavers, Re-Restating the Conflict of Laws: The Chapter on Contracts, XXth Century Comparative and Conflicts Law 349, 350 (1961) and Cavers, The Choice-of-Law Process 9 (1965).

60. See Seeman v. Philadelphia Warehouse Co., 274 U.S. 403 (1927); Ehrenzweig, Conflict of Laws § 182, at 482-85 (1962).

61. Land, Trusts in the Conflict of Laws 74 (1940). See generally Dean, Conflict Avoidance in Inter Vivos Trusts of Movables, 21 Law & Contemp. Prob. 483 (1956).

62. See text accompanying note 51 supra.

siderations that produce lack of predictability in choice of law. These are well illustrated by two claims to security which constantly compete against each other—security of titles and security of transactions (unauthorized transfers of title). No conflicts rule can completely protect both interests simultaneously, any more than can a single rule of substantive law. When interests represented by the predictability consideration fight to a draw, the balance of interests which leads to a decision will have to be based on other considerations. That will often be the case where contradictory claims to movable chattels, as between an owner and a bona fide taker from a bailee, are at issue.[63] Even more clearly, predictability might not be the major consideration if title claims be pitted against interests of some other character.[64]

B. Maintenance of Interstate and International Order

Most countries have single nation-wide systems of law on most subjects, so that in them the formulation of conflicts law requires only international accommodations. In the United States, accommodations to a unique system of federalism must be added. International accommodations may be quite meager where chauvinistic nationalism prevails, but as chauvinism recedes treaties or other agreements dealing with conflicts matters are likely to develop side by side with domestic conflicts law. As "one world" gradually becomes reality, both of these side-by-side methods of international accommodation will serve to match its growing reality. They will appear in this country both from Washington as federal statutes, treaties, and executive agreements and from the states as common law and statute. Increasing accommodations to our federal system will similarly appear, for the most part in statutes[65] enacted in Washington, but in state law as

63. See Leary, Horse and Buggy Lien Law and Migratory Automobiles, 96 U. Pa. L. Rev. 455 (1948); Vernon, Recorded Chattel Security Interests in the Conflict of Laws, 47 Iowa L. Rev. 346 (1962). Compare the discussion of Forgan v. Bainbridge, 34 Ariz. 408, 274 Pac. 155 (1928), in M. Traynor, Conflict of Laws: Professor Currie's Restrained and Enlightened Forum, 49 Calif. L. Rev. 845, 862-67 (1961), with that in Currie, The Disinterested Third State, 28 Law & Contemp. Prob. 754, 774-75 (1963). Views expressed in Leflar, Constitutional Jurisdiction Over Tangible Chattels, 2 Mo. L. Rev. 171 (1937), failed to take some of the relevant choice-of-law considerations adequately into account.

64. E.g., Shanahan v. George B. Landers Constr. Co., 266 F.2d 400 (1st Cir. 1959), discussed in Cavers, The Conditional Seller's Remedies and the Choice-of-Law Process—Some Notes on *Shanahan*, 35 N.Y.U.L. Rev. 1126 (1960).

65. That the accommodation is not always statutory is illustrated by the current development of a "federal common law" for essentially federal problems under the so-called Clearfield rule. Clearfield Trust Co. v. United States, 318 U.S. 363 (1943). Despite this, the assumption is that most federal choice-of-law decisions will purport to apply state law under Klaxon Co. v. Stentor Elec. Mfg. Co., 313 U.S. 487 (1941). See Friendly, In Praise of *Erie*—And of the New Federal Com-

well, as centralization persistently changes the character of our federalism.

Specific clauses in the federal constitution (full faith and credit, due process, privileges and immunities, equal protection, interstate commerce, and perhaps others) as well as the inherent federal control over foreign and national affairs, all as interpreted by the United States Supreme Court, have imposed outer limits on the states beyond which they must not go in interfering with basic requisites to international and interstate orderliness. The latest area for which these limits have been established concerns escheat to the states of choses in action abandoned by their owners.[66] Previously, either a plural escheat or a first-claiming-state-takes-all theory appeared to prevail, with resultant injustice either to the debtor or to the less diligent state. The new due process rule on escheat assures that the debtor will pay once, and only once, to a state mechanically selected on a basis that is fair to all states. The imposition of such outer limits constitutes a proper function of a court interpreting a constitution. But there are factors affecting relationships between states and nations, in choice-of-law cases, that ought to be taken into account yet which ought not (not yet, at least) to be hardened into constitutional limitations.[67] These are properly considerations in the common-law judicial process.

The concern with claims to sovereignty that enters into international choice of law ought not to be very important where the choice is between laws of the states of the United States. The political concern of the states, apart from mere preference for local law and local persons, is primarily with a need for systematization, for an orderliness that will make our federal system work with reasonable efficiency in the complicated choice-of-law field.

The free and unpenalized movement of people and goods from state to state,[68] and freedom in commercial intercourse, are essential to the success of our federal system, and it is part of the law's task to assure them. Deference to sister state law in situations in which the sister state's substantial concern with the problem gives it a real interest in having its law applied, even

mon Law, 39 N.Y.U.L. Rev. 383, 401-02, 407-12 (1964). There will be occasional federal choice-of-law cases coming up under independent federal grounds, such as Siegelman v. Cunard White Star Ltd., 221 F.2d 189 (2d Cir. 1955) (admiralty).

66. See Texas v. New Jersey, 379 U.S. 674 (1965).

67. Cf. Leflar, Constitutional Limits on Free Choice of Law, 28 Law & Contemp. Prob. 706 (1963).

68. Crandall v. Nevada, 73 U.S. (6 Wall.) 35, 43-44 (1868). Cf. Matter of Estate of Thornton, 1 Cal. 2d 1, 33 P.2d 1 (1934); Depas v. Mayo, 11 Mo. 314 (1848).

though the forum state also has an identifiable interest, will sometimes usefully further this aspect of the law's total task. This will sometimes be a deference to what has been called the "stronger law," meaning the law of the state that is in the best position to insist upon ultimate enforcement of its rule, as is the state of situs when title to a tangible res (movable or immovable)[69] is in question, or possibly the state of the domicile when the existence of a familial status[70] is the issue. The sixth of the Cheatham-Reese list of policies,[71] "favoring application of the law of the state of dominant interest," ties in functionally with this deference to the primarily concerned state. It must be recognized that if nearly all of a transaction's significant contacts are with one state (*X*), yet the forum state (*F*) applies its own law to the transaction despite its lesser contacts, resentment in *X* may induce later retaliation in kind. Avoidance of the interstate friction that can develop from this sort of retaliatory comity[72] is a proper choice-of-law objective.

The regulation of forum shopping, both by permitting it within reasonable limits and by barring it under forum non conveniens rules, has bearing on this consideration since it affects choice of law at least as to so-called procedural matters and, where a court employs forum preference among substantive rules, as to them also. Any deliberate employment of forum preference is suspect, since on its face it leaves interstate and international concerns out of account. The balancing process here, however, is particularly delicate, since discrimination against the interests of other governments can be a subtle thing, and the interests of other governments in private litigation are seldom large enough by themselves to dictate the choice of law that a court should make. The most that can be safely said of them is that they constitute a relevant factor for consideration, and that failure to consider them may produce results that, though within the permissible limits of constitutionality as now defined, are troublesome and unfortunate. A neat and orderly system of choice of law, with states' rights clearly identified and allocated, is in our federalism an unrealizable ideal, yet one that should not be discarded.

69. Griswold, Renvoi Revisited, 51 Harv. L. Rev. 1165, 1194-95 (1938).

70. See Williams v. North Carolina, 325 U.S. 226 (1945) (full faith and credit to divorce); Meisenhelder v. Chicago & N.W. Ry., 170 Minn. 317, 213 N.W. 32 (1927) (validity of marriage). But see Estate of Lund, 26 Cal. 2d 472, 159 P.2d 643 (1945) (legitimation).

71. Cheatham & Reese, Choice of the Applicable Law, 52 Colum. L. Rev. 959, 972-76 (1952).

72. Hilton v. Guyot, 159 U.S. 113 (1895), is the classic example of this in the international area. See Nadelmann, Reprisals Against American Judgments?, 65 Harv. L. Rev. 1184 (1952).

C. Simplification of the Judicial Task

An easy cliché is that law does not exist for the convenience of the court that administers it, but for society and its members; therefore, simplification of the judicial task should be a minor consideration in determining what any rule of law should be. The statement is true enough. But overcrowded dockets can become a real problem, and complicated rules of law may encourage the delay in decision that is sometimes a reason why dockets lengthen. Also, complex rules are sometimes difficult to apply, especially to complex facts, and even reasonably competent courts, both trial and appellate, may misapply them. The danger of this is multiplied when juries have to deal with foreign law. The strange handling which some good courts have given to renvoi[73] furnishes a convincing illustration. Simplicity in law is a virtue. Judicial efficiency often depends upon it.

It has been argued that a court should apply its own local law unless there is good reason for not doing so.[74] No one can deny the propriety of this argument so long as the "unless" clause is adequately emphasized. It will usually be easier for the forum court to apply its own law than any other. The court is presumably already familiar with it and is already accustomed to administering it.

That is without question a good reason for a court's applying its own procedural rules, since it would be utterly impracticable for a court in *F* to import the whole procedural machinery and technique of *X* even in a case that is otherwise clearly governed by *X* law. But the reasons of practicality which justify that generalization stop short when the rule in question is an outcome-determinative one that would be no harder for the *F* court to apply than any other *X* rule of substantive law.[75] If the procedure concept is broadened to cover such matters as statutes of frauds,[76]

---

73. See Ellis v. Crowe, 193 Ark. 255, 99 S.W.2d 568 (1936); University of Chicago v. Dater, 277 Mich. 658, 270 N.W. 175 (1936).

74. Both Currie and Ehrenzweig urge application of the forum's law in the mass of situations, when other social or governmental interests do not clearly overshadow the forum's interests. See their summaries of their views in Cheatham, Griswold, Reese & Rosenberg, Cases on Conflict of Laws 477-79 (5th ed. 1964). See Baxter, Choice of Law, 42 Can. B. Rev. 46, 54-56, 75-77 (1964), generally accepting Ehrenzweig's forum preference.

75. See Sedler, The Erie Outcome Test as a Guide to Substance and Procedure in the Conflict of Laws, 37 N.Y.U.L. Rev. 813 (1962).

76. Marie v. Garrison, 13 Abb. N. Cas. 210 (N.Y. Super. Ct. 1883). Compare Bernkrant v. Fowler, 55 Cal. 2d 588, 360 P.2d 906, 12 Cal. Rptr. 266 (1961), in which the possibility of characterizing a statute of frauds question as procedural was rejected by deliberately ignoring it.

measure of damages,[77] and the survival of tort claims,[78] one may suspect that the real reason for the decision is some consideration other than the one that supports a forum court's application of its own procedural rules. The true reason may be outright chauvinistic preference for forum law, or an effort to select what is regarded as the sounder of the two competing rules of law, or an effort to do justice in the individual case, or something else. Whatever the true reason is, it ought to be brought out in the open and either accepted or rejected on its own merits. The procedure-substance dichotomy has real justification, but use of it as a cover-up gimmick affording technical legal support for results justifiable only by other real reasons is wrong.

Preference for forum law is of course not the only approach that can simplify the judicial task in choice-of-law cases. Any simple mechanical rule, such as that the law of the place of contracting governs in contract cases and the law of the place of first harmful impact governs torts, is also easy to apply. That is a virtue, and was some justification for these purported rules. Their ultimate rejection did not deny this virtue, but was based rather on a recognition that other relevant considerations were more important. Yet simplicity and ease of application remain a significant consideration that is properly taken into account in passing upon the utility of any choice-of-law rule that may be suggested for any area of law.[79]

Minimization of conflicts problems by weeding out "false conflicts,"[80] a technique not yet adequately developed, should be one of the most fruitful and expandable methods of simplifying choice of law. The method will not be useful in cases where one state's contacts with a set of facts are few and relatively insignificant as compared with those of another state whose law is

77. Kilberg v. Northeast Airlines, Inc., 9 N.Y.2d 34, 172 N.E.2d 526, 211 N.Y.S.2d 133 (1961).

78. Grant v. McAuliffe, 41 Cal. 2d 859, 264 P.2d 944 (1953).

79. In branches of law, such as mercantile law, where the influence of lay opinion has been felt, it has been exerted towards simplicity. Should similar considerations not apply in regard to a person's status? Is it not desirable that a lawyer should be able to advise a client on his status with reasonable confidence that the advice will be correct? The fact that two or three systems of law may have to be resorted to, in order to advise a client if he is living in sin, or if he is legitimate—yielding a hesitant opinion—is not a desirable result; and less so if the opinion indicates that the client may be lawfully married by the law of X but not married by the law of Y.

Baxter, Recognition of Status in Family Law: A Proposal for Simplification, 39 Can. B. Rev. 301, 348 (1961). This is obviously a plea for predictability as well as for simplification. Sometimes the two considerations will coincide in their operative effects.

80. See R. Traynor, Is This Conflict Really Necessary?, 37 Texas L. Rev. 657 (1959).

different; in that situation a choice of law still has to be made even though the choice may be a comparatively quick one. That is an easy conflicts case, not a false one. But if the laws of both states, relevant to the set of facts, are the same, or would produce the same decision in the lawsuit, then there is no real conflict of laws at all, and the case ought to be decided under the law that is common to both states. Some of the strangest decisions with some of the lengthiest and most convoluted opinions in the books[81] could have been handled simply and easily if the false conflict analysis had been understood and accepted. This of course is a facet of Professor Cavers' extremely helpful emphasis on the conflicts problem as one of "choice of laws" rather than "choice of jurisdictions."[82]

D. Advancement of the Forum's Governmental Interests

Entirely apart from the simplification of judicial tasks that comes from a forum court's application of its own rather than some other state's law, a court has a natural and largely justifiable primary concern with advancement of the governmental interests of its own state. These interests are not always clearly reflected, or even reflected at all, by the state's private law, either legislative or judge-made, but they often are. If they are, it is reasonable that in a choice-of-law situation a court will, and should, endeavor to effectuate these interests and purposes insofar as it can identify them. To the extent that the elusive concept "local public policy" can be correlated with local positive law, it constitutes an affirma-

81. E.g., Scheer v. Rockne Motors Corp., 68 F.2d 942 (2d Cir. 1934), holding that a defendant bailor's liability for his bailee's negligent auto driving might be defeated even though both states provided for such liability; Marie v. Garrison, 13 Abb. N. Cas. 210 (N.Y. Super. Ct. 1883), in which the conclusion was asserted that a contract should be sustained even though it was bad under the Statutes of Frauds of both connected states, New York and Missouri; Escrow Serv. Co. v. Cressler, 59 Wash. 2d 38, 365 P.2d 760 (1961), which used community and common-law marital property intricacies to hold that an Oregon creditor could not reach his debtor's interest in Washington property even though the law of either Oregon or Washington, taken separately, would have subjected the property to the claim. On Marie v. Garrison, supra, see Currie, Ehrenzweig and the Statute of Frauds: An Inquiry Into the "Rule of Validation," 18 Okla. L. Rev. 243, 253-57 (1965). On the Scheer case, supra, see Cavers, The Two "Local Law" Theories, 63 Harv. L. Rev. 822, 826-28 (1950).

82. In Cavers, Oral Contracts To Provide by Will and the Choice-of-Law Process: Some Notes on ***Bernkrant***, in Perspectives of Law: Essays for Austin Wakeman Scott 38, 67-68 (1964), it is suggested that even Bernkrant v. Fowler, 55 Cal. 2d 588, 360 P.2d 906, 12 Cal. Rptr. 266 (1961), may have presented the same sort of situation as the cases cited in note 81 supra, since the Nevada dead man's act might have operated to preclude recovery on the contract, just as the California Statute of Frauds would, so that this may have been another case in which recovery was allowed even though it would have been denied under the laws of both connected states.

tive pull on any court to prefer its own law over any foreign law.[83] This is a reasoned basis for forum preference. It differs sharply from that "counsel of despair"[84] which is said to be the last resource of puzzled critics who ignore true choice-of-law considerations, give up the effort to effectuate them, and take instead an easy way out by a selection of forum law which gets by as long as the forum state has the minimum fact contacts required by the federal constitution.[85]

Such an unreasoning fall-back on forum preference as a substitute for choice-of-law thinking is not calculated to advance the governmental interests of the forum or any other state, nor is it what the commentators have been talking about in that context. True governmental interests of a state are not discoverable by blind matching with any old law that may be on the state's books. They can be identified, and in turn implemented, only by thoughtful and intelligent analysis of the legal materials in the light of current socio-economic, cultural, and political attitudes in the community. Ascertainment of a state's governmental interests is no small task, not one to be solved by locating a statutory section or a paragraph in an old judicial opinion. Courts should not lightly undertake the task, but it is a task sometimes within the judicial function.

Too often the search for governmental interests in a particular case, especially for the purpose of sustaining application of forum law, is artificial. It turns into something like the argument of amateur debaters who seek as many "points" as possible to support their side without recognizing that one really relevant consideration can outweigh a dozen "points."

A governmental interest in a choice-of-law case, in its simplest sense, is discoverable by putting together (a) the reasons supporting the rule of law in question (*F*'s or *X*'s law) and (b) the state's (*F*'s or *X*'s) factual contacts with a case, or the issue in a case, to see if they match. Since some reasons, usually a variety of them, can be called up in support of almost any rule of law that is on the books anywhere, it is nearly always possible for a good lawyer to conjure up governmental interest in just about any state that has any connection with a set of facts.

83. "As justice can be administered only in accordance with the sense of what is right existing in the community in which the court sits, the feelings of the local community cannot be disregarded altogether." Lorenzen, Territoriality, Public Policy and the Conflict of Laws, 33 Yale L.J. 736, 748 (1924).

84. Yntema, The Objectives of Private International Law, 35 Can. B. Rev. 721, 735 (1957).

85. See note 20 supra. No one, it is assumed, would seriously advocate a rule under which a forum would apply its own law in every case in which it is constitutionally permissible to do so.

It is not at all unusual for one state to discover that it has such interests in a set of facts though another state's courts would say otherwise. A court is usually more discriminatingly hard-boiled in analyzing another state's interests than in analyzing its own.[86] It has been suggested, for example, that in *Babcock v. Jackson*[87] New York was the only state that had a governmental interest in the operation of host-guest laws because all the parties were domiciled in New York and were riding in a New York car on a trip that was to begin and end in New York even though the accident occurred in Ontario.[88] Yet an Ontario court could well say, if the action were before it, that its guest statute was designed to prevent collusive suits directed against insurance companies (not just Ontario insurance companies) in Ontario courts, at least on Ontario facts.[89]

The original policy that underlay the Statute of Frauds was at least arguably stated in its title "An Act for the Prevention of Frauds and Perjuryes,"[90] which would tend to locate the interest behind the statute at the place where fraud and perjury might occur—the forum where suit is brought on an oral contract. Yet most courts today tie their search for interest in oral contracts cases to other connecting factors.[91] As to a recent case involving effect of a time-for-suit limitation in an Illinois personal property insurance contract on a Florida action for losses suffered after the insured and his property had moved to Florida, Professor Currie thought that the interest of Illinois was exclusive[92] while Michael Traynor, certainly a perceptive analyst, thought Florida's interest was superior.[93] Probably the difficulty in all these cases is one of definition. The simple definition at the beginning of the preceding paragraph does not cover all that must be taken into

86. This is the sort of uneven view that presumably would not occur in Professor Currie's "restrained and enlightened forum."

87. 12 N.Y.2d 473, 191 N.E.2d 279, 240 N.Y.S.2d 743 (1963).

88. See Currie, Comments on *Babcock v. Jackson*, A Recent Development in Conflict of Laws, 63 Colum. L. Rev. 1233, 1238 (1963), agreeing in this respect with the court's opinion, 12 N.Y.2d at 482-83, 191 N.E.2d at 284, 240 N.Y.S.2d at 750.

89. Compare Dym v. Gordon, 16 N.Y.2d 120, 209 N.E.2d 792, 262 N.Y.S.2d 463 (1965), discussed at notes 162-68 infra and accompanying text.

90. 1676, 29 Car. 2, c. 3.

91. See notes 76, 82 supra.

92. Currie, The Verdict of Quiescent Years: Mr. Hill and the Conflict of Laws, 28 U. Chi. L. Rev. 258, 290-94 (1961).

93. M. Traynor, Conflict of Laws: Professor Currie's Restrained and Enlightened Forum, 49 Calif. L. Rev. 845, 867-71 (1961). The United States Supreme Court finally sustained Traynor's view, at least to the extent of holding unanimously that Florida's interest was sufficient to withstand an attack on the constitutionality of applying Florida law. Clay v. Sun Ins. Office, Ltd., 377 U.S. 179 (1964).

account. Governmental interest is too large a notion to be narrowly defined or rigidly confined. It must include all the relevant concerns that the particular government, not only as a sovereign entity but also as a repository of justice, may have in a set of facts or an issue.[94] A different legal entity, even though it has a differing statute or judicial precedent on its books, might have about the same total governmental interest in reference to the facts of a particular case.

Use of the connecting factor of domicile[95] as a base for discovering or denying the existence of governmental interests illustrates this. A state of course has some special interest in its domiciliaries, and there are a number of choice-of-law purposes for which domicile is traditionally relevant or even controlling. In many of these areas, however, factors other than a state's concern with protecting its domiciliaries are involved. Where intestate succession to movables is the issue, or marital property titles in movables, or assignments of such property, it is desirable to have some single law to govern so that unity of results can be assured, and domiciliary law is chosen for the sake of convenience. The motivating considerations are predictability of results and simplification of the judicial task more than governmental concern for domiciliaries. The once powerful concern of the domiciliary state with matters of familial status is weakening. In the United States, increasing mobility of the citizenry is decreasing the importance attached to the socio-political idea of each person's having a preeminent headquarters at some one place. The fact that in this country the states are becoming more alike, less chauvinistic in their eccentricities, contributes to this. Most of the states are becoming accustomed to the fact that a large proportion of the human beings who at any given moment are working or playing within their borders will have ties with other states as well. An effect of this is that the states are less concerned than they once were with protection of the local citizen as distinguished from the "stranger," and more inclined than they once were to promulgate and enforce laws that apply to both equally, well beyond the minimum equalities prescribed by the federal constitution.[96] Visitors as well as residents may be protected by "good" local laws. The domicile of parties in one state or another has less significance today, and may well have far less in another

94. Cf. Kramer, Interests and Policy Clashes in Conflict of Laws, 13 Rutgers L. Rev. 523 (1959).

95. See Weintraub, An Inquiry Into the Utility of "Domicile" as a Concept in Conflicts Analysis, 63 Mich. L. Rev. 961 (1965).

96. The trend exists even as between nations, but this paragraph is written primarily with reference to domiciliaries of states in the United States.

generation, than it once had as a basis for locating true governmental interests.

It has been remarked that a state's governmental interests in a given multistate set of facts may be contrary to the state's own law. An obvious response is that a court should be reluctant to find that this is so. It is said that courts should take their social policy from their legislatures, not make it themselves. That is sound enough where the law from which the policy is to be derived is enacted law, or at least enacted law that is to a fair extent in tune with the times. But suppose, as is most often the case, that the opposing rules of states *F* and *X* are judge-made. In that case must the court find that the governmental policies of the states are as surely opposed to each other as their judge-made laws are?

This is a situation in which if either state had a clean slate today, instead of precedent, it might now for good socio-legal reasons adopt the other state's rule as its own. True, there are some states whose mores are actually far apart, as Nevada's and Kansas' probably are on gambling transactions. But that is exceptional. Ordinarily differences in common-law rules between states do not represent deep and genuine differences in social policy. They may result from the accident of court membership (the accidents of politics, or sometimes the deliberate schemings of politics),[97] the accident of timing (the early social era when litigation produced a precedent in *F* as against the middle or later era when one was produced in *X*), or the accidents of legal education. As far as social policy in the two states is concerned, despite the differing decisions, it is apt to be about the same. There are likely to be in each state two, or possibly more than two, opposing sets of socio-economic interests, one favoring one rule of law, with the other or others to the contrary. These differing interests are not much more likely to be bounded by state lines today than is the air we breathe. The fact that one set of interests has at some past period prevailed in *F* is relevant, but only as a precedent for deciding cases clearly governed by *F* law. This precedential effect does not have anything to do with governmental interests in their choice-of-law sense. The prior decision is not a choice-of-law precedent. And a real search for governmental interest relevant to choice of law may or may not reveal that a result opposite to the local precedent is really preferable.

97. The underlying explanations of legislative enactments may of course involve events and influences just as accidental as (or more connived than) those that underlie judge-made law. The separation-of-powers concept attaches a different significance to legislative influences, however, or tends to ignore them just as it ignores other aberrations from a theoretical ideal.

It does no harm to say that this policy analysis is a continuing search for governmental interests, provided we recognize that what we ought to do in any event is to analyze the problem in terms of all the relevant choice-of-law considerations, of which the interest behind the forum's internal rule is only one. If we classify the process as a search for and effectuation of the state's governmental interests, we should think of them in terms of the total governmental concerns of a justice-dispensing court in a modern American state. Despite the increasingly common character of the states of the United States, there are still significant differences among them on some but not on most matters. If two states really have opposing governmental interests, then advancement of the forum's interests as against those of the other state must be accepted as a legitimate part (but not all) of the choice-of-law process.

E. Application of the Better Rule of Law

At one time judges deciding choice-of-law cases would have self-consciously denied that they gave any weight to the quality of the rules of law between which choice was made. A vested rights approach called for a choice between states,[98] not between laws, and there was thought to be some tinge of the unethical in the conduct of a judge who, unlike blind Justice, deliberately opened his eyes to see the consequences of his choice. Even today some jurists assert the blind ideal, though none would deny the reality, sometimes partially concealed but readily discoverable,[99] of weight given to the content of rules and the results they produce. Choice of law, as distinguished from choice of jurisdictions, is accepted by the courts more by deed than by word,

98. So long as deduction from territorial postulates could indicate only one jurisdiction as a source of law in a given case, the content of that law would be logically irrelevant. Again, so long as the court was in search of a "foreign-created right," it would seek an appropriate jurisdiction, not an appropriate substantive rule, for metaphorical consistency demands that the creation or non-creation of rights be attributed only to states and not to their legal rules.

Cavers, A Critique of the Choice-of-Law Problem, 47 Harv. L. Rev. 173, 178 (1933).

"In earlier times, legal systems were not regarded as anchored to jurisdictions to the same extent as now. Some laws were associated with persons (with a consequent mobility), while others were connected with physical things (such as land)." Baxter, Choice of Law, 42 Can. B. Rev. 46, 54 n.17 (1964).

99. Professor Cavers deplores the fact that the Restatement (Second) is expressed altogether in terms of "jurisdiction-selecting rules," but points out that many of the so-called rules, such as the one making choice of law dependent on "most significant relationship," can be employed indirectly as a means to selection of what may be regarded as the better law. Cavers, Re-Restating the Conflict of Laws: The Chapter on Contracts, XXth Century Comparative and Conflicts Law 349, 350, 358 (1961).

but it is accepted, within limits. It is easiest to accept when the laws of two involved states are substantially identical, or give the same result in the pending dispute, so that a court can apply the rule or reach the result, perhaps as against the contrary rule of a third state, without having to choose between the first two.[100] But choice between laws as such is a common element in ordinary conflicts cases today. Superiority of one rule of law over another, in terms of socio-economic jurisprudential standards, is far from being the whole basis for choice of law, yet it is without question one of the relevant considerations.[101]

"Justice in the individual case" has always been one of the objectives of law, and it has at times been suggested as the best ultimate that could be aimed at in choice-of-law cases.[102] Cheatham and Reese, on the other hand, placed it ninth on their list of nine policies. Yntema identified it as "justice of the end results" in his enumeration of objectives, and then included it as an aspect of "comparative justice," one of the two heads ("security" is the other) under which he subsumed all the policy considerations that he deemed essential in conflicts law.[103] In a sense, justice in a particular case calls for individualization of decisions, a choice of the better party in the litigation rather

100. The importance of doing this as a means of avoiding "false conflicts" when the laws of all involved states would produce the same result in the litigation is evident. See notes 81, 82 supra. In the more difficult situation, where the laws of some of the states are different, the Restatement (Second) takes a timid step in this direction by proposing that if the relevant rules in two or more states which have contacts with a contract are the same, "the case will be treated . . . as if these contacts were grouped in a single state." Restatement (Second), Conflict of Laws § 332b, comment c (Tent. Draft No. 6, 1960). Compare Judge Frank, discussing a choice between Saudi-Arabian and "American" law in Walton v. Arabian Am. Oil Co., 233 F.2d 541, 545 n.14a (2d Cir. 1956): "As the tort rules, pertinent here, of New York, Delaware, and Arkansas are doubtless substantially similar, there would be no need to choose one or the other."

101. This occurs not only when choice of law is by the courts, but even more specifically when the rule has been laid down by a legislature. See notes 43-46 supra.

102. Harper, Policy Bases of the Conflict of Laws: Reflections on Rereading Professor Lorenzen's Essays, 56 Yale L.J. 1155, 1174 (1947): "Subject to other policy considerations, a court may with complete propriety, exploit the flexibility of the legal situation to produce a result in conformity with the merits of the case." Cavers, A Critique of the Choice-of-Law Problem, 47 Harv. L. Rev. 173, 193 (1933): "The choice . . . would not be the result of the automatic operation of a rule or principle of selection but of a search for a just decision in the principal case." But see the qualifying explanation of this language in Cavers' Cooley Lectures. Cavers, The Choice-of-Law Process 75-81 (1965).

103. Yntema, The Objectives of Private International Law, 35 Can. B. Rev. 721, 735 (1957). See text accompanying note 51 supra. Yntema's identification of the content of the policy favoring "comparative justice" gives it a meaning similar to preference for the "better law," and it is believed that the latter is susceptible to somewhat more exact and helpful implementation in specific cases and areas than is the broad policy of "comparative justice."

than of the better law. Such individualization is not outside the function of law, and judges sometimes properly take pride in it, but it at the same time is a bit frightening to one who, remembering that *P*'s justice may be *D*'s damnation, is anxious to maintain "the rule of law as against the rule of men." A choice made between competing rules of law is more impersonal, less subjective, more in keeping with the traditional law-discovering functions of a common-law court. When the choice is deliberately made in favor of applying what by the forum's standard is the better of the competing rules of law, it is likely that justice between the litigating parties, according to the forum's standards, will be approximated too. The larger consideration seems to serve all the purposes of the narrower one, and to serve them more acceptably.

The fifth Cheatham-Reese policy, "protection of justified expectations," will likewise be implemented in part, though only in part, by a court's deliberate choice of the better law. The protection of expectations generally is a facet of consideration (A), "predictability of results." Expectations in general should be realizable, predictable, and reliable, but only to the extent that they are "justified" expectations. The existence of an expectation that given legal results will ensue may depend upon a variety of connecting factors in a case, including the location of elements in the transaction and the intention of the parties. Whether the expectation will be deemed a "justified" one, worthy of the law's protection apart from the fact that it exists, is a different matter. As to that, it is proper to look to what appears to the forum court to be the better law. This may well be the forum's own law. It is especially apt to be the forum's own law if the foreign law that might be applied would somehow interfere with fundamental local policies, but that should not often be true.

More often the better law, for any given set of facts, will be the law which undertakes to uphold a fair transaction entered into by the parties in good faith. This of course is Ehrenzweig's "basic rule of validity," already referred to as applicable to many contracts, trusts, wills, commercial instruments, marriages, legitimations, and other socially favored arrangements.[104] The usurious contract cases[105] are the ones most often cited to illustrate this

104. Note 58 supra.

105. E.g., Seeman v. Philadelphia Warehouse Co., 274 U.S. 403 (1927). The opinion, written by Justice Stone, is discussed in Freund, Chief Justice Stone and the Conflict of Laws, 59 Harv. L. Rev. 1210, 1214 (1946): "The decision is noteworthy for renouncing a geographical test in favor of a teleological one in choice of law. Not place but purpose was decisive. *Ut res magis valeat quam pereat* was implicitly recognized as a pertinent basis of decision in multistate no less than in domestic law."

operation of the choice-of-the-better-law process, but the others are almost as familiar. This process, while it normally leads to validation, could equally well lead to invalidation, if the subject matter of the contract were deemed grossly immoral or antisocial by the forum court,[106] or if its form or method of execution, as in the case of some sorts of adhesion contracts,[107] savored of what that court regarded as unfair advantage. In choosing between a relevant law that would sustain the transaction and another that would defeat it, the court will almost surely be influenced by its strongly held views on these matters;[108] if it has no strongly held views the policy favoring validation will presumably win out.[109]

It is evident that the search for the better rule of law may lead a court almost automatically to its own lawbooks. The idea that the forum's own law is the best in the world, especially better than fancy new sets of laws based on such nontraditional approaches as research and policy analysis, is unfortunately but understandably still current among some members of our high courts.[110] There are good reasons why a court should prefer its own state's law, both for the sake of simplifying its judicial job and in order to advance the forum's governmental interests, if it has any, in the litigation. These two relevant considerations have already been discussed. Furthermore, it is altogether pos-

---

106. See Paulsen & Sovern, "Public Policy" in the Conflict of Laws, 56 Colum. L. Rev. 969, 980 (1956).

107. Ehrenzweig, Adhesion Contracts in the Conflict of Laws, 53 Colum. L. Rev. 1072 (1953).

108. Cf. Reese, Conflict of Laws and the Restatement Second, 28 Law & Contemp. Prob. 679, 698 (1963):

> But it must be remembered that there are many kinds of contracts and that some of them may be deemed socially undesirable or at least less desirable than others. Likewise, all states have laws which, largely for the purpose of protecting the weak against the strong, limit the parties' freedom to contract by invalidating certain kinds of contractual provisions. Whether a court will seek to apply a validating law in a given case will depend upon the kind of contract or contractual provision involved and also upon the degree of interest which the state of the validating law has in the parties and the transaction.

109. This can be true, obviously, only for cases in which it has first been determined that there was a real transaction to which the validating law can be applied. Professor Cavers has pointed out the significant limitation that a preference for validation cannot be usefully employed if the question is whether the transaction was actually entered into at all. Cavers, Oral Contracts To Provide by Will and the Choice-of-Law Process: Some Notes on *Bernkrant*, in Perspectives of Law: Essays for Austin Wakeman Scott 38, 52 (1964).

110. For an illustration of overemphasis on forum policy, see Lilienthal v. Kaufman, 239 Ore. 1, 395 P.2d 543 (1964), where Oregon law was applied to invalidate a contract made by a spendthrift resident of Oregon with a California resident. The contract was both made and to be performed in California, and the California party had no reason to suspect that Oregon's spendthrift laws had any bearing on the transaction.

sible, and perhaps more likely than not, that a court may conscientiously conclude, after intelligent comparison, that its local rules of law are wiser, sounder, and better calculated to serve the total ends of justice under law in the controversy before it than are the competing rules of the other state or states that are involved in the case. Such a conscientious conclusion is to be respected. But it does not amount to an automatic preference for local law, nor is an automatic preference justifiable. Most courts today do not employ any such automatic preference. What has been called the "result-selective approach" in choice-of-law cases,[111] frequently covered up by a facade of reference to conventional conflicts rules, is too clear in its persistent manifestations, including frequent determination that nonforum law is controlling, to be denied. In every case, however, it can be shown that the choice is directed to the rules of law that produce the result rather than to the result as such.

Judges can appreciate as well as can anyone else the fact that their forum law in some areas is anachronistic,[112] behind the times, a "drag on the coat tails of civilization,"[113] or that the

111. Documentation of the "result-selective principle," often partially concealed by labored characterizations, appears at length in Morse, Characterization: Shadow or Substance, 49 Colum. L. Rev. 1027 (1949), and is to some extent repeated in Ehrenzweig, Characterization in the Conflict of Laws: An Unwelcome Addition to American Doctrine, XXth Century Comparative and Conflicts Law 395 (1961). See also Hancock, Three Approaches to the Choice of Law Problem: The Classificatory, the Functional and the Result-Selective, XXth Century Comparative and Conflicts Law 365, 372, 373 (1961):

> When the laws of two states, functionally construed, compete for application in a conflicts case . . . . judges are very likely to be influenced, consciously or unconsciously, by the same consideration which would guide their judgment in the domestic analogue. They are likely to consider which of the two competing rules will produce the most rational, convenient and just decision in the litigation before them. . . . The result-selective approach rarely rises to the surface in an opinion . . . .

Compare the language of Lord Reid in Starkowski v. Attorney-General, [1954] A.C. 155, 170, in dealing with a problem of legitimacy and successive marriages in different countries: "To my mind the best way of approaching this question is to consider the consequences of a decision in either sense. The circumstances are such that no decision can avoid creating some possible hard cases, but if a decision in one sense will on the whole lead to much more just and reasonable results, that appears to me to be a strong argument in its favour."

112. "What if we strongly dislike the policy of one state, the forum, believe it outmoded, irrational, an anachronism, a relic of the past, as compared to the modern enlightened policy of the other state? Will there not be a strong temptation, by hook or by crook, somehow to prefer the policy of the latter state? Certainly this cannot be denied." Kramer, supra note 94, at 546.

113. Cheatham & Reese, Choice of the Applicable Law, 52 Colum. L. Rev. 959, 980 (1952). Sunday laws, the fellow-servant rule, and married women's incapacity to contract are cited as illustrations. See Freund, supra note 105, at 1216:

> If one of the competing laws is archaic and isolated in the context of the laws of the federal union, it may not unreasonably have to yield to the more prevalent and progressive law, other factors of choice being roughly

law of some other state has these benighted characteristics. When a court finds itself faced with a choice between such anachronistic laws still hanging on in one state, and realistic practical modern rules in another state, with both states having substantial connection with the relevant facts, it would be surprising if the court's choice did not incline toward the superior law. A court sufficiently aware of the relation between law and societal needs to recognize superiority of one rule over another will seldom be restrained in its choice by the fact that the outmoded rule happens still to prevail in its own state. One way or another it will normally choose the law that makes good sense when applied to the facts.

"One way or another." That suggests manipulation of conflicts rules, the deliberate employment of conflicts concepts as gimmicks to enable courts to reach desired results, as "cover-up" devices designed to conceal the real influences that dominate the judicial process in choice-of-law decision. Such deceits are normally regarded as bad. We praise the great judge who knows how to use precedents narrowly or broadly, build up constructive analogies and explain others away, use fictions wisely and reach results that society approves yet clothe them in the garb of traditional law. That is the method, the technique of our common-law system as good lawyers learn and practice it. It is a method that calls for cleverness but not for deceit. At least we do not like it when there is less than the appearance of intellectual integrity in the process, and we ask that the process be purified as soon as possible. That is definitely our attitude today in viewing manipulative gimmicks in choice of law. We do not in general disagree with results that these deceits have enabled courts to achieve in the past, but we do ask that real reasons and not cover-up devices be given now as explanations of past decisions and guides to future ones.

That choice-of-law concepts are susceptible to manipulation has been openly recognized for a long time. The process of characterization, once seriously regarded as the key to many choice-of-law problems,[114] was particularly easy to turn into gimmick functioning because it was based on traditional analytical classifications long honored in Austinian jurisprudence yet never much more exact than a key-numbered descriptive word index. The distinction between substance and procedure has been ma-

equal. A married woman's disability to make a contract, imbedded in the law of one state, may be carried away by the current if contact is made with the main stream in another state. Perhaps one of the functions of conflict-of-laws decisions is to serve as growing pains for the law of a state, at all events in a federation such as our own.

114. See Robertson, Characterization in the Conflict of Laws (1940); Sumner, Choice of Law Governing Survival of Actions, 9 Hastings L.J. 128, 138 (1958).

neuvered back and forth a hundred ways:[115] personal injury cases usually given a tort characterization are sometimes classified as presenting contract problems,[116] survival cases traditionally deemed to sound in tort have been called matters of estate administration,[117] trespass cases can be classified as involving either tort law or land titles,[118] land sale disputes can be characterized as either title or contract problems,[119] and the same dichotomy is possible as to numerous sorts of transactions concerning chattels.[120]

Nor is characterization the only or even the principal gimmick employed to cover up actual choice-of-law reasons. Definitions of domicile and residence as well as fact findings calculated to suit a given definition of one or the other may shift from court to court.[121] Renvoi has been employed to move a case over to another governing law when this was thought desirable.[122] The multiple rules available in contract cases have been picked over and chosen from so as usually to apply a law that would sustain

---

115. Grant v. McAuliffe, 41 Cal. 2d 859, 264 P.2d 944 (1953), got by with characterizing survival as a procedural matter, as did Kilberg v. Northeast Airlines, Inc., 9 N.Y.2d 34, 172 N.E.2d 526, 211 N.Y.S.2d 133 (1961), with a similar characterization for measure of damages. Home Ins. Co. v. Dick, 281 U.S. 397 (1930), held, however, that characterization of contractual time limitations on suit as procedural went too far, and violated the due process clause.

116. Levy v. Daniels' U-Drive Auto Renting Co., 108 Conn. 333, 143 Atl. 163 (1928); Dyke v. Erie Ry., 45 N.Y. 113 (1871).

117. Grant v. McAuliffe, 41 Cal. 2d 859, 264 P.2d 944 (1953); Herzog v. Stern, 264 N.Y. 379, 191 N.E. 23 (1934).

118. See Caldwell v. Gore, 175 La. 501, 143 So. 387 (1932) (flooding upper land in Arkansas by building dike on subjacent Louisiana land). "This case . . . was decided as a question of property law, on the basis that the land in Louisiana owed an easement to the land in Arkansas. It seems to present a nice problem of primary characterization, on whether the question was one of tort or property law." Robertson, supra note 114, at 228 n.24.

119. Compare Selover, Bates & Co. v. Walsh, 226 U.S. 112 (1912) (law of place of contracting applied), with Kryger v. Wilson, 242 U.S. 171 (1916) (law of situs applied), in which substantially identical problems were presented.

120. Compare Shanahan v. George B. Landers Constr. Co., 266 F.2d 400 (1st Cir. 1959), with Thomas G. Jewett, Jr., Inc. v. Keystone Driller Co., 282 Mass. 469, 185 N.E. 369 (1933), both Massachusetts cases.

121. The famous cases in which both Pennsylvania and New Jersey levied death taxes on the theory that the deceased, Dr. Dorrance, was domiciled in their respective states afford the classic example. Dorrance's Estate, 309 Pa. 151, 163 Atl. 303 (1932); In re Dorrance's Estate, 115 N.J. Eq. 268, 170 Atl. 601 (Prerogative Ct. 1934). See also McDonald v. Hartford Trust Co., 104 Conn. 169, 132 Atl. 902 (1926), and Matter of Newcomb, 192 N.Y. 238, 84 N.E. 950 (1908), as analyzed in Reese, Does Domicil Bear a Single Meaning?, 55 Colum. L. Rev. 589, 592-95 (1955); Weintraub, supra note 95, at 961.

122. In Richards v. United States, 369 U.S. 1 (1962), the Court read into the Federal Tort Claims Act a renvoi-type reference to the "whole law" of "the State where the act or omission occurred" in order to avoid what would otherwise have been an unfortunate choice-of-law rule. See text accompanying notes 36-38 supra.

contracts entered upon in good faith.[123] The flexibility of the "center of gravity" or "predominant contacts" rule proposed by the Restatement (Second) for contract and tort cases constitutes one of the major arguments for approving it. Similar flexibility is present in the "specificity" test for statute of limitations cases.[124] Trusts, especially charitable ones, have regularly been sustained by applying to them first one rule as to governing law and then another.[125] The "presumed intent of the parties" as a choice-of-law guide is usually no more than a judicial selection of the law that will most nearly effectuate the socio-economic purposes of the parties' transaction. Many other illustrations could be given. All of them are of courts actually choosing one set of laws over another, rather than choosing one state and then finding out afterward what its law is.

There is nothing new or strange in this choice of law rather than choice of jurisdictions. Every judge and lawyer knows that our courts have engaged in it from time immemorial, and that it was right for them to do so. Some courts probably have engaged in a choice of parties, but that will scarcely be defended. The urge to do justice in the individual case is amply cared for by a wise choice of the better law to govern the parties' claims.[126] The difficulty is in the cover-up, the pretense that the courts do not make a choice of laws but only a choice of jurisdictions. Our experience tells us that it was (and is) better for the courts to reach the results they have reached, choosing the better law by means of the manipulative devices they have employed, than for them to disregard superiority in rules of law altogether. It would

123. See notes 57, 58 supra and accompanying text. See generally Leflar, Conflict of Laws §§ 121-26 (1959).

124. See Bournias v. Atlantic Maritime Co., 220 F.2d 152 (2d Cir. 1955).

125. See Land, Trusts in the Conflict of Laws 74, 80 (1940).

126. It would clearly be a mistake to assume that every court's choice of better law will always be the same as that of every other court. That would be as wrong as an assumption that wise men will always agree with each other. Compare an analysis of a policy-weighing approach:

> [I]t places on the court at the forum the responsibility of weighing in its own scales the competing policies of the interested states. This is indeed a dangerous jurisdiction if no further standards of judgment are available than that an activity should be upheld wherever reasonably possible. This standard has diminishing relevance as one moves away from the realm of consensual or commercial transactions. Even in that realm, the danger is that the judge may be encouraged to indulge a general preference for a permissive rather than a prohibitory rule, or for common rather than statutory law. Having been attuned to the themes of nineteenth-century philosophy, he may prefer to march to the familiar strains of Herbert Spencer rather than to the cacaphonies, shall we say, of the New York legislature.

Freund, supra note 105, at 1215. Needless to say, judicial choice between competing rules of law, whether in conflict of laws or any other field, has never been guaranteed to please everybody.

be worse for them to make mere mechanical choices of governing law, or to follow any other system that disregards this and other proper choice-influencing considerations. That would be as bad, or almost as bad, as a simple and outright "choice of preferred parties."

The lawyer representing one side or the other in a case starts, at least approximately, with the result he wants to reach, whether the case involves choice of law or something else. That we expect. In nonconflicts cases he first endeavors to characterize his problem, to determine what field it falls in; then, when he finds that the governing rule is unsettled he builds an argument for the rule that for his purposes seems the better one. At the same time he seeks a characterization under which he can with reasonable hope of success argue for the preferred rule. In choice-of-law cases the customary process is much the same, up to a point. The typical lawyer, knowing the result he wants to reach and having characterized his problem sufficiently to know what rules of law he is concerned with, checks the laws of the connected states and ascertains those favorable to him. Then he looks at the mechanical conflicts rules which choose a state rather than a law, and selects anew a characterization or a conflicts theory (gimmick) that will, under the mechanical rules, lead him to the previously chosen law with its desired result. When he comes before the court, he reverses the reasoning process and argues first for his ultimate characterization and conflicts theory, then leads on to the concluding result which was in fact his starting point. Since both sides normally present their choice-of-law reasoning in this final form, it is understandable that courts accept the form, and in their decisions adopt it as presented by one side or the other. But it is also expected that a court will see through what the lawyers have done, follow the order of their unstated as well as of their stated argument, and weigh it also in the judicial balance. The court's desire to achieve justice is just as real as that of the opposing lawyers, the difference being that the court's definition of justice is not controlled by the identity of the lawyers' clients. The court can concern itself with the quality of the opposing laws between which it has to choose, and there is plenty of evidence that courts do concern themselves with this question of quality even though they do not often phrase their opinions in terms of it. The lawyer who omits argument on the inherent superiority of the opposing laws, apart from their territorial origins, is crediting the average court with less understanding and wisdom than it really possesses. Argument presented under the label "strong public policy" may serve the purpose, but it would be more to the point if the cover-up were played down and the discussions were directed specifically, as in non-conflicts cases, to the question of which rule of law deserves preference.[127]

No one can sensibly contend that this fifth consideration, favoring application of the better rule of law, outweighs the other four considerations. It is given special emphasis here because in years gone by the other considerations, or at least their content, were more often discussed while this fifth one was overlooked or not clearly identified. The fact remains that it is only one of the five, more important in some types of cases than in others, almost controlling in some but far in the background in others.

IV

Correlating the Considerations

Is there enough definiteness to the five considerations taken together to enable them to serve usefully as guides to solution of specific cases? Or can they be helpful only in the broad reaches of choice-of-law jurisprudence rather than in the down-to-earth processes of judicial decision?[128]

Obviously, the considerations do not furnish rules of thumb, but we are not looking for rules of thumb. The considerations tie in with the common law as it has already developed, and they assume that the mass of developed common law on choice of law will continue to serve its normal precedential function. Wiser judicial opinions and more thoughtful analysis of the relevant reasons for decision may be expected if the considerations are given proper weight, and different results in the decisions may occasionally be hoped for in areas where mechanical rules have in the past crowded out practical reasoning. The function of the considerations, when they are consistently noticed by the courts, should be to assure a continuing reexamination of precedents, a

127. To some extent "choice of law rather than choice of jurisdictions" implies that the common law, or the law generally, *is* "a brooding omnipresence in the sky," contrary to Holmes' insistence in Southern Pac. Co. v. Jensen, 244 U.S. 205, 222 (1917), that it is *not*. Despite Holmes, it is undeniable that, in a common-law system, law does exist (in accepted theories, principles and standards, in treatises, and in the law reviews) as an operative force which has potency entirely apart from its technical connection with any particular organized government. That is the basis on which all of our national law schools are conducted. Still, a forum court is not free to choose as governing any preferred rule of law that it finds anywhere, but may only choose among rules that are supposed to have tangible existence in states substantially connected with the facts. Home Ins. Co. v. Dick, 281 U.S. 397 (1930). The due process clause preserves that much of a Holmesian concept of territoriality.

128. See note 51 supra.

readiness to lay aside old mechanical rules that turn out to be without support in the considerations or to contradict them, yet at the same time to promise a reaffirmation of old rules, or at least of old results, that conform to and implement the considerations.

In most land title cases, for example, the choice of situs law as governing is as clearly demanded as ever. Analysis in the light of the five considerations reemphasizes the reasons that have always been given for the situs rule. Predictability of results, maintenance of interstate and international order, and simplification of the judicial task in all their aspects point toward this answer, while advancement of the nonsitus forum's governmental interests and forum preference for superior rules of property law weigh but lightly. For similar reasons, title problems involving tangible chattels will often be resolved by a situs reference and title problems involving intangibles by reference to a domiciliary law, though the balance of weight among the considerations will operate less certainly where personalty, either tangible or intangible, is concerned than where land titles are at issue. In some situations, even land title questions will not be referred to situs law if the greater weight among the considerations, measured with particularity, calls for application of some other law. This may well be true, for example, in so-called equitable conversion cases[129] where the same substantive reasons that in nonconflicts cases justify the flexibility of the conversion doctrine, permitting emphasis upon either the title or the contract[130] (or perhaps upon testamentary provisions),[131] may justify corresponding flexibility in choice of law. Tort cases involving land afford comparable opportunities.[132] In such situations, however, the choice

129. This problem is dealt with realistically in Hancock, Equitable Conversion and the Land Taboo in Conflict of Laws, 17 Stan. L. Rev. 1095 (1965). Cf. Matter of Estate of Plasterer, 49 Wash. 2d 339, 301 P.2d 539 (1956) (death tax on decedent's interest in extrastate land he had contracted to sell held collectible at his domicile). And consider cases such as Selover, Bates & Co. v. Walsh, 226 U.S. 112 (1912) (contract law governs), and Kryger v. Wilson, 242 U.S. 171 (1916) (situs law governs), where contract cancellation was the issue; and Polson v. Stewart, 167 Mass. 211, 45 N.E. 737 (1897), in which specific performance was granted in Massachusetts of husband's North Carolina contract to convey interest in Massachusetts land to wife, when the contract was valid by North Carolina but not by Massachusetts law.

130. See Williams, Land Contracts in the Conflict of Laws—Lex Situs: Rule or Exception, 11 Hastings L.J. 159 (1959); Note, Choice of Law for Land Transactions, 38 Colum. L. Rev. 1049 (1938).

131. It has been asserted, in a leading conversion-by-will case, that the doctrine of equitable conversion has no place in the conflict of laws. Toledo Soc'y for Crippled Children v. Hickok, 152 Tex. 578, 261 S.W.2d 692 (1953). The case is effectively criticized in Hancock, "In the Parish of *St. Mary le Bow*, in the Ward of *Cheap*," 16 Stan. L. Rev. 561 (1964).

132. As in Irving Trust Co. v. Maryland Cas. Co., 83 F.2d 168 (2d Cir. 1936) (tort characterization employed as reason for sustaining reference to superior rule

should not rest on a pretense that a title characterization or a tort or contract characterization controls the result, with reasons for the choice of characterizations muddied by conceptual analysis. The reasoning ought to be stated honestly, in terms of the actual choice-of-law considerations that call for reference either to situs law or to some other law under the specific circumstances. It makes no difference whether the conceptually supporting characterization be mentioned or not, though it is probably too much to expect that most judges, seeking support for their conclusions from every traditional quarter, will omit this one.

The reasoning ought to be essentially the same as that which has induced legislatures to enact statutes[133] sustaining wills of land if the will be validly executed either by the law of the situs or by the laws of other enumerated states. The selection of the better rule of law, the one sustaining the will, is appropriate, especially if the situs will go along with the selection. The use of a kind of renvoi in land cases serves the same purpose.[134] The prime purpose in these cases is the assurance of predictably uniform results, but weight is given also to any other considerations that appear significant to the forum court. The renvoi technique itself furnishes no reason for reference to the whole law of another state, but is only a tool that facilitates that reference in situations where the relevant considerations call for it.

Determination of whether the forum state's own statutes are applicable to out-of-state facts is no different. When a statute is silent as to its extrastate applicability, as is usually the case, a court may and should as appropriately look to all the relevant choice-of-law considerations as if it were choosing between common-law rules.[135] Legislative silence is as indicative of lack of legislative thought about choice of law as is judicial silence or the silence of parties to a private transaction. All three silences

---

of law). Compare Caldwell v. Gore, 175 La. 501, 143 So. 387 (1932) (situs law employed in land tort case), discussed in note 118 supra.

133. See text accompanying note 46 supra.

134. See Matter of Schneider, 198 Misc. 1017, 96 N.Y.S.2d 652 (Surr. Ct. 1950). See also Restatement (Second), Conflict of Laws § 8, comment b (Tent. Draft No. 12, 1965).

135. See Proctor v. Frost, 89 N.H. 304, 197 Atl. 813 (1938), in which a New Hampshire statute invalidating certain mortgages by married women was held inapplicable to a mortgage executed outside the state by a Massachusetts domiciliary on her New Hampshire land. See discussions of this case in Cavers, The Choice-of-Law Process 184-85 (1965); Harper, Policy Bases of the Conflict of Laws: Reflections on Rereading Professor Lorenzen's Essays, 56 Yale L.J. 1155, 1172 (1947). Cavers sees new choice-of-law rules and principles emerging from the process of applying statutes which are silent as to their territorial reach. Cavers, supra at 97, 108-10.

leave the choice-of-law problem squarely up to the court which has to decide it.

In tort and contract cases common-law courts have always felt free to take socio-economic considerations into account because precedents were less rigid. In *Babcock v. Jackson*[136] and its successors,[137] for instance, the "dominant contacts-most significant relationships" test used to choose governing law is by its nature not an exact one,[138] and room is left under it for a court to weigh such considerations either explicitly or, too often, without mentioning them as fully as they are in fact taken into account. Current social attitudes about host-guest statutes, especially in states that enacted them a long time ago,[139] are relevant not only to judicial reinterpretation of the statutes but also to choice-of-law decisions concerning them, and may well influence a court in deciding which state has the most significant relationship to a complicated fact situation. This is almost as real a possibility as when the characterization process is the purported basis of choice, as it was in *Kilberg v. Northeast Airlines, Inc.*,[140] *Grant v. McAuliffe*,[141] *Levy v. Daniels' U-Drive Auto Renting Co.*,[142] and a host of other cases. The choice-of-law policy that frankly favors sustaining certain types of contracts[143] and deliberately selects a preferred law, often that of the forum,[144]

136. 12 N.Y.2d 473, 191 N.E.2d 279, 240 N.Y.S.2d 743 (1963) (New York host-guest rule applied though injury was in Ontario), commented on by Cavers, Cheatham, Currie, Ehrenzweig, Leflar & Reese in 63 Colum. L. Rev. 1219 (1963).

137. Dym v. Gordon, 16 N.Y.2d 120, 209 N.E.2d 792, 262 N.Y.S.2d 463 (1965), discussed in text accompanying notes 162-68 infra, is the leading later case. See also LaChance v. Service Trucking Co., 215 F. Supp. 162 (D. Md. 1963), discussed in Currie, The Disinterested Third State, 28 Law & Contemp. Prob. 754, 768-72 (1963). It is interesting that Lowe's No. Wilkesboro Hardware, Inc. v. Fidelity Mut. Life Ins. Co., 319 F.2d 469 (4th Cir. 1963), the first case to follow the Babcock v. Jackson approach expressly, was criticized for its assertedly inaccurate evaluation of the significance of contacts in the case. Note, 1964 Duke L.J. 377; Note, 42 N.C.L. Rev. 419 (1964). Cf. Griffith v. United Air Lines, 416 Pa. 1, 203 A.2d 796 (1964). See also Friday v. Smoot, 211 A.2d 594 (Del. 1965); Long v. Pan Am. World Airways, Inc., 16 N.Y.2d 337, 213 N.E.2d 796, 266 N.Y.S.2d 513 (1965) (forum as "disinterested third state").

138. See Restatement (Second), Conflict of Laws § 8, comment j at 30 (Tent. Draft No. 12, 1965), speaking of this rule as promulgated in §§ 332 (contracts) and 379 (torts): "Uniformity of result can hardly be hoped for with so vague a rule. Undoubtedly, there will be situations where on the same facts different courts would reach different conclusions as to which is the state 'of most significant relationship.' "

139. See note 49 supra.

140. 9 N.Y.2d 34, 172 N.E.2d 526, 211 N.Y.S.2d 133 (1961).

141. 41 Cal. 2d 859, 264 P.2d 944 (1953).

142. 108 Conn. 333, 143 Atl. 163 (1928).

143. Seeman v. Philadelphia Warehouse Co., 274 U.S. 403 (1927) (usury). See note 58 supra and accompanying text.

144. E.g., the holding in Sun Ins. Office, Ltd. v. Clay, 133 So. 2d 735 (Fla. 1961), finally sustained in Clay v. Sun Ins. Office, Ltd., 377 U.S. 179 (1964), that

illustrates the practical reality of decision in terms of the broad but relevant choice-of-law considerations that have been listed here. Thus, in child custody cases the welfare of the child and not any rule concerning choice of jurisdictions controls the courts' decisions.[145]

The Supreme Court's recent decision in *Texas v. New Jersey*,[146] concerning what states may escheat intangibles, illustrates overtly the reasoning processes in which other courts sometimes engage covertly. While the Court identified its problem as one of "which State has ***jurisdiction*** to take title . . . through escheat,"[147] the question could also have been stated, without changing the problem, as one of which state's law of escheat should govern.[148] The property consisted of some 1,730 small debts, totaling $26,461.65, owed by the Sun Oil Company, a New Jersey corporation whose principal place of business was in Pennsylvania, to persons who for seven to forty years had not appeared or been located to receive payment. Most of the debts had arisen out of Texas transactions, and the Texas position was that it should be allowed to escheat them because under the currently popular "center of gravity" approach it had "the most significant contacts" with the debts. New Jersey claimed because it was the domicile of the debtor corporation, and Pennsylvania's theoretically comparable claim was based on the idea that the corporate debtor's preeminent headquarters (commercial domicile) was really at its principal place of business rather than in the state of incorporation. The State of Florida, to which several of the creditors had moved before they disappeared, was per-

---

Florida law could be used to defeat a twelve-month limitation-on-time-for-suit clause in an Illinois property insurance contract, valid by Illinois law, when the insured owner had moved with his insured chattels from Illinois to Florida during the period of the policy's coverage and before the chattels were destroyed. Florida's reasons for preferring its own law could well have been a restatement of the choice-influencing considerations that are relevant to the whole of conflict of laws. See M. Traynor, Conflict of Laws: Professor Currie's Restrained and Enlightened Forum, 49 Calif. L. Rev. 845, 867-69 (1961), discussing the case in its earlier stage. See Case (7), p. 316 infra.

145. See Ratner, Child Custody in a Federal System, 62 Mich. L. Rev. 795 (1964); Note, 49 Iowa L. Rev. 1178 (1964); Note, 73 Yale L.J. 134 (1963).

146. 379 U.S. 674 (1965). A final decree implementing the Court's opinion appears in 380 U.S. 518 (1965).

147. 379 U.S. at 675. (Emphasis added.)

148. The test for judicial jurisdiction and that for choice of law would, it seems, coincide in most cases if Ehrenzweig's "forum conveniens" test for jurisdiction, Ehrenzweig, Conflict of Laws § 30, at 106-07 (1962), combined with his or Currie's preference for forum law in most choice-of-law cases, were accepted. Compare Leflar, The Converging Limits of State Jurisdictional Powers, 9 J. Pub. L. 282, 290-91 (1960). The correlation between jurisdiction and choice of law on grounds for divorce is similar. See Case (11), p. 322 infra.

mitted to intervene, with the argument that escheat should be to the state of each creditor's last known address.[149]

The Court first submitted the whole problem to a master, to secure from him an appraisal of its practicalities. The ultimate decision substantially followed his recommendations. The decision was that (a) escheat goes to the state of each creditor's last known address as shown on the company's books, but that (b) as to creditors for whom there was no address or whose last address was in a state that has no applicable abandoned property law, escheat is to the state where the debtor is incorporated, subject to the condition that (c) if the state of a creditor's previously unknown address should subsequently be ascertained or if the state of last known address should subsequently enact an applicable escheat statute, such last state has the right to retake the amount escheated from the state in which the debtor is incorporated.

The result is important apart from the escheat problem for the reasons, frankly stated by the Court, that support it. They are largely realistic practical reasons rather than theoretical ones of the traditional choice-of-law sort. The principal objective that the Court states is to set up a rule that is clear and easy to apply, assuring in every contingency that one state, and one state only, can be selected to take. The "significant contacts" test does not meet this standard, because more than one state might conclude that its contacts with the debt-creating transaction were the most significant ones. The "last known address as shown by the debtor's books and records" test, on the other hand, "involves a factual issue simple and easy to resolve," one which "will tend to distribute escheats among the States in the proportion of the commercial activities of their residents. And by using a standard of last known address, rather than technical legal concepts of residence and domicile, administration and application of escheat laws should be simplified."[150] The Court makes the express point that logic is not the basis of the decision. "It is fundamentally a question of ease of administration and of equity. We believe that the rule we adopt is the fairest, is easy to apply, and in the long

149. Under Western Union Tel. Co. v. Pennsylvania, 368 U.S. 72 (1961), it was clear that no single claim could be escheated to more than one state. For a debtor to be subjected to multiple escheat was held to be violative of due process of law. It is interesting to compare this holding with cases permitting multiple death taxes, such as State Tax Comm'n v. Aldrich, 316 U.S. 174 (1942), and with those permitting multiple findings of the tax-sustaining fact of domicile, as in the Dorrance litigation, note 121 supra.

150. 379 U.S. at 681. On this point, compare the Dorrance litigation, note 121 supra.

run will be the most generally acceptable to all the States."[151] The alternative allocation of escheat rights, in the absence of last known address, to the state of incorporation was based even less on logic,[152] and almost completely on the idea that this result was the second best one available in terms of simplicity, singleness of taking, ease of administration, general fairness, and acceptability to all states and parties likely to be involved in escheat of intangibles. That completes a perfect analysis not only based upon but explained in the language of relevant choice-influencing considerations broken down so that they were intelligently related to the specific problem that had to be solved.

Similar analysis for other fact situations is worth attempting, even though exact answers cannot be forthcoming and each court must make its own analysis as the cases come before it. Several illustrative cases will be examined. For each of them, it is arbitrarily assumed that the five choice-influencing considerations previously described sum up, with varying weights for each consideration, the major reasons for making one choice-of-law decision or another in the case.

Case (1). *O*, a resident of State *F*, drives his car negligently in State *X* and there injures *P*, also an *F* resident. *O* then dies, and *P* sues *O*'s administrator in *F*. *F* has a survival statute but by *X* law a tort right dies when the tortfeasor dies. Traditional law would say that the law of *X*, the place of the tort, controlled.[153] Other cases using a procedural[154] or an administration-of-decedent's-estate[155] characterization would hold *F*'s law applicable. In a more gimmick-disdaining vein, recent commentators would say that *F*'s law should apply because *F* was the only state having a real "governmental interest" in the facts,[156] so that the case involved only a "false conflict," though the courts of *X*, if the suit were brought there, might dispute that conclusion. How would the case stand if analyzed in terms of the relevant choice-influencing considerations?

(A) Predictability of result, in the sense of serving as a guide to the conduct of the parties, is completely irrelevant. Parties do

151. 379 U.S. at 683.

152. Justice Stewart, the lone dissenter, thought that the state of incorporation, as domicile of the debtor, ought to have the sole right of escheat in all situations. Unlike the majority view, this conclusion was based almost entirely on logic. Ibid.

153. Ormsby v. Chase, 290 U.S. 387 (1933); Orr v. Ahern, 107 Conn. 174, 139 Atl. 691 (1928).

154. Grant v. McAuliffe, 41 Cal. 2d 859, 264 P.2d 944 (1953).

155. Ibid.; Herzog v. Stern, 264 N.Y. 379, 191 N.E. 23 (1934).

156. See Currie, Survival of Actions: Adjudication Versus Automation in the Conflict of Laws, 10 Stan. L. Rev. 205 (1958); R. Traynor, Is This Conflict Really Necessary?, 37 Texas L. Rev. 657, 670 (1959).

not plan this sort of tort with reference to survival rules. Predictability of the territorial scope of liability might have had bearing on liability insurance premiums, but a check on insurance company practices shows that it did not.[157] After the event, if the governing law were clearly known, forum shopping would be inhibited, which is of some importance.

(B) In respect to maintenance of interstate order, neither state will be much affected or annoyed by what the other state does, nor will interstate automobile movement be affected. The court can select either law without harming any socio-economic or political interest that inheres in our system of federated states.

(C) As to easing the judicial task of trying the case, there is little choice between the competing rules. Apart from the fact that under the *X* rule it would not be necessary to try the case at all, both rules are simple, easily ascertained, and easy to apply. Neither one affects efficiency in judicial administration.

(D) *F*'s interests in the transaction and in the outcome of the litigation are evident, and its interests are greater than *X*'s. *F* is especially concerned with the protection of its injured domiciliaries and their families (though it may as a modern humanitarian state in a mobile society have about equal concern for nonresidents) and it is also concerned with the distribution of its other domiciliary's estate. In contrast, *X*, despite its no-survival rule, probably has no very substantial concern with protecting even its deceased domiciliaries' estates, let alone those of nondomiciliaries, from automobile tort liabilities, especially since payment will normally be made by a liability insurance company. *X*'s governmental interest in its own rule has declined as the rule has become increasingly inappropriate to the current socioeconomic situation, even though *X*'s legislature has not yet bothered to replace it.

(E) No state in *X*'s position can be very proud of such a remnant of outmoded law as its no-survival rule. The superiority of *F*'s rule is pretty clear, regardless of which state the action was brought in.

Admittedly, there is room for disagreement with some parts of this analysis, and some courts would reject parts of it. It is nevertheless a reasonable analysis, and it leads quite definitely to the application of *F*'s survival law. If the forum were changed to *X*, the facts remaining the same, *F*'s law probably would still be applied if *X* reached its decision on the basis of the same

157. See Morris, Enterprise Liability and the Actuarial Process—The Insignificance of Foresight, 70 Yale L.J. 554 (1961); Peck, Comparative Negligence and Automobile Liability Insurance, 58 Mich. L. Rev. 689 (1960).

choice-influencing considerations. If *F* were the forum but the facts were changed so that one of the parties to the accident was a resident of *X*, or of *Y*, the other a resident of *F*, it would still be possible, and reasonable, to reach the same result, though evaluation of the considerations for those cases would necessarily be somewhat different. If both actors were residents of *X*, and *F* were the forum only, *X*'s rule would normally be applied, though *F* might still apply its own survival rule in deciding whether the decedent *O*'s assets, located in *F*, should be subjected to *P*'s claim. The only good reason for *F*'s not applying its own law to any of these sets of facts would be that the facts have no substantial connection with *F* at all.

Case (*2*). State *F* has a dramshop law, State *X* does not. *O* operates a dramshop in *F*, near the *X* line. In violation of the *F* law *O* sells liquor to *T*, who is already drunk, then *T* drives his car drunkenly into *X* where he injures *P*. *P* sues *O* in *F*. (a) *P* is a resident of *F*. (b) *P* is a resident of *X*, or of *Y*. (c) *T* is a resident of *F*. (d) *T* is a resident of *X*, or of *Y*.

The traditional place-of-the-wrong rule for tort cases would apply the law of *X*, permitting no recovery.[158] What happens if the relevant choice-influencing considerations are taken into account?

(A) The significance of predictability of results as a consideration is about as small in most respects here as in Case (1), in terms of the *X* accident at the time it happened. There is some significance, however, to be attached to predictability at the time of the liquor sale. Tavern keepers subject to the statute would like to know what sales come under it. This could not mean much on these facts, however, unless *O* could know in advance the direction in which *T* would drive after he left the tavern.

(B) Interstate relationships will not be much affected by any choice of law that may be made. No American state has much sovereign concern with exclusive control over its drunks.

(C) Either state's rule is simple and easy to apply.

(D) Each state presumably likes its own law, but *F* by enacting its dramshop act has taken an affirmative position on the matter. *F* has a clear concern with the regulation of dramshops that operate within its borders, and the nature of its concern, which includes the prevention of harm to third persons, has little or no relation to the residence of the drunk to whom the liquor is sold nor to that of the injured person. *F*'s civilized concern is with protecting people, not just people who live in *F*. Nor is

158. Eldridge v. Don Beachcomber, Inc., 342 Ill. App. 151, 95 N.E.2d 512 (1950).

the concern of *F*, as one of a closely bound federation of sister states, limited to harms inflicted within its own borders. The standard tort principle that imposes liability for harms within the area of appreciable risk is as applicable geographically as it is in other tort senses.

(E) An *F* court is likely to regard its own enactment as the better of the two laws unless the dramshop act has over the years been so ineffectual that disillusionment has set in. Although it is possible that the *F* court might regard the *F* act as bad law and think that *X*'s no-law is better, this is unlikely.

Under this analysis it is probable that *F* will conclude that on balance the choice-influencing considerations call for application of *F*'s dramshop law to the case in all the listed variations of the facts.[159]

Case (3). Take exactly the same facts as in Case (2), but let the action be brought in State *X*.

Considerations (A), (B), and (C) seem to operate no differently than in Case (2). As to (D), the forum's governmental interest in its own no-law is apt to be negligible. Under (E), *X* will have no aversion to *F*'s dramshop law unless *X* too has been disillusioned by what it has seen of the law's operation across the border. Probably the same substantive law will be applied here as in Case (2).[160]

Case (4). Suppose that the dramshop and the liquor sales were located in *X*, near the State *F* line, but *P*'s injury was in *F*, and *F* is the state that has the dramshop act. Will an *F* court, having acquired personal jurisdiction over *O*, the *X* dramshop keeper, hold him liable under *F*'s law?

In the first place, it would be constitutionally permissible, *i.e.*, not a violation of the due process clause, for *F* to apply its law against *O* on these facts. *O*'s sale of liquor to *T* at a place near *F* was a cause (created an appreciable risk) of harm to persons such as *P* from *T*'s subsequent and nearby drunken driving. As *Young v. Masci*[161] held, *O* may be liable under *F* law for harms in *F* caused by his acts in *X*. It is like shooting across the state line and hitting *P* in *F*.

With the constitutional question out of the way, we fall back on the choice-influencing considerations to help answer the common-law choice-of-law question. They are inconclusive. The

159. This goes only slightly beyond the result in Schmidt v. Driscoll Hotel, Inc., 249 Minn. 376, 82 N.W.2d 365 (1957). See also Zucker v. Vogt, 200 F. Supp. 340 (D. Conn. 1961) (injured man was resident of X).

160. See Osborn v. Borchetta, 20 Conn. Supp. 163, 129 A.2d 238 (Super. Ct. 1956).

161. 289 U.S. 253 (1933).

predictability consideration, (A), is different from what it is in cases (2) and (3), but only in respect to *O*'s conduct, not *T*'s and *P*'s. It may seem a bit odd to require *O* to regulate his liquor selling in *X* by *F*'s law, but *O* should anticipate that some of his customers will drive into nearby *F*. If *P*'s claim were based on a theory of common-law negligence in *O*'s sale to the drunken *T*, without any dramshop act in the case, the fact that the sale to *T* was in nearby *X* would be no bar to liability under *X* law. Some ruffling of interstate relations, (B), within very limited circles, might ensue from application of the *F* law. These must be balanced, if they can be, by (D), the concern of *F* for persons injured in *F* by drunks whose irresponsibility has been increased by excessive liquor sales to them. This concern cannot be measured by any court save *F*'s, and the *F* court can go either way. The weight of considerations (C) and (E) seems to be about the same as in Case (2). The ultimate answer depends on *F*'s weighing of considerations (D) and (E) against (A) and (B).

Case (5). Two residents of *F* decide independently to go to a university in *X* for the fall semester. *O*, one of them, invites *P*, the other one, to ride to *X* with him in his car, and to return with him from *X* to *F* at the Christmas vacation. *P* accepts, and they drive to *X*. During October a class exercise requires them both to go to a place in *X* six miles from the university campus. *O* again invites *P* to ride with him, which she does. On this trip *O* negligently collides with a car driven by *T*, a tourist from State *Y*, and *P* is injured. *O*'s car is licensed in *F*, and his liability to *P*, if any, is covered by a liability policy issued to him in *F* by an *F* insurance company. The standard for liabilty in such cases fixed by *F* law is ordinary care under the circumstances, but *X* has a guest statute which bars liability except for injuries wilfully and wantonly inflicted. *P* sues *O* in *F*.

The relevant precedents are too mixed to be very helpful. The old place-of-the-tort cases would of course apply *X* law,[162] but the newer center-of-gravity cases are not so clear. Judge Fuld, who wrote for the New York court in *Babcock v. Jackson*[163] and dissented in *Dym v. Gordon*,[164] would probably prefer *F*'s law. Judge Burke, who wrote for the majority in *Dym v. Gordon* would probably apply *X*'s law, but some of his colleagues who helped form the majority might desert him on these facts. Chief Judge

162. Loranger v. Nadeau, 215 Cal. 362, 10 P.2d 63 (1932); Fessenden v. Smith, 255 Iowa 1170, 124 N.W.2d 554 (1963).

163. 12 N.Y.2d 473, 191 N.E.2d 279, 240 N.Y.S.2d 743 (1963).

164. 16 N.Y.2d 120, 129, 209 N.E.2d 792, 797, 262 N.Y.S.2d 463, 470 (1965).

Desmond would prefer *F*'s law.[165] Will analysis in terms of the choice-influencing considerations be any more helpful?

The fact that *T*, from State *Y*, may have a claim against *O* arising from the same accident can be disregarded since that case is in all respects separable and separated from the present one.

Predictability of legal result, (A), has about the same importance here between *O* and *P*, as in Case (1), with putative bearing on liabilty insurance premiums and after-the-event bearing on forum shopping. Interstate relationships, (B), in the federal system, including interstate travel by residents of various states, will not be appreciably affected whichever law is applied. As for (C), an *F* court can apply *X*'s law or its own with about equal ease. But what of *F*'s governmental interest, (D), in its own residents who were driving and riding in a car licensed and insured in *F* and whose host-guest relationship in a sense had its inception in *F*? The contacts with *F* are certainly sufficient to give it a real interest, though not an overriding one. It would be possible for *F* to take the view that it does not have much more concern with local domiciliaries who have moved to another state for an extended stay than it has with persons who are domiciled in the other state, and that *F*'s contact as home base for the car is an incidental, almost mechanical, fact that has little qualitative relevance. The evaluation of *F*'s state interest here is a process on which an *F* court can go either way. But on (E), the selection of the superior law, there is not much doubt about the reaction of a modern court in *F*. *F* has never succumbed to the insurance lobby's propaganda for host-guest statutes, and current doubts about such statutes in the states that did succumb will make *F* all the more certain that its rule is the better one. It seems that if an *F* court were to go through this analysis, and base its decision upon it, it would conclude that *F*'s law should be applied.[166]

Case (6). Take exactly the same facts as in Case (5), but let the action be brought in State *X*.

Considerations (A), (B), and (C) operate no differently here than in Case (5). Consideration (D), the forum's governmental interest, is different since *X* is a different forum. But the fact that *X* has a host-guest statute does not automatically establish a clear interest in applying the statute in all possible circumstances. For one thing, the statute was probably enacted in the

165. Desmond's dissent in Dym v. Gordon emphasized what he regarded as New York's strong public policy in favor of applying its own host-guest rule where New York citizens are the parties. Id. at 134, 209 N.E.2d at 800, 262 N.Y.S.2d at 474.

166. This was essentially what Chief Judge Desmond did in his Dym v. Gordon dissent. See note 165 supra.

1930's, and the "don't bite the hand that feeds you (or gives you a ride)" argument which induced the legislature to enact it is obsolete today. On the other hand, the risk of collusion between plaintiff guest and defendant host to mulct the insurance company is today more real than ever, and a court can have strong feelings about this, especially when the threat of collusion is in its own courtrooms. As to the parties, *X* is concerned with them about as much as if they were permanent residents. As to consideration (E), only the *X* court itself can tell what its reaction will be. The fear of collusion might induce a hard-boiled preference for *X*'s law, but it is at least possible that disillusionment with the law, now seen to protect only insurance companies rather than the good-hearted Samaritans on whose behalf it was enacted, would induce an *X* court to prefer *F*'s law. The recent tendency to interpret guest statutes narrowly[167] confirms this possibilty. A court of *X* is likely to lean the same way on both considerations (D) and (E), and the direction of this leaning should decide the case.[168]

Case (7). *P*, a resident of State *X*, contracted in *X* with the *I* Company, an *X* insurance corporation, for insurance against loss or destruction of *P*'s manuscript collection, then located at *P*'s home in *X*. The policy included a clause limiting *I*'s liability to losses of which *I* is notified within sixty days after the insured learns of the loss, a limitation valid under *X* law. When *P* applied for the policy, he told *I*'s agent that he intended a year hence to move to State *F* and take the manuscript collection with him. The agent assured *P* that this would be all right. Later *P* did move to *F* with the insured collection, and so notified *I*, which changed his address record accordingly. Then *P*'s wife, in a family quarrel, tore up some of the manuscripts in *F*. *P* did not notify *I* at once because he wanted to patch up the quarrel with his wife without publicity, but three months later she sued him for divorce, whereupon he filed his insurance claim which *I* promptly disallowed. *P* then brought action against *I* Company on the policy in *F*. By *F* law the sixty-day notice clause in the policy would be void.

The notice clause was clearly valid at the contract's inception, when *X*'s law was the only law that had anything to do with the transaction. The later removal to *F*, with related facts, made it constitutionally permissible for *F*'s law to be applied and to in-

167. See note 49 supra.

168. Compare Friday v. Smoot, 211 A.2d 594 (Del. 1965), in which F (Delaware), the residence of the parties from which a trip in a Delaware car was started, refused to apply its own guest statute and applied instead the law of the place of the tort, New Jersey, which had no guest statute.

validate the clause.[169] But should *F* (or *X*, if it were the forum) reach that result?

Predictability, (A), is far more important in contract than in tort cases. It is most important, however, when the validity of an entire transaction, rather than a single clause, is at issue, especially when the clause is itself a contract-defeating provision.[170] Still, the insurer relies on the clause as one facilitating quick investigation of claimed losses, and the insured has after a fashion agreed to it. There would be some advantage, but not a tremendously important one, if both parties knew from the beginning whether the clause would be upheld regardless of subsequent removals. On the other hand, useful predictability is achieved if the parties know that validity of the clause will be governed by the law of the place where the risk is located at the time of the loss. That may well be the place where the insured has to act under the clause.

Considerations (B) and (C) do not weigh very importantly in this case. Federal concerns with interstate order, such as with ready mobility of persons and property from state to state, are not much involved. The opposing rules are so simple that the judical task is merely one of deciding which rule applies and going on from there.

F's governmental interests, (D), though real, are not very strong. Nor are *X*'s. Each state has significant contacts with the parties and the transaction, but neither's contacts overshadow the other's. Each has policy reasons behind its legal rule, *F*'s favoring protection of the insured against unreasonably short notice requirements, *X*'s favoring the insurer's investigative needs. Each state of course weighs the significance of its own interests, but neither much outweighs the other unless the forum court itself concludes that its own state's interests are of real importance. That could happen. Or the forum could take the attitude that it would protect its own state's interests and disregard the other state's, even though its own were no greater than the other's. That is even less likely to happen.

The turning point in this case may well come under consideration (E). *F* is apt to feel that the sixty-day notice provison is

169. Clay v. Sun Ins. Office, Ltd., 377 U.S. 179 (1964), discussed at note 144 supra.

170. Validation of transactions entered into in good faith by the parties is an ideal that ordinarily relates to entire transactions, not to isolated clauses. This is especially true as to defeasance clauses in adhesion-type contracts. Validation of such clauses tends to defeat the ideal. It is only in the entire transaction context that the validity ideal serves the useful purposes ascribed to it under the predictability consideration.

so harsh and unreasonable that it ought to be avoided if *F*'s rule of law can reasonably be applied, as obviously it can be. Upholding the contract against unfair defeasance, especially since this corresponds with *F*'s own governmental interests, such as they are, will probably lead to choice of *F*'s law as governing. If *X* were the forum, and were not dominated by insurer influences, it might reach the same result. It might rate its own rule, as applied to these facts, about as low as *F* would rate it.

Case (8). *S* has been officially adjudicated a "spendthrift" at his State *F* domicile. One effect of this under *F* law was to make his contracts voidable. *S* went to State *X* where he borrowed money from *P*, giving *P* a promissory note executed in *X* for the amount borrowed. The stated purpose of the loan was to enable *S* to finance a business venture in *X*. *P* knew nothing of *S*'s "spendthrift" status. Under *X* law the whole transaction would be valid. *S* later returned to *F* without paying *P*, and *P* now sues *S* in *F* on the note. *S* sets up avoidance as authorized by *F* law.

An easy answer would be to say, with Beale, that the law of the place of making governs. That would achieve the ends of justice on the facts of this case. Or it could be said that it was the implied intent of the parties to have *X* law govern, since that was the law that would sustain their contract, which would give the same beneficent answer as the place-of-making rule. Perhaps a "law of the place of performance" rule would also give the same answer, as would a center-of-gravity approach. The trouble with all these approaches is that they do not speak in terms of real reasons.[171] Another approach could be characterized as one of status (capacity) which could establish the law of *S*'s domicile as governing. But that too would be mechanical, ignoring real reasons. If real reasons for one result or the other are to be identified and stated, it will have to be in terms of the choice-influencing considerations.

The problem is one of overall contract validity, as to which predictability, (A), at the inception of the contract is of first importance. This means predictability by both parties, presumably acting in good faith. It is possible here that *S*, knowing his status under *F* law, anticipated avoidance of the contract, but that sort of one-sided, deceptive predictability is not what motivates choice of law. *P*'s intention was to achieve a valid contract, and good faith imputes that intention to *S* also. The only choice of law that will effectively further this end is the choice of *X*'s law which will sustain the contract.

171. See Leflar, Conflict of Laws, Contracts, and the New Restatement, 15 Ark. L. Rev. 163 (1961).

The needs of the federal system, (B), call for the same result. To permit *S* to get by with invalidation of the contract by applying *F*'s law to it would be to put a real strain on the interstate economic order, on the easy and practical conduct of business in a federation of states that should be one economic unit. The judicial task will not be complicated, (C), by application of either state's rule. It might cause less judicial commotion to enforce the contract than to defeat it, but that is a minor matter.

It is clear that *F* has a governmental interest, (D), in the protection of its own spendthrifts and their estates. That the interest is a very strong one, when opposing extrastate interests enter the picture, is doubtful. *F* itself has very real opposing interests which favor the validation of contracts made in good faith—the protection of innocent parties from fraud and the encouragement of citizens of other states to do business with citizens of *F*. It could be well concluded that *F*'s own interests, on balance, call for application of *X* law. Also, most lawyers and laymen would regard *X*'s as the preferable law, (E), as applied to an innocent party such as *P* on these facts. Analysis in the light of all these considerations clearly points toward selection of *X*'s law as governing.[172]

If the action had been brought in a court of State *X*, similar analysis would have led all the more clearly to the same result.

Case (9). *P*, a resident of State *X*, and *O*, a resident of State *F*, contracted orally in *X* for *O* to render certain services for *P* in both *X* and *F* over a period of two years. *O* did not perform, and *P* sues him in *F* on the contract. *X* has no applicable statute of frauds rule for such contracts, but the *F* statute is that "no action shall be brought on any contract not to be performed within a year unless it be in writing, signed . . . ."

The traditional rule would have led to the decision that no action was maintainable in *F* because of the procedural phrasing of *F*'s Statute of Frauds. [173] Most modern courts, however, would conclude that all statute of frauds sections operate substantively to determine whether there is an enforceable contract, either rejecting the procedure-substance dichotomy[174] based on statu-

172. In Lilienthal v. Kaufman, 239 Ore. 1, 395 P.2d 543 (1964), discussed in note 110 supra, the law of F (Oregon) was applied on similar facts, as against the law of X (California), by a divided court. It is possible, however, that the majority judges, or some of them, felt that their spendthrift law was an unfortunate one and that the best way to get the legislature to repeal or modify it was to apply it as rigorously as possible. That, however, would not be a real judicial objective in very many cases.

173. Leroux v. Brown, 12 C.B. 801, 138 Eng. Rep. 1119 (1852).

174. Lams v. F. H. Smith Co., 36 Del. 477, 178 Atl. 651 (1935).

tory phrasing or, as Chief Justice Traynor did in *Bernkrant v. Fowler*,[175] ignoring the phrasing test as being too silly to notice in this context. That leaves the question of which substantive law governs.

Since the validity of a contract is the issue, the predictability consideration, (A), has the same genuine importance that it had in Case (8). The desired certainty can be achieved by letting the contract be governed by *X* law, with support drawn from the fact that *X* was where the contract was made, or from an implied intent that *X* law govern, or from a preference for validation over invalidation. Interstate economic orderliness, (B), is not so vital here as in Case (8) since this transaction is further from the mainstream of the nation's commerce. Simplification of the judicial task, (C), which is the great reason for applying a forum's procedural rules, is almost irrelevant here since both rules are simple and easy to apply—the contract is either valid and enforceable or invalid and unenforceable. The conclusion has practically no bearing on the court's efficiency in its administration of judicial business. A forum's interest, (D), in its statute of frauds rule consists of a concern for preclusion of possibly faked claims, especially if fraudulent or perjured testimony in *F*'s own courts may be involved. That the interest may not be a very strong one, however, is indicated by the tendency to regard statutes of frauds as relics from another century that ought to be updated by major amendments or even repealed.[176] This is a matter as to which judicial attitudes concerning what rule is preferable, (E), are not likely to be controlled by state lines. They are more likely to be controlled by whether the court has thought much about the supertechnicality, the refinements, and the ambiguities that inhere in the statute. With contacts as evenly divided as they are in Case (9), there is no need for an enlightened court in *F* to apply *F*'s contract-defeating statute. If the lawsuit were tried in *X*, an *X* court would almost surely not apply the *F* rule.

Case (10). *M*, age twenty-five and *W*, age fourteen, both domiciled in State *F*, wished to marry, and had the consent of *W*'s parents, but marriages of girls under fifteen were forbidden by *F* law (void, not merely voidable). *M* and *W* went to State *X* whose law permitted such marriages, and were married in *X* after com-

175. 55 Cal. 2d 588, 360 P.2d 906, 12 Cal. Rptr. 266 (1961). See notes 76, 82 supra.

176. Willis, The Statute of Frauds—A Legal Anachronism, 3 Ind. L.J. 427, 528 (1928). The repeal of the English statute, parent of the American enactments, is noted in 68 Harv. L. Rev. 383 (1954); 70 L.Q. Rev. 441, 442 (1954) ("This is the way the Statute ends/Not with a bang but a whimper"). See Note, 41 Cornell L.Q. 472 (1956) (judicial restriction of the statute).

plying with all the relevant laws of that state. (a) *W* brings an annulment suit in *F*. (b) *W* sues *M* for divorce and alimony in *F*, and *M* defends on the ground that they were never validly married. (c) *M* died shortly after the marriage, and his sister *S* seeks an adjudication in *F* that *W* was not *M*'s wife and is therefore not entitled to a widow's share in his estate.

Most of the authorities say that the validity of a marriage will be determined by the law of the place of the ceremony (normally selected by the parties because it would validate their marriage) unless the domicile, or intended matrimonial domicile, has a *strong* public policy against such marriages. This means that the law of the domicile should basically control but that the domicile will ordinarily, though not always, refer the question to the law of the state of celebration.[177] The choice of law may also vary with the purposes and circumstances of the particular lawsuit.

Probably there is no area of the law in which predictability, (A), is more important than in this one. The parties need to know, and at once, whether they are married. The "place of ceremony" rule facilitates this certainty especially if local officials check on the facts before they issue a license. The retention of control by the domiciliary state normally interferes with certainty. It should be noted, however, that the predictability consideration is more important to the parties themselves, and their issue, than to others, even including collateral heirs.

Interstate order, (B), is also a significant consideration in this type of case. It is messy to have a couple married in one state and not in another, or to be uncertain what law determines if they are married or unmarried. A mobile society such as ours needs clear and uniform answers to validity of marriage problems.

Comparative difficulty of the judicial task, (C), seems to be of not much importance here. If the question were presented to the courts of *X*, or of a third state, it would be easier to apply the law of *X*, place of celebration, and end the matter there, than to seek the strong public policy rule of *F*. But our case is in an *F* (domiciliary) court, as most cases presenting the question will be, and *F* will find it as easy to apply its own law as to apply *X*'s, other considerations apart.

F's governmental interests, (D), are bound up with the strengths of its public policies, already mentioned, and with the interests of its domiciliaries. The strongest single governmental concern is probably the latter, and the domiciliaries' strongest interest is in knowing for sure and at once whether they are or

177. Taintor, Marriage in the Conflict of Laws, 9 Vand. L. Rev. 607 (1956).

can be married, (A). The state has almost as much interest in that certainty as the parties have. As to the strengths of policies that underlie particular marital prohibitions and requirements, only *F*'s courts can give authoritative answers, and different states will come up with different strengths behind essentially similar rules. The policy strengths can vary also from one fact situation to another. As to judicial preference for what may be regarded as the better law, (E), it may be assumed that *F* will prefer its own law unless it is anachronistic, as it clearly is not in the present case, but the importance of this preference is relatively small as against the genuine significance of considerations (A), (B) and (D).

Since the weight of (D) can be evaluated only by the *F* court, and not by any outside commentator, it is unrealistic now to suggest what *F*'s answers would be, but it should be evident that *F*'s concerns, (D), will match more evenly with *W*'s in her annulment suit, (a), than with *M*'s in his divorce defense, (b), or *S*'s in her effort to defeat *W*'s claim as widow, (c). The *F* court may well reach different conclusions depending on which of the three lawsuits it has to decide.

Case (11). *H* and *W*, husband and wife, were domiciled in State *X* where *W* committed acts of cruelty toward *H*. *H* then moved his domicile to State *F* and there, after complying with *F*'s jurisdictional requirements, sued *W* for divorce. *W* appears and defends on the merits. Cruelty is a ground for divorce by *F* law but not by *X* law.

It is so well settled that a court having divorce jurisdiction will apply its own state's law on grounds for divorce,[178] regardless of where the facts occurred or where the spouses were domiciled when the facts occurred, that the question of what law governs in such cases is almost never raised.

Predictability, (A), is completely defeated by this rule, since it cannot be known where a divorce suit may later be brought, but this seems to be of small importance. Divorce suits nowadays are brought for the most part because one or both spouses are dissatisfied with the marriage. "I want a divorce" rather than "I have grounds for divorce" not only is the usual reason for initiating divorce proceedings but also has become a socially acceptable reason, almost a legally acceptable one, in the easy divorce states. Furthermore, the extrastate divorce system has become a part of the American way of marital life. It furnishes the safety valve that enables New York and other states with limited

178. Goodrich, Conflict of Laws § 128 (4th ed. Scoles 1964); Leflar, Conflict of Laws § 168 (1959).

grounds for divorce to retain substantive divorce laws which are called for by local political expediency but which are unrealistically impractical for many of their citizens. The fact that extrastate divorces are available on extrastate grounds definitely furthers interstate and international order, (B), under our present social system. Simplification of *F*'s judicial task, (C), is facilitated since *F* applies its own laws, but that is a minor consideration in these cases. *F*'s governmental interests, (D), are presumably furthered by application of its own law, not only as to *F*'s long-time domiciliaries but as to any one who has recently established the jurisdictional requisites prescribed by *F*. This appears to be an instance in which the forum state is truly interested in the welfare of people, not just that of its own people. In the so-called "quickie states," the strong governmental interest of *F* may even embrace economic factors—the divorce-seekers' money—and the governmental interest in money is not limited to what it can get from domiciliaries. Finally, the effort to achieve justice by applying what *F* regards as the better law, (E), is apparently not very significant here. *F* presumably regards its own broad grounds for divorce as socially preferable to the narrower ones in *X*, and this may be a part of its reason for preferring to apply them, along with the furtherance of its own governmental (sometimes including economic) interests mentioned under (D). But general acceptance of the rule that grounds for divorce are controlled by the law of the forum state (which has judicial jurisdiction) is justifiable primarily because it best serves the multistate needs of our federal system, (B), in the troubled social field in which divorce laws operate.

Case (12). *H* and *W*, husband and wife domiciled in State *X*, were traveling together by auto, *H* driving a car owned by *H*, registered and insured in *X*, when *H* by his negligent driving in State *F* injured *W*. By the law of *X* a wife may not recover from her husband in tort; by the law of *F* a wife may so recover. *W* sues *H* in *F*.

There are many cases saying that husband-wife rights in tort are governed by the law of the place of the injury under a tort characterization,[179] while others use a family law characterization to say that the law of the parties' marital domicile should govern.[180] But the characterization technique does not get at the real issues here any more than in other problems.

179. See Hancock, The Rise and Fall of *Buckeye v. Buckeye*, 1931-1959: Marital Immunity for Torts in Conflict of Laws, 29 U. Chi. L. Rev. 237 (1962).

180. E.g., Haumschild v. Continental Cas. Co., 7 Wis. 2d 130, 95 N.W.2d 814 (1959). But see McSwain v. McSwain, 215 A.2d 677 (Pa. 1966) (comparison of

Predictability, (A), is practically unimportant here, as in cases (1), (2), and (5). Negligent injuries are not planned in reliance on one law or another. The interstate order, (B), is not particularly affected by the choice of law in husband-wife injury cases. Spouses will travel together across state lines regardless of choice-of-law rules. The forum court can apply the other state's law as easily as its own; both are simple. No problem of efficiency in judicial administration, (C), is presented. It might be said that *F* has no governmental interest, (D), in applying its law to protect an *X* wife against her *X* husband (or, more realistically, to protect an *X* husband and wife against the insurance company that issued a liability policy to *H* in *X*), when the only *F* contact was the accidental occurrence of negligent injury in *F*. The fact is, however, that *F* as a typical American state is about as much interested in the welfare of visitors from sister states as in that of its own domiciliaries, especially when the visitors seek aid from *F*'s courts on an *F* set of facts. The conflicting interest in preventing collusive raids on insurance companies, if *F* attaches importance to this interest, has about the same weight for extrastate insurance contracts in an *F* court as for local ones. On this kind of case the nonresidence of the parties would not make much difference to *F*. As to which state's law is better, (E), each court is entitled to its own opinion, and there is a real difference of opinion among courts on this kind of law. Probably *F* will believe that its own law is preferable, though it might not. It would be quite possible for a good court to go either way on the balance of choice-influencing considerations on these facts, though probably most courts in *F*'s situation would apply their own law and permit *W* to maintain the action.[181]

V

Conclusion

The most evident thing about choice-of-law analysis in terms of reasonable choice-influencing considerations is not only that it does not lead to many exact choice-of-law rules—at least not permanent ones—but also that the controlling considerations cannot themselves be stated very exactly. Every listing of them is an incomplete, overlapping, and tentative effort at generalization. The plain fact is that the considerations have been present and

state interests); Wilcox v. Wilcox, 26 Wis. 2d 617, 133 N.W.2d 408 (1965) (most significant contacts approach).

181. Compare Haynie v. Hanson, 16 Wis. 2d 299, 114 N.W.2d 443 (1962), in which F held that the law of X, the domicile, should govern under a family law characterization in an action for contribution by a third party tortfeasor against husband's liability insurer.

operative all along, and have been motivating reasons behind every choice-of-law rule that was ever formulated and every case that was ever decided. New types of transactions and new conditions in society give rise to new factors in the considerations, or change the thrust of old ones. Better insight also brings changes. The process of listing and weighing is one for the centuries. That does not mean, however, that we need not work at it today, or that we should reject the task in favor of some mechanical approach. Above all, it does not justify our concluding that the whole effort is too difficult, or too important, for courts to engage in and that they should abdicate their concern with reasons either in favor of the legislative branch of government or in favor of anybody else who may be assumed to be better equipped than courts are to deal with reasons, *i.e.*, with choice-influencing considerations. Reasons, realistic reasons, are still the life of the common law and of common-law adjudication. They have constituted the basic judicial approach to cases since the common law began.

The common-law system works better when reasons are clearly identified and correlated than when they run wild. That justifies methodism, but without any pretense that everlasting truth is being revealed. The relevant considerations balance out to one result in one type of case, to another in a different type. The results they call for have already been pretty well calculated in some types of cases. In others, such as the tort cases, there has been merely some exploration of the ground, and in some special areas such as defamation there has hardly been any exploration. The results produced will not always be the same even in quite similar cases, because different courts will weigh the considerations on different scales. The results, however, should be more uniform than would be produced by unfettered forum preference, and certainly more rational, but there will still be much room for diversity. The choice-influencing considerations are not eternal; neither are the answers they produce.

Nor do they necessarily bar gimmicks, which are the enemies of honesty. Not at once anyway. Reliance on tricks of characterization, for example, to lead the court's choice to a state which has a preferred rule of law, is apt to continue. It is equivalent to the use of fictions to achieve growth in the law. Any such indirect means to a good result is likely to mark a transitional stage in the law's development. Even after jurists have identified anew the ends that the law should serve in conflicts cases, *i.e.*, the relevant choice-influencing considerations, common-law courts committed to precedential techniques will feel bound to maintain their formal ties with the past by pretending that nothing has changed. The gimmicks facilitate this pretense and at the same time enable judges to satisfy their social consciences by giving under-cover weight to newly recognized principles and considerations. We have always had these less-than-admirable devices in all branches of the law, and conflict of laws has had its full share of them. All that we can do with them is to recognize as soon as possible and as best we can what should be the true choice-influencing considerations, and thus keep moving through the transitional stage.

Does ultimate reliance upon the choice-influencing considerations, rather than upon more exactly stated mechanical rules or upon simple forum preference, leave too much room for variety in decision, more flexibilty than it is good for courts to have? Some will answer this question "Yes." There is room for difference of opinion. But all must agree that there is virtue in flexibility for at least some areas of choice of law.

For one thing, there are a good many cases, like those dealing with land titles, in which the relevant considerations generally support rules of choice that are already formulated and pretty well agreed upon. Such rules deal adequately with the flexibility problem, either by giving the needed flexibility or by avoiding flexibility where none is desired. For those areas little more flexibility is in prospect. But there are other areas in which the rules are not already clear. We can be sure that in any area in which a variety of purported choice-of-law rules has developed, as for contracts, torts, and inter vivos trusts of personalty, that alone proves that no one of the various rules deals with the problem adequately. The variety of available rules enables the parties, and later the judges, perhaps by employing one of the gimmicks so the result will seem logical, to pick one from among the rules, or devise some combination of them, that will somehow take care of the situation's needs. Thus flexibility is available, even with so-called rules, because there really is no rule. It is in such areas that the search for truly relevant considerations, and frank recognition of their controlling effect, is particularly needed. The variety is already there, presumably as it should be, but what is lacking is a reasonably clear explanation of what it is that justifies now one choice of law and next a different one. Intelligent analysis in terms of the choice-influencing considerations should produce that explanation. Even in these areas it seems that no more flexibility than before is in prospect. The difference should be not in greater variety of results or more judicial freedom to reach various results, but in more realistic reasoning, more openly stated, behind the results. Even the frequent preference for forum law, normally expectable in many but by no means in all cases, will ordinarily be explained in terms of a preference for what is honestly regarded as the better law as well as one designed to advance the forum's governmental interests and to simplify the judicial task in administering the dispute.

This is not a "free law" proposal, not a suggested system of adjudication that would leave it to courts to reach what is conceived to be a "just result" in the particular case regardless of rules and precedents. Nor is it a new program for choice-of-law adjudication in any other sense. Rather, it is a somewhat idealized description of the present system of choice-of-law decision designed to accept substantially what happens now, together with current trends, and to give the real reasons (which on the whole are good reasons) for the law as it currently operates. There is less of "free law" in the system when real reasons, however broadly and generally formulated, are recognized and given than when opinion language is forced, circuitous, and false. The movement should be away from "free law" rather than toward it.

It is not too much to hope that emphasis upon real (and good) reasons—valid choice-influencing considerations, as distinguished from the cover-up of sometime rules and manipulative gimmicks—can produce some improvement in the results of adjudication along with a substantial improvement in understanding the results. That is the only sense in which this study contemplates major changes in the law of choice of law.

[14]

INTEREST ANALYSIS AND THE MYTH OF LEGISLATIVE INTENT

*Lea Brilmayer**

Modern conflict-of-laws scholarship is the victim of a well-intentioned misrepresentation. Proponents of "governmental interest analysis" have marketed their theory as a species of legislative interpretation, indeed as the definitive approach to construing legislative intent.[1] But while promoted by Brainerd Currie as an antidote to the pernicious metaphysical assumptions that afflicted Beale and the *First Restatement*,[2] interest analysis is in fact nothing of the kind. Interest analysis merely substitutes one set of metaphysical premises for another, leaving the body of conflicts law with a remedy every bit as distressing as the disease it was designed to cure.

Thus far, the interest analysts have been allowed to argue, in effect, "Our method may seem shortsighted and parochial, but it is not the courts' business to second-guess a state legislature." The avowed goal is precise, case-by-case implementation of state statutory policies — loyalty to state policy concerns rather than to "first principles" such as uniformity or predictability. By neglecting to challenge the interest analysts' claims of fidelity to legislative intent,[3] tradition-

---

* Assistant Professor of Law, University of Chicago Law School. B.A. 1970, J.D. 1976, University of California at Berkeley; LL.M. 1978, Columbia University. —Ed. I would like to thank my research assistant, Brenda Lyons, as well as many colleagues, including David Currie, Doug Laycock, Bill Powers, Gary Simson, and Russell Weintraub. The Article arose out of a very valuable intellectual interchange with Professor Maurice Rosenberg, whose influence is evident throughout.

1. B. CURRIE, SELECTED ESSAYS ON THE CONFLICTS OF LAW (1963) [hereinafter cited as CURRIE ESSAYS] is the seminal work. "It is explicitly an attempt to determine legislative purposes. . . ." *Id.* at 727. "[T]he method I advocate is the method of statutory construction. . . ." *Id.* at 627. In addition, see Currie, *The Disinterested Third State*, 28 LAW & CONTEMP. PROB. 754, 760-61 (1963); Hancock, *"In the Parish of St. Mary le Bow, in the Ward of Cheap" Choice-of-Law Problems Resolved by Statutory Construction: The Charitable Testamentary Gift Cases*, 16 STAN. L. REV. 561 (1964). Currie once attempted to distinguish between "intention" and "purpose." The difference he saw is not altogether clear, although it may be the distinction proposed in the text below, between actual and constructive intent. He did concede that legislatures did not have any particular intent about how certain cases ought to be decided. 28 LAW & CONTEMP. PROB. at 761-62.

2. Currie, *The Disinterested Third State*, 28 LAW & CONTEMP. PROB. 754 (1963). *See also* CURRIE ESSAYS, *supra* note 1, at 613: "Almost all constructive writing on conflict of laws in this century has been in revolt against this heritage . . . ."

3. One author who has disputed these claims is Professor Robert Leflar:

> This process [of statutory construction] involves discovering in a statute something that the legislature did not put into it. . . . Even if called "statutory construction," this is really an independent and essentially extraneous process, depending on facts not cited in the statute itself and in the interests growing out of them. . . . The term "statutory con-

ally minded conflicts theorists have by implication left themselves espousing the proposition that a court should decline to honor valid legislative wishes. That posture is unnecessarily vulnerable, conceding the interest analysts far too much. This Article attempts to strip away the defense of mock judicial deference and to criticize governmental interest analysis on its own merits.

My critique begins with a brief analysis of the principles underlying the Currie school's calculations of whether a state has an interest in having its law applied; it seeks to expose the unarticulated biases inherent in that calculus.[4] I then argue that Currie's principles cannot be justified as expressions of actual legislative intent regarding a statute's territorial scope.[5] Indeed, the discrepancy between governmental interests and actual legislative intent has been overlooked only because, in the vast majority of cases, legislatures *have* no actual intent on territorial reach with which to contrast Currie's results.

But without actual legislative endorsement, interest analysis must fall back on constructive intent — on a theory that a rational legislature would, upon reflection, prefer the results of interest analysis to those of competing conflicts methodologies.[6] In the most detailed discussion of this Article, I take issue with this theory. Interest analysis is simply too unpredictable and parochial to be a plausible theory of constructive intent.[7] Furthermore, it is highly doubtful that substantive intent can by itself provide a sufficient basis for conflict of laws decisions.[8] I conclude with a short survey of conflicts statutes to demonstrate that when legislatures treat conflicts problems explicitly, they ordinarily do not follow the interest analysts' approach to territorial reach.[9] Interest analysis no more reflects actual or constructive legislative intentions than did the *First Restatement*. It is a metaphysical system, and a remarkably flawed one at that.

I. The Calculus of Interests

Any study of the method proposed by Brainerd Currie must be-

struction" is no more than a pretentious disguise for application of the court's conflicts law.

Leflar, *Choice-of-Law Statutes*, 44 Tenn. L. Rev. 951, 954 (1977). *See also* Reese, *Conflicts of Laws and the Restatement Second*, 28 Law & Contemp. Prob. 679, 686 (1963).

4. *See* text at notes 10-35 *infra*.

5. *See* text at notes 36-47 *infra*.

6. *See* text at notes 48-87 *infra*.

7. *See* text at notes 48-87 *infra*.

8. *See* text at notes 88-97 *infra*.

9. *See* text at notes 100-16 *infra*.

gin with the concept of a "governmental interest."[10] An "interest" is, essentially, a prima facie claim that a state's law should apply. It is generally thought, for instance, that a forum's interest will trump the interests of other involved states because of the court's duty to follow legislative commands.[11] And while other factors may override an interest, commentators disagree over when an interest should yield. For instance, some authorities believe that it is desirable to mediate conflicts between two or more competing interests by reexamining those interests. Closer examination may show one interest to be weightier than the other,[12] one to be more consistent with modern trends in substantive law than the other,[13] or one to be more jeopardized by neglect.[14] But lengthening the process of accommodating and implementing those state interests already recognized will not remedy all defects inherent in the initial "identification" of interests. Among other things, injustice may result precisely because a state *fails* to find an interest;[15] subsequent steps do not remedy this problem. For this reason, and because the identification of "interests" in theory determines whether the legislature would wish to have its law applied, "interest" is the key concept in the critical discussion below.

Whether a state is thought to have an interest in having its law applied to a particular case is a function of the multistate elements present in a case, the precise statutes involved, and the policies underlying those statutes. These policies can be categorized as protective, compensatory, and regulatory, for in drawing multistate implications from statutes, Currie relied upon their protective, compensatory, and regulatory aspects. His treatment of the married women's contract cases exemplifies the interest analyst's approach to a statute that furthers a protective policy. The court in *Milliken v.*

10. *See* CURRIE ESSAYS, *supra* note 1, at 189.

11. *See, e.g.*, CURRIE ESSAYS, *supra* note 1, at 181-82, 610, 617.

12. Currie argued that a court should not weigh interests. *See id.* at 182, 606, 610, 617. Apparently, however, he thought balancing was intimated by the *Second Restatement* approach, which asked which contacts were "more significant." *See also* Currie, *supra* note 2, at 759 (criticizing Cavers's proposal to weigh interests to decide which is "greater").

13. Leflar thought that it was relevant to ask which rule of law was substantively more sound. *See* Leflar, *Conflicts Law: More on Choice-Influencing Considerations*, 54 CALIF. L. REV. 1584 (1966). *See also* Weintraub, *The Future of Choice of Law for Torts: What Principles Should Be Preferred?*, 41 LAW & CONTEMP. PROB. 146, 163 (1977).

14. Professor Baxter has espoused an approach based on "comparative impairment." *See* Baxter, *Choice of Law and the Federal System*, 16 STAN. L. REV. 1 (1963).

15. The parochialism problems which arise when the state fails to find an interest in assisting nonresidents are discussed in the text at notes 64-87 *infra*. Other problems, which arise when a court tries to limit the unpredictable application of forum law under interest analysis, are discussed in the text at notes 59-61 *infra*.

Pratt[16] had to choose between a Massachusetts statute invalidating married women's agreements to act as guarantors for their husbands' debts and a Maine statute that did not; Pratt, the defendant, had guaranteed her husband's credit. In an early article, Currie analyzed the possible relevance of four multistate elements: the place of contracting, the domicile of the defendant, the domicile of Milliken, the merchant who sought to enforce the agreement, and the location of the suit.[17]

Currie found the place of contracting irrelevant.[18] Furthermore, if suit was brought in Massachusetts, the wife's domicile was the only important element. According to Currie, Massachusetts had enacted its law invalidating contracts for the protection of Massachusetts married women; it had no reason to invalidate an agreement by a woman from Maine, which had emancipated its married women. "Never mind, for the time being, exactly what we mean by 'Massachusetts' married women — whether citizens, domiciliaries, residents. For the sake of convenience, until we must decide that question, let us say that it is *residence* in Massachusetts that defines the ambit of the state's protective policy."[19] Herein lies the first general principle of Currie's analysis: If a state has a protective policy, then its interest in applying its law depends upon the residence of the defendant.[20] State protective policies are designed to benefit resident defendants alone.[21]

16. 125 Mass. 374 (1878).

17. Discussed in chapter two of his *Selected Essays*, Currie, *Married Women's Contracts: A Study in Conflict-of-Laws Method*, in CURRIE ESSAYS, *supra* note 1, at 77.

18. CURRIE ESSAYS, *supra* note 1, at 109: "To apply the law of the place of making would be to make the result in each case depend upon an irrelevant factor, determined by chance."

19. *Id.* at 86 (emphasis original).

20. This principle is illustrated also by Currie's attitude toward guest statutes, which are protective laws. *See id.* at 690-742. Objecting to New York's application of the Ontario guest statute in a case involving a New York defendant, he wrote, "Ontario has no interest at all in the application of its guest statute. . . . The guest statute expresses a policy for the protection of defendants. The defendant here, however, is not a citizen or resident of Ontario, he is a citizen of a state that holds him accountable for injuries to his guests." *Id.* at 724.

21. On several occasions, Currie qualified this rule by saying that Massachusetts should also invalidate the contract if the defendant's state invalidated such contracts. *See, e.g., id.* at 111-13. This qualification was apparently designed to limit the parochial effects of his theory and to thwart constitutional objections. Yet his compromise does nothing for the woman who is not from a state that invalidates married women's agreements; she is still treated differently from forum residents. Currie's compromise was not recognizing a forum interest in having its law applied so much as applying the protective law of the other state. CURRIE ESSAYS, *supra* note 1, at 113 (indicating that it is her home law which protects her). He still could not imagine that the Massachusetts legislature would care about anyone other than Massachusetts women. He also suggested that, even without the qualification deferring to the other state's protective law, his parochial plan would be a rational way to maximize interests and would be acceptable if "higher authority" need not be consulted. *Id.* at 89. In his subsequent discussions of interests, he often did not mention the qualification.

Compensatory interests are the second classification implicit in Currie's analytical approach. As we have noted, protective interests favor defendants and are keyed to the defendant's residence or domicile. Compensatory interests, in contrast, favor plaintiffs and are triggered by the plaintiff's residence. The nature of compensatory interests is demonstrated by Currie's treatment of *Grant v. McAuliffe*,[22] in which an Arizona protective statute competed with a California compensatory statute. In *Grant*, a California car had collided with another California car in Arizona, and the administrator of a deceased driver's estate brought suit in a California court. Under Arizona law, no tort suit could begin after the death of the tortfeasor; California, however, allowed such actions to survive. The California Supreme Court held the California statute applicable and allowed the action to proceed to trial.

Currie applauded this result.[23] Damages for personal injury, he argued, are intended to compensate the injured party. The California statute evidenced concern that if tort law did not provide compensation, the injured person would become a public charge. Thus it subordinated the interests of the tortfeasor's estate to the interests of the injured person and of the citizens at large who would pay for public assistance. As with protective policies, Currie asserted that this compensatory policy was intended to benefit only injured residents.[24]

A compensatory statute, favoring the plaintiff in a particular case, may of course have effects beyond the confines of that case. The price it exacts from the defendant may make the conduct that caused the harm unprofitable. If the statute is in fact *designed* to change incentives by making previously profitable conduct too costly, it may evidence a regulatory policy as well as a compensatory one. Occasionally, protective statutes also regulate conduct; while a contributory negligence standard favors defendants, it is also supposed to discourage negligent activity by plaintiffs. Currie found these "conduct-regulating" interests — the third class implicit in his analysis of legislative policies — to be triggered by territorial con-

22. 41 Cal. 2d 859, 264 P.2d 944 (1953).

23. CURRIE ESSAYS, *supra* note 1, at 132.

24. *Id.* at 144-45. Although he also said there might be an interest when the plaintiff was present in the state at the time of injury, he dropped this suggestion thereafter, presumably because it reinforced the "state of wrong" rule.

Currie applied a similar analysis to cases involving other compensatory statutes, such as the New York child support statute in Haag v. Barnes, 9 N.Y.2d 554, 175 N.E.2d 441, 216 N.Y.S.2d 65 (1961). In *Haag*, he asserted, New York had an interest in applying its law because the mother and child were New York residents. CURRIE ESSAYS, *supra* note 1, at 732.

necting factors rather than domiciliary factors. The most significant territorial connection with the forum was presence of the complained-of activity, but sometimes one could find a connection in the possibility of foreseeable harm within the jurisdiction.[25]

When the sole purpose of the statute is to regulate conduct, its scope seems clearly limited to conduct with territorial connections. Currie mentioned traffic rules as obvious examples: "We all know that the rule of the road varies from place to place. It is perfectly apparent that the rule in New York is not intended to have any application to Saudi Arabia, but is designed solely to regulate traffic on the streets and highways of New York."[26] He also cited Sunday blue laws. Discussing a Georgia case concerning a contract formed in Kansas on a Sunday, he argued that the Georgia law invalidating Sunday contracts had no rational application to transactions in Kansas:

> Georgia invalidates domestic Sunday contracts because (A) the criminal laws of the state prohibit the pursuit of one's ordinary calling on that day, and (B) the courts have decided that, in addition to the penal sanctions provided by statute, a contract made in violation of the prohibition should be made unenforceable. But the Georgia court would hardly have taken the position that the parties, in entering into this transaction in Kansas, had committed an offense against the criminal laws of Georgia.[27]

As even Currie recognized, the reason Georgia would not want its Sunday blue laws to apply to contracts made in Kansas is that expectations are important in governmental efforts to influence conduct, and expectations are largely territorial.

Because statutes embodying only regulatory policies are so obviously territorial, their conflict of laws implications are rarely litigated.[28] Regulatory policies, however, are important in conflicts

---

25. Frequently in the text below, and solely for the purpose of convenience, it will be stated simply that conduct-regulating rules apply to activities within the state, and the qualification "or causing foreseeable harm there" will be omitted.

26. CURRIE ESSAY, *supra* note 1, at 58.

27. *Id.* at 59-60 (footnotes omitted).

28. One interesting example, however, is People v. One 1953 Ford Victoria, 48 Cal. 2d 595, 311 P.2d 480 (1957). California police had confiscated an automobile used for transporting narcotics, and the Texas mortgagor sought its return. Under California law the owner of a security interest had to inquire into the debtor's character in order to preserve that interest if the security was confiscated. Under Texas law, however, no such inquiries were necessary. The California court held forum law inapplicable.

> In the absence of a plain legislative direction to the contrary, . . . the statute cannot reasonably be interpreted as requiring such investigation when the sales are financed in other states and the vehicles are taken to California, not only without the knowledge of those financing the sales, but in violation of express contractual prohibitions. . . . A person financing the sale of an automobile in Texas for use exclusively in that state will look to the laws of Texas for the determination of his rights and duties.

litigation because they are often joined with compensatory or protective policies in a single statute. Regulatory policies are triggered by territorial connecting factors, and protective or compensatory policies by domiciliary ones. The difficult issue, therefore, is what to do when a fact situation triggers one of the interests behind a statute but not the other. What, in other words, should be done when conduct within the state injures a nonresident or when a resident is hurt by conduct outside the state? Apparently, the interest analysts would answer that either the compensatory or the conduct-regulating interest is a sufficient reason to apply forum law.[29] Thus, if the plaintiff is a resident *or* the tortious conduct occurred within the state, the state has an interest in having its statute applied. This is apparently the reason Currie would have allowed a New Yorker to benefit from New York negligence law even though the accident occurred out of the state: the New York compensatory interest was sufficient.[30] Various cases purporting to apply interest analysis are consistent with this view,[31] and it has been explicitly urged by at least one commentator.[32]

Implicit in this calculus of interests are three discernible biases: pro-resident, pro-forum-law, and pro-recovery. The pro-resident bias results from the assumption that protective and compensatory policies of the forum can be invoked only by forum residents. Residents thus have the best of both worlds: they can claim the benefits of these policies in multistate cases without incurring the corresponding costs. The pro-recovery and pro-forum-law biases stem from the assumption that when a statute embodies several policies, any one of them may trigger the finding of an "interest." Thus, a forum statute that embodies regulatory and compensatory policies gives rise to a governmental interest if the plaintiff is a resident of the

48 Cal. 2d at 598-99, 311 P.2d at 482 (citations omitted).

29. At least, when dealing with statutes evidencing both types of policies they seem content merely to cite one as justification for a finding of "interest." There seems to be no sentiment that if a court finds a compensatory policy, it should ask whether there are other policies involved and whether they are satisfied. *See* notes 59-61 *infra* and accompanying text.

30. *See* CURRIE ESSAYS, *supra* note 1, at 725.

31. *See, e.g.*, Brown v. Market Dev., Inc., 41 Ohio Misc. 57, 322 N.E.2d 367 (1974) (act providing civil damages held applicable where activity occurred within borders, even if nonresident defrauded); Johnson v. Spider Staging Corp., 87 Wash. 2d 577, 555 P.2d 997 (1976) (allowing unlimited wrongful death recovery on a deterrence theory); Kilberg v. Northeast Airlines, 9 N.Y.2d 34, 172 N.E.2d 526, 211 N.Y.S.2d 133 (1961) (allowing unlimited wrongful death recovery on a compensation theory).

32. "For purposes of interest analysis, a rule of substantive law should be presumed to reflect *all* legitimate policies that it could possibly serve." Sedler, *The Governmental Interest Approach to Choice of Law: An Analysis and Reformulation*, 25 UCLA L. REV. 181, 199 (1977) (emphasis original). *See also* Note, *False Conflicts*, 55 CALIF. L. REV. 74, 76-78 (1967) (state has an interest when one of a number of alternative grounds is satisfied).

forum or if the offensive conduct occurred there.[33] This splintering of policies increases the likelihood that the state will have an interest and predisposes the method toward forum law. Furthermore, it creates a bias toward recovery because pro-recovery statutes are the most likely to serve several different policies, namely compensatory and regulatory ones. The plaintiff's power to choose the forum contributes further to the pro-recovery bias; interest analysis permits different courts to reach different results by honoring their respective states' interests, and the plaintiff naturally selects the most favorable forum.

These biases do not bother the interest analysts too much, for the abiding purpose of their theory is case-by-case implementation of state policies. For members of the Currie school, deference to the laws of other jurisdictions and even-handed treatment of nonresidents do not warrant disregard of state substantive goals.[34] Since they think "interests" are the perfect embodiment of legislative intent, the sacrifice of mundane system-coordinating concerns does not distress them. And if their premise is truly sound, their conclusion may be compelling;[35] if interest analysis really holds the key to legislative intent, the sacrifice is not only worthwhile but arguably necessary.

II. Interest Analysis and Legislative Intent

Why do the interest analysts claim that their theory satisfies legislative desires? Saying it's so doesn't make it so. Most traditionally minded theorists would agree that any explicit legislative instructions should be followed;[36] but the problem is what to do when the face of the statute is silent. What sort of evidence would interest analysts use to justify their inferences?

Currie did not envision extensive reliance upon legislative history. Many states do not even publish legislative histories, and those that do rarely document the legislators' views on territorial reach. Currie reached his solutions by generalizing about classes of statutes

33. This must include conduct which causes foreseeable harm within the jurisdiction. *See* note 25 *supra* and accompanying text.

34. Currie conceded that uniformity and protection of expectations were desirable, Currie Essays, *supra* note 1, at 100-01, 186-87, but claimed that they did not justify substantial sacrifices of substantive interests. *Id.* at 118 (only where substantive policies weak).

35. One objection that might still be made is that many substantive law doctrines are judge made. If legislatures may specify the territorial reach of statutes as they please (within constitutional limits), courts should be equally free with common law. The policies are judicially created, and could be modified or overruled by later courts.

36. *See, e.g.*, Restatement (Second) of Conflicts of Laws § 6(1) (1971).

(married women's contract laws, for instance), apparently assuming that unless otherwise indicated in the statute the policies behind all such statutes could be treated as identical.[37] This assumption alone should make us suspicious about whether Currie was deducing true legislative intent, which one might expect to vary from state to state. It suggests that Currie's principles of inference were rather a product of his own normative beliefs about how far certain policies *ought* to reach.

Two pieces of evidence bolster this suspicion. The first is the willingness of Currie and his followers to criticize legislative choice when it contradicts the principles of interest analysis. Currie, for example, strenuously opposed efforts to change the result in *Grant v. McAuliffe*[38] by legislation, writing that "a more mischievous piece of legislation . . . would be difficult to imagine."[39] This is a strange posture for one who criticized traditional analysis for disregarding legislative preference. Currie apparently felt that legislatures should not participate in choice-of-law problems by expressing their wishes about the territorial reach of their statutes, at least not by enacting traditional rules.

> [T]he California Legislature, and all others, would do well to avoid enacting choice-of-law rules in general. This is intended as a very narrow statement. It does not mean that legislatures should not concern themselves with problems of conflict of laws. There is a body of highly desirable legislation in the field. The statement means only that the legislature would be well advised not to express its will concerning conflict-of-laws problems in the form of traditional choice-of-law rules . . . .[40]

Since Currie did favor legislative action when it coincided with his views,[41] what mattered to him was not whether the courts or the legislature should decide territorial reach, but whether the end result was application of interest analysis. Moreover, the interest analysts' willingness to criticize actual legislative choice manifests a conviction that a given statute has a "natural" territorial reach. This is, of

37. Currie did acknowledge that substantive law specialists should have the final say. CURRIE ESSAYS, *supra* note 1, at 592. But unless legislators give some indication of their wishes, there is nothing for such specialists to go on, and the courts facing conflicts problems are left speculating about types of statutes.

38. 41 Cal. 2d 859, 264 P.2d 944 (1953).

39. CURRIE ESSAYS, *supra* note 1, at 131 n.18.

40. *Id.* at 170. This seems particularly anomalous given that one supposed benefit of interest analysis is that it "invites legislative revision" if courts err. *Id.* at 604, 728. Currie was also opposed to legislatures adopting interstate treaties, on the ground that trading away the rights of state citizens was troubling. *Id.* at 121-22, 190 n.5. Apparently their role was to be limited to specifying the substantive policies involved, and letting the "natural law" of interest analysis take its course.

41. *Id.* at 171, 114.

course, the familiar Bealean metaphysics in a new garb — although the content of the *a priori* principles has changed, they are *a priori* principles nonetheless.

The second piece of evidence that betrays the value-laden posture of interest analysis is Currie's promotion of the concept of "interest" as a constitutional test. Borrowing from Supreme Court decisions that chanced to use the word "interest"[42] before it became a term of art, Currie argued that the Constitution would be offended if and only if a court applied the law of a state without an interest.[43] The significance of using the same term both to signify actual intent and to serve as a constitutional test is that the tests for actual intent and constitutionality are thereby equated. This jeopardizes the status of "interests" as actual intent, since to make actual intent dispositive of constitutionality would be to allow a state legislature to apply its law in its courts whenever it so desired. The legislature would need only to specify its intent clearly to create an "interest" and satisfy the Constitution. Indeed, since state courts are the final interpreters of state policies in our federal system,[44] a test of actual intent would leave no federal question and, *a fortiori*, no jurisdictional basis for Supreme Court review.[45]

But Currie clearly did not intend to repose such awesome discretion in the hands of state legislators when he described his constitutional test. He devoted a complete article to a discussion of the constitutional limits that interest analysis puts on legislative author-

42. Currie cites, for instance, Carroll v. Lanza, 349 U.S. 408 (1955); Watson v. Employers Liab. Assurance Corp., 348 U.S. 66 (1954); Pacific Employers Ins. Co. v. Industrial Accident Commn., 306 U.S. 493 (1939). CURRIE ESSAYS, *supra* note 1, at 145 n.64.

43. *See* CURRIE ESSAYS, *supra* note 1, at 188-282.

44. The Supreme Court has no authority to correct state court errors in state law, even when there is an alternate federal basis for review. Murdock v. City of Memphis, 87 U.S. (20 Wall.) 590, 635 (1875).

45. Another area in which interest analysis has served to confuse constitutional issues is full faith and credit, in which it is sometimes argued that a second state ought not to have to enforce the first state's judgments when to do so would be contrary to the second state's "interests." Magnolia Petroleum Co. v. Hunt, 320 U.S. 430, 419 (1943) (Douglas, J., dissenting); Brief of the Solicitor General's Office in Thomas v. Washington Gas Light Co., *cert. granted*, Docket No. 79-116, 48 U.S.L.W. 3356 (Nov. 26, 1979). Ordinarily, the second state's "interests" are irrelevant with regard to enforcement of sister-state judgments; Fauntleroy v. Lum, 210 U.S. 230 (1907) (no defense that gambling contract would have been held void as contrary to public policy); Milwaukee County v. White, 296 U.S. 268, 277 (1935) ("considerations of policy in the forum which would defeat a suit . . . are not involved"). *See also* Cheatam, *Res Judicata and Full Faith and Credit*, 44 COLUM. L. REV. 330, 336 (1944); R. CRAMTON, D. CURRIE & H. KAY, CONFLICT OF LAWS 681 (2d ed. 1975) (state may not invoke public policy as a defense to enforcement of judgments).

If this test were adopted, and if "interest" is understood as actual intent, then, as with choice-of-law problems there would be no federal question. It is possible that proponents of this test mean "interest" as Justice Stone did; see cases cited in note 42 *supra*. The confusion of terms is extremely unfortunate and use of the word might best be abandoned.

ity regarding choice of law.[46] Thus, either he was intending to create a second constitutional type of interest analysis — and if he had such an independent theory he never developed it in print[47] — or else "interests" do not involve *actual* intent at all.

Interest analysis must therefore be some species of constructive intent: a calculus of *a priori* principles that a court may fall back on when the legislature gives no guidance. Only if this conclusion is correct do interest analysts have a normative base from which to criticize conflicts statutes — for one's approach to constructive intent would probably be to choose what one finds to be the most coherent and convincing theory. This interpretation forces the interest analysts to concede that they reason from *a priori* assumptions, but at least it explains how they are able to draw inferences from a seemingly silent statute, like rabbits from a hat.

III. CONSTRUCTIVE INTENT

The law contains many maxims of statutory construction; penal laws, for instance, are supposed to be narrowly construed, as are statutes in derogation of the common law. If interest analysis is a plausible way of thinking about conflict-of-laws problems, it should be able to join those maxims as a basis for making inferences when no actual intent has been manifested. To avail itself of this opportunity, however, it must be convincing on its own merits, for it no longer has the legislative imprimatur. In this Section, I hope to demonstrate that the features that have made interest analysis unpalatable to many commentators — in particular, its unpredictability and parochialism — also leave it unconvincing as a species of constructive intent.

A. *Unpredictability*

Opponents of interest analysis have frequently objected that the theory allows unpredictable results:[48] that persons who act in reliance on one state's laws may be unfairly surprised by application of another's. One cause of this unpredictability is the assumption that

46. *See* Currie, *The Constitution and the Choice of Law: Governmental Interests and the Judicial Function*, 26 U. CHI. L. REV. 9, 43-44, 75-76 (1958), *reprinted in* CURRIE ESSAYS, *supra* note 1, at 232-33, 271.

47. His constitutional discussion follows and refers back to the nonconstitutional discussion, without offering a second definition of "interest." *But see* note 21 *supra*.

48. *See, e.g.*, Hill, *Governmental Interest and the Conflict of Laws — A Reply to Professor Currie*, 27 U. CHI. L. REV. 463, 463, 503-04 (1960) (interest analysis too "ad hoc"); Reese, *Choice of Law: Rules or Approach*, 57 CORNELL L. REV. 315 (1972) (rules allow predictability, an obvious benefit, but "approach" does not).

when a statute evidences both a regulatory policy and a compensatory or protective policy, either would suffice to justify application of forum law.[49] Thus, a statute that embodies a strong regulatory policy together with a compensatory policy may be applied on the ground that the plaintiff is a forum resident, a fact that the defendant might well have been unable to ascertain at the time of conduct. This is problematic, since in enacting a regulatory statute a legislature manifests a belief that most people will change their behavior in contemplation of the law. It seems unjust to apply such a law to persons who could have had no notice of the applicable standards, since the legislature could not have expected them to change their conduct to conform. The resulting unfairness can be demonstrated by two hypothetical situations.

Dram-shop acts are statutes that prohibit the sale of liquor to inebriates; some states have interpreted them also to authorize recovery of civil damages from the tavern owner if the inebriate negligently injures someone later.[50] It seems clear under interest analysis that dram-shop acts, so interpreted, embody both regulatory and compensatory policies. The compensatory policy seems implicit in the reasoning courts have used to justify imputing civil liability.[51] The regulatory policy is evident both because the statutes make sale of liquor to inebriates illegal and because presumably anyone, resident or nonresident, could sue a tavern owner who made such a sale within the state.[52]

If either of the two policies is a sufficient basis for applying a dram-shop act, then civil liability is appropriate whenever the sale occurs within the state *or* a state resident is injured. Interest analysis would thus seem to imply that if while on vacation in a state with no dram-shop act, a forum resident is hit by an auto careening out of a local bar's parking lot, then he may return home, sue, and recover from the tavern owner. There may be interest analysts who would

---

49. *See* text at notes 29-32 *supra*.

50. *See, e.g.*, the statutes involved in Bernhard v. Harrah's Club, 16 Cal. 3d 313, 546 P.2d 719, 128 Cal. Rptr. 215, *cert. denied*, 429 U.S. 859 (1976); Graham v. General U.S. Grant Post, 43 Ill. 2d 1, 248 N.E.2d 657 (1969).

51. *See* Vesley v. Sager, 5 Cal. 3d 153, 486 P.2d 151, 95 Cal. Rptr. 623 (1971). *But see* Hamon v. Carson City Nugget, Inc., 85 Nev. 99, 450 P.2d 358 (1969). The reasoning in Bernhard v. Harrah's Club, 16 Cal. 3d 313, 546 P.2d 719, 128 Cal. Rptr. 215, *cert. denied*, 429 U.S. 859 (1976), which relied upon the plaintiff's California residence, strongly suggests that the California dram shop act as extended by *Vesley* demonstrated an interest in resident plaintiffs.

52. *But see* Graham v. General U.S. Grant Post, 43 Ill. 2d 1, 248 N.E.2d 657 (1969).

Interest analysts cannot explain nonresident recovery under dram-shop acts by compensatory policies. Rather the explanation must be that it is desirable to discourage all sales of this sort, since the tavern owner had no way of knowing that a mere resident would be injured.

not flinch at this result, since the forum has an "interest" in seeing its plaintiff compensated. These theorists would not mind that the tavern owner was surprised by application of forum law, since state courts are not in business to take pity on dismayed nonresidents, but rather to do as their legislature bids. The legislative command, presumably, is "Thou shalt compensate forum residents."

A second hypothetical, however, indicates that residents, too, may be trapped by the interest analysts' logic. Assume that the forum legislature has learned that installing a special safety guard would reduce the number of accidents caused by power lawn mowers. It orders manufacturers to install the guard on all new mowers and provides that noncompliance shall be negligence per se. A resident manufacturer diligently complies when manufacturing lawn mowers to be sold within the state. The safety guard is expensive, however, and he decides not to put himself at a competitive disadvantage by installing them on mowers he manufactures for sale and use in other states. "After all," he reasons, "my state legislature would have no desire to regulate my sales in other jurisdictions. That's interstate commerce."[53] Will the forum nevertheless apply the negligence per se provision if the person injured in an out-of-state accident turns out, coincidentally, to be a resident? It is unlikely that an interest analyst scholar or a court would go so far. But if not, why not?

Traditional theory would have no problem with this case, since one of its goals was predictability, and a foreseeability test would preclude the law's application to situations where reliance upon another state's law was this likely. Interest analysts, however, are not noted for their fondness for foreseeability tests.[54] They would probably prefer something other than an across-the-board foreseeability test to explain why the supposed compensatory policy should not be honored. The interest analysts might, for instance, assert that when

53. *But cf.* Sligh v. Kirkwood, 237 U.S. 52 (1915) (statute penalizing sale of shipping of unripe citrus fruit valid as applied to interstate commerce, despite argument that state had no valid concern for health of persons in other states). *See also* Brown v. Market Dev., Inc., 41 Ohio Misc. 57, 322 N.E.2d 367 (1974). In some cases, a legislature may desire to prohibit any manufacture within the state, regardless of the place of sale. In the hypothetical example this seems unlikely and the manufacturer's inference seems reasonable. The rationale for *Brown* was that fraud within the state remained fraud regardless of the fact that it was directed against outsiders: The rationale in *Sligh* was that the state had a right to protect the reputation of its citrus products.

54. Currie, as noted earlier, did concede predictability to be a virtue, but did not find that it warranted sacrificing substantive interests. *See* note 34 *supra*. One commentator who has emphasized both analysis of interests and foreseeability is Professor Russell Weintraub. R. WEINTRAUB, COMMENTARY ON THE CONFLICT OF LAWS 208-10 (1971). For Leflar's choice-influencing considerations, see Leflar, *supra* note 13.

a statute has a significant regulatory purpose, then the statute is not designed to be triggered by domiciliary factors, except perhaps when the plaintiff's residence is known at the time of conduct. In other words, satisfaction of the regulatory policy would be a necessary precondition to assertion of the concurrent compensatory interest.

No doubt, this accommodation to foreseeability would be an improvement. It could, furthermore, be readily subsumed under either a "comparative impairment" or a "moderate and restrained interpretation" approach to interest analysis.[55] But interest analysts who find themselves sympathetic to such an accommodation should ask whether a more radical revision is not in order. In particular, this strategy suggests that there are dangers in merely spotting a compensatory interest in a case with a resident plaintiff and then applying forum law. A concern with foreseeability makes it important to ask whether the statute does not also embody a regulatory policy and, if it does, whether that policy also gives rise to an interest.

It is easy to think of situations where this question should have been asked. With married women's contract statutes, it seems reasonable to impute to the legislature an awareness that merchants would not enter into unenforceable contracts. It also seems reasonable to assume that the legislature deliberately intended to discourage merchants from the overreaching that such contracts were conclusively presumed to demonstrate. In fact, many of the statutes that interest analysts call protective or compensatory alter incentives in a way that suggests that the legislature was aware of, and probably approved of, their regulatory effects.[56] Treating married women's contract statutes as protective rather than regulatory seems arbitrary — they are both. Limiting concern to a statute's protective aspects is reminiscent of the Bealean system's arbitrary process of characterization, which Currie deplored.[57]

Moreover, recognizing that satisfaction of a regulatory purpose is a *necessary* condition to application of a law with both regulatory

55. *See* articles cited in notes 12-14 *supra*.

However, it would be preferable to accommodate foreseeability in the initial stages of interest determination rather than merely taking a sober second look once a conflict was identified. If the foreseeability test is delayed until this latter stage, it may never be brought to bear since the other state may not have an "interest" under Currie's definitions.

56. Spendthrift trust statutes may influence conduct, *but see* Lilienthal v. Kaufman, 239 Or. 1, 395 P.2d 543 (1964); so also may vicarious liability statutes for loan of automobiles, which also have the compensatory purpose of providing a solvent defendant, *see* Young v. Masci, 289 U.S. 253 (1933) (upholding application of New York vicarious liability law after foreseeability analysis); Levy v. Daniels' U-Drive Auto Renting Co., 108 Conn. 333, 337, 143 A. 163, 164 (1928) (vicarious liability statute provides incentive to person renting vehicle to rent only to competent and careful drivers).

57. CURRIE ESSAYS, *supra* note 1, at 133.

policies and compensatory or protective policies means that, for such statutes, domiciliary factors are completely irrelevant. The reason is that interest analysts seem to feel that the regulatory purpose is also a *sufficient* condition.[58] If this is true, then Currie's theory has made significant concessions to territorialism, which emphasized predictability and looked ordinarily to the places where the conduct at issue occurred while disregarding unpredictable domiciliary factors. Returning to the problem of dram-shop acts, and to an actual case decided according to Currie's principles, it is clear that treating the regulatory interest as both necessary and sufficient would require significant departures from the Currie school's analysis.

The case is *Bernhard v. Harrah's Club*.[59] In *Bernhard*, a Nevada casino owner sold liquor to a patron who then drove into California and collided with a Californian on a motorcycle. In using interest analysis to apply the California dram-shop act, the California Supreme Court emphasized the plaintiff's California residence, as well as the foreseeability of application of California law. The Court found that the California statute embodied a regulatory policy and that "[d]efendant by the course of its chosen commercial practice has put itself at the heart of California's regulatory interest, namely to prevent tavern keepers from selling alcoholic beverages to obviously intoxicated persons who are likely to act in California in the intoxicated state."[60]

Given such a finding, however, it is difficult to see the relevance of the plaintiff's California residence or even the California location of the accident. All of the facts that triggered the regulatory interest would also be present if the patron had happened to collide with a nonresident in California — or, for that matter, with a Nevada resident in Nevada. Perhaps the answer is that *both* regulatory and compensatory interests must be present before a court applies forum law: recovery only if a resident plaintiff is struck by an inebriate driving foreseeably through California. But this rule would prevent application of California law where the sale and accident occur there, but a nonresident is hurt. It is hard to believe that the interest analysts would wish that result, especially since the California stat-

58. *See* text at notes 29-32 *supra*.

59. 16 Cal. 3d 313, 546 P.2d 719, 128 Cal. Rptr. 215, *cert. denied*, 429 U.S. 859 (1976).

60. 16 Cal. 3d at 322, 546 P.2d at 725, 128 Cal. Rptr. at 221. One possible test to explain this result, which would match the rationale fairly well, while avoiding the problems outlined in the text, would be to ask whether there was a foreseeable injury within California, disregarding the actual residence of the plaintiff. This probably places too much emphasis on foreseeability and location of the accident, and too little on "compensatory" interests to please the interest analysts.

ute was presumably intended to regulate all sales inside the state by making such sales illegal.[61]

These examples illustrate some basic points about the value of predictability. First, predictability is crucial where the statute regulates conduct. If a state court believes that its state's statutes can be triggered by the location of conduct, it imbues the statute with a regulatory purpose. All unforeseeable applications should then be foreclosed. Second, if there is no way of determining in advance whether particular conduct will be covered by a statute, residents and nonresidents alike are put to a difficult choice between forgoing conduct that may later turn out to have been permissible and risking sanctions. This is the typical "vagueness" problem: a statute with uncertain boundaries discourages permissible conduct if people are aware of the possible penalties. And if they are unaware of the penalties because the possibility of applying the statute seems too remote, then application surprises individuals after the fact.[62] Third, it is simply inefficient to govern activity through the *in terrorem* effect of overly broad laws. Regulations that are applied on an unpredictable basis impose costs that cannot be justified by social necessity, since by hypothesis they discourage conduct needlessly. The additional cost of lawnmower safety shields illustrates this inefficiency. Surely all concerned are better off if there is a predictable basis for deciding which lawnmowers need shields: the forum obtains its safe product; people in other jurisdictions can buy cheaper lawnmowers; and manufacturers are not put to the cost of installing shields on all mowers.[63]

---

61. 11 Cal. 3d 574, 522 P.2d 666, 114 Cal. Rptr. 106 (1974). *See also* Johnson v. Spider Staging Corp., 87 Wash. 2d 577, 555 P.2d 997 (1976).

62. *See* Amsterdam, *The Void-for-Vagueness Doctrine in the Supreme Court*, 109 U. PA. L. REV. 67 (1960).

It is an inadequate response to say that in a mobile society like our own, application of any state's law is foreseeable. This position would require every individual in the United States to ascertain and conform his conduct to the most stringent of the fifty states' laws, regardless of whether there is any apparent connection between that state and the conduct. It would give any state the right to regulate any conduct it wished merely by announcing that it intended its law to apply. The problem is reminiscent of the fourth amendment test of "reasonable expectations of privacy" established in Katz v. United States, 389 U.S. 347 (1967). The test is not only one of actual expectations, since the government might condition expectations by announcing a far-reaching wiretap program, just as a state might declare an intent to apply its law to all cases tried in its courts. Instead, it includes normative elements of what an individual ought to have to expect. *See* Smith v. Maryland, 99 S. Ct. 2577, 2580 n.5 (1979). *See also* Hague v. Allstate Ins. Co., No. 47874 (Minn. Aug. 19, 1979), *cert. granted*, No. 79-983, 48 U.S.L.W. 3535 (1980) (finding that automobile insurance companies accept the risk that insured may be subject to the law of states other than where the policy was written); World-Wide Volkswagen Corp. v. Woodson, 48 U.S.L.W. 4079 (1980) (insufficient contacts for personal jurisdiction that automobile sold by defendants would predictably be driven into other states).

63. The forum with the plaintiff-favoring rule may be able to effectuate its policies without making concessions to other states, although this would still leave the problem of surprising

B. *Parochialism*

A second objection to the interest analysts' methodology is its parochialism, for interest analysis assumes that protective and compensatory policies are intended to benefit residents alone. The consequences of such an assumption are scarcely even-handed. For example, suppose the forum has an automobile guest statute — one requiring a passenger to demonstrate reckless or willful misconduct in order to recover from a host driver. Interest analysis holds that in a negligence action brought by a passenger who is a resident of the forum, a nonresident driver cannot claim the benefit of forum law and require a showing of reckless or willful misconduct. If, however, the nonresident had been the passenger and the resident had been driving, the forum would have an "interest" in applying its guest statute. The out-of-stater must pay if he is the driver but cannot collect if he is the passenger.

Limiting the reach of protective and compensatory statutes to precisely those cases where they benefit residents can lead to other obnoxious results. Suppose, for example, that state *A* has a statute of frauds provision: according to interest analysis, it was designed to protect the residents of *A*. Anderson, a merchant from state *A*, contracts with Becker from state *B*; the contract does not satisfy *A*'s statute of frauds, but under the law of *B* it would be binding. Suppose Anderson wants to know if the contract is valid in state *A*. An interest analyst could not give a straight answer. The contract could be either valid or invalid since *A*'s "interest" in having its statute of frauds applied depends upon which party is seeking to enforce the contract. If Anderson is suing Becker, then *A* has no interest in supplying a protective defense. If, on the other hand, Becker sues Anderson, state *A* will have an interest in asserting its statute of frauds on his behalf. State *A* has, in effect, given its residents the power to

forum defendants. Otherwise all jurisdictions might achieve their goals better by specifying the law governing each case. Furthermore, although Currie disparaged the search for uniformity of result as comparable to a psychological need to make all substantive laws identical, precisely the opposite is true. Diversity of laws is protected when one state cannot undercut another's rules of conduct. If unlimited forum-shopping were allowed, only states with plaintiff-favoring rules would be able to enforce their standards.

Currie pointed out that, even if uniformity were important, no state could unilaterally attain it. *See* CURRIE ESSAYS, *supra* note 1, at 178-79. A state might sacrifice its interests only to have other states selfishly pursue their own. This demonstrates an important function that documents such as the *Restatement* should, ideally, fulfill. By coordinating expectations through suggesting voluntary compliance with known standards, the *Restatement* could induce cooperation by making it more likely that other states will reciprocate. As Schelling has argued, where all parties stand to gain through cooperation, but have no mutually binding way to agree, it may be sufficient that a third party suggest a compromise which focuses the necessary coordination. *See* T. SCHELLING, THE STRATEGY OF CONFLICT (1960).

bind parties from out of state to a contract without being bound themselves.[64]

In other situations, faithful adherence to interest analysis would require a court to browse through the laws of the states involved in the controversy to pick the one that best served the resident party. Assume that Anderson is injured by a toy designed and manufactured by Billings in state *B*. Anderson thinks Billings was negligent in designing the product. An *A* statute provides tort compensation for damages from negligent manufacture, which has been interpreted to include defective design. Does *A* have an interest in having its law applied? As in the previous example, the answer must be "it depends." If *B* law excludes recovery for defects in design, then *A* has an interest in securing compensation for Anderson under its own law, for *A*'s law appears to have a compensatory purpose that makes it applicable to help Anderson. But if *B* is a strict liability state with no exclusion for design defects, *A*'s interest would vanish since it is no longer to Anderson's advantage that *A* law apply.[65] In comparison to strict liability, a negligence system appears designed to protect manufacturers, and in this case the manufacturer is from out of state. "Interest" under the Currie approach amounts to an "interest" in getting the best deal possible for the resident party by choosing the most favorable law.[66]

The difficulty with Currie's approach is not its reference to domiciliary factors. If a state declared that its products liability law ap-

64. This bears a superficial resemblance to the Uniform Commercial Code statute-of-frauds provision, which makes a contract enforceable only against the party who signed the writing. That rule, however, has an obvious evidentiary explanation.

65. Or at least some courts have so reasoned when forced to choose between forum negligence law and a strict liability law of the state of manufacture. *See, e.g.*, Foster v. Day & Zimmerman, 502 F.2d 867 (8th Cir. 1974).

66. Selective browsing through the statute books and case reports, to compile the most advantageous package for the resident party, is implausible given the factual assumptions underlying protective statutes. Legislatures enact guest statutes to prevent fraudulent claims against defendant drivers and their insurers. These statutes codify the legislative determination that host/guest claims are so likely to be fabricated that the forum should not honor them without proof of gross negligence. Currie assumed that the legislature would want a guest statute to benefit resident drivers only; if the driver was from a state without a guest statute, Currie would allow a resident plaintiff to recover. *See* text at note 30 *supra*. But it is not reasonable to believe that claims against nonresident drivers are less likely to be fabricated than claims against resident drivers. Interest analysis thus seems to impute to the guest statute state's legislature the rather cynical position that its courts should enforce fraudulent claims when the defendant is a nonresident. Since similar legislative determinations underlie other protective statutes (married women's laws or the statute of frauds, for instance), sensitive analysis of legislative history might lead courts to apply such statutes in all cases involving a forum cause of action, not just those with resident defendants. This solution would be akin to the traditional one of characterizing the issue as procedural. In the alternative, a court might limit application of the forum's guest statute out of some sentiment, such as comity, unrelated to what the court perceived as the substantively appropriate result.

plied to all injured residents, the problem outlined above would be avoided. Either there would be an interest or there would not, and it would not depend upon comparison with other states' laws. But such a statute would not always benefit forum residents. It would benefit them in some cases and harm them in others. Thus, such a rational statute is irreconcilable with the superficially plausible syllogism that seems to underlie Currie's approach: if a statute is designed to benefit forum residents, it should be applied only when a resident will benefit.

Why should a court accept the suggestion that protective and compensatory policies should be applied only when a forum resident will benefit? The blatant parochialism evidenced by these examples surely imposes costs. It jeopardizes a principle essential to smooth functioning of federal systems: treating nonresidents as fairly as residents.[67] It also raises difficult problems of whether an individual ought to be able to get a change of law by deliberately acquiring a

---

67. Some courts have justifiably balked at carrying this parochialism to its ultimate conclusion. *See, e.g.*, Frummer v. Hilton Hotels, Intl., Inc., 19 N.Y.2d 533, 227 N.E.2d 851, 281 N.Y.S.2d 41, *cert. denied*, 389 U.S. 923 (1967), where a New York court rejected an argument that England had no interest in applying its comparative negligence rule merely because the plaintiff was from New York and the defendant from England. While denying that English law served a regulatory purpose, the *Frummer* court nevertheless gave the New Yorker the benefit of the more lenient standard of recovery:

> With regard to the compensatory policy of the comparative negligence statute, it may be contended that, since the plaintiff is a New York resident, England might well prefer New York law, which would benefit its domiciliary in this case. But it is difficult to conceive of England having such a parochial viewpoint. The statute by its language is not limited to any particular class of plaintiffs.

Concededly, the New York court may have been influenced in its decision to apply English law broadly by the New York residence of the beneficiary even though it purported to be analyzing English interests.

In McCrossin v. Hicks Chevrolet, Inc., 248 A.2d 917 (D.C. Ct. App. 1969), however, a District of Columbia court rejected a similar argument calling for application of Maryland's privity-of-contract doctrine to a Maryland resident. "The rule in the District," the court explained, "dispensing with the requirements of privity in implied warranty cases, is for the benefit and protection of all who buy in the District, not for residents of the District alone." 248 A.2d at 921. *Cf.* Gravina v. Brunswick Corp., 338 F. Supp. 1 (D.R.I. 1972) (where the court found the interests of the state of plaintiff's residence and the state of defendant's principal place of business equivalent and therefore applied the "better" rule of law). The obvious problem with the *Frummer* strategy is that if there is an interest when the plaintiff is a resident, but we prefer not to treat nonresidents differently, then the law is applicable to all cases.

Another way of avoiding limiting compensatory statutes is by discovering a simultaneous regulatory interest. *See, e.g.*, Hurtado v. Superior Court, 11 Cal. 3d 574, 522 P.2d 666, 114 Cal. Rptr. 106 (1974), in which a resident of Zacatecas, Mexico, was killed in an automobile accident in California by a California resident. The California Supreme Court held that California had an interest in applying its unlimited recovery rules, because unlimited damages deterred negligent driving:

> It is manifest that one of the primary purposes of a state in creating a cause of action in the heirs for the wrongful death of the decedent is to deter the kind of conduct within its borders which wrongfully takes life. . . . It is also abundantly clear that a cause of action for wrongful death without any limitation as to the amount of recoverable damages strengthens the deterrent aspect of the civil sanction . . . . Therefore when the defendant is a resident of California and the tortious conduct giving rise to the wrongful death action

new domicile after the transaction in question occurs.[68] Moreover, these costs might easily be avoided through a more comprehensive investigation of legislative intent, one that projects into the legislative mind some sensitivity to system-coordinating values. There are four possible justifications for the pro-resident bias of interest analysis: an analogy to welfare, protection of state resources, the nonresident's consent to his own state's laws, and pure favoritism.

It has been urged that restricting the benefits of forum law to residents is just like restricting the payment of welfare payments to residents. One author claims, "[A] state is interested in having its tort law applied to implement the compensatory policy reflected in that law in the same manner as it would be interested in applying its social insurance law."[69] This analogy fails, however, because tort compensation is not state largesse; it is paid by private individuals.[70] The funds for welfare, medical benefits, and unemployment insurance are amassed from state residents, and only those who could be required to contribute are eligible to make claims on the available money. Similarly, low tuition at state universities has been limited to residents because only residents support state universities through

---

occurs here, California's deterrent policy of full compensation is clearly advanced by application of its own law.

11 Cal. 3d at 583-84, 522 P.2d at 672, 114 Cal. Rptr. at 112 (citations omitted). While this reasoning has some appeal, the problems arising when concurrent regulatory interests are found are discussed in the text at notes 48-63 *supra*.

Confusion prevailed in Labree v. Major, 111 R.I. 657, 306 A.2d 808 (1973), which applied Rhode Island negligence law despite the guest statute of the state where the accident occurred. The court found that Rhode Island had an interest in holding its citizens to its own standard of care, and that there was no problem of unfair surprise because "no driver alters his manner of driving when he crosses into a state which holds him to a lesser degree of care towards his passenger." 111 R.I. at 671, 306 A.2d at 817. The court should have been consistent: negligence law either influences behavior, or it does not.

68. After-acquired domicile is a difficult problem for Currie's theory, and one which is likely to become more frequent. *See, e.g.*, Hague v. Allstate Ins. Co., *cert. granted*, No. 79-938, 48 U.S.L.W. 3535 (Feb. 19, 1980); *cf.* Rush v. Savchuk, 100 S. Ct. 580 (1980) (declaring unconstitutional Minnesota's assertion of quasi in rem jurisdiction over defendant; plaintiff moved to Minnesota after the accident that prompted the suit).

Currie argued that a state should be able to limit application in cases of after-acquired domicile. *See* CURRIE ESSAYS, *supra* note 1, at 620-21, 644. His explanation based upon "vested rights" seems peculiar in a theory decrying the metaphysics of the *First Restatement*.

An interesting question is the likely effect of the durational residency requirement cases on after-acquired domicile should Currie's residency test be universally explained as social welfare. Shapiro v. Thompson, 394 U.S. 618 (1969), held that discouraging migration into the state through waiting periods for welfare eligibility was an impermissible restriction on the right to travel. If application of state tort law is comparable to social insurance, then forum shopping through change of domicile might be equally protected in the conflicts setting.

69. Sedler, *supra* note 32, at 192.

70. *Cf.* Magnolia Petroleum Co. v. Hunt, 320 U.S. 430, 442 (1943) (full faith and credit case, "no constitutional question would be presented if Louisiana chose to be generous to the employee out of the general funds in its Treasury").

taxes.[71] In contrast, when an interest analyst finds a compensatory policy in a multistate case, only in-staters are entitled to collect and only out-of-staters are required to pay. The result is a windfall to residents involved in multistate accidents: a benefit without a corresponding burden.[72]

In a related vein, Currie justified his parochial view of compensatory policies by suggesting that they are enacted to minimize the drain on state welfare funds.[73] Presumably, nonresidents would never drain such funds.[74] This rationale exemplifies a problem with Currie's methodology that interest analysts have never adequately faced. Currie seems to have been suggesting that the plaintiff's residence could be used as a proxy for other legislative concerns, such as the likelihood that the plaintiff would be thrown back upon public assistance or would default on local medical bills, thus harming the interests of local creditors. The domiciliary factor would, under this rationale, not be important in and of itself. But obviously, there will be some cases in which the plaintiff is wealthy enough that eventual recourse to welfare is unlikely. Should one nevertheless treat residence as conclusive? Or should one look beyond the plaintiff's residence to the presence or absence of these true concerns?

Currie vacillated on this issue,[75] but appeared to conclude that

71. A state university today is an establishment with capital costs of many millions of dollars of investment. Its annual operating costs likewise may run into the millions. Parents and other taxpayers willingly carry this heavy burden because they believe in the values of higher education. It is not narrow provincialism for the State to think that each State should carry its own educational burdens. Until we redefine our system of government — as we are free to do by constitutionally prescribed means — the States may restrict subsidized education to their own residents.

Vlandis v. Kline, 412 U.S. 441, 459-60 (1973) (Burger and Rehnquist, JJ., dissenting). Since the majority opinion invalidated a presumption regarding out-of-state residency, it would, *a fortiori*, have been sympathetic to the argument expressed in the text.

72. In some cases, if application of forum law is predictable, then residents bear a burden which makes the benefit fair. For example, in the married women's contract cases the statute imposes a disability as well as a benefit, since married women will be unable to enter into such contracts even if they want to. There is a benefit without a burden if and only if the merchant is unable to distinguish which women are residents, and thus deals with all women.

73. CURRIE ESSAYS, *supra* note 1, at 61. Currie, of course, realized that not every plaintiff was on the verge of welfare, but never reconciled that fact with his asserted need for precision. Currie, *supra* note 2, at 760.

74. However, a single accident's effect on the size of a welfare budget is insignificant. Or, at least, so the interest analysts have responded to arguments regarding the increased insurance costs of compensatory policies; they claim that the price of a single catastrophic accident is absorbed by the loss-spending mechanism, not passed on. CURRIE ESSAYS, *supra* note 1, at 724-25, 725 n.118 (citing Morris, *Enterprise Liability and the Actuarial Process — The Insignificance of Foresight*, 70 YALE L.J. 544, 565 (1961)); *see* Ehrenzweig, *Guest Statutes in the Conflict of Laws — Towards a Theory of Enterprise Liability Under "Foreseeable and Insurance Laws"* (pt. 1), 69 YALE L.J. 595, 603 (1960).

75. At certain points he seemed to realize that complete precision was unattainable and that it was not desirable to look behind the named variable even though it might be a fiction. CURRIE ESSAYS, *supra* note 1, at 145; Currie, *supra* note 2, at 760. But in his analysis of cases

one should go beyond the mere fact of residence to determine whether the crucial variables support a state interest. This is the only way to account for his attitude toward liability insurance. In analyzing what would have happened if *Grant v. McAuliffe* had been brought in Arizona, Currie argued that the Arizona interest in protecting the tortfeasor's estate "evaporates completely" if the tortfeasor is fully insured.[76] If the estate would not bear the loss, a court would subvert no Arizona interest whatsoever by applying the California survival statute.[77] Thus, Currie apparently thought that even if the proxy seems to require application of a law (the tortfeasor was from Arizona, suggesting that we apply the Arizona law), we should look behind it to determine whether the crucial variables also point to that law.

This is surely nothing like ordinary statutory construction. In purely domestic cases, the Arizona courts would not look to the presence of insurance to determine whether the Arizona abatement law should apply. While such an inquiry would be entirely consistent with Currie's reasoning, it is not permissible under any currently held theory of domestic interpretation of statutes.[78] In fact, the existence of insurance is supposed to be kept as much out of the process of adjudication as can be arranged.

More can be gleaned from this hypothetical variation of *Grant* than the simple observation that Currie was willing to consider factors that he would have thought illegitimate in a domestic case. We should also notice exactly what triggered this kind of illegitimate inquiry. What facts made it appropriate for Currie to take insurance into account in conflict cases but not in purely domestic cases? The

---

he commonly cited variables not specified in the statute, ones which would presumably not be important in domestic cases. His treatment of Grant v. McAuliffe, 41 Cal. 2d 859, 264 P.2d 944 (1953), discussed in text at note 22 *supra*, is one example. *See also* his evaluation of Home Ins. Co. v. Dick, 281 U.S. 397 (1930), *discussed in* CURRIE ESSAYS, *supra* note 1, at 232-33 (Texas party was only an assignee of original contracting party and thus not entitled to application of Texas law), and of Bradford Elec. Light Co. v. Clapper, 51 F.2d 992 (1st Cir. 1931), *discussed in* CURRIE ESSAYS, *supra* note 1, at 210-13 (deceased left no dependents, for whose benefit wrongful death act had been intended).

If interest analysis relies on these "substantive" factors that would not be considered relevant in domestic disputes, it runs into the problems outlined in the text. Even where it relies upon substantive variables that *are* relevant in domestic cases, it causes courts serious difficulties when alluding to them as justification for applying another state's law. These are spelled out in the text at notes 88-97 *infra*.

76. CURRIE ESSAYS, *supra* note 1, at 159-60.

77. Currie qualified this view only by conceding that the Arizona statute might have been designed to protect the insurance industry. In this unlikely event, he thought there might be an Arizona interest in cases involving an Arizona insurance company. *Id.* at 160.

78. *But see* Jess v. Herrmann, — Cal. 3d —, 604 P.2d 208, 161 Cal. Rptr. 87 (1979) (mandatory set-off rule not applicable in comparative fault setting where parties are insured).

only multistate connecting factor that Currie thought an Arizona court should find relevant was the tortfeasor's residence. Yet that could not have been the triggering factor, for in both the purely domestic case and in Currie's hypothetical the tortfeasor was from Arizona. No, *other* multistate elements in the case must have led Currie to perceive the dispute as a conflicts case and thus to apply this unusual mode of reasoning. In particular, Currie must have perceived this variation of *Grant* (with its Arizona tortfeasor carrying Arizona insurance) as a conflicts case because the plaintiff was a nonresident plaintiff, the accident took place out of the state, or something of that sort. Yet such elements are supposed to be formally irrelevant within Currie's theory.

It is easy enough for present day interest analysts to avoid such an embarrassing result by denying that it is ever appropriate to look behind the fact of residence to determine whether there are local creditors, whether the defendant was insured, or whether either the plaintiff or the defendant is likely to end his days on welfare.[79] But if interest analysis does not look behind the domiciliary factor to these supposedly crucial variables, then it falls prey to the same objections Currie made to the Bealean system. It treats one crude geographical factor as talismanic.

In effect, the interest analysts have made three incompatible claims for their theory:

1) The legislative policy responsible for restricting the benefit of protective and compensatory laws to residents is a policy of avoiding dissipation of state welfare resources;

2) Interest analysis, unlike Bealean theory, allows precise case-by-case enforcement of legislative policies; and

3) Interest analysis is just like ordinary statutory interpretation in a purely domestic setting.

As we have seen, these three claims cannot all be correct. Currie tried to remain faithful to the first two in his discussion of *Grant* but was left with a clear contradiction of the third. Present day analysts who cling to the first and third claims must abandon the key second

79. The Supreme Court has indicated, in support of this position, that excessive particularization is uncalled for. *See* Carrol v. Lanza, 349 U.S. 408, 413 (1955). Currie realized the Court's view, but never took it into account. *See* CURRIE ESSAYS, *supra* note 1, at 145 n.64. *See also* Barret v. Foster Grant Co., 450 F.2d 1146, 1153 (1st Cir. 1971):

> Plaintiff argues that New Hampshire has a "strong legislative policy" at stake in this case in that the New Hampshire legislature has expressed an intention that its workmen's compensation act not bar suits against tortious third parties. . . . Plaintiff's further assertion that New Hampshire law should control "because plaintiff was the sole support of five minor children" is not only a jury argument, but an improper one at that. We cannot believe that a rule of conflict of laws is to depend upon the affluence, vel non, of the parties.

claim. The best alternative is to renounce the first claim and to search for another justification for interest analysis as a species of constructive intent.[80]

A third defense of parochialism might be that restricting benefits to residents is not unfair since a nonresident should not complain of being held to his own state's law.[81] Thus, when the state of residence of a defendant-driver decides not to enact a guest statute, it indicates a willingness to have its residents pay such claims. This justification raises issues of reciprocity. The nonresident is held to his state's law when it imposes a burden, but cannot recover under that law when he attempts to reap its benefits in a suit against a forum resident. It makes more sense to view the other legislature's decision not to enact a guest statute as a compromise — a regulation of the legal relationship between drivers and passengers. The extra burdens a guest statute imposes on plaintiffs are justified by corresponding advantages to defendants and to the insurance-buying public; a given individual may as easily end up on the plus side as on the minus. The legislature of a state without a guest statute probably did not intend to burden its residents when they drive without allowing them benefits when they ride along.

Interest analysis projects into multistate cases the other legislature's willingness to have its residents pay claims but fails to consider its own demonstrated willingness to have the injured guest go uncompensated. If interest analysis respected such a legitimate "noncompensatory" policy, it would apply the forum guest statute and deny recovery. Instead, the interest analysts would have the forum court make a very curious sort of concession to other states: "Yes, we realize that you prefer to see your rule of decision applied. You

80. These three claims might, in fact, all be incorrect. Much tort law could not have been designed to protect the welfare rolls since it predated welfare legislation. Rather it reflected a sense of who ought to bear the cost of particular accidents. Whether one defines "ought" in terms of ethics or economics, *compare* R. POSNER, ECONOMIC ANALYSIS OF LAW (2d ed. 1972) ("ought" in terms of economics), *with* R. DWORKIN, TAKING RIGHTS SERIOUSLY (1977) ("ought" in relation to the general welfare), plaintiff's residence attains no particular relevance as it might with a welfare rationale. In addition, "precision" is not pursued singlemindedly even in purely domestic cases. The very act of codification — of selecting one group of factors out of a large variety of possible relevant ones — entails some sacrifice of precision. *See* Powers, *Formalism and Non-formalism in Choice of Law Methodology*, 52 WASH. L. REV. 27 (1976). *See generally* Kennedy, *Form and Substance in Private Law Adjudication*, 89 HARV. L. REV. 1685 (1976). In domestic cases this loss of precision is justified in part by increased predictability and ease of administration. Thus, to the extent that interest analysis downgrades these values, it ceases to resemble ordinary methods of interpretation. *See* Twerski & Mayer, *Toward a Pragmatic Solution of Choice of Law Problems — At the Interface of Substance and Procedure*, 74 NW. U. L. REV. 781, 790 (1979) (in domestic case, individualized justice subordinated).

81. CURRIE ESSAYS, *supra* note 1, at 720.

think it the best way to decide cases. Our compromise will be to apply the rule of decision you find appropriate in some, but not all, cases: exactly those cases in which your rule would work to the advantage of a resident of our state." This is obviously not much of a concession. As a justification for the inherent inequity in selectively deferring to the laws of a nonresident's home state it is disingenuous at best.

A final justification for the interest analysts' belief that legislatures are or should be parochial might be that such legislatures are predisposed to line the pockets of their constituents. From a purely abstract standpoint, such a predisposition is at least coherent. Perhaps it is even plausible. It is, however, an impermissible basis for a conflict-of-laws theory. In commerce clause cases, the Supreme Court has consistently held naked preference for local commercial enterprise to be invidious. For example, in *Baldwin v. Seelig*[82] the Court invalidated a New York statute prohibiting the sale of milk for less than a fixed minimum price, even if the milk was originally purchased outside the state. The statute, the Court held, could not be justified as an economic measure designed to protect local farmers from competition, since such favoritism is impermissible.[83]

A conflicts methodology based only on favoritism for local residents would surely run counter to the established principles of the American federal system.[84] It seems directly contrary to the spirit of the privileges and immunities clause and the equal protection

82. 294 U.S. 511 (1935). *See generally* Simson, *State Autonomy in Choice of Law: A Suggested Approach*, 52 S. CAL. L. REV. 61 (1978); Simson, *Discrimination Against Nonresidents and the Privileges and Immunities Clause of Article IV*, 128 U. PA. L. REV. 379 (1979); Note, *Unconstitutional Discrimination in Choice of Law*, 77 COLUM. L. REV. 272 (1977). The extent to which this rationale can rely upon political underrepresentation is in doubt after Holt Civic Club v. City of Tuscaloosa, 439 U.S. 60 (1978) (individual residents of outlying unincorporated community do not have constitutionally guaranteed right to vote in municipal elections, despite municipality's power to regulate).

83. More recent cases have reaffirmed the *Baldwin* result. *See* Dean Milk Co. v. City of Madison, 340 U.S. 349 (1951); Polar Ice Cream & Creamery Co. v. Andrews, 375 U.S. 361 (1964) (principles of *Baldwin* "as sound today as they were when announced").

In *Baldwin*, New York had attempted to justify the statute as a health measure, arguing that the dairy farmers' health was endangered if they could not make a living. This argument seems curiously to anticipate the "social welfare" justification of interest analysis discussed immediately above. *See* text at notes 73-74 *supra*. Yet the Court rejected the argument:

> Economic welfare is always related to health . . . . Let such an exception be admitted, and all that a state will have to do in times of stress and strain is to say that its farmers and merchants and workmen must be protected against competition from without, lest they go upon the poor relief lists or perish altogether . . . . The Constitution was framed under the dominion of a political philosophy less parochial in range.

294 U.S. at 523 (1934). *See also* Simson, *State Autonomy*, *supra* note 82.

84. For instance, prejudice against out-of-staters was an original motivation for the establishment of diversity jurisdiction. *See* C. WRIGHT, FEDERAL COURTS 85 (3d ed. 1973).

clause.[85] The point is not that any statute that incidentally favors local residents (or any conflict-of-laws method that does likewise) is unconstitutional. The point is that the increased advantages for state residents at the expense of outsiders cannot serve as a justification. There must be some other legitimate rationale for the rule.[86] The interest analysts have yet to present one.[87]

IV. Are Substantive Policies Enough?

Underlying the analysis of governmental interests is the assumption that conflict-of-laws reasoning is no different from ordinary substantive interpretation of statutes. In both cases, the job is allegedly to determine whether the policies behind the statute make the statutory remedy appropriate in the particular case. Therefore, it makes no sense to say that a law "applies" apart from the sense that its substantive policies "apply."[88] In this Section, I will argue that there are two very different meanings to the word "apply," and that they cannot be equated, even if one is committed to Currie's theory. One is the domestic meaning, asking whether the statute's policies are satisfied; the other is the conflicts meaning, asking whether the rule of decision supplied by the statute is pertinent. By analyzing examples taken from the section on parochialism, I hope to show that domestic interpretation and conflicts interpretation are different enterprises altogether.

The first example is based upon the guest statute cases. Currie argued that a state with a guest statute has an interest in applying that statute only in suits against a resident defendant. But what hap-

85. *See* Simson, *State Autonomy, supra* note 82; Simson, *Discrimination, supra* note 82. Currie demonstrated some awareness of this problem. *See, e.g.*, Currie Essays, *supra* note 1, at 619. *See also* note 21 *supra*.

86. Many statutes provide different substantive results depending on the fact of residence. *See* Simson, *State Autonomy, supra* note 82; Simson, *Discrimination, supra* note 82. These, perhaps, provide the strongest support for the suggestion that legislatures would treat residents more favorably than nonresidents when choosing whether their law should apply. However, an established principle of statutory interpretation is to avoid constructions that exacerbate constitutional infirmities. If courts interpret state legislation on the theory that it is designed to benefit locals at the expense of out-of-staters, they are choosing, instead, the most provocative interpretation.

87. Perhaps at the root of the restriction of benefits to state residents is the fact that when it enacted protective or compensatory legislation, the legislature "had in mind" cases where a resident would benefit. The legislator voting for a guest statute, for example, visualizes cases with a resident defendant. However, this mental picture undoubtedly also featured a resident *plaintiff*— as well as an accident which occurred within the state. A too literal fidelity to what the legislature "had in mind" ultimately leads to the conclusion that forum law should not apply in cases with any multistate elements.

88. Currie consistently argued that interest analysis was identical to substantive policy analysis of whether the law applied. *See* Currie Essays, *supra* note 1, at 183; Currie, *supra* note 2, at 757.

pens, for an interest analyst, if the state repeals its guest statute? The repeal is undoubtedly "for the benefit" of state residents, helping resident guests to be better compensated for their injuries. Would an interest analyst therefore limit the repeal's application to cases where a resident thereby benefits? That would leave the guest statute standing when a nonresident guest sues a resident driver, and surely such a result would be absurd. Members of the Currie school would agree that the territorial reach of the repeal must be identical to the territorial reach of the original statute. But if the scope of the guest statute is defined in terms of benefiting residents, the repeal must perversely work to the residents' disadvantage.[89]

More generally, interest analysis shifts the geographical reach of forum law as substantive law is first enacted and then repealed. The boundaries of forum law shift in ways that the Currie school would find hard to explain in terms of substantive policies alone. These fluctuations may be illustrated with a matrix. Since Currie felt that the domiciles of the two parties were the only relevant features in guest statute cases, only a two-by-two matrix is required.[90] In the matrix below, which represents all two-party cases that might be brought in the forum's courts, the upper left rectangle represents the purely domestic cases; the lower right rectangle the purely foreign cases; the upper right rectangle the cases where the defendant is a resident and the plaintiff a nonresident; and the lower left rectangle the cases where the plaintiff is a resident and the defendant a nonresident.

		Residence of Plaintiff	
		resident	nonresident
Residence of Defendant	resident	domestic cases	resident D nonresident P
	nonresident	nonresident D resident P	foreign cases

DIAGRAM A

89. A similar argument might be made that if a statute creates a new defense for an old cause of action, it probably intends that defense to apply to all cases involving the original cause of action, although the conclusion is less obvious than in the repeal context. The idea would be that it "repeals" the statute in a substantively specified group of cases, not just where the resident would benefit by application of the defense. This argument could be used regarding guest statutes.

90. While Currie also took forum into account in his diagrams depicting married women's contracts, these matrices reflect only cases in a particular forum.

For an interest analyst, the cases in the left half of the matrix will trigger any forum interest in advancing a compensatory policy, and those in the upper half will trigger any interest in advancing a protective policy. The domestic cases are covered whether compensatory or protective policies are involved, and the foreign cases are not. These domestic and foreign cases pose no conflicts issues.

Interests Generated

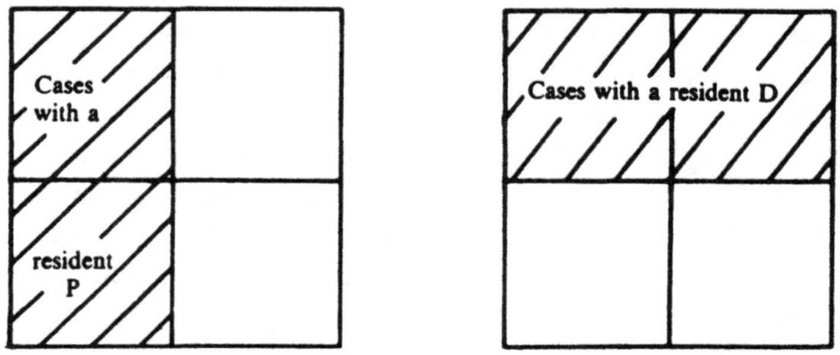

Compensatory Policy

Protective Policy

DIAGRAM B

Before a state enacts a guest statute, its negligence laws presumably promote a compensatory policy. Thus, over the period of time during which its substantive policies change, the forum law's intended scope fluctuates in the following manner:

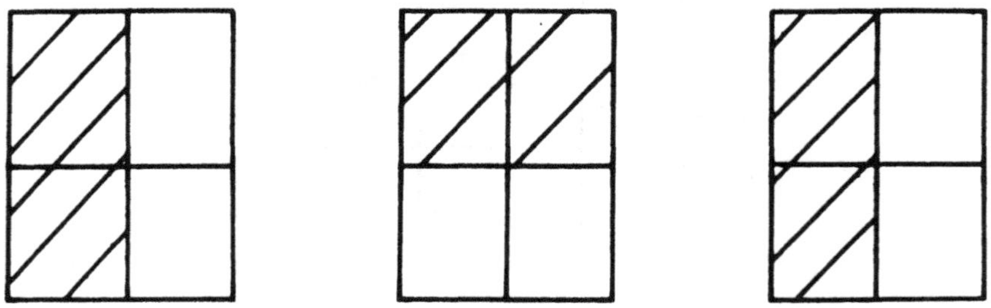

before enactment

during

after repeal

DIAGRAM C

We have already seen one problem with this conception of interests: a repeal *must* apply to all cases previously covered by the statute, including those cases in the upper right corner of the matrix. It is entirely reasonable to say that the repeal has both conflicts and substantive implications for the cases in the lower left corner, but only conflicts implications for those in the upper right corner. The repeal could be said to entail a *lack of concern* with this last group of cases, referring the forum court to the laws of other concerned jurisdictions.

But this intent to disavow any interest in that group of cases cannot be explained in terms of benefiting forum residents, for it probably does not have that effect. Indeed, it cannot be explained as a substantive policy at all, for the legislature has no substantive wish for those cases. Rather, it resembles a traditional choice-of-law rule — an "odd creature" in Currie's words "which never tells us what the result will be but only where to find the result."[91] Thus, in passing laws, a legislature necessarily makes conflicts decisions, *even under the Currie analysis*. Some laws have implications for the territorial reach of forum law that cannot be explained in substantive terms.

That legislatures have — indeed, must have — such unsubstantive intent at times does not necessarily jeopardize any particular conclusions Currie might have reached about when a forum should apply its own law; rather, in this instance, it derives from them. But while this particular nonsubstantive intent is not threatening, generalized searching for nonsubstantive intentions regarding a statute's scope might lead a court to different conclusions than Currie's methodology would dictate. A court might, for instance, discern a legislative intent that the law of the place of wrong should govern, therefore refusing to apply forum law even though interest analysis would deem the law's substantive policies satisfied. Or it might use forum law to settle cases that did not fulfill Currie's interpretation of the statute's substantive policy. Currie found this last possibility absurd, insisting that a law "applied" if and only if the substantive policies underlying it applied.[92]

Currie was demonstrably mistaken on this point. His attempts to treat geographical connecting factors in exactly the same way that ordinary domestic factors are treated were doomed to failure. Apparently, the idea was that for any particular statute, some geographical connecting factors would be relevant and some would not, just as some facts that might be found in local cases are relevant and

91. CURRIE ESSAYS, *supra* note 1, at 170. Compare also his remark that "a choice-of-law rule is an empty and bloodless thing. Actually, instead of declaring an overriding public policy, it proclaims the state's indifference to the result of the litigation." *Id.* at 53.

92. For instance, he derided the public policy exception because it provided "a basis for not applying the 'applicable' law." CURRIE ESSAYS, *supra* note 1, at 181, 212, 736.

some are not. In both domestic and conflicts cases, the court's job is supposedly to identify the necessary preconditions for the result specified in the statute. In a domestic guest-statute case, a court might have to decide whether it was relevant that compensation was offered and thus whether failure to pay was a prerequisite for application of the guest statute.[93] Similarly, in a multistate case, Currie would have the court consult the underlying policies to determine whether it was relevant that the accident occurred in another state. In Currie's view, the substantive and conflicts prerequisites for using the guest statute to require a showing of reckless misconduct were not qualitatively different.

The fallacy in this idea can be illustrated by classifying cases according to three criteria: a) whether the relevant substantive preconditions for domestic law are satisfied, b) whether the supposedly relevant conflicts preconditions for domestic law are satisfied, and c) whether there are any other elements that link the case with a foreign state but that Currie would have declared irrelevant. Consider a case where the substantive criteria *are* satisfied, the conflicts criteria are *not* satisfied, and there are no other multistate connecting factors in the case. Does the forum legislature intend its law to apply?

It seems the interest analysts would say that forum law should not apply. The crucial conflicts test has not been met. The fact that all other connecting factors point toward domestic law is by hypothesis irrelevant. Interest analysts would presumably also say that this case is indistinguishable from one where the substantive test is satisfied, the conflicts test is not satisfied, and all the "irrelevant" connecting factors point toward the other state's law. The reason is precisely that other connecting factors are supposed to be irrelevant. To express this point diagramatically, the argument is that cases (1) and (2) are equivalent:

substantive test	conflicts test	irrelevant connecting factors
(1) satisfied	foreign	all foreign
(2) satisfied	foreign	all domestic

But the interest analysts claim that conflicts preconditions are just like substantive preconditions. Since there is no difference between the two sorts of variables, a failure to satisfy one should have the same result as a failure to satisfy the other.[94] Therefore, cases (2)

93. *See, e.g.*, W. Prosser, Handbook of the Law of Torts 382-85 (4th ed. 1971).

94. *See, e.g.*, Currie's treatment of Bradford Elec. Light Co. v. Clapper, 286 U.S. 145

and (3) are identical:

substantive test	conflicts test	irrelevant connecting factors
(2) satisfied	foreign	all domestic
(3) not satisfied	domestic	all domestic

However, if (1) and (2) are identical, and (2) and (3) are identical, then so are (1) and (3). Yet (1) is a foreign case, with no domestic aspects at all, and (3) is a domestic case, with no multistate elements. Surely, if there is anything that all conflict-of-laws theorists would agree upon, it is that the legislature intends its law to apply to (3) and not to (1).[95]

The problem that leads to this paradox is the assumption that conflicts preconditions are just like substantive preconditions, that is, that case (2) is identical to case (3). This assumption leads the interest analysts to conclude that a case's failure to meet a statute's substantive preconditions will keep the state from finding an interest, presumably even if the "crucial" conflicts variable points toward forum law. In cases with other multistate features, that conclusion is difficult to refute since we have no clear evidence about legislative intent; but in a purely domestic case, it is clearly false. Moreover, the only factors that the interest analysts might employ to distinguish between those two classes of cases are multistate features that are supposed to be irrelevant.[96] If we assume that those features are indeed irrelevant, then we must abandon the prior assumption that conflicts preconditions are just like substantive preconditions.

In truth, there is no reason why substantive requirements should be like conflicts requirements. Failure to satisfy the substantive requirements of forum law does not in domestic cases provide a reason for turning to the law of another state; nor does it mean that the forum no longer wants to use its own rule of decision. The paradox outlined above arises because the interest analysts have lumped to-

(1932), in which he concluded that New Hampshire had no interest and Vermont law should apply because the substantive preconditions for application of the wrongful death statute were not satisfied. CURRIE ESSAYS, *supra* note 1, at 210.

95. In precisely the same way, it can be demonstrated that a fourth case: substantive test, not satisfied; conflicts test, domestic; irrelevant connecting factors, all foreign; is equivalent to both (1) and (3).

96. This anomaly is similar to the problem that arose from Currie's treatment of insurance. *See* text at notes 76-77 *supra*. In cases with a variety of multistate elements, Currie asserted that facts such as the existence of insurance might be relevant to the satisfaction of substantive criteria, and thus defeat an interest based on a defendant's residence. Yet in purely domestic cases courts would never consider insurance.

gether two different uses of the word "applies." They argue that if a conflicts prerequisite is not met, the statute fails to apply in the same sense as when a substantive prerequisite is not met. But in a purely domestic case, domestic law "applies" under any conflict of laws theory; the word means that domestic law supplies the pertinent rule of decision. Once we "apply" that law, however, the issue may go either way, depending upon whether the substantive preconditions are satisfied. In the conflicts-of-laws sense, a domestic guest statute "applies" to all domestic accidents; but in the substantive sense of prohibiting recovery, it "applies" in only some of those cases, namely those in which the driver was not compensated. To say that a standard applies may mean either that it is pertinent, or that it is satisfied.

Interest analysts have attended only to the latter use of the word. Yet a single meaning is necessarily insufficient. At least three different situations require different treatment: the purely domestic case with all substantive preconditions satisfied, the purely domestic case with some deficiency in the substantive preconditions, and the purely foreign case. To insist on only one meaning, and therefore only one test, forces cases in the middle category to be treated as falling into either the first group or the third group. But they are not identical to the first, since they require a different substantive outcome. Nor should they be equated with the third group, since purely domestic cases call for domestic law and purely foreign cases call for foreign law. A two-step inquiry about the pertinence of the standard and then about whether it is satisfied, would give cases in the middle group the special treatment they deserve. If forum law is pertinent, the second step is to apply it, thus dividing the group to which the forum law applies into two more groups: those that satisfy the standard and those that do not.

Courts resolve problems involving both state and federal law by using this same two-stage process. The decision about whether federal law supplies the rule of decision is independent from and prior to the decision about what substantive result is appropriate.[97] This method is particularly clear where a federal question is the only basis for subject matter jurisdiction; the jurisdictional issue is decided before the substantive issue. A subsequent finding that the federal law's substantive purposes do not mandate recovery does not make that law any less dispositive; the court need not then turn to state law or dismiss for want of jurisdiction.

97. *Cf.* Suchomajcz v. Hummel Chem. Co., 524 F.2d 19 (3d Cir. 1975) (court made its conflict-of-laws decision before passing on the merits of a disputed substantive issue).

V. Actual Legislative Intent Revisited: A Glance at Selected Statutes

The traditional methodology aspired to predictability, simplicity, and evenhandedness. The interest analysts claim that these methods risked sacrificing substantive policy goals in the process. Interest analysis, in contrast, allows parochial, unpredictable, and chaotic results. Nonetheless, the interest analysts argue, the results are at least faithful to legislative wishes. And Currie's confidence that state legislatures would agree with him was remarkable. At one point he wrote:

> [There] is [a] growing tendency of legislators to specify how their enactments are intended to affect mixed cases. The task of drafting such provisions forces attention to the interests and objectives involved. *A legislature is not likely to append to any statute dealing with a specific problem any such rule as that the law of the place where the contract is made shall control.*[98]

Even a casual glance at choice-of-law statutes shows that he was wrong. Existing choice-of-law statutes demonstrate that simplicity, predictability, and multistate harmony motivate state legislatures just as they have motivated all conflicts theorists except the interest analysts.[99] Indeed, given the two senses of the word "applies," this is entirely sensible. In enacting a substantive statute, the legislature considers the competing substantive claims on both sides and strikes a balance. In drafting a conflicts provision to accompany it, the legislature must choose between making its own standards pertinent or referring to the law of other states. Again, a balance must be struck: but the substantive values were already accommodated in the first decision. The other decision — about when to make the statute pertinent — reflects values such as comity and predictability.

In the statutes cited below, explicit legislative adoption of the Currie school methods seems to be lacking. Almost wholly absent, for example, is support for the premise that compensatory and protective policies are designed to benefit only forum residents. If Currie's inferences about legislative intent were correct, this premise would be reflected in two ways. First, statutes motivated solely by a protective or compensatory policy would limit their own scope to cases where the forum rule would benefit a resident. Second, when

98. Currie Essays, *supra* note 1, at 116 (emphasis added). *Cf. id.* at 703: "In any realistic setting . . . , we are likely to find that the concern of the state is with the people involved rather than the scene of the activity."

99. For a survey and discussion of choice-of-law statutes, see W. Reese & M. Rosenberg, Conflict of Laws 553-56 (7th ed. 1978); Leflar, *supra* note 3.

such policies were conjoined with regulatory policies in a single statute, they would supply an alternative ground for its application.

Instead, a search through conflict-of-laws statutes reveals mostly Bealean conflicts rules. We find statutes that make the rule of lex loci govern the permissible interest on loans,[100] statutes that make forum law apply to all torts or crimes committed in airplanes over forum territory,[101] and statutes that make the law of the place of execution or performance govern interpretation of wills.[102] None of these statutes is phrased in terms of benefiting forum residents, although many serve protective or compensatory purposes. The effect on forum residents is never mentioned as either a sole or an alternative basis for applying forum law. Other conflict-of-laws statutes establish the relevance of different geographical factors, but also in the style of traditional conflicts rules: certain securities problems are to be decided according to the law of the issuer's residence,[103] mergers are controlled by the law of the state where the survivor is incorporated,[104] and bank deposits are governed by the law of the bank's

100. *See, e.g.*, GA. CODE ANN. § 57-106 (Harrison 1977); MICH. COMP. LAWS § 438.154 (1970); NEB. REV. STAT. § 45-158 (1978).

101. *See* ARIZ. REV. STAT. ANN. § 28-1704 (1976); MICH. COMP. LAWS § 259.177 (1970); N.C. GEN. STAT. § 63-16 (1975); PA. STAT. ANN. tit. 2, § 1470 (Purdon 1963).

102. *See* ARIZ. REV. STAT. ANN. §§ 14-2506 (1975), 14-2602 (Supp. 1979); CAL. CIV. CODE § 1646 (West 1973); CAL. CIV. PROC. CODE § 1857 (West 1955); CAL. PROB. CODE § 26 (Deering 1974); DEL. CODE ANN. tit. 12, § 1306 (Supp. 1978); LA. CIV. CODE ANN. art. 10 (West 1952); LA. CODE CIV. PRO. ANN. art. 2888 (West 1961); MASS. ANN. LAWS. ch. 191, § 1A (Michie/Law Co-op. Supp. 1979); MICH. COMP. LAWS ANN. § 700.133 (West Supp. 1979). NEB. REV. STAT. § 30-2340 (1975); N.D. CENT. CODE § 30.1-08-06, -09-02 (1976); OR. REV. STAT. § 112.230, .255 (1977); S.D. COMP. LAWS ANN. § 53-1-4 (1967); WIS. STAT. ANN. § 853.05 (West 1977).

103. *See* ALA. CODE § 7-8-106 (1975); ARIZ. REV. STAT. ANN. § 44-3006 (1967); ARK. STAT. ANN. § 85-8-106 (1961); CAL. COM. CODE § 8106 (West 1964); COLO. REV. STAT. § 4-8-106 (1973); CONN. GEN. STAT. ANN. § 42a-8-106 (West 1960); DEL. CODE tit. 6, § 8-106 (1974); FLA. STAT. ANN. § 678.8 -106 (West 1966); ILL. ANN. STAT. ch. 26, § 8-106 (Smith-Hurd 1974); IOWA CODE ANN. § 554.8106 (West 1967); KAN. STAT. ANN. § 84-8-106 (1965); KY. REV. STAT. § 355.8-106 (1970); ME. REV. STAT. ANN. tit. 11, § 8-106 (1964); MD. COM. LAW. CODE ANN. § 8-106 (1975); MASS. ANN. LAWS ch. 106, § 8-106 (Michie/Law Co-op. 1976); MICH. COMP. LAWS § 440.8106 (1970); MINN. STAT. § 336.8-106 (West 1974); MISS. CODE ANN. § 75-8-106 (1972); MO. REV. STAT. § 400.8-106 (1969); MONT. REV. CODES ANN. § 87a-8-106 (1947); NEB. REV. STAT. U.C.C. § 8-106 (1971); NEV. REV. STAT. § 104.8106 (1973); N.H. REV. STAT. ANN. § 382A:8-106 (1961); N.M. STAT. ANN. § 55-8-106 (1978); N.C. GEN. STAT. § 25-8-106 (1965); OHIO REV. CODE ANN. § 1308.05 (Page 1979); OKLA. STAT. ANN. tit. 12a, § 8-106 (West 1963); OR. REV. STAT. § 78.1060 (1973); PA. STAT. ANN. tit. 12A, § 8-106 (Purdon 1970); R.I. GEN. LAWS § 6A-8-106 (1969); S.C. CODE § 36-8-106 (1976); S.D. COMP. LAWS ANN. § 57-31-19 (1967); TENN. CODE ANN. § 47-8-106 (1979); TEX. BUS. & COM. CODE ANN. tit. 1, § 8.106 (Vernon 1968); UTAH CODE ANN. § 70A-8-106 (1979); VA. CODE § 8.8-106 (1965); WASH. REV. CODE § 62A.8-106 (1966); W. VA. CODE § 46-8-106 (1966); WIS. STAT. § 408.106 (1977); WYO. STAT. ANN. § 34-21-806 (1977).

104. *See* ALASKA STAT. § 10.05.408 (1968); CAL. CORP. CODE § 1108 (West 1977); COLO. REV. STAT. § 7-7-107 (1973); CONN. GEN. STAT. ANN. § 33-482 (1960); ME. REV. STAT. ANN. tit. 13-B, § 906 (1977); NEV. REV. STAT. § 78.475 (1977); N.M. STAT. ANN. § 53-14-7 (1978); N.Y. NOT-FOR-PROFIT CORP. LAW § 908 (McKinney 1970); N.C. GEN. STAT. § 55A-42.1

location.[105]

Even when a conflict-of-laws statute relies on a party's residence, we do not find the parochialism Currie anticipated. Connecticut determines the status of children born after artificial insemination by the law of the place of birth, but it apparently does not matter whether the child would be helped or harmed by Connecticut law on the subject.[106] The Uniform Probate Code determines spousal elective share by reference to the law of the parties' residence, but apparently either a resident or a nonresident may invoke that law, whoever would benefit by having it applied.[107]

We also find the familiar "alternative reference" rules, which uphold wills or contracts if they would be valid under the law of any one of several states (state of making, state of execution, etc.).[108] No doubt legislatures adopt these rules to vindicate reasonable expectations. But once again, they make no mention of who will benefit under any of the laws in question.[109] A number of conflicts statutes

---

(1975); OHIO REV. CODE ANN. § 1701.79 (Page 1978); PA. STAT. ANN. tit. 40, § 459a (Purdon 1971); TEX. BUS. CORP. CODE ANN. art. 5.07 (Vernon 1956); UTAH CODE ANN. § 16-10-72 (1953); VA. CODE § 13.1-71 (1978); WASH. REV. CODE § 23A.20.070 (1969); W. VA. CODE § 31-1-38 (1975); WIS. STAT. § 180.68 (1977); WYO. STAT. ANN. § 17-1-406 (1977).

105. *See* ALA. CODE § 7-4-102 (1975); ARIZ. REV. STAT. ANN. § 44-2602 (1967); ARK. STAT. ANN. § 85-4-102 (1971); DEL. CODE ANN. tit. 6, § 4-102 (1974) (Delaware annotations to this provision cite the *Restatement* with approval); FLA. STAT. ANN. § 674.4-102 (1966); ILL. REV. STAT. ch. 26, § 4-102 (1963); IOWA CODE ANN. § 554.4102 (1967); KAN. STAT. ANN. § 84-4-102 (1965); LA. REV. STAT. ANN. § 10:4-102 (West Supp. 1978); ME. REV. STAT. ANN. tit. 11, § 4-102 (1964); MD. COM. LAW CODE ANN. § 4-102 (1975); MASS. ANN. LAWS ch. 106, § 4-102 (Michie/Law Co-op 1976); MINN. STAT. § 336.4-102 (1966); MISS. CODE ANN. § 75-4-102 (1977); MO. REV. STAT. § 400.4-102 (1969); MONT. REV. CODES ANN. § 87A-4-102 (1947); NEB. REV. STAT. § 4-102 (1971); NEV. REV. STAT. § 104.4102 (1973); N.H. REV. STAT. ANN. § 382-A:4-102 (1961); N.M. STAT. ANN. § 55-4-102 (1978); N.C. GEN. STAT. § 25-4-102 (1975); OHIO REV. CODE ANN. § 1304.02 (Page 1979); OKLA. STAT. ANN. tit. 12A, § 4-102 (1963); OR. REV. STAT. § 74.1020 (1977); PA. STAT. ANN. tit. 12A, § 4-102 (Purdon 1970); R.I. GEN. LAWS § 6A-4-102 (1969); S.C. CODE § 36-4-102 (1976); TEX. BUS. & COM. CODE ANN. tit. 1, § 4.102 (Vernon 1968); UTAH CODE ANN. § 70A-4-102 (1953); VA. CODE § 8.4-102 (1950); WASH. REV. CODE § 62A.4-102 (1966); W. VA. CODE § 46-4-102 (1966); WIS. STAT. § 404.102 (1977); WYO. STAT. ANN. § 34-21-402 (1977).

106. CONN. GEN. STAT. ANN. § 45-69k (West Supp. 1979).

107. *See* N.D. CENT. CODE § 30.1-05-01 (1976); *accord*, 20 PA. CONS. STAT. ANN. § 2203 (Purdon Supp. 1979).

108. *See* ARIZ. REV. STAT. ANN. §§ 14-2506, 25-112 (1975); CAL. CIV. CODE § 63 (West 1954); CAL. PROB. CODE § 26 (West Supp. 1979); DEL. CODE ANN. tit. 12, § 1306 (1975); IDAHO CODE § 32-203 (1963); LA. CODE CIV. PRO. ANN. art. 2888 (West 1961); N.D. CENT. CODE §§ 14-03-08, 30.1-08-06 (1976); OR. REV. STAT. § 112.225 (1977); UTAH CODE ANN. § 30-1-4 (1976); WIS. STAT. § 853.05 (1977).

109. *But see* the discussion of borrowing statutes in notes 113-16 *infra* and accompanying text. Some examples of statutes that do not mention who will benefit include:

Rules that real property may be governed by the law of the situs. CAL. CIV. CODE § 755 (West 1954); N.D. CENT. CODE § 47-04-01 (1978); S.D. COMP. LAWS ANN. § 43-1-6 (1967).

Rules that personal property may be governed by the law of domicile. CAL. CIV. CODE

explicitly mention the "conflicts rules" of other jurisdictions,[110] thus approving renvoi, a practice Currie found irrational.[111] Legislatures also typically define personal jurisdiction by facts such as location of the accident,[112] finding that factor relevant to whether the state has an interest in adjudicating the case. Statutes of limitation also define willingness to adjudicate by whether the cause of action arose within the state. Where will such irrationality stop?

Perhaps the only example of a statute reflecting Currie's views is the borrowing statute, which allows residents but not nonresidents to take advantage of a forum statute of limitations that is longer than the statute that would otherwise apply.[113] However, borrowing statutes are intended primarily to prevent forum shopping, a goal the Currie school does not consider important.[114] If there were no such provision, many courts would always apply the forum statute of limitations[115] and this might draw litigants to a forum with a long statute. The borrowing statute prevents forum shopping but allows forum law to apply when there is no danger — when the cause of action accrued in the forum or the plaintiff is a resident.[116]

---

§ 946 (West 1954); IDAHO CODE § 55-401 (1979); N.D. CENT. CODE § 47-07-01 (1978); S.D. COMP. LAWS ANN. § 43-1-7 (1967).

Rules that marital property may be governed by the law of the state where acquired. ARIZ. REV. STAT. ANN. § 25-217 (1976).

110. ARIZ. REV. STAT. ANN. § 44-3006 (1967); CONN. GEN. STAT. ANN. § 42a-8-106 (West 1960); DEL. CODE ANN. tit. 6, § 8-106 (1975); *see* statutes cited in note 103 *supra*.

111. CURRIE ESSAYS, *supra* note 1, at 184.

112. Other factors, of course, include residence of the defendant, place of incorporation, place of doing business, etc.

113. There are, of course, many statutes which turn on the residence of one party in the substantive sense. *See generally* Simson, *State Autonomy*, note 82 *supra*; Simson, *Discrimination*, note 82 *supra*. Such, for instance, are those tolling statutes that specify that the statute of limitations shall not run in favor of nonresidents. *See* MINN. STAT. ANN. § 541.13 (West Supp. 1979); N.J. STAT. ANN. § 2A:14-22 (West 1952); OKLA. STAT. ANN. tit. 12, § 98 (West Supp. 1979); PA. CONS. STAT. ANN. tit. 42, § 5532 (Purdon 1975); R.I. GEN. LAWS § 9-1-18 (1970); W. VA. CODE § 55-2-17 (1966); WIS. STAT. ANN. § 893.30 (1974). These are not, however, conflicts statutes since the statutes supply rules of decision regardless of the parties' residence. The statute of limitations does not apply in the substantive sense with regard to nonresidents (because it is tolled), but it does apply in the conflicts sense, because the court does not conclude that there is no interest and then turn to foreign law. As indicated in the accompanying text, this last result has been changed in some states by borrowing statutes; but tolling statutes are not by themselves an exception to the general principle. *But see* note 86 *supra* and accompanying text.

114. The purpose of avoiding forum shopping is demonstrated by the common proviso that the resident must have held the cause of action since it accrued. *See* CAL. CIV. PROC. CODE § 361 (West 1954); KAN. STAT. ANN. § 60-516 (1976); NEB. REV. STAT. § 25-215 (1975); N.C. GEN. STAT. § 1-21 (1969); UTAH CODE ANN. § 78-12-45 (1953); WIS. STAT. § 893.205 (1977); *cf.* ALASKA STAT. § 09.10.220 (1973); LA. CIV. CODE ANN. art. 3547 (West 1953); OR. REV. STAT. § 12.260 (1977); WASH. REV. CODE § 4.16.290 (1974) (all barring two nonresidents who are injured out of state from using this forum's statute of limitation).

115. Leflar, *supra* note 3, at 960.

116. Such borrowing statutes were held constitutional in Canadian N. Ry. v. Eggen, 252

Interest analysts might offer three explanations for the dearth of statutes reflecting their views. First, they might suggest that these statutes shed no light on what should be done in the absence of a statute, the problem with which Currie primarily concerned himself. They might grant the significance of these laws in the situations explicitly covered, but refuse to extend them by analogy. This response would undercut somewhat their pretensions to "ordinary statutory interpretation," for ordinary statutory interpretation takes advantage of available analogies. Moreover, these statutes demonstrate serious legislative concern with system values, such as predictability and uniformity, in multistate cases.

Perhaps most disturbingly, the Currie school asks us to draw a strange inference from legislative silence. Many substantive statutes were enacted before interest analysis was popular, against a presumption that the applicable rule was "lex loci."[117] When conflicts statutes were formulated, they codified that Bealean principle by and large, adapting it where appropriate to reflect new connecting variables, such as place of incorporation for the law of mergers. It seems odd to assume that the legislature intended implicitly to change whatever was not codified and wanted the change to reflect governmental interest. A somewhat more plausible explanation would be that the legislatures left to the wisdom of the courts the decision whether to modify any uncodified territorialist conflicts rules. Even that position is troublesome when used to justify a theory that stresses strict obedience to legislative intent. The most sensible deduction from legislative silence is that the legislature expected everything it took for granted at the time of enactment to remain unchanged.

The second response to the preponderance of Bealean statutes is that legislatures have simply been blinded by territorialist dogma. Many conflict-of-laws statutes are, after all, state-adopted uniform legislation; the drafters of such legislation are undoubtedly pecu-

U.S. 553 (1920). While holding only that the shorter statute of limitations was reasonable, the Court also noted that the plaintiff's sole purpose for selecting the forum was to take advantage of the longer period. 252 U.S. at 563.

117. Historically, it is most probable that legislatures contemplated territorial approaches to conflicts problems. Courts have recognized this legislative predilection when declining to adopt "modern" approaches. *See, e.g.*, Friday v. Smoot, 58 Del. 488, 211 A.2d 594 (1965); Marmon v. Mustang Aviation, 430 S.W.2d 182 (Tex. 1968). After *Marmon*, the Texas legislature acted to permit application of whichever substantive law the courts think appropriate. TEX. REV. CIV. STAT. ANN. arts. 4671, 4678 (Vernon Supp. 1976-1977). Texas courts subsequently rejected lex loci and adopted the approach of the *Second Restatement* in a case that arose between *Marmon* and the revision of the statute, on the theory that the old statute did not apply to common-law causes of action, and that the new theories were virtually interchangeable. Gutierrez v. Collins, 583 S.W.2d 312 (Tex. 1979).

liarly susceptible to the charms of predictability and interstate harmony.[118] This explanation of statutory conflicts rules may be accurate. Even if it is, however, it is not an argument that can be addressed to courts by adherents of a "mine is not to reason why" approach to conflicts. Unless the interest analysts are able to convince state legislators to cast off such "outmoded" and "overly altruistic" inclinations, their hands are tied.

A third explanation is that these apparently territorialist statutes are really entirely consistent with interest analysis. Most of the provisions that refer to the location of activity — such as the one requiring the law of a bank's location to control bank deposits — can be termed "regulatory," making it natural to apply the law of the place where the conduct occurs. But this solution involves an important concession to the traditionalist perspective; it means abandoning concurrent "protective" or "compensatory" policies, and focusing solely on territorial connecting factors. The residence of one party can no longer trigger application of forum law, and interest analysis is thereby made more predictable (as well it should be, especially in matters of commercial law). In short, analysis of governmental interests is made consistent with existing manifestations of legislative intent by rejecting one of the characteristics that distinguish it from traditional analysis: the premise that residents receive favored treatment.

Conclusion

I have adduced a fair number of instances in which principles of interest analysis are contrary to the expressed or reasonably imputed wishes of legislatures. Perhaps this only pushes back the scope of interest analysis to cases where absolutely no legislative intent is demonstrable; perhaps it can still be argued that Currie's principles govern there. This tactic preserves the appearance of consistency with legislative intent, but only by retreating from cases that offer evidence on the question. Moreover, the situations where the interest analysts' imputations of intent are most convincing are precisely those where interest analysis and traditional approaches agree. Currie's most persuasive argument about legislative intent was that a New York rule of the road is not intended to have any application to Saudi Arabia, "but is designed solely to regulate traffic on the streets

118. Currie typed traditionalists as "probably among the strong advocates of uniform state laws." Currie Essays, *supra* note 1, at 708. He also expressed concern that drafters of uniform legislation or interstate compacts would be influenced by settled conflict-of-laws doctrine. *Id.* at 190 n.5. *But see* note 63 *supra*.

and highways of New York."[119]

Perhaps by tinkering with the calculus of interest it will be possible to avoid some of the other problems set out in this Article. At a certain point, however, the excessive complexity of a system may cause it to collapse. The Bealean system accommodated itself to larger and larger numbers of more and more serious counter-examples until eventually it was no longer convincing or even intelligible. Interest analysts can hardly cite methodological sponginess, enabling courts to circumvent their method's absurd results, as one of the methodology's virtues.[120] Currie was quick to make the analogous point when criticizing the *First Restatement*.[121]

Some may think that this is not tinkering at all, that it is honest development of a single principle: a court should follow legislative intent, and if there is no actual intent, then the court should turn to constructive intent. Interest analysts could then accept this Article's criticisms as a tool to hone their methods. This may even be acceptable, so long as they realize that their talk about "intent" is a fiction and their premises are metaphysical.

It should not be surprising that a theoretical approach to "constructive intent" reflects the value preferences of the theoretician. Where there is no objective evidence, one falls back to one's own conception of the best arrangement. This is particularly likely in conflict-of-laws cases, where evidence of actual legislative intent is rare. Thus in reasoning about conflicts problems, scholars and courts can and should heed some of the values that interest analysts condemned as "metaphysical," such as evenhandedness and predictability. In doing so, a court would not disregard its duty to follow the commands of its legislature. Legislatures, like conflicts theorists, have frequently concerned themselves with systems values. And this is entirely appropriate; respect for these values may benefit residents as well as nonresidents.

When a legislature has not indicated the territorial scope of a

119. CURRIE ESSAYS, *supra* note 1, at 58.

120. Currie did not dispute the method's considerable flexibility:

> To one of Mr. Hill's charges I plead guilty without reservation. In the first sentence of his essay he attributes to me the proposal that traditional methods of choice of law be abandoned in favor of a method "involving the effectuation of relevant governmental policies on what appears to be an *ad hoc* basis." "*Ad hoc*" has a deprecatory connotation that was no doubt intended. But the method I advocate is the method of statutory construction, and of interpretation of common-law rules, to determine their applicability to mixed cases. . . . The distinctive virtue of the common-law system is that it also proceeds on an *ad hoc* basis. I am proud to associate myself with the common-law tradition.

CURRIE ESSAYS, *supra* note 1, at 627.

121. *Id.* at 181.

statute in either the words enacted or in the legislative history, it is a fiction to speak of "legislative intent." If my analysis of what the calculus of interests requires is erroneous, the interest analysts should clarify the a priori principles upon which their theory necessarily rests. Even better, they would do well to cease making extravagant claims about fulfilling legislators' wishes, and get to work on a theory of constructive interpretation that at least comports with demonstrated legislative concerns.

[15]

LEGAL CERTAINTY VERSUS EQUITY IN THE CONFLICT OF LAWS†

PAUL HEINRICH NEUHAUS*

INTRODUCTION

The struggle between legal certainty and equity is as old as the law itself. Only the labels have changed: while formerly discussion proceeded in terms of *ius strictum* and *ius aequum*, the expressions currently preferred, especially in Germany, are "legal certainty" and "justice (in individual cases)." Whatever terms are used, they refer to two different aspects of the law. One is the public interest in clear, equal, and foreseeable rules of law which enable those who are subject to them to order their behavior in such a manner as to avoid legal conflict or to make clear predictions of their chances in litigation. The other is the need for deciding current, concrete disputes adequately, by giving due weight to the special and perhaps unique circumstances of each case. The former aspect calls for legislation, the latter for judicial decision.

It has often been said that legislation corresponds to the abstract and systematic mode of thought of continental Europeans, while judge-made law is more suited to the practical and empirical style of Britons and Americans. Indeed, in England as well as in the United States, even statutes are generally directed not so much to general regulation in comprehensive terms, but rather to case-by-case solutions of separate situations. It is for this reason that a German lawyer who had just written a report on the latest English legislation, complained that when compared with English statutes, the labyrinth of Minos would look like a formal garden.[1] On the other hand, continental judges are so accustomed to decide not on the basis of precedents but on that of general statutes that they incline to express their own decisions in general terms resembling the style employed in legislation. Thus, the German Supreme Court once remarked, with respect to public policy:[2]

> Although the question as to the compatibility of the application of a rule of foreign law with the purposes of our legislation cannot be decided in an abstract manner but only in accordance with the circumstances of each individual case, still the decision of the individual case must be based on a rule which, when generalized, deserves approval.

† Authorized translation from the German by the Editor.

* Dr. rer. pol. Münster (1939); Dr. iur. Tübingen (1945). Research Associate, Max-Planck-Institut für ausländisches und internationales Privatrecht, Hamburg; Academic Member, Max-Planck-Gesellschaft; Honorary Professor of Law, University of Hamburg.

[1] Letter of Hans A. Schwarz-Liebermann von Wahlendorf to the author, accompanying the manuscript of Schwarz-Liebermann & Daig, *Die englische Gesetzgebung auf dem Gebiete des Privatrechts 1945-1950*, 17 RABLES ZEITSCHRIFT FÜR AUSLÄNDISCHES UND INTERNATIONALES PRIVATRECHT [hereinafter cited as RABELSZ] 56 (1952).

[2] 80 Entscheidungen des Reichsgerichts in Zivilsachen 129, 132-33 (1912). *Cf.* SWISS CIVIL CODE art. 1, § 2: "If the Code does not furnish an applicable provision, the judge shall decide . . . according to the rule which he would establish as legislator" (English translation in RUDOLF B. SCHLESINGER, COMPARATIVE LAW 318 (2d ed. 1959)).

On the other hand, this difference between the civil law[3] and the common law (*i.e.*, the preference of the former for general statutes serving legal certainty, and the emphasis of the latter on judicial decisions purporting to do justice to the individual circumstances) should not be exaggerated. For instance, ancient Roman law, the root of all continental legal systems, was primarily case law. On the other hand, American law is partly based on continental European canon law and on regional codifications; furthermore, there is the stabilizing effect of stare decisis. Especially in recent times, civil law and common law have come closer to each other. On the continent, judicial decisions have constantly gained in importance as against the codes, which are more and more recognized to be full of gaps and which are partially outmoded. Recently, an Austrian author, in a much noticed book entitled *From the Legislative to the Judicial State*, has deduced by purely philosophical and systematical considerations the superiority of judge-made law to legislation.[4] And on the other side of the Channel and of the Atlantic, judge-made law is frequently replaced by statutes. At least the gap between present-day German and American legal method is much smaller than that between English and French or Italian law.[5] Furthermore, the geographical (horizontal) differences are substantially mitigated in significance by (vertical) movements in time. Just as there are parallels between the epochs of European and American cultural history since the Enlightenment, there have been many similarities in the history of law on both sides of the Atlantic; and we may well expect the intensification of economic and political ties between the two continents to contribute to a further synchronization of the respective legal systems.

But the conflict between legal certainty and justice (equity) will never come to an end. In different countries and at different times, the one or the other of these twin objectives of the law will dominate; there is no permanent solution. Especially neither goal can replace the other. Thus, it cannot be maintained that real legal certainty is the certainty that justice will prevail[6]—just as there is no merit to the assertion that in some technical branch of the law (*e.g.*, civil procedure) the sole purpose of justice is to guarantee the certainty of the law.

All that has been said above also applies to the conflict of laws. In this area as well, legal certainty and justice are struggling for supremacy; and the predominance of the one over the other differs in point of time as well as place. In the following, an attempt will be made to show how in our century, the trend (in Europe somewhat earlier than in America) was from the predominance of legal certainty to the

[3] As herein used, "civil law" or "continental European law" does not include the law of the communist states. The to some extent quite different problems arising in connection with the latter cannot be discussed within the scope of this article.

[4] RENÉ MARCIC, VOM GESETZESSTAAT ZUM RICHTERSTAAT especially 231-52 (1957).

[5] See Rabel, *Deutsches und amerikanisches Recht*, 16 RABELSZ 340, 342, 349 (1951), referring to German and American law as "the most telling examples of modern progressive development" and showing by several examples "how closely related the trends are today in Germany and in the United States."

[6] This was claimed by Hermann Göring in his speech, *Die Rechtssicherheit als Grundlage der Volksgemeinschaft*, 1 ZEITSCHRIFT DER AKADEMIE FÜR DEUTSCHES RECHT 233 (1934).

emphasis on justice, and how today, at least in Europe, there is once more a significant tendency in favor of certainty in the law. It is, of course, impossible to write a full modern history of private international law in this paper. We have to limit ourselves to mentioning some typical points of the development, and will not always be able to avoid seemingly perfunctory observations.

I

THE PREDOMINANCE OF CERTAINTY

At the beginning of the twentieth century, the idea of certainty of the law was in its heyday. While the natural sciences, philosophy, and the fine arts were already in various stages of rebellion against the dominant ideas of the last century, legal theory continued to reflect the constancy of economic development and international peace which existed until 1914—at least so far as Western Europe and America are concerned. There was little cause for a re-examination of traditional modes of thought. The promotion of legal certainty with a view to eliminating the legal risks of business and of other transactions by making them clearly predictable was regarded more important than the struggle for justice and for equity, which were largely not considered to be in danger, anyway. Even after World War I, the tendency towards legal certainty continued to be dominant in many instances. To a large extent, this was probably due to two reasons. First, many persons were inclined to ignore, as much as possible, the basic transformation of their environments, and to return to the old standards (*e.g.*, the gold standard) as soon as practicable. Secondly, lawyers often consciously tend to oppose revolutionary change and to defend traditional values (a typical example is the preparatory work that went into the Italian Civil Code of 1942; here, the Italian legal profession defended the traditional legal doctrines of nineteenth century liberalism against revolutionary fascism[7]). In the field of private international law, the strong predilection for legal certainty is apparent in the point of departure (A), in the method adopted (B), and, finally, in the objective sought (C).

A. The Point of Departure

The conflicting schools of private international law at the turn of the century—internationalists, nationalists, adherents of the theory of "vested rights," proponents of domicile or nationality, partisans and enemies of renvoi, and so on—all proceeded from certain general principles (*e.g.*, comity, national sovereignty, global renvoi) from which they attempted to deduce their theses with compelling logic. This applies not only for the realm of the civil law, but for English and American authors as well. The internal consistency and the consequent clarity of the various theories appeared to be more important to their proponents than mere practical considerations.

[7] See Neuhaus, *Das internationale Privatrecht im italienischen Zivilgesetzbuch von 1942*, 15 RABELSZ 22, 32 (1949).

B. The Method

The formal fixing of choice-of-law rules by statutes or—preferably—by international agreements was regarded as the method best suited to increase legal certainty in this area. Especially the attempts at the international unification of conflict-of-law rules undertaken by the Hague Conference on Private International Law, which convened four times between 1893 and 1904, were accompanied by great optimism in this regard. The theoretical groundwork for the Hague Agreements was laid to a large extent by the guidelines and drafts elaborated by the Institut de Droit international (since 1873) which included Anglo-American lawyers ever since its establishment, and by the International Law Association which was established through American initiative.

C. The Goal

At the beginning of this century, the highest aim of conflict-of-laws rules, and the specific objective of international agreements, was considered to be the guaranteeing of the uniformity of decisions. Friedrich Carl von Savigny had already described this ideal to be "that, in cases of conflict of laws, the same legal relations (cases) have to expect the same decision, whether the judgment be pronounced in this state or in that"; he had spoken of "the desirable and gradually approaching accord in deciding cases of conflict in different states."[8] Franz Kahn coined the term, "harmony of laws" ("Gesetzesharmonie")[9]; Dicey and Pillet preferred a more subjective expression for the same ideal: protection of "duly acquired rights"[10] or of "droits acquis."[11]

II

TRANSITION TOWARDS EQUITY

The political, economic, and social changes brought about by two world wars have had some influence on legal thinking, as had the progressive influence of the methods of the natural sciences. On the one side, the quest for security and continuity had to make room for attempts to attain a new equity. For when confronted with massive currency depreciations, the principle of *pacta sunt servanda* lost its absolute effectiveness; the idea of the completeness of existing legal orders was destroyed and numerous gaps were revealed by confrontation with a world which was undergoing drastic changes; and in the face of a lawgiver who himself was a criminal, it could no longer be maintained that even the worst law was better than rebellion because it provided at least for an orderly state of affairs. On the other

[8] 8 FRIEDRICH CARL VON SAVIGNY, SYSTEM DES HEUTIGEN RÖMISCHEN RECHTS 27 and 129 (1849); the English translation here used is WILLIAM GUTHRIE, PRIVATE INTERNATIONAL LAW, AND THE RETROSPECTIVE OPERATION OF STATUTES 69-70 and 145 (2d ed. 1880).

[9] Kahn, *Gesetzeskollisionen* (1891), reprinted in 1 FRANZ KAHN, ABHANDLUNGEN ZUM INTERNATIONALEN PRIVATRECHT at 122 (1928).

[10] ALBERT VENN DICEY, A DIGEST OF THE LAW OF ENGLAND WITH REFERENCE TO THE CONFLICT OF LAWS 22 (1896) (General Principle no. I).

[11] ANTOINE PILLET, PRINCIPES DE DROIT INTERNATIONAL PRIVÉ 33-34 (1903).

side, a more sociological and realistic attitude towards the law led to increased awareness of the law in action ("Rechtstatsachen") and of relevant interests instead of abstract terms.

Private international law did not remain unaffected by these changes. Again, we shall distinguish between the point of departure, the method, and the objective.

A. The Point of Departure

Instead of rigid principles, the modern authors of private international law cultivate a realism that is free from ideologies, and a sober respect for actual circumstances and interests—especially for the purpose of the rules of substantive law which are ultimately at issue. A critical analysis of judicial decisions with a view to discovering the real reasons hidden behind conventional opinions is much in vogue, as evidenced, for instance, by the discovery of the "homeward trend."[12] In the preparation of statutes and of international agreements, the national interests affected are disclosed point blank. Thus, immigrant countries favor the domicile principle for questions of personal status and relations in order to assimilate immigrants who still retain their old nationality, and to keep them from becoming a foreign-law based state within the state.[13] Countries of emigration, on the other hand, choose the nationality principle, asserting that the emigrants want to retain their ties to their homeland even when abroad.[14] Furthermore, in a debtor state, it is suggested that the personal law of the debtor should govern loan contracts, because this will lead to the more frequent application of the *lex fori*.[15] German authors speak of "internationally typical interests,"[16] and generally of a "jurisprudence of interests" in private international law.[17] In the United States, a large portion of learned comment deals with the question as to which state has the predominant interest in the application of its laws to various fact situations. The doctrinal dispute as to the nature of the applicable foreign law between the adherents of the "fact" and the "law" theories loses its significance because the several questions relating to pleading, proof, and application of foreign law (judicial notice or proof by the parties; determination by the judge or by the jury; reviewability on appeal or *cassation*) are increasingly decided not in accordance with a paramount principle, but with a view to procedural convenience and expediency.[18]

[12] The term was coined by ARTHUR NUSSBAUM, DEUTSCHES INTERNATIONALES PRIVATRECHT 43 (1932); see also ARTHUR NUSSBAUM, PRINCIPLES OF PRIVATE INTERNATIONAL LAW 37 (1943).

[13] Joint Declaration of the delegates of Colombia and Costa Rica at the signing of the Código Bustamante, SEXTA CONFERENCIA INTERNACIONAL AMERICANA, ACTA FINAL 83 (1928).

[14] See, for instance, Maridakis, *Les principaux traits de la récente codification hellénique touchant le droit international privé*, 85 ACADÉMIE DE DROIT INTERNATIONAL, RECUEIL DES COURS 107, 159 (1954-I): "The Greek, wherever he may be, has only one dream: to return and to hear again the bell of the humble church of his hamlet" (translated from the French by the Editor).

[15] This suggestion is made in the Official Explanation of draft Hungarian Statute on Private International Law (1947) (not published; quoted in PAUL HEINRICH NEUHAUS, DIE GRUNDBEGRIFFE DES INTERNATIONALEN PRIVATRECHTS 36 n.82 (1962)).

[16] Zweigert, *Nichterfüllung auf Grund ausländischer Leistungsverbote*, 14 RABELSZ 283, 291 (1942).

[17] Especially Kegel, *Begriffs- und Interessenjurisprudenz im internationalen Privatrecht*, FESTSCHRIFT HANS LEWALD 259 (1953); *cf.* GERHARD KEGEL, INTERNATIONALES PRIVATRECHT 28 *et seq.* (1960).

[18] See, *e.g.*, Dölle, *Über die Anwendung fremden Rechts*, [1957] GEWERBLICHER RECHTSSCHUTZ UND

B. The Method

In the period of transition from certainty to equity, the most popular path pursued by private international lawyers no longer leads to codification and to the conclusion of treaties. While there still are some codifications, these are not representative of the new era, but rather stragglers from times past.[19] Most of the newer multilateral agreements are not ratified.[20] It is even suggested, on occasion, that existing laws be repealed and everything be left to adjudication.[21] Courts as well as academic authors prefer elastic formulae such as "the proper law," "the spatially closest law," "grouping of contacts," and "center of gravity," and neglect fixed choice-of-law rules. It is explicitly pointed out that the decisions of conflict-of-law cases by mechanized rules have not even promoted certainty and uniformity.[22] Indeed, it is the very fact that these rules often lead to inequitable results that militates against their gaining general recognition. A European author even says that the difficulties facing private international law are "so complicated and so extensive that it is completely impossible to draft general rules... in anticipation of conflicts."[23] And an American commentator asserts repeatedly: "We would be better off without choice-of-law rules."[24]

In more concrete terms, the fixed connecting factors of nationality or domicile are frequently replaced by "domicile in fact" (*résidence habituelle*). Especially nationality as a connecting factor is abandoned wherever it would lead to unjust decisions: for instance, with respect to refugees who are nationals of their countries of origin in form only;[25] to spouses of different nationality but common domicile;[26]

URHEBERRECHT 56; Schlesinger, *Die Behandlung des Fremdrechts im amerikanischen Zivilprozess*, 27 RABELSZ 54 (1962).

[19] *E.g.*, the Polish law of 1926 and the Czechoslovak law of 1948, both of which are based on an Austrian draft of 1913; articles 17-31 of the *Disposizioni sulla legge in generale* of the Italian Civil Code of 1942, see Neuhaus, *supra* note 7, especially at 34-35; and the to some extent quite similar articles 5-33 of the Greek Civil Code of 1940, see Gogos & Aubin, *Das Internationale Privatrecht im griechischen Zivilgesetzbuch von 1940*, 15 RABELSZ 240, especially 247 (1949). All legislative texts may be found, in German and French translations, in ALEXANDER N. MAKAROV, QUELLEN DES INTERNATIONALEN PRIVATRECHTS (2d ed. 1953 *et seq.*).

[20] *E.g.*, the agreement for the enacting of a uniform statute on private international law in the Benelux states, signed on May 11, 1951. Of the eight Hague Agreements on Private International Law drafted in the fifth through ninth sessions in The Hague (1925-1960), only one agreement was in force as of April 1, 1963, and that only as between 5 of the 18 Member States of the Conference. Note, *Conférence de La Haye de droit international privé, Etat actuel des travaux*, 52 REVUE CRITIQUE DE DROIT INTERNATIONAL PRIVÉ 138, with tables at 139-41 (1963).

[21] See, with respect to Austria, Wahle, Book Review, 12 ÖSTERREICHISCHE JURISTEN-ZEITUNG 614, 615 (1957).

[22] See Judge Frank in Siegelman v. Cunard White Star Ltd., 221 F.2d 189, 206 (2d Cir. 1955), observing, in reliance upon writings by Cavers, Rheinstein, and Goodrich: "It is generally agreed that the decisions of conflict-of-laws cases by mechanized rules... cannot be defended on the ground that they have promoted certainty and uniformity, since such results have not been thus achieved."

[23] GEORG COHN, EXISTENZIALISMUS UND RECHTSWISSENSCHAFT 119 (1955).

[24] Currie, *Notes on Methods and Objectives in the Conflict of Laws*, 1959 DUKE L.J. 171, 177; Currie, *The Verdict of Quiescent Years: Mr. Hill and the Conflict of Laws*, 28 U. CHI. L. REV. 258, 259 (1961).

[25] Especially article 12 of the Geneva Convention of July 28, 1951, Relating to the Status of Refugees, 189 U.N.T.S. 150.

[26] See, *e.g.*, the famous decision of the French Cour de cassation in the Rivière case, 42 REVUE CRITIQUE DE DROIT INTERNATIONAL PRIVÉ 412 (1953) with note Batiffol and 20 RABELSZ 519 (1955) with note Francescakis.

and to the support claims of children not residing in the country of their nationality.[27] The principle of the "immutability" of the regime of matrimonial property is rejected because the necessity of blending in with changed circumstances is thought to outbalance the difficulties of changing the matrimonial property regime during coverture.[28] The applicability of foreign conflict-of-laws rules and the relevance of party autonomy are not rejected out of hand as illogical, but appropriate solutions are sought for each distinctive fact pattern. Foreign conflict-of-laws rules are taken into consideration especially when the international recognition or effectiveness of a judicial decision is dependent upon them.[29] Party autonomy is fully recognized except in cases of evasion of statutes or other instances of abuse. *Ordre public* or public policy, one of the fundamental principles of private international law according to the Franco-Italian theory, metamorphoses into an escape valve for particularly unusual foreign law even in France and Italy; and the "relativity" of public policy is frequently emphasized.

C. The Goal

The goal of choice-of-law rules in more recent days appears to be not the international harmony of decisions but the best substantive solution of all cases—the appropriate decision in terms of substantive law. There is direct talk of a "result-selective approach."[30] The judge is to apply the "more progressive" or the "better" substantive law in case of doubt, and generally to take into account the "policy" of his state; the latter notion far transcends the most extreme theory of *ordre public*. When parts of different legal orders are applicable to a set of facts, it is suggested that the judge avoid an unjust decision through a process of discretionary "adaptation," the outcome of which cannot be predicted.[31]

Generally speaking, there appears to be a crisis in private international law, for both the possibility and the willingness to apply foreign law have decreased as a consequence of the enhanced importance of normative legal principles and of general clauses.[32] It is pointed out again and again that the application of foreign law is not the only means for the approximate solution of "international" fact situations. Traditional choice-of-law rules ("Verweisungsrecht") are challenged by a new issue:

[27] Especially the Hague Convention on the Law Applicable to Obligations to support Minor Children, of Oct. 24, 1956, 5 AM. J. COMP. L. 656 (1956).

[28] See, *e.g.*, the recommendation of the Commission on Family Law of the German Council on Private International Law, in VORSCHLÄGE UND GUTACHTEN ZUR REFORM DES DEUTSCHEN INTERNATIONALEN EHERECHTS 2-3 (1962) (comment, *id.* at 22), also reprinted in 25 RABELSZ 340 (1960); *cf.* Kegel, *Reform des deutschen internationalen Eherechts*, *id.* at 201, 208.

[29] The leading article on this subject was Melchior, *Die Selbstbeschränkung des deutschen internationalen Privatrechts*, 3 RABELSZ 733 (1929).

[30] Hancock, *Three Approaches to the Choice-of-Law Problem*, XXTH CENTURY COMPARATIVE AND CONFLICTS LAW (LEGAL ESSAYS IN HONOR OF HESSEL E. YNTEMA) 365 (1961).

[31] See especially Lewald, *Règles générales des conflits de lois*, 69 ACADÉMIE DE DROIT INTERNATIONAL, RECUEIL DES COURS 1, 136-45 (1939-III); JOCHEN SCHRÖDER, DIE ANPASSUNG VON KOLLISIONS- UND SACHNORMEN (1961); and, with respect to the latter, Neuhaus, Book Review, 26 RABELSZ 753 (1961).

[32] For details, see Neuhaus, *Die Krise im internationalen Privatrecht*, 3 DEUTSCHE RECHTS-ZEITSCHRIFT 86 (1948); *cf.* Neuhaus, *op. cit. supra* note 15, at 18-20.

decisional law ("Entscheidungsrecht") which regulates these fact situations directly[33] —and not only in the shape of internationally uniform rules, *i.e.*, a "private law on the international level,"[34] but also in the form of a purely national body of separate rules for the decision of cases with foreign elements.

III

THE NEW SEARCH FOR LEGAL CERTAINTY

Perhaps the tendency of subordinating legal certainty to justice in individual cases has not as yet reached its peak; and legislation as well as adjudication still frequently continue to employ the traditional, rigid formulae. But in some places, there already appears again a reversion (or, rather, a new progress) towards a novel kind of legal certainty; and it is the most important aim of the present paper to call attention to this new trend. Again, the political and economic development of the leading countries may have been decisive. A certain stabilization after the changes and disturbances wrought by World War II and its immediate aftermaths; the integration of Europe and, generally, of the free world; and finally, increasing contacts with underdeveloped countries—these are the factors that may contribute today or in the near future to strengthening the quest for legal certainty. But the real reasons go deeper: the search for certainty in the law is an essential function of law as such, and therefore cannot be suppressed for any length of time.

A. The Point of Departure

While the past started from more or less abstract principles and the present regards the relevant interests as most significant, the lawyer of the future will have to devote his chief attention to generally recognized values or standards. A radical "jurisprudence of interests" is revealed to be logically deficient and impracticable once it is realized that the interests in conflict cannot always be quantified but often are of different quality, so that a choice between them requires a value judgment. (Even "interests" is prone to be a misleading label, for it tends to falsify this value judgment by an overemphasis of the material and otherwise tangible interests and a corresponding neglect of higher, spiritual values.) In a democratic and pluralist society, the standards for judgment cannot be purely personal or irrational; the judge must be guided by generally recognized standards capable of rational cognition. This is the essential difference between a democratic legal order and a so-called Khadi justice which decides individual cases in accordance with the judge's sense of equity and without reliance on any objective standards.[35] The practical need for

[33] The term was coined by Dölle, *Gegenwärtige Aufgaben der deutschen Wissenschaft vom internationalen Privatrecht*, DEUTSCHE RECHTS-ZEITSCHRIFT, Supplement 5, p. 3, at 5 n.10 (1948). In substance, this is also the tendency of Baade, Book Review, 10 JAHRBUCH FÜR INTERNATIONALES RECHT 330 (1962).

[34] The expression was coined by Rabel, *Privatrecht auf internationaler Ebene*, UM RECHT UND GERECHTIGKEIT (FESTGABE FÜR ERICH KAUFMANN) 309 (1950).

[35] For a discussion of Khadi justice, see 2 MAX WEBER, WIRTSCHAFT UND GESELLSCHAFT 571 (4th ed. Johannes Winckelmann, 1956); also the English translation of MAX RHEINSTEIN, MAX WEBER ON LAW IN ECONOMY AND SOCIETY 351 (1954): it "decides cases . . . non-formalistically and in accordance with concrete ethical or other practical value-judgments; . . . there are no 'rational' bases of 'judgment.' "

uniformity and predictability of decisions and the dignity of the individual, which is incompatible with arbitrary judicial fiat, create an abiding need for objective standards of law.

Whether these standards are contained in laws or in precedents, in constitutions or in international declarations of the rights of man, is a matter of subsidiary importance. The main thing is that the judge must be able to find the answer to the question not yet specifically provided for by discovering the spirit and the purpose of those texts through taking into consideration the interaction of their various norms. It is the special task of the science of the law to bring out these interactions between individual legal norms. The method required for this task will continue to be the development of clear terms and the construction of a system. This does not imply a return to antiquated notions of analytical jurisprudence, or *Begriffsjurisprudenz*, for terms and construction now have a different significance. The past has made us suspicious of a purely logical-deductive and stationary approach to terminology and systematic analysis. The development and the adaptable application of the law must remain possible in a changing world, and each value judgment must proceed from an exact analysis of the facts. But despite the myriad of actual fact situations and possible points of approach to the decision of concrete cases, the lawyer should always strive to express the solution of individual cases in clear terms, and seek to fit them into a larger framework. In Ernst Rabel's words, there should be "system construction from below."[36]

As regards our field, the conflict of laws, there are two reasons for thinking that firm standards that help to avoid confusion and arbitrary actions are especially needed here. First, the judge himself needs such standards. For a choice-of-law problem—the question as to the law to be applied and as to the rules for its application—incites so little spontaneous legal reaction and occurs so seldom in the experience of most lawyers that a judge will be relatively helpless when faced with these complicated problems, and will have to obtain guidance from clear rules if he is to avoid decision by chance. Secondly, in transnational controversies, the parties are particularly dependent upon the service of attorneys and judges, for they often live under different legal systems and therefore have no common legal or extra-legal customs and expectations. While in internal law, a legal reference to "good faith" or to the "custom of trade" will occasionally suffice, private international law always requires more precise rules. It is therefore a matter of profound regret that some authors become the victims of a certain "pointillisme" that recommends decisions which vary from case to case (or even from edition to edition) without supplying either solid paths for the courts or a guideline to students.[37] And above all, lawyers should avoid the appearance of surrendering to the power of the stronger party or state, and of seeing their function in the mere "transformation of power into law."[38]

[36] Rabel, *Die Fachgebiete des Kaiser Wilhelm-Instituts für ausländisches und internationales Privatrecht 1900-1935*, 3 25 JAHRE KAISER WILHELM-GESELLSCHAFT 77, 109 (1937).

[37] Batiffol, Book Review, 48 REVUE CRITIQUE DE DROIT INTERNATIONAL PRIVÉ 775, 777 (1959).

[38] See the criticism of Kollewijn against this misleading formula, Book Review, 7 NEDERLANDS TIJDSCHRIFT VOOR INTERNATIONAAL REICHT 384, 385 (1960).

B. The Method

Between the extremes of rigid general rules and the lack of any rules, there is a middle way (unfortunately, it is not superfluous to state such a triviality). This middle way consists of refined and elastic rules that provide for specified solutions for different types of cases and also allow for exceptions in special situations. Thus, already in 1908, the Institut de Droit international resolved that the proper law of contracts be determined by a catalogue of choice-of-law rules for specific types of contracts, and by a supplementary general clause.[39] Similarly, in more recent times it was recommended that the choice of law in torts be diversified by adding to the traditional rule (applicability of the *lex loci delicti commissi*) a general clause for exceptional circumstances as well as a catalogue of choice-of-law rules for typical cases.[40] There might be dispute over the relative importance of the general rule, the escape clause, and the detailed rules for typical transactions or events. But in any case, there is no need for doing away with definite rules altogether, so long as the various rules are not simply derived from abstract notions such as contract and tort, but are based on a comparative legal analysis of different kinds of typical events and relations.[41]

However, such a differentiation becomes problematical where a series of relationships in actual life are loosely interconnected, as for instance in the area of family law and succession. The form of marriage as well as its personal and property effects, parentage, relations of parents to legitimate and illegitimate children, divorce, and the order of succession are always somehow interrelated. Yet it appears impossible to subject the personal and family affairs of a man from cradle to grave, or yet all legal interrelations of an entire family, always to the same law. This observation holds true as regards the three distinct relationships involved in a guarantee contract or the old and the new contractual relationship in the case of a novation. Here it is often possible to create choice-of-law rules for the various facets of the basic relationship which, while not identical, are nevertheless similar and will in many cases lead to the application of the same legal order. At least, it should not be left entirely to the discretion of the judge who chances to hear his case to determine the "proper law of a person." Quite to the contrary, there always should be a careful effort not to destroy unnecessarily a more comprehensive relationship by an over-refined *ad hoc* analysis of that facet which happens to be at issue.

On the positive side, the need for prudent differentiation is well illustrated by a recurring problem of transnational contracts law. Here, it is increasingly realized that choice-of-law rules for economic-regulatory law (including currency control

[39] 22 ANNUAIRE DE L'INSTITUT DE DROIT INTERNATIONAL 289-92 (1908); see in this connection Makarov, *Die Resolution des "Institut de Droit international" über das internationale Obligationenrecht und deren Einfluss auf die nationalen Kodifikationen des Kollisionsrechts*, FESTSCHRIFT HANS LEWALD 299 (1953).

[40] Binder, *Zur Auflockerung des Deliktsstatuts*, 20 RABELSZ 401, 498-99 (1955).

[41] Rabel, *Das Problem der Qualifikation*, 5 RABELSZ 241, 258 (1931): "There is a healthy and promising tendency towards discovering inductively the choice-of-law rules which are appropriate to each individual legal type."

and antitrust) cannot be identical with the rules determining the law of the contract itself.[42] For these rules transcend the conflicts law of private contracts which is based on the principle of freedom of contract and the search for the "proper" law, and lead into the realm of public law where considerations of "policy" are more relevant. It would be just as unreasonable to let the parties choose their own currency control law as it would be to determine rules for the protection of private interests (*e.g.*, the permissibility and the extent of contractual limitation of liability) in accordance with the "interests" of the enacting state and to apply them, for instance, only to its citizens. The area of conflicts of public law, which has up to now been beclouded by the ambiguous slogan of the "territoriality" of public law, still needs a substantial amount of analytical and systematic spadework before we can see more clearly the parallels to, and the deviations from, choice-of-law norms pertaining purely to private law.[43]

C. The Goal

The duty of the judge "to do right to all manner of people"[44] requires not only that he avoid personal arbitrariness in deciding transnational cases, but also that he shun any attitude suggestive of nationalistic bias. If the judge should attempt to apply the best substantive law after comparing the relative merits of all possible relevant foreign and indigenous legal rules, he will all too readily prefer his own law because he is not trained to appreciate the reasons and the advantages of the rules to be found in foreign legal systems. Therefore, private international law has to be based, in principle, on the equality of foreign and domestic substantive law. Furthermore, the economy of the process of adjudication dictates that the great volume of civil cases be decided according to clear-cut rules without a judicial repetition of the frequently quite involved legislative thought processes; this precludes a weighing of all possibly relevant interests (the situation may be different in criminal litigation or in public international law cases). Consequently, general rules placing limits on justice in individual cases are a necessary element of private law, including choice-of-law rules; if need be, an inequitable result in an individual case has to be accepted so that the stability of the legal order may be preserved. Thus, choice-of-law rules must, instead of selecting that substantive law which has the "best" rules for the disposition of a particular case, limit themselves to referring to that legal order which, judging by external circumstances, seems most appropriate.

[42] See especially Wengler, *Die Anknüpfung des zwingenden Schuldrechts im internationalen Privatrecht*, 54 ZEITSCHRIFT FÜR VERGLEICHENDE RECHTSWISSENSCHAFT 168 (1941); Zweigert, *supra* note 16; Neumayer, *Autonomie de la volonté et dispositions impératives en droit international privé des obligations* (2 pts.), 46 REVUE CRITIQUE DE DROIT INTERNATIONAL PRIVÉ 579 (1957); 47 *id.* 53 (1958).

[43] Franz Gamillscheg has pioneered this field in three incisive parallel studies: FRANZ GAMILLSCHEG, INTERNATIONALES ARBEITSRECHT 7-13, 185-210 (1959); Gamillscheg, *Gedanken zu einem System des internationalen Arbeitsrechts*, 23 RABELSZ 819 (1958); *id.*, *Les principes du droit du travail international*, (3 pts.), 50 REVUE CRITIQUE DE DROIT INTERNATIONAL PRIVÉ 265, 477 and 677 (1961). Two or three studies by other German authors are in the making.

[44] As provided in the oath sworn by English judges, quoted from Wortley, *The Concept of Man in English Private International Law*, 33 THE GROTIUS SOCIETY, TRANSACTIONS 147, 154 (1947). (Note by the Editor: the oath formula reads in full: "to do right to all manner of people after the laws and usages of this realm, without fear or favour affection or ill-will.")

(This, incidentally, not only goes for the primary selection of the applicable law, but also for the decision as to which law is to be applied if the contents of the proper law cannot be determined or if it cannot be applied for some other reason; the "Ersatz" law need not necessarily be the *lex fori.*)

But even this view of choice-of-law rules will not avoid the dangers of nationalistic bias. For instance, a country with a patriarchal family law will regard the choice of the father's personal law as quite natural, while a country where the equality of the sexes has been realized and where the welfare of the child is paramount, may select a different choice-of-law rule. But efforts should be made to avoid such partialities. More particularly, choice-of-law rules should not be tied to the internal constitutional law of the forum state any more than is absolutely necessary. The Institut de Droit international rightly proclaimed the following guideline at its 1952 session:[45]

> The rules of private international law should, generally speaking, use criteria which are capable of internationalisation, *i.e.*, which lend themselves, in particular, to adoption in international conventions, thus avoiding the danger of conflicting solutions of given cases in different countries.

For a different decision of the same case from country to country subjects the reputation of the law and public faith in its inviolability to especially great strains. It is in this sense—and not as a criticism of the multitude of different legal orders as such—that the much cited saying of Blaise Pascal seems justified:[46]

> Plaisante justice, qu'une rivière ou une montagne borne!
> Vérité au deçà des Pyrénées, erreur au delà.

Furthermore, divergent decisions are often frustrating justified expectations. In the worst cases, there are even conflicts of duties, as when one judgment orders what another judgment forbids (*e.g.*, the performance of a contract despite a moratorium or the outbreak of war, or the restitution of conjugal rights in a marriage recognized in one state but not in another jurisdiction with which the parties also have connections).

The danger of "conflicting solutions of a given case in different countries"—in the most extreme instance, the danger of the abuse of this possibility by "forum shopping" in bad faith—cannot be eliminated merely by procedural rules on international jurisdiction that confer power to decide a particular controversy on the courts of only one state: that state the substantive law of which should be applied (*forum legis*). For in many cases, where due to circumstances such as extreme distance, war, and the like, the plaintiff has no access to the courts of such a state, this would lead to a denial of justice; furthermore, the rule would not be practicable for mere preliminary questions. The avoiding of conflicting decisions thus remains as the specific task of choice-of-law rules.

Surely, the complete internationalization of private international law is unattainable in the foreseeable future. All the more is it important that some consideration

[45] 44 ANNUAIRE DE L'INSTITUT DE DROIT INTERNATIONAL pt. 2, at 477 (1952).
[46] BLAISE PASCAL, PENSÉES no. 108 (Lafuma ed., Paris 1951).

be given to foreign choice-of-law rules, particularly in cases of renvoi and preliminary questions. In other words, there must be an attempt to achieve "coordination des systèmes."[47] Especially countries which seek to keep their choice-of-law rules free from any predilection in favor of their own substantive law and which attempt to "use criteria which are capable of internationalisation" are tempted to enact rigid choice-of-law rules, and not to make any concessions to less ideal foreign conflicts systems.[48] But the fact is that there will never be an integral realization of the postulates of justice; and here, too, there is the danger of *summum ius, summa iniuria*. The optimum attainable is a fair compromise between equity—or what one believes to be equity in the particular case—and legal certainty: between national law and international cooperation.

CONCLUSION

More than a hundred years ago, Friedrich Carl von Savigny wrote in the introduction to his famous treatise on the conflict of laws:[49]

> Germans, Frenchmen, English, and Americans, often stand in marked opposition to one another; but all agree in evincing the most lively interest in the questions which ... [this book] embraces, in an effort after approximation and agreement, such as is found in no other department of jurisprudence.

We read these words not without a feeling of shame. For today, even after the heyday of nationalism characteristic of earlier decades has passed, a practical, resigned nationalism or at least regionalism remains dominant. There are especially few contacts between American and continental European private international law, although the relations between our countries are closer than ever before. Part of the explanation for this situation may be found in the fact that in the United States, the international conflict of laws is relatively insignificant as compared to the interstate conflict of laws. The latter is necessarily more limited in scope because the differences between the legal systems of the various states of the American Union are not nearly as great as are those between some national legal systems, and because these differences are, in the main, limited to matters regulated by statute while the remaining portions of private law in the United States still consist of a more or less homogeneous common law. Furthermore, it has to be said in apology for the current state of mutual ignorance that even the best-equipped law library on the European continent cannot subscribe to all American law reviews that publish articles dealing with the conflict of laws, and that European law is relatively inaccessible to Americans, if only for reasons of language. It is to be hoped that the present symposium will increase the contacts between European and American thinking on private international law, thus contributing towards a reciprocal accommodation.

[47] This idea of the "coordination des systèmes" is especially emphasized by HENRI BATIFFOL, TRAITÉ ÉLÉMENTAIRE DE DROIT INTERNATIONAL PRIVÉ 356-58 (3d ed. 1959), and HENRI BATIFFOL, ASPECTS PHILOSOPHIQUES DU DROIT INTERNATIONAL PRIVÉ 102-141 (1956).

[48] This has already been observed by Melchior, *supra* note 29, at 733-34, with respect to the Italian Civil Code of 1865. A more recent example is Greek private international law which, while generally refraining from a preference in favor of Greek substantive law, expressly forbids taking into account a foreign renvoi, see Gogos & Aubin, *supra* note 19, at 243-46.

[49] SAVIGNY, *op. cit. supra* note 8, at iv; p. 43 of GUTHRIE's translation.

The Pragmatic Tradition in England

VOLUME 64 APRIL 1951 NUMBER 6

HARVARD LAW REVIEW

THE PROPER LAW OF A TORT

J. H. C. Morris *

FEW sections of the *Restatement of Conflict of Laws* have provoked more adverse criticism than Section 332, which lays down in general terms that the validity of a contract is governed by the law of the place of contracting. Whether this rule is applied more frequently than any other by American courts is, to say the least, highly doubtful. By contrast, the English rule appears to be well settled: the validity of a contract is governed by its proper law, that is, ". . . the law, or laws, by which the parties intended, or may fairly be presumed to have intended, the contract to be governed. . . ."[1] An American writer has described the elaboration of this proper law doctrine as "among the outstanding contributions of English learning to the general theory of private international law."[2] As a matter of history the doctrine seems to have been formulated[3] because of the impossibility of reconciling decisions applying the law of the place of contracting[4] with

* Fellow and Tutor of Magdalen College, Oxford, and All Souls Lecturer in Private International Law; Visiting Professor of Law, Harvard Law School. B.A., Oxford, 1931, B.C.L., 1932, D.C.L., 1949.

[1] DICEY, CONFLICT OF LAWS 579 (6th ed. 1949).

[2] NUSSBAUM, PRINCIPLES OF PRIVATE INTERNATIONAL LAW 168 (1943). Contrast Beale's sardonic remark that "[t]he remarkable fact which is noticed after reading many of the [English] cases is the great regularity with which the English courts find, by various methods, that it was the law of England which was intended by the parties." 2 BEALE, CONFLICT OF LAWS 1102 (1935). This remark ignores the fact that London was the center of world trade until 1914, possibly later, and that English law was as much an invisible export as English shipping, insurance and finance.

[3] Lloyd v. Guibert, L.R. 1 Q.B. 115, 122, 122 Eng. Rep. 1134, 1146 (1865) (Willes, J.).

[4] *E.g.*, Peninsular & Oriental Steam Nav. Co. v. Shand, 3 Moo. P.C. (N.S.) 272, 16 Eng. Rep. 103 (1865).

decisions applying the law of the place of performance [5] or some other law.[6] To those who hanker after certainty in their rules of law, this may seem like taking refuge behind a verbal formula in order to avoid the necessity of following precedent. But as a practical matter, the proper law doctrine works well in a jurisdiction where respect for precedent assumes exaggerated proportions, and both the final [7] and intermediate [8] courts of appeal are bound by their own decisions.

To those who are more interested in the adequacy of decisions from the social and economic points of view than they are in stare decisis, the chief merit of the English rule is its flexibility, an advantage that is gained on two distinct planes. In the first place, the rule enables proper weight to be attributed in a particular case to factors of constantly varying significance like the place of contracting, the place of performance, the nationality of the ship, the situs of the land, the domicil, residence and place of business of the parties, their reasonable expectations, the currency in which the obligation is expressed, and countless others. In the second place, the rule enables attention to be concentrated, not so much on the question, what law governs the validity of the contract, as on the question, what law governs the particular question before the court. This enables different answers to be given to such questions as offer and acceptance, reality of consent, formalities, necessity for consideration or "cause," agency, capacity of parties, essential validity, illegality, interpretation, scope, performance, discharge, remedies, and so forth. We have here a practical experiment in doing what Cook so often insisted should be done, namely, breaking the problems down into smaller groups.[9]

At this point critics of the proper law doctrine will probably object (if they have been reading Beale [10] and Goodrich [11]) that

[5] *E.g.*, Burgess v. Richardson, 29 Beav. 487, 54 Eng. Rep. 716 (Rolls Ct. 1861).

[6] *E.g.*, Lloyd v. Guibert, L.R. 1 Q.B. 115, 122 Eng. Rep. 1134 (1865) (law of the flag).

[7] London Street Tramways Co. v. London County Council, [1898] A.C. 375 (House of Lords).

[8] Young v. Bristol Aeroplane Co., [1944] K.B. 718 (Ct. of Appeal). This rule is subject to exceptions which are stated in the case cited.

[9] "The problems in the field under consideration [contracts] need to be broken down into smaller groups and dealt with so as to meet the needs of society." Cook, Logical and Legal Bases of the Conflict of Laws 431 (1942). See *id.* at 417–18.

[10] 2 Beale, Conflict of Laws 1083–86.

[11] Goodrich, Conflict of Laws 326–27 (3d ed. 1949).

it may take a lawsuit to determine the validity of the contract, and that this is commercially undesirable in a consensual transaction, since business men require to know in advance of litigation whether their contracts will be valid or not. There is force in this objection, but two factors prevent it from becoming decisive. One is that the fact (if it be a fact) that it may take a lawsuit to determine the validity of the contract is not peculiar to this situation, but is of the essence of a great deal of law in general, and is indeed necessary in the interests of justice. We do not hesitate to say that a contract is void for mistake or is discharged by frustration merely because courts sometimes have difficulty in deciding whether the mistake or the frustrating event is sufficiently material to produce these results. The other factor is that if the parties seek certainty, they can achieve it by an express selection of the governing law. Provided the selection is confined to the law of a country with which the contract has a close factual connection, the court will give it nearly decisive effect.[12]

The object of this paper is, however, not to argue the merits of the English proper law doctrine as applied to contracts, but to suggest that there is room for a similar approach in the field of torts. English courts have reached results which, on the whole, seem commercially convenient and sound by applying the proper law doctrine to the question whether the defendant is liable for breach of contract. Why should we not reach results which are socially convenient and sound by applying the proper law doctrine to the question whether the defendant is liable for tort? To a foreign observer, it seems extraordinary that there should be so much uncertainty in the United States as to what law governs the validity of a contract,[13] and so much uncritical acceptance of the rule that tort liability is governed by the law of the place of wrong. Such criticism as there is [14] seems to be concentrated on the *Re-*

[12] The King v. International Trustee for the Protection of Bondholders, [1937] A.C. 500, 529; Vita Food Products, Inc. v. Unus Shipping Co., [1939] A.C. 227 (P.C.). In order not to overstate the case, the statement in the text is deliberately made more cautious than dicta in these cases would suggest. On this aspect of the matter, see Mann, *The Proper Law of a Contract*, 3 INT'L L.Q. 60 (1950), and Morris, *The Proper Law of a Contract: A Reply*, 3 INT'L L.Q. 197 (1950).

[13] "The question of what law determines the validity of a contract . . . is the most confused subject in the field of Conflict of Laws." GOODRICH, CONFLICT OF LAWS 321. "There is no topic in the conflict of laws in regard to which there is greater uncertainty than that of contract." LORENZEN, SELECTED ARTICLES ON THE CONFLICT OF LAWS 261 (1947).

[14] COOK, *op. cit. supra* note 9, c. 13; STUMBERG; CONFLICT OF LAWS 201–12

statement's rule that "[t]he place of wrong is in the state where the last event necessary to make an actor liable for an alleged tort takes place."[15] Cook nowhere suggests that the tort problems, like the contract problems, "need to be broken down into smaller groups and dealt with so as to meet the needs of society."[16] And yet the matters discussed in a textbook on the domestic law of torts are probably as various, and certainly more heterogeneous, than those discussed in a textbook on the domestic law of contracts. To take a few illustrations only, is it inherently probable that courts will achieve socially desirable results if they apply the same conflicts rule to liability for automobile negligence, radio defamation, escaping animals, the seduction of women, economic conspiracies, and conversion? The present writer suggests that it is not: the social factors involved differ too fundamentally for that. A proper law approach, intelligently applied, would furnish a much-needed flexibility. It may be conceded that in

(2d ed. 1951); Rheinstein, *The Place of Wrong: A Study in the Method of Case Law*, 19 TULANE L. REV. 4, 165 (1944). Lorenzen's article (now reprinted as chapter 13 of his SELECTED ARTICLES ON THE CONFLICT OF LAWS) is mainly an attack on the English rule that the act must be actionable by the lex fori as well as not justifiable by the lex loci. HANCOCK, TORTS IN THE CONFLICT OF LAWS c. 3 (1942), accepts without question the place of wrong rule for tort liability.

[15] RESTATEMENT, CONFLICT OF LAWS § 377 (1934).

[16] See note 9 *supra*. In discussing how the tort sections of the *Restatement* should be rephrased in order to bring them into harmony with Section 7 of the *Restatement of Conflict of Laws* (the renvoi section), Cook says that if all the events which together constitute the alleged tort have occurred in a single foreign state, then the forum should determine whether by the law of this single foreign state there is a right of action for tort: "If so, the forum will ordinarily and subject to certain possible exceptions to be noted later, recognize that by its law a similar but not necessarily identical right of action exists." COOK, *op. cit. supra* note 9, at 341–42. The "exceptions" are referred to in a footnote on the following page and cover such familiar matters as public policy and the lack of a form of action in the forum for enforcing the foreign right. *Id.* at 343 n.57. If the group of events in question is factually connected with more than one state, Cook says that the forum should model its rule of decision "upon the domestic rule of the state in which the decisive portion of the events has occurred. . . ." *Id.* at 342. Elsewhere, however, he expresses his preference for the German Reichsgericht rule that the forum should apply whichever of the two or more domestic rules is most favorable to the plaintiff. *Id.* at 345. His former suggestion is in line with a suggestion which is developed later in this article, see pp. 888–92 *infra*. A criticism of a more general character is advanced by LORENZEN, *op. cit. supra* note 13, at 366–67, who says: "Much may be said in favor of greater elasticity in the rules of the conflict of laws. Just what the qualifications to the *lex loci delicti* should be it is difficult to say. What is wanted are decisions that appeal to one's sense of justice." Needless to say, the present writer is in entire agreement with this observation.

many, perhaps most, situations there would be no need to look beyond the law of the place of wrong, so long as there is no doubt where that place is. But we ought to have a conflict rule broad and flexible enough to take care of exceptional situations as well as the more normal ones, or else we must formulate an entirely new rule to cope with the exceptional situations. Otherwise the results will begin to offend our common sense.

Consider, for example, the following situation. An American co-educational school establishes for its students a summer vacation camp in the lake and forest country of northern Quebec. The camp is entirely self-contained and self-supporting and there is no other human being within 50 miles. One of the girls is seduced by one of the boys so that she becomes pregnant; another is bitten by a dog kept in the camp by another boy. Neither incident would have happened but for the negligence of the camp organizers, who are instructors in the school. The girls, the boys, and the organizers are all residents of State *X*, an American state, where also the school is located. Does it make sense to say that the question whether the girls or their parents can sue the boys or their parents or the camp organizers in State *X* "must" be governed by the law of Quebec, merely because the incidents happened there? To the present writer it does not.

Now consider the following more typical situation. An automobile owned and driven by *P* collides with an automobile owned and driven by *D* in State *X*, and *P* sustains personal injuries for which he sues *D* in State *F*. It seems obvious that the question whether *D* is liable in damages to *P* should be governed by the law of *X*. But if we begin to change the facts, the answer seems to be far less obvious. Suppose (1) that *P* and *D*, both residents of *F*, were only temporarily in *X* and that *D*'s insurance company does business in *F* and the policy was effected there; (2) that *P* is not a motorist but a pedestrian on the highway; (3) that *P* is a guest occupant in *D*'s car who was offered a ride in *X*; (4) that *P* is a guest occupant, a resident of *F*, who was offered a ride in *F*; (5) that *P* is the wife of *D*, both of them being residents of *F* and in the car at the time of the accident, the obstacle to *P*'s success being a rule in *X* that a wife cannot sue her husband in tort. In these varying fact situations, surely there comes a time when common sense would revolt at the application of the law of *X* in a court in *F*. Many lawyers would agree with Cook's suggestion [17]

[17] COOK, *op. cit. supra* note 9, at 346.

that (5) is a distinct and separate problem, since it involves questions of policy concerning domestic relations, and that the matter should be governed by the law of the domicil, in this case *F*. It seems at least arguable that in (4) also we should reach more sensible results by applying the law of *F* rather than the law of *X*, since all of the significant factors are *F* factors except the fortuitous place of harm.

There is one tort to which courts seldom apply the law of the place of tort, and that is the tort of conversion. That this is so abundantly appears from typical leading cases. In *Cammell v. Sewell*,[18] lumber belonging to *P*, an Englishman, was shipped to England from a Russian port on board a Prussian ship. The ship was wrecked off the coast of Norway and the master sold the lumber to *D*, a Norwegian, in circumstances which conferred a good title on *D* by Norwegian but not by English law. *D* brought the lumber to England and refused to deliver it to *P* on demand. *P* brought an action of trover against *D* in England, claiming damages for conversion. The action was dismissed on the ground that *D*'s Norwegian title prevailed. Yet the conversion (demand and refusal) undoubtedly took place in England. Again, in *Goetschius v. Brightman*,[19] *P*, a California corporation, conditionally sold a car in California to one Oesting, a California resident, on the usual terms that no title was to pass to Oesting till the price was fully paid, and that the car was not to be removed out of the state without *P*'s consent. Oesting drove the car to New York and sold it there to *D*, a bona fide purchaser. *P* replevied the car in New York. By California domestic law, *P*'s title prevailed, but by the domestic law of New York (assuming it was applicable), *D*'s title prevailed, since *P* had not recorded the conditional sale contract in New York.[20] The New York court held that California law governed. The New York recording statute was held to be inapplicable to a California conditional sale contract. There is no reference in the opinion to New York having been the place of tort. Yet if *D* committed the tort of conversion, it must have been in New York: so far as appears he never was in California, and he never had possession of the car outside of New York state.

It is obvious that the results in these cases could not have been

[18] 5 H. & N. 728, 157 Eng. Rep. 1371 (Ex. Cham. 1860).

[19] 245 N.Y. 186, 156 N.E. 660 (1927).

[20] N.Y. Laws 1904, c. 698, §§ 1, 2.

reached on the basis that liability for the tort of conversion is governed by the law of the place of wrong. Indeed, it is doubtful whether they could have been reached on the basis that liability for conversion is governed by the proper law of the tort, unless that phrase is to be very broadly interpreted. Their true explanation, it is suggested, is that the courts realized that, from the standpoint of the conflict of laws, they were not really dealing with a question of tort liability at all but with a question of title to property. True it is that in the common law title to property has to be tried through forms of action which have been labeled tortious. But there is no jurisprudential necessity for this, and in civil law countries an owner out of possession of a chattel recovers possession (or damages) by asserting his ownership and right to possession, not by alleging that the defendant has done him a wrong.[21] Thus, the common law courts rightly disregard the label when faced with conflicts problems and raise the question to the plane of title where it obviously belongs, just as they discard the common law distinction between realty and personalty in conflicts cases in favor of the more universal and natural distinction between movables and immovables. The conversion cases do, however, demonstrate that one kind of tort at least is not referable to the law of the place of wrong; and they suggest the reflection that other kinds may not be.

Another advantage of the proper law of the tort doctrine is that it would facilitate a more rational approach to the interstate tort problem than the *Restatement's* mechanistic last event doctrine. Attempts to justify that doctrine have seemed unsatisfying because they fail to take account of the policy factors involved. Thus, Judge Goodrich says:

> Suppose the defendant carelessly does an act in state *A* which results in harm to the plaintiff in state *B*. The law of *B* controls. The plaintiff does not sue the defendant for the latter's negligence, but because the negligence has caused the plaintiff harm.[22]

But if the rule had been settled the other way, that the place of tort is where the negligent act is done and not where the resulting harm occurs, it would be just as convincing to argue that the plaintiff does not sue the defendant for causing him harm but because

---

[21] *E.g.*, French Civil Code art. 2279 (1804); German Civil Code art. 932–35 (1900); Swiss Civil Code §§ 934, 936 (1912).

[22] Goodrich, Conflict of Laws 263.

the defendant caused it negligently. Of course, the negligence and the harm are both necessary ingredients in the tort. We are told [23] that the German Reichsgericht rule is to adopt whichever law is most favorable to the plaintiff; but why not choose whichever law is most favorable to the defendant? If we adopt the proper law of the tort, we can at least choose the law which, on policy grounds, seems to have the most significant connection with the chain of acts and consequences in the particular situation before us. The task might not be easy, but at least we should be asking the right questions. In order to see how this might work in practice, let us consider one of the cases which is most frequently cited for the last event doctrine.

In *Alabama Great Southern R.R. v. Carroll*,[24] *P*, a resident of Alabama, was employed by *D*, an Alabama corporation, as a brakeman on freight trains operated by *D* and running from Birmingham, Alabama, to Meridian, Mississippi. The contract of employment was made in Alabama. *P* was injured in Mississippi because of the breaking of a link between two freight cars in that state. It was proved that the link was defective when the train left Birmingham, and that it was the duty of *D*'s servants to inspect the link in Alabama; and it was inferred that their failure to discover the defect was the result of negligence. By the law of Mississippi the common law fellow-servant rule applied and *P* could not have recovered if the negligence as well as the harm had occurred there. But by the Alabama Employers Liability Act *P* could have recovered if the harm had been sustained in Alabama.[25] The Alabama court denied recovery on the ground that "there can be no recovery in one state for injuries to the person sustained in another unless the infliction of the injuries is actionable under the law of the state in which they were received." It is a reasonable deduction from the court's opinion that if the train had been travelling in the opposite direction, and the negligence had occurred in Mississippi and the harm in Alabama, the decision would have been otherwise and *P* would have recovered. It seems difficult to sustain such results on any reasonable basis. The place where the defective link finally worked loose and caused the injury could hardly have been more fortuitous. Perhaps the

[23] LORENZEN, *op. cit. supra* note 13, at 368–70; 2 RABEL, THE CONFLICT OF LAWS: A COMPARATIVE STUDY 304–06 (1947).

[24] 97 Ala. 126, 11 So. 803 (1892).

[25] Ala. Laws 1884–85, No. 51, p. 115.

Alabama court should have inquired whether the Alabama Employers Liability Act modifying the common law fellow-servant rule was intended to apply (1) to injuries sustained outside Alabama by an Alabama resident through the negligence of fellow servants of an Alabama corporation, or (2) to injuries sustained in Alabama by foreign residents through the negligence of fellow servants of foreign corporations. If the court had asked itself these questions, it seems almost certain that it would have answered question (1) in the affirmative and highly probable that it would have answered question (2) in the negative. If *P* had been claiming compensation in Alabama under an Alabama workmen's compensation act, we should probably agree that Alabama had sufficient interest in the economic welfare of Alabama residents and employees to make it reasonable for the Alabama court (or board) to allow recovery under the Alabama statute, although the accident occurred outside the state. Certainly it would not be unconstitutional for it to do so.[26]

The mechanical last event doctrine appears to be so firmly embedded in American case law that courts are sometimes driven to tortuous processes of reasoning in order to escape from its consequences when common sense revolts. In *Levy v. Daniels' U-Drive Auto Renting Co.*,[27] the defendant company rented a car to one Sack in Connecticut. While *P* was a passenger in the car, Sack parked it so negligently on a Massachusetts highway that the defendant Meginn negligently ran into the car and *P* sustained injuries. If all these facts had occurred in Massachusetts, the defendant company would not have been liable in the absence of proof that it had been negligent; but Connecticut had a statute which provided that "any person renting or leasing to another any motor vehicle owned by him shall be liable for any damage to any person or property caused by the operation of such motor vehicle while so rented or leased." [28] The Connecticut court held the defendant company liable under this statute, apparently on the theory that *P* was an indeterminate third-party beneficiary under a contract made in Connecticut, the term in respect of which he sued being implied by Connecticut law.[29] Of course this

[26] Alaska Packers Ass'n v. Industrial Accident Comm'n of Cal., 294 U.S. 532 (1935).

[27] 108 Conn. 333, 143 Atl. 163 (1928).

[28] Conn. Acts 1925, c. 195, § 21.

[29] A similar argument, minus the fiction that the plaintiff was a third-party

is in the highest degree unrealistic: the plaintiff was claiming damages for a tort, not for a breach of contract. As a tort case the decision cannot be reconciled with the last event doctrine, and not unnaturally it seems incorrect to those who advocate that doctrine.[30] But under the more elastic doctrine advocated in this article, might it not have been said that Connecticut had sufficient interest in the business of renting cars in Connecticut to justify the application of Connecticut law,[31] that the place where the car was rented was of more significance than the place where the accident happened, and that therefore Connecticut was the proper law of the tort? To be sure, the court did examine the purpose of the Connecticut statute. "The purpose of the statute" it said, "was not primarily to give the injured person a right of recovery against the tortious operator of the car, but to protect the safety of traffic upon highways by providing an incentive to him who rented motor vehicles to rent them to competent and careful operators by making him liable for damages resulting from the tortious operation of the rented vehicles." [32] If the court had pushed its inquiry one stage further, it would have asked "what highways" and "what renters of motor vehicles;" in other words, it would have asked whether the Connecticut statute was intended to apply to renters renting cars in Connecticut to persons who cause injury in other states, or whether it was intended to apply to renters renting cars outside Connecticut to persons who cause injury in Connecticut. If it had asked itself these questions, it might have concluded that the former was the correct answer, unless indeed Connecticut is so provincial that its courts are indifferent to the safety of traffic upon highways outside Connecticut.

This case, and others like it, suggest that the problem of vicarious liability cannot be solved by a mechanistic application of the last event doctrine, but only by a more sophisticated inquiry into problems of causation and foreseeability coupled with a balancing of the interests of the states whose law is involved. In *Scheer*

beneficiary, was advanced and rejected in Alabama Great Southern R.R. v. Carroll, 97 Ala. 126, 11 So. 803 (1892).

[30] *E.g.*, 2 BEALE, CONFLICT OF LAWS 1296 n.2, where the citation of the case is preceded by the laconic "But see;" GOODRICH, CONFLICT OF LAWS 279–80, where after stating the case in the text the author comments: "This decision seems incorrect. . . ."

[31] STUMBERG, *op. cit. supra* note 14, at 204.

[32] 108 Conn. at 336, 143 Atl. at 164.

v. Rockne Motors Corp.,[33] for instance, the trial court held a New York bailor of a car liable for his bailee's negligent act in Ontario under an Ontario statute which provided that "the owner of a motor vehicle shall be liable for loss or damage sustained by any person by reason of negligence in the operation of such motor vehicle on a highway unless such motor vehicle was without the owner's consent in the possession of some person other than the owner. . . ."[34] But the Court of Appeals for the Second Circuit ordered a new trial on the ground that the bailor did not give the bailee permission to go into Canada merely by giving him possession of the car. Under the "last event" doctrine, of course, the bailor should have been held liable. Then why was the new trial ordered? As Professor Cavers has convincingly demonstrated,[35] it cannot have been on the ground that the bailor's express or implied permission for the bailee to take the car to Ontario was required in order to give "legislative jurisdiction" to Ontario to apply its law. For New York has a statute, similar in scope to the Ontario statute, which imposes liability on the bailor of a car for the negligence of his bailee.[36] It can hardly be the law that if an Ontario bailment, followed by a negligent act in Ontario, imposes liability on the bailor, and a New York bailment, followed by a negligent act in New York, imposes liability on the bailor, yet a New York bailment, followed by a negligent act in Ontario, leaves the bailor scot free. For if that were the reason why the new trial was ordered, then the accident of geography becomes decisive in a case where there was no true conflict of laws at all. The new trial can only have been ordered, then, on the supposition that the jury's finding was consistent with the bailor having expressly prohibited the bailee from driving into Canada: for only then would a true conflict between the laws of Ontario and New York have been presented. But if that was the reason why the new trial was ordered, why was the Pennsylvania owner of the dog in *Fischl v. Chubb*[37] liable for its bite in New Jersey? The answer can only

[33] 68 F.2d 942 (2d Cir. 1934).

[34] Ont. Highway Traffic Act § 41-A (1930).

[35] Cavers, *The Two "Local Law" Theories*, 63 HARV. L. REV. 822 (1950).

[36] "Every owner of a motor vehicle . . . operated upon a public highway shall be liable . . . for . . . injuries to person or property resulting from negligence in the operation of such motor vehicle . . . by any person . . . operating the same with the permission, express or implied, of such owner." N.Y. VEHICLE AND TRAFFIC LAW § 59. This was the statute applied to a New Jersey bailment in Young v. Masci, 289 U.S. 253 (1933).

[37] 30 Pa. D. & C. 40 (1937).

be that it is reasonable to expect a human being, but not a dog, to obey a domestic restriction on its radius of action. But this takes us into the realms of foreseeability and far beyond the scope of the place of harm or even the place of wrong.

A third advantage of the proper law of the tort doctrine is that it would enable the problems to be broken down into smaller groups and thus facilitate a more adequate analysis of the social factors involved. The questions that may arise in the field of torts are, no doubt, less various than those that arise in the field of contracts. But they are numerous enough to suggest doubts as to whether the application of a single formula — the law of the place of wrong — can possibly produce socially adequate results. The following questions have been suggested by random perusal of a well-known handbook [38] and a well-known casebook [39] on the conflict of laws: [40] Is the infliction of harm actionable without proof of negligence or intent? [41] Is the plaintiff's contributory negligence a defense? [42] Does the fellow-servant rule bar recovery? [43] Was the person causing the harm a servant or an independent contractor? [44] Is the bailor of a car liable for the negligence of his bailee? [45] Is it tortious to cause the death of a human being? [46] If so, who can sue [47] and among whom should the damages be distributed?[48] Does the cause of action survive the death

---

[38] GOODRICH, CONFLICT OF LAWS.

[39] CHEATHAM, DOWLING, GOODRICH & GRISWOLD, CASES AND MATERIALS ON CONFLICT OF LAWS (2d ed. 1941).

[40] The list is of course illustrative and not exhaustive.

[41] Connecticut Valley Lumber Co. v. Maine Central R.R., 78 N.H. 553, 103 Atl. 263 (1918); Dallas v. Whitney, 118 W. Va. 106, 188 S.E. 766 (1936); Hunter v. Derby Foods, Inc., 110 F.2d 970 (2d Cir. 1940); *cf.* Le Forest v. Tolman, 117 Mass. 109 (1875); Fischl v. Chubb, 30 Pa. D. & C. 40 (1937).

[42] Fitzpatrick v. International Ry., 252 N.Y. 127, 169 N.E. 112 (1929); *cf.* Levy v. Steiger, 233 Mass. 600, 124 N.E. 477 (1919); Sampson v. Channell, 110 F.2d 754 (1st Cir. 1940).

[43] Alabama Great Southern R.R. v. Carroll, 97 Ala. 126, 11 So. 803 (1892); Walsh v. New York & New Eng. R.R., 160 Mass. 571, 36 N.E. 584 (1894).

[44] Venuto v. Robinson, 118 F.2d 679 (3d Cir. 1941).

[45] Levy v. Daniels' U-Drive Auto Renting Co., 108 Conn. 333, 143 Atl. 163 (1928); Young v. Masci, 289 U.S. 253 (1933); Scheer v. Rockne Motors Corp., 68 F.2d 942 (2d Cir. 1934).

[46] Slater v. Mexican Nat. R.R., 194 U.S. 120 (1904); Loucks v. Standard Oil Co. of New York, 224 N.Y. 99, 120 N.E. 198 (1918); Rose v. Phillips Packing Co., 21 F. Supp. 485 (D. Md. 1937).

[47] Ghilain v. Couture, 84 N.H. 48, 146 Atl. 395 (1929); Rose v. Phillips Packing Co., *supra* note 46.

[48] Pennsylvania R.R. v. Levine, 263 Fed. 557 (2d Cir. 1920).

of the tortfeasor[49] or the injured party?[50] Can a wife sue her husband in tort?[51] Is a husband liable for his wife's torts?[52] It seems extraordinarily unlikely that all these questions can be satisfactorily answered by mechanically applying the law of the place of wrong without reference to the social factors involved, particularly if the wrongful act and the consequential harm occurred in different states, one of which has to be arbitrarily selected as the place of wrong.

No doubt courts have applied the law of the place of wrong more often than any other rule in most of these situations, except when considerations of public policy and the like have intervened to bar recovery.[53] But the question is whether the results are socially sound. In one situation at least it is believed that they are not. It is often said that damages for wrongful death should be distributed in accordance with the law of the place of wrong.[54] Suppose that a court in *F* is dealing with an action for wrongful death inflicted in *X*, and that the *X* wrongful death statute distributes the damages among the dead man's wife and children. If *F* refers to the law of *X* to determine who the wife and children are, it would seem too clear for argument that the reference must be to the conflicts rules of *X*, since to insist that the wife and children must qualify as such under the domestic law of *X* would often produce fantastic results. Yet this reference to the conflicts rule of *X* would seem contrary to the *Restatement's* rule[55] that renvoi is ordinarily to be rejected. Is it not at least arguable that the question who are the dead man's wife and children should be determined in accordance with the conflicts rule, not of *X*, but of *F*? We have here what some writers on the conflict of

[49] Orr v. Ahern, 107 Conn. 174, 139 Atl. 691 (1928); Ormsby v. Chase, 290 U.S. 387 (1933).

[50] Potter v. First Nat. Bank, 107 N.J. Eq. 72, 151 Atl. 546 (Ch. 1930).

[51] Buckeye v. Buckeye, 203 Wis. 248, 234 N.W. 342 (1931); Gray v. Gray, 87 N.H. 82, 174 Atl. 508 (1934); Mertz v. Mertz, 271 N.Y. 466, 3 N.E.2d 597 (1936); Bogen v. Bogen, 219 N.C. 51, 12 S.E.2d 649 (1941).

[52] Siegmann v. Meyer, 100 F.2d 367 (2d Cir. 1938).

[53] See Mertz v. Mertz, 271 N.Y. 466, 3 N.E.2d 597 (1936); Slater v. Mexican Nat. R.R., 194 U.S. 120 (1904); and the wrongful death cases before Loucks v. Standard Oil Co. of New York, 224 N.Y. 99, 120 N.E. 198 (1918).

[54] RESTATEMENT, CONFLICT OF LAWS § 393 (1934); 2 BEALE, CONFLICT OF LAWS 1312; GOODRICH, CONFLICT OF LAWS 302. HANCOCK, *op. cit. supra* note 14, at 125, says that the courts are divided on this question, and that decisions applying the law of the place of wrong have proceeded on the basis of assumption rather than conscious determination.

[55] RESTATEMENT, CONFLICT OF LAWS § 7 (1934).

laws have termed the preliminary [56] or incidental [57] question. In some situations, at least, it would appear that constitutional considerations would compel the forum to apply its own conflicts rule. Suppose that a court in Massachusetts is dealing with a wrongful death inflicted in Ontario, that the Ontario wrongful death statute distributes the damages among the dead man's wife and children, and that two women, *W1* and *W2*, are each claiming to be his wife. The deceased may have been a Canadian citizen, domiciled in Ontario. His first wife, *W1*, may have obtained a divorce from him while domiciled (in the American sense) in Florida. The divorce may well be invalid in Ontario, since under the law of that province *W1* was incapable of acquiring a domicil separate from that of her husband.[58] But how can the Massachusetts forum hold that the Florida divorce, and therefore the second marriage to *W2*, is invalid, without violating the full faith and credit clause of the Federal Constitution? [59]

When the present writer first suggested [60] that the application of the proper law of the tort might be a desirable way of handling tort problems, the suggestion was immediately stigmatized [61] as "absurd" on account of the difficulty of determining what is the proper law of a tort; but the critic did not explain why the difficulty of determining the proper law of a tort should be any greater than that of determining the proper law of a contract. In fact, the difficulty would appear to be somewhat less, because the factors to be taken into consideration are likely to be less various, and because in many, perhaps most, cases there would be no need to look beyond the law of the place of wrong. It should also be noted that the proper law of the tort theory is not open to one objection which has been raised to the proper law of the contract

[56] ROBERTSON, CHARACTERIZATION IN THE CONFLICT OF LAWS c. 4 (1940).

[57] WOLFF, PRIVATE INTERNATIONAL LAW c. 16 (2d ed. 1950); DICEY, CONFLICT OF LAWS 73–76.

[58] Attorney-General for Alberta v. Cook, [1926] A.C. 444 (P.C.). It is of course conceivable that the Ontario courts would estop *W1* from contesting the validity of the divorce on the ground that she had procured it. But the estoppel doctrine has not been elaborated in Canada to the same extent that it has, for instance, in New York. See *In re* Graham Estate, 52 Bri. Col. 481 (1937).

[59] See *In re* Degaramo's Estate, 33 N.Y. Supp. 502 (1895), where the New York court applied its own conflicts rule and not that of Ohio (the place of tort) to determine the validity of a Michigan divorce in order to determine who was entitled to the damages under the Ohio wrongful death statute.

[60] See Morris, *Torts in the Conflict of Laws*, 12 MOD. L. REV. 248 (1949) (comment on McElroy v. McAllister, [1949] S.C. 110).

[61] See Gow, *Delict and Private International Law*, 65 L.Q. REV. 313, 316 (1949).

theory,[62] namely, that it produces grave uncertainty in commercial matters. A shipping company or an insurance company may legitimately need to know what law will govern its contracts before it makes them. But a tort is not a consensual transaction. Tort liability is nearly always unexpected. A motorist does not legitimately need to know what law will determine his liability to pay damages if he runs down a pedestrian. His social duty is not to run the pedestrian down; he ought not to be concerned (at least until after the accident) with the questions whether the law imposes on him a strict liability or only a duty of care, or whether his liability is to be governed by the law of State *X* or the law of State *Y*. A duty not to cause harm is a good rule socially, though it may not always hold good in the domestic law of torts.[63]

[62] This objection is discussed and (I hope) answered earlier in this article at pp. 882–83 *supra*.

[63] I express my indebtedness to my class in the conflict of laws at the Harvard Law School, whose interest in and criticism of the ideas herein expressed encouraged me to develop them further.

[17]

IS AMERICAN GOVERNMENTAL INTEREST ANALYSIS THE SOLUTION TO ENGLISH TORT CHOICE OF LAW PROBLEMS?

By

J. J. FAWCETT*

THE unique contribution of American conflict of laws to modern ideas on choice of law is the introduction of governmental interest analysis to solve the perennial problem of which law to apply. Whilst this approach has been used extensively in several areas of choice of law in America it is only in tort choice of law that it has found favour in England. In this particular sphere interest analysis is advocated not only by English academics[1] but, even more importantly, by at least one Law Lord in the leading case of *Boys* v. *Chaplin*.[2] With the likelihood of reform of our tort choice of law rules in the near future it is appropriate to consider whether it is desirable or even possible to apply interest analysis in England to this area. In answering these questions it is proposed first to look at interest analysis as a means of arriving at particular decisions and secondly to consider the wider consequences for us in England of adopting interest analysis.

1. INTEREST ANALYSIS AS A MEANS OF ARRIVING AT PARTICULAR DECISIONS

A. What Interest Analysis Involves

Interest analysis requires the court to ascertain the content of the different competing laws in a choice of law case. It must then be asked what the purposes underlying these laws are and, having determined this, the court must decide whether each State has a legitimate interest in giving effect to its purpose on these particular facts. Where only one State is interested in having its law applied there is a false conflict and the law of that State is applied. Where both States are interested (a true conflict) then the strength of their respective interests must be weighed and the state which is more interested has its law applied.[3] One of the leading American cases, *Babcock* v. *Jackson*,[4] serves as a

*Lecturer in Law, University of Bristol.

My colleague, Nigel Lowe, read the draft of this article and I am grateful to him for the suggestions he made.

1. Jackson, *The Conflicts Process* (1975), chap. 17; Karsten, (1970) 19 *I.C.L.Q.* 35; Morse, *Torts in Private International Law* (1978), chap. 10; see also for Australian support, Nygh, (1977) 26 *I.C.L.Q.* 932.

2. [1969] 2 All E.R. 1085, *per* Lord Wilberforce at pp. 1097-1105, Lord Hodson at pp. 1088-1094 favoured the American most significant relationship test which involves an element of interest analysis but in applying his approach to the facts in front of him looked only at contacts.

3. Currie, (1963) 63 *Colum. L. Rev.* 1233, at 1242-3; Weintraub, *Commentary on the Conflict of Laws* (1971), chap. 6. In a true conflict situation Currie said the *lex fori* should apply but there are numerous instances of the courts weighing interests.

4. 191 N.E. 2d 179 (1963).

good illustration of the working of this approach. Both the plaintiff and defendant were New York residents, the defendant was injured by the plaintiff in an automobile accident in Ontario. This State has a guest statute preventing a guest suing his host. New York had no such law. Trial took place in New York. The New York Court of Appeals found that the purpose behind the Ontario statute was to prevent collusive claims against insurance companies. New York's purpose was to compensate plaintiffs. Which of these states was interested in having its law applied? Ontario was not concerned with protecting New York defendants or insurers whereas New York was interested in compensation New York plaintiffs. It was a false conflict and New York law was accordingly applied as the law of the only interested State.

B. *The Attractions of Interest Analysis*

The main merit of interest analysis is that it has, at first glance at least, a conceptual attractiveness which is in marked contrast to the traditional *lex loci delicti* rule, as espoused in America, or its English counterpart, the general rule of double actionability by *lex fori* and *lex loci delicti*. In any case involving a multistate tort a choice has to be made between different laws rather than between different jurisdictions. It seems only sensible to look at the purpose behind the competing laws and ask whether each law, given its purpose, has a claim to be applied in the particular circumstances of the case. When a State wants and can reasonably expect to have its law applied it is said to be interested in the dispute. There is something odd about applying the law of State X. when that State is not concerned that its law should be applied.

Admittedly, terminology which refers to "governmental" or "State" interests is not well chosen.[5] Any State's interest in private law litigation, if it exists at all, is indirect to say the least,[6] particularly where the law in question is a common law rule with no legislative origin. But defects in terminology should not on their own be a reason for excluding an approach which has something new and valuable to offer.

Compare the exciting originality of interest analysis with the undeniably mechanical line taken under the *lex loci delicti* rule or the English double actionability rule. In America one looks for the place of the tort and having found that jurisdiction its law is applied, regardless of the content of the other laws which are potentially applicable, and of whether the *locus delicti* is bothered about having its law applied. In England the *lex loci delicti* plays the same part but recovery under it will be cut down by the *lex fori* and only the overlap between the English law and the *lex loci delicti* will be recoverable.

5. Cavers, *The Choice of Law Process* (1965), pp. 100-102.

6. Kegel, (1964) II *Hag. Rec.* 95 Ch. 12. It can be argued that in a broad sense a State is always interested in having its purpose effectuated, see Cavers, *op. cit supra, n. 5.*

The second virtue of interest analysis is its flexibility. By refusing to give contacts any significance except in so far as they show whether a State is interested in having its law applied, interest analysis is able to deal with any fact situation regardless of the distribution of the contacts. Contrast this with the rigid *lex loci delicti* rule whose application inevitably means that the law of a fortuitous *locus delicti* is sometimes applied. Although the proper law of the tort[7] as adopted in America and as introduced in England in *Boys* v. *Chaplin* may help to avoid this particular difficulty that rule will only work where all the contacts are heavily on one side, as, for instance, where both parties reside in the same State. What is more, the imprecise nature of the search for a purpose and the wide discretion allowed to the court when weighing the interests of both States in a true conflict situation means that a judge can reach a result which he considers to be just. The development of interest analysis in America can be seen to be not just dictated by an attractive theory but also partly a pragmatic response to the many difficult and varied law fact situations facing the courts there.

C. The Problems in Applying Interest Analysis

1. The American Experience

Finding the purpose behind a law lies at the heart of interest analysis and it is this aspect of the approach which has caused the major headaches in America. This in itself should act as a warning when it comes to considering whether one should adopt interest analysis in England. There is no guarantee that in every case all would agree on a single clearly defined purpose underlying the law in question. The purpose may be unclear[8] in that it may be the result of contradictory arguments (since the passing of the statute would be the result of conflicting interests in the legislature and the result of skill in lobbying) or there might be more than one clear purpose.[9]

Added to these inevitable difficulties are problems which arise because the courts have not always properly carried out the search for the purpose, even though academic proponents of the approach have stressed that it should be carried out scientifically and not by guesswork.[10] There is a definite lack of consistency in the courts' behaviour when finding the purpose. In some cases the courts have looked for this in the light of modern day conditions,[11] neatly avoiding the problem of legislative intent, whereas in others the actual purpose

7. There is some ambiguity in the meaning of this phrase, in this article it is being used to connote a rule which looks at contacts, analogously to the objectively determined proper law of the contract, and does not pay any attention to the interests of States.

8. Rosenberg, (1967) 67 *Colum. L. Rev.* 459-464; Reese, (1969) 8 *Columbia J.* of *Transnational Law*, 182, at 186.

9. Currie, *Selected Essays on Conflict of Laws* (1963), pp. 85, 702; Frank (1947) 47 *Colum. L. Rev.* 1259; Brimlmayer, (1980) 78 *Mich. L. Rev.* 392, at 405.

10. Weintraub, *Commentary on the Conflict of Laws* (1971), pp. 201, 202; Shapira, *The Interest Approach to Choice of Law*, (1970), pp. 134-137.

11. See *Offshore Rental Co.* v. *Continental Oil Co.*, 138 Cal. Rptr. 838 (1977).

at the time of enactment has been sought. Sometimes the courts have made assumptions as to the purpose without giving any authority for their decision.[12] Where authority is cited this may involve direct evidence of legislative intent, using the aids to interpretation available to them.[13] Alternatively, the court may resort to indirect evidence of intent such as statements from the courts of the State whose law is being considered. Both of these are good evidence of the legislature's purpose. However, the courts have not always acted as scientifically as this and the authority cited may be suspect. The evidence of intent may merely be a student note in a law journal in which no authority is given to back up the student writer's opinion.[14] Even worse, a court may simply rely on a textbook or article which considers purposes in general and not the particular States, even though there is authority readily available from the State in question.[15] Courts may even "find" the purpose underlying State A's guest statute by quoting cases which deal with the purpose behind state B's guest statute, assuming incorrectly that the purposes are the same.[16]

The consequence is a whole range of different objectives being stated for the same statute.[17] Even the well-known Ontario guest statute has had its purpose alternatively described as being protection for insurance companies from fraudulent claims and preventing collusion, or that ungrateful guests should not bite the hand that feeds them.[18] Choosing one purpose rather than another can mean that a State is not interested and the choice of applicable law is thereby affected.[19] Uncertainty as to purpose will inevitably lead to uncertainty as to outcome. Even more fundamentally this shows that if a single clear purpose behind a law cannot be found then interest analysis becomes quite unworkable.

Once the purpose is "discovered" the next stage is to ask whether the respective States have an interest in having their law applied. Again, this is a matter in which there may be no objective truth. For example, it has been claimed that the State where injury occurred has an interest in having its compensatory law applied to plaintiffs resident outside that State because the

12. See *e.g. Kuchinic* v. *McCrory*, 222 A. 2d 897 at 899-900 (1966); *Griffith* v. *United Airlines*, 203 A. 2d 796 at 807 (1964); *Tramontana* v. *S.A. Empresa*, 350 F. 2d 468 at 471 (1965); *Challoner* v. *Day and Zimmermann, Inc.* 512 F. 2d 77 (1975), (the last two were international cases).

13. See nn. 31-39 *infra* and text accompanying them.

14. *Babcock* v. *Jackson*, 191 N.E. 2d 279 at 284.

15. See *e.g. Mullanc* v. *Stavola*, 243 A. 2d 842 at 845 (1968), several purposes underlying the Florida guest statute found by quoting *Prosser on Torts*. Yet a quick glance in *American Jurisprudence* (8 Am. Juris. 2d (1963) s. 471), reveals a Florida case of *Nelson* v. *McMillan*, 10 So. 2d 565 which states only one of these purposes, preventing ingratitude of guests. See also *Doiron* v. *Doiron*, 241 A. 2d 372 at 374 and *Clark* v. *Clark*, 222 A. 2d 205 at 209-210.

16. See *Heath* v. *Zellmer*, 151 N.W. 2d 526, 527 (1966) on the South Dakota guest statute and then the South Dakota case of *Schlim* v. *Gau*, 151 N.W. 2d 664, 669 (1967).

17. Reese, (1971) 71 *Colum. L. Rev.* 548 at 559. Compare *Chila* v. *Owens*, 348 F. Supp. 1207 at 1210 (1972) with *Mellk* v. *Saranson*, 229 A. 2d 625 (1967) on the purposes underlying the Ohio guest statute. In the former the court looked at the forum decisions and in the latter solely at Ohio decisions.

18. Compare *Babcock* v. *Jackson*, 191 N.E. 2d 279 at 283-284 (1963), with *Neumeier* v. *Kuehner*, 285 N.E. 2d 454 at 455 (1972). See also Trautman, (1967) 67 *Colum. L. Rev* 465 at 468-469.

19. See *Neumeier* v. *Kuehner*, *ibid.* at p. 455.

locus delicti is either concerned with deterring negligent conduct or it wants to protect State authorities from bearing the expense of medical treatment,[20] or because it wants to protect medical creditors,[21] or because it even wants altruistically to protect plaintiffs who are resident abroad.[22] But others have argued that any plaintiff will probably leave the State of injury, altruism does not apply and deterrence is outdated in this day and age.[23] There is therefore an inherent uncertainty of outcome whenever interest analysis is used, even if the purpose behind a law can be found accurately.

Where only one State is interested the theory of interest analysis works well and that State's law is applied. Although a great variety of different approaches are applied in those States which have rejected the *lex loci delicti* rule, most States begin by using interest analysis to weed out false conflicts. Where it is not a false conflict then there is much more disagreement amongst courts and commentators as to how one should proceed.

The theory of interest analysis is much less convincing where both States are interested in the dispute and some States have abandoned interest analysis at this point and adopted Leflar's choice influence considerations approach to solve the problem.[24] In those States where interest analysis is still applied in these true conflict cases it is asked how strong is each State's interest. This is a matter not only of factual contacts but also of the strength of policy and is generally anyone's guess. Then the interests have to be weighed. The outcome of the case is unpredictable but what tends to happen is that the weighing process becomes a weighing of the laws and not merely of the policies underlying them and there is a temptation for the forum to prefer its own law, at least if it is the more modern pro-plaintiff law. A court will be unwilling to admit to this and so dishonesty is fostered. Where Leflar's choice influencing considerations are used the process is much more open since one of the considerations (and in practice this is the most important one) is to consider which is the better rule of law.

The theory of interest analysis has never really developed to provide a satisfactory answer where neither state is interested (a zero interest case). The New York Court of Appeals in the recent case of *Neumier* v *Kuehner* was faced with this problem and solved it by replacing their ad hoc interest analysis approach with a number of narrow rules to be applied in guest statute cases.[25]

20. *Wilcox* v. *Wilcox*, 133 N.W. 2d 408 at 415 (1965); *Heath* v. *Zellmer*, 151 N.W. 2d 664 at 675; Cavers, (1970) III *Hag. Rec.* 75 at pp.154-156.
21. *Watson* v. *Employers Liability Assurance Corp. Ltd.*, 248 U.S. 66 at 72, (1954).
22. Martin, (1976) 61 *Cornell L. Rev.* 185.
23. Sedler, (1973) 61 *Kentucky L.J.* 378, 383.
24. Leflar, *American Conflicts Law*, (3rd edn.) (1977) pp. 193-195.
25. 285 N.E. 2d 454 (1972).

2. The Problems in England

The only justification for applying interest analysis in England is if it is conceptually attractive and stands up on its own merits. The flexibility it allows the court is not as necessary here as it is in America and so must be discounted when considering the advantages of adopting interest analysis in England. One of the striking characteristics of English tort choice of law has been the dearth of cases facing the courts. This is very different from the American position where the courts have been faced with hundreds of very different tort choice of law cases since the landmark decision in *Babcock* v. *Jackson* and have had to adopt a flexible approach to deal with these. Interest analysis loses its attractions if, as European critics contend,[26] it is harder or even impossible for one to find purposes scientifically or to discover and weigh the interests of the States involved. Whatever the failings of contact based rules they do at least produce a workable approach. The crucial question therefore is how would English lawyers fare in applying the process required by interest analysis and developed largely in interstate cases in the very different English context?

(a) Problems in using a teleological technique

According to Brainerd Currie, the father of governmental interest analysis, the approach involves the usual process of construction and interpretation of statutes.[27] American lawyers, brought up on a diet of sociological jurisprudence and used to a loosely phrased constitution, are accustomed to thinking in terms of the purposes behind internal laws.[28] The language of interest analysis and even some of its basic propositions were lifted by Currie from Supreme Court decisions on choice of law.[29] This is the real significance of development of interest analysis taking place within an interstate political unit. The Supreme Court may have withdrawn from the choice of law field in recent years but before it did so it provided the inspiration for interest analysis. It was natural that the Supreme Court, which was concerned with mutual respect between, and rights and duties of, all the States as political entities in a union, should adopt the language of the interests of States.

Regrettably, the usual process envisaged by Currie simply does not exist in England. Lawyers have not generally used a teleological technique when engaging in statutory interpretation. The literal meaning is all important and whilst English law has its mischief rule this has usually only been resorted to in the event of ambiguity in the wording.[30]

26. See Zweigert, (1973) 44 *U. Col. L. Rev.* 283 at 289.
27. Currie, *Selected Essays on Conflict of Laws* (1963), pp. 183-184.
28. Frankfurter, (1974) 47 *Colum. L. Rev. 527;* Hancock, (1964) 16 *Stan. L. Rev.* 561; *Erwin* v. *Thomas*, 506 P. 2d 494 at 469 (1973).
29. Currie, *Selected Essays on Conflict of Laws* (1963), pp.87, 204-205, 228.
30. Cross, *Statutory Interpretation* (1976), pp. 132-133; MacCallum, (1965) 75 *Yale L. J.* 754.

American lawyers not only have the practice in using a teleological technique but also their courts are well equipped to find the purpose accurately and are often able, if they go about it in the right way, to find the single clear purpose behind a law that interest analysis requires. Cases using interest analysis show the many aids to interpretation available to American judges. They have looked at law reform reports,[31] at failed attempts to repeal a statute barring recovery (to gauge the strength of the policy)[32] and at failure to enact a statute which does bar recovery[33] (although this can only be relevant if the legislature was invited to enact such a law and even then could be equally due to inertia).[34] They have read the statute as a whole,[35] looked at the preamble[36] and at the wording of earlier statutes dealing with the same topic.[37] In assessing the strength of a policy the courts have looked at the earlier repeal of a State law which limited recovery[38] and at State Constitutions which bar particular laws.[39]

Compare this wealth of available aids to interpretation with the English position. Where the courts are allowed by the canons of interpretation to look at the purpose underlying a statute, there are further rules which severely limit the extent to which legislative history can be studied.[40] The reports of law reform bodies cannot normally be looked at but if there is ambiguity can be used to ascertain the mischief against which the Act was directed[41] and so would presumably be applicable when using interest analysis. Records of parliamentary debates are precluded[42] and probably also the changes in an Act as it passed through Parliament, as are drawing implications from the fact that Parliament has not acted.[43] When it comes to internal aids the rules which allow

31. *International Planning* v. *Daystrom*, 248 N.E. 2d 576 at 582 (1969); *Farber* v. *Smolack*, N.E. 2d 36 at 39 (1967).

32. *Fuerste* v. *Bemis*, 156 N.W. 2d 831 at 834 (1968); *Satchwill* v. *Vollrath*, 293 F. Supp. 533 at 537 (1968).

33. *Babcock* v. *Jackson*, 191 N.E. 2d 279 at 284 (1963), there was evidence it was invited to do so. In the following cases there was no such evidence, *Wilcox* v. *Wilcox*, 133 N.W. 2d 408 at 416 (1965); *Bolgrean* v. *Stich*, 196 N.W. 2d 442 at 444 (1972); *Doiron* v. *Doiron*, 241 A. 2d 372 at 374 (1968).

34. Hart and Sachs, *The Legal Process* (1942), 1394-1395; Leflar, (1966) 41 *N.Y.U.L. Rev.* 267 at 306; *Halvering* v. *Hallock*, 309 U.S. 106 at 119 (1940). For conflicts cases making the point, see *Gravina* v. *Brunswick Corp.*, 338 F. Supp. 1 at 5 (1972); *Clark* v. *Clark*, 222 A. 2d 205 at 208 (1966).

35. *Tooker* v. *Lopez*, 249 N.E. 394 at 397 (1969).

36. *Macey* v. *Rozbicki*, 221 N.E. 2d 380 at 382 (1966); *Tooker* v. *Lopez*, 249 N.E. 2d 394 at 398 (1969); *Chila* v. *Owens*, 348 F. Supp. 1207 at 1211 (1972).

37. In *Re Estate of Clark*, 236 N.E. 2d 152 at 157 (1968).

38. *Tramontana* v. *S.A. Empressa*, 350 F. 2d 468 at 470 (1965).

39. E.g. limitations on damages in wrongful death actions: *Kilberg* v. *North-East Airlines Inc.*, 172 N.E. 2d 526 at 528 (1961); *Miller* v. *Miller*, 237 N.E. 2d 877 at 880 (1968); *Rosenthal* v. *Warren*, 457 F. 2d 438 at 443 (1973); *Griffith* v. *United Airlines Inc.*, 203 A. 2d 796 at 807 (1964); *Fox* v. *Morrison Motors*, 267 N.E. 2d 405 at 406 (1971).

40. See generally Cross, *Statutory Interpretation* (1976) Ch. 6.

41. Walker and Walker, *The English Legal System* (5th edn.) (1980), p.108; *Black-Lawson* v. *Papierwerke* [1975] 1 All E.R. 810; *Wachtel* v. *Wachtel* [1973] 2 W.L.R. 366 at 375. See also the Law Commission Report on "The Interpretation of Statutes" *Law Comm.* No. 21, which recommends the use of Law reform reports in all cases and more emphasis on purposes, and the Renton Report on The Preparation of Legislation (1975) *Cmnd.* 60, 53, at pp. 135, 148.

42. *Craies on Statute Law* (7th ed.) (1971) 128-130. The Law Commission recommends that this rule should remain, *op. cit. supra* n.41, pp. 36-37.

43. *Per* Lord Reid in *Knuller Ltd.* v. *D.P.P.* [1972] 2 All E.R. 898 at 903.

recourse to particular aids may not be very different in England from in America but in practical terms some of the aids in question are simply not available here. For instance, English statutes, unlike American, rarely contain a preamble.[44]

The limitations placed on the search for intent are self-imposed by the judges and thus there is a problem of judicial attitudes to be faced. There are thought to be good reasons why English courts should not go beyond certain rudimentary steps in interpretation of statutes. The courts are reluctant to use aids like Hansard as a guide to Parliament's intention because of a genuine scepticism about whether this intention can ever really be found whatever aids are used. The questions debated and reported in Hansard are often not the ones that occur before the courts. Promoters of a bill may never have thought of the issue before the court.[45] There is also the matter of judicial efficiency and the time involved in looking at external aids has been put forward as a reason against their use.[46] These arguments against a teleological interpretation of statutes can be put forward against the adoption of interest analysis in conflict of laws and show the extent to which that approach goes against the whole practice and philosophy of English lawyers. Because the courts do not favour a teleological approach they will not favour the basic concept at the root of interest analysis and will not have the tools to allow the purpose to be ascertained.

(b) Problems of technique in construction of foreign law

English courts would also face problems of technique in construction of foreign law which an American court operating in an interstate context would not have. Are the forum's methods and techniques of interpretation to be adopted or those of the State whose law is in question? Would we use foreign cases as authorities on the purpose if this was only revealed in that country by using methods not allowed by English courts? In American interstate cases, because of the uniform techniques of interpretaton throughout the nation, this problem has not arisen. But in an international choice of law case it can clearly arise.

If English courts, as is likely, were to adopt English techniques[47] then the purpose would be unlikely to be revealed. If Continental techniques were to be used when interpreting Continental law, the courts would face problems of proving, understanding and applying these techniques to be added to their existing problems of proving the content and purpose of foreign law.

44. For the American position see H. F. Stone, (1936) 50 *Harv. L. Rev.* 4 at 15.
45. *Per* Lord Reid in *Black-Lawson* v. *Papierwerke* [1975] 1 All E.R. 810 at 814-815.
46. *Ibid., per* Lord Simon at 842.
47. See a case where this was done, *Re Marshall* [1957] Ch. 507.

(c) Lack of Continental case law authority on the purpose

The American experience shows that it is extremely useful when searching for the purpose behind a law to look at judicial statements from cases decided in the state whose law is being considered. If the rule is a case law development this will be the only good evidence there is. However, an English lawyer would be less likely to have this invaluable source available to him than an American. Where courts think in teleological terms they will also talk in these terms but, as has been shown, English courts do not tend to do this. It would be over-optimistic to assume that if interest analysis were introduced English Courts would suddenly start talking in terms of purposes in internal cases, when they have not done so in the past, or that Parliament would put clauses in declaring the territorial reach of particular statutes.[48] Even if all this did happen, it would still take many years for an abundant case law to be there revealing underlying purposes.

An English court looking at the case law of a Continental country would encounter problems not met in an interstate context. Although a teleological interpretation of laws may be used in civil law systems, the way that judgments abroad are given and reported will mean that the purpose is not so abundantly clear to us as it would be if the judgment were that of a court in another common law jurisdiction. The terse style of Continental judgments[49] is not conducive to a case by case development which is what interest analysis is built upon and requires.

(d) The significance of similarity in the laws potentially applicable

Because of the similarity of laws in an interstate system ideas circulate throughout the nation and if, for example, one State does not have a guest Statute it may well have considered whether it ought to have one.[50] It will be easy therefore to understand what the purpose behind it is.

In an international context there is the problem of a common lawyer having to ascertain and understand the purpose behind a civil law rule, which may be totally different from anything ever encountered in the home State. Faced with a concept totally unknown to him, an English lawyer could not hope truly to ascertain the purpose behind the foreign law and he would be even harder pushed to gauge the strength of the interest of the foreign State.

It must also be remembered that there is always a risk of either being unable to prove foreign law or of making a mistake as to the content of that law and this risk will rise sharply if it is the law of an unfamiliar legal system that is being considered especially if the content includes something as vague as underlying

48. Cf. Gorman, (1968) 5 *U.C.L.A. Rev.* 605 at 617.

49. Court of Justice of the European Communities Judicial Academic Conference of Sept. 27-28, 1976, II-20.

50. Lipstein, (1972) *Hag. Rec.* 97 at 161-163.

purposes.[51] The American experience in international cases is revealing here. No problems have been encountered when the other country involved is another common law nation with similar economic and social conditions to those in America, for example Canada.[52] But a federal court, after looking at the relevant Civil Code and the affadavit of an expert witness, was unable to ascertain whether the law of Mozambique required a higher or lower standard of care in negligence cases than Illinois law and had to ask the parties to provide more evidence as to this.[53] It is also noteworthy that American courts, no doubt because of necessity, have made assumptions as to the purposes underlying Vietnamese and Cambodian law and, coming closer to home, Spanish, Netherlands and Scots law.[53a]

Furthermore, the English method of proving foreign law by using expert witnesses is particularly inappropriate where something as vague as the purpose underlying a Statute is being sought. The expert witnesses, since they are appointed by the parties, tend to disagree with each other and there will be plenty of scope for this when looking for a non-existent purpose or where there are perhaps two purposes.

(e) No purpose and the content of the law

Hitherto, it has been assumed that there is a clear purpose behind a law, although there may be problems in discovering what it is. But an English court may well have to consider a law which simply does not have a clear purpose behind it and this problem is much more likely to arise in English international choice of law problems than in American interstate conflict of laws because of the variety and origins of the different laws we are likely to come across.

In America the courts have been lucky in that frequently they have had to analyse a few relatively modern concepts like guest statutes and wrongful death limitations on damages. There were clear social purposes behind these laws, although the variety of possible purposes has caused trouble in particular instances. A more acute problem is where the rule in question is an old established case law development and the English courts are bound to encounter this. A rule may have evolved as a matter of historical accident rather

51. In interstate cases research has also shown that the courts often make mistakes as to the territorial reach of statutes e.g. that compensatory statutes are only for the benefit of forum residents, Brilmayer (1980), 78 *Mich. L. Rev.* 392.

52. See the Ontario guest statute cases starting with *Babcock* v. *Jackson*, 191 N.E. 2d 279 (1963). Nor, suprisingly, have there been problems in proving the content of Mexican law, see *Kasel* v. *Remmington Arms Co.*, 101 Cal. Rptr. 304 (1972).

53. *Pancotto* v. *Sociedade des Safaris de Mocambique S.A.R.L.*, 422 F. Supp. 405 at 409 (1976). See however the optimistic view of Baade that a "few idle hours work with foreign law books and pocket dictionaries" will reveal governmental interests in an international case, (1972) 72 *Colum. L. Rev.* 329 at 378.

53a. See In *Re Air Crash Disaster Near Saigon*, 476 F. Supp 521 (1979) (Vietnamese law); *Challoner* v. *Day and Zimmerman, Inc.*, 512 F. 2d (1975) (Cambodian law); *Jackson* v. *K.L.M. N. V.*, 459 F. Supp. 953 (1978) (Spanish and Netherlands law); *Reyno* v. *Piper Aircraft Co.*, 479 F. Supp. 727 (1978) (Scots law).

than as a deliberate policy decision, for example, the concept of separate matrimonial property as opposed to community of property.[54]

(f) Impossible exercises in comparison

When purposes have been discovered interest analysis always requires a weighing of the two disparate purposes in true conflict cases and this is an appalling task.[55] The result of an historical accident may have to be compared with a system of community of property which has a clear policy basis and has been strongly influenced by religious tradition.[56] The measure of this problem in Europe is shown by the difficulties that confronted an American court in an international choice of law case involving contributory negligence rules in England and New York.[57]

Comparing the merits of two laws and not merely their purposes is an even more difficult task. It is possible to use interest analysis yet to avoid looking for direct or indirect evidence of the purpose by doing as some American courts have done and look for the purpose in the light of modern conditions. But by avoiding one problem another one instantly springs up to replace it. What is really being asked is whether a law serves a useful purpose nowadays, whatever the original underlying intent. So a court is inevitably going into the merits of particular law. If the court considers, for example, that a law which allows a guest to sue his host is better than one which does not then it will say that a guest statute serves no useful purpose. Even where legislative intent has been found, in true conflict cases comparing underlying policies often degenerates into comparing the laws themselves. It is hard enough doing this in the interstate context where laws are similar and background conditions are virtually indistinguishable but the task of comparison may be quite impossible where what is being compared are two laws which have evolved against entirely different backgrounds. An English court might have to consider the French law of vicarious liability of a parent in respect of a child, unless the parent could have prevented the accident. The purpose of the law seems to be that children should be supervised and given a good education.[58] The rule is different in England but in French society the role of the parent and amount of supervision exercised by the parent may be very different from that in England and other countries. Who is then to say that French law is not as good as English law?

54. Friedmann, *Matrimonial Property Law* (1955), pp. 435, 436.
55. Reese, (1971) 71 *Colum. L. Rev.* 548 at 559.
56. See Friedmann, *op. cit. supra* n. 54, at p.434.
57. *Frummer* v. *Hilton Hotels International Inc.*, 304 N.Y.S. 2d 335 at 341 (1969).
58. Tunc, (1965) 14 I.C.L.Q.1089 at 1093; Amos and Walton, *Introduction to French Law*, (3rd edn., 1967), pp.227-228.

3. *Application in England: an Arbitrary, Parochial and Uncertain Approach*

It has been shown how American courts in interstate cases have yielded to the temptation to make assumptions as to the purposes underlying laws even when they could have found them with some degree of accuracy. Because they would be operating the approach in a different context, English courts, if they are able to prove the content of the foreign law in the first place, will often be unable to find the purpose scientifically and will be forced into making guesses in order to produce an answer to the case in front of them. This is already clear from the attempts made by some writers to use interest analysis to explain *Boys* v *Chaplin* and factual variants of its theme.[59]

One can look in more detail at the conclusions of one of the advocates of interest analysis, Dr. Karsten, to show how assumptions are made and why they should not be. He has said that there would be a true conflict if the facts were as in *Boys* v. *Chaplin* but with an English plaintiff and a Maltese defendant.[60] He reached this result by saying that England is concerned with compensating English plaintiffs so it is interested. He assumes that because Maltese law does not allow recovery for pain and suffering its policy is to protect defendants and since the defendant is Maltese it is also interested. If one adopts Karsten's analysis of the purpose underlying Maltese law it is a true conflict and, according to Karsten, Maltese law would have to be applied under the general rule of double actionability by the *lex fori* and *lex loci delicti,* the exception being in effect confined to cases where there is a false conflict.[61] But is Malta interested? If Maltese lawyers were asked about damages for medical expenses they may well say the purpose is to compensate the plaintiff. If then asked about damages for pain and suffering their reply could be that the Maltese legislature has never been asked to bring in recovery for this. In other words, the failure to allow recovery may be for many reasons other than a deliberate policy to protect the defendant. The only accurate way of putting it is to say that Malta has not shown the concern with compensating the plaintiff that England has. On this new analysis England is interested. Malta is not interested in the defendant at all, regardless of where he comes from. It is a false conflict and therefore English law, as the law of the only interested state, would be applied.

Even if purposes can be found accurately assumptions may have to be made at the next stage in the process when determining whether a state is interested in applying its law on these facts. Where the plaintiff is only temporarily resident in the *locus delicti* then it is unlikely that it could be said with certainty whether

59. Nygh, (1977) 26 *I.C.L.Q.* 932 especially at pp. 950-951 (1977); Karsten, (1970) 19 *I.C.L.Q.* 35; Morse, *Torts in Private International Law* (1978), Ch. 10. See also the Victoria case of *Corcoran* v. *Corcoran* [1974] V.R. 164 at 171 where the same fault is evident.

60. Karsten, *op. cit. supra* n. 59.

61. Note that Karsten very confusingly uses the language of interest analysis to describe the very different English approach which has a general rule with an exception and the general rule does not look at State interests.

that state is interested in having its compensatory law applied and this very question has led two academics who both favour interest analysis to reach different results on the same given set of facts[62]

The application of interest analysis in the English context has involved using a technique which is even less satisfactory than that adopted in America. Laws have been put into one of two crudely drawn categories; the first is those whose purpose is to compensate plaintiffs and the second is those whose purpose is to protect defendants. The more generous law is said to be designed to compensate plaintiffs and the less generous is automatically classified as being designed to protect defendants. There is not even the semblance of a search for actual legislative intent whereas in America in interstate cases there is usually the semblance of this and in many cases the reality as well. However, in international cases the American courts have been forced to adopt the same unrefined technique.[62a] The variety of purposes behind laws revealed by the American cases and the above analysis of Maltese law show the over simplistic nature of such a two fold division.

The clear conclusion from the examples given is that making assumptions destroys the sole justification for us using interest analysis, its conceptual attractiveness. What is being done is to apply one State's law in preference to another's when there is no valid criterion for so doing. And if one cannot prove the content of foreign law or if one has to assume the purpose underlying it then parochialism is likely to become increasingly important as an underlying consideration in tort choice of law cases, with English law being all too frequently applied as the only or most interested State. This nationalistic tendency is clearly evident in American cases involving international choice of law problems. There is always a tendency towards forum preference in international cases because of a basic mistrust of foreign law[63] and where there are practical difficulties in operating interest analysis then the court will automatically end up applying forum law and may not even enquire into the content of the foreign law[64] There has been for many years a heavy and much criticised reliance on the *lex fori* in English conflict of laws and so an approach which allows massive scope for this is singularly inappropriate here, especially when there is no English equivalent of the American constitutional checks in deterring excessive parochialism.[65]

62. Compare Karsten, *op. cit supra* n. 59 at p. 42 with Nygh, *op. cit. supra* n. 59 at p. 950.

62a. See *Jackson* v. *K.L.M.N.V.* 459 F. Supp. 953 (1978); *Reyno* v. *Piper Aircraft Co.* 479 F. Supp. 727 (1979).

63. See international cases asserting the forums interest *qua* forum in having it law applied; *Kasel* v. *Remmington Arms Co.*, 101 Cal. Rptr. 304 at 327 (1972).

64. See *Re Paris Air Crash of March 3, 1974*, 399 F. Supp. 732 (1975), decedents from 24 countries. Californian forum law was said to have the greatest interest in having its law applied, the content of the other applicable laws not being ascertained. Cf. *Tramontana* v. *S.A. Empressa*, 350 F. 2d 468 (1965), the content and purpose of Brazilian law discovered and that law applied.

65. Morse, *Torts in Private International Law* (1978), p. 226; Lipstein, (1972) I *Hag. Rec* 97 at 161-163; Morris, *The Conflict of Laws*, (2nd edn., 1980), p.515; Graveson, (1960) I *Hag. Rec.* 21 at 112.

One final point about operating interest analysis is that a guesswork process renders the outcome in a particular case completely uncertain. Reverting to the situation where a tort is committed in Malta and there is an English plaintiff and a Maltese defendant two separate legal advisers could give totally different advice and who can predict what a judge would decide!

II. THE WIDER CONSEQUENCES OF ADOPTING INTEREST ANALYSIS

APART from the problems already mentioned there are disadvantages of a more general nature which would be an inevitable result of applying interest analysis in England and which are sufficiently great to rule out its adoption.

A. The Burden on the Legal Profession

Interest analysis is undeniably complex and requires a lot of both practitioner and judge. This new complexity would be imposed upon an existing system which in the tort choice of law sphere is noteworthy for its simplicity of operation; if there is no actionability by English law no more need be said and the plaintiff's claim fails and where there is actionability by English law the plaintiff does not have to plead the foreign *lex loci delicti.*

Inevitably, the complexity created by interest analysis would be resented by the legal profession who would be required to undertake roles to which they are not accustomed. The role of judges would have to be altered. They would be required openly to acknowledge that they are lawmakers, which they have been reluctant to do for fear of impinging on the sovereignty of Parliament.[66] The practitioner would be required to expend enormous effort in assimilating this new approach and in applying it would have to become much more involved in comparative law than at present.[67] He would have to advise a client despite the uncertainty of outcome inherent in the process and this uncertainty would be resented much more by an English lawyer than by an American.

Sociological jurisprudence and American realism have convinced many American lawyers that certainty has been overvalued, that absolute certainty is never attainable and therefore should not be sought at the price of other objectives such as flexibility to give justice in the individual case.[68] The English philosophy sets more store by certainty in the law. When it comes to conflict of laws the importance of certainty can be seen from the frequent references in *Boys* v. *Chaplin* to its value and from the limited nature of the changes in the English tort choice of law rules in that case.[69]

66. Devlin, *Samples of Lawmaking* (1962), pp. 20-22.
67. Drion, *Festchrift für Otto Riese* (1964), p. 236.
68. Pound, *An Introduction to the Philosophy of Law* (1921), p. 71; Holmes, *Collect Legal Papers* (1920), 180; Frank, *Law and the Modern Mind* (1930), Ch. 1; Cardozo, *Nature of the Judical Process* (1932), p. 75.
69. *Boys* v. *Chaplin* [1969] 2 All E.R. 1085, per Lord Wilberforce at 1102, 1103, Lord Pearson at 1111, Lord Guest at 1095, Lord Donovan at 1097, Lord Hodson at 1092.

B. The Burden on the Client

The client would have to bear the burden of the lack of predictability which is inevitable with an approach as inherently uncertain as interest analysis. This would mean his not knowing what his legal rights and duties are and an increased likelihood of litigation.

The client would have to bear a greater expense both because of the complexity of the process and the cost involved in proving the content and purpose of foreign law. Unlike the English rule in *Phillips* v. *Eyre*, interest analysis, if it is to be carried out properly and not in a parochial way requires an enquiry into the content and purpose of not just one foreign State's law but into the laws of all of those foreign States which are connected with the problem. In an interstate context this heavy reliance on comparative law [70] does not present enormous difficulties. If interest analysis is to be adopted, it is important that English lawyers should, like American, be equipped with rules that make proof of foreign law a cheap and easy matter and there is a ready availability of sources of foreign law. Unfortunately for the client, English lawyers lack these essentials.

In America judicial notice is taken of the content of the others State's law. This means that the judge, often assisted by written testimony of expert witnesses employed by either party, will ascertain the content of foreign law. Most importantly, the judge can look at materials which have not been formally admitted into evidence, such as digests and textbooks. [71] One consequence of development against an interstate background is that the law is stated in nationally used digests, textbooks and a national reporter system (all of which are available to lawyers) and it is easy for a judge to prove sister State law. Furthermore, American lawyers are used to looking at sister State law in conflicts cases, indeed they have to because of the Constitution.

In England the first limb of the rule in *Phillips* v. *Eyre* and the rules of pleading mean that sometimes foreign law is never even looked at in tort choice of law cases. This is perhaps just as well since foreign law has to be proved as a fact and the method employed is usually the costly and lengthy process of proof by expert witnesses. [72] Even if the rules were changed to allow judicial notice the problem is not over. English lawyers are not comparative lawyers and even university law libraries seldom contain much in the way of civil law legal materials. So it would be difficult for lawyers to advise their clients without paying for expert witnesses on foreign law.

Finally, when considering the expense of applying interest analysis it must be remembered that in America expense does not provide a real handicap for the

70. Von Mehren, (1975) 23 *Am. J. Comp. Law* 751.

71. See Leflar, *American Conflicts Law* (3rd edn., 1979), s. 130.

72. See generally, Delaume, *Transnational Contracts* (1979), s. 4:1; Jackson *The Conflicts Process* (1975), pp. 329-332.

client because the contingency fee system takes away the financial deterrent against litigation. The client in England is going to object to paying out large sums of money simply in the cause of alleged conceptual attractiveness.

C. *The Reaction of Other Member States in the E.E.C.*

One of the obvious disadvantages of interest analysis wherever it is operated is that it leads to a lack of uniformity, with the outcome depending on which State applies the approach. In England uniformity takes on a new significance with the future possibility of an E.E.C. Convention on Tort Choice of law.[73] Yet it would be hard to think of an approach which is less likely to produce uniformity of law than interest analysis.

To reach agreement amongst nine member States any rules adopted must be non-controversial which can hardly be said of interest analysis. Neither does interest analysis produce the certainty, predictability and fulfilment of the parties' expectations which are regarded as being such important values in civil law systems,[74] so it is likely to be as unpopular with other member States as it would in England. Agreement can only be reached by looking for the bare minimum of common ground and this would point to a basic *lex loci delicti* rule with perhaps a proper law of the tort exception. There is not only this practical consideration of actually reaching agreement but it does seem entirely inappropriate when seeking to harmonise rules on private international law throughout Europe to adopt an approach which is likely to lead to dishonesty and which allows free rein for nationalism and provincialism.

To achieve the subsequent uniformity of interpretation which an E.E.C. Convention requires, the approach adopted must be such as to give a certain and predictable result and this is manifestly not true of interest analysis. Even identical laws may have different purposes and different strengths of interest in being applied, as the American experience with the guest statutes of different States shows. The choice of forum for trial would be vital since the unscientific search for the purpose, the necessity to make assumptions and the tendency to give the forum an interest *qua* forum would mean that an English court may well give a different answer on a given set of facts from say a French or German court. In England it has already been realised that a teleological approach will lead to a lack of uniformity. The Court of Appeal has gone as far as saying that when interpreting International Conventions, in order to achieve uniformity, a method should be adopted which looks at what has actually been said rather

73. See the E.E.C. preliminary Draft Convention on the Law Applicable to Contractual and Non-Contractual Obligations and the Law Commissions Consultative Document of August 1974.

74. Drion, *op. cit. supra* n. 67 p. 236.

than using a teleological method of interpretation which leads to different views in different countries.[75]

CONCLUSION

Interest analysis has nothing to offer the English or Continental lawyer. The process presupposes a set of background conditions which enable it to operate properly, all of which are simply absent in the English context. These include the presence of a "Supreme Court", a similarity in the laws of the forum and the other concerned States, an availability of aids to statutory interpretation, a wealth of materials on comparative law and a contingency fee system. Yet without these essential prerequisites the outcome in any individual case becomes arbitrary, nationalistic and uncertain. And to make things worse, whilst striving to do the impossible a crippling burden would be cast on English lawyers, their clients and possibly our relations with fellow member States of the E.E.C. The way ahead lies in refining and improving our contact based rules rather than dangerously over-reacting to the defects in these by introducing interest analysis.

75. *Ulster-Swift Ltd.* v. *Taunton Meat Ltd.* [1977] 1 W.L.R. 625 at 632.

[18]

THE FOUNDATIONS OF RULES FOR THE CHOICE OF LAW

A. J. E. Jaffey*

This article is concerned with the objectives which underlie choice of law rules in the conflict of laws. The discussion will be confined to aspects of contract, tort and marriage law. In the United States, particularly, much is made of the interests which countries or legal systems are said to have in the application of their rules to the question in issue, and, for some, choice of law mainly consists of an investigation into the presence or absence of such interests. It will be suggested, however, that the question of a country or legal system having an interest or concern in its rules being applied really only arises if the purpose of the rules in question is to protect or advance the public interest of that country. As regards such domestic rules, the relevant choice of law rules may well have as their object the protection of the interest of the country concerned. For the most part, however, the purpose of rules of contract and tort, and to some extent of marriage law also, is to do justice to individuals, and as regards those domestic rules, the idea that a country or legal system can have an interest or concern in their application in some cases, but not in others, is misconceived. Similarly, if the policy of a rule is to do justice to parties to a dispute, that policy can tell us nothing about the scope of the rule's application in cases involving foreign elements. Rather, the applicability of such a rule in conflict cases depends on principles of justice germane to the conflict of laws. What we shall be concerned with then is, firstly, to identify the limited areas where the advancement or protection of interests of countries is a factor which influences choice of law rules, and then to see what general principles of justice can be identified as the foundation of choice of law rules.

1. THE INTERESTS OF COUNTRIES

Although the advancement or protection of the interests of countries is widely thought of as relevant in choice of law, in the areas we are considering—marriage, contract and tort—the interests of countries are affected only to a limited extent. For present purposes, domestic rules of law may be divided into those whose purpose is to protect or advance the public interest of the country concerned, those whose purpose is to do justice to, or between, individual litigants or parties to a transaction or relationship, and those whose purpose is both of these. As we shall see below, the interests of countries are not relevant to the applicability of domestic rules whose primary purpose is to do justice to the parties.[1] When,

*Senior Lecturer in Law, University of Exeter.

1 See 376–377.

however, the English court, in a conflicts case, applies a domestic rule whose purpose is to protect the public interest of the country whose rule it is, it is a plausible assumption that the reason for applying that domestic rule, or the policy of the choice of law which leads the court to apply it, is the desire to protect the public interest of the country concerned. That is not necessarily so, however, for although the *effect* of applying the domestic rule in question may be to protect the public interest of the country, the reason for applying it may be different, for example to do justice to the parties, or to try to ensure uniformity of decision or status in different countries. So it is necessary to examine the extent to which the policy behind the choice of law rule is the protection of the public interests of countries. We shall begin with the law of marriage.

(*a*) *Marriage*

Some rules of domestic marriage law have the purpose of protecting the public interest rather than the interests of the parties. In the field of essential validity there are the rules which invalidate a marriage that the parties themselves freely agreed to contract, and perhaps have ever since wished to continue, for example rules laying down prohibited degrees of relationship or requiring monogamy, and rules prohibiting marriage between members of different religions or races. Such rules invalidate the marriages in question as being harmful to the moral, religious, social and perhaps even physical well-being of the community,[2] as seen by the legal system of that community, even though the parties themselves desire the marriage. Rules laying down a minimum age for marriage, on the other hand, in addition to advancing the public interest in stable marriages, no doubt also have the purpose of protecting a young person against his own possible immaturity and want of judgment.[3]

It needs no arguing that the reasons for an English court's application of an English rule invalidating a marriage on the grounds of the public interest will include the protection of that public interest. When in *Brook* v *Brook*[4] the House of Lords held that a marriage between a man and his deceased wife's sister, both domiciled in England, was governed by English law and thus invalid, even though celebrated in Denmark, by the law of which the marriage was valid, the protection of the English public interest was obviously in the minds of the judges. Lord Campbell LC said,[5] 'It is quite obvious that no civilized State can allow its domiciled subjects or citizens, by making a temporary visit to a foreign country, to enter into a contract to be performed in the place of domicile, if the contract is forbidden by the law of the place of domicile as contrary to religion, or morality, or to any of its fundamental institutions.'

2 For a comprehensive list of such public purposes see P. M. North, *Recueil des Cours* (1980) I, 54–55.

3 *Pugh* v *Pugh* [1951] P 482, 492; Hartley, 'The Policy Basis of the English Conflict of Laws of Marriage' 35 *Mod L Rev* 571, 577 (1972); North, loc cit 59–60.

4 (1861) 9 HLC 193.

5 P 212.

The more difficult question is whether the reason for the application of a foreign rule of essential validity can be the protection of the public interest of the foreign country concerned. Suppose that Ruritanian first cousins marry each other in England and then return to Ruritania, where they live as man and wife, and that by Ruritanian law the marriage is void for consanguinity. There is no doubt that if the parties subsequently move to England, and the issue arises in an English court, the marriage will be held void, even though it is valid by English law. Why? The reason for applying the Ruritanian rule which invalidates the marriage cannot be in order to promote the interests of the parties. The interests of the parties cannot lead the English court to hold void a marriage which the parties themselves freely chose to contract and, let us assume, desire to continue, and which is perfectly valid and unobjectionable in the eyes of English law. Even if we assume that a subsidiary purpose of the Ruritanian rule is to protect the interests of the parties by saving them from sin or wrong doing, that cannot be of any consequence for the English court, in whose eyes they are doing nothing wrong, or against which it could be in their own interests to be protected.

If then Ruritanian law is applied to invalidate the marriage, it seems that the reason can only be the wish to protect the Ruritanian public interest as defined by Ruritanian law. As against this, however, it might be argued that the protection of the Ruritanian public interest is not the purpose of the English choice of law rule, but merely the accidental consequence of its application, its purpose being in general the promotion of the interests of the parties to marriages. The choice of law rule, that capacity to marry is governed by the parties' domicile, is designed in the interests of spouses, not countries, for to apply say the *lex fori* or the *lex loci celebrationis* to invalidate a marriage which is valid by the law of the parties' domicile would indeed be unjust to the parties. But then consistency requires that the law of the domicile should also be applied when it makes the marriage invalid. A general rule inevitably leads to hard cases. But a mere desire for conceptual consistency is hardly a good reason for invalidating a marriage. If the attitude of the English conflict of laws was that the application of a Ruritanian rule invalidating a marriage could not be justified by the desire to protect the Ruritanian public interest, and that the proper foundation of a choice of law rule in this sphere was only the interests of the parties (or the English public interest), then the appropriate choice of law rule would be that a marriage is valid if it is valid by either English law or the law of the parties' domicile.

Another explanation, apart from the advancement of the Ruritanian public interest, which might be given for applying the Ruritanian invalidating rule in the case under discussion, is that of producing uniformity of status in different countries. It is obviously undesirable that parties should be regarded as validly married in one or more countries and not married in another or other countries. The choice of law rule that a marriage is invalid if it is so by the law of the parties' domicile does to some extent promote uniformity, even if many other countries use different connecting factors for their corresponding rules. This is because most people are nationals of the country in which they are domiciled, remain domiciled in the same country after marriage as before, and are married to spouses who have the same domicile and nationality as their own. In our case of two Ruritanian cousins, domiciled in Ruritania, who marry each other, very probably they would both be Ruritanian citizens and would remain such, as well as domiciled in Ruritania, after the marriage. In such a case choice of law rules by which prohibited degrees of relationship are governed by the law of the antenuptial domicile of each of the parties, or by the law of the intended matrimonial home, or by the law of the nationality of each party would all produce uniformity of status, for in every case Ruritanian law would govern. But as soon as the parties' domicile is different from their nationality, or the domicile or nationality of the one differs from that of the other, or changes after the marriage, then, because the choice of law rules of different countries are not the same, uniformity of status can of course no longer be achieved.

It seems reasonable then to conclude that the choice of law rule by which the applicability of domestic rules of essential validity of marriage whose purpose is to promote the public interest of the country concerned is governed by the law of the domicile, is based on two policy factors: (*a*) the desire to promote the public interest of the country concerned, as defined by that country's law, and (*b*) the desire to achieve uniformity of marriage status.

When, however, we come to consider how these policy factors help to identify precisely what the choice of law rule should be, for example, as between a dual domicile or intended matrimonial home approach, we find that the factor of promoting uniformity does not help at all,[6] because for uniformity to be achieved it is necessary, but only necessary, that the choice of law rules of different countries should be the same; any rule will do, so long as it is applied by all. This reinforces the view that the promotion of the public interest of countries, even foreign ones, must be accepted as a policy factor in the choice of law rules we are considering, otherwise there would be no criterion at all for selecting one possible choice of law rule in preference to another.

If then the reason for applying a domestic rule invalidating a marriage on, say, the grounds of degree of relationship, or polygamy, is the wish to promote the public interest of the country concerned, it is clear that the choice of law rule must use a connecting factor which will ensure that only marriages capable of damaging the public interest in question are caught by the invalidating rule. If for instance the public interest which a particular country's domestic rule is designed to protect can only be affected if the matrimonial home after the marriage is in that

6 But the desire for uniformity no doubt influenced the court in *R* v *Brentwood Marriage Registrar* [1968] 2 QB 956, when renvoi was used in relation to capacity to marry, and the incidental question of the validity of a divorce was referred to the *lex causae* rather than the *lex fori*; so also, as regards the incidental question, in *Padolecchia* v *Padolecchia* [1968] P 314 and *Schwebel* v *Ungar* (1963) 42 DLR (2d) 622, (1964) 48 DLR (2d) 644. But the *Brentwood Registrar* decision has been partly overruled by s 7 of the Recognition of Divorces and Legal Separations Act 1971, and for the rest not followed in *Perrini* v *Perrini* [1979] 2 WLR 472.

country, then a choice of law rule which requires the application of that domestic rule on the basis that one of the parties was domiciled in the country before the marriage, although the parties do not live there after it, will nullify marriages quite unnecessarily. It seems pretty clear that the public interest protected by rules relating to prohibited degrees of relationship, and polygamy, for instance, can only be damaged by a relationship connected with the country in question after the celebration of the marriage, so that a matrimonial home rule, as applied in *Radwan* v *Radwan* (*No. 2*),[7] rather than an antenuptial domicile rule, is appropriate.[8]

What is the justification for an English court's having regard to the public interest of a foreign country, whether friendly or not? Why should an English court ever subordinate the interests of parties, or justice between them, to the public interest of a foreign country, as it will be doing when, for example, it holds invalid a marriage which the parties desire to be valid, and which is valid by English law, by the application of foreign law? The only possible answer to this puzzling question is that it is done of out of comity[9] (discredited though this reason for the application of foreign law is with some writers), in the hope that other countries will adopt the same approach, as of course they do, though not necessarily using exactly the same criteria.

It will have been observed that, in this area of essential validity of marriage, the only domestic rules we have considered as having the function of protecting a public interest are invalidating rules. It may be asked whether a country's rules by which marriages are valid, as opposed to invalid, may not have as a purpose the protection of the public interest, which might, in a conflict case, have to be weighed against the public interest of another country in its invalidation. It is of course true that all countries have a public interest in the well-being of the institution of marriage, and all legal systems work on the premise that marriages should be valid unless there is some good reason for invalidating them. Conflict rules must reflect this by ensuring that no country's invalidating rule is applied without sound reason. It would be unreal, however, to regard a country as having a public interest in upholding the validity of any particular marriage (as opposed to marriages in general) in competition with the public interest of another country in its invalidation. What may have to be weighed against a country's interest in invalidating a marriage is not the interest of another country, but, as we shall see,[10] the interest of the parties, or one of them, in its validation.

Other choice of law rules in marriage, outside the area of essential validity, may also have the protection of the public interest of countries as one of their underlying policy factors. Domestic rules laying down the formalities of marriage

7 [1973] Fam 35.

8 See 'The Essential Validity of Marriage in the English Conflict of Laws' 41 Mod L Rev 38 (1978).

9 Or 'the needs of the interstate and international systems' in the words of Cheatham and Reese, 'Choice of the Applicable Law' 52 *Col L Rev* 959, 962 (1952) and the Restatement (Second) of the Conflict of Laws, s 6 (1971).

10 See 380–381 *infra*.

have, for instance, among their purposes, the proper recording of marriages, and this public interest is no doubt one of the reasons why formal validity is governed by the *lex loci celebrationis*. Domestic rules of divorce also of course reflect the public interest of the country or countries where the parties reside,[11] as well as protecting the interests of the parties. The English court quite appropriately applies English law when it exercises jurisdiction in a divorce case, for the grounds of jurisdiction are such that, except when the artificial rules of domicile work badly, at least one of the parties resides in England, whose public interest is thus involved.

(*b*) *Contract*

Some domestic rules of contract, like those of marriage, have the purpose of protecting the public interest. While for the most part the function of the rules of contract is to settle disputes between individuals in a manner thought by the legal system in question to be fair or expedient, some contracts, or contractual provisions, are regarded as being injurious to the public interest, for instance because immoral, criminal or damaging to the national economy. The rules which invalidate such contracts exist to protect the public interest, not to advance the parties' interests or to do justice between them. When the English court applies a foreign rule of this kind it would seem on the face of it that the policy behind the English choice of law rule must be to promote the public interest of the foreign country concerned. Suppose two parties of full capacity and equal bargaining power make a contract by correspondence which contains no express or implied choice of law by the parties. One party is English, the other French, and the contract is to be wholly performed on both sides in Italy. By no system of law is the contract objectionable on the score of being unfair as between the parties, but by a rule of Italian law, designed to protect the Italian economy, the contract is invalid. Very possibly the English court would hold Italian law to be the governing law, with the result that the contract would be held invalid at the instance of one of the parties who is sued by the other. What would be the justification for applying Italian law to invalidate the contract, rather than English law to uphold it? Since the purpose of the Italian rule is not to do justice between the parties—which requires the enforcement of the contract—but to protect the Italian public interest, it seems to follow that the reason for the English court's application of the Italian rule must be the protection of the Italian public interest, as defined by Italian law.

To this it might be objected that the reason why Italian law would be applied in the case in question is simply that, in the absence of a choice by the parties, a contract is governed by the law of the country with which it is most closely connected, the reason for that rule being that there should be a single law governing most aspects of, or issues arising from, contracts, and the most appropriate law for that purpose is that of the country with which the contract is

11 Wolff, *Private International Law* 2nd ed, 373–374; North, *Recueil des Cours* (1980) I, 27–30.

most closely connected. Even, however, if we assume the need for a single governing law for a contract, there is no basis at all for suggesting that the law of the country with which the contract is most closely connected is more likely to do justice between the parties, or serve their interests, than any other law. From the point of view of the court itself, the *lex fori* represents what is just, while for each of the parties probably justice is to be identified with his own law. Factors such as where the contract was to be performed and where it was made shed no light at all on which country's rules are appropriate from the point of view of justice to the parties. Nor can such a vague formula as the law of the country with which the contract is most closely connected serve the parties' interests in having a certain, predictable and uniform law, which we shall consider further below.[12] The only possible rationale for the law of the country with which the contract is most closely connected (as opposed to the legal system with which the contract is most closely connected, which is another way of describing the implied intention of the parties) is that it is a rough and ready way of selecting the country whose public interests are most likely to be affected by a contract. In the case of our hypothetical contract between an English and a French party entirely to be performed in Italy, the fact that it is to be performed in Italy, as we have seen, is no reason at all for an English court to use Italian standards of justice to solve a dispute between the parties, but if the performance of the contract was prohibited by Italian law as being contrary to the public interest then clearly the fact that performance is to take place in Italy is relevant in deciding whether Italian law should be applied. The conclusion must be that this choice of law rule for contract, that the governing law is that of the country of closest connection, primarily serves the purpose of protecting those public interests of countries, foreign as well as the forum, which are reflected in their invalidating rules. The misplaced desire to have a single governing law for contractual matters generally then leads to the law of the country of closest connection being used for other issues, for which it is not appropriate at all.

We see then that in this sphere of legality and essential validity of contracts the policy factor of the choice of law rule is to promote the public interests of countries in cases where their invalidating rules are designed to protect such interests. (An invalidating rule may of course be designed to protect the interests of a weaker party, but we are not concerned with such rules at the moment.) It is immediately clear, however, that this policy factor, and incidentally also the interests of the parties, would be better served by a more refined rule.[13] It is not really a question of how closely a contract is connected with a particular country, but rather whether it is connected with that country in the precise way which will affect the public interest which the invalidating rule is designed to protect. If, for

12 See 387–389 *infra*. These points are more fully discussed in P M North, ed, *Contract Conflicts* (1982), chapter 2.

13 See 'Essential Validity of Contracts in the English Conflict of Laws' 23 *Int'l and Comp LQ* 1 (1974).

instance, a particular kind of conduct is regarded as damaging to the public interest, then usually it will only be so damaging if it occurs in the country in question; in such a case it would be pointlessly destructive of the parties' agreement to apply that rule if the conduct in question is to take place outside that country, no matter how closely in other respects the contract is connected with that country. So, for example, an English court should not apply an English rule to invalidate a provision ousting the jurisdiction of a foreign court, or which is collusive or champertous of foreign litigation, or which restricts trade abroad, and mutatis mutandis with regard to foreign rules.[14] If the formula of closest connection is to be used, only relevant connections should be taken into account. (As will be indicated in the next section, connections may be relevant not only on the score just mentioned, but also in weighing the public interest of the country concerned against justice as between the parties.)

As with essential validity of marriage, it is only rules which invalidate contracts, not those which validate them, whose applicability can depend on the public interest of countries. Certainly it is in the public interest of a country to promote the effectiveness of contracts, so it should be a basic choice of law principle that contracts are prima facie valid. Choice of law rules must be formulated and applied so as not to invalidate contracts without good reason. There is no call, however, to regard a country as having a public interest in the validation of any particular contract, to be weighed against the interest of another country in its invalidation. Rather, as we shall see below,[15] the interest of a country in invalidating a contract may have to be weighed against the interests of the parties, or one of them, in its validation.

(c) *Tort: speculative or non-existent interests*

The next inquiry is whether the protection of the public interest of a country is, or should be, a policy factor in choice of law rules for tort. It is ironical that in the area of law where the interests of countries (or governments, as it is sometimes put) have perhaps been most strongly advocated as the criteria for the applicability of domestic rules, the proper conclusion seems to be that such interests should not normally be taken into account. The topic cannot be fully discussed here,[16] but the following points can briefly be made:

1. The primary purpose of domestic rules of tort is to achieve justice between the litigants, not to protect the public interest. While some tort rules may perhaps have secondary purposes, involving the protection of the public interest, such as deterring harmful conduct, the existence and precise nature of such purposes are so difficult to identify in relation to individual rules that they make far too uncertain and speculative a foundation for choice of law rules.

14 23 *Int'l and Comp LQ* 9 (1974).

15 See 378–379 *infra*.

16 For a full discussion, see 'Choice of Law in Tort: a Justice-Based Approach' 2 *Legal Stud* 98 (1982).

2. If the purpose of domestic tort rules is to do justice between the parties, the promotion of the interests of countries cannot be a factor in the choice of law rules. While a country has, of course, an interest in its courts doing justice (though of course this does not necessarily require, in conflicts cases, the application of its own standards of justice), and indeed a country has an interest or claim that its inhabitants should obtain justice when they litigate in a foreign court, a country clearly cannot have an interest or claim that its own domestic standards of justice should be applied in a foreign court.
3. These propositions cannot be evaded by regarding the purpose of a domestic tort rule as being to protect the one party or the other—the plaintiff or the defendant—and then going on to assert that the country has or has not an interest or concern in its rule being applied, meaning that the policy of the rule requires or does not require its application, depending on whether the party whom the rule is designed to protect does or does not belong to the country. A given tort rule is not designed to protect one party rather than the other, but to do justice between them, and the justice of the rule is not conditional on either party belonging to the country whose rule it is, or the facts having any particular connection with that country. The rule simply represents that legal system's notion of what is fair. If a court refrains from applying its own or another country's tort rule, the reason cannot be that its application is outside the policy of the rule, for that policy is to do justice between the parties. How can any case be outside the purpose or policy of such a rule? The real question, as we shall see, is which country's standards of justice ought to be applied in the light of principles of justice operating at the choice of law level? This point incidentally applies equally to choice of law in contract, outside the area of those invalidating rules which truly are designed to protect the public interest.
4. It is possible that the application of a country's rule will benefit the country, even though it is not the purpose of the rule to bring about that benefit. To rely on that benefit as a basis for saying that the country in question has an interest in its rule being applied, as has sometimes been done, is to use the rule for a purpose alien to it, and therefore unjustifiably at the expense of justice between the parties. This applies to such supposed interests as the provision of a fund out of which those who rendered assistance to the victim of an accident can recover payment for their services, or the avoidance of the victim becoming a charge on the public purse.[17] Making the point general, we can say that the interest of a country cannot be a factor in the choice of its rule, whether in tort, contract or marriage, unless the rule is one which is designed to protect the public interest.

We may sum up so far by saying that the promotion of the public interest of a country, as defined by that country, may be a policy factor behind a choice of law rule, but this can only be so in relation to domestic rules whose purpose it actually is to protect the public interest, that in the spheres of contract and marriage the

17 See e.g. *Bray* v *Cox* 333 NYS 2d 783 (1972).

domestic rules in question will generally be invalidating rules, and that tort rules are best regarded as not being designed to protect the public interest.

In those instances where the protection of the public interests of countries is a policy factor in a choice of law rule, it is important that the rule should accurately select cases where the public interest of a country is likely to be affected.

2. JUSTICE TO THE PARTIES

Just as the purpose of most domestic rules of marriage, contract and tort is to serve the interests of the parties to the relationship, transaction or occurrence, or to do justice in a dispute between them, so also is that normally the purpose of choice of law rules in these areas. Sometimes the emphasis is on the common interest of the parties, as where at the time of making a contract or celebrating a marriage there is a common desire by the parties that legal effect should be given to that transaction or relationship; sometimes the emphasis is on doing justice between the parties, as in tort, or when the parties to a contract or a marriage are in dispute.

When the purpose of the domestic rules of the different countries which may possibly be applicable to an issue is to do justice to, or between, the parties, rather than to serve the public interest, then, as we have seen,[18] the interests of those countries cannot be relevant for the choice of law. Rather, the policy behind the choice of law rules will be, as with the domestic rules themselves, to do justice to the parties. In tort, as we have seen, the dominant purpose of domestic rules is to do justice to the parties. In contract, the purpose of rules other than those invalidating rules that are designed to promote the public interest, discussed above, is to achieve justice between the parties. This includes not only non-mandatory rules, whose function is to fill the gaps in the parties' agreement, but also mandatory rules (applying irrespective of the parties' agreement to the contrary) designed to protect the interests of a weaker party, whether by invalidating terms or imposing compulsory terms, and rules relating to the formation of the contract, or to its avoidance on such grounds as mistake, misrepresentation and undue influence. In the sphere of marriage, examples of rules designed to do justice between the parties, rather than to promote the public interest, are those which entitle a party, at his option, to have a marriage annulled on such grounds as physical incapacity or lack of consent. Rules as to a minimum age for marriage, formal validity and divorce have the purposes both of protecting the public interest and doing justice between the parties.

When we speak of justice to the parties, we must distinguish between justice at the domestic level and justice at the choice of law level.[19] The former is concerned

18 See 376 *supra*.

19 Kegel speaks of 'the concept of a specific *justice of conflict of laws*, as distinguished from the justice of substantive law' in *Recueil des Cours* (1964) II, 185. Cf von Mehren, 'Choice of Law and the Problem of Justice' 41 *Law and Contemporary Problems* 27 (1977), whose approach is different.

directly with the merits of the dispute between the parties: domestic rules whose function is to do justice to the parties provide a fair solution to the dispute. The difficulty of course is that the domestic rules of different countries reveal different views as to what is fair, and the function of the choice of law rules which we now come to consider is to decide which country's standards of fairness are to be applied. In deciding which domestic standards of justice are the appropriate ones, standards of justice of a different kind, not necessarily concerned directly and immediately with a fair solution to the dispute, which is a matter for the chosen domestic rules, come into play. These we shall have to identify and examine. This view of the function of choice of law rules of course rejects a 'better law' approach,[20] which is hardly consistent with the existence of legal rules at all, whether domestic or choice of law; for if it is proper for a court to select the rule of one country rather than another on the ground that it is better, why stop short of inventing ad hoc a rule which seems to the court even better than any existing one?

We shall proceed now to examine some principles of justice at the choice of law level.

(a) In favorem validatis—implementing the parties' wish that their transaction or relationship should be legally effective

It is of course the policy of all domestic systems that contracts and marriages should be valid unless there is some reason to the contrary. That is also the policy of the conflict of laws: domestic invalidating rules should not be applicable without good reason. This principle of choice of law justice, that effect should be given to the parties' common intention that their contract or marriage be legally valid, operates primarily to control the application of invalidating rules in the public interest. As we have seen,[21] a policy factor in a choice of law rule relating to the essential validity of contracts may be the protection of the public interest of a country. But the application of an invalidating rule in furtherance of that public interest will deprive the party who is seeking to enforce the contract of his bargain. As between the parties that is unjust. While it is true that the domestic rules of all legal systems at times subordinate fairness as between the parties to the public interest, in the case of an international contract it may be that the party who will be deprived of his bargain by the application of an invalidating rule has no connection with the country in question nor had, at the time he made the contract, any reason to suppose that a rule of that country would intervene to his detriment.[22]

Though comity leads the court, as we have seen, to apply invalidating rules to protect the public interest of foreign countries, it does not follow that that interest should without question prevail over the private interest of the litigants. For

20 Leflar, *American Conflicts Law* 3rd ed, 212–215.

21 See 373–375 *supra.*

22 23 *Int'l and Comp LQ* 10, 24 (1974).

instance, the public interest of a country, as defined by its law, may require the application of its invalidating rules to conduct beyond its borders, for example exchange control or anti-trust legislation. English conflict rules can well take the view, however, that in such a case justice to the parties requires that regard for the public interest of the foreign country be confined to conduct or events occurring within its own territory, unless, perhaps, the party who will be adversely affected by the application of the invalidating rule belongs to that country or, perhaps, unless he made the contract there. Thus the English court was willing to protect the Spanish public interest as regards conduct in Spain in *Ralli Brothers* v *Compania Naviera Sota y Aznar*[23] but not the Hungarian public interest as regards conduct in England in *Kleinwort* v *Ungarische Baumwolle Industrie A/G.*[24]

Under the vague English choice of law rule for contracts, the applicability of the invalidating rule depends on whether the contract is most closely connected with the country in question. In examining the closeness of the connection, the principle of choice of law justice we are now considering demands that the court should be concerned not only with whether the links are such that the public interest of the country is capable of being affected, but also, if it is, whether there are such links between the performance of the contract, or the party who will be affected, and that country as to justify subordinating the interests of the party to those of the country. Another way of balancing the interest of the country and that of the party would be to give effect to the former only if it is of fundamental importance. Although such an approach has been advocated for some purposes in the United States,[25] it is suggested that it is too subjective to be practicable. It is of interest here to note that under Article 7 of the EEC Convention on the Law Applicable to Contractual Obligations,[26] a court may apply mandatory rules of a law which is not the governing law; in considering whether to do so 'regard shall be had to their nature and purpose and to the consequences of their application or non-application'. This no doubt requires firstly consideration of whether the public interest of the country concerned can be affected by the contract, secondly perhaps an evaluation of the importance of that public interest, and thirdly the effect which the application of the rule will have on the party who will be prejudiced thereby.

Does the principle of choice of law justice by which effect should be given to the parties' common intention that their contract be legally effective have any relevance to the applicability of domestic mandatory rules whose object is to protect not the public interest but the interest of one of the parties? Since the reason for the protection in such a case is likely to be that the consent of the party was unreal, or obtained by improper means, or not freely given because of the

23 [1920] 2 KB 287.

24 [1939] 2 KB 679.

25 E.g. Restatement (Second) of the Conflict of Laws, s 187 (2)(*b*) (1971).

26 OJ 1980 L266.

inequality of bargaining power or similar factors, it would beg the question to apply a presumption *in favorem validatis*.

In the case of essential validity of marriage also, as we have seen,[27] a policy factor of the choice of law rule may be the protection of the public interest of a country. Again this may lead to the interests of the parties being subordinated to the public interest of a country, where the parties have always desired their marriage to be valid, but it is invalid by an applicable foreign law. The question of balancing the relevant public interest against the interests of the parties is perhaps less difficult than with contracts because, whether the choice of law rule invokes the antenuptial domiciles or the matrimonial home, the possibility does not really arise of the parties having no connection with the country in question or having no reason to suppose that the law of that country may intervene.

The supposed injustice of subordinating the interest of an English person in the validity of his marriage to the public interest of a foreign country in its invalidation is, however, the basis of the rule in *Sottomayor* v *De Barros* (*No. 2*).[28] Under this exception to the dual domicile rule the validity of a marriage celebrated in England by a person domiciled in England is governed by English law. It is clear from the dictum in *Sottomayor* v *De Barros* (*No. 1*),[29] which is the origin of the rule, that its rationale is the injustice which would be done to an English party who celebrates in his own country a marriage which is valid by his own law if the marriage were held invalid on the application of the foreign rule.

> Our opinion in this appeal is confined to the case where both the contracting parties are, at the time of their marriage, domiciled in a country the laws of which prohibit their marriage. . . . No country is bound to recognise the laws of a foreign State when they work injustice to its own subjects, and this principle would prevent the judgment in the present case being relied on as an authority for setting aside a marriage between a foreigner and an English subject domiciled in England on the ground of any personal incapacity not recognised by the law of this country.

This refusal to subordinate the interests of a party to that of a country with which he has no connection, if it is justified, should be extended to a foreign party marrying in his own country. It is doubtful, however, whether it can be justified,[30] for the party marrying in his own country will normally be aware of the foreign domicile of his spouse, so it can hardly be said that he could not reasonably have anticipated the relevance of a foreign law.

Where the governing law is the law of the intended matrimonial home, as in the case of capacity to contract a polygamous marriage, there are two situations where the public interest of a country should give way to the interests of the spouses. In the first place, the public interest of a country against an objectionable

27 See 369–372 *supra*.

28 (1879) 5 PD 94.

29 (1877) 3 PD 1, 6–7.

30 Though it is well established, and has recently been extended by the Court of Appeal to the question of consent, *Vervaeke* v *Smith* [1981] Fam 77, 122. (This point was not dealt with in the HL, [1982] 2 WLR 855.)

marriage is affected not only if the parties set up their home there immediately after the celebration of the marriage, but also if they do so later, having in the meantime lived, perhaps for many years, in another country by whose law the marriage is valid. Justice to the parties obviously requires that their change of country should not result in a change of status. Secondly it is arguable that when a marriage is valid by the law of the domicile of both parties at the time of the marriage, but invalid by the law of the matrimonial home immediately after the marriage, the parties' expectation that their marriage, unobjectionable by the *mores* of their own community, will be legally effective should be upheld.[31] In other words, the line between the protection of the public interest of the intended matrimonial home and the protection of the interests of the parties should be so drawn that the marriage is valid if it is so by either the law of the intended matrimonial home, or by the law of the parties' antenuptial domicile.

Domestic rules relating to the formalities of marriage have as one of their purposes the protection of the public interest, and of course if a marriage is held invalid for want of form, the interest of the spouses in the validity of their marriage is overridden. It is arguable that the choice of law rule which makes compliance with the formalities of the *lex loci celebrationis* necessary as well as sufficient gives too little weight to the principle of justice under discussion, even taking into account the statutory and common law exceptions.[32] Certainly greater scope is given to the interests of the parties in relation to the formal validity of contracts and of wills.[33]

The next point for consideration is whether any distinction should be made between the forum and other countries in balancing the public interest with justice between the parties. It is accepted by the English conflict of laws that even the English public interest may be subordinated to the interests of the parties: for instance it is accepted that not every rule of English law which strikes down a contractual provision in the public interest is necessarily applicable to a case with foreign elements. Yet it is only to be expected that greater regard will be given to the forum's own public interests than those of foreign countries. For instance, foreign extra-territorial legislation invalidating a contract may not be applied, but English legislation, where the public interest is important, will be applied without regard to any injustice to the party who will be deprived of his contractual rights.[34]

We turn now briefly to a different aspect of the principle of choice of law justice under discussion. The parties to a contract may by express provision, or impliedly, select a law to govern their contract, and the principle that effect should be given to the parties' intention means that generally their choice of law is decisive. But there is no reason why greater effect should be given to the parties' intention that

31 41 *Mod L Rev* 40 (1978).

32 See Dicey and Morris, *The Conflict of Laws* (Vol I) 10th ed, 261–262, Rule 32.

33 See Dicey and Morris, op cit 784, Rule 148, and 617, Rule 100.

34 *Boissevain* v *Weil* [1950] AC 327.

their chosen law should govern than to their intention that their contract should be valid, so that the former should not to any greater extent than the latter prevail over the public interests of a country whose law invalidates the contract.[35] The converse problem arises when there is an apparent conflict between the parties' intention that a specified law should govern their contract and their intention that their contract should be valid, in that the specified law invalidates their contract. The answer to the problem should nearly always be that the parties' choice of the specified law was not intended to include provisions of it which would invalidate their contract.[36] In other words, questions as to the essential validity of a contract should not be subjected to a law chosen by the parties. Thus by section 27 of the Unfair Contract Terms Act 1977 the choice of English law as the proper law of a contract does not of itself bring into operation the mandatory provisions of the Act, nor can the parties freely avoid those provisions by the choice of a foreign law. The English conflict of laws would benefit by the generalization of this approach.

The principle of choice of law justice which we have just been considering operates principally to give due weight to the interests of the parties in competition with the public interest of a country. The situations where the public interest of a country is relevant, involving mainly the possible applicability of some invalidating rules in marriage law or contract, are few, however. Most issues do not involve the public interests of countries, and the main function of the principles of choice of law justice which we now turn to examine is to select which country's standards of substantive justice should be applied in a given case.

(*b*) *Justice is done to a party if the law of his own country is applied*

Where no question of the public interest arises, so that the problem is only one of selecting which country's standards of justice should be used, it will nearly always be sensible and reasonable to attribute to a party as his own the standards of justice of the country to which he belongs. With only a few possible exceptions, a party in an international dispute cannot complain of injustice if the justice given to him is that of his own country. The difficulty of course is that the parties will often belong to different countries, whose standards of justice may differ. We shall first deal, however, with cases where the parties belong to the same country.

(i) ***Where both parties belong to the same country.*** Where both parties belong to the same country, the law of that country will usually be the appropriate law. In contract, the law of the country to which both parties belong should be the governing law in any case where no question arises of the applicability of mandatory rules designed to protect the public interest of the country. Where the question is which country's standards of justice are the appropriate ones, the objective connections which a contract (as opposed to the parties) has with

35 But of course this proposition is not fully accepted by the English conflict of laws.

36 23 *Int'l and Comp LQ* 4 (1974); Restatement (Second) of the Conflict of Laws, s 187, 565–566 (1971).

countries—such as the making of the contract or its performance—are quite without significance, as we have already seen.[37] It is however entirely appropriate that the standards of justice of the country to which both parties belong should be used.

In marriage law, among the relevant domestic rules here are those which entitle a party, if he wishes, to avoid the marriage on such grounds as physical incapacity or lack of consent. That such rules are not designed to protect the public interest of the country in question is shown by the fact that it is at the option of the party whether to have the marriage annulled or not. If not, it is a perfectly good marriage in all respects. Whether in justice to the parties the marriage should be capable of being annulled on one of these gounds is most appropriately left to the standards of justice of the country to which both parties belong at the time of the marriage. In English law this is established with regard to consent.[38] As regards impotence and wilful refusal to consummate the marriage, the weight of authority[39] is that a party's power to avoid the marriage is governed either by the law of the husband's domicile at the time of the marriage or the law of the intended matrimonial home. If the latter is the correct alternative, the law of the country to which both parties belong at the time of the marriage might in a rare case not apply.

Finally, as regards tort, although it would not even be mentioned in any possible official formulation of the choice of law rule in England, there is now no doubt of the significance of the law of the country to which both parties belong. It seems as appropriate here as in the instances in contract and marriage just mentioned that the standards of justice of the parties' own country should be used to decide the dispute between them. The fact that both parties were English was the decisive fact in *Boys* v *Chaplin*[40] which led to the application of English law rather than the Maltese *lex loci*. In other legal systems also, the cases where most often it has been thought right to depart from the *lex loci* in a tort case are those where the parties belong to the same country. So also the cases in which the application of the *lex loci* has been most severely criticized are those in which both parties belonged to the same country. The only difficulty in the way of the law of the country to which both parties belong is the argument that a party who acts in a particular country ought not to be held liable if he is not liable by the law of that country, a possible principle of justice at the choice of law level which will be examined below.[41]

An extension of the principle that the standards of justice of the country to which both parties belong should be applied, following from the same notion that there ought to be attributed to a person the standards of justice of his own

37 See 374 *supra*.

38 *Szechter* v *Szechter* [1971] P 286, 294–295.

39 *de Reneville* v *de Reneville* [1948] P 100, *Way* v *Way* [1950] P 71, *Ponticelli* v *Ponticelli* [1958] P 204.

40 [1971] AC 356.

41 See 385–387 *infra*.

country, is that where the parties belong to different countries, but the relevant rules of their respective laws are the same, then those rules should be applied.[42]

Finally in this section it is necessary to define what is the appropriate connection between party and country to enable the court to regard the former as belonging to the latter. In marriage no doubt it must be domicile. In contract and tort it should be habitual residence, or in the case of a person acting in the course of business, his place of business (and, if more than one, the place of business relevant to the transaction or accident in question).[43]

(ii) *Where the transaction or event is entirely domestic as regards one party.* Among the most difficult though frequent choice of law problems are those where no public interest of any country is involved and the parties belong to different countries, the rules of which differ on the issue in question. In one class of case, however, it is clear which party's law should be applied, for there is an important principle of justice at the choice of law level which protects a person who, in his own country, acts or participates in a transaction or event that is entirely domestic to his country, except for the fact that the other party is, without the knowledge, or without the choice, of the first party, a foreigner. The only foreign element in the case, in other words, is the foreign residence, place of business or domicile of the one party, which fact is unknown to the other party, or if known to him, the situation was not of his choosing. In such a case it would be unjust to the party who belongs to the country in question if his legal position was to be the worse merely because the other party happens to be a foreigner. Although this principle of justice protects the expectations of a party, it is not based on that idea, because it applies in the absence of any expectation, for example in favour of a party whose act was inadvertent, or who was the victim of another's act. The foundation of the principle is rather that to treat like cases differently is unjust—what Lord Simon, in a different context, recently described as 'the injustice of different results in fundamentally analogous circumstances.'[44] In the situations we are considering, the fact that the one party happens to be a foreigner is immaterial, and to diminish the other party's rights on account of it would contravene this principle.

This principle of choice of law justice is fundamental in tort.[45] A defendant who acts in his own country so as to cause injury to a plaintiff who is in the defendant's country should not be held to any greater liability than he is under by his own law merely because the plaintiff happens to be a foreigner.[46] A plaintiff who is injured in his own country by a defendant acting there should not have any lesser remedy

42 A good example is *Reich* v *Purcell* 67 Cal 2d 551 (1967). See discussion in 2 *Legal stud* 110–112 (1982).

43 This is in effect the connection used in Article 4(2) of the EEC Convention on the Law Applicable to Contractual Obligations.

44 *National Carriers Ltd* v *Panalpina Ltd* [1981] AC 675, 701.

45 2 *Legal Stud* 102–103, 105–106 (1982).

46 *Cipolla* v *Shaposka* 439 Pa 563, 566–567 (1970), *Neumeier* v *Kuehner* 286 NE 2d 454, 457–458 (1972).

than he would have by his own law merely because the defendant happens to be a foreigner.[47] It is these instances which point to the *lex loci delicti* as being normally the governing law in tort.

The principle is also important in contract. If a person makes a contract in his own country, which is to be entirely performed in that country, then the mere fact that, unknown to him, the other party is a foreigner, should not place him in a worse position than he would be under his own law. By English conflict of laws, of course, the law of that party's country would clearly be the proper law. A problem arose here at one time from the possibility that a party's capacity to contract was governed by the law of his domicile,[48] but it seems now accepted that an incapacity by the law of the domicile will not prevail over the proper law.[49]

The operation of this principle in the sphere of the essential validity of marriage—the rule in *Sottomayor* v *De Barros (No. 2)*[50]—has already been referred to.[51]

This principle of justice is sometimes given a wider scope, by extending it to cases where the foreign connection of the one party is known to the other, or where that connection is not the only foreign element. Thus by section 27(2)(*b*) of the Unfair Contract Terms Act 1977 the provisions of the Act are to be applied if 'in the making of the contract one of the parties dealt as consumer, and he was then habitually resident in the United Kingdom, and the essential steps necessary for the making of the contract were taken there . . .'. Similarly, under Article 5 of the EEC Convention on the Law Applicable to Contractual Obligations a consumer is not to be deprived of 'the protection afforded to him by the mandatory rules of the country in which he has his habitual residence:—if in that country the conclusion of the contract was preceded by a specific invitation addressed to him or by advertising, and he had taken in that country all the steps necessary on his part for the conclusion of the contract . . .'.

Presumably the rationale of such provisions is that it would be unjust to the consumer in the circumstances specified to deprive him of the protection conferred on him by the law of his own country. The weaker bargaining power of the consumer no doubt accounts for the extension for his benefit of this principle of justice.

(*c*) *A party should not be held liable to a greater extent than he is liable by the law of the country where he acted*

This principle of justice at the choice of law level is relevant primarily to tort. We have already seen that if a person acts in his own country so as to cause damage or

47 *Tooker* v *Lopez* 249 NE 2d 394, 404 (1969).

48 *Re Cooke's Trusts* (1887) 56 LJ Ch 637, 639, *Cooper* v *Cooper* (1888) 13 App Cas 88, 99, 100 and 108.

49 Dicey and Morris, op cit (Vol 2), 778 Rule 147; *Bodley Head Ltd* v *Flegon* [1972] 1 WLR 680, 689.

50 (1879) 5 PD 94.

51 See 380 *supra*.

injury there to a plaintiff, an important principle of justice requires that he should not be held liable if he is not so by the law of that country. What of a person who acts in a country which is not his own? Is there any principle of justice which would limit his liability to that, if any, imposed by the law of that country? Such is in fact the result of the second branch of *Phillips* v *Eyre*,[52] as interpreted by the majority of the House of Lords in *Chaplin* v *Boys*;[53] the former interpretation in *Machado* v *Fontes*[54] reflected a narrower notion that there would be injustice in holding such a defendant liable only if his conduct was not wrongful in any sense by the *lex loci*. The rationale of this principle, based on the expectations of the parties, particularly the defendant, was explained by the late Sir Otto Kahn-Freund:[55] the defendant 'should be able to feel safe in Rome if he does as the Romans do' and if he sees that his 'insurance policy covers the risks against which Romans insure'. This principle will be satisfied to the extent that the governing law is the *lex loci delicti*, but difficulty will arise where the parties belong to the same country or to different countries whose relevant rules are the same. Should the defendant in such a case be held liable under the parties' law, even though he is not liable by the law of the country in which he acted? In other words, which principle should prevail, (*b*)(i)[56] or the present one, when they conflict? Kahn-Freund[57] argued in favour of the present principle, except when the parties share a relationship connected with the country other than the *locus delicti*, or an environment insulated from the *locus delicti*, or perhaps when the issue is other than liability itself. The contrary can also be argued, that the law common to the parties should normally prevail.[58] At any rate here is an example of a possible clash between two of our principles of justice at the choice of law level; normally they supplement rather than conflict with each other.

The principle of justice under discussion will rarely be apt for contract or marriage, where the place of making the contract or celebrating the marriage, if it is not the country of either party, is of little significance, because the rights and obligations spring from the relationship rather than from an act. An example of a similar principle, however, operating in relation to capacity to contract, can be found in Article 11 of the EEC Convention on the Law Applicable to Contractual Obligations: 'In a contract concluded between persons who are in the same country, a natural person who would have capacity under the law of that country may invoke his incapacity resulting from another law only if the other party to the contract was aware of this incapacity at the time of the conclusion of the contract or was not aware thereof as a result of negligence.'

This provision seems to fall between the present principle and the immediately

52 (1870) LR 6 QB 1.
53 [1971] AC 356.
54 [1897] 2 QB 231.
55 *Recueil des Cours* (1968) II, 43–44.
56 See 383 *supra*.
57 Loc cit, 64ff, 92–93, 123–124.
58 See 2 *Legal Stud* 107–110 (1982).

preceding one. Under the previous principle the provision would have been confined to the case of one party concluding the contract in his own country. It is extended here to apply even when he is concluding the contract in another country, if the party seeking to rely on the incapacity is also present in that country.

(d) Certainty and predictability

Certainty and predictability are frequently mentioned[59] as desirable aims of choice of law rules, for it is obviously in the interests of the parties to a relationship or transaction that they should know, or be able to ascertain, without the necessity for litigation, which is the governing law. In contract the parties may need to know this from the time of making their contract, for the purpose of performing their obligations and, if a dispute arises, in order to decide whether to sue, defend or settle. In tort also it is advantageous for the parties to know, after the alleged tort has been committed, which law will govern. It is obviously also desirable that spouses should be able to ascertain the law governing their marriage.

This principle of justice is relevant to the nature of the choice of law rule which should be adopted, rather than as indicating which domestic law should govern. Certainty and predictability require the existence of definite, fixed choice of law rules rather than, for instance, choice-indicating factors or ad hoc analyses of interests or policies which are supposed to lead to the decision of the particular case without the intervention of choice of law rules at all. Furthermore, certainty cannot be provided by vague or flexible choice of law rules such as 'a contract is governed by the law of the country with which it is most closely connected' or 'an issue in tort is governed by the law of the country with which it has its most significant relationship'.

It is sometimes said that certainty and predictability can be bought at too great a price, but in fact they are not inconsistent with any other principle of justice which we have considered or will consider, because all that they require is that the choice of law rule should point with certainty to a definite law. None of our principles of justice conflict with that. The only area where the interests of the parties in certainty and predictability may have to be sacrificed, and hence where a vague and flexible choice of law rule may be necessary, is where the public interest of a country is a factor in the choice of law in contract, i.e. as regards domestic invalidating rules which are designed to protect the public interest of the country concerned.[60] Because contractual invalidating rules are so varied in their objectives, it is not possible to have a fixed choice of law rule which will indicate with certainty that the rules of a particular country, and no other, will be applicable to a contract, as regards essential validity. Just as the interest of the parties in the effectiveness of their transaction must yield, to the extent we have

59 E.g. Cheetham and Reese, 'Choice of the Applicable Law' 52 *Col L Rev* 959, 969 (1952); Restatement (Second) of the Conflict of Laws, s 6 (2)(*f*).

60 See 373–375 *supra*.

considered above,[61] to the public interest of a country, so also must their interest in having their contract governed by a predictable law. The vague and uncertain formula of 'the law of the country with which the contract is most closely connected' is tolerable then as regards the applicability of contractual rules which protect the public interest, so long as the formula is understood to raise the criteria discussed earlier.[62] The vagueness is inappropriate however in other aspects of contract where, as we have seen, the public interests of countries do not intrude, the contract's connections with countries are therefore irrelevant, and certainty ought therefore to be attainable. Similarly in tort, where, as suggested earlier, supposed public interests are of little consequence, a vague rule that the tort, or the particular issue, is governed by the law of the country with which it has the closest or most significant connection should be avoided. All the relevant principles of justice can be provided for by a definite[63] rather than a vague and flexible choice of law rule for tort. The point need not be argued as regards marriage, where the prevailing rules are definite, except that the law of the intended matrimonial home as the governing law can lead occasionally to a measure of uncertainty when the parties delay in establishing a home after their marriage. That small degree of uncertainty, however, which can be mitigated by additional rules,[64] is a lesser evil than invalidating the marriage by the application of the law of an antenuptial domicile abandoned immediately after the celebration of the marriage.

(*e*) *Uniformity*

Justice between the parties makes it desirable that the same law be applied to decide a case in whatever country the proceedings are brought. This is necessary if predictability is to be fully achieved; a party to a contract for instance cannot decide whether an event is such as to excuse him from performance if different laws, with different rules on the matter, may govern the issue in the different courts where the other party may sue. Also uniformity is necessary to avoid the injustice to the defendant which would flow from the plaintiff's ability to choose to sue in the forum where he is likely to succeed, or will enjoy the better remedy.[65] In marriage of course the uniformity of status in different countries is highly desirable.

The problem is of course that uniformity cannot be achieved,[66] except by means

61 See 378–379 *supra*.

62 See 374–375 and 379 *supra*.

63 For instance, that issues in tort are governed by the *lex loci*, with an exception in favour of the law of the country to which both parties belong or the laws of the different countries to which they belong, if those laws are the same on the relevant issue.

64 Cheshire and North, *Private International Law* 10th ed, 334; 41 *Mod L Rev* 41 (1978).

65 Thus uniformity, like our principle (*b*)(ii) above, is based on the principle of justice that like cases should be treated alike. Cf von Mehren, 'Choice of Law and the Problem of Justice' 41 *Law and Contemporary Problems* 27, 32 (1977).

66 Renvoi has sometimes been justified as promoting uniformity but the doctrine is not used in relation to contract or tort, and rarely in relation to marriage. *Supra* n 6.

of conventions between countries by which they adopt identical choice of law rules in the areas of law in question. In the absence of such a convention, the only practical influence the desire for uniformity can normally have in the formulation of choice of law rules is to exclude the *lex fori* as the governing law, for that is the one law which makes uniformity impossible. Also, as with certainty and predictability, a vague choice of law rule reduces the chance of uniformity being achieved: even if the choice of law rule is nominally the same in different countries, it may lead different courts to apply different laws.

(f) Convenience

It is in the interests of a party that the law governing his dispute, transaction or relationship should be a convenient one. This means primarily one to which he has easy access for professional advice, so this principle of justice again points to the law of the party's own country. Convenience in another form becomes a consideration for parties who enter into many contracts of the same kind, i.e. those who regularly provide goods or services or employment under contracts which have foreign elements. It is convenient for such parties that all their transactions should be governed by the same law, again preferably their own law.[67]

We must now look at examples of the way in which these last mentioned principles of choice of law justice—certainty, uniformity, convenience—can help in the formulation of choice of law rules in cases not involving public interests of countries, in which the parties belong to different countries and the transaction or event is not domestic as regards one party.

As regards contract we have already seen[68] that, in the absence of any question of the public interest of a country, the objective connections which a contract has with a country—where it was made, where it is to be performed—are without significance. Also excluded, where the applicability of mandatory rules in the public interest does not arise,[69] is the vague formula of the country with which the contract is most closely connected, not only because it brings in those factors just mentioned which are without significance in the search for the appropriate domestic standards of justice, but also because it offends against the requirements of certainty and predictability. The only possible rule which provides for certainty is one which points to the law of one of the parties. But which party? Here convenience may provide the answer. Which party should enjoy the advantage of

67 This consideration was regarded as important by the Court of Appeal in *Sayers* v *International Drilling Co NV* [1971] 1 WLR 1176, where one of the factors which was relied on by the majority of the Court in holding that the proper law of the contract was the law of the employer's country was the fact that the employer engaged employees from various different countries under similar contracts; see 1183–1184, 1185–1186.

68 See 374 *supra*.

69 This means of course that a different law may govern, depending on whether or not the issue is the applicability of mandatory terms in the public interest. For further justification of this limited degree of dépeçage, see 23 *Int'l and Comp LQ* 7 (1974), and P M North, ed, *Contract Conflicts* (1982), chapter 2, 44–45.

his own law being the governing law? It can be argued that it should be the party who is likely, or likely more often, to have to consult the law, i.e. the party whose performance is more complicated. In the ordinary bilateral contract, whereby a thing or a service is exchanged for money, it is the obligations of the party who is to provide the thing or the service, rather than of the party who is to pay money, which are usually the more complicated. Moreover it is the party whose obligation is to provide the goods or services, rather than he who pays for them, who is the more likely to make many similar contracts, which convenience requires should all be governed by the same law.[70] So when all our other principles of justice have brought us to the point where the law of one of the parties should govern, convenience indicates the law of the party who, in the phrase adopted by the EEC Convention on the Law Applicable to Contractual Obligations,[71] is to render the characteristic performance.[72]

On the other hand, since many legal systems today seek to protect the weaker party to a contract against the greater bargaining power of the stronger, it can be urged that it is the convenience of the weaker party, whose resources and opportunities to obtain legal advice about, and ability to adapt his expectations to, the rules of foreign legal systems are less than those of the business concern with which he deals, which should be preferred. On this basis, again using examples from the EEC Convention,[73] consumer contracts can be singled out for different provision by making it the consumer's law which governs, as well as employment contracts, where the law of the country in which the employee normally works is the one most accessible to him.

It must be borne in mind that the choice of one party's as the governing law on the basis of convenience, whether that of the party rendering the characteristic performance or that of the weaker party, is subject to the principle of justice (*b*)(ii) above, i.e. that where the transaction or event is entirely domestic as regards one party, that party should not be placed in a worse position than he would be under his own law. So where a consumer purchases goods while on a visit to a foreign country, the law of the latter country must govern, not the consumer's.

(*g*) *The lex fori*

The most intractable problems in the choice of law are those where no question of the public interest of a country arises, and where no general principle of choice of law justice seems apposite. Sometimes some consideration of justice or convenience peculiar to the issue in question may be found to supply the

70 Ole Lando, *International Encyclopaedia of Comparative Law* (Vol III) Chap 24, 89; *RabelsZ* 38 (1974) 6, 30–32.

71 Article 4. Even greater certainty can be achieved by legislation that specifies for each class of contract that is commonly made which party's law shall be the governing law, as is proposed by the Swiss Draft Federal Statute on Private International Law.

72 And uniformity will be achieved to the extent that this approach is adopted by various countries, whether as a result of the Convention or otherwise.

73 Articles 5 and 6.

appropriate choice of law rule. Otherwise, where no consideration of justice or convenience seems to point to one party's law rather than the other's, the natural approach is to fall back on the *lex fori*. Where no principle of choice of law justice favours the application of the standards of substantive justice of one foreign country rather than another, the court's own standards of justice remain undisplaced as the appropriate ones to apply. Of course uniformity and predictability will suffer to the extent that the *lex fori* is the governing law, but sometimes that cannot be helped. An example of this problem is to identify the law which should determine whether the parties to a purported contract ever reached agreement, in a case where they belong to different countries whose laws differ on the point, and where the transaction is not one which is domestic to one of the parties. No principle of justice seems available to prefer the law of one party to the other. The criterion of convenience, which indicated for other contractual matters that the law of the party rendering the characteristic performance, or the law of the consumer, should govern, hardly applies to a case where it is disputed whether a contract was ever made. Should we not then fall back on the *lex fori*?

Another area of difficulty is the law to govern the annulment of a marriage on grounds not involving the public interest of a country, for example, lack of consent or physical incapacity. Is there any basis for preferring one party's law to the other's, or should it be sufficient that there is a remedy by either law, or should the court fall back on its own law?[74] Of course there are many other areas raising particular difficulties, but they will not be pursued here. The main purpose of this article is to try to identify general principles of justice, not to point out all the cases where none seems to be available. It is important to emphasize, however, that the appropriate questions to be asked, in deciding upon the appropriate choice of law rule in a problem area, will much less often relate to the interests of countries than to justice, at the choice of law level, between the parties.

(*h*) *Public policy—justice and morality*

The well-established principle that foreign law will not be applied when it is contrary to public policy serves two distinct purposes. One aspect is the protection of the public interest of the forum, and its use is exemplified in contract, where, for instance, even though a contract is valid by its foreign governing law, it may be held invalid by a rule of English law which is designed to protect the public interest. A similar device is to rely on the construction of an English statute as making it applicable even though the contract is governed by a foreign law. Such

74 As regards consent, it is unsettled in English law whether a party can rely on his lack of consent by the law of the other party's domicile or only by the law of his own domicile. See Dicey and Morris, op cit, 305. If the marriage is celebrated in England, and one party is domiciled there at the time of the marriage, the issue of consent is to be decided exclusively by English law: *Vervaeke* v *Smith* [1981] Fam 77, 122. This seems to be an inappropriate application of principle of justice (*b*)(ii) *supra*. As to physical incapacity, see 383 *supra*.

uses of public policy are only necessary because of the inadequacy[75] of the ordinary choice of law rules. If these were so formulated and applied as to give due regard to the public interests of countries in the first place, as discussed above, the invocation of public policy in this sense would be unnecessary.

The other aspect of public policy is concerned with justice and morality as between the parties. Normally the standpoint of choice of law is that the standards of justice of different legal systems, including the court's own law, are of equal value. The principles of justice at the choice of law level, which we have been considering, do not select as between them on the grounds of some being better than others. The fact remains that for a court its own law represents justice, and certain foreign rules, which grossly offend those domestic standards, must be rejected. So a final and overriding principle of justice at the choice of law level is, after all, that no foreign rule which grossly offends English standards of justice will be applicable.[76]

75 The rules are defective mainly because they subject questions as to the applicability of even mandatory rules to the law expressly or impliedly chosen by the parties.

76 A well known example in contract is *Kaufman* v *Gerson* [1904] 1 KB 591. In marriage, foreign rules invalidating marriages between persons of different races or religious groups would no doubt be held contrary to public policy. Dicey and Morris, op cit, 86–87.

Name Index

www.ingramcontent.com/pod-product-compliance
Lightning Source LLC
LaVergne TN
LVHW081343011026
849161LV00013BB/2994